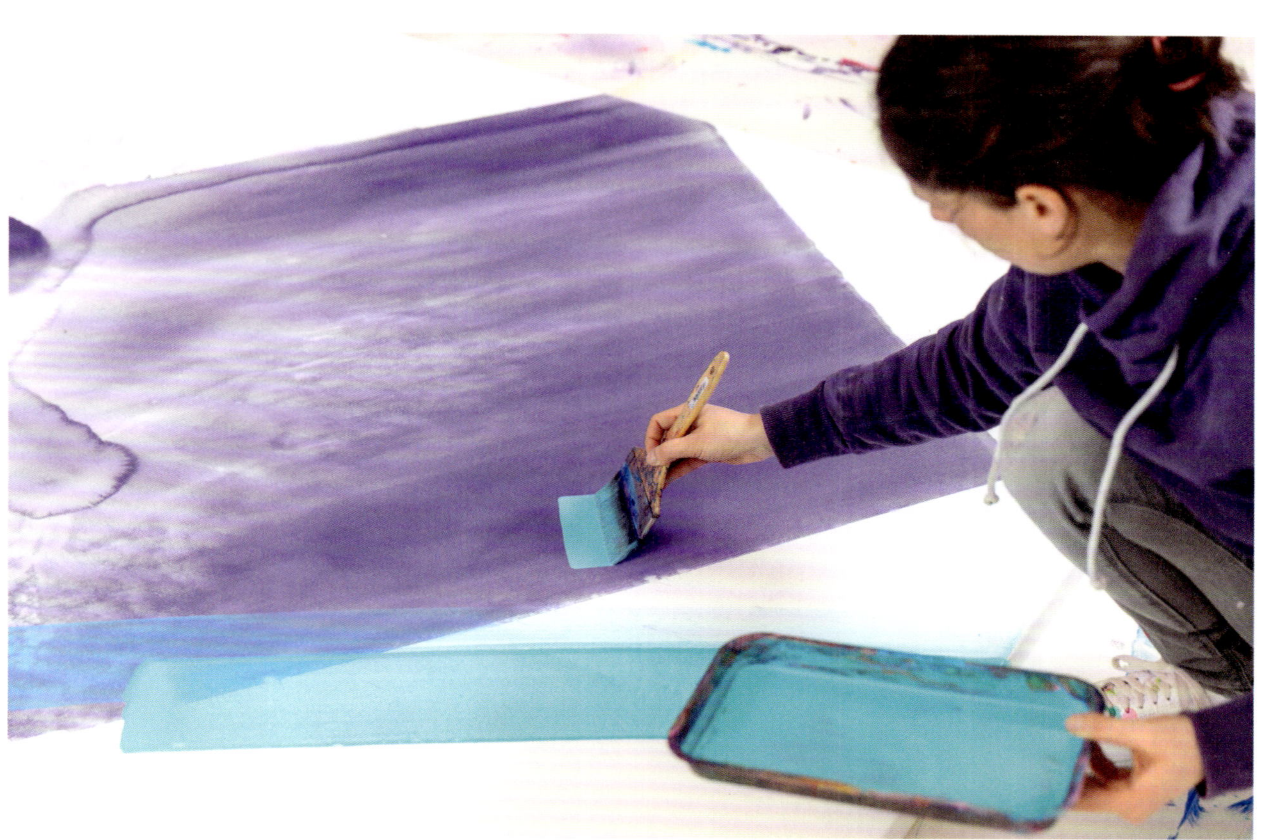

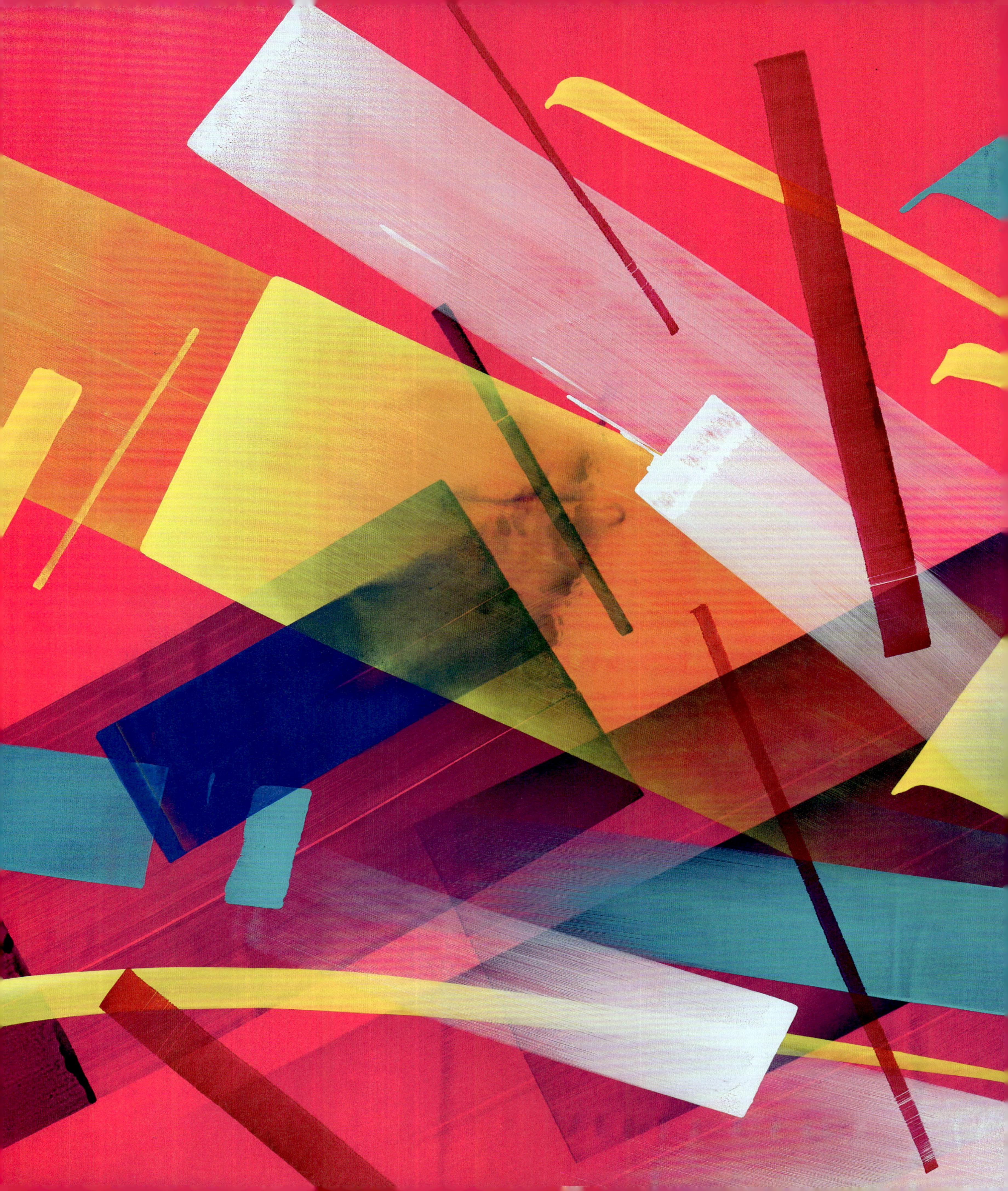

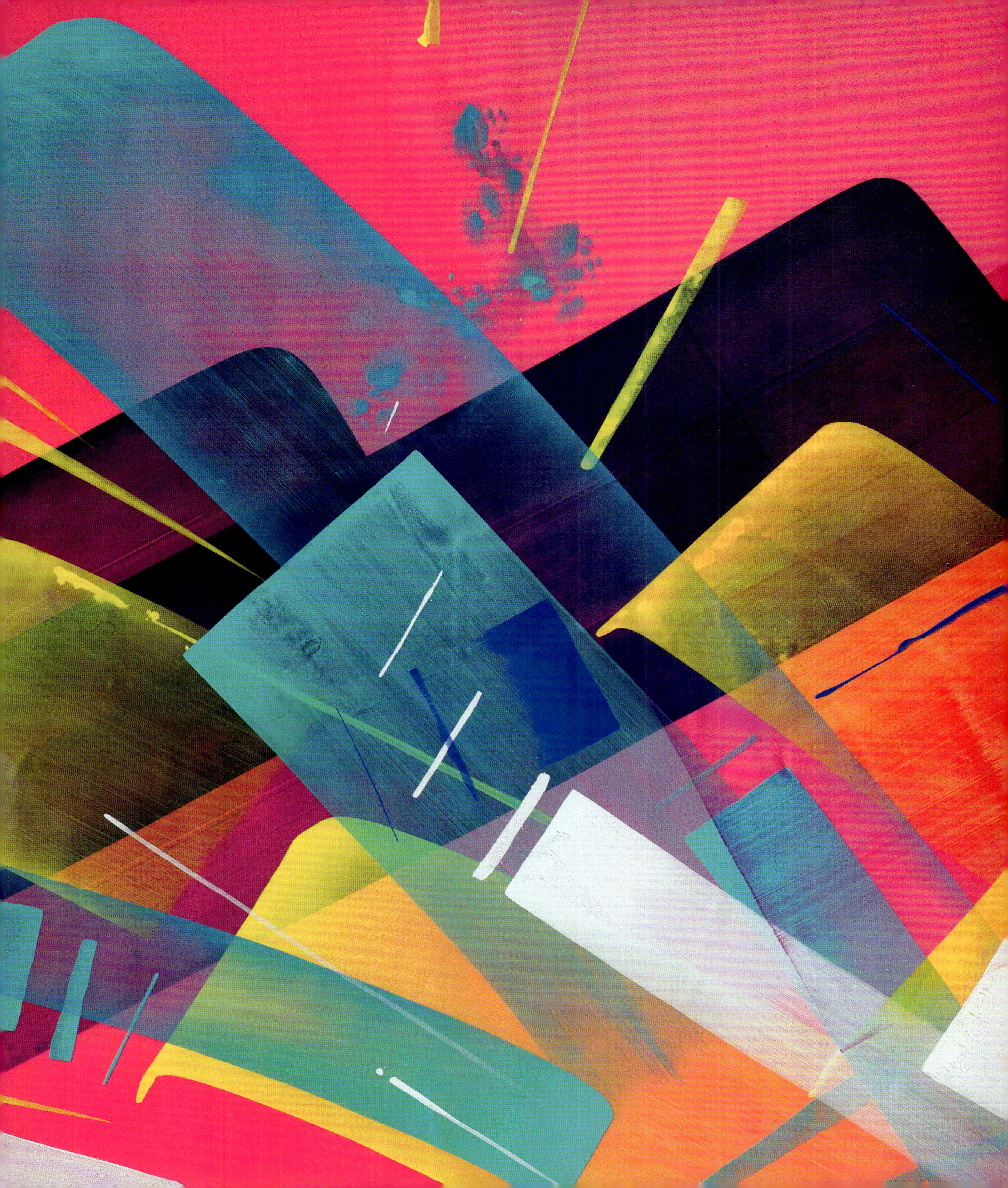

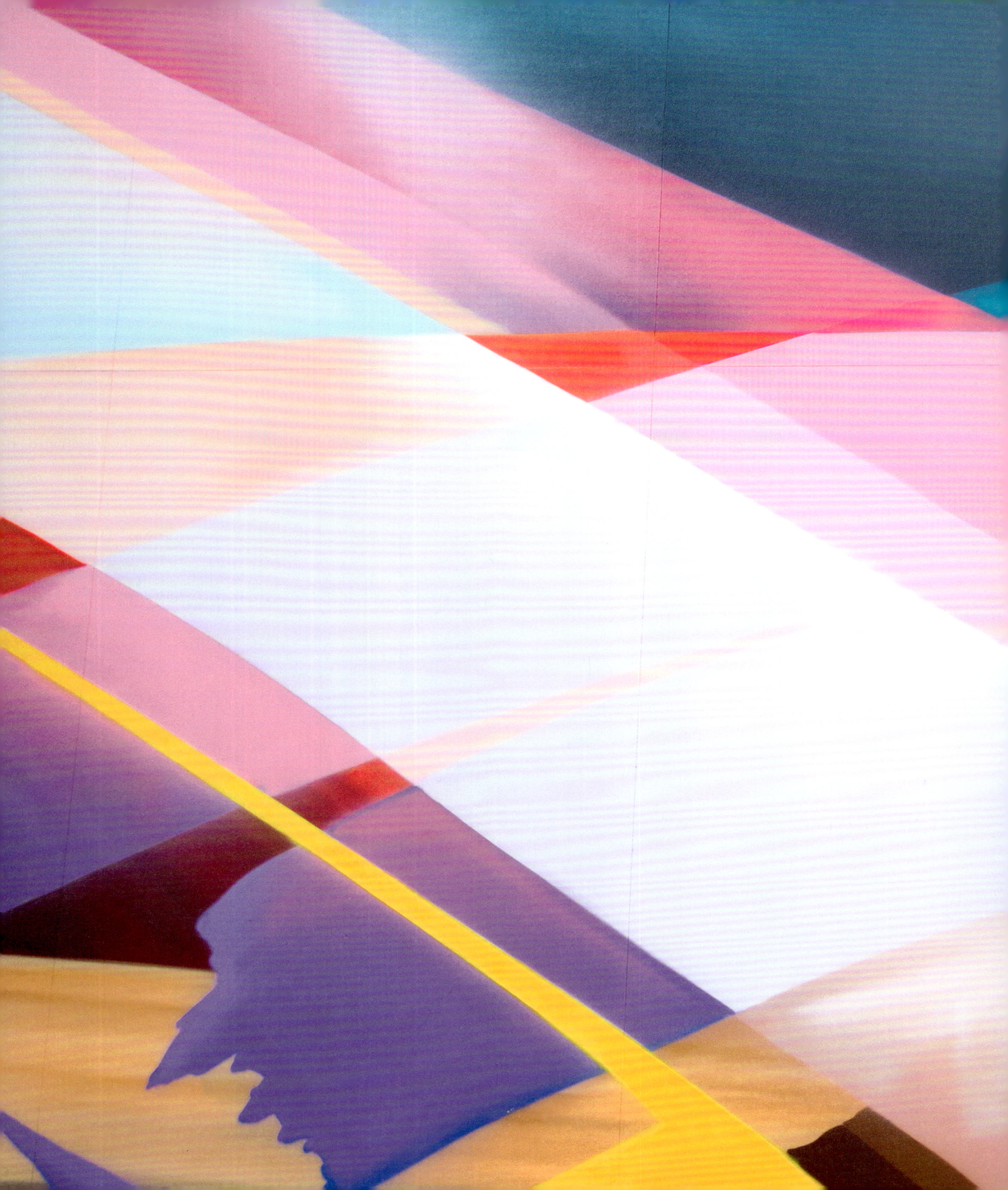

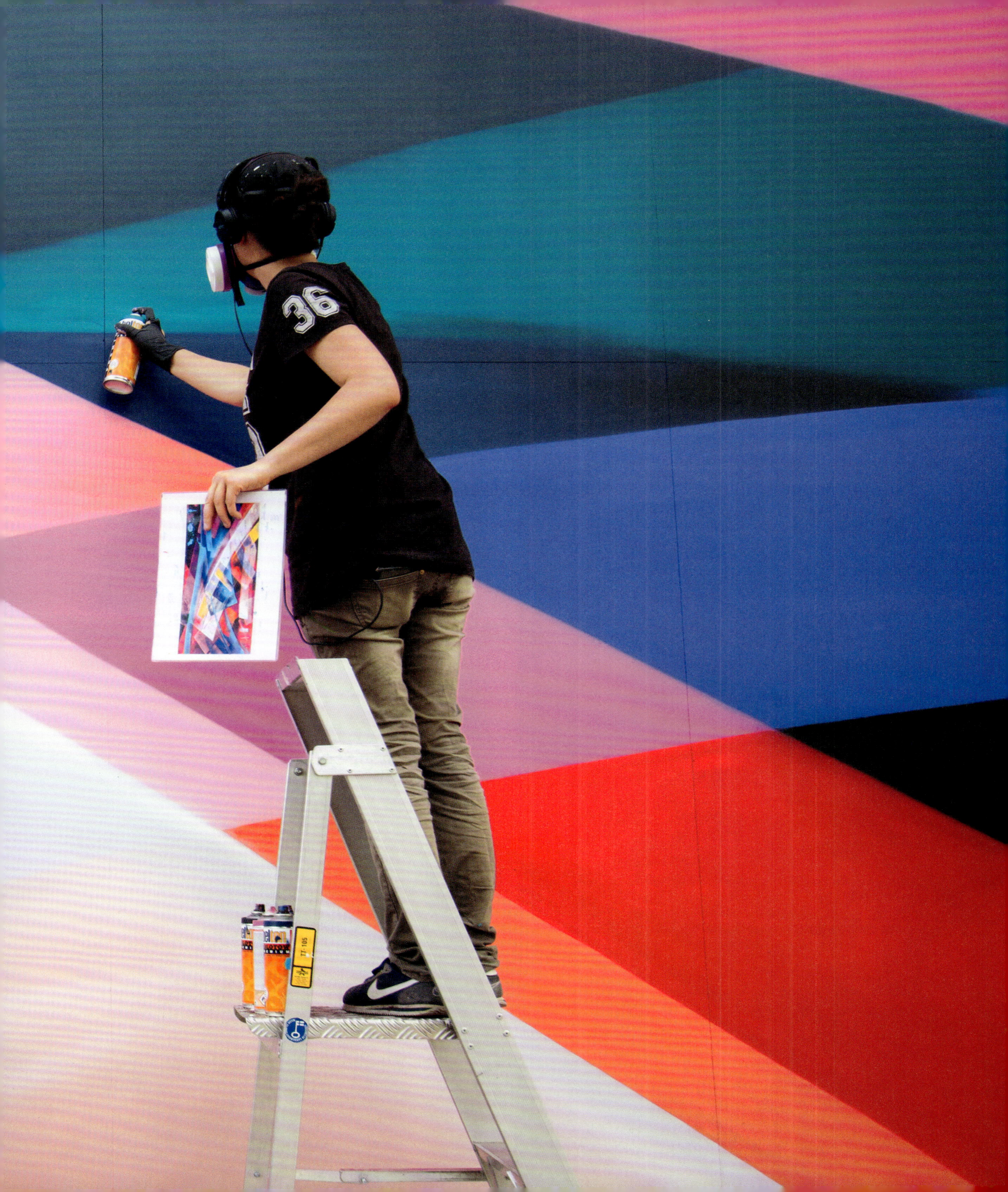
36

Front cover: MadC working on *The 1000 Wall*, Wabash Arts Corridor, 1326 South Michigan Avenue, Chicago, USA, 2018
Back cover: *13:47-21102017*, 100 x 100cm, acrylic, watercolour and spray paint on canvas, 2017

p. 1: MadC studio, Halle, Germany, 2018
pp. 2–3: *20:06-23022021*, 200 x 450cm, acrylic, watercolour and spray paint on canvas, 2021
pp. 4–5 and 234: *Free at Last*, Art and Museum Centre Sinkka, Kerava, Finland, August 2017
pp. 8–9 and 240: Pullman Maldives, Maamutaa Island, September–October 2019
pp. 10–11: MadC, Dresden Airport, Germany, 2019
pp. 12–13: *JC 180*, 627 Summit Avenue, NJ 07306, Jersey City, USA, June 2019
pp. 236–237: Detail from *May The Force Be With You*, 180 x 160cm, acrylic, watercolour and spray paint on canvas, 2018
pp. 238–239: *Reading between the Lines*, Philadelphia Mural Arts Program, 26th Street and Girard Avenue, Philadelphia, USA, May 2016

ISBN 978-1-912122-43-1

Translated by Eva Ruschkowski
Edited by Miranda Harrison
Designed by Sylvia Ugga
Editorial Assistant Kirsty Watling
Printed and bound by Gomer Press

MadC

STREET TO CANVAS

Luisa Heese

Translation by Eva Ruschkowski

HENI PUBLISHING, LONDON

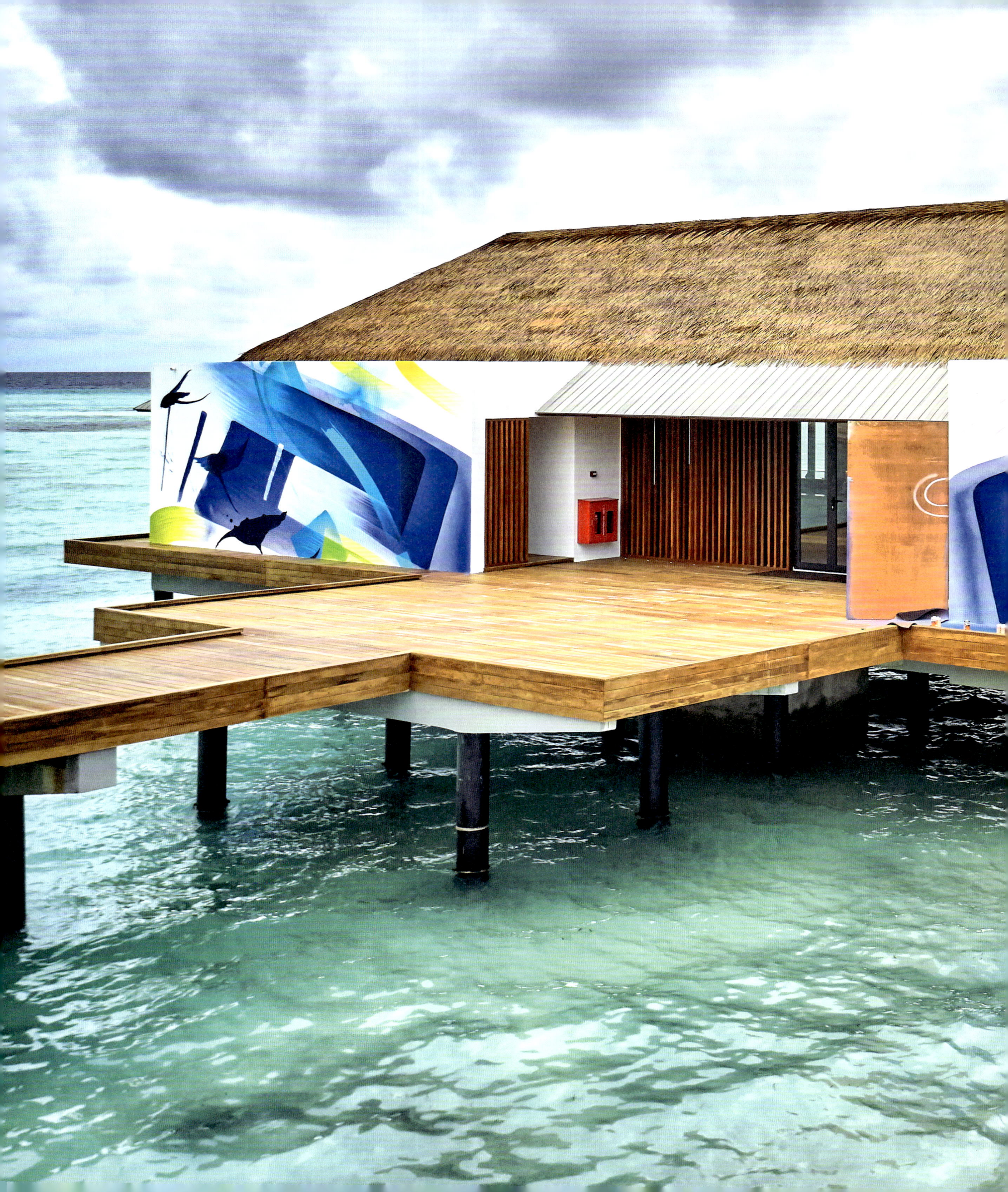

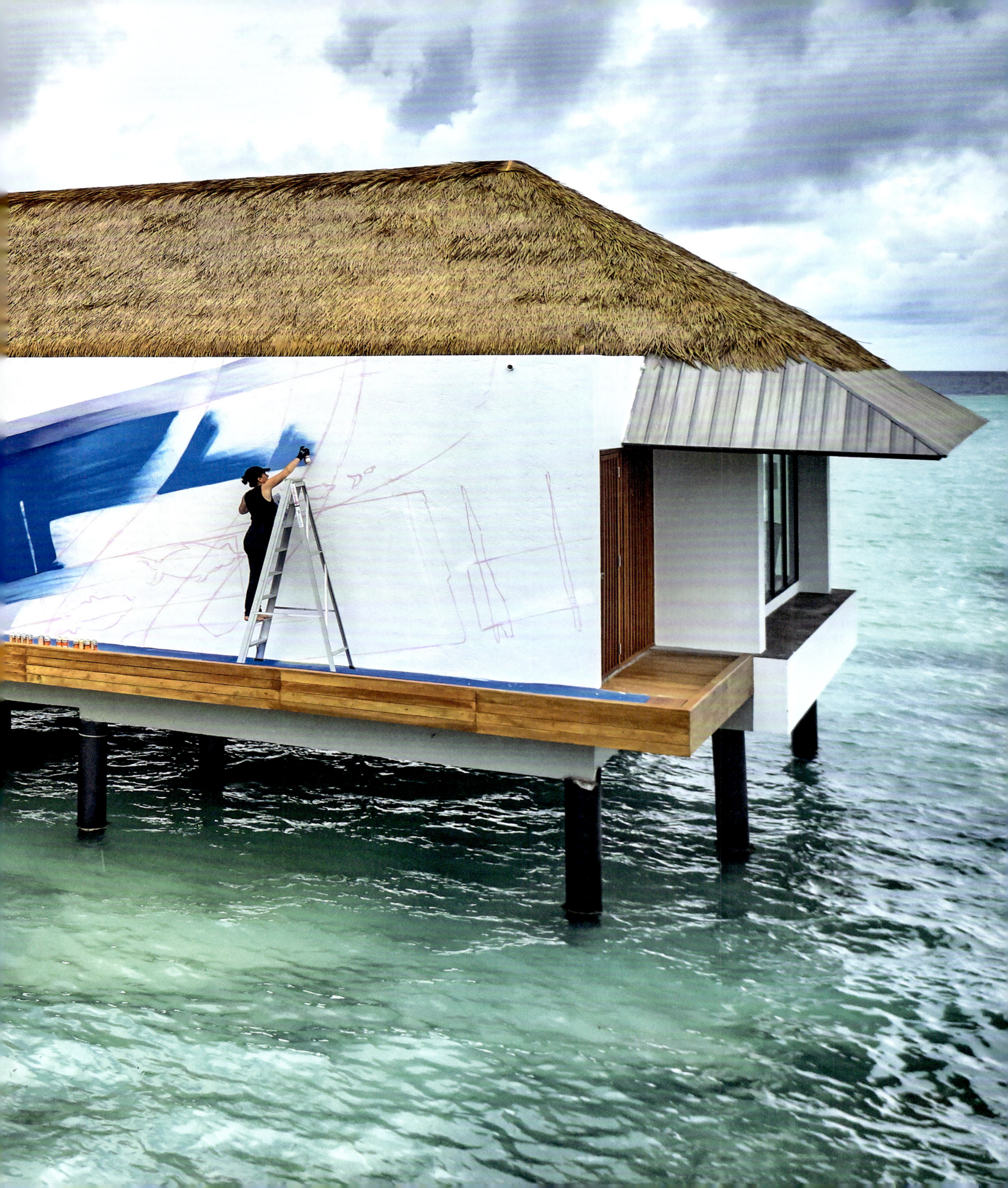

CONTENTS

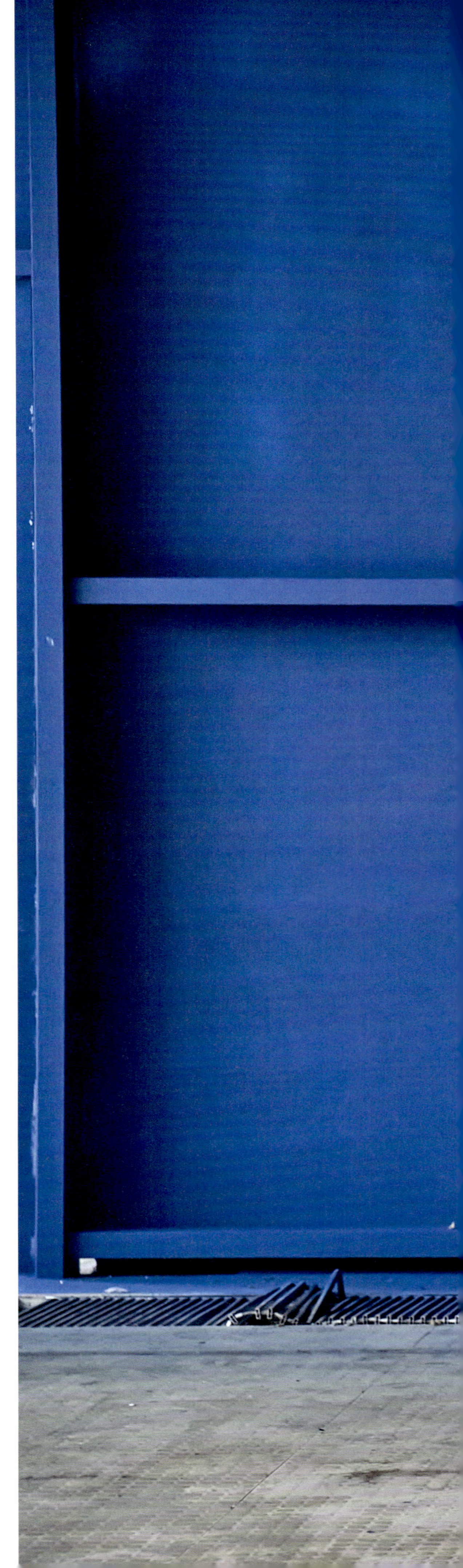

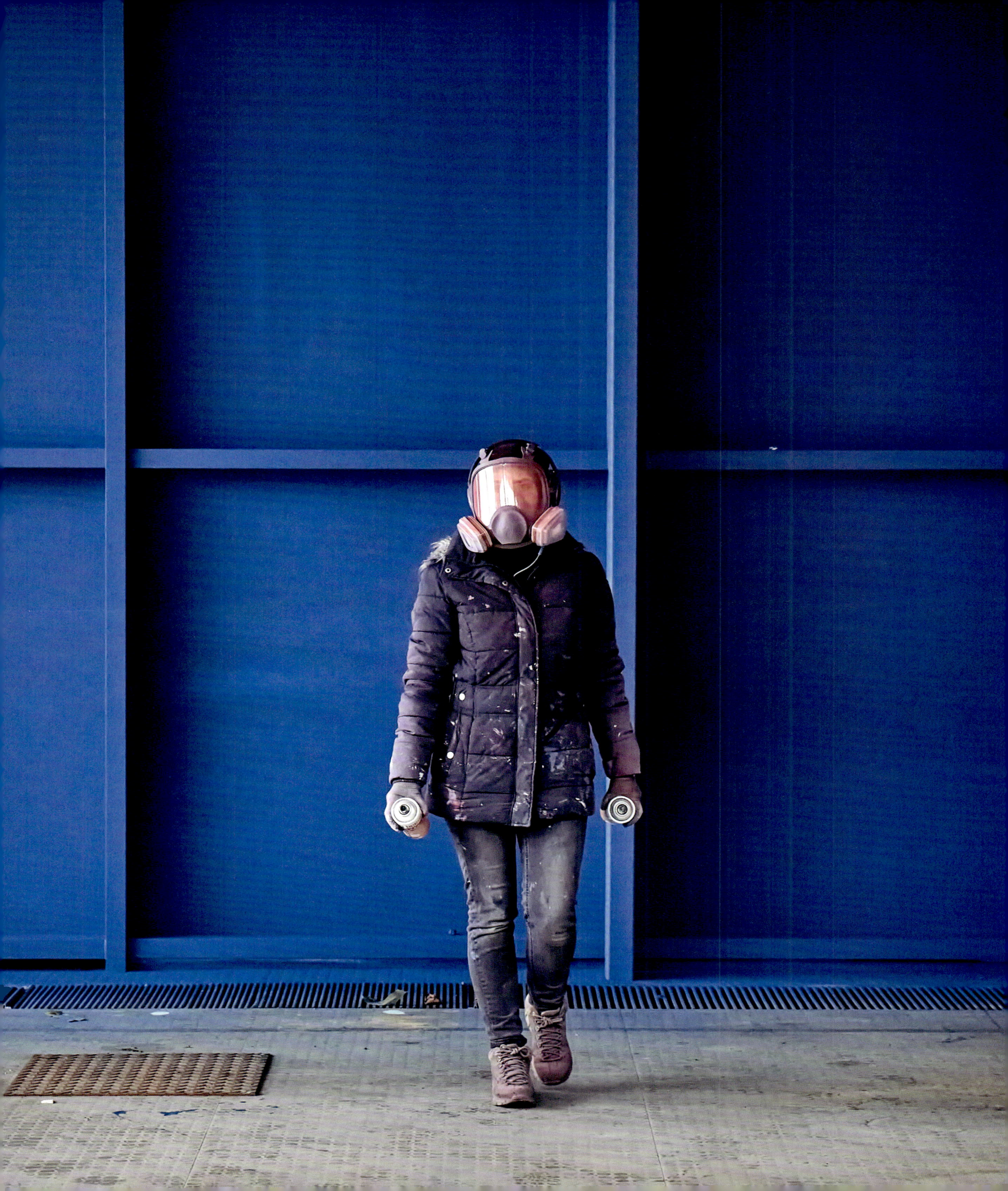

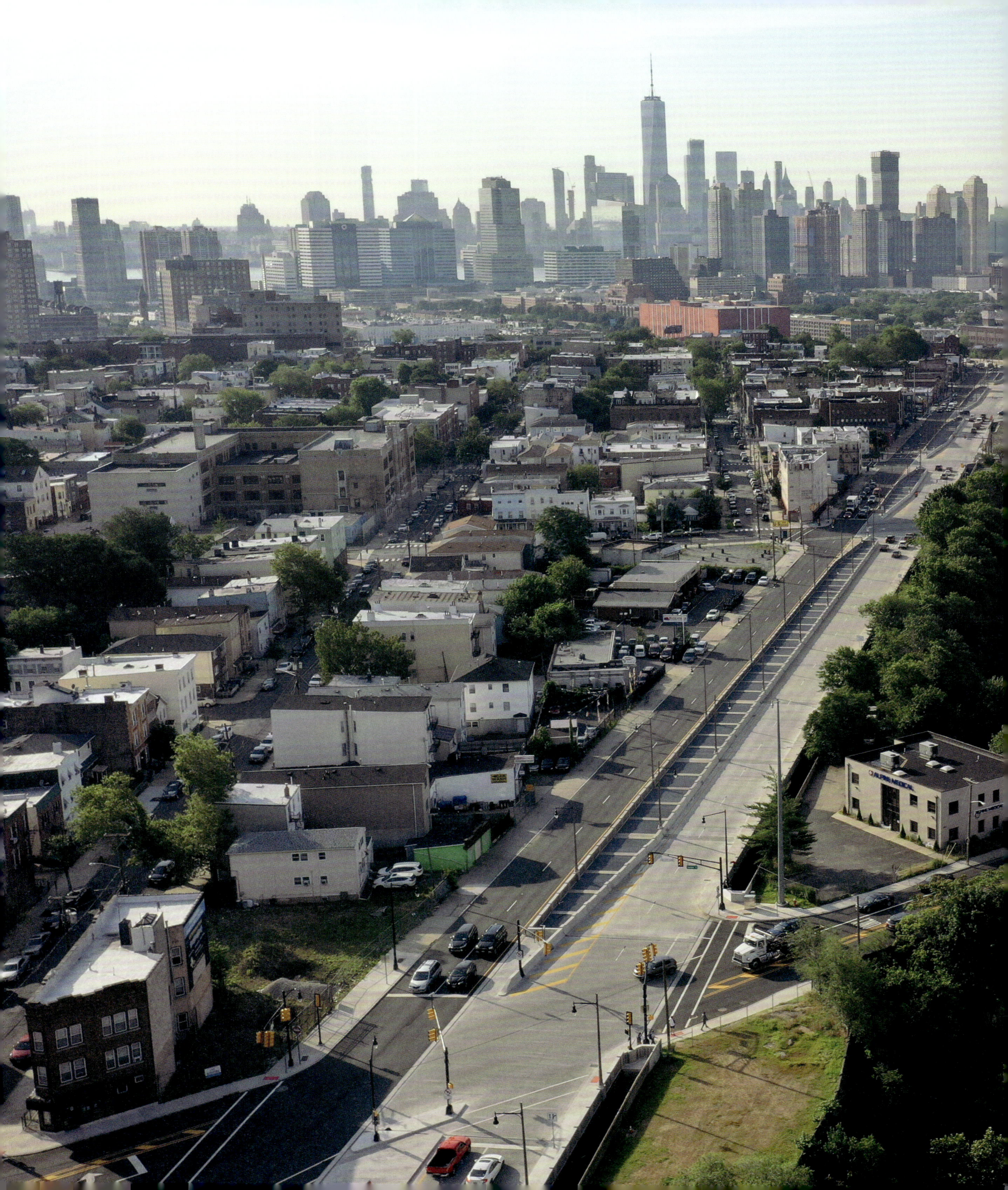

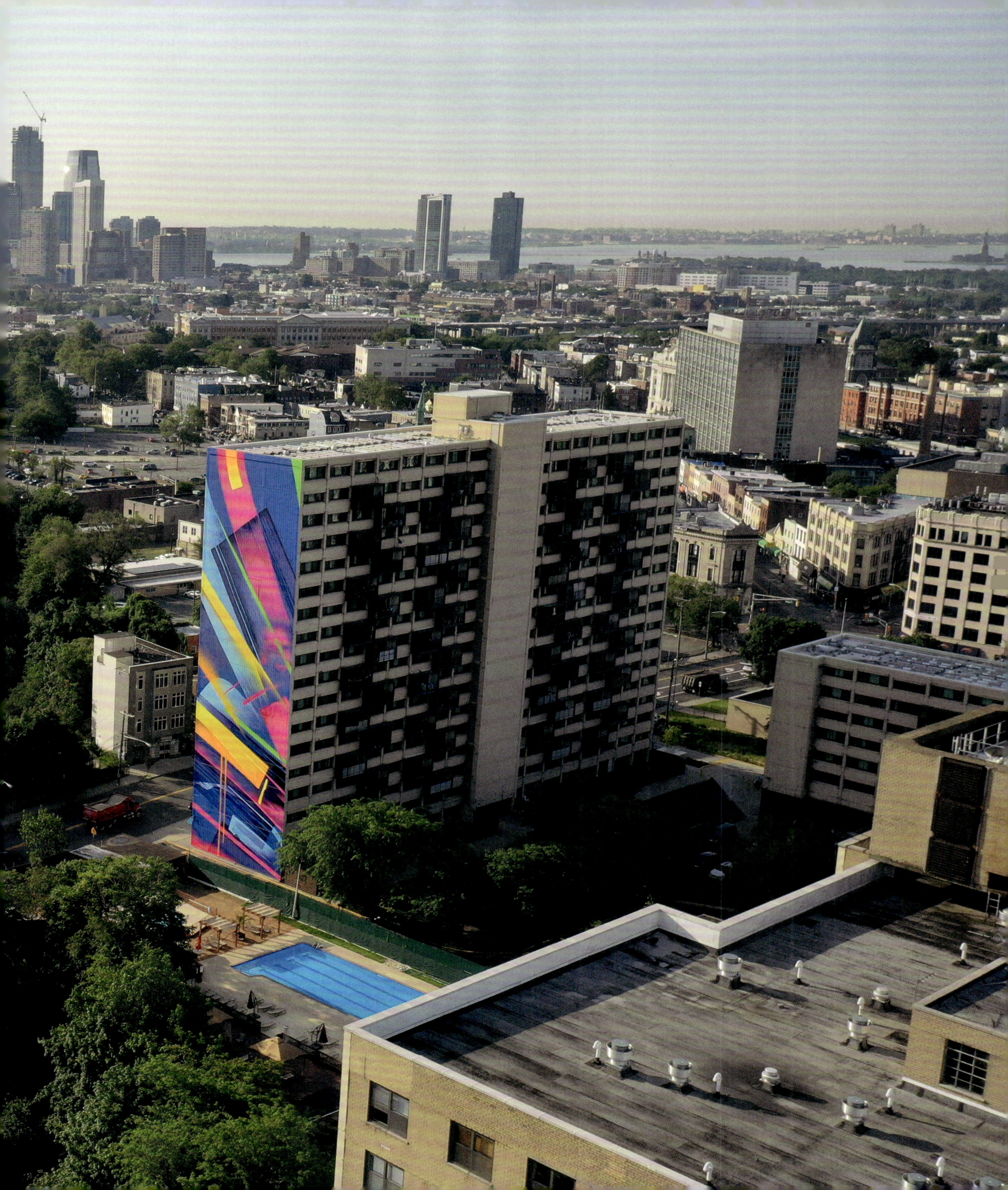

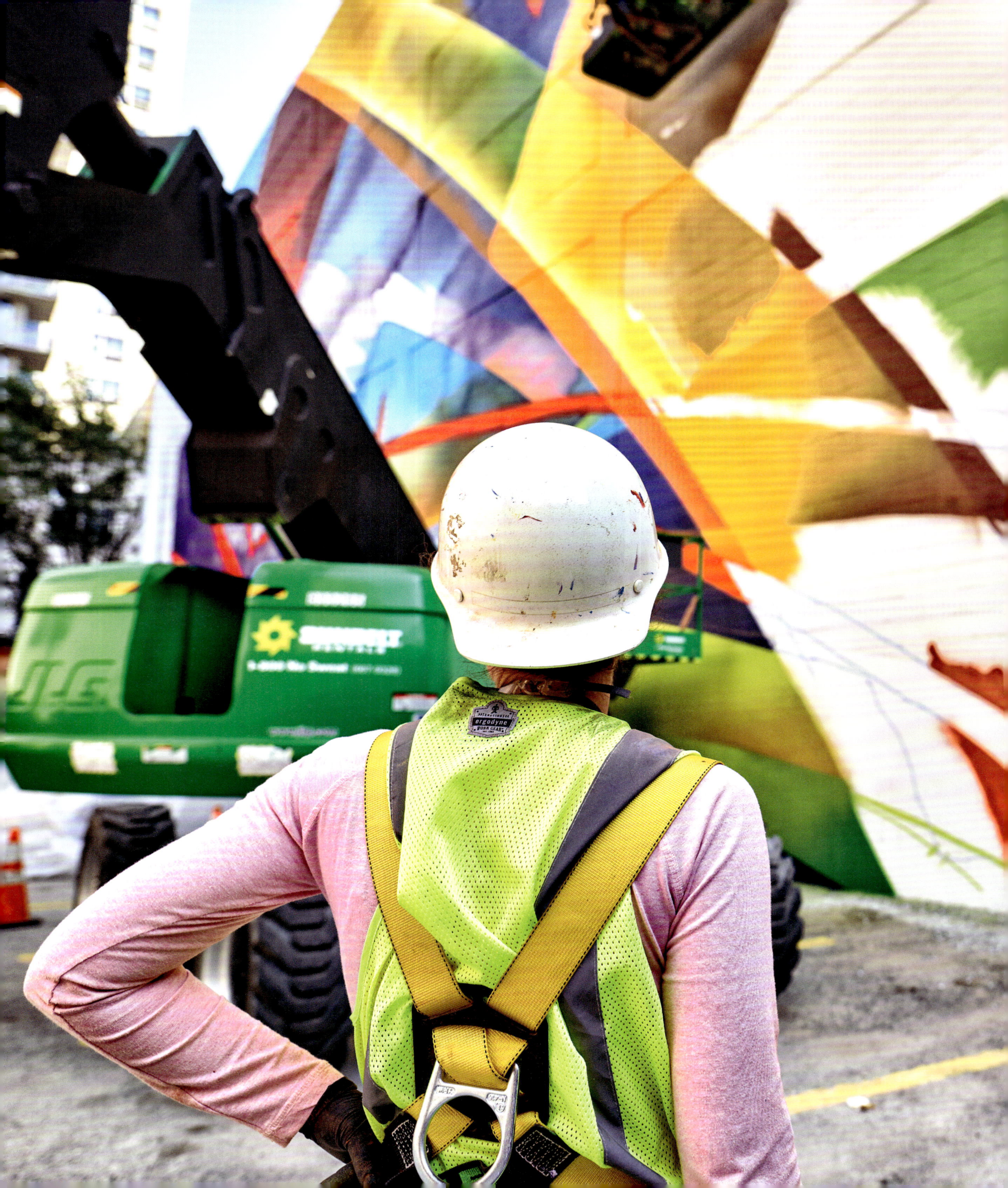
ergodyne

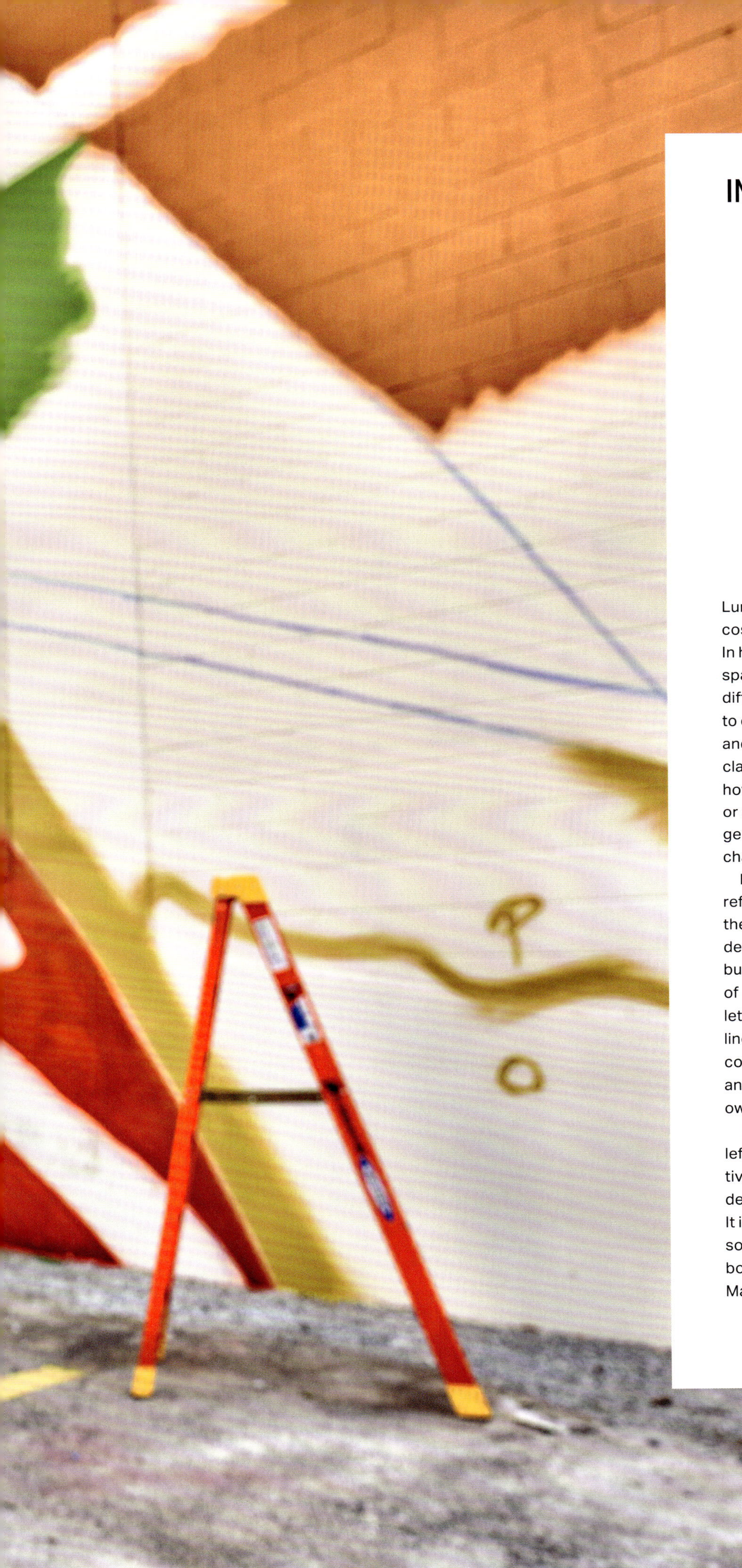

INTRODUCING MadC

Luminous colours, dynamic lines, translucent layers creating their own cosmos in space and time – these are the characteristics of MadC's work. In her choice of materials and references she acts freely and is unorthodox, spanning the divide between art genres. Her universe finds expression in different shapes and formats. From the classic canvas to graffiti-style writing to oversized wall paintings – all of these are closely related to one another, and together make up a body of work that successfully eludes clear-cut classification. While art historians and theorists are still arguing about how the worlds of graffiti, street art and contemporary visual arts should or should not be related to one another, MadC crosses the boundaries of genres and discourses, the rules of milieus and aesthetic conventions, with charming ease to create a distinctive work that exists in between.

Her works are created in the studio as well as on the street. The pieces reference each other but also stand for themselves. Initially situated in the genre of graffiti art, with its cultural and visual codes, MadC began to develop a visual language in the 2000s that preserved the essence of graffiti but refrained from elements such as fonts. From then on, using techniques of calligraphy, she has created swinging lines, only vaguely reminiscent of letters (which disappeared out of the works). The individual components, lines, shapes and layers are united in an overall composition, brimming with colours that, through transparent coats of paint, fan out into numerous layers and give a spatial depth to the abstract images. She creates art that sets its own standards and requires new approaches to interpretation.

MadC is now one of the most sought-after mural artists worldwide, and has left her works in numerous countries. This publication is the first retrospective in book form. It not only shows the work of today, but also the artistic development of a unique protagonist in the art world – or rather, art worlds. It is an attempt to trace MadC's path from 'writing' into abstraction and, in so doing, to convey the energy and dynamics of her work as it transcends boundaries. Thus, in this book, we will move not only through the story of MadC but also through the many art genres that she touches upon.

1. *The 1000 Wall*, Wabash Art Corridor, 1326 South Michigan Avenue, Chicago, USA, 2018

A WORLD OF GRAFFITI

The origins of the phenomenon known as graffiti go back over a decade before the birth of Claudia Walde. In the late 1960s, kids in Philadelphia and later in New York begin to inscribe themselves into the urban landscape by leaving their names as quick tags, wherever possible, or by spraying more sophisticated 'style writings' onto walls or 'rolling canvases' (trains). The artist's name took centre stage from the very beginning. With its legibility exhausted to the utmost, writing remained the key to generating an individual style and recognition factor.

Fame, as well as acknowledgement by other 'writers', is one of the most important incentives in the scene. It can be gained through aiming for omni-presence in the public space, and through having an original style within the prescribed set of rules. The rules originated in the 1970s and in large parts are still valid today. A common way to spray the pieces also established itself as early as the 1970s. Firstly, letters and other picture elements are indicated by outlines, then larger areas are coloured in. This is followed by individual designs, consisting of ornaments and effects, with lastly the contours as second outlines. The train is considered to be one of the most important carriers for graffiti, the most ambitious discipline of the art form. It was Lee Quiñones and his Fabulous 5 crew who sprayed the first 'running whole subway train' in 1976, and thus created one of the foundations for a visual culture that has been practised ever since.[1] In the 1970s and '80s in New York, the subway system offered unprecedented visibility, expanding the audience over several districts (fig. 2).

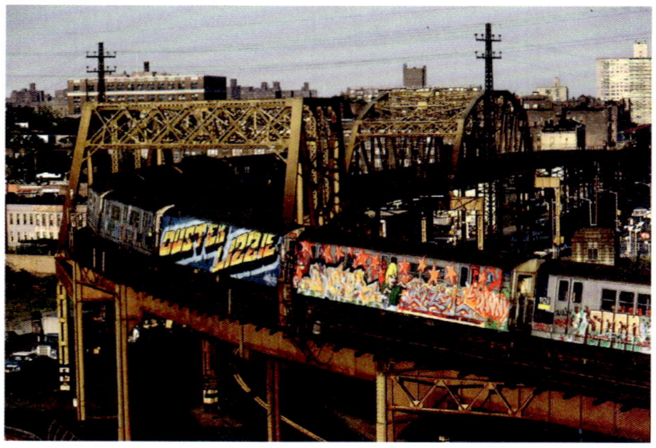

Graffiti was a phenomenon born out of youth culture, which quickly intermingled with hip hop, breakdance and skateboarding, but also evolved as an art form in its own right. It did not do this, however, as an inherent part of the art establishment, despite big overlaps, especially in 1980s New York where the scenes were in close proximity. With Neo-Expressionism at its zenith, young artists discovered on the streets an urgency of expression which was sought after in the visual arts. The legendary *Times Square Show*, held in a former massage parlour in 1980, brought graffiti artists together with the downtown art scene, allowing for publicity and exchange. For artists like Jean-Michel Basquiat, Keith Haring and Kenny Scharf, this was one of the first important exhibitions of their works which had been shaped by street influences and work in the studio alike. Numerous other exhibitions, gallery openings and institutional presentations followed. Thus, in the early 1980s, graffiti was briefly embraced by the art establishment, only to be dropped shortly afterwards. The languages, discourses and attitudes differed too much, after all. Artists like Basquiat, who managed to walk the tightrope between street and gallery, paved the way for future generations of artists – not least for MadC and her work between genres.

With the art and graffiti communities in New York drifting apart again, the city's anti-graffiti campaign was reinforced. Heavily illegalised, the exuberantly vibrant graffiti scene had to change a lot. This did not stop the movement, however. In 1989, the city's transport companies proudly announced that all sprayed trains in New York would be cleaned within 24 hours – but the graffiti movement was already in full swing worldwide.[2] From Berlin to London to São Paulo, graffiti artists (mostly teenagers) established local expressions of an international language in a very short time, claiming their cities for their creative outlet. The canon that had been shaped in New York, with its specific aesthetic and social rules, laid the foundation for the emerging international networks. As Lady Pink, one of the legends of the New York scene, aptly said: 'This isn't just random scribbling on the wall. We have protocol, we have ethics, we have a code of conduct, we have a hierarchy. It's a very well-constructed subculture.'[3]

Aside from pop-culture media (such as the famous music video *Rapture* by Blondie and films like *Wildstyle*, *Style Wars* and *Beat Street*), it was mainly books, passed on among friends from Paris to Bautzen, which enabled the worldwide dissemination of the content and aesthetic of the international graffiti style. The tireless photographic documentation by Martha Cooper (fig. 2) and Henry Chalfant, in particular, ensured that the ephemeral works had an afterlife even after their often rapid disappearance, immortalised in books such as the legendary *Subway Art* from 1984.

2. *Two whole cars painted by Duster and Lizzie running through South Bronx*, 1982.
Photograph. © Martha Cooper

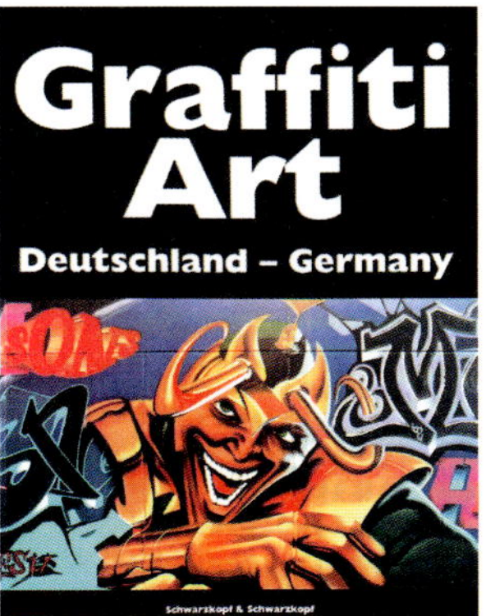

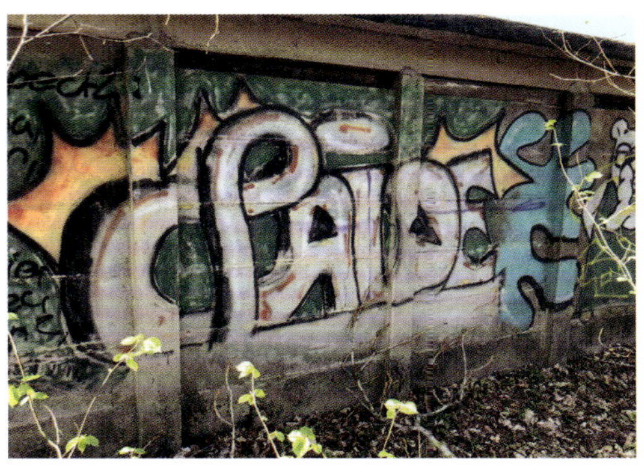

It was a book that brought the teenage Claudia Walde to graffiti art. She was 15 years old when a friend gave her *Graffiti Art: Deutschland – Germany* (fig. 3). In the mid-1990s, graffiti culture could already look back on a lively decade in Germany, with centres formed in Berlin, Dortmund and Munich. Tags and pieces had become part of everyday life in the metropolitan landscape of West Germany, and there were comprehensive exhibitions such as the show *Spray City: Graffiti in Berlin* (1994), organised by Berlin's Academy of Arts. The first whole train had already been sprayed by a few kids in a suburb of Munich in the 1980s, causing a sensation and encouraging imitators. The 1990s was an exciting time, as the scene became more established and internationally connected. Festivals and competitions, often in combination with hip hop jams, skating and breakdance contests, were increasingly being held in every major city, and legal walls were made available for graffiti writers. In Bautzen, however, where Claudia Walde spent her youth, the situation was rather different. Even though there was already an active scene in the GDR, Bautzen was far away from the nearest big city and, only a few years after the fall of the Berlin Wall, many movements took their time to arrive in the town, whose name is more associated with the Stasi prison than a thriving art scene.

In contrast to most people in the GDR, Claudia spent a childhood with relative freedom of movement. Her father worked as a seconded engineer for agricultural machinery in Addis Ababa, Ethiopia, and from the ages of three to eight Claudia only knew the GDR from visiting her grandparents. During the years in Addis Ababa, she enjoyed an international environment in a lively apartment building in the centre of the city. In 1988, however, the family had to leave the country because of the Eritrean War of Independence. At the time of their return to Bautzen, a sense of impending doom prevailed within the GDR. Shortly afterwards the GDR collapsed, creating a rift between two systems.

Claudia discovered art at a young age. In the early 1990s she took courses with local artists, and used her talent to work intensively with various techniques such as charcoal and watercolour. By the age of 15 she had already exhibited her drawings, worked for a sculptor in Dresden, and won an art prize. But the art scene that surrounded her was rather depressing; nobody could make a living from their artistic work. The high-class art world, on the other hand, appeared elitist and unreachable. For Claudia, the *Graffiti Art* book not only gave her a broader insight into the activities of the graffiti scene, but also offered her space for her own artistic work in which she could realise her ambitions. She read the book in one night, and was gripped by the world that opened up to her. The very next day, she began her first attempts. This was 1995. She sprayed her first piece – a still untrained lettering with a cute Ottifantin[4] in a green dress next to it – on the back wall of a garage with car spray paint from the hardware store (fig. 4). Her artist's name was found after some trial and error, as she was always called 'crazy Claudia' by her friends as a child. The moniker turned into MadC.

Joining the world of graffiti is hard work. In order to be able to deal with the conventions, and to survive in them, the artist has to acquire their own language, using an existing canon and following a specific system of rules. The graffiti scene appears to be liberal and anarchic to outsiders, but ultimately it has as many rules as the society that it counteracts subversively. The art historian Ilaria Hoppe explains this well:

> In its gesture [graffiti] is directed against the establishment, but internally it reproduces many of its norms. Surprisingly, this includes the evaluation of the styles and their writers. Within the scenes, a standard of assessment has emerged that has developed in art history since the Renaissance (Vasari) and solidified in the 19th century. It starts with the naming of the piece, which is derived from masterpiece, and goes as far as the distinction between *toys* and *kings*, i.e. between apprentice and master.[5]

In order to gain recognition within the scene, it is important to play by the rules – which were developed in an extremely male-dominated environment. MadC had already experienced the role of the outsider, both as a white child in Ethiopia and through the return to a foreign country. Thus, the Boys Club of graffiti was not a big deterrent and she did not expect recognition (which eventually she received anyway). In the early years, MadC acted like a tomboy and avoided any recognisable femininity in her works. She mostly worked alone and only revealed herself to a few people – she wanted her works to stand for themselves and not be linked to her persona. The colour pink did not appear at all yet. MadC experimented with her techniques mainly on places like bridge piers. While the Berlin senate set up a 'graffiti investigation group' in 1994 and graffiti writers feared increased persecution, in Bautzen the situation was different, with greater freedom to experiment. The scene here in the 1990s was smaller – along with one or two other sprayers, MadC was one of the pioneers of writing. Role models were not on-site but were to be found in magazines. Trains were stored in openly accessible depots; police prosecution was still in its infancy. MadC thrived in this freedom and left behind illegal pieces, but also early on she took advantage of opportunities to work on legal walls and upon invitation in order to develop further.

For her, it was less about quantitative tagging or quick throw-ups and more about complex style writings with artistic aspirations. The cultures of hip hop, breakdance and skateboarding, so much an integral part of graffiti, were only

3 (top left). *Graffiti Art: Deutschland-Germany*, vol. 1, ed. Oliver Schwarzkopf (Berlin: Schwarzkopf & Schwarzkopf, revised edition 2002)
4 (top right). MadC's very first graffiti, Germany, 1995

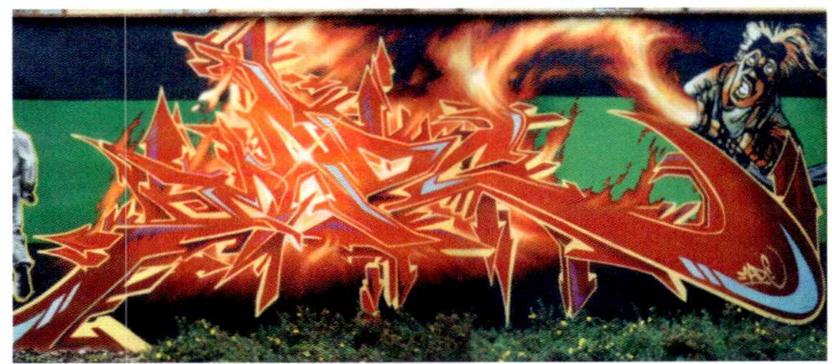

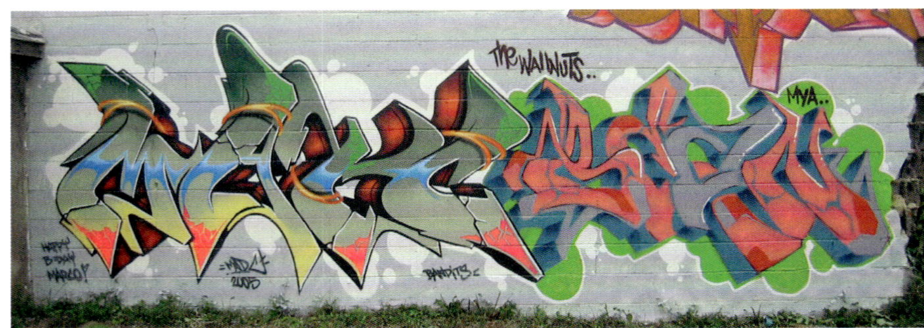

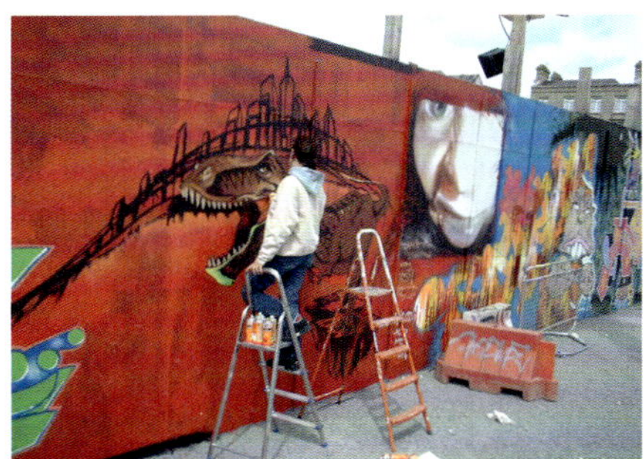

taken on to a limited extent by MadC. She did not use them as a distinguishing feature of her work – although some skateboarders belonged to her circle of friends. She looked for a connection to the nationwide scene early on, and established her network beyond the city by travelling to Dresden, Berlin and Munich, meeting other writers there. While she benefitted from the strong sense of community that is one of the unwritten rules of the scene, initially she remained a loner who earned her own fame. She only became a member of a crew in 2001, having met the Bandits founded by Slider at the *Urban Syndromes Jam* in Dresden. The chemistry was right, and joint projects followed. But in principle, MadC remained independent, maintaining a certain distance that enabled her to develop further without being restricted.

In the 1990s and early 2000s, MadC explored all the possibilities of graffiti, acquiring a rich repertoire and developing her own original style, characterised by dynamic wild-style pieces and detailed scenes, often with motifs from fantasy and science fiction. Dragons and dinosaurs appeared, as well as characters from films like *The Matrix*. Her works show meticulous accuracy; even the smallest detail is excellently crafted. The handling of artistically difficult elements such as fire, water, clouds or lightning is remarkable (**fig. 5**). This is how the figurative elements of her works often get a hyper-realistic touch.

Despite the importance that art had in her life, MadC decided not to study the visual arts and instead, in 2000, enrolled for design at the Burg Giebichenstein University of Art and Design in Halle. At that time in Germany, graffiti and street art were still largely viewed as vandalism in broader society, and perceived rather disparagingly in the art scene. The field of design, however, being closely aligned to everyday life, seemed for MadC to be the right path for her own development, and it also offered her the opportunity to stay creative for herself. Years later, she explained in an interview that she 'didn't dare to study art', because she had seen so many art graduates being forced to teach art in adult education and not having the time to make their own work.[6] As a graffiti artist, she was already known in the German scene at this time; her works were present in many cities. She received her first invitation to an international graffiti jam in Dublin (**fig. 6**) and travelled to numerous major European cities from Barcelona to Prague, where she left her increasingly elaborate works.

In 2005, MadC spent three months in New York on a scholarship, at the centre of the early graffiti movement, which had a lasting impact on her perception of art and her own self-image. There she quickly got to know artists who showed her new lifestyles that did not accept the boundaries drawn between art and design, between high and low, pop and concept, street and gallery, and who found their own way in between; for example, Shepard Farey, who a few years later would gain worldwide fame with his iconic poster for Barack Obama's election campaign. During these months, MadC was immersed in the New York street art and graffiti scene, meeting many of the old and new stars in person. Whereas some New York sprayers relied on the fame they achieved during the 1970s and '80s, she found an interesting and open-minded group of writers in the Wallnuts crew, roaming the streets with them and joining them as a crew member. Together they worked on pieces in New York and other cities in the US, such as Atlantic City (**fig. 7**).

In 5Pointz, the New York mecca for graffiti and street artists, MadC finally met Lady Pink – one of the few women among the early greats of the international graffiti scene and who is still very active today. When Lady Pink saw MadC at work, she invited her to a joint session on a wall in Queens (**figs. 8, 9**). MadC went on to produce several works on the walls of the legendary 5Points, which goes down in history not only because of the illustrious list of artists who worked there, but also because the pieces on the upper floors of the facade (which had remained untouched sanctuaries since the 1990s), would prove to be of great importance for the status of the art movement (**fig. 10**). After the owner of the site had been supportive of the artists for a long time and made the place available for their activities, he decided to sell the property to investors and hastily had the works whitewashed overnight without prior notice. Thereupon he lost a legal dispute against the artists, whose works now legally belonged to the category of fine art, according to the verdict. This was an important step in the recognition of murals as art, even if they are attached to someone else's property. Ultimately, however, 5Pointz was completely demolished a few years later.

After her time in New York, MadC completed her studies in Halle by exploring the book as a medium for herself. Compiling what was later published as *Sticker City: Paper Graffiti Art*, she looked at a topic that – similar to graffiti in the past – had spread rapidly across the globe within a few years and represented a separate genre of public art. The medium was not painting anymore, but stickers, paper and posters, mostly made by hand and attached (and above all glued) to walls, telephone boxes, street signs and other objects of public space. In *Sticker City*, she put into a historical context a trend that she had observed on her travels in the world's metropolises, and she documented the

5 (top left). Bautzen, Germany, 2002
6 (bottom left). *Out to Burn Jam*, Dublin, Ireland, 2003
7 (top right). Atlantic City, MadC and Been3, USA, 2005

8 (opposite, top left). Meeting Lady Pink in New York City, USA, 2005
9 (opposite, top middle). Cycle, Daze, Dalek, Lady Pink, Sane, Shiro and MadC, Queens, New York City, 2005
10 (opposite, top right). 5Pointz, New York City, USA, 2005
11 (opposite, bottom). Koura, Lebanon, December 2006

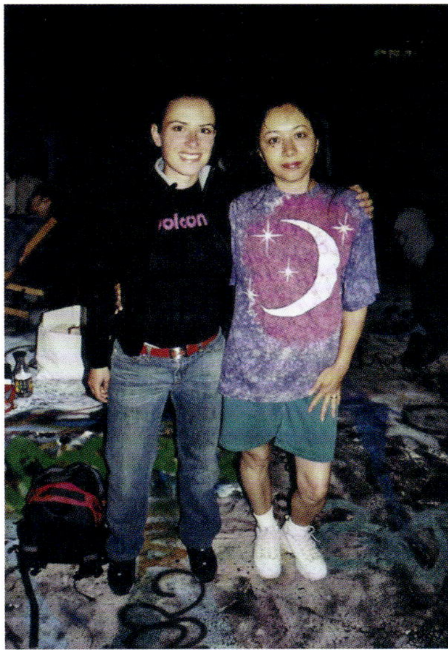

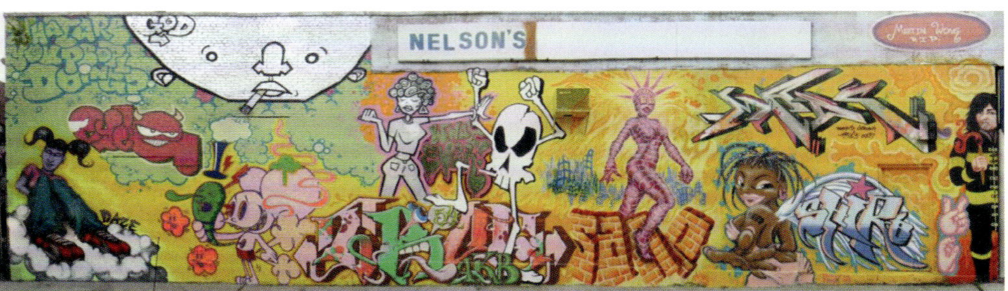

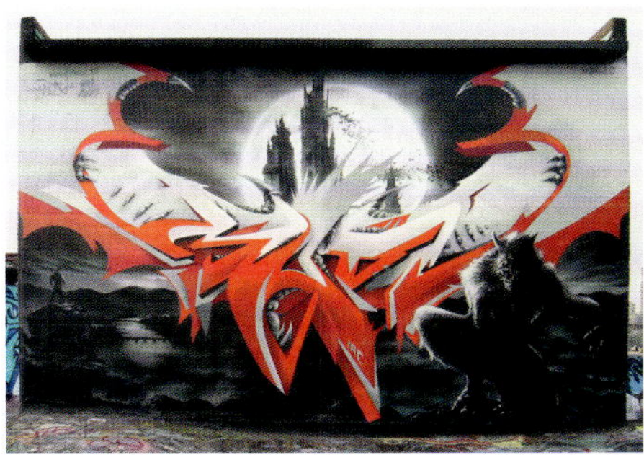

works and techniques of important protagonists like Shepard Farey, Swoon or Invader. This was one of the first overviews written on the phenomenon, and it was later published in large numbers by Thames & Hudson.

During a postgraduate course at the famous Central Saint Martins College of Art and Design in London, MadC continued her travels and received an increasing number of invitations to places that expanded her terrain of activity – and also her imagination, such as Lebanon. In 2006 she received an invitation from the Goethe-Institut to give workshops for students at the University of Tripoli and to develop works for public spaces together, although the country was still in the midst of war at that time. The mood within the country was tense, and the power that words have in the public space was experienced by MadC through the sceptical reactions that her work on the street initially triggered (fig. 11). Writings on a wall were seen as having much more of a political nature, staking out territories and marking affiliations. The idea in American graffiti that the letters only stand for an – albeit highly aesthetic – 'I was here' without conveying a directed political message is deeply rooted in Western youth culture, and is by no means a universal world language. Experiences like these were also part of the development of her own artistic self-understanding.

Back in London, MadC finished her studies and made a far-reaching decision. Before she graduated, she had received an offer to join a major London agency as an art director – but she declined, in order to fully devote herself to her own art. Encouraged by her experiences in the big urban centres of the world, she decided to return to Germany, rent a studio, and take a waitress job in order to survive financially. Years of struggle to find her own expression and path as an artist followed, driven by the search for something new, something her own, something that was beyond the set rules.

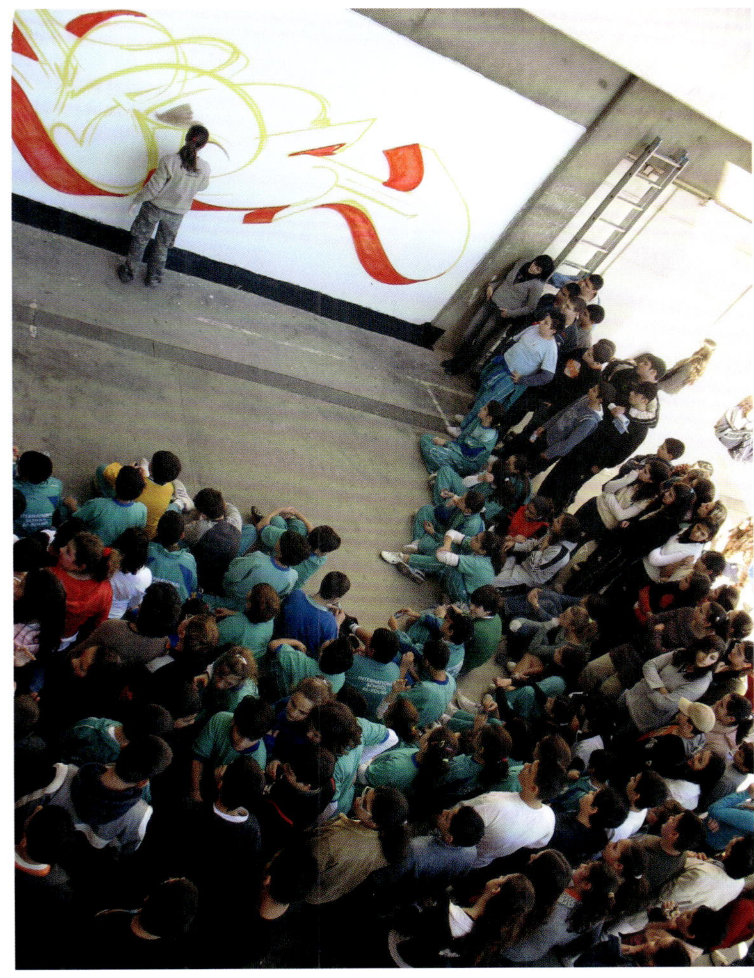

1 Deitch, Jeffrey, 'Art In The Streets', in Jeffrey Deitch, Roger Gastman, Aaron Rose (eds), *Art in the Streets*, exh. cat., New York and Los Angeles: Museum of Contemporary Art 2011, pp. 10–18, here p. 11.
2 Ibid., p. 13.
3 Lady Pink cited in Cascone, Sarah, '"I Was a Feminist and I Didn't Know It": How Lady Pink Made a Space for Herself in the Boys Club of New York's Graffiti Scene', *Artnet*, 18 July 2019, https://news.artnet.com/exhibitions/lady-pink-interview-1602208 (accessed 11 February 2021).
4 Ottifant is a cartoon character in the shape of an elephant by the German comedian Otto Waalkes. It fuses the words 'Otto' and 'Elefant'. Ottifantin means that it was a female character.
5 Hoppe, Ilaria, 'Konservativ, maskilistisch und reaktionär: Sind Graffiti wirklich tot?', in Jo Preußler, Oliver Kuhnert (eds), *The Death of Graffiti*, Berlin: Possible Books 2017, pp. 105–112, here p. 108. Extract translated by Eva Ruschkowski.
6 MadC cited in Haeming, Anne: 'Ich darf das!', *Spiegel*, 3 April 2014, https://www.spiegel.de/karriere/graffiti-spruehen-als-job-kuenstlerin-madc-erzaehlt-von-ihrem-beruf-a-962185.html (accessed 14 March 2021). Extract translated by Eva Ruschkowski.

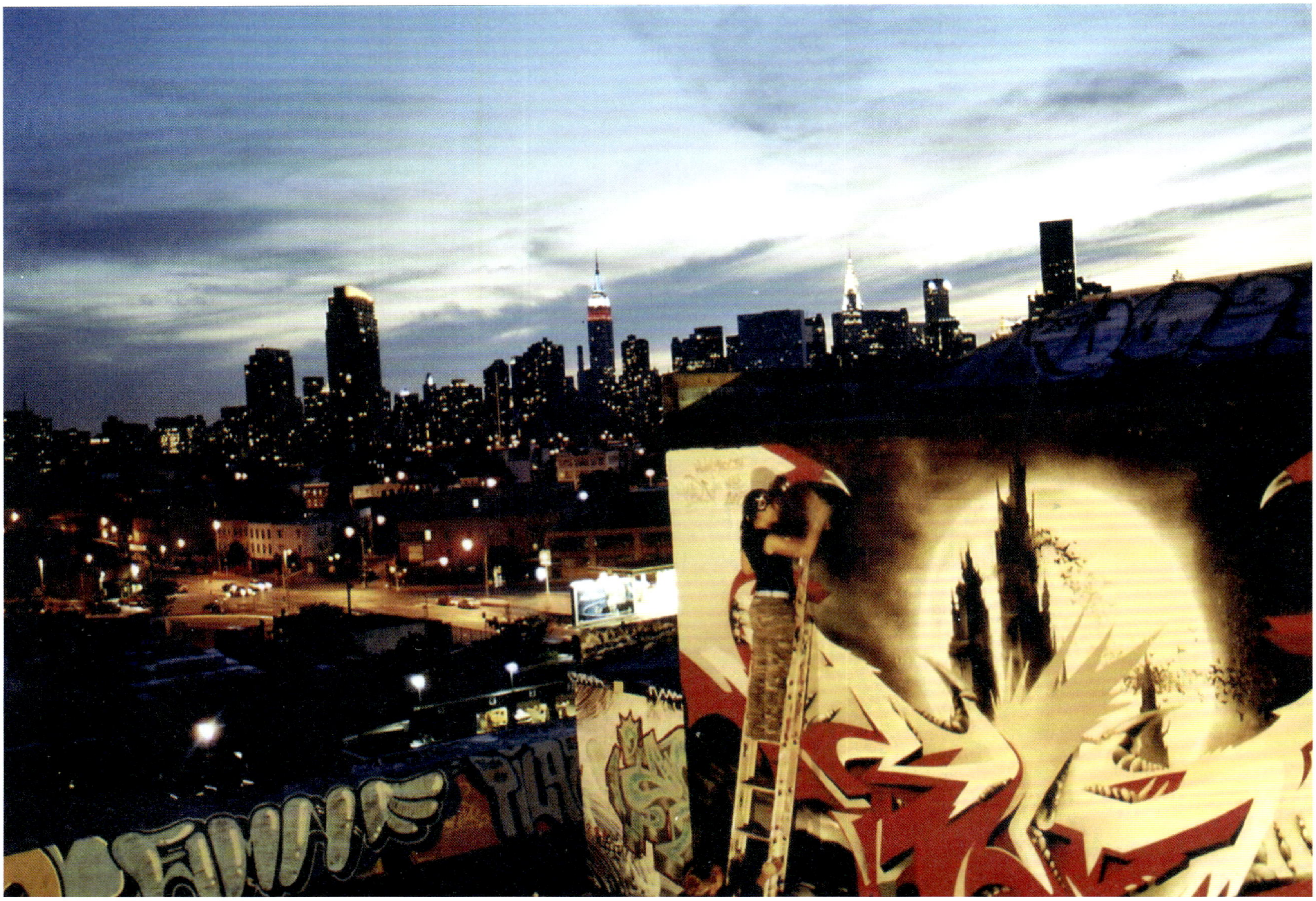

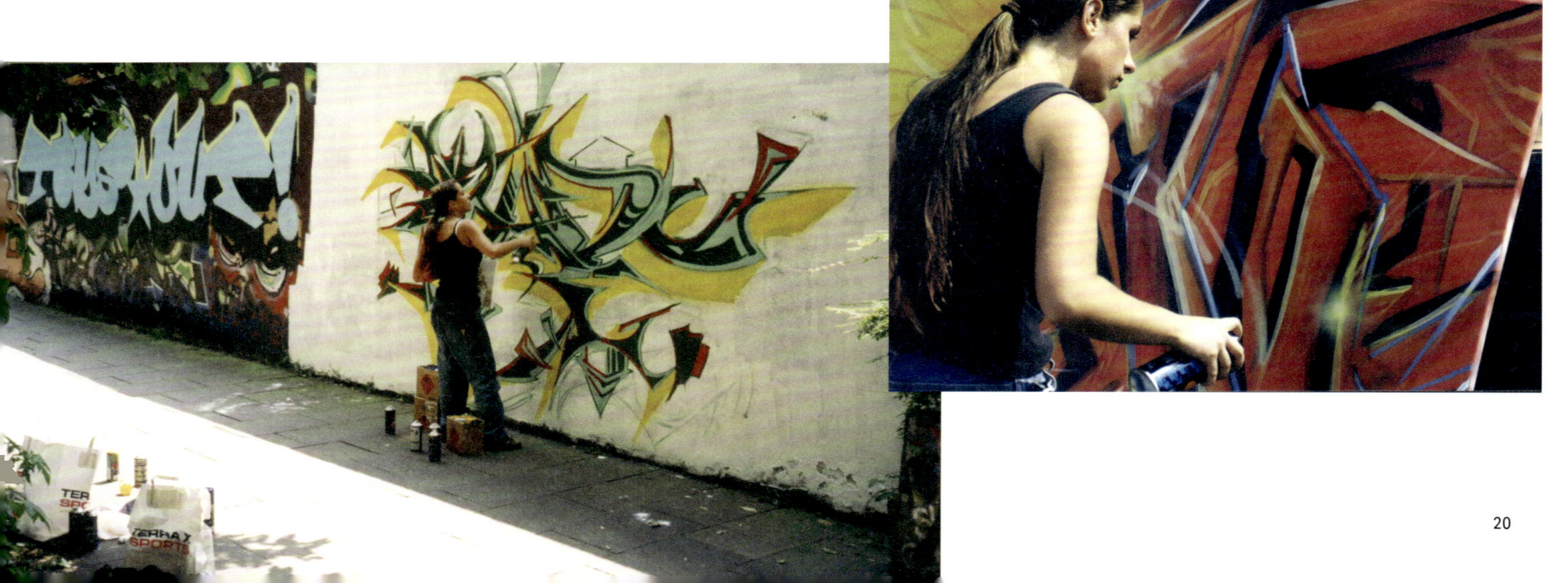

12 (opposite, top). 5Pointz, New York City, USA, 2005
13 (opposite, bottom left). Munich, Germany, 1999
14 (opposite, bottom right). MadC painting a canvas in Bautzen, Germany, 2000
15 (top right). Bautzen, Germany, 2004
16a–c (bottom, top row). Grossenhain, Germany, 2000; Mauerpark, Berlin, Germany, 2001; Neukirch, Germany, 2001
16d–f (middle row). Vienna, Austria, 2003; MadC and Mogi, Braunschweig, Germany, 2004; Halle, Germany, 2006
16g–i (bottom row). Halle, Germany, 2007; London, UK, 2007; MadC and Karl Toon, Leipzig, Germany, 2007

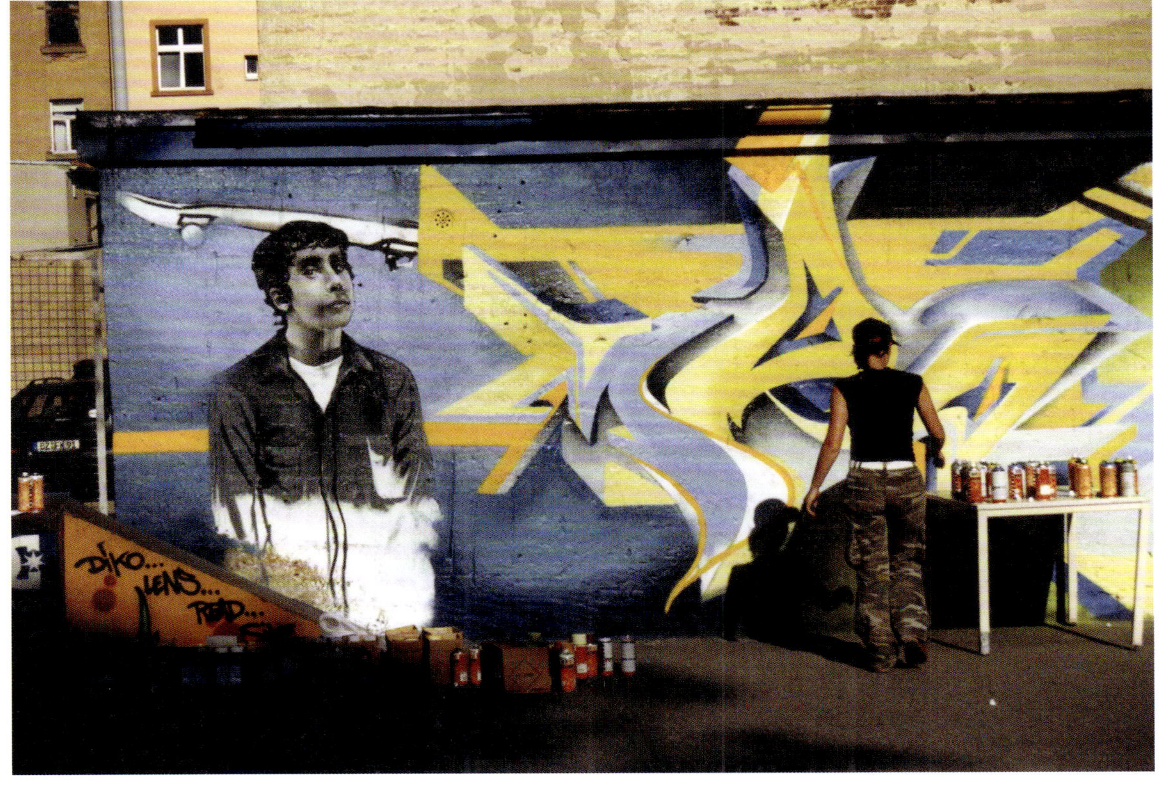

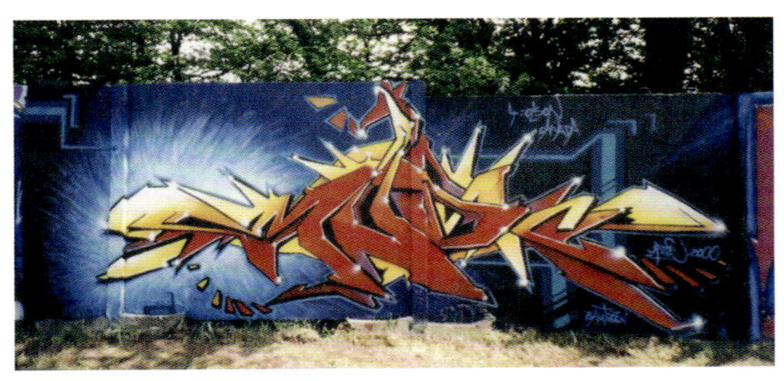

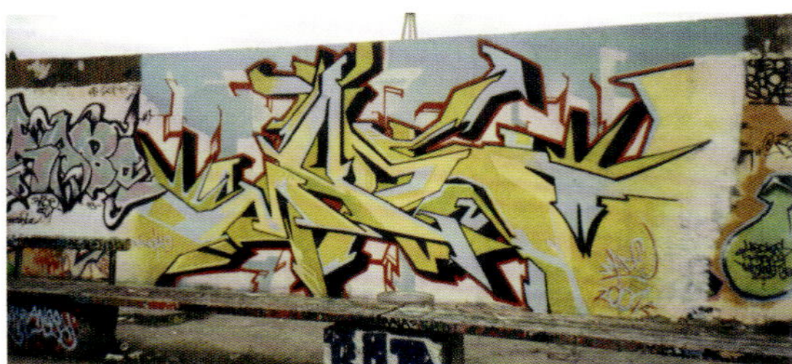

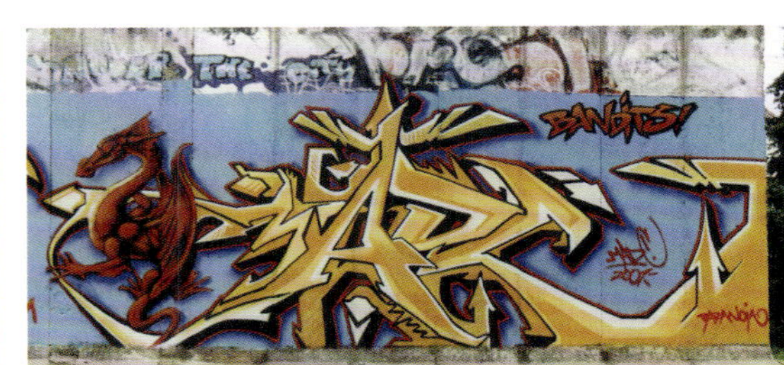

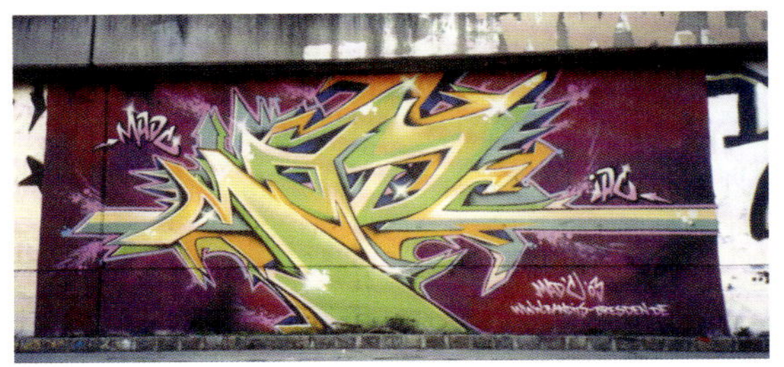

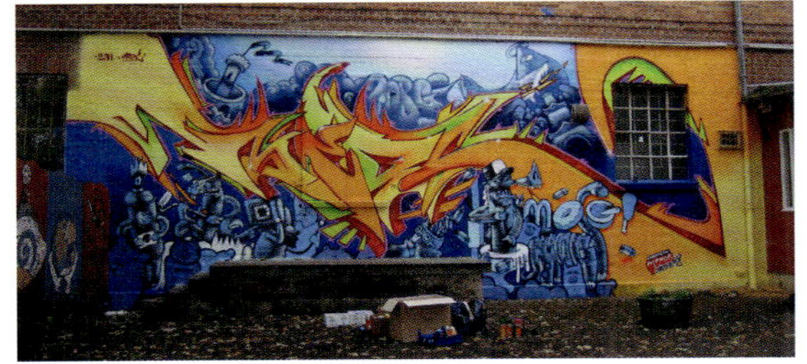

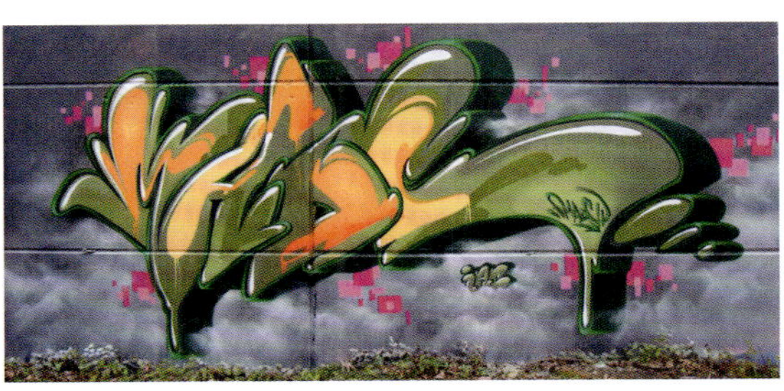

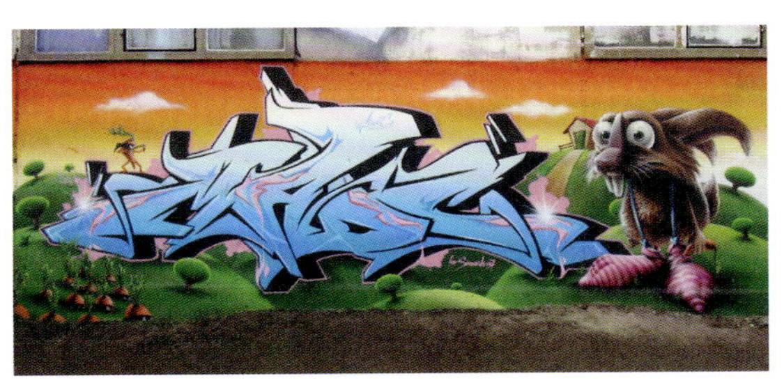

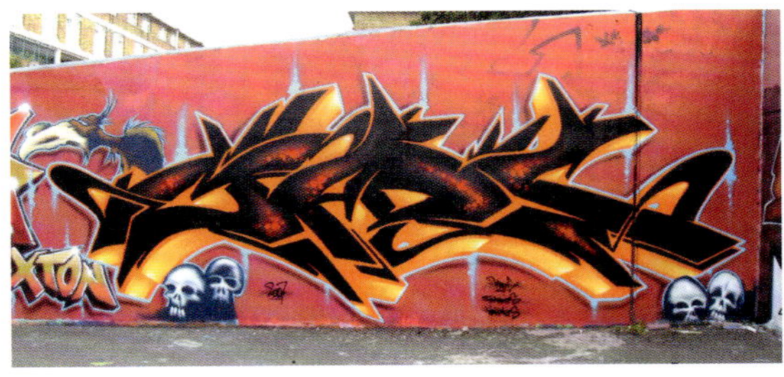

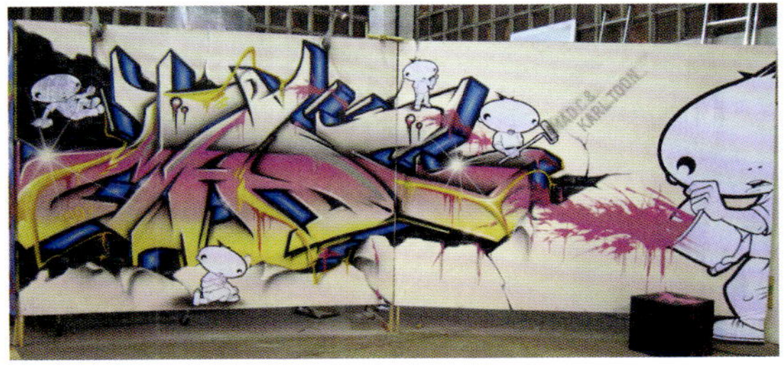

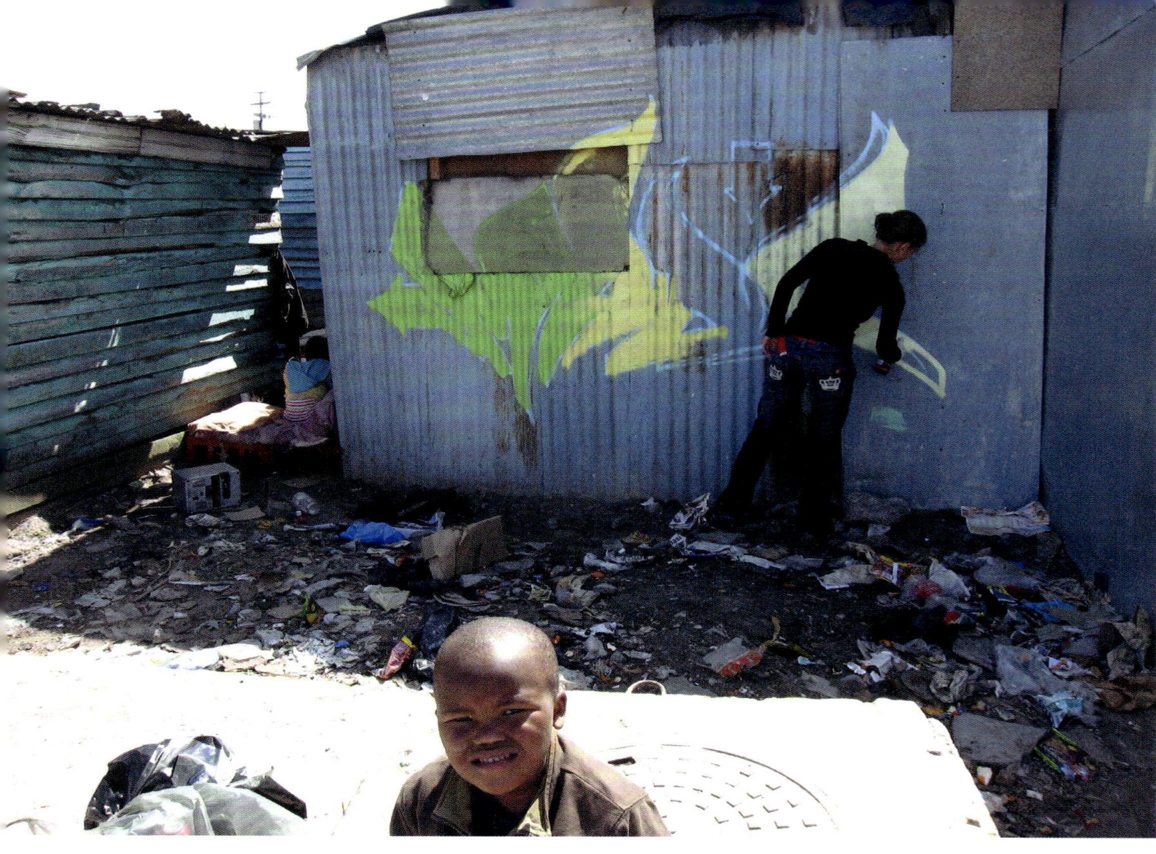

17 (top left and middle). South Africa, 2008
18 (bottom left). Lebanon, 2006
19 (opposite, top left). Lebanon, 2006
20 (opposite, top right and bottom). Cape Town, South Africa, 2008

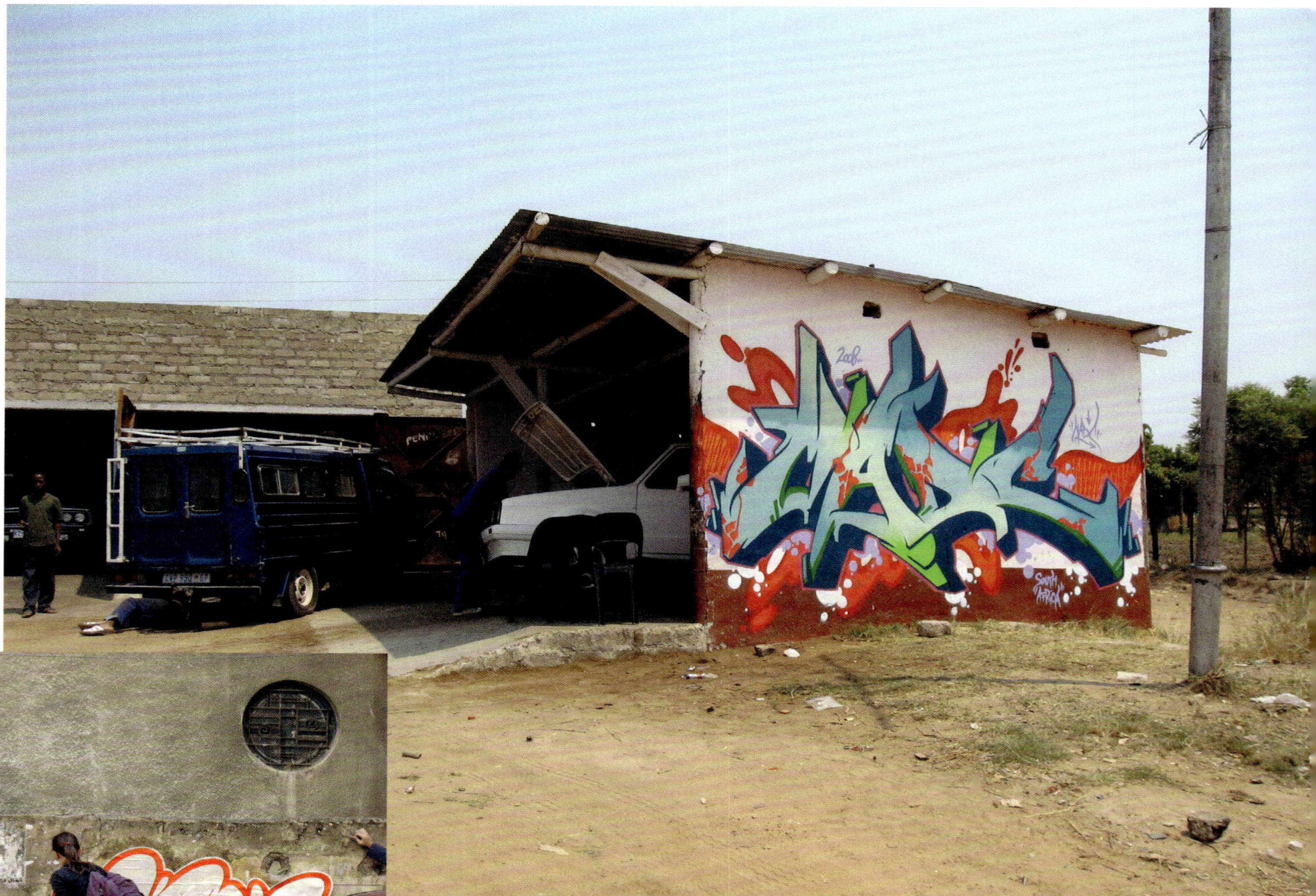

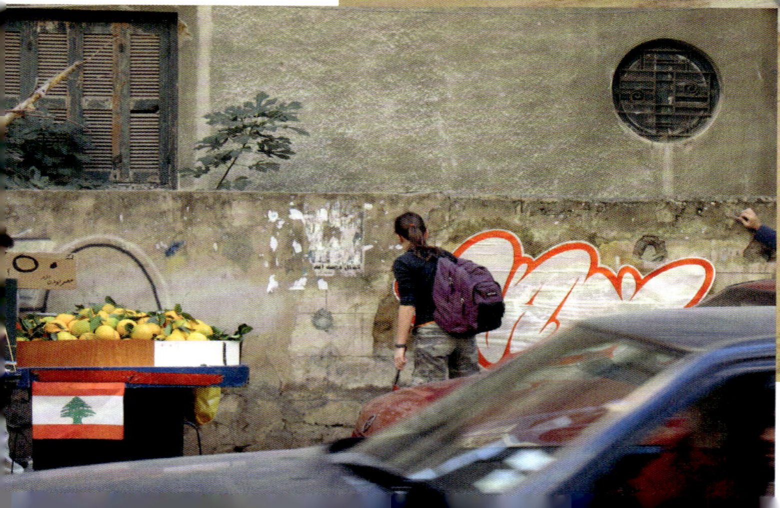

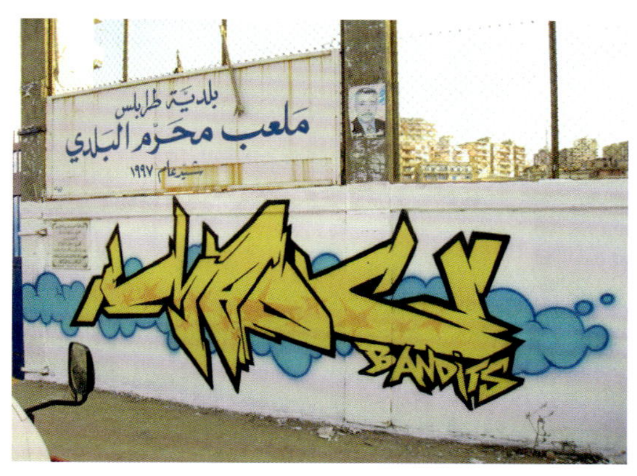
بلدية طرابلس
ملعب محرم البلدي
شيد عام ١٩٩٧
BANDITS

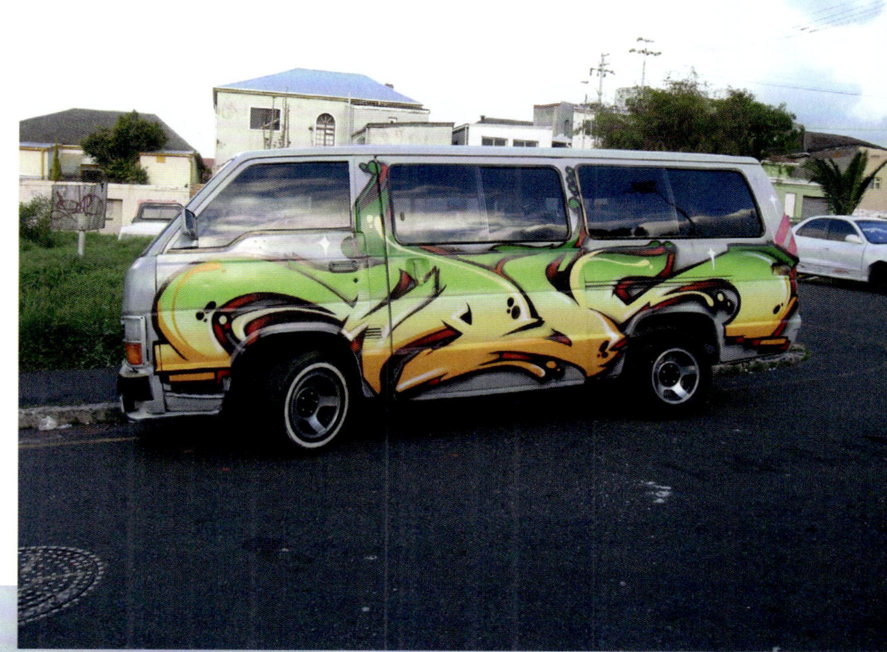

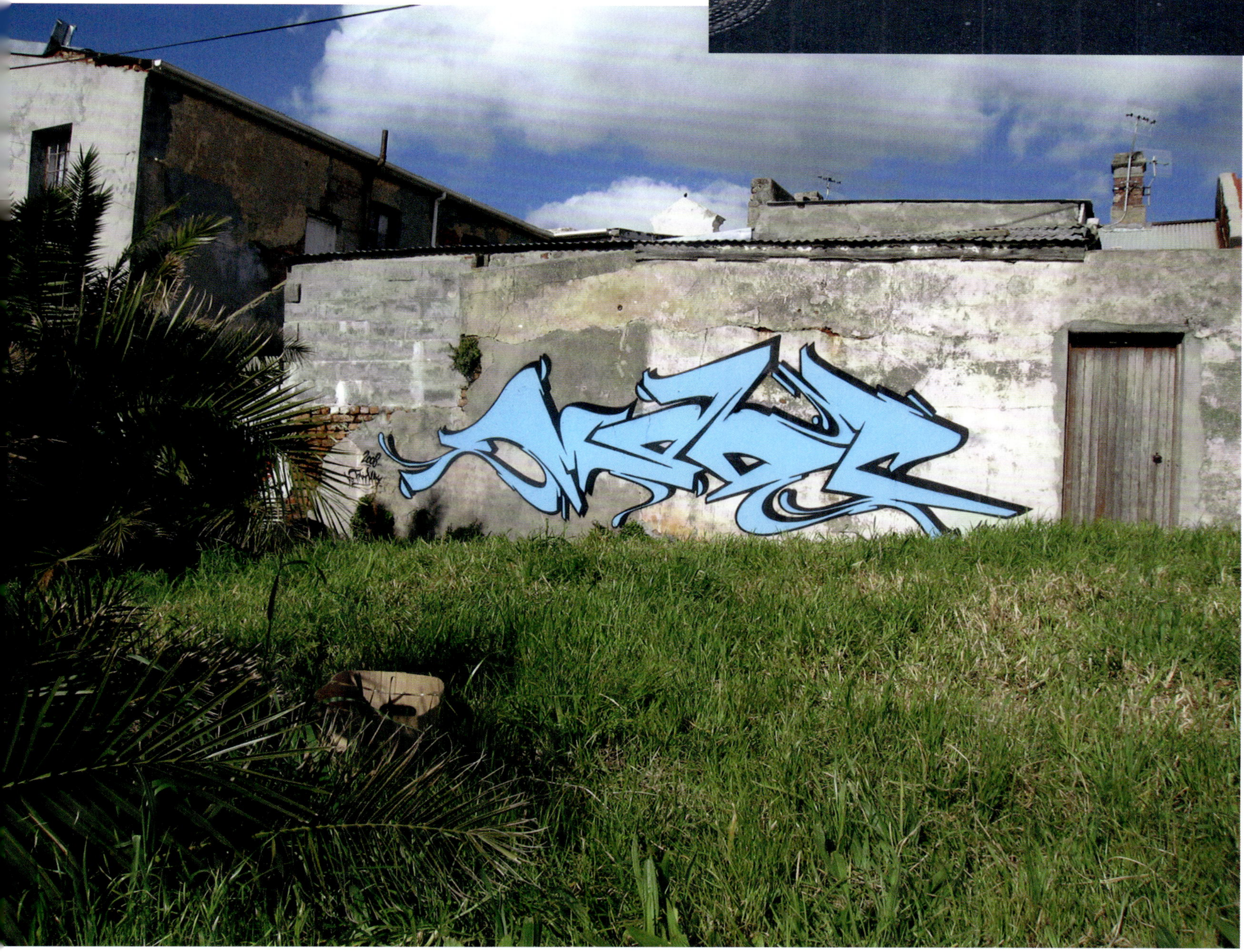

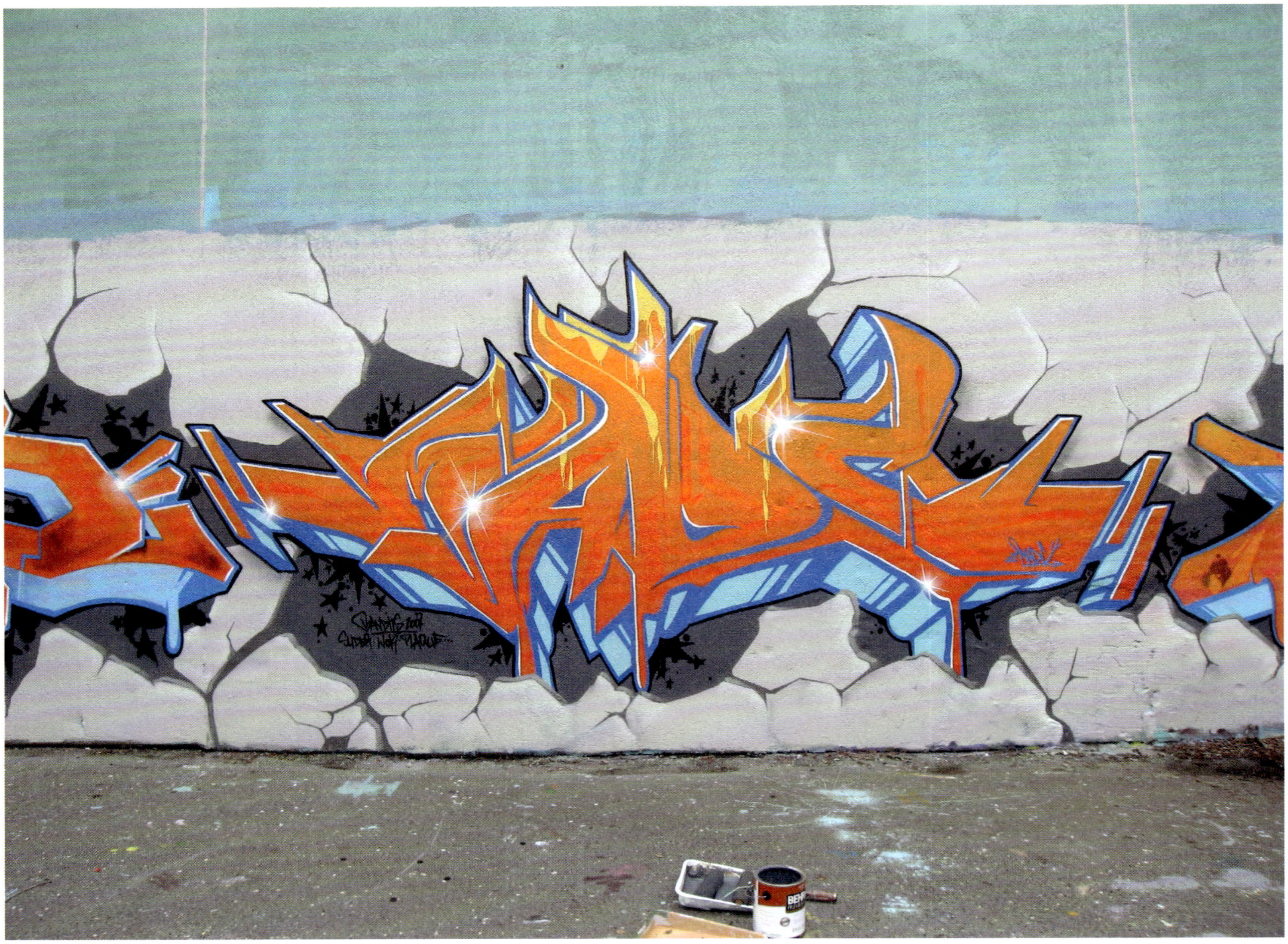

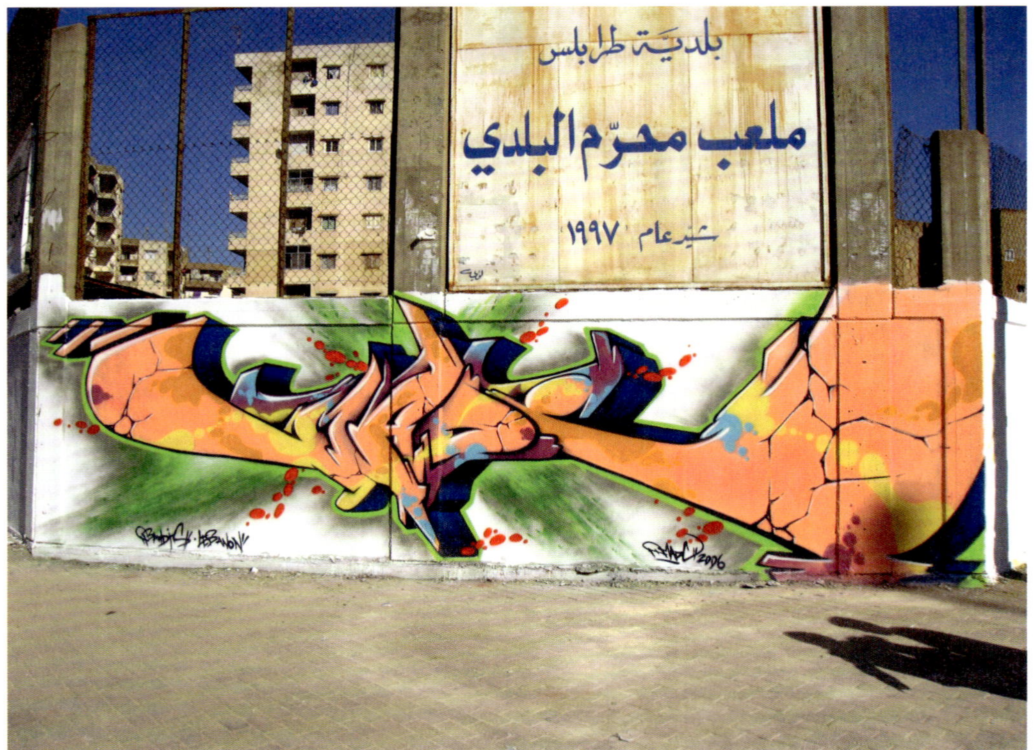

21 (top). New Jersey, USA, 2007
22 (bottom). Lebanon, 2006
23 (opposite, top left). Leipzig, Germany, 2009
24 (opposite, top right). Poland, 2008
25 (opposite, middle). *Heart* by MadC, Leipzig, Germany, 2008
26 (opposite, bottom). MadC and Swet, Copenhagen, Denmark, 2007

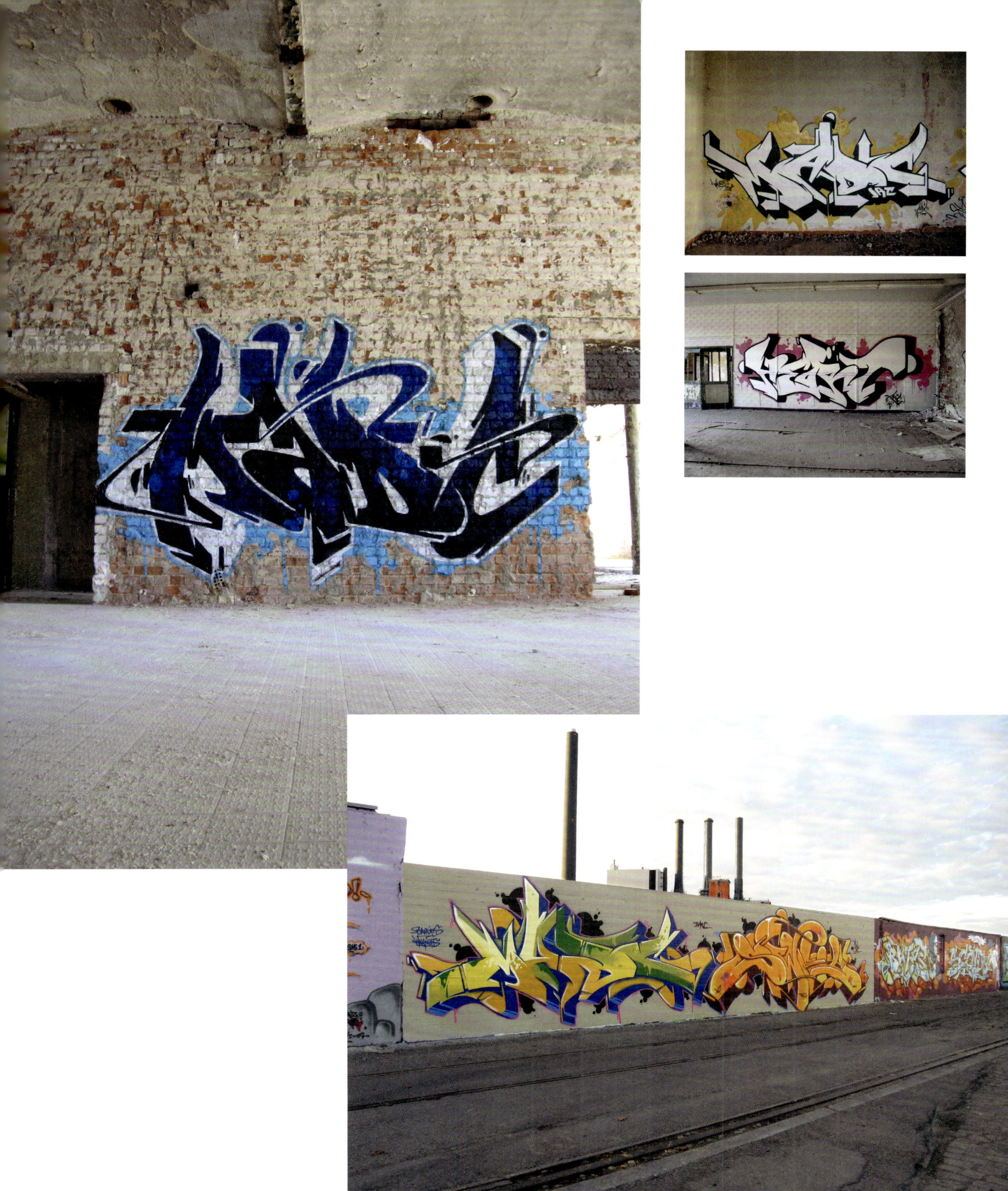

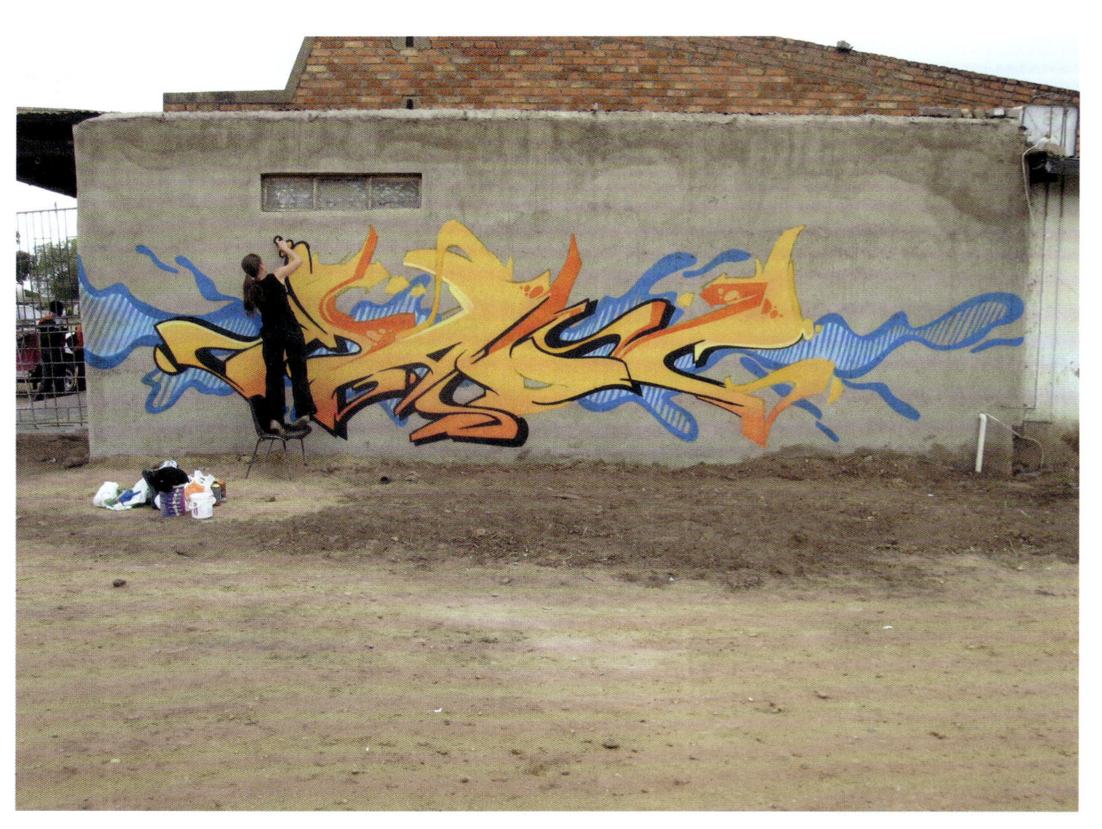

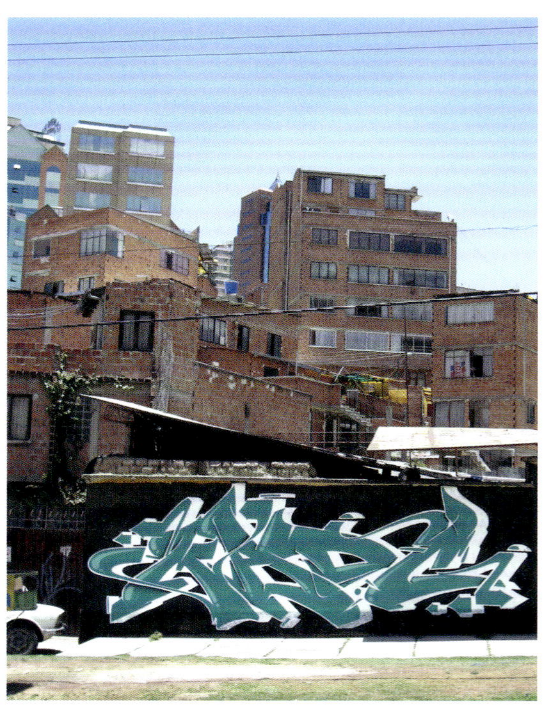

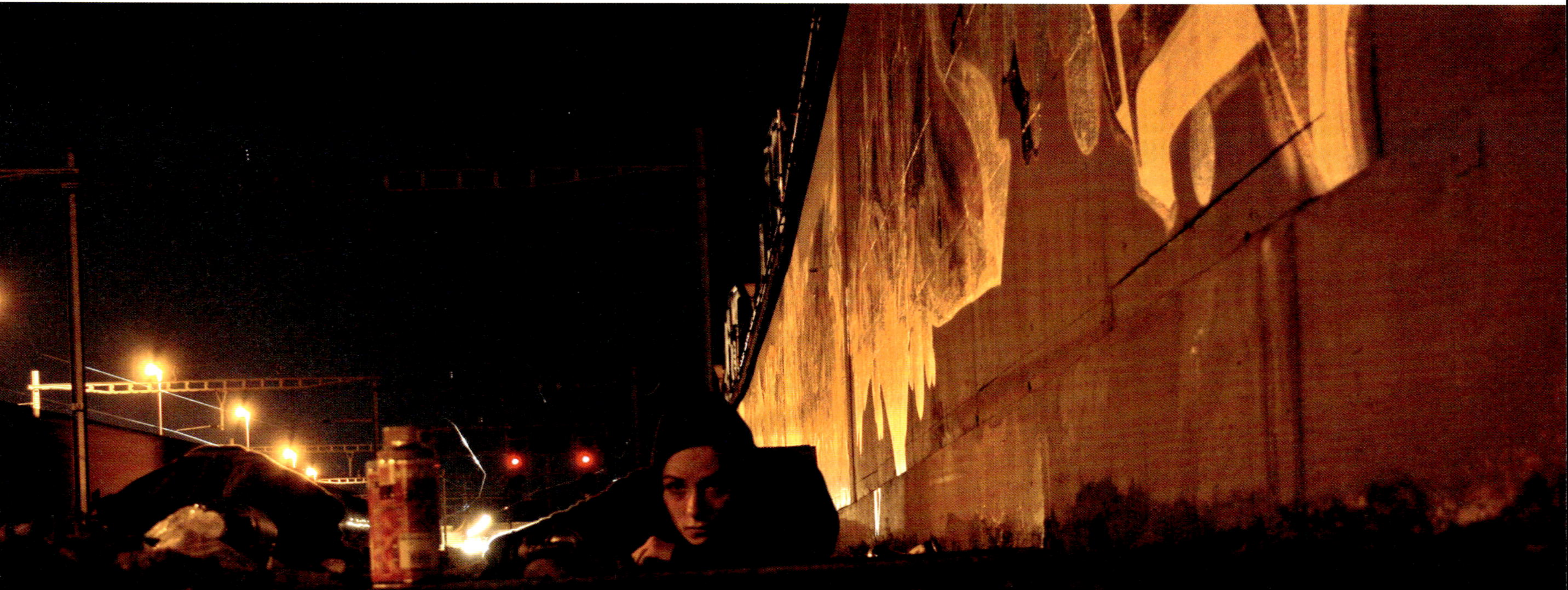

27 (opposite, top left). Tzaneen, South Africa, 2008
28 (opposite, top right). La Paz, Bolivia, 2009
29 (opposite, bottom). Photo taken by Dare in Basel, 2008
30 (top and left). La Paz, Bolivia, 2009
31 (bottom right). Halle, Germany, 2008

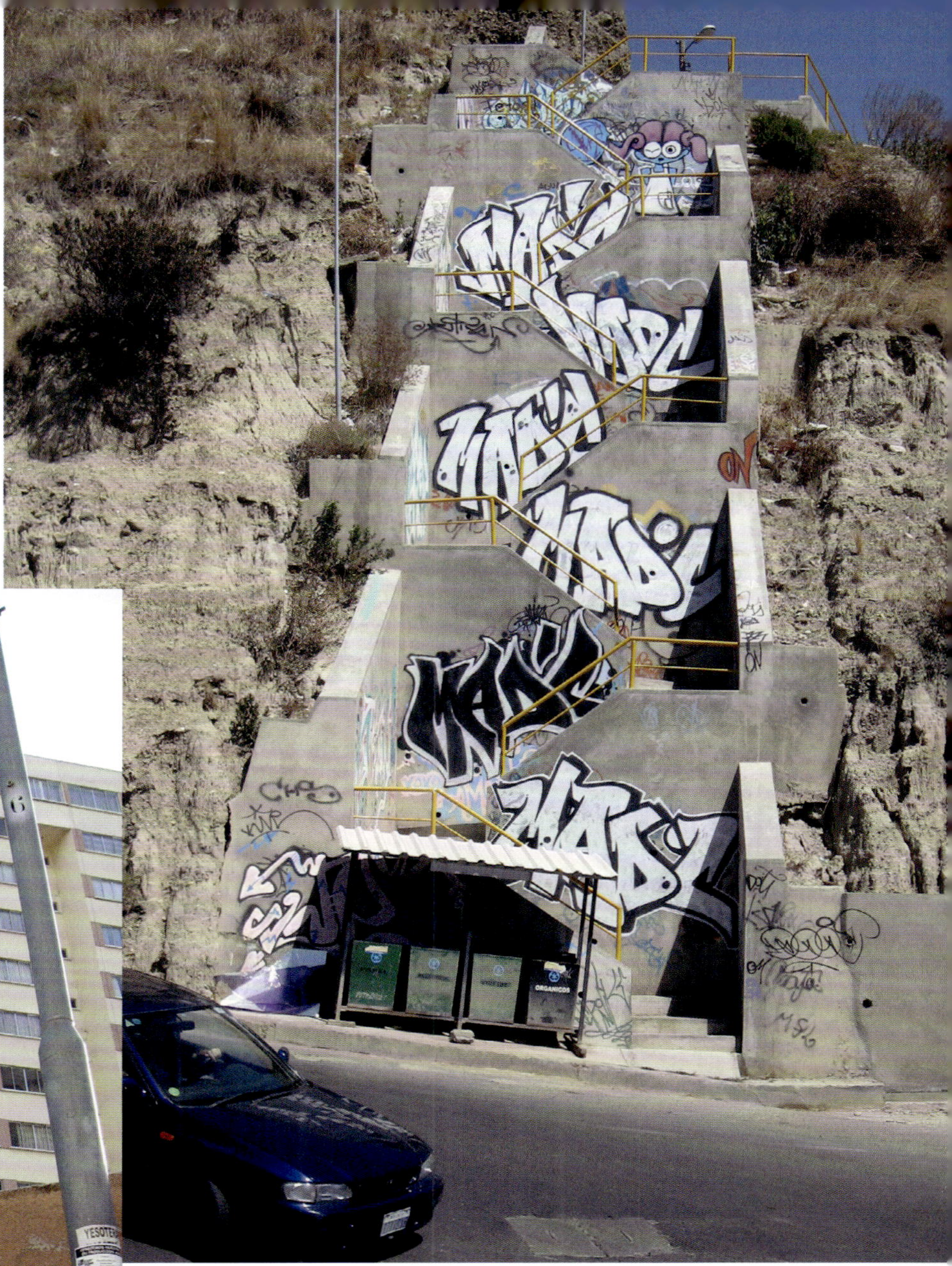

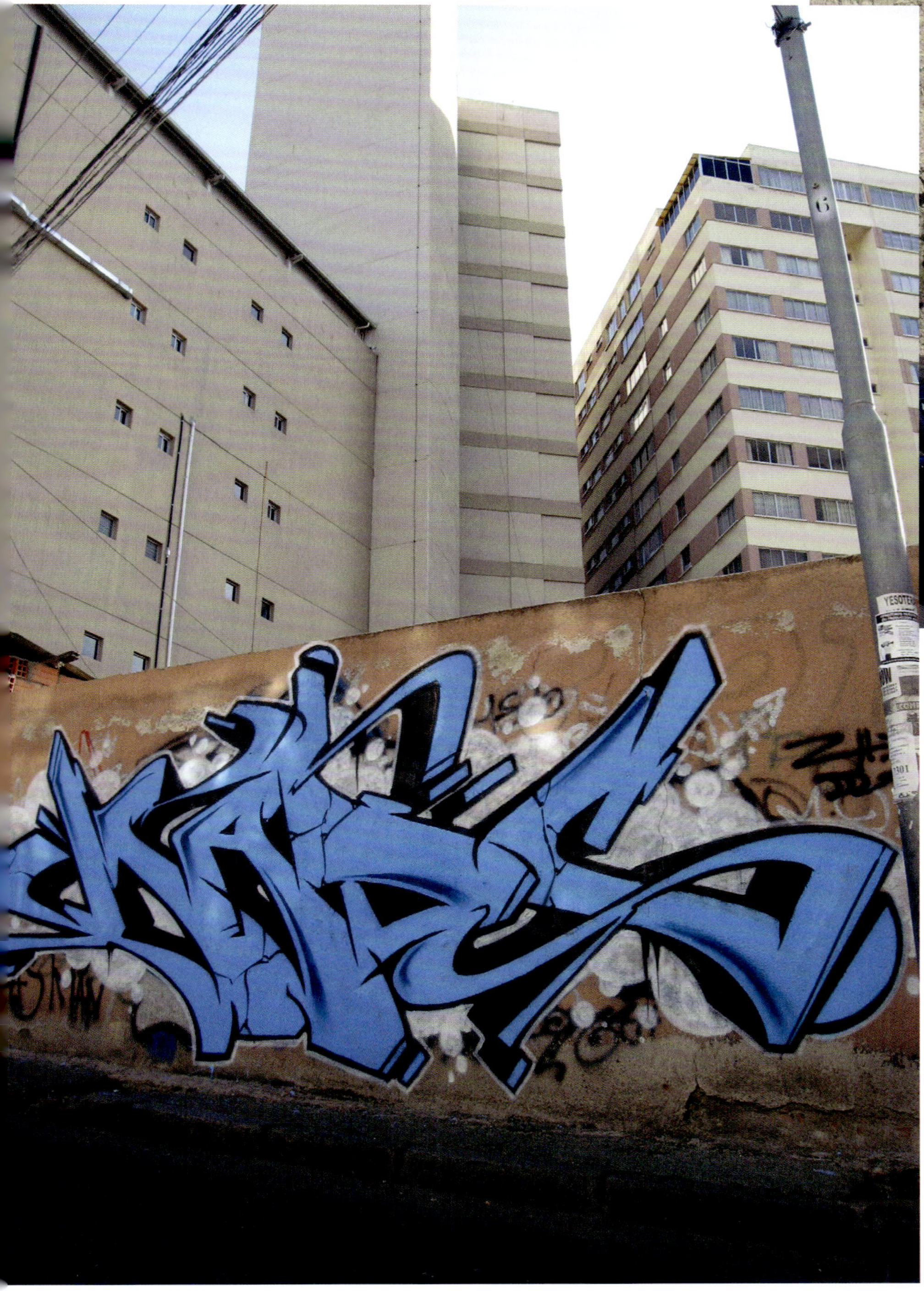

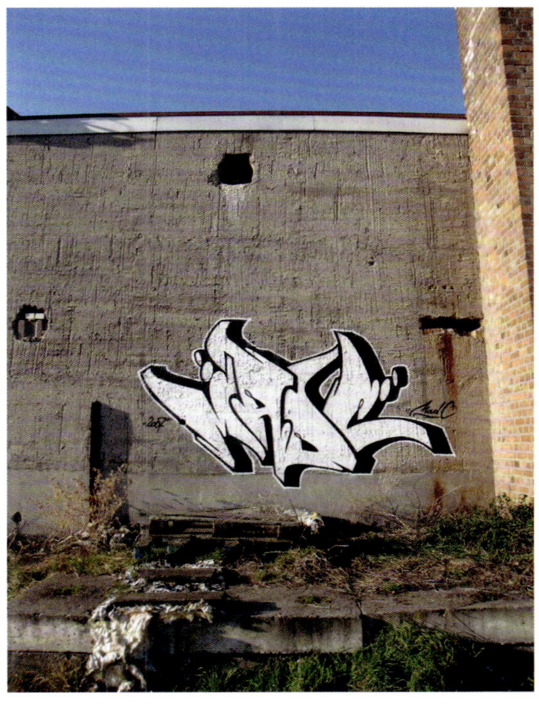

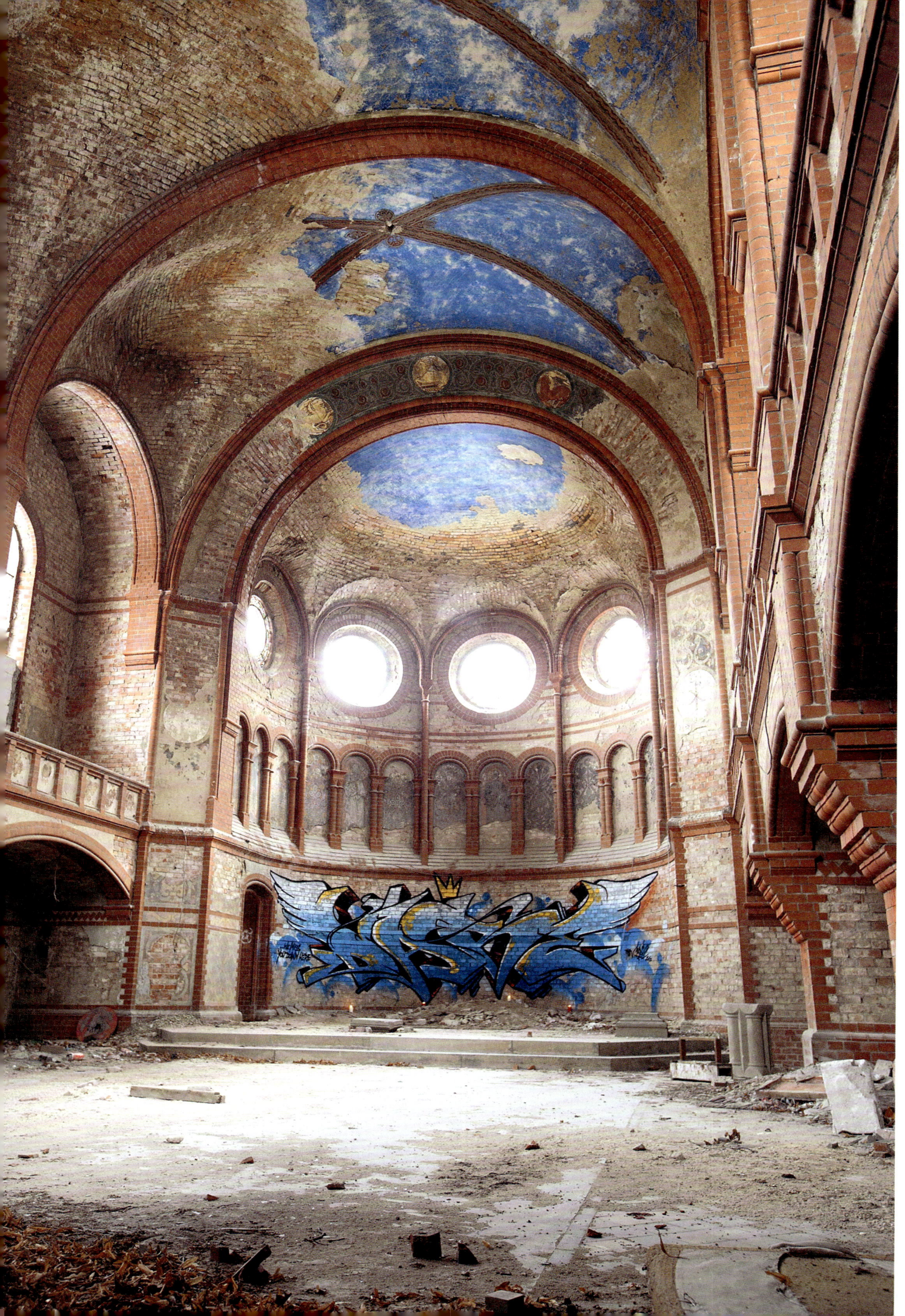

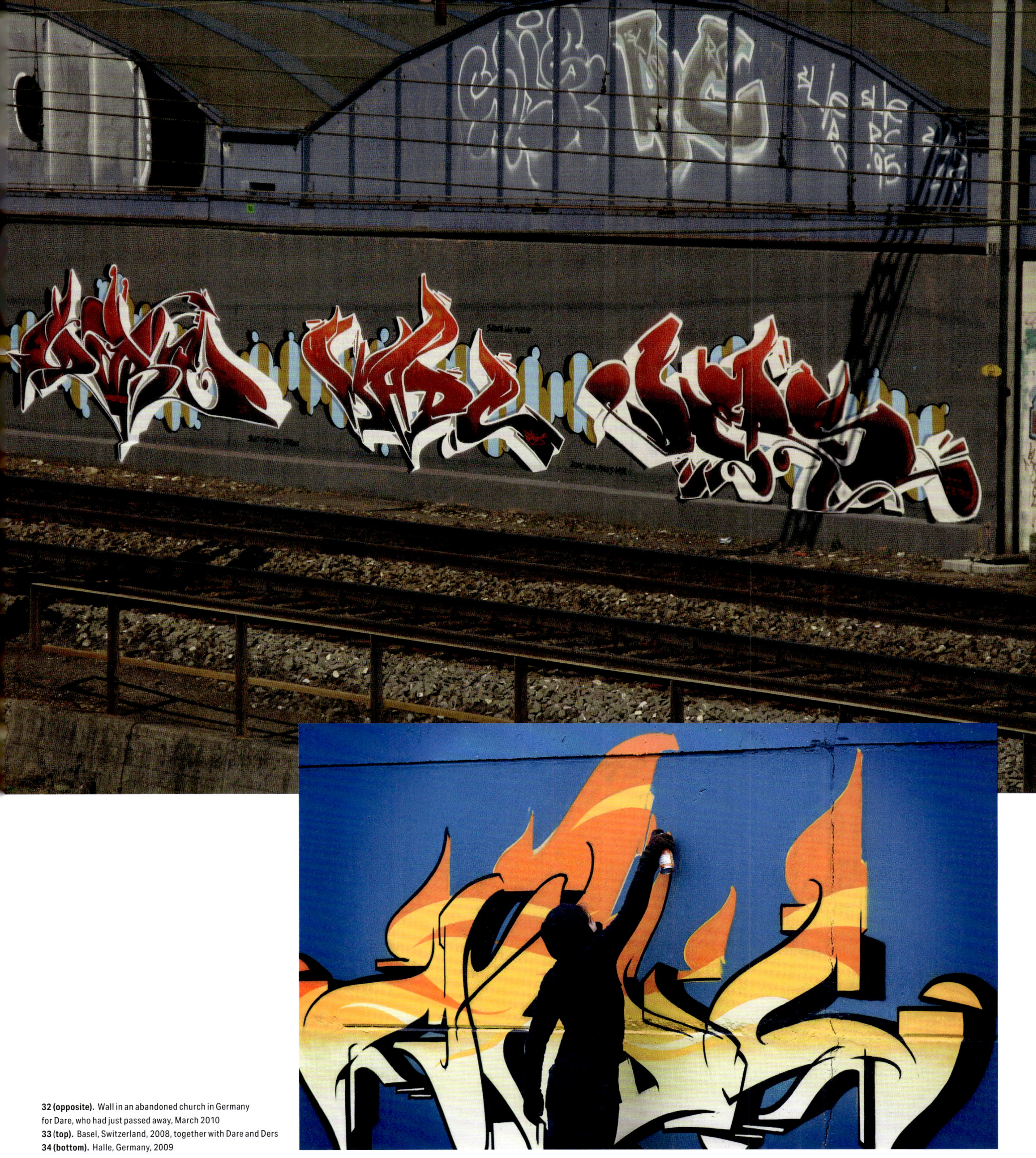

32 (opposite). Wall in an abandoned church in Germany for Dare, who had just passed away, March 2010
33 (top). Basel, Switzerland, 2008, together with Dare and Ders
34 (bottom). Halle, Germany, 2009

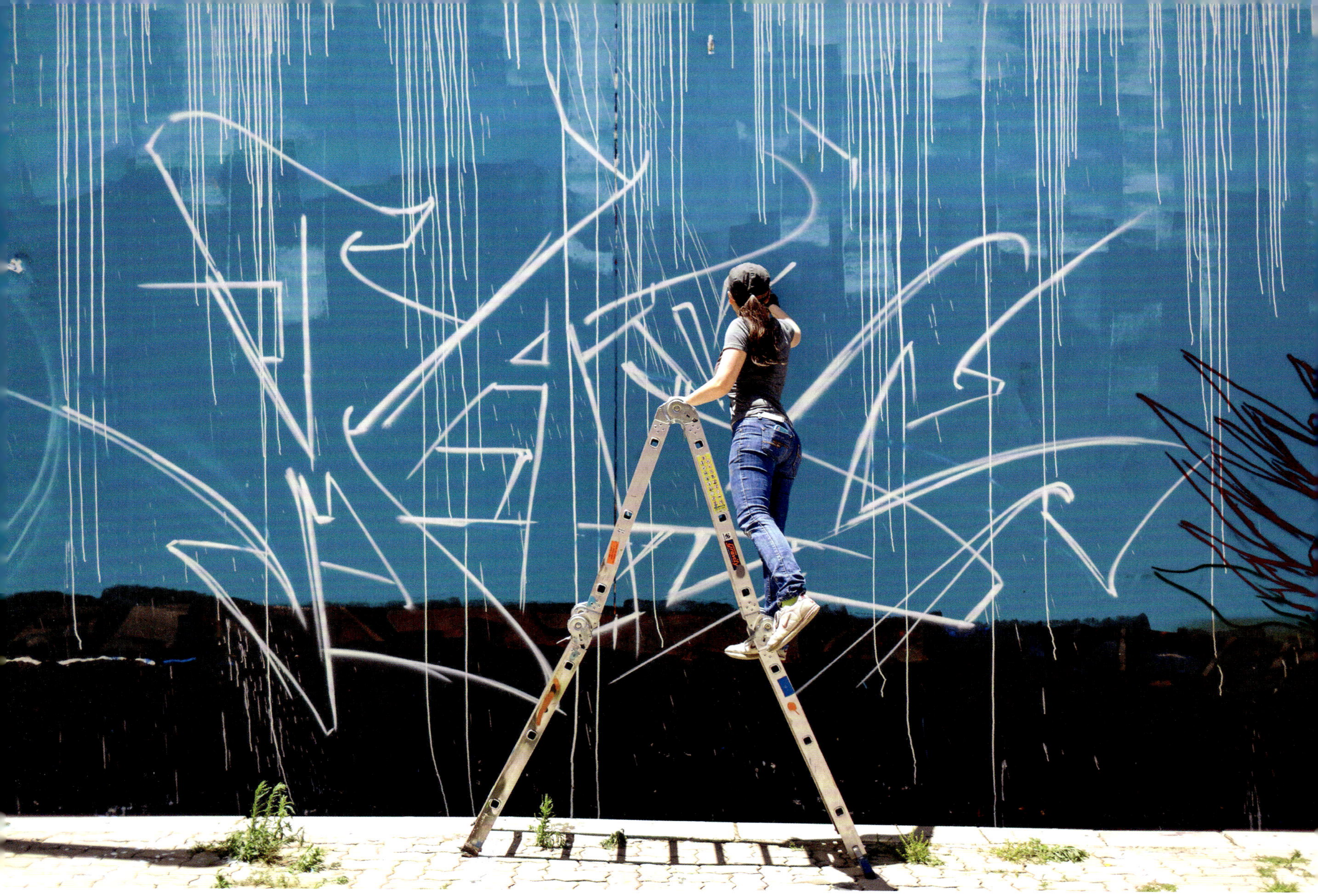

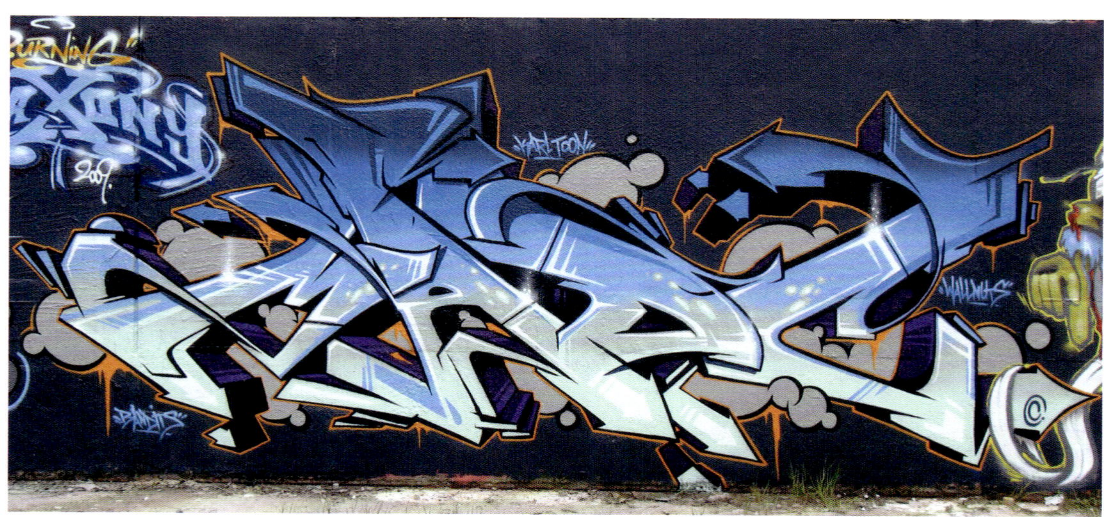

35 (top). Johannesburg, South Africa, 2013
36 (bottom). Itzehoe, Germany, 2009
37a–c (opposite, top). Trains and railway wall
38 (opposite, bottom). Halle, Germany, 2009

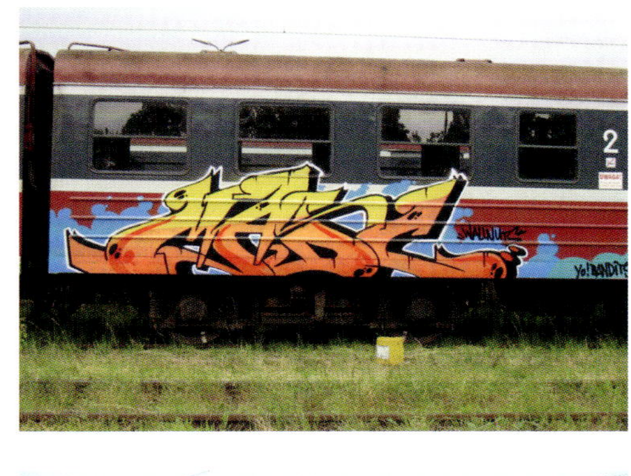

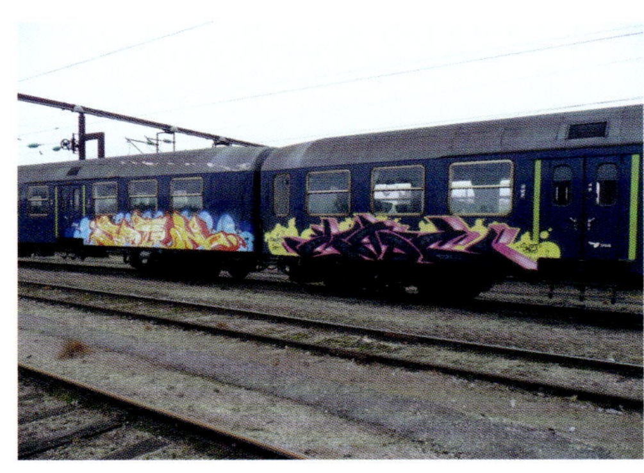

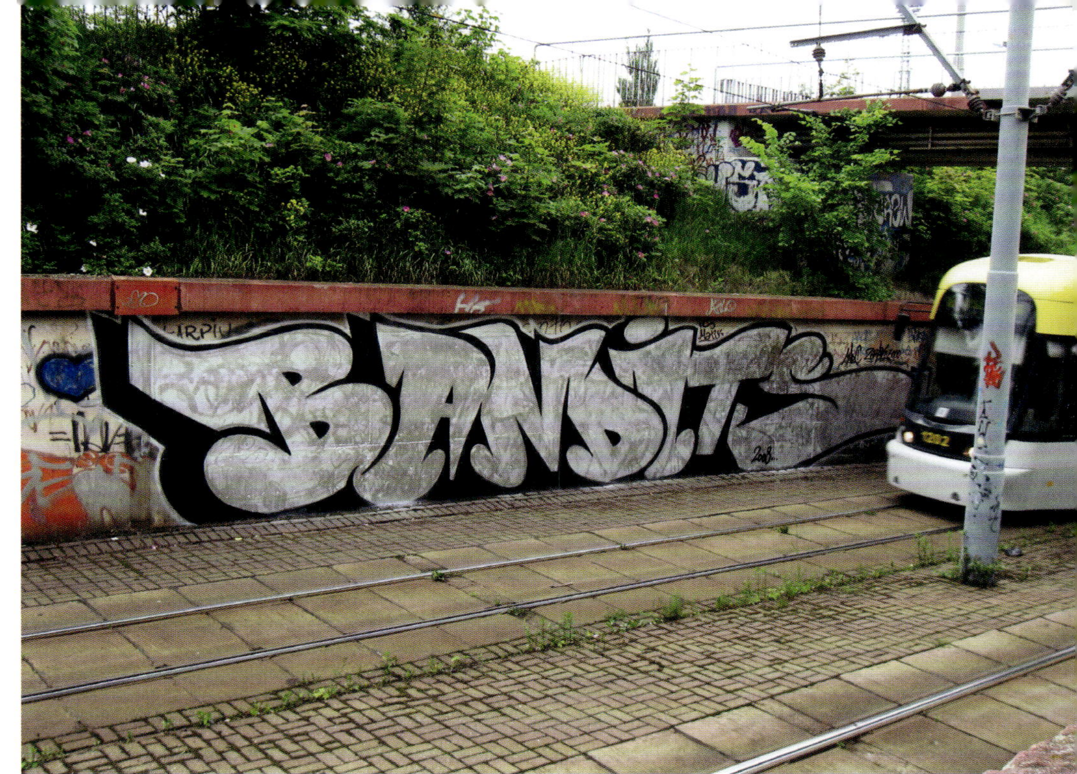

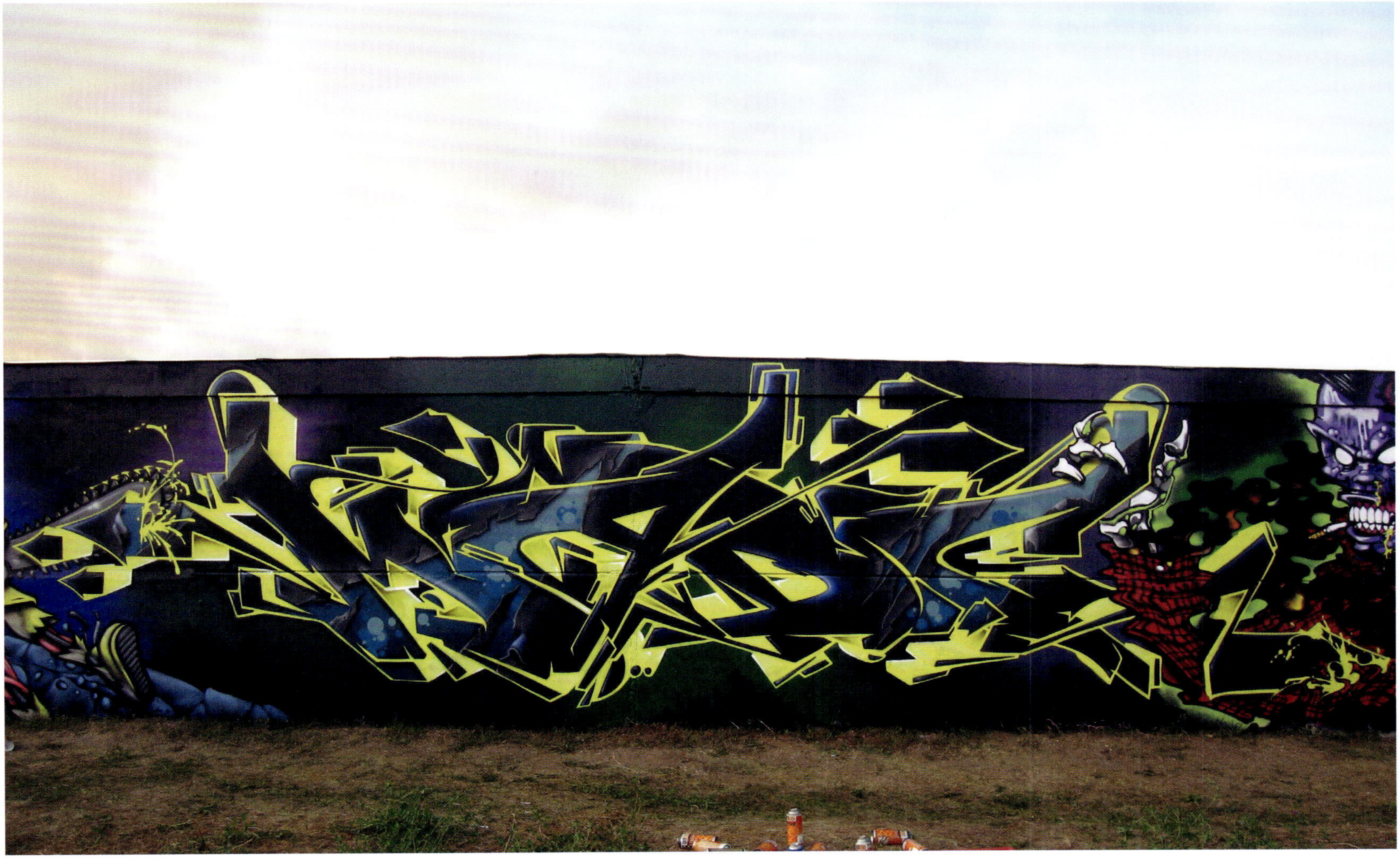

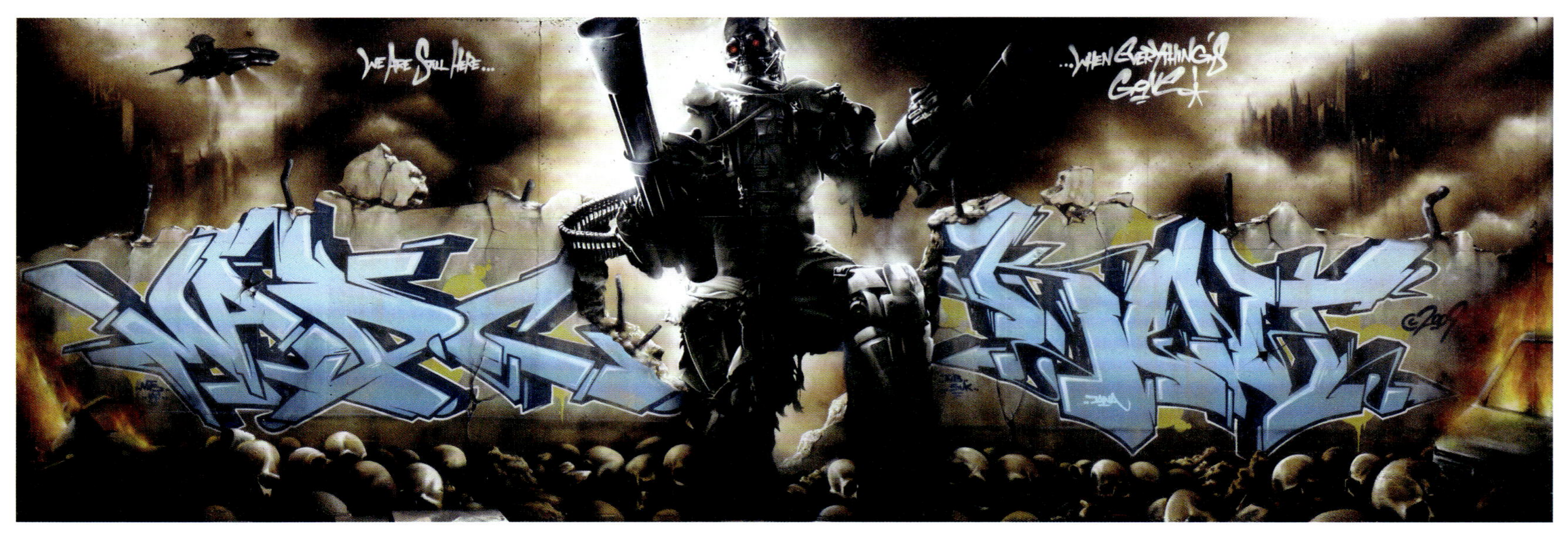
WE ARE STILL HERE...
...WHEN EVERYTHING'S GONE

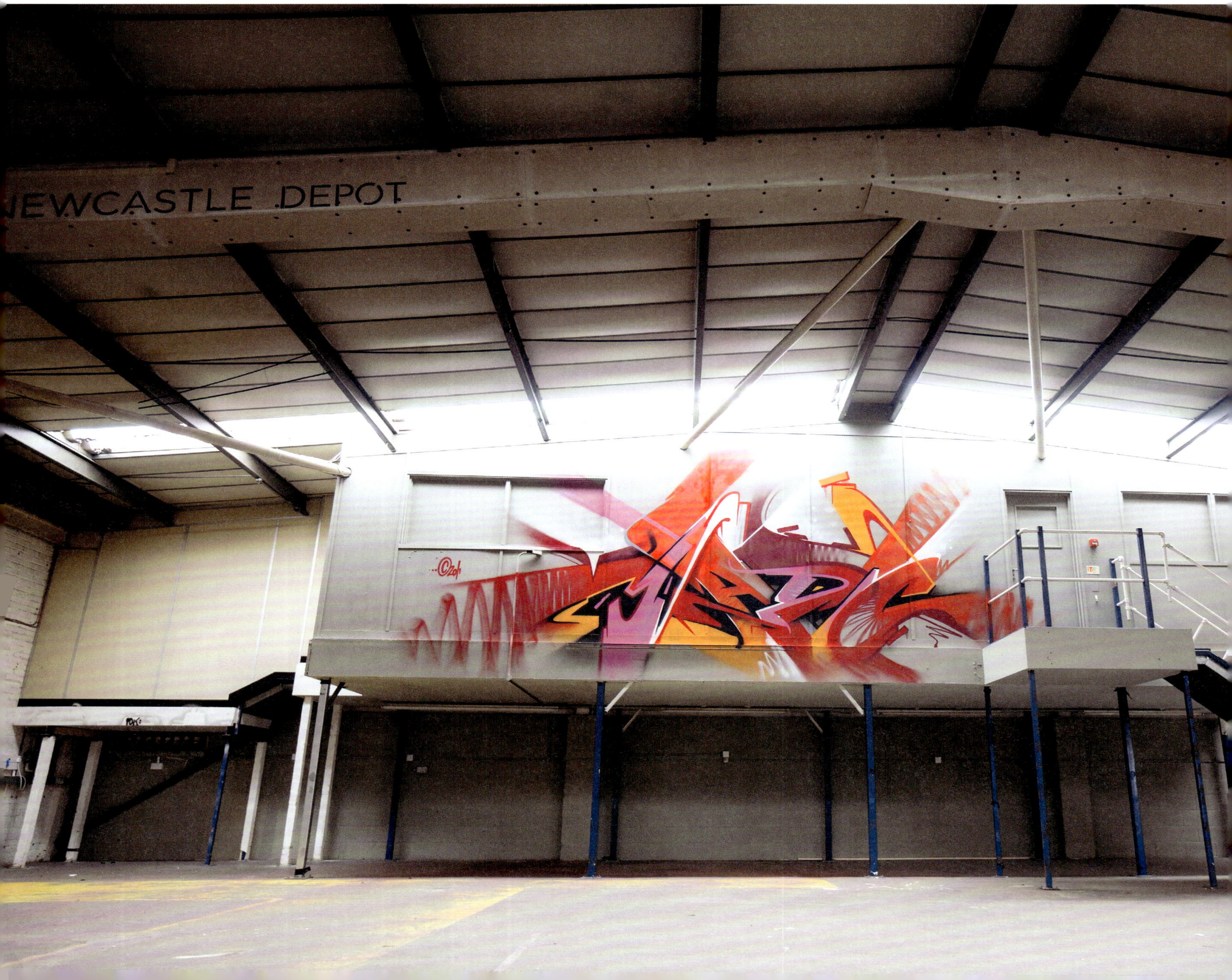

39 (opposite, top). *The Terminator Wall*, Frankfurt, Germany, 2009, together with Klark Kent
40 (opposite, bottom). An old East London warehouse, painted inside and outside by MadC as an off-site location for the show *MadABC* at Pure Evil Gallery, 2011
41 (top and bottom). Germany, 2012
42 (middle). Germany, 2011

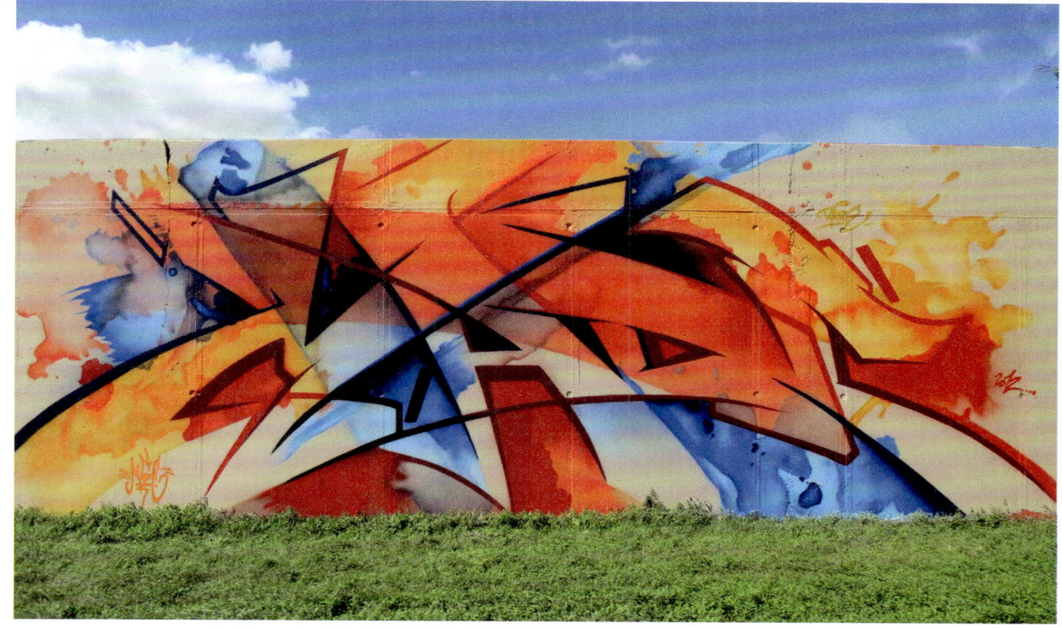

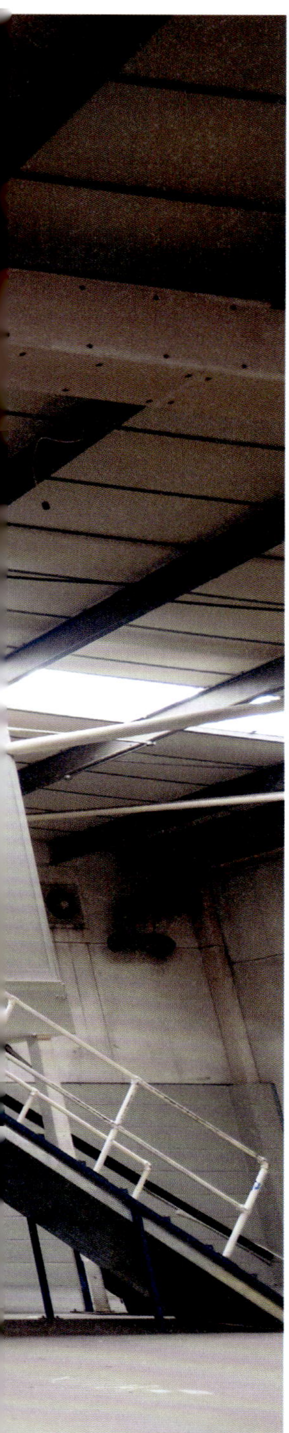

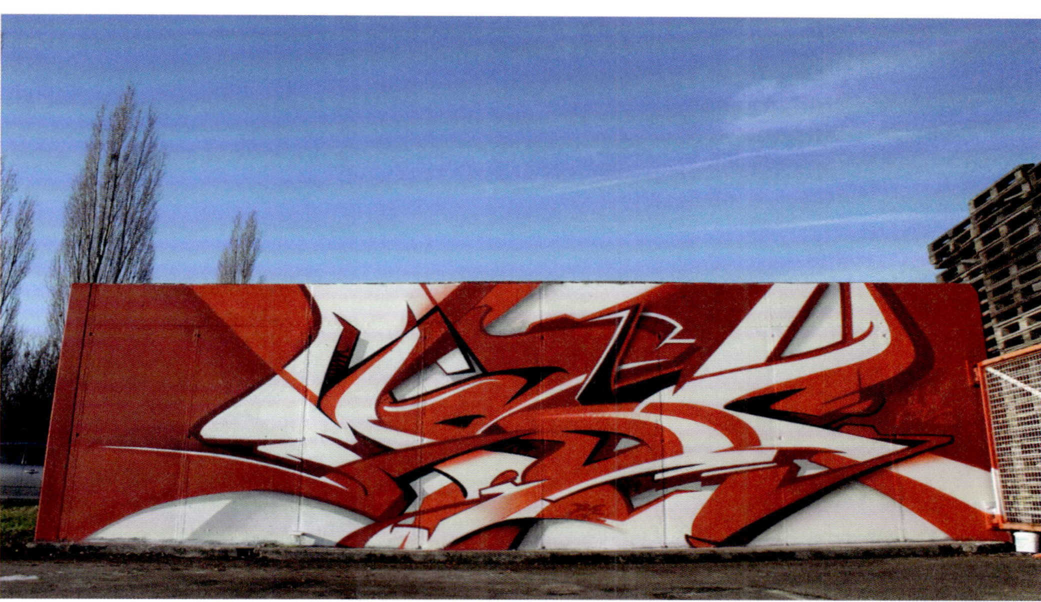

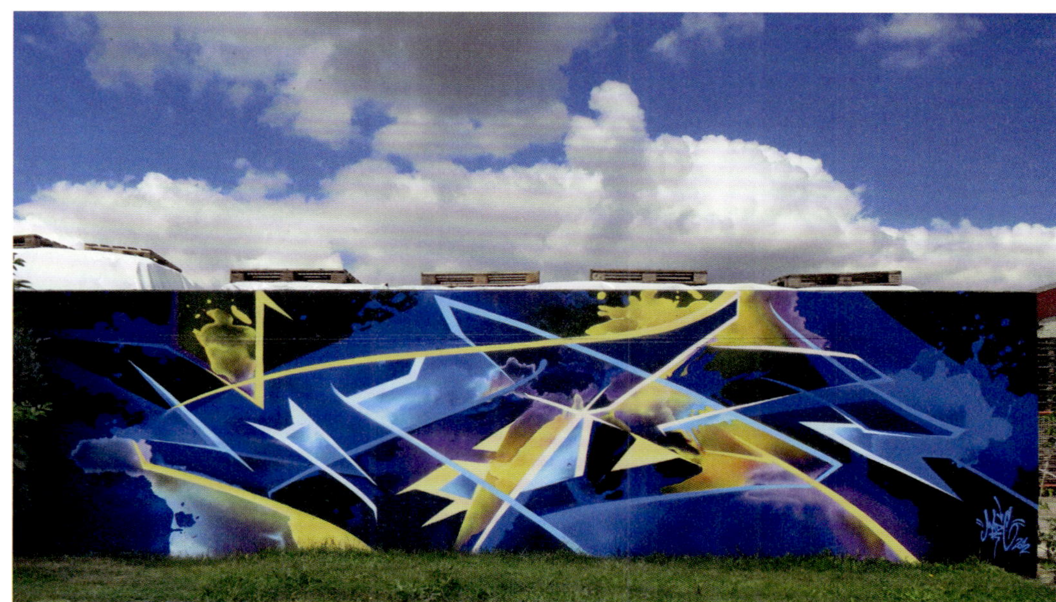

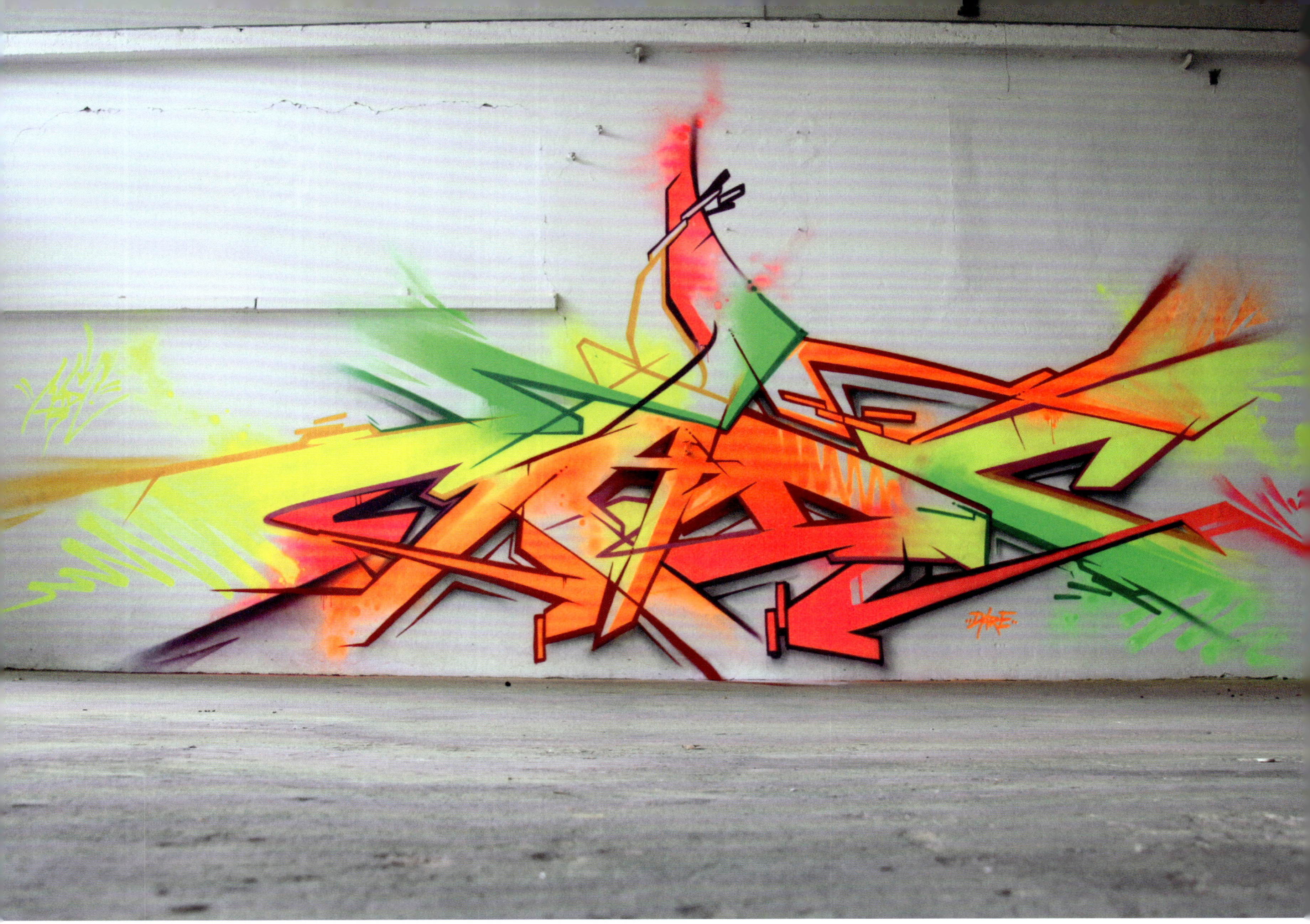

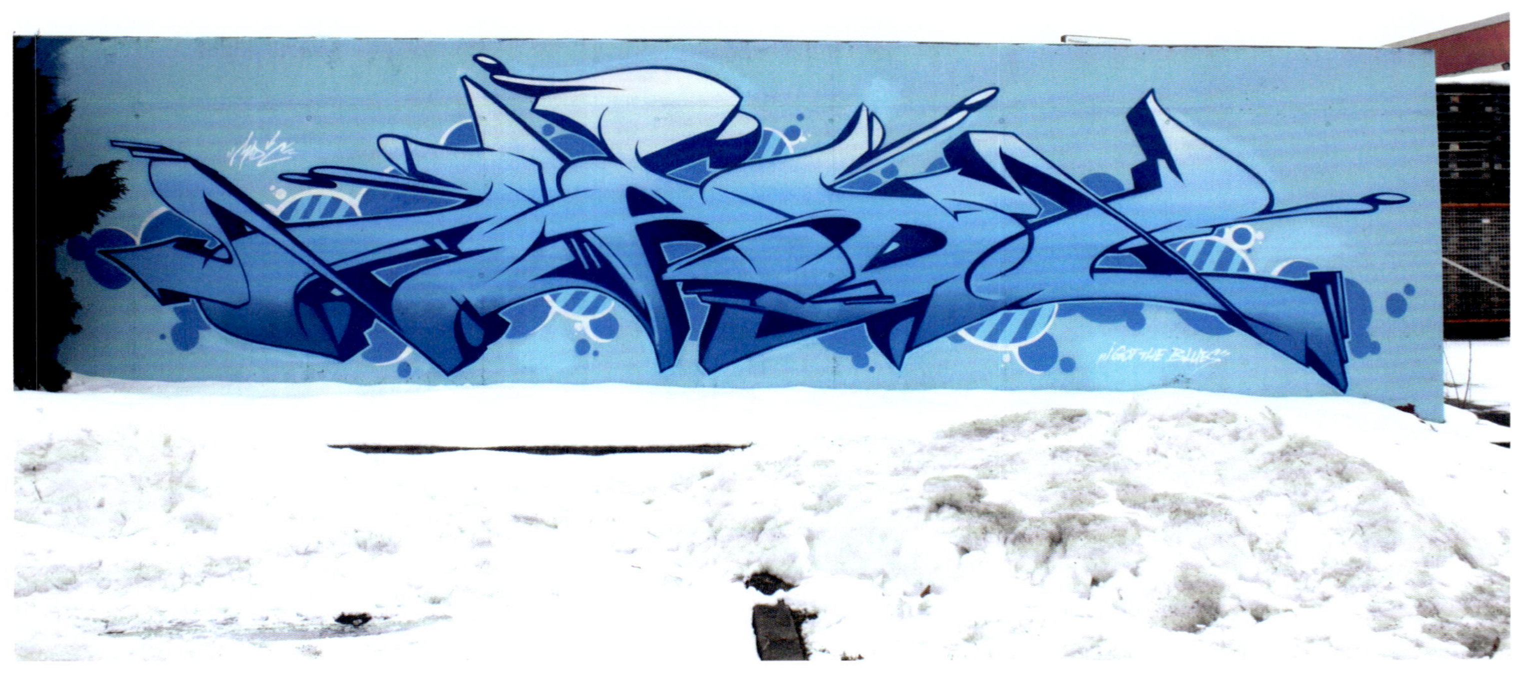

43 (opposite, top). *The Neon Wall*, Lahr, Germany, 2011
44 (opposite, bottom). Germany, 2009
45 (top). Landsberg, Germany, January 2015
46 (bottom). Halle, Germany, August 2020

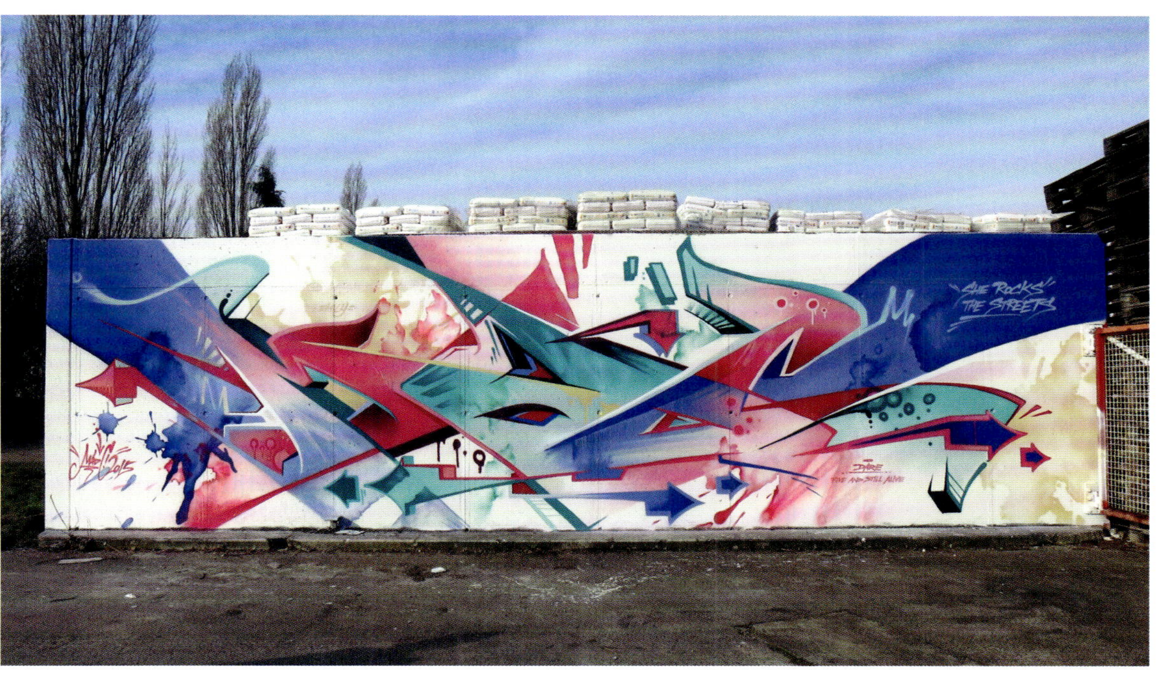

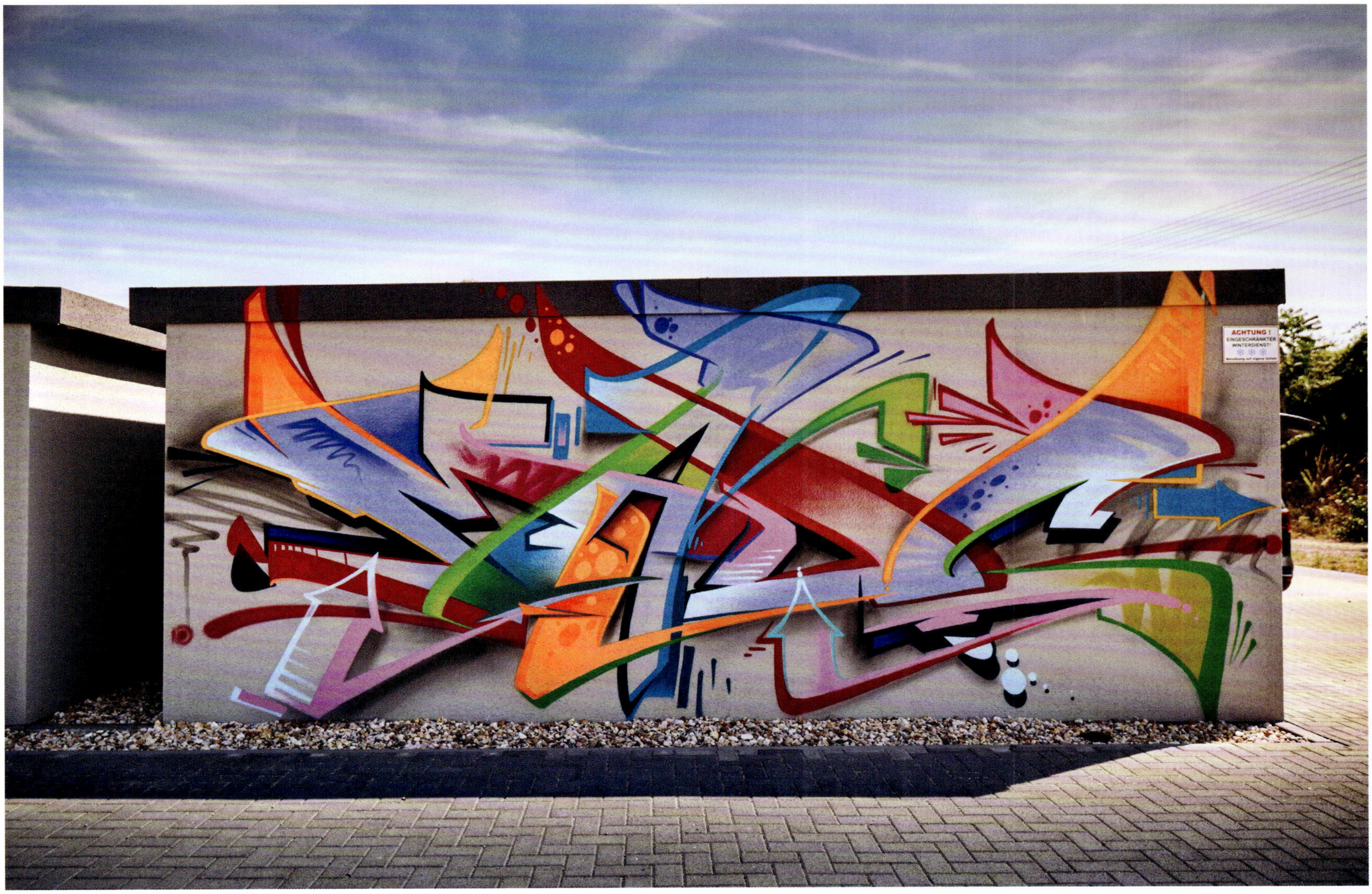

47 (top). San Francisco, USA, 2012
48 (bottom). *The Sugar Rush Wall*, Copenhagen, Denmark, 2013, together with Soten
49 (opposite, top). Landsberg, Germany, 2015
50 (opposite, bottom). Mural Oasis, 32100 Las Vegas Boulevard South, Primm, Nevada, USA, 2019

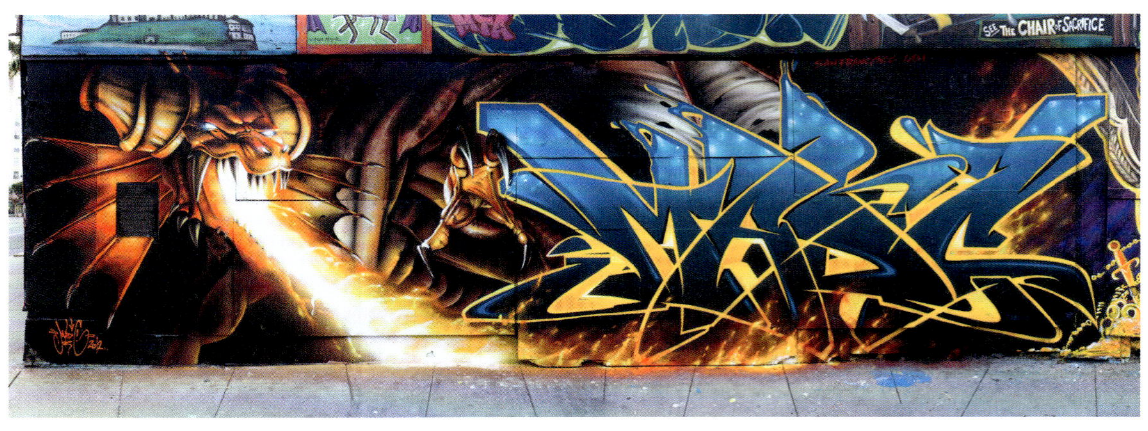

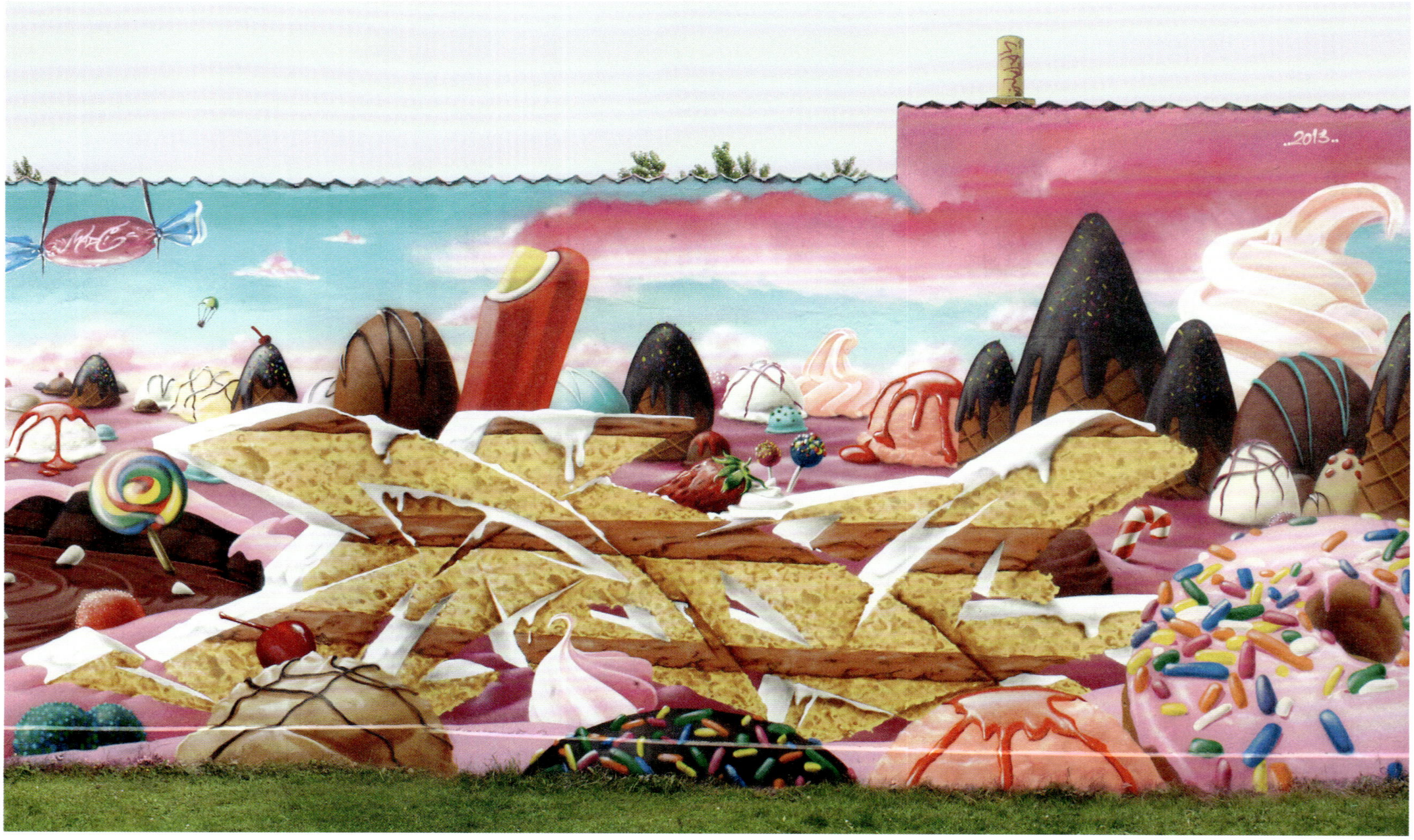

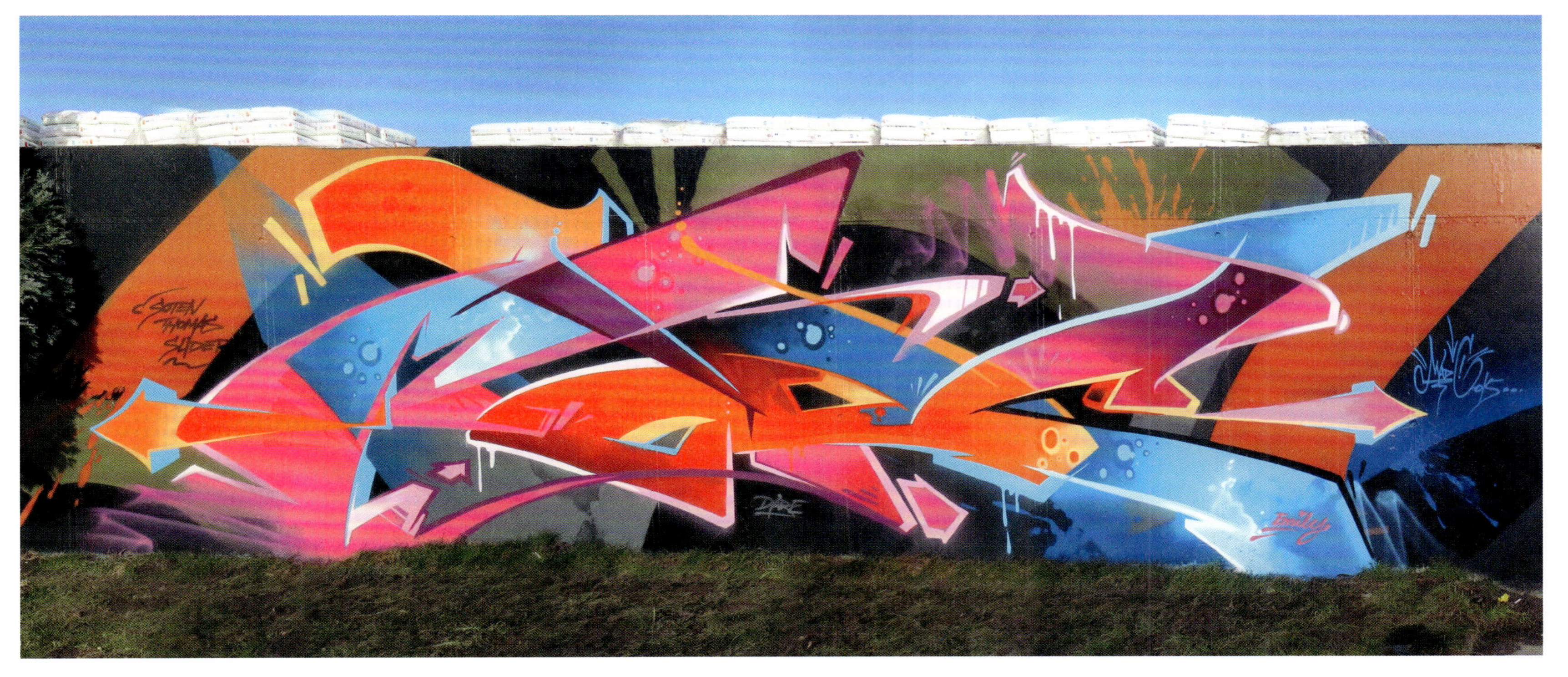

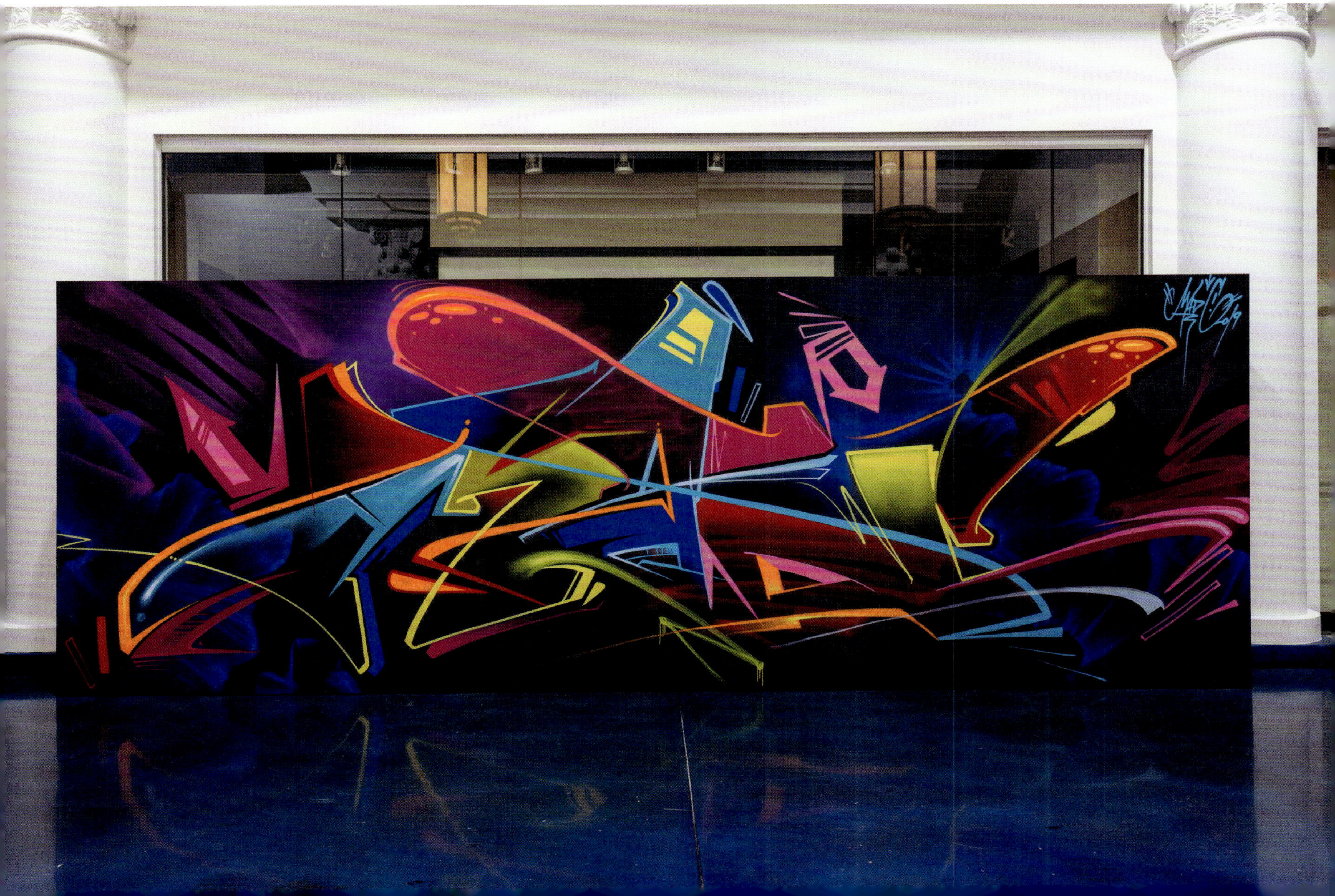

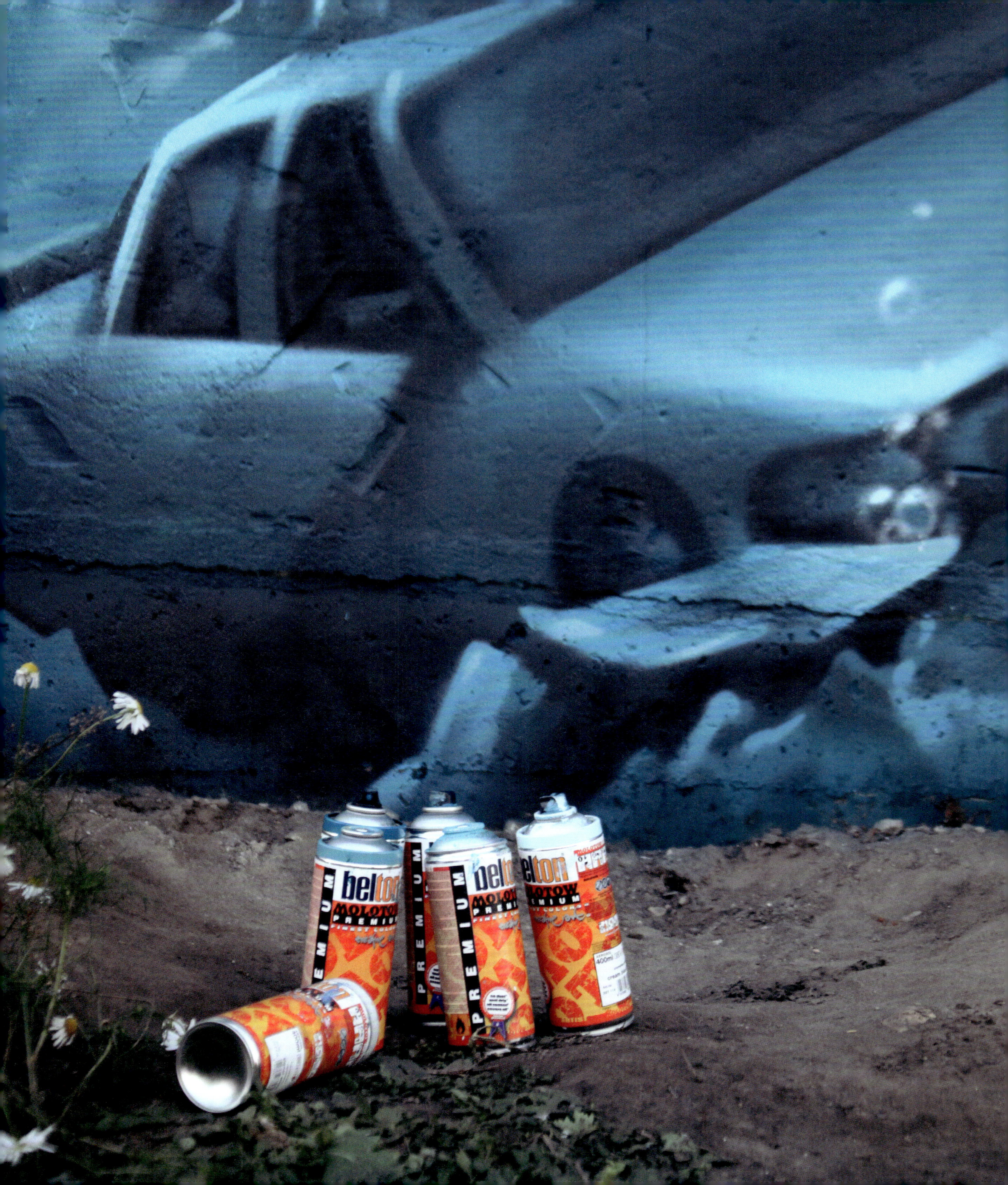
belton
MOLOTOW
PREMIUM

EXPERIMENTS BEYOND GENERIC BOUNDARIES

Some days I went up and down the ladder more than 500 times; fell off the ladder 4 times; counted in days, I painted more than 4 months every day at least 10 hours; I used 1489 cans; 158 different colours; 600+ caps; 3 different kind of caps, 100 litres primer; 140 litres exterior paint; painted at temperatures from +2C° to +38C° in sunshine, rain, storm, day and night; painted my biggest and smallest piece so far and overall painted my name far more than 100 times on this wall.[7]

There is no better way to describe the magnitude of *The 700 Wall* in Peissen near Halle than with these facts. This project, which MadC realised in 2010, marked a turning point. It was a milestone not only for her, but also for the history of graffiti. Enabling a sense of looking back and pausing to reflect, MadC used visual metaphors along the wall to describe the journey that she had embarked on, just like any other graffiti artist, and that still continued: 'My Stylemachine idea was based on the life of a dedicated graffiti writer. It's a wall for all of us who paint 10+ years and who put all their energy and heart into it.'[8]

Starting in a bizarre laboratory situation, somewhere between Frankenstein and Dr Phibes, two rats sneak through the foreground, nicking pickled cheese in a jar and also a sketch on paper that reveals the name of MadC. A figure, resembling Frankenstein's monster from the 1931 film, crouches on the floor between paper sheets and draws in a black book in the middle of an elongated room with an arched glass roof. It is the first visualisation of what is carried out into the world from the interior of the laboratory, what transpires out of the inner life of the Creator. The name MadC as a sketch or as a piece forms the bracket between inside and outside. It can be found on the arched glass roof as a piece, another on the inner wall, and as tags in the form of inlays on the round arches of the roof and on the floor of the room. It stands for one thing above all – the experiment. Trying. Brewing, simmering and mixing ideas is the starting point of every artistic process, and always accompanies its development **(fig. 53)**. The picture slides into a kind of factory hall in which a machine is installed – the 'style machine' – with extravagant dimensions. A colossus made of metal with countless entanglements, melting furnaces, cranks and surveillance screens, the machine is a huge production facility in which ideas are implemented and produced, to be spat out as finished pieces on a treadmill at the end **(fig. 54)**. A sea port is directly connected; the pieces are stacked like containers by robots and wait to be shipped across the sea. No modern container ships are sailing there; instead we see historical sailing ships that remind us of the times of so-called explorers and pirates.

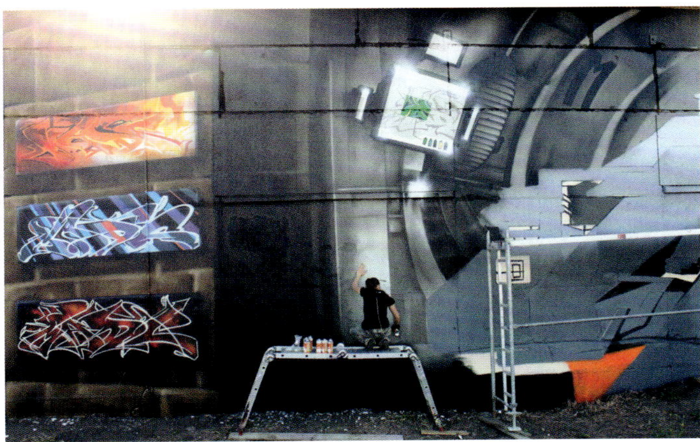

51 (opposite). Detail of *The 700 Wall*, Peissen, Germany, 2010
52. MadC working on *The 700 Wall*, Peissen, Germany, 2010

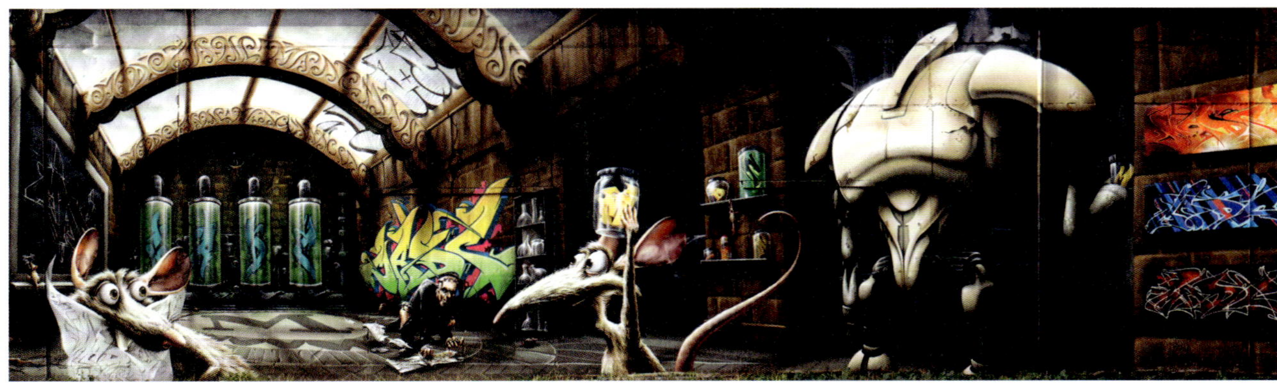

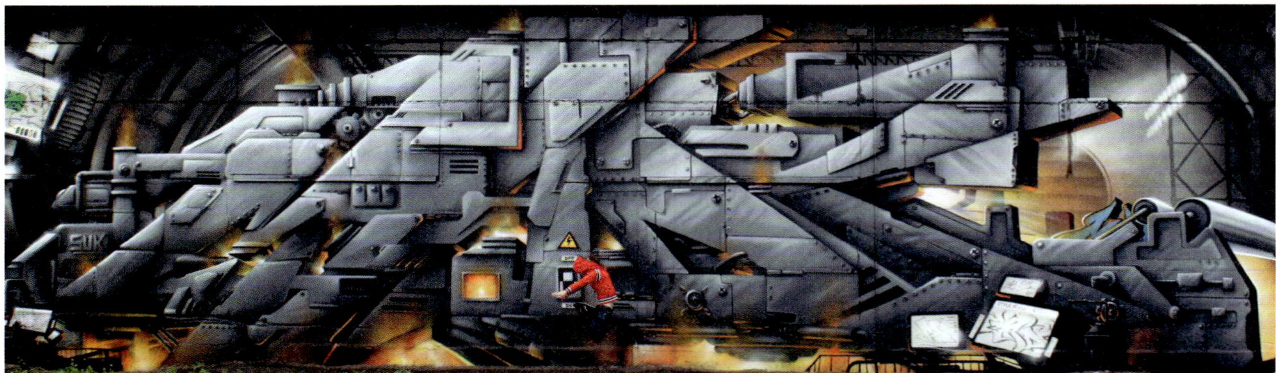

MadC's ships have to withstand difficult journeys on choppy seas, attacked by monsters that pull names down with their long tentacles **(fig. 57)**. This serves as a metaphor for the hard work of the writer in achieving recognition and visibility in a genre that is based on an ephemeral concept; the disappearance of the work is countered by producing more and more. The journey ends in the city (the resemblance to the New York skyline is, of course, no coincidence) – the place to be, the melting pot for artistic ideas and the place where the works can be seen as much as possible. This visibility is not least due to the train that rushes through the scenery on an elevated railway line – of course, marked with the name MadC **(fig. 59)**.

The self-imposed challenge of the sheer size of the area significantly shifts the performative aspect within the realisation of the work. While graffiti is traditionally about reaching inaccessible areas and quick executions, about the energy that feeds on the rule violation of the endeavour, MadC shifted the focus with *The 700 Wall* to the testing and exceeding of her physical limits through the spatial dimensions of the work – a focus that she goes on to maintain elsewhere. With *The 700 Wall*, MadC stylistically took the world of characters (in the graffiti world's sense of the word, meaning people rather than letters) to extremes and refined it – perhaps also exhausted it. After this project, she created only a few narrative murals with detailed scenes.

53–68 (this spread and next three spreads)
The 700 Wall, Peissen, Germany, 2010

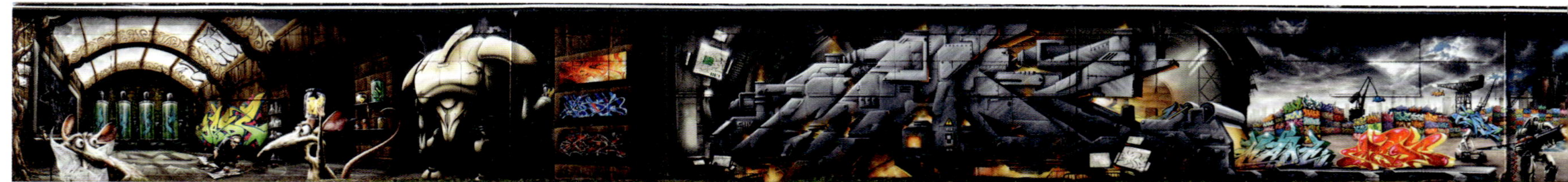

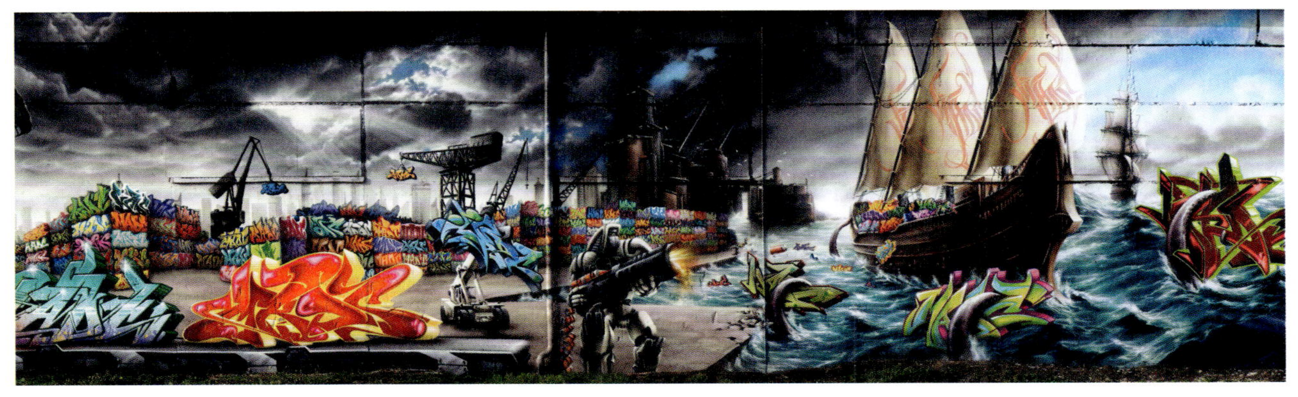

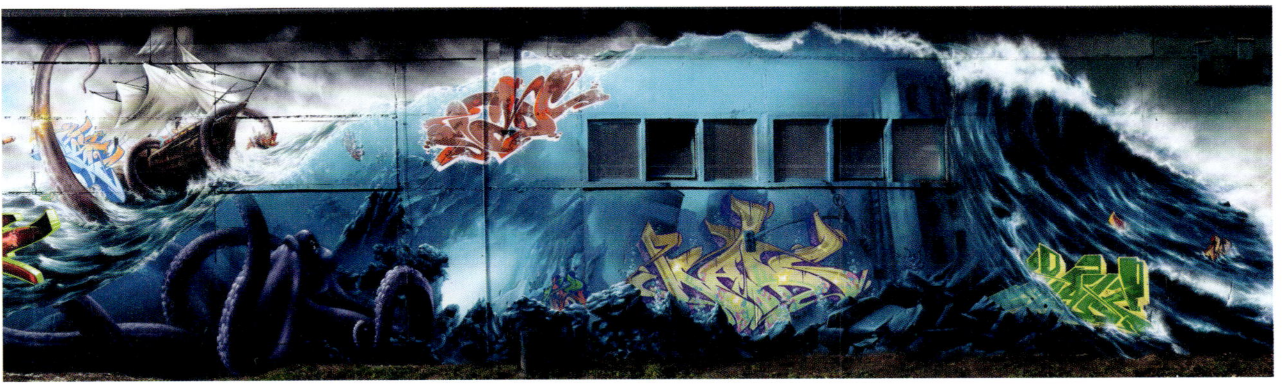

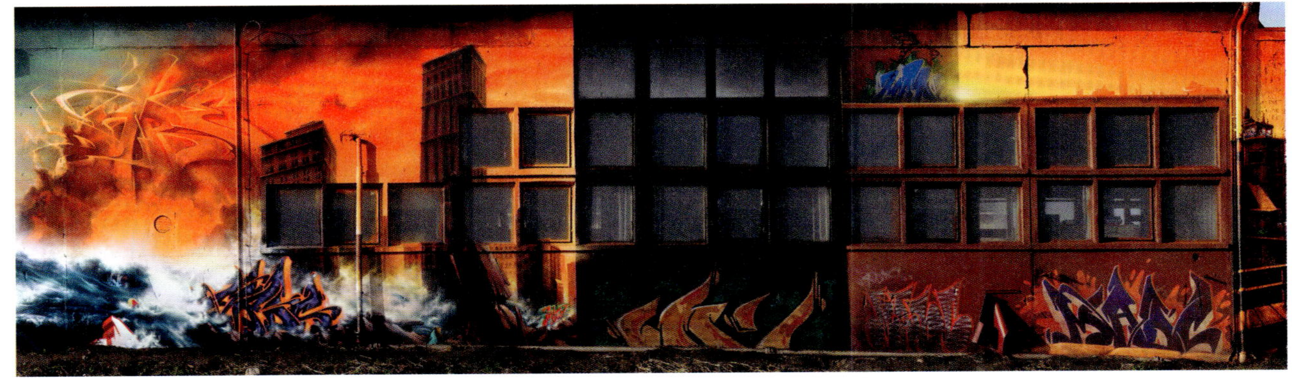

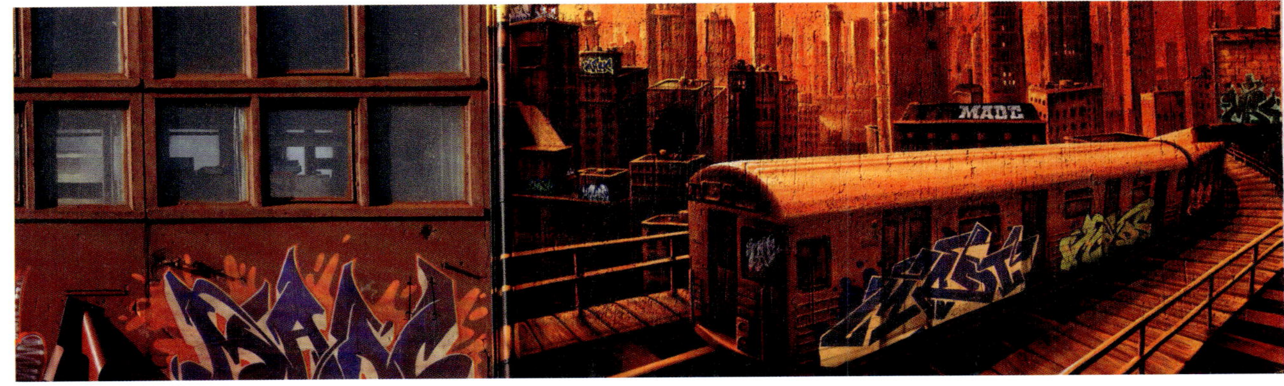
MADC

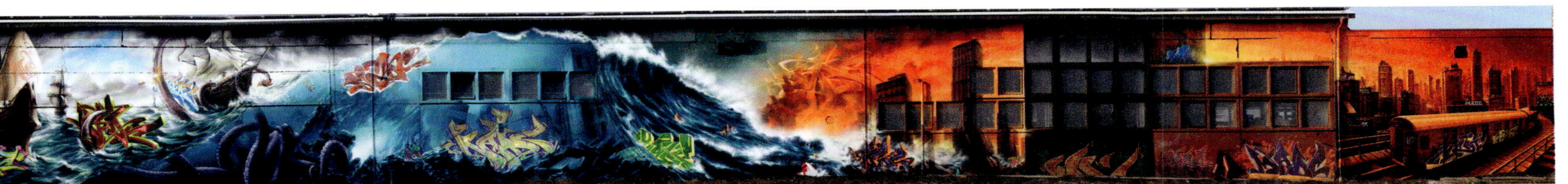

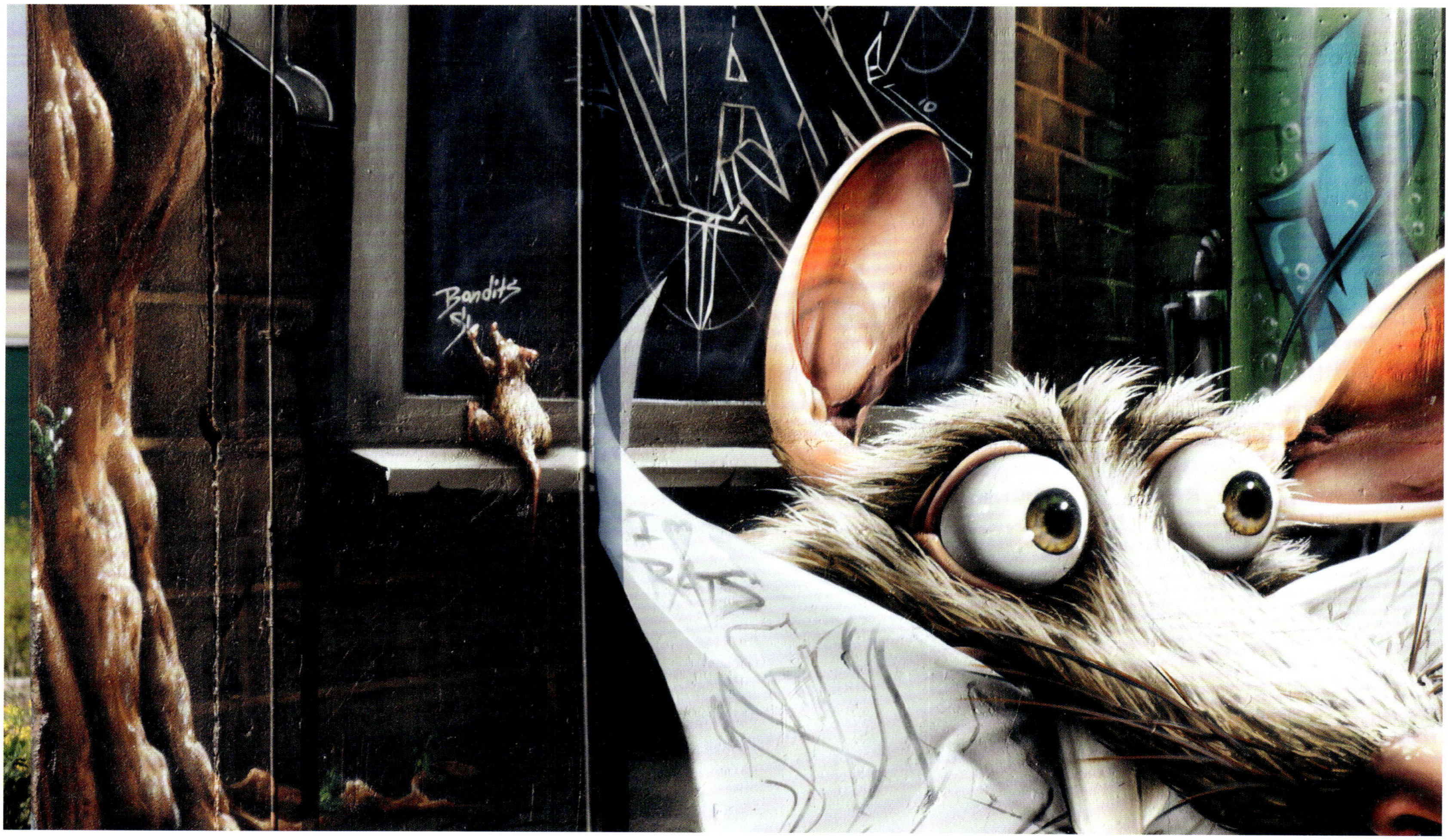

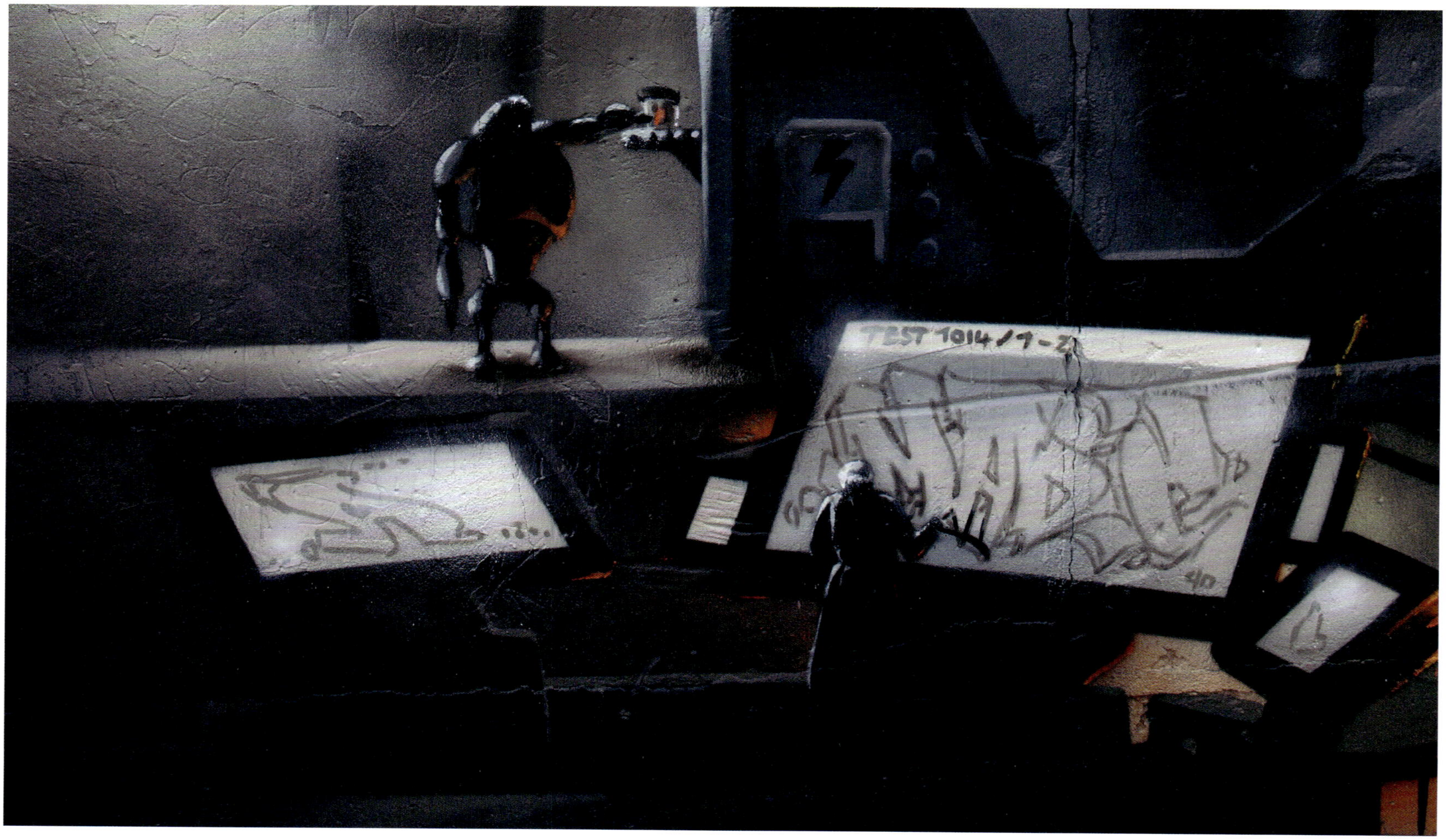

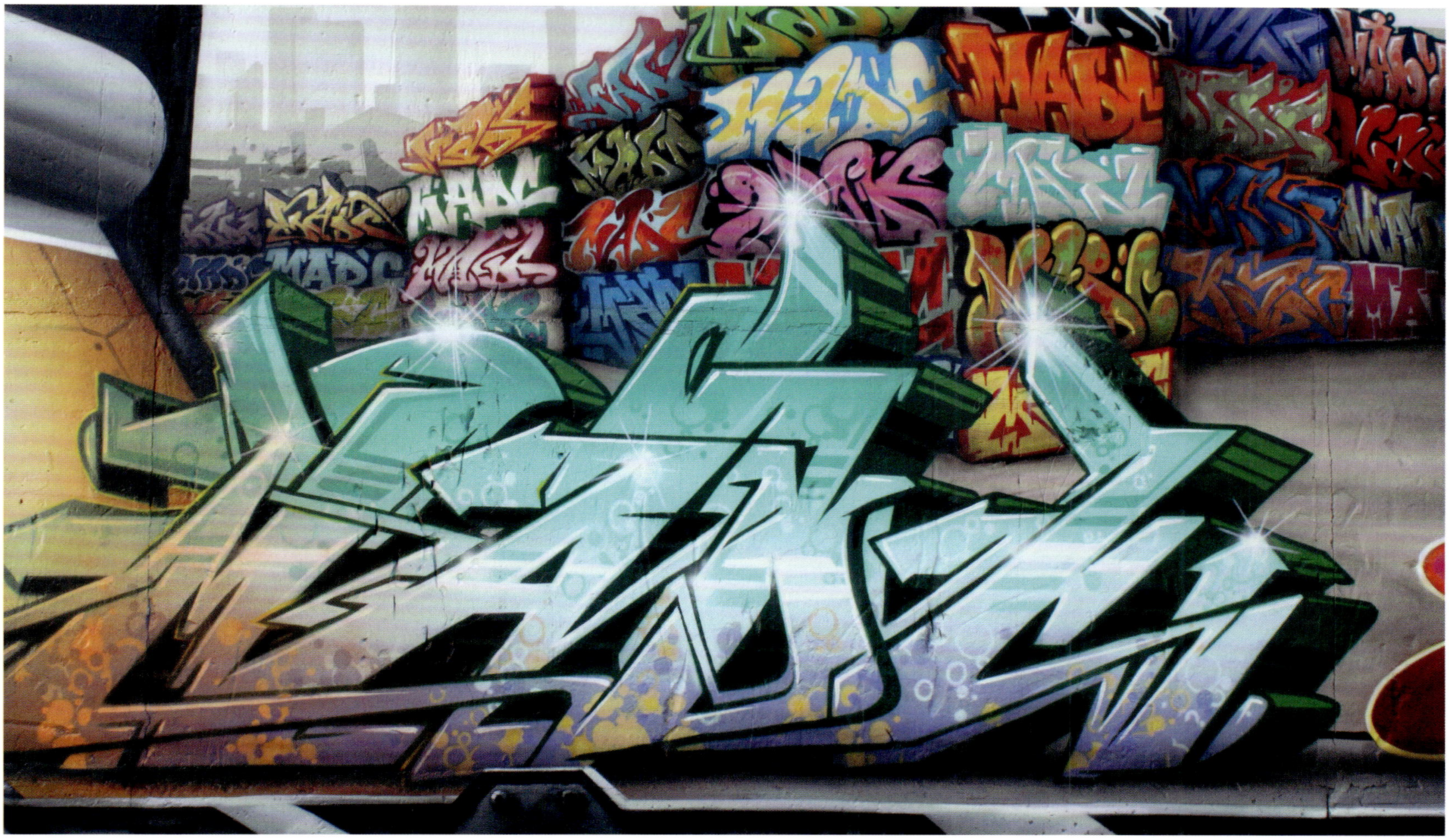

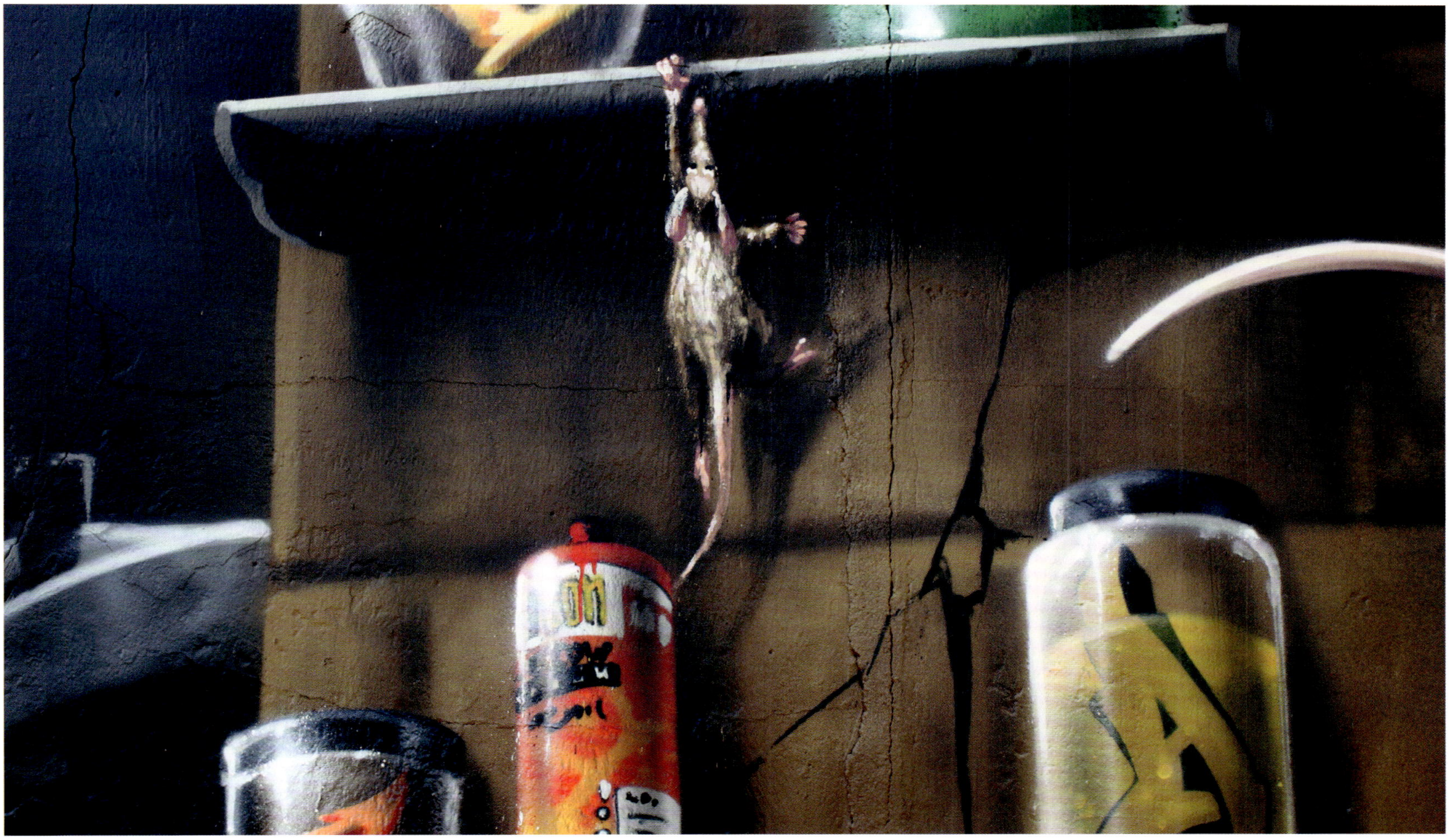

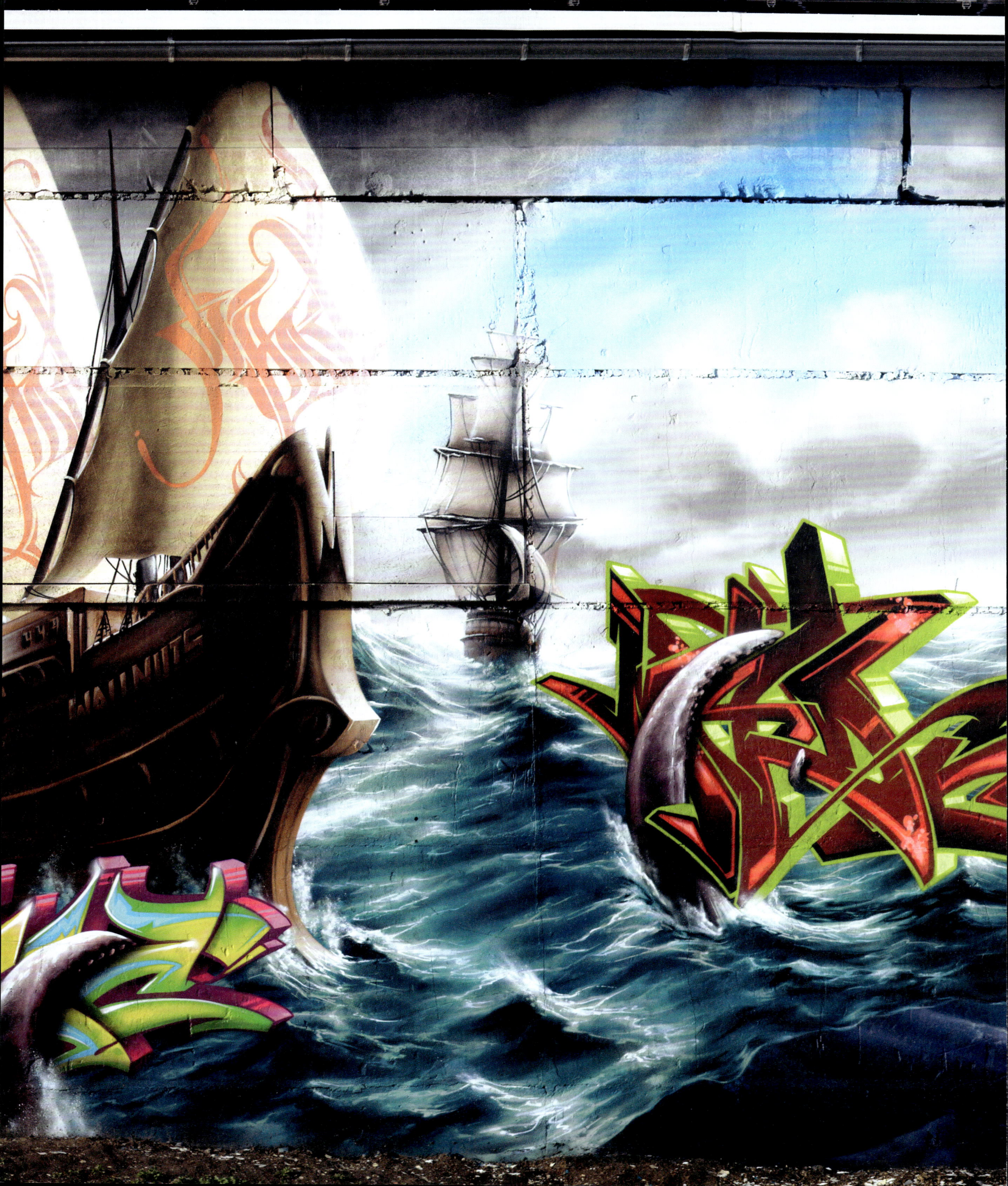

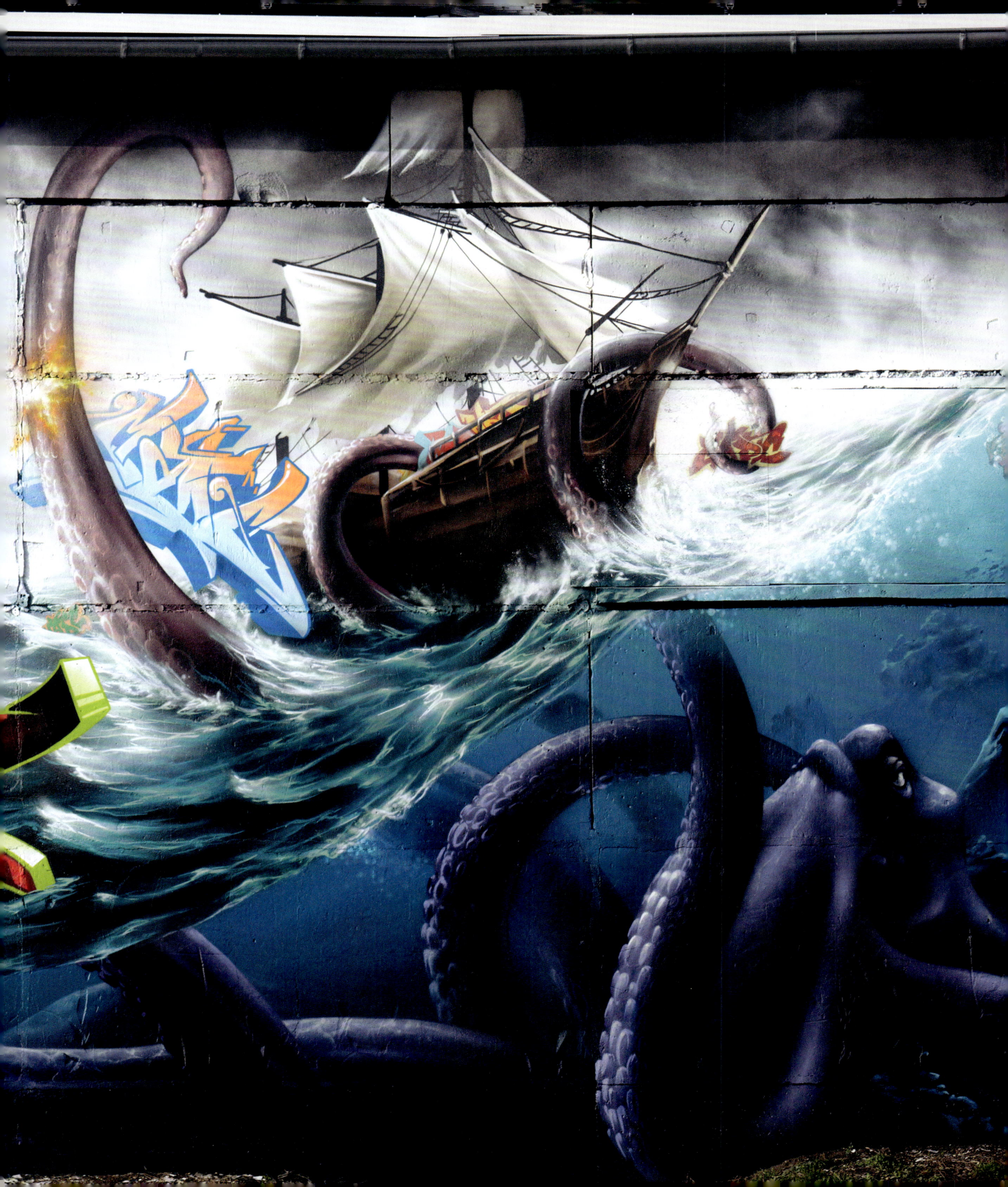

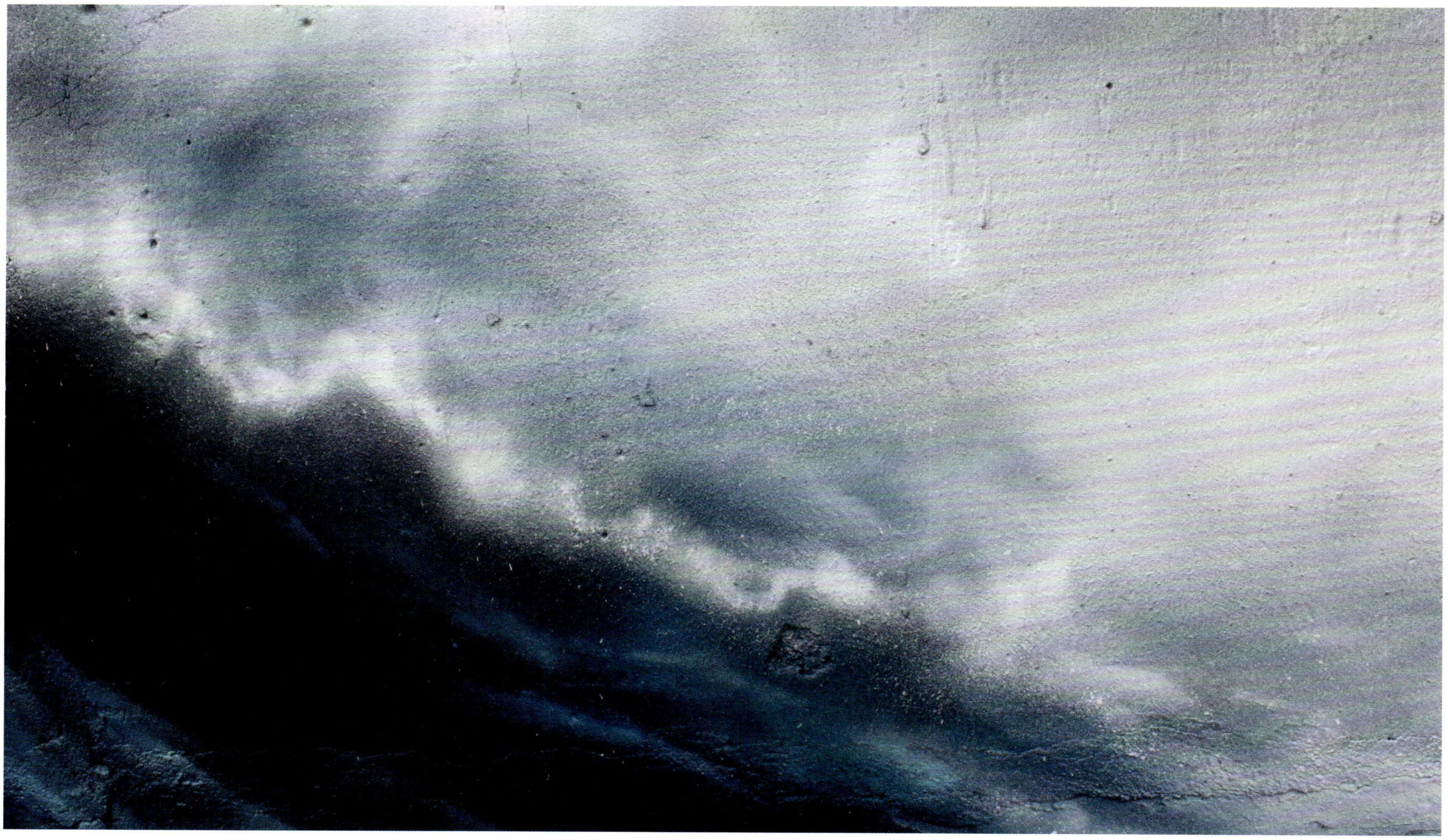

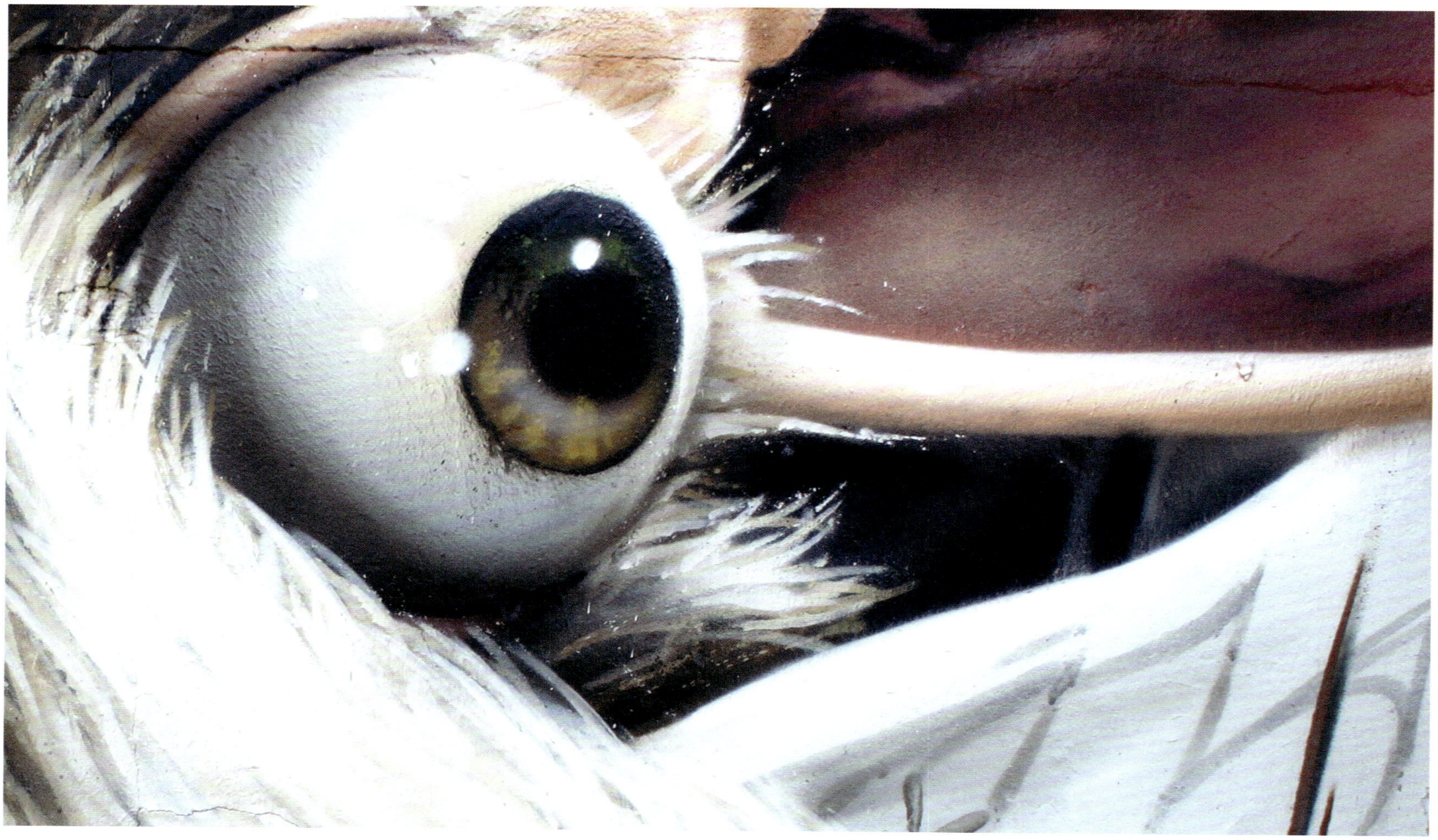

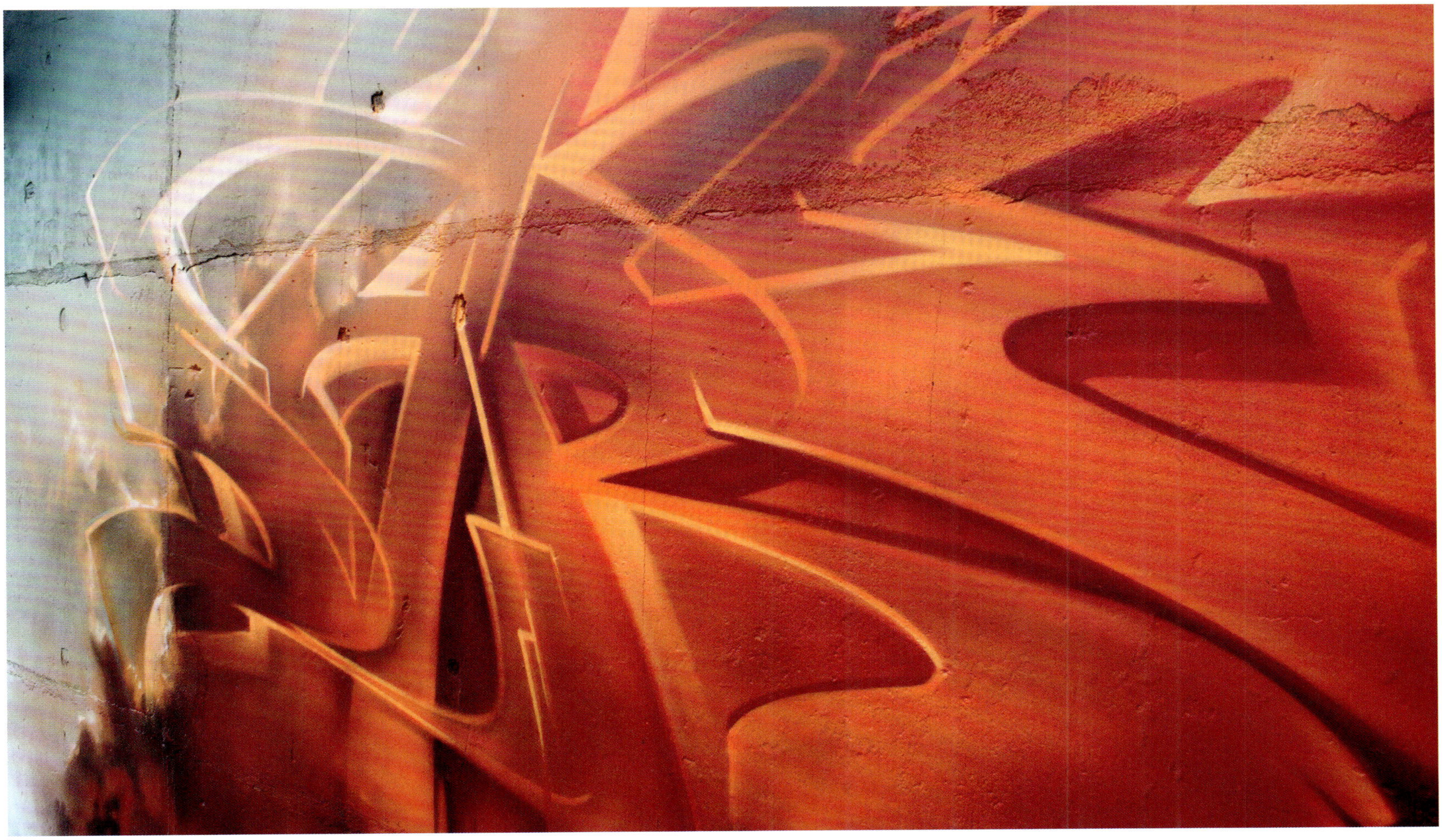

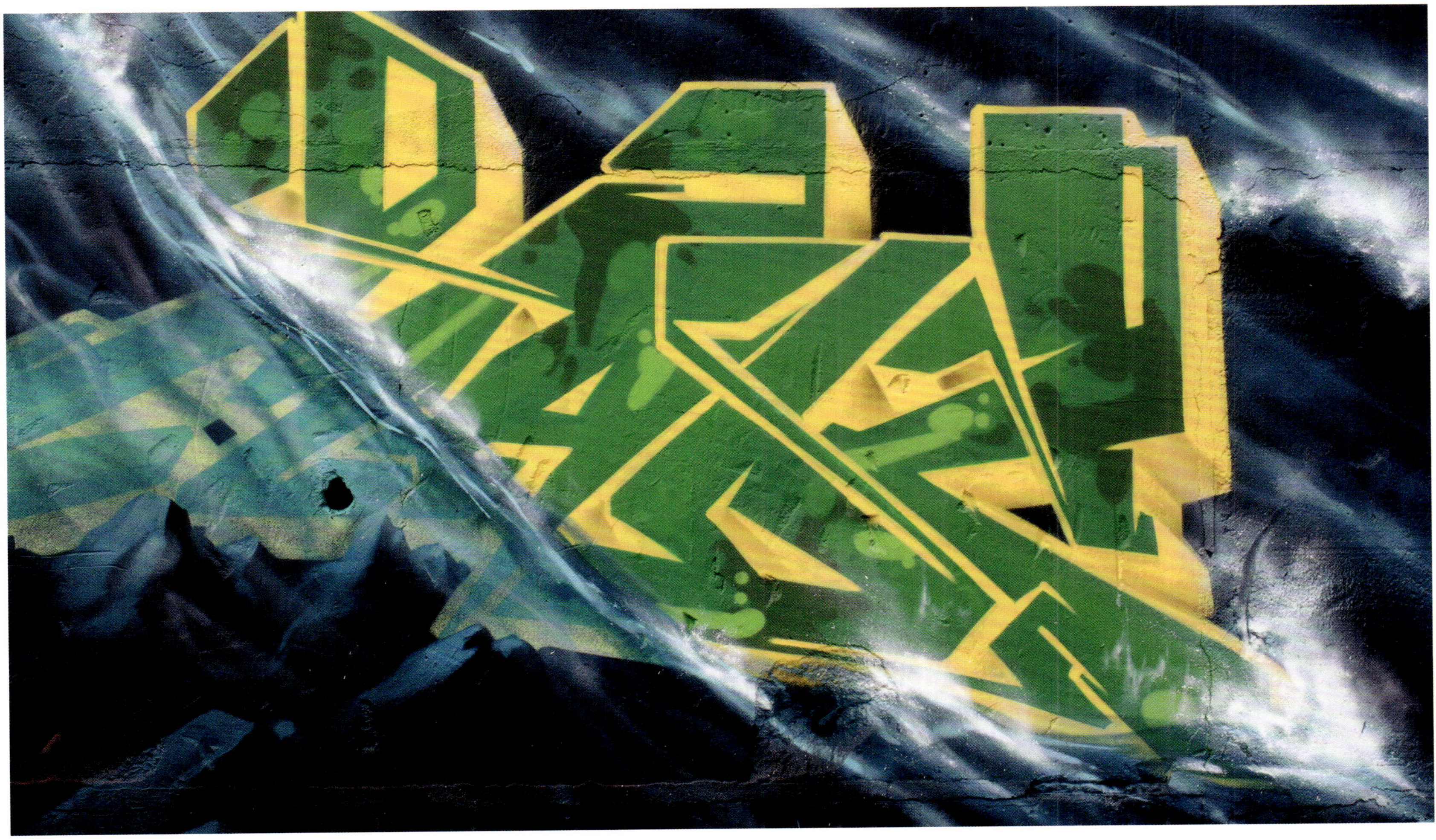

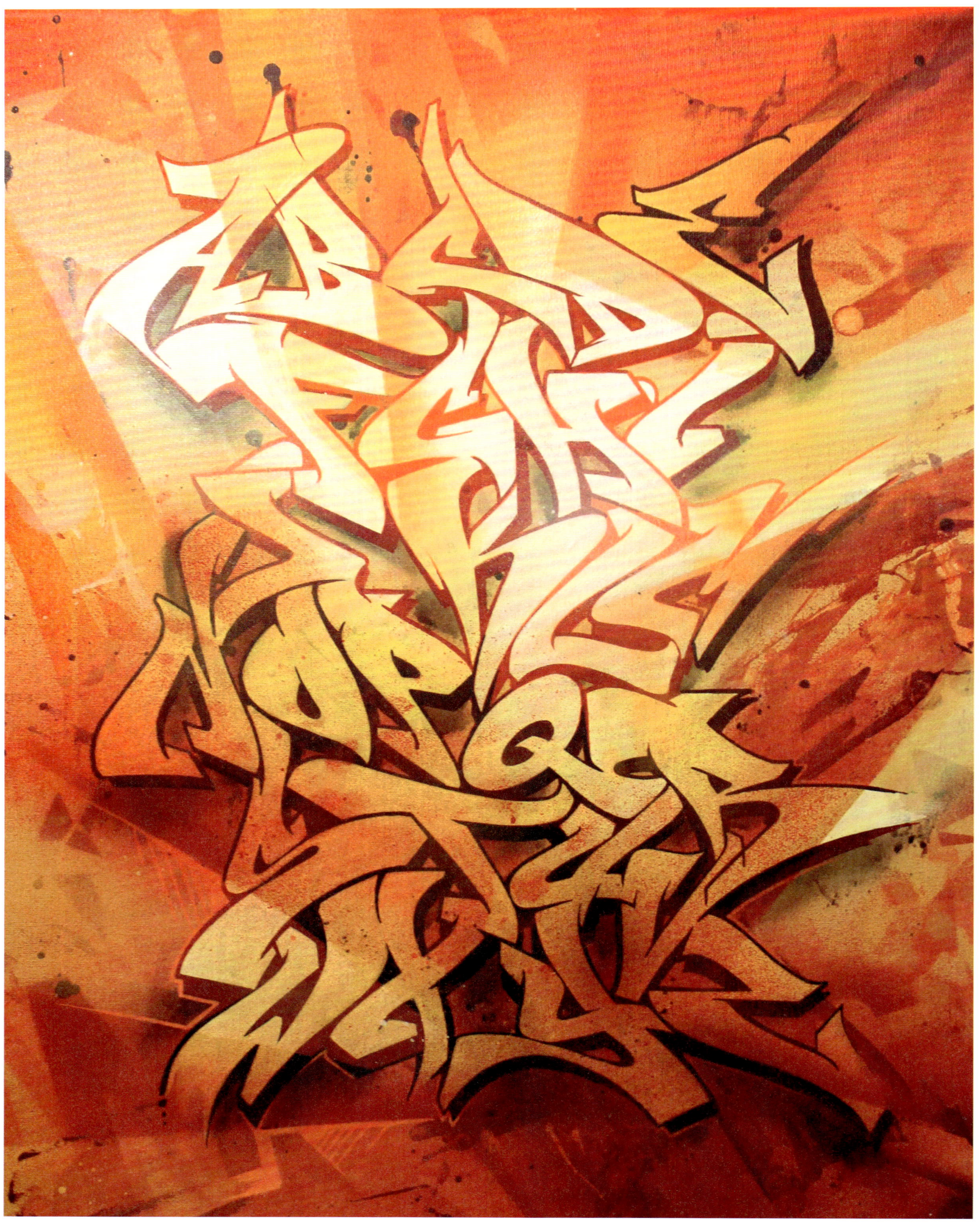

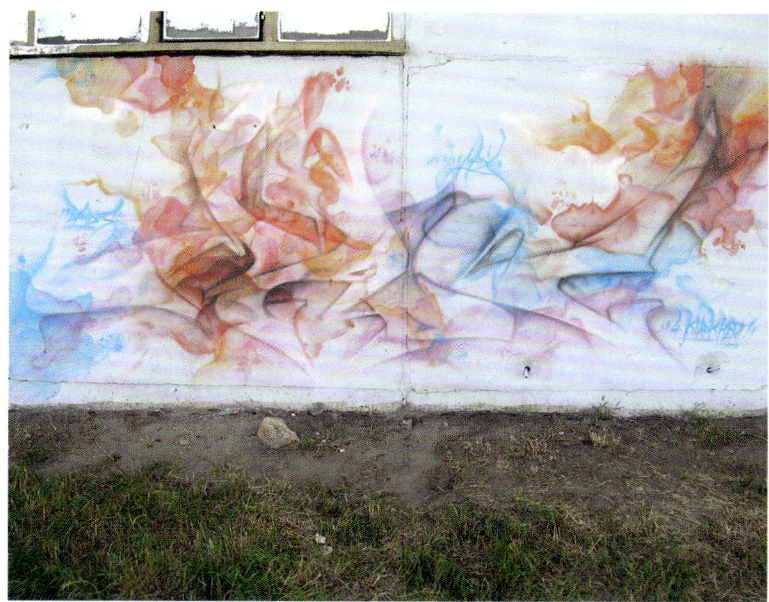

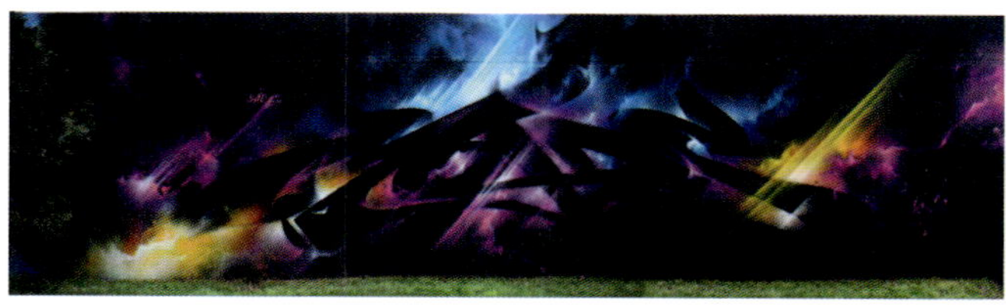

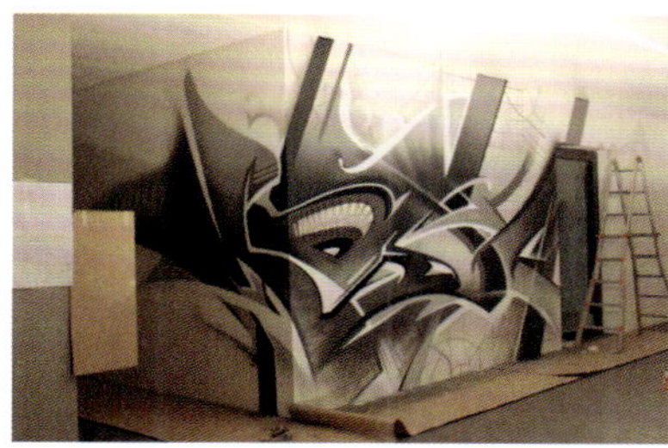

What remains are letters, the design of which has formed the core of graffiti writing for well over half a century. The degree of abstraction is possible up to the point at which legibility is still preserved, even if it is already difficult to recognise for strangers to the scene. At the same time, this exhaustion gives expression to one's own style. MadC was increasingly concerned with precisely the point at which alphabetical characters dissolve into abstraction. With the book *Street Fonts: Graffiti Alphabets from Around the World*, which was published by Thames & Hudson in 2011, MadC once again chose the book form to approach the subject of characters from a wider direction and also to document a moment in the history of graffiti art. She invited over 150 writers to design the 26 letters of the Latin alphabet in their respective styles. This was a challenge, in that many writers usually only use the letters that are part of their name. Those invited were free to use their choice of medium. Entire walls, as well as small paper sketches, were submitted, capturing an impressive range of styles. MadC herself also contributed an alphabet, which was strongly representative of her dynamic style and which already bore an essential characteristic that pointed to her future development – she shaped the alphabet on canvas **(fig. 69)**.

In retrospect it seems that these two extensive projects, *The 700 Wall* and *Street Fonts*, which dealt intensively with the two areas of 'classic' graffiti art, also meant a kind of liberation for MadC from precisely these areas, which she was now able to leave behind. The handling of fonts continued to play a major role, but MadC explored more and more how far she could break them up into dynamic lines before they disappeared. Where is the limit of letters as signs, as objects – when do they become abstract? In precisely this abstraction, a new field opens up that leads in a direction beyond classic writing.

Since her return to Germany, MadC had intensified her work in the studio in order to successfully embark on a path on which many writers before her had failed: to translate the presence and energy of graffiti writing from the street onto the canvas and to let the result flow back onto the street. Since the public spaces of a city form a charged context for graffiti that is not available in white gallery spaces, graffiti characters quickly run the risk of losing their aesthetic appeal without this context. By simply translating – spraying pieces on canvases – their 'distinctive difference to conventional visual production',[9] based above all on connotations of freedom, risk and anarchy, can quickly disappear, and thus the entire conceptual foundation disappears. MadC saw the large gap between the street and the canvas, and bridged this gap by incorporating her early experiences with the visual arts. The focus of her search was the transfer of energy and dynamics from one medium to another, and it ultimately constituted the greatest challenge. It called for a radical step outside the rules of graffiti, but without completely cutting off the references. Acrylic and watercolour paints, brushes and scrapers were used in addition to the spray can.

For a long time, MadC was not satisfied with the outcome, working through the night just to dispose of the work in the morning. She delved into a meticulous investigation of the visual properties of her mediums – how do watercolours behave on paper compared to canvas? Which visual effects can be created with which means? Finally, coloured watery splodges, translucent brushstrokes and overlapping image layers found their way onto the canvas, forming together with hard-edged remnants of letters – a visual language that MadC, in turn, carried outside onto the walls. Transparent spray paints, which she had used for the first time in 2008 **(fig. 70)**, were an important tool for enabling her highly water-based, translucent painting methods. In addition to spray cans, she also increasingly used paint spray guns. The interplay of the mediums gave the works a particular depth, and the gap between the worlds became smaller, creating a connection between the painterly and gestural energy of the studio with the performative–actionist dynamics of the street. In MadC's experiments on canvas, characters as a supporting element dissolved further and further into complete illegibility, but the dynamism of the wild style remained in the lines. The works were still structured on a compositional architecture based on letters; however, they increasingly gave way to an autonomous aesthetic. By 2012 at the latest, classic outlines and fill-ins disappeared, and increasing abstraction could be traced with every work. The canvases became works of art in their own right.

69 (opposite). *Street Fonts Alphabet*, 50 x 40cm, ink, spray paint and acrylic and canvas, 2010
70 (top left). First wall painted only with transparent spray paint, Germany, 2008
71 (top right). *The Transparent Wall*, Landsberg, Germany, 2010
72 (bottom right). Munich, Germany, 2010

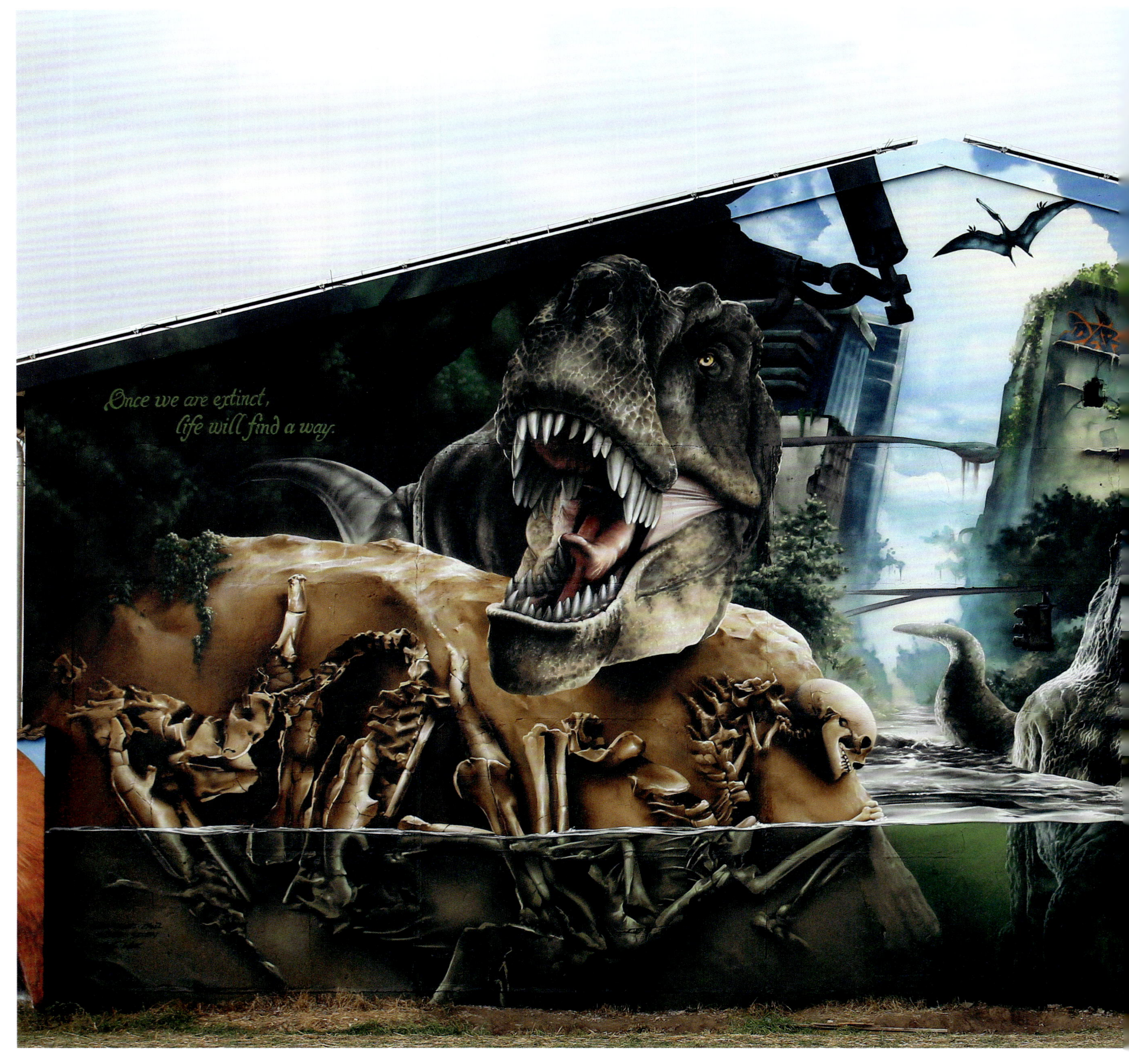

73–76. *The Jurassic Park Wall*, Peissen, Germany, 2012

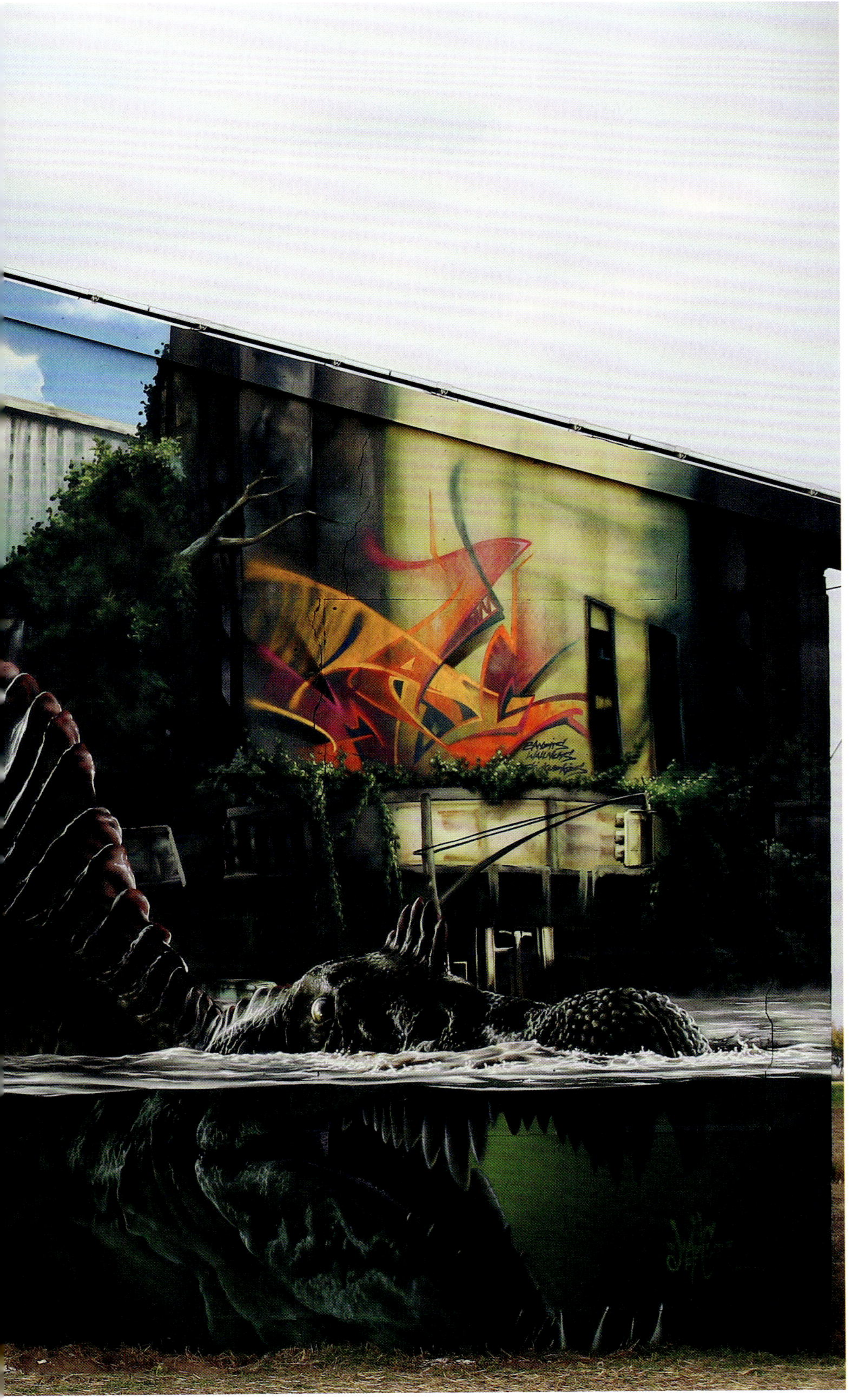

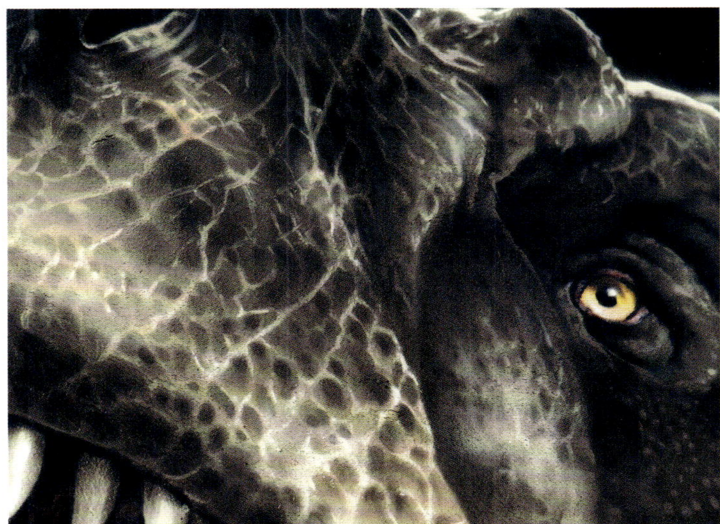

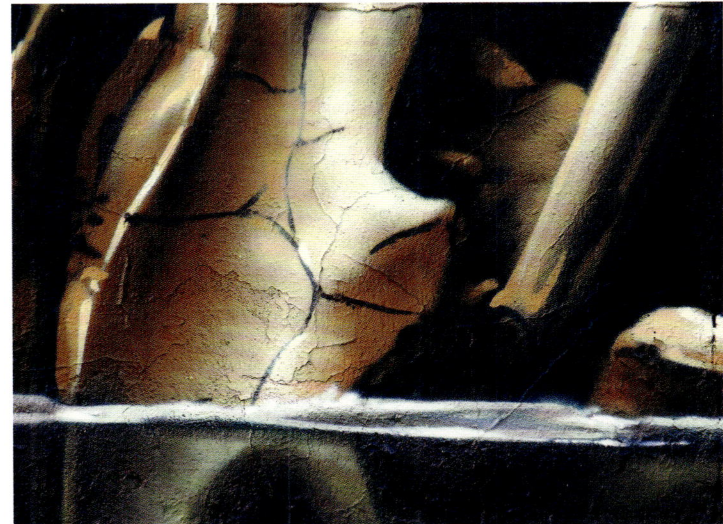

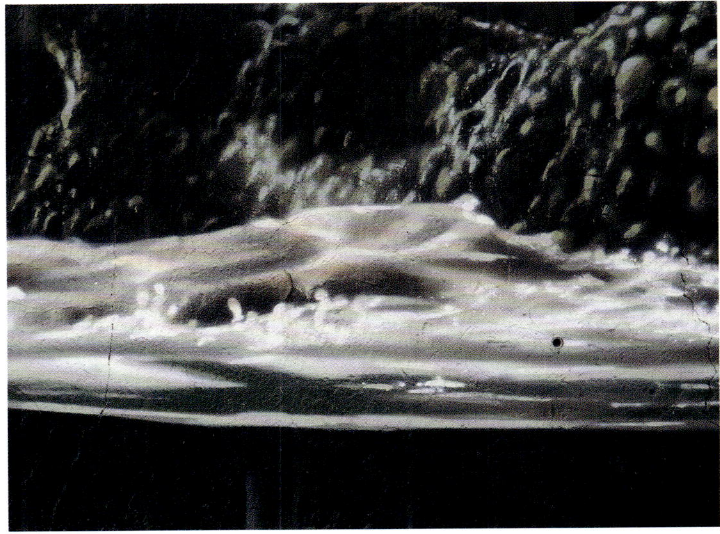

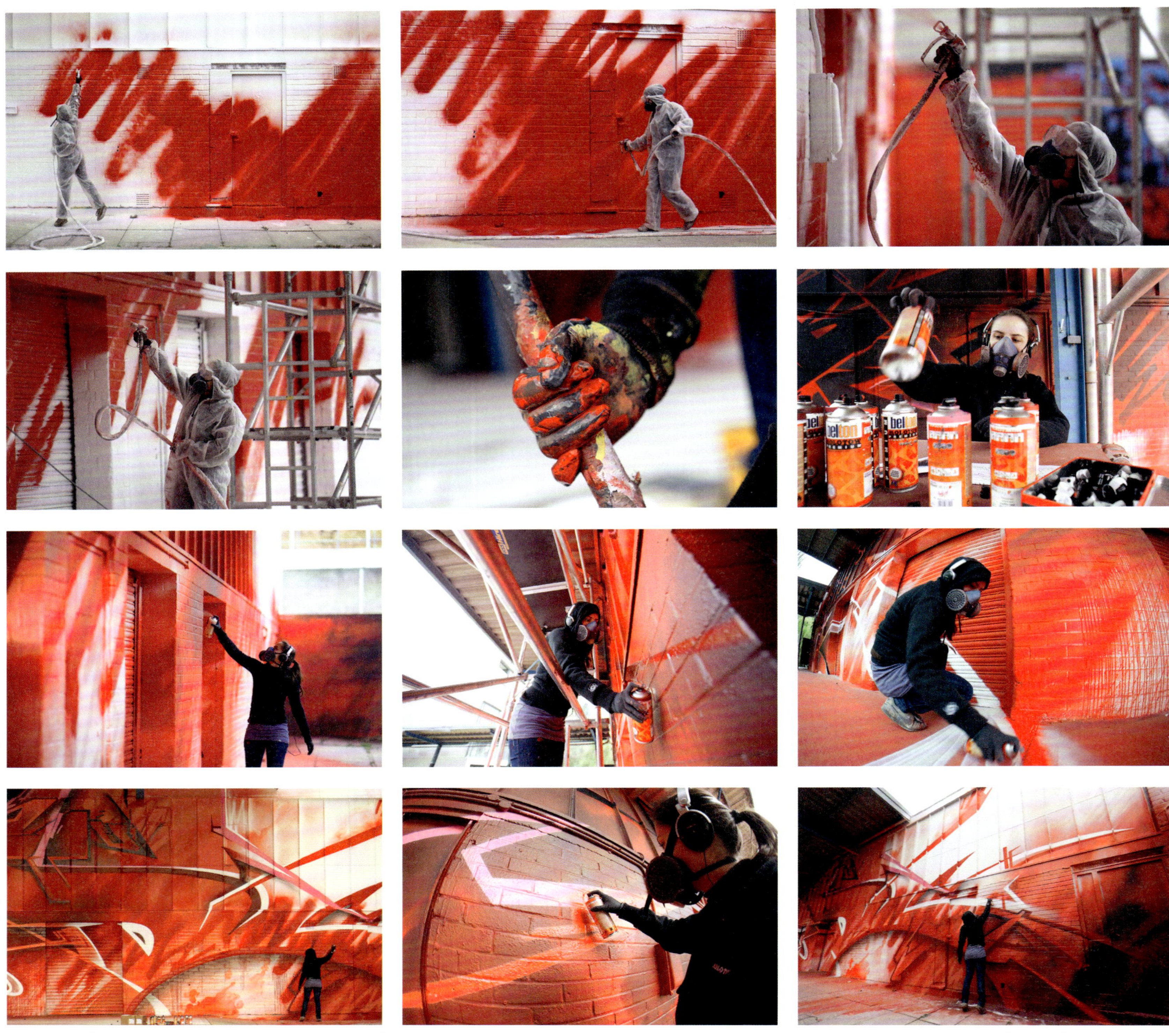
belton

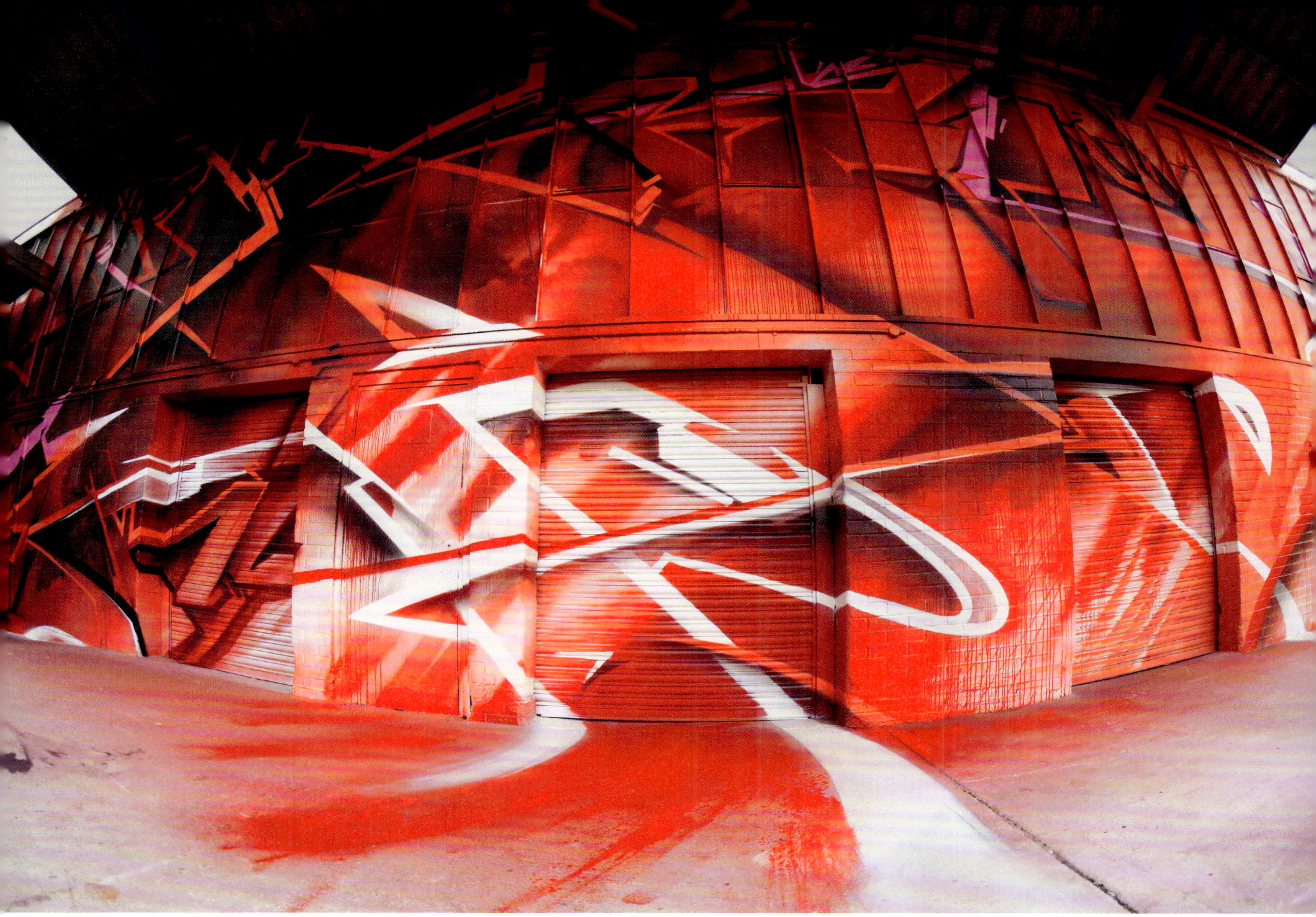

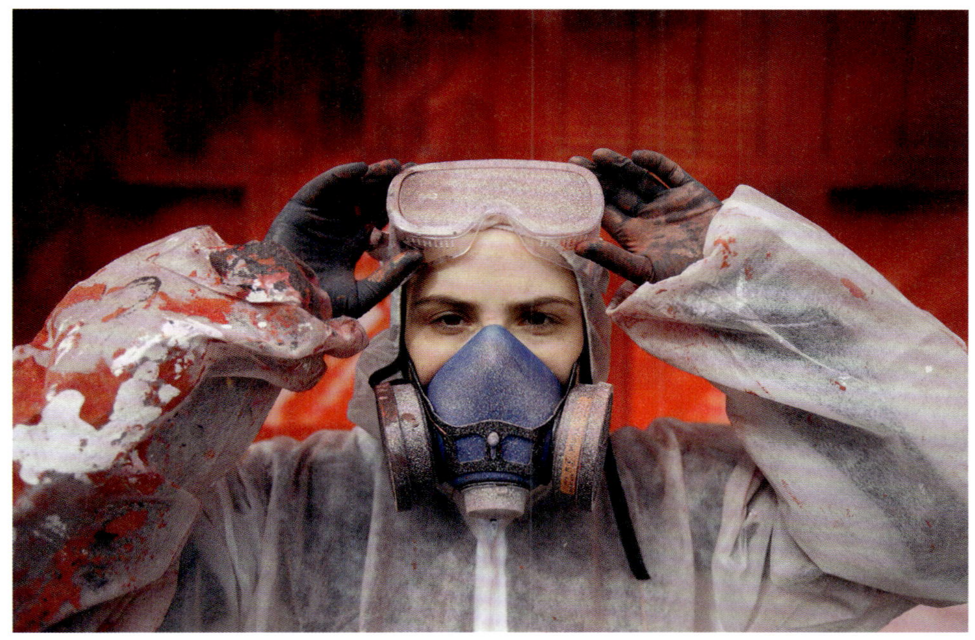

77–79 (this spread). *The ABC Wall*, painted as part of the solo show *MadABC* at Pure Evil Gallery, London 2011. The old warehouse was an off-site location for the show; people were able to shuttle between the two locations on the opening day in April 2011

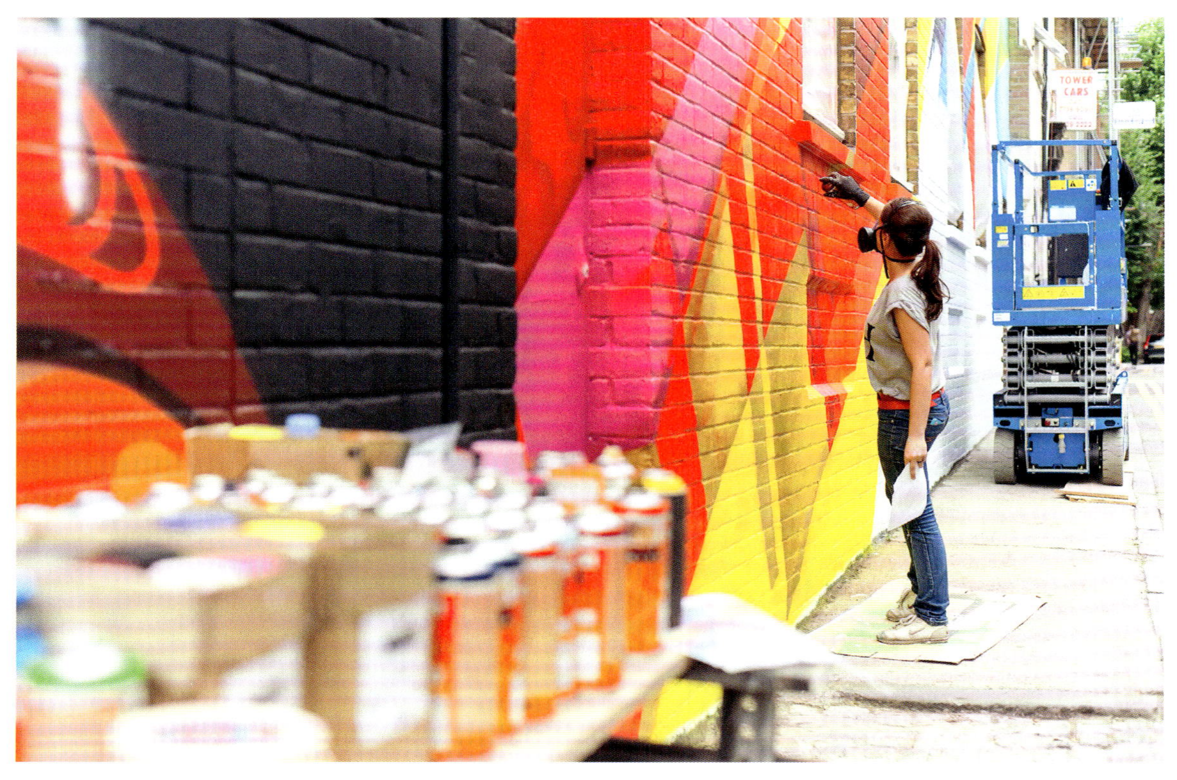
TOWER
CARS

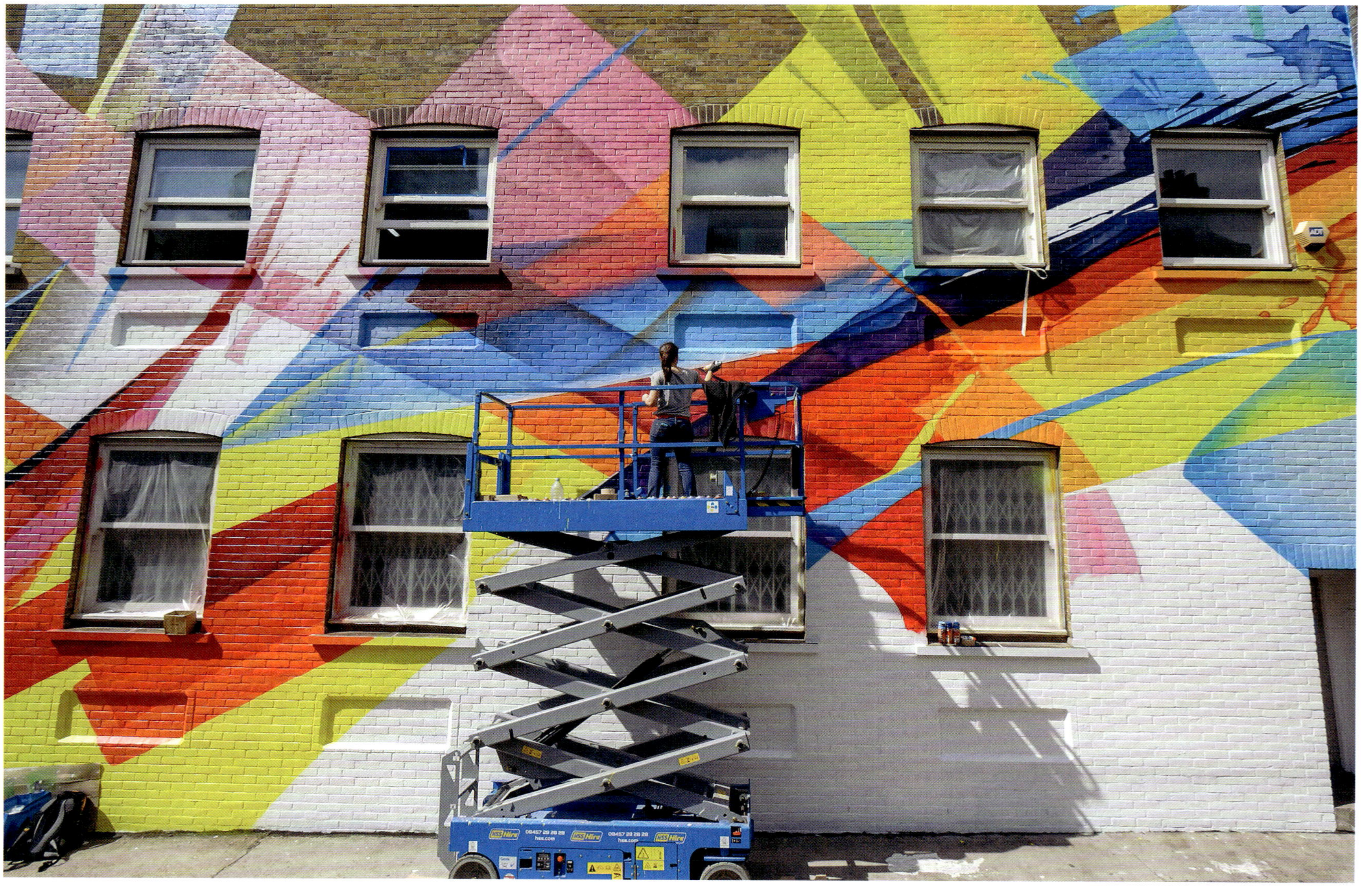

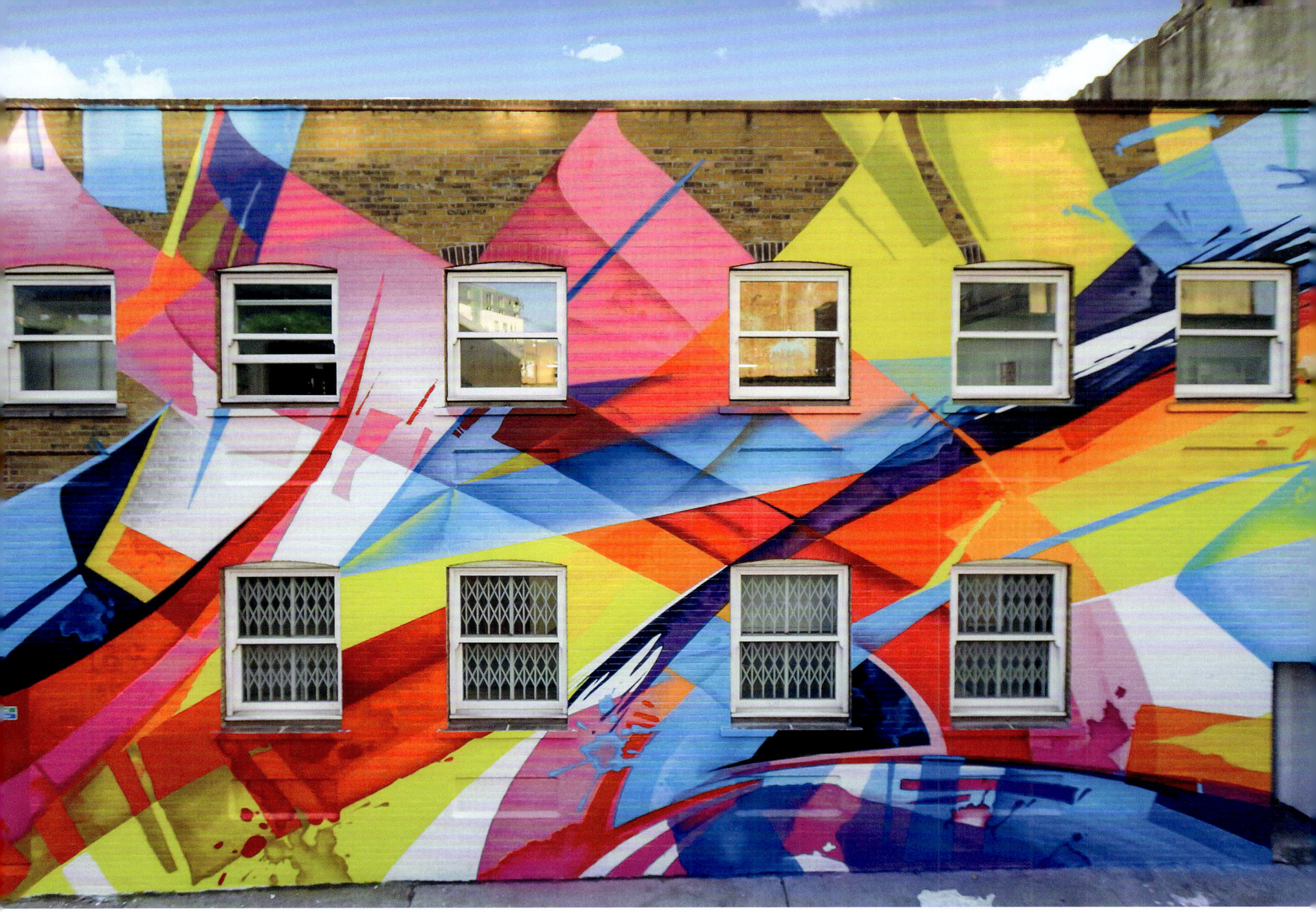

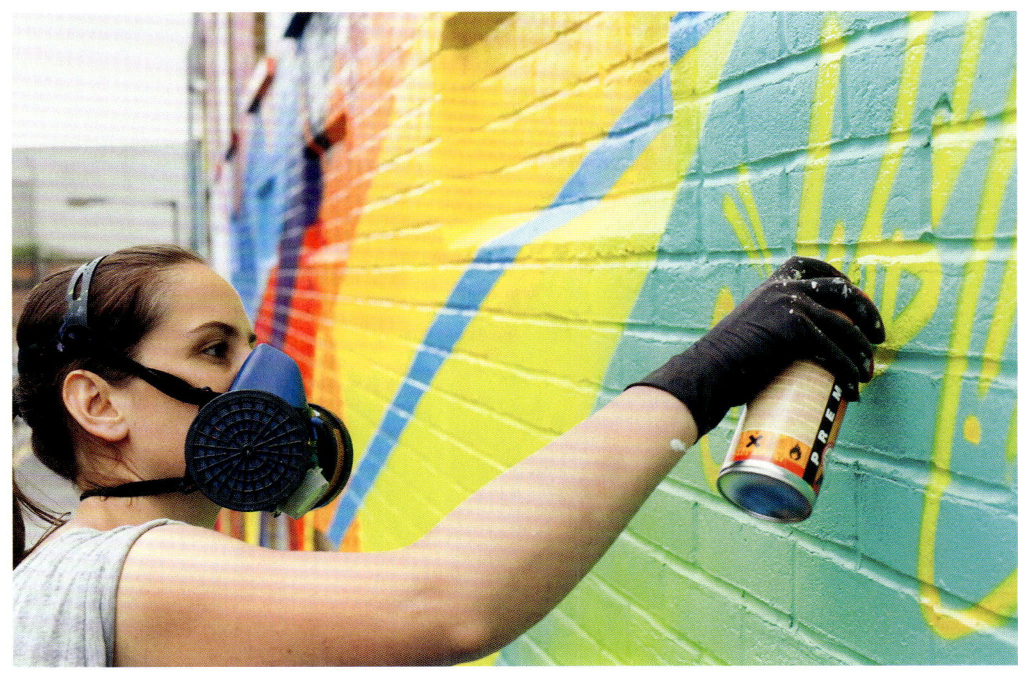

80–83 (this spread). Chance Street, Shoreditch, London, UK, August 2013

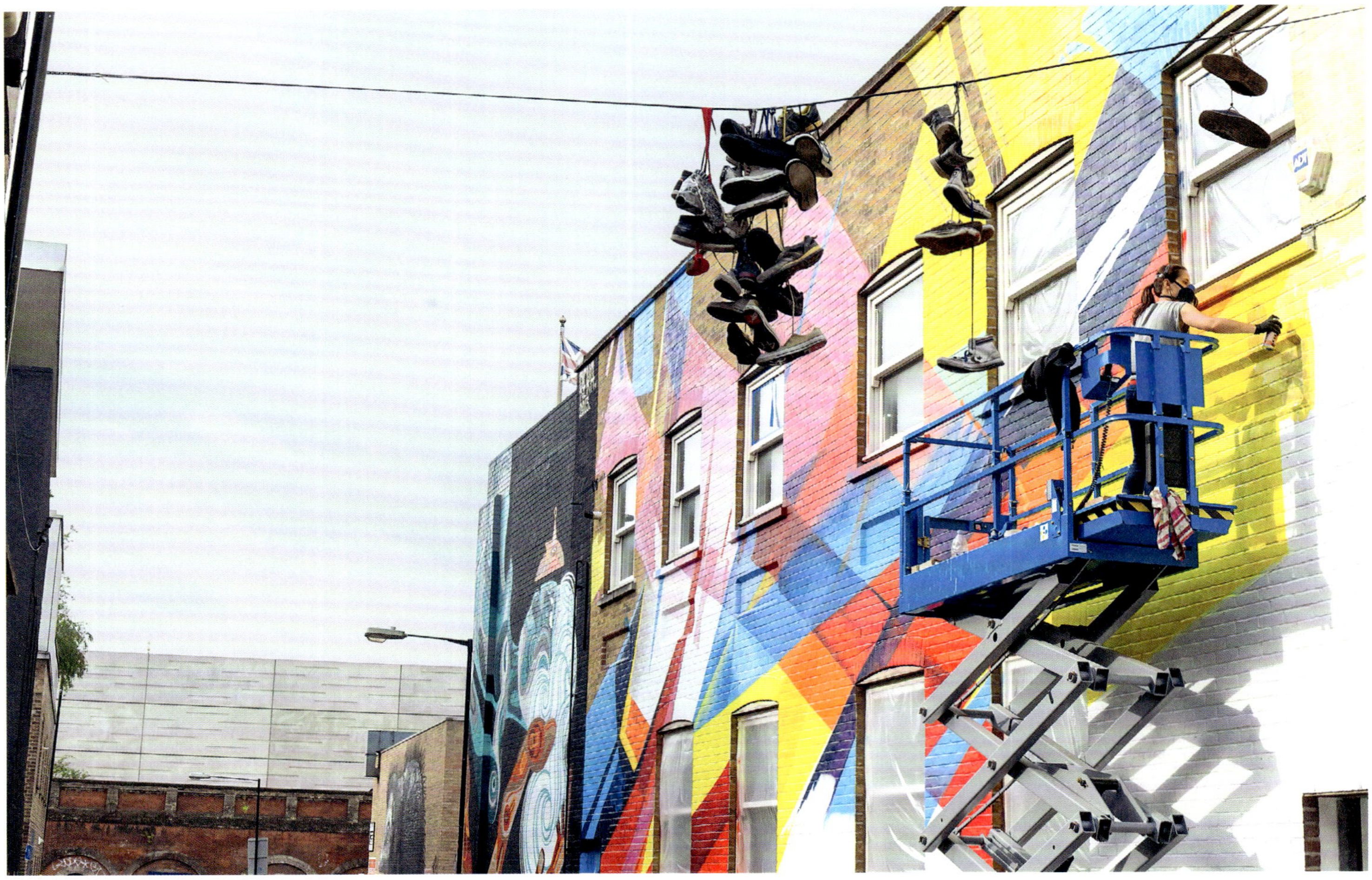

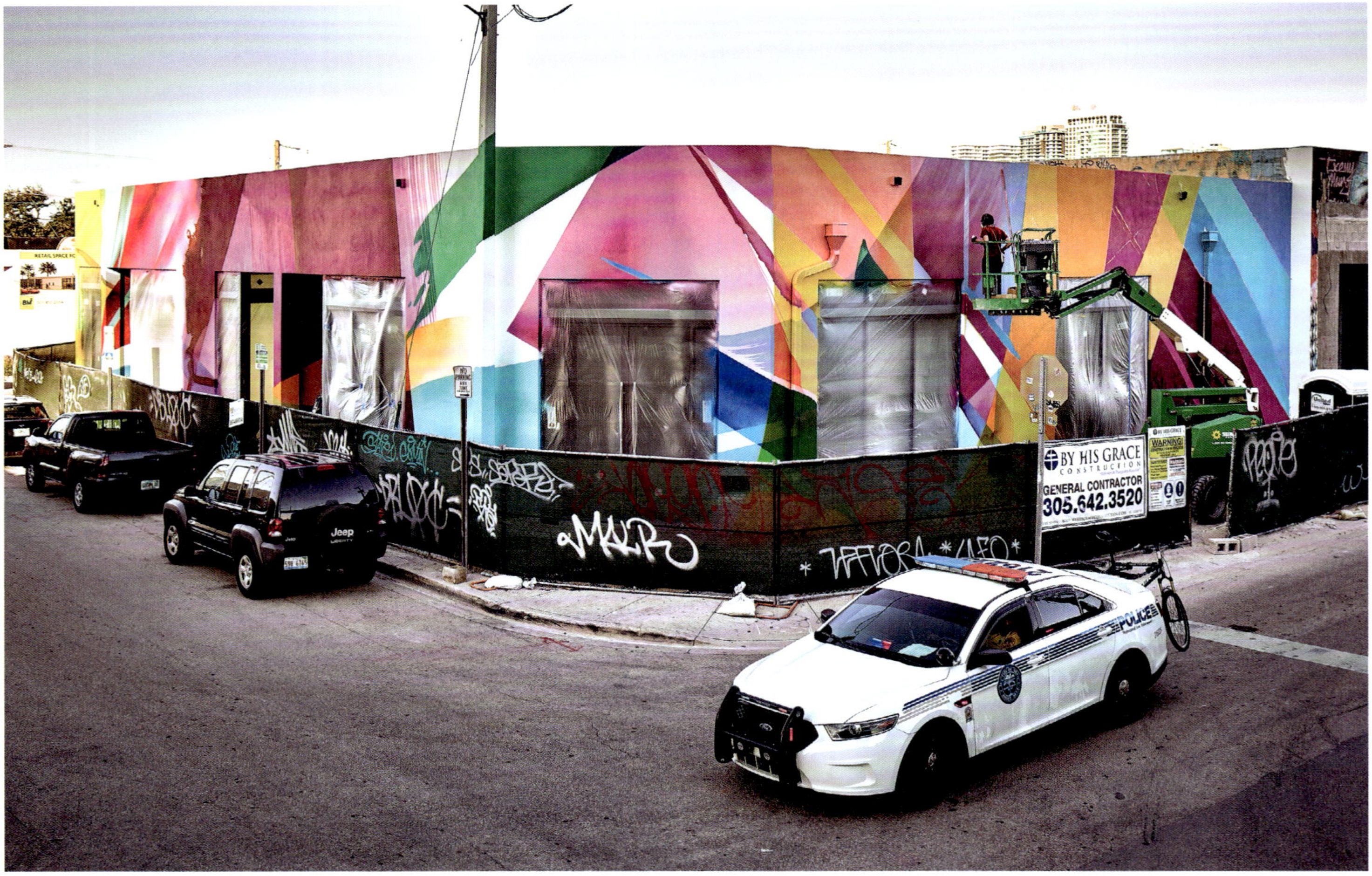
BY HIS GRACE
CONSTRUCTION
GENERAL CONTRACTOR
305.642.3520
WARNING
POLICE

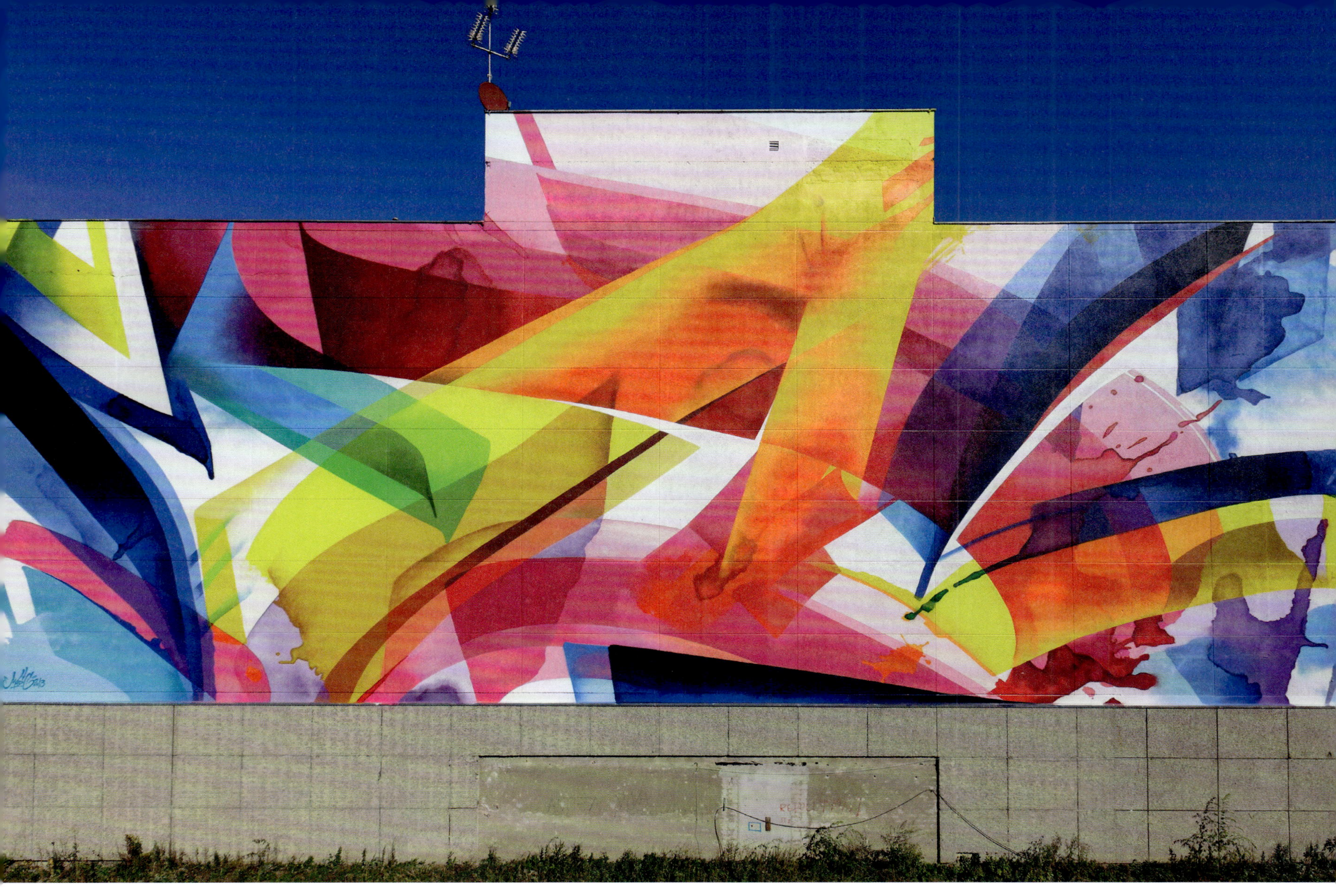

On the street, MadC's development towards abstraction progressed at a slower pace. She held on to the classic basics of style writing and returned to them repeatedly, and then again at later points. An important project that brought her newly developed visual language into the world was her work in London's Chance Street, created in 2013 **(figs. 80–84)**. It is probably the first work by MadC for which the term 'graffiti writing' is no longer sufficient and 'mural' seems more appropriate. The change of direction in her artistic expression could clearly be seen in this typical London brick house in Shoreditch. The location was – in an old graffiti manner – well chosen. While she still had to carry the costs for the equipment and paint herself, it offered so much visibility that MadC subsequently received numerous invitations for further murals, for example in Miami **(fig. 85)**.

Another milestone followed in the same year with *The 500 Wall* at the Alte Messe (Old Fair) in Leipzig **(fig. 86)**. On this occasion MadC did not have several months to fill this huge area, as she had done for *The 700 Wall*, so she developed a method that enabled the realisation of the work within a few days, and that she continued to use for future projects. A work on canvas that she previously made in the studio served as a model **(fig. 87)**. She divided it into grids according to the individual panels of the cladding that covered the wall. For the first time, she hired a cherry picker, which pushed her slight fear of heights beyond certain limits. This physical challenge remained an important element in MadC's work, which was also anchored in its gestural dynamics. Within seven days, she had painted the work all by herself, using over 1,000 spray cans and many litres of wall paint.

The composition was characterised by calligraphic lines that unfurled across the surface in different directions. Mostly transparent, they overlapped in numerous layers and created their own space. In contrast to the neatly closing edges, some surfaces and specific areas appeared like oversized, water-soaked splashes of watercolour paint. Together these elements paid testimony to the production process that the motif had gone through, and referred to the artistic act that had taken place in the studio. Nevertheless, the mural can by no means be understood as a large-format copy of the canvas. Especially through the play with visual means, each work stands for itself and its specific context.

84 (opposite, top). Chance Street, Shoreditch, London, UK, August 2013
85 (opposite, bottom). Wynwood, Miami, November 2017
86 (above). *The 500 Wall*, Alte Messe, Leipzig, Germany, September 2013
87 (next spread). *thirteen-thirty-one*, 180 x 250cm, acrylic, watercolour and spray paint on canvas, 2013. This was the sketch for the mural in Leipzig, Germany

7 MadC cited in https://sojomojo.art/700-wall (accessed 17 March 2021).
8 Ibid.
9 Wuggenig, Ulf, 'Kunst-Kunst, Street Art und "Kreativität". Annäherungen mit Hilfe von Feld- und Systemtheorie', in Daniel Suber, Hilmar Schäfer, Sophia Prinz (eds), *Pierre Bourdieu und die Kulturwissenschaften*, Konstanz: UVK Verlag 2011, pp. 217–251, here p. 221. Extract translated by Eva Ruschkowski.

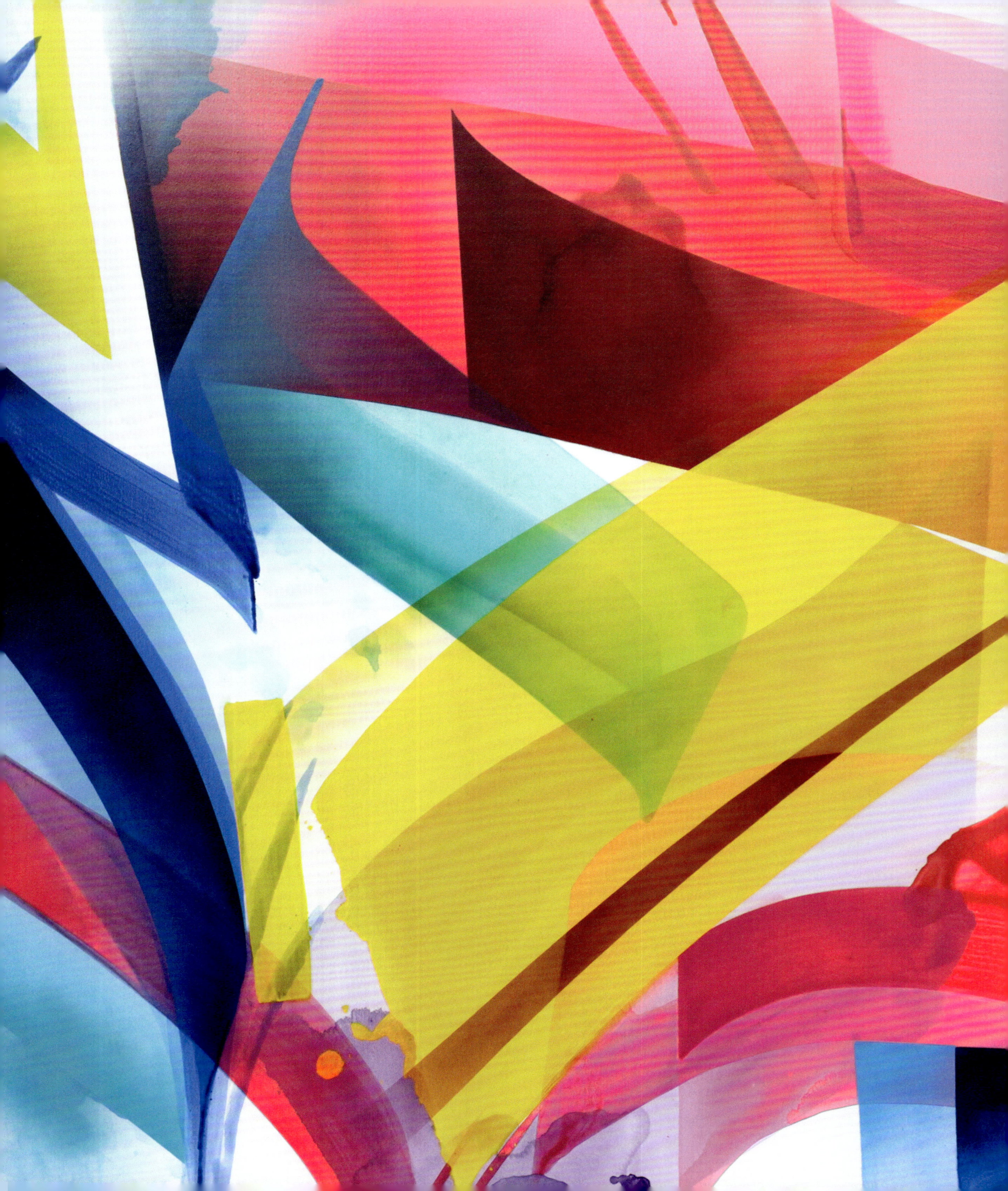

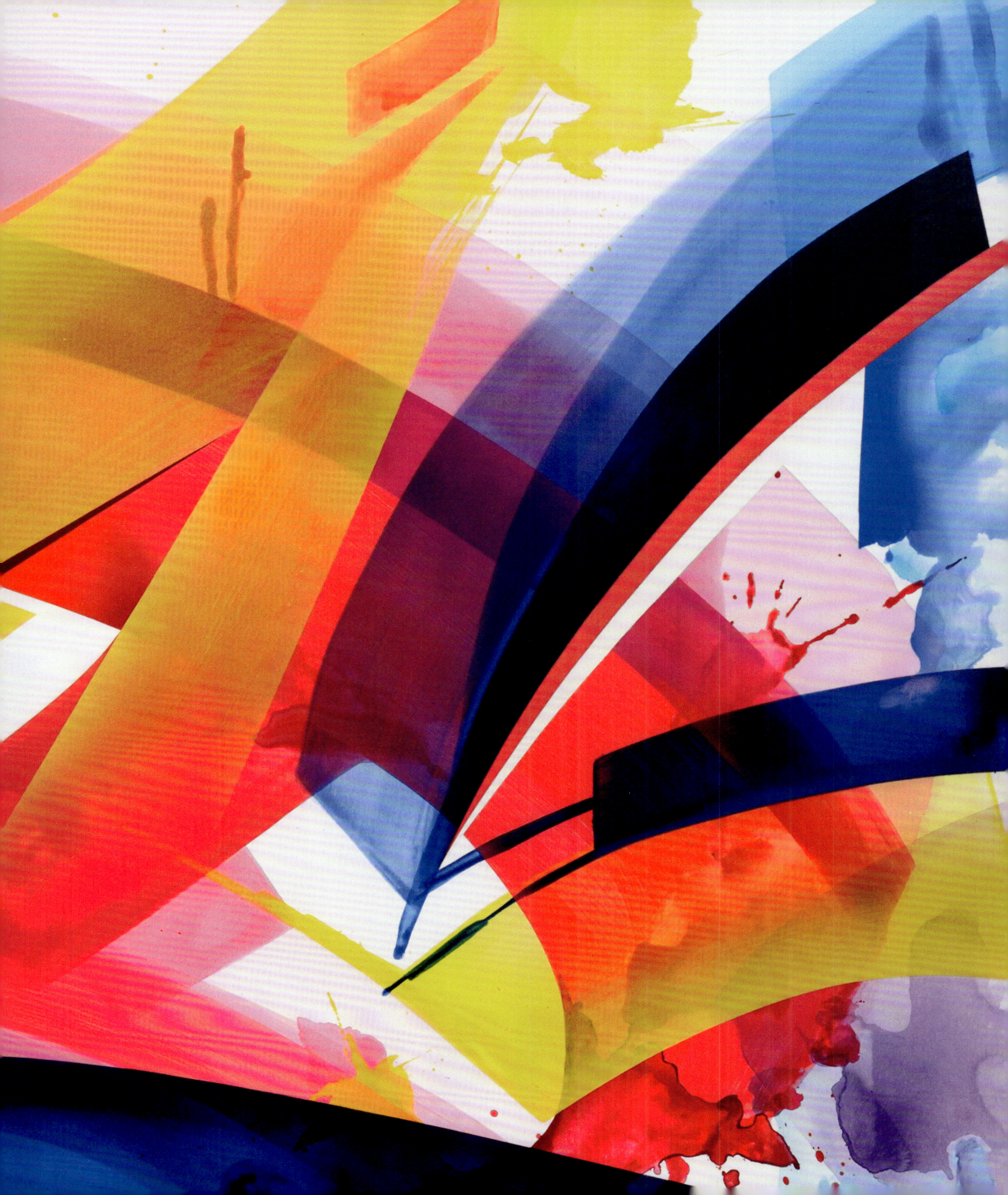

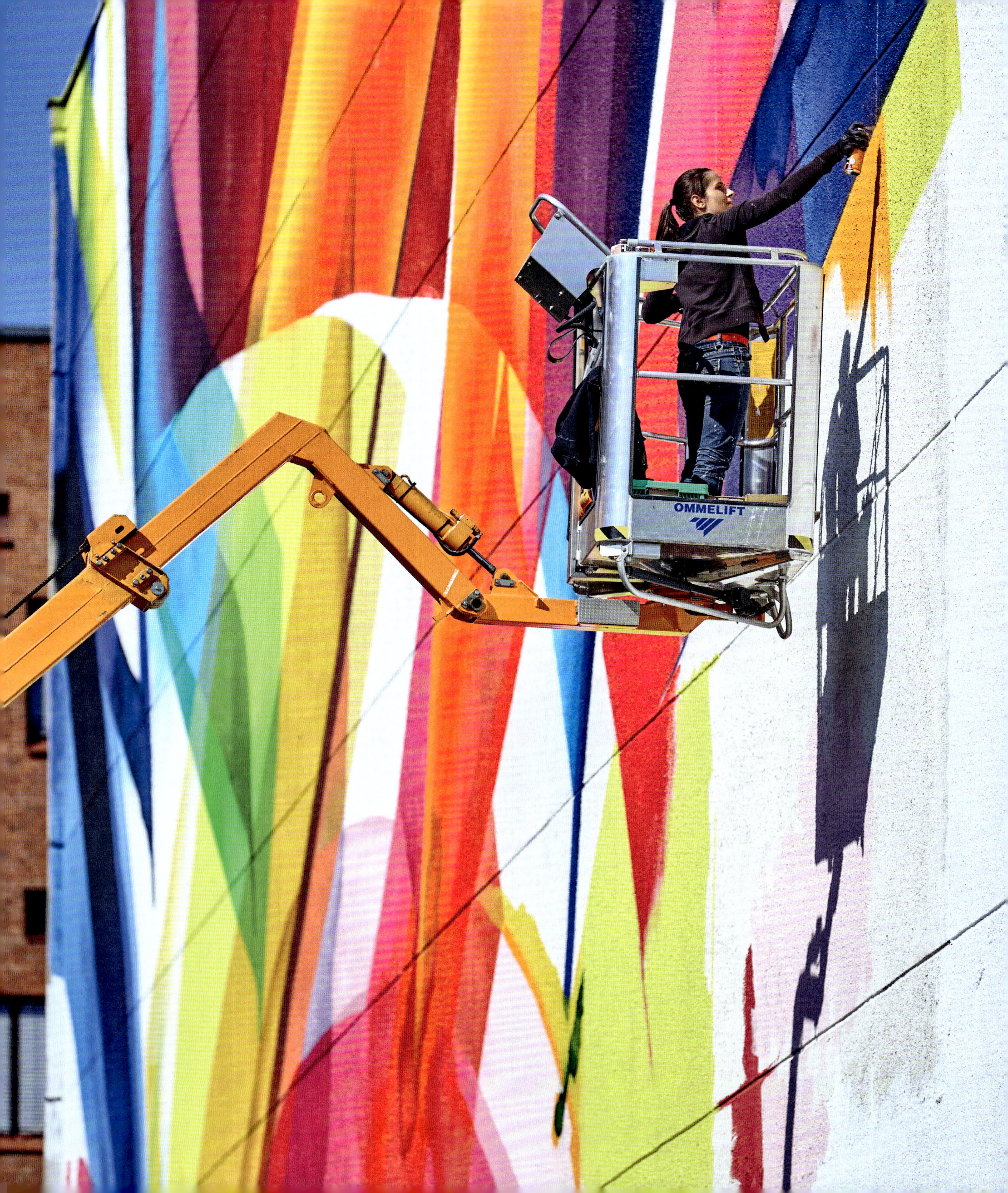
OMMELIFT

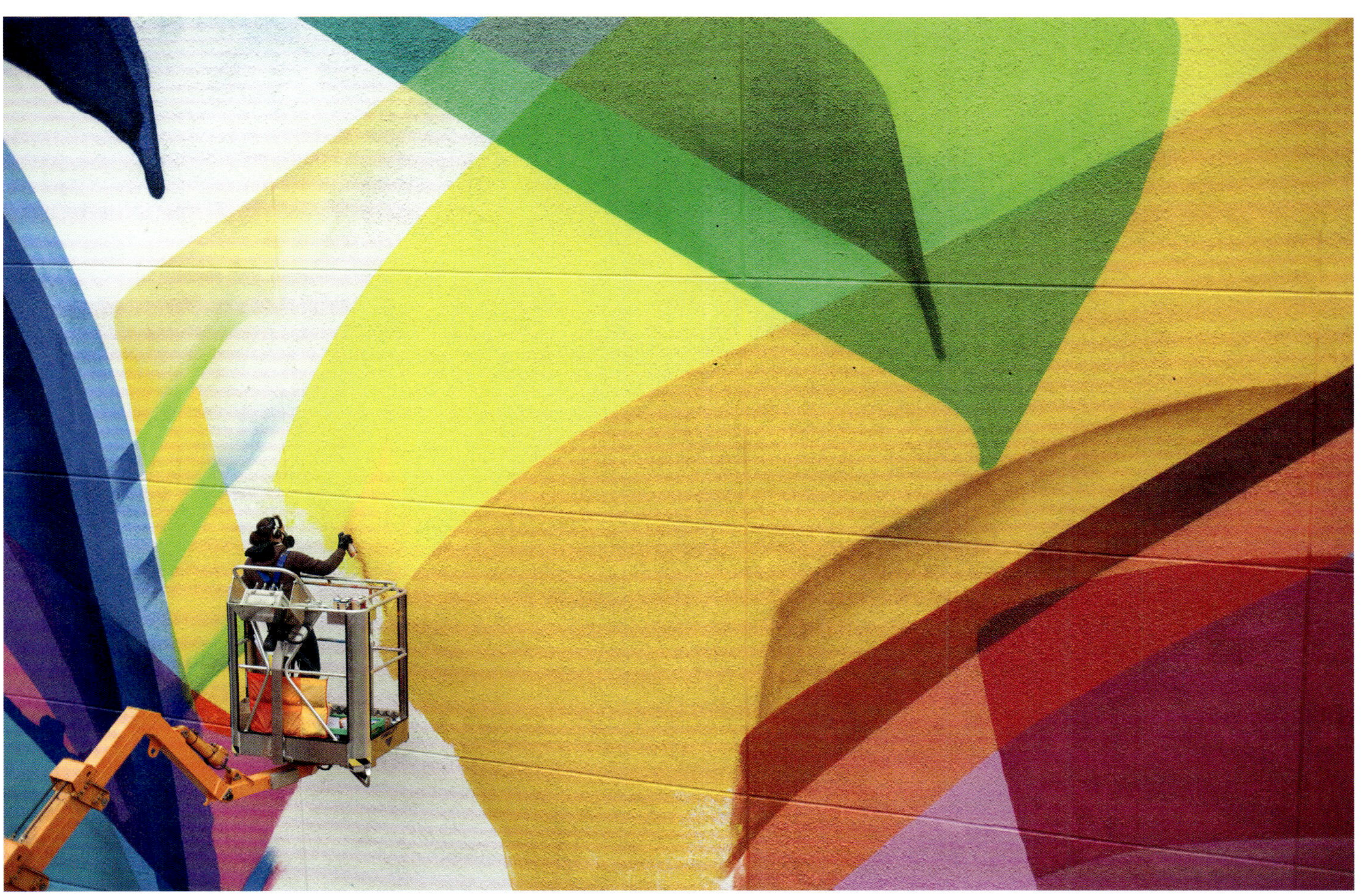

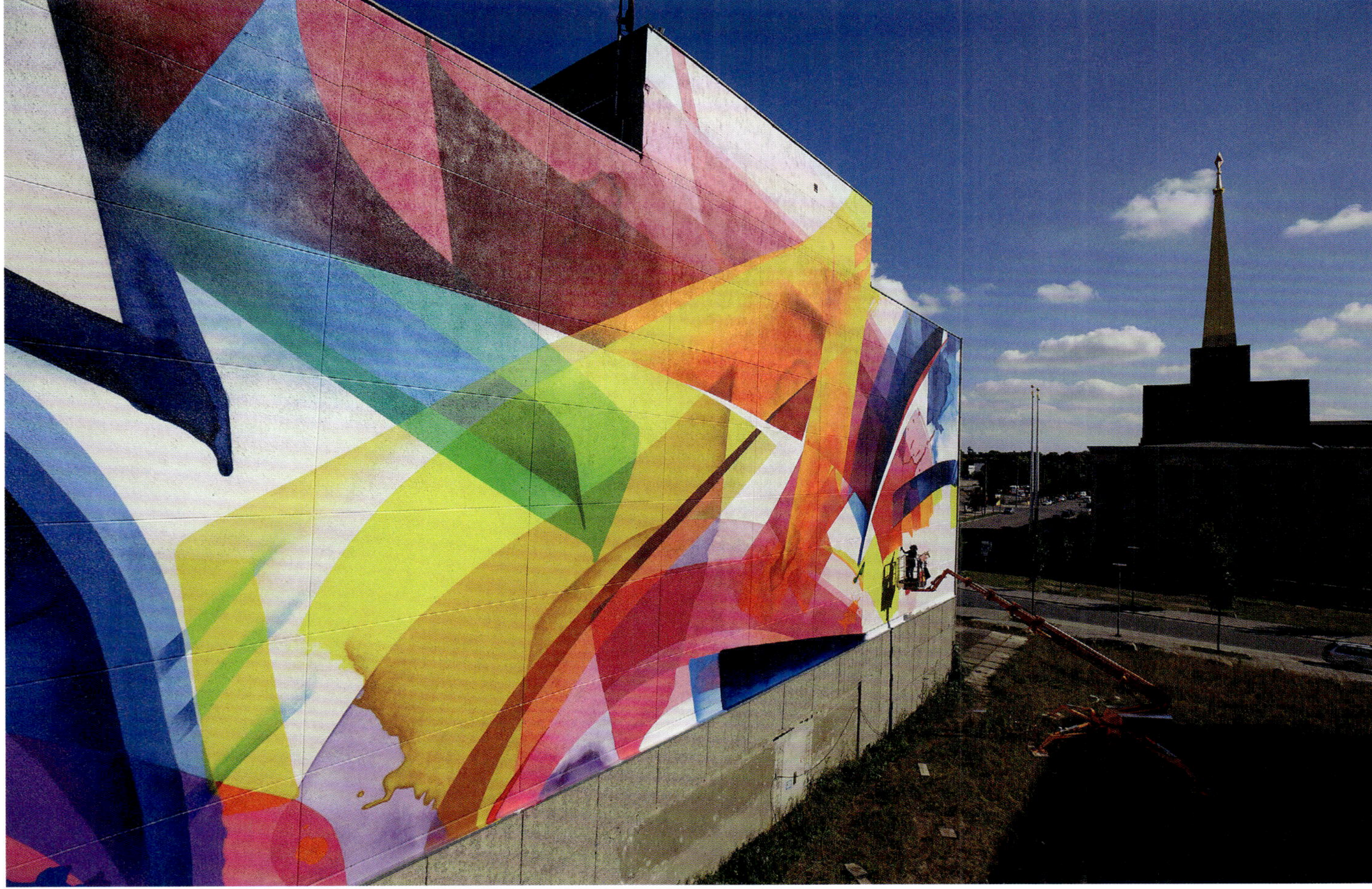

88–91 (this spread and next). *The 500 Wall*, Alte Messe, Leipzig, Germany, September 2013

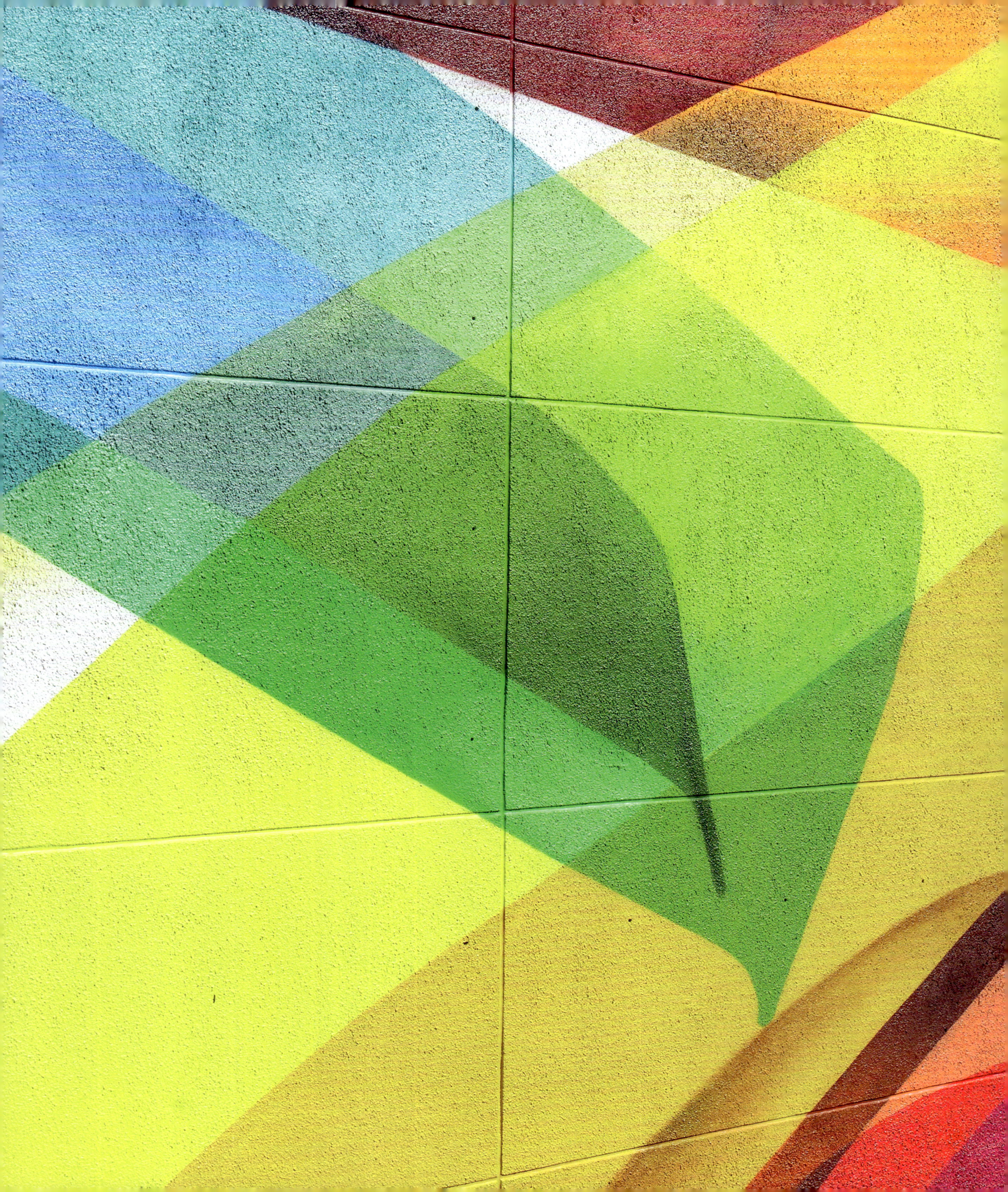

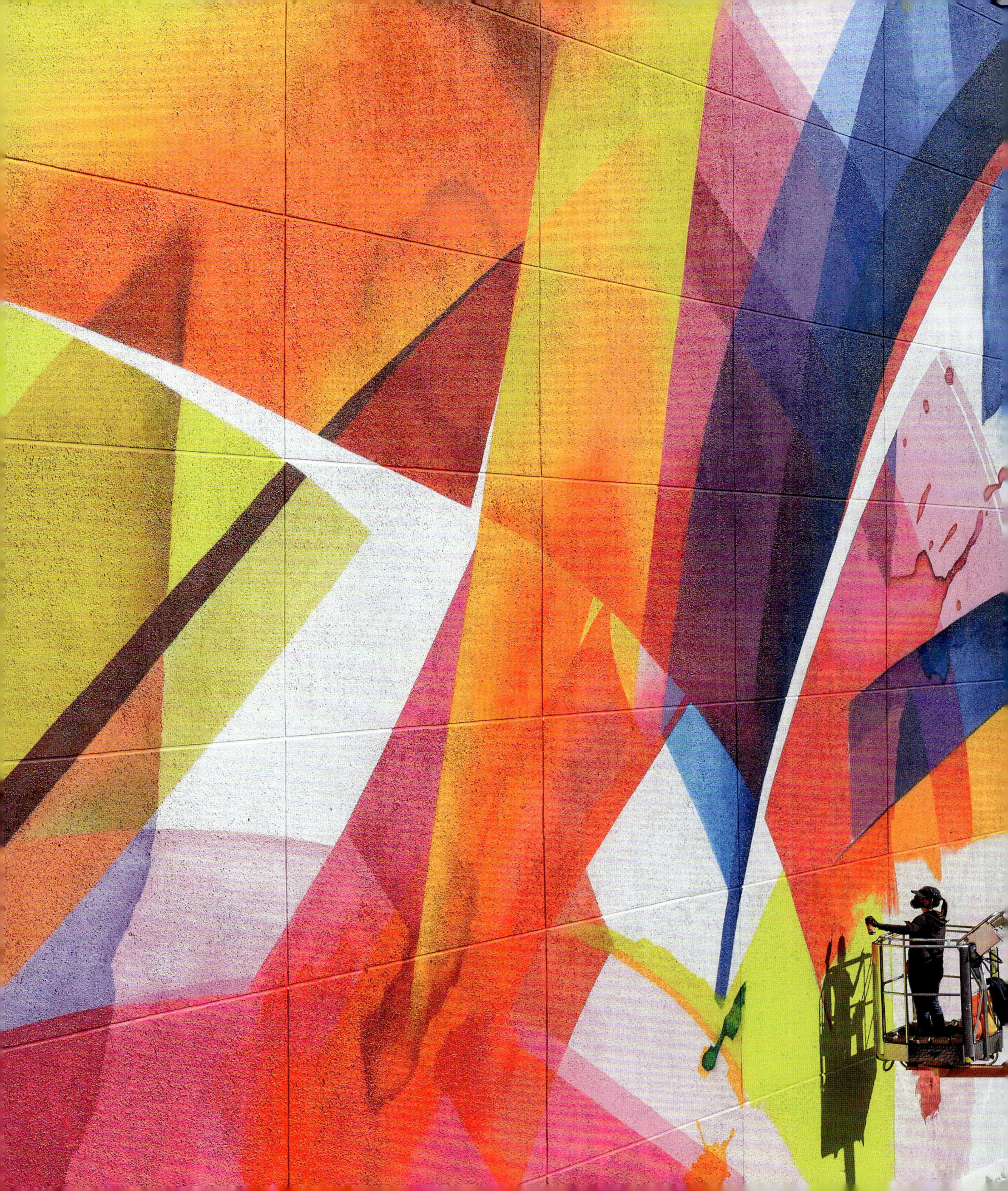

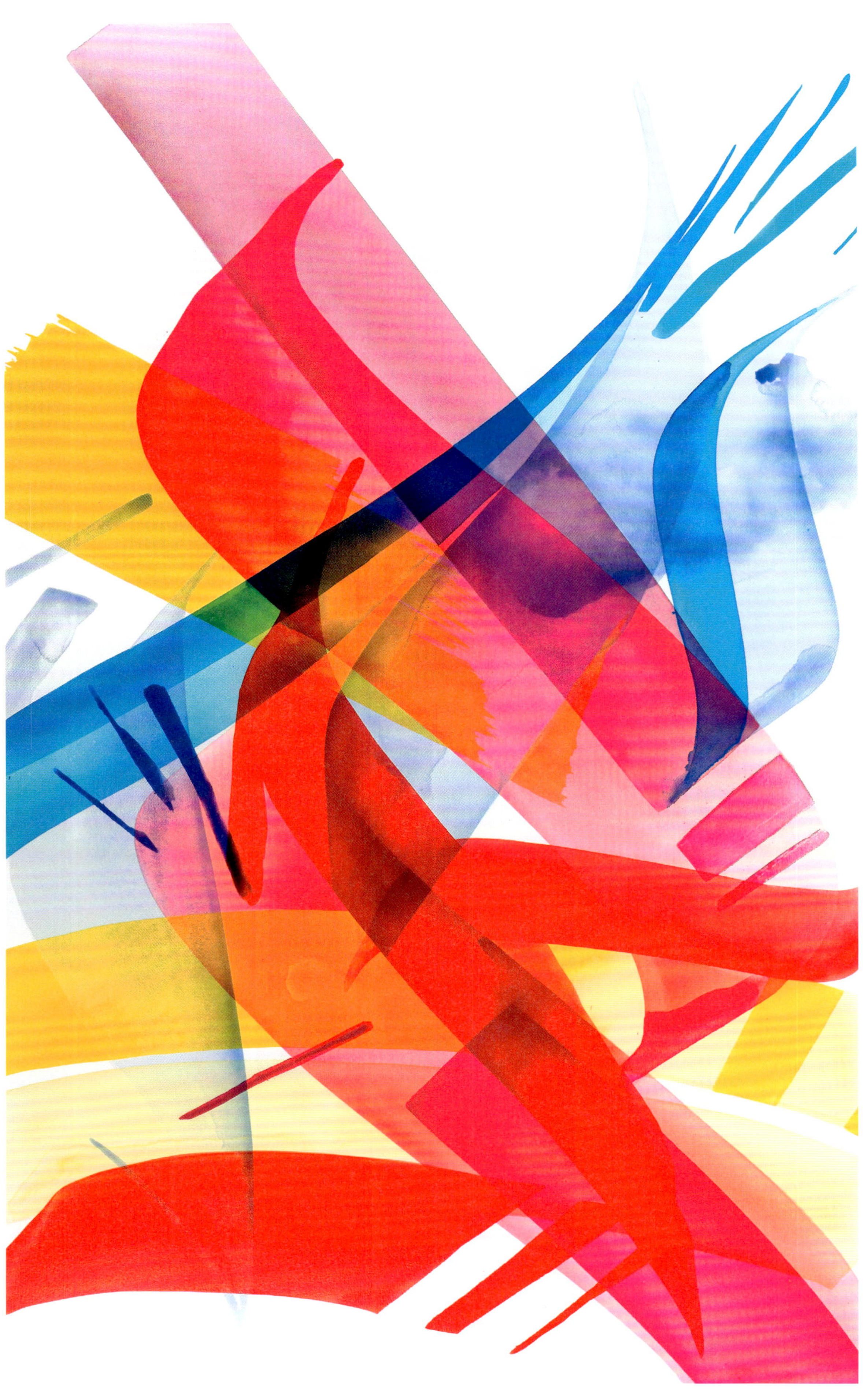

92. *eleven-thirty*, 180 x 110cm, acrylic and spray paint on canvas, 2014.
This was the sketch for the mural in Papeete, Tahiti, French Polynesia

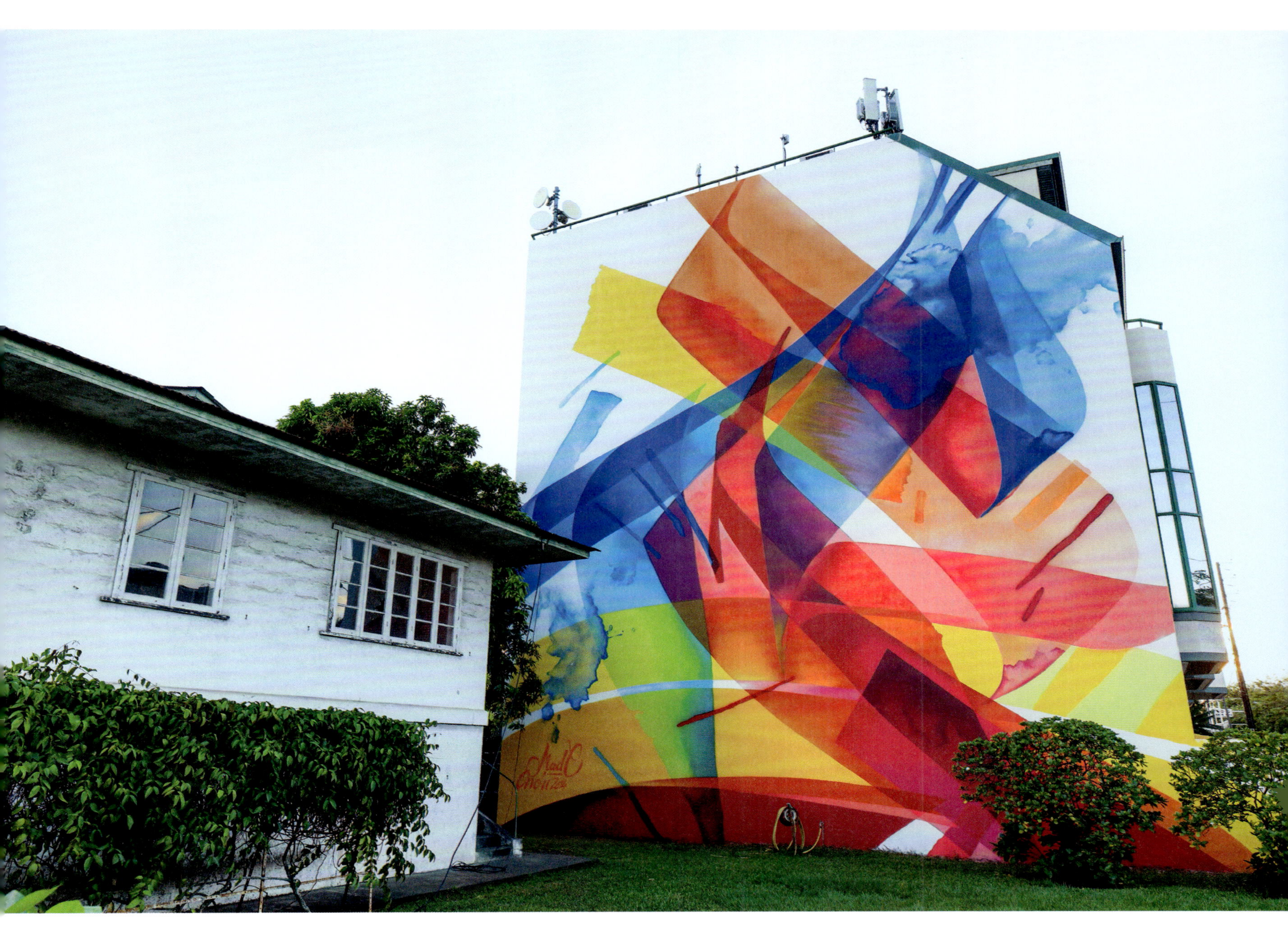

93–94 (above and next spread). Ono'u Festival, Avenue du Prince Hinoi, Papeete, Tahiti, French Polynesia, May 2014

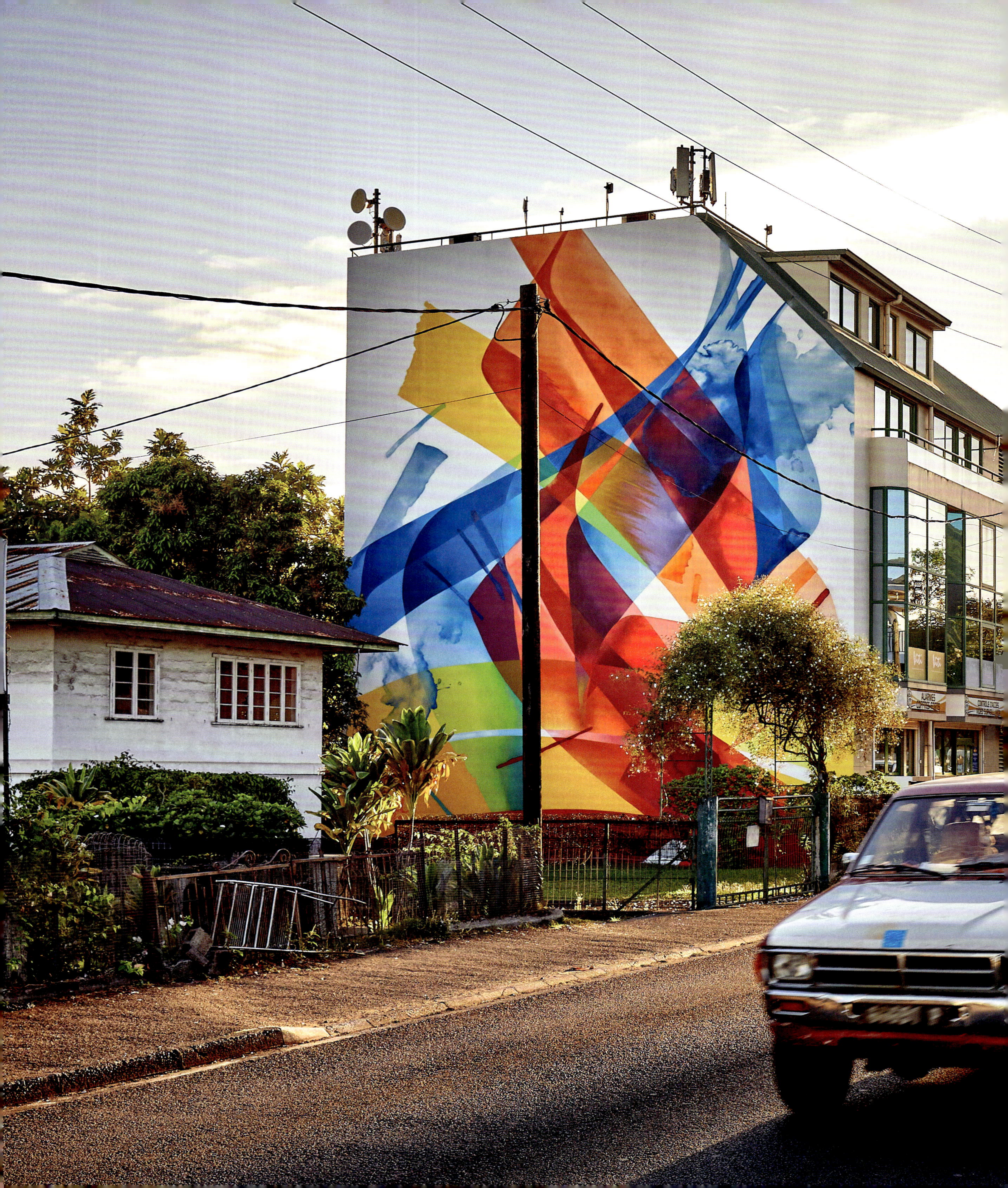

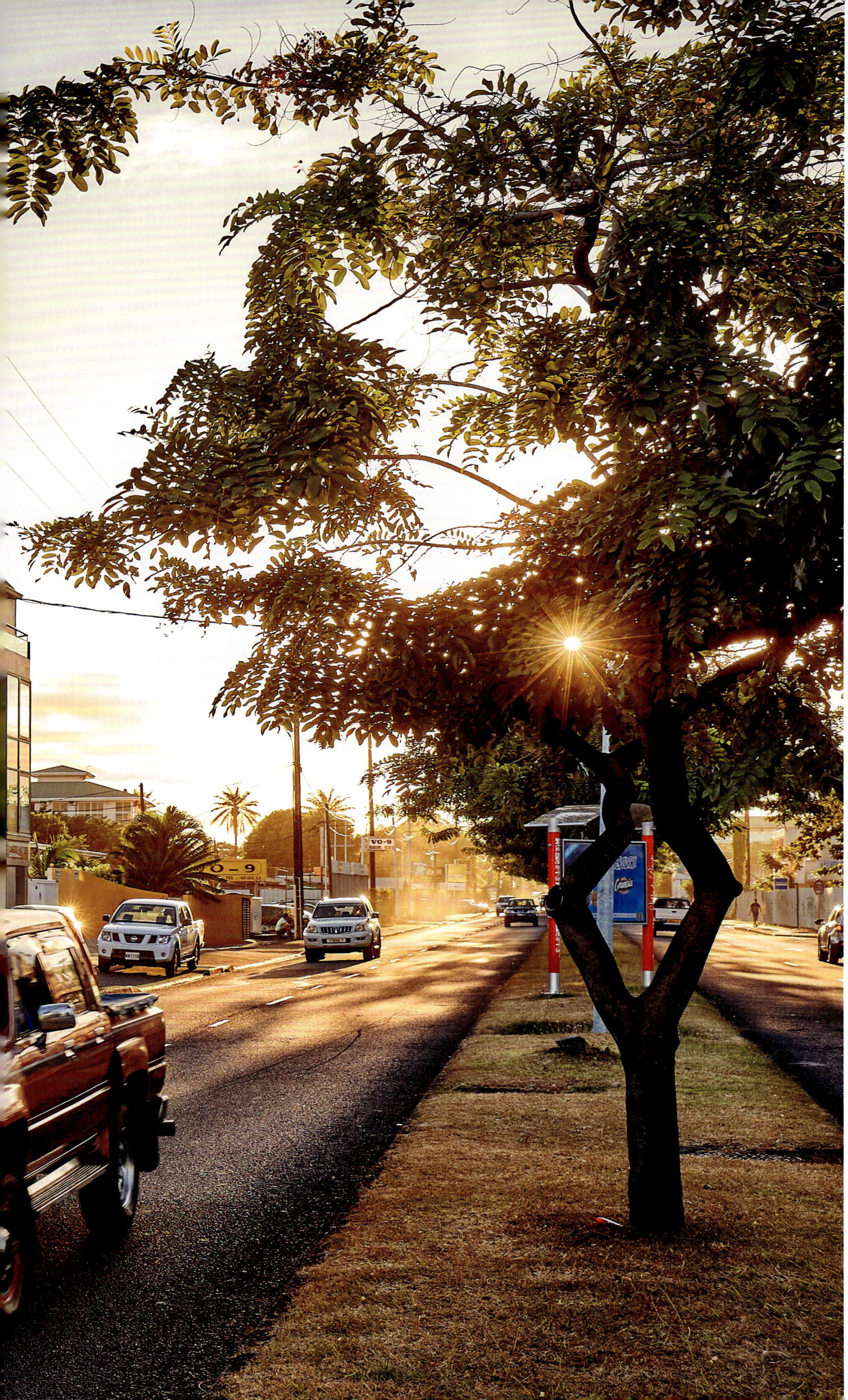

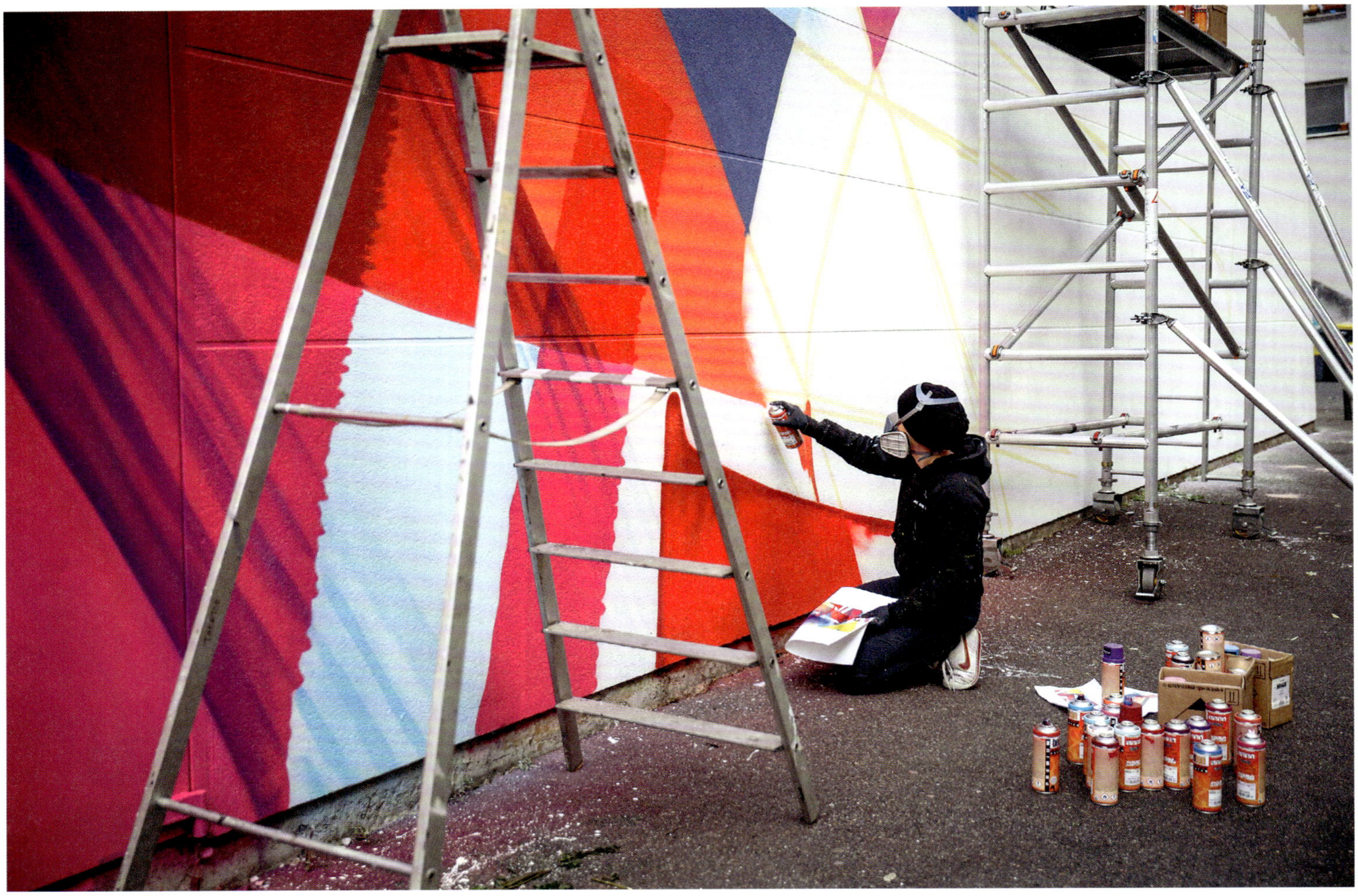

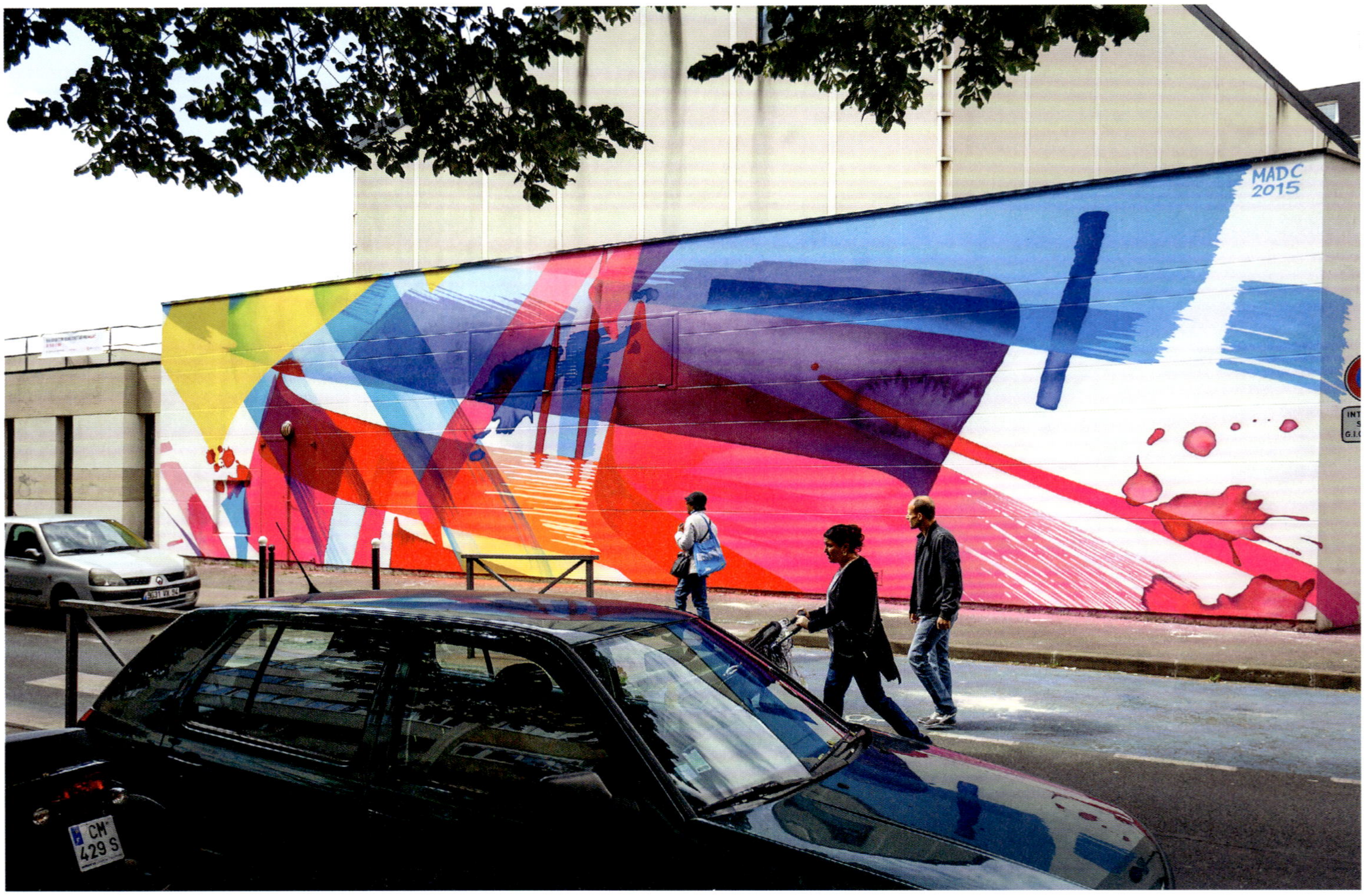

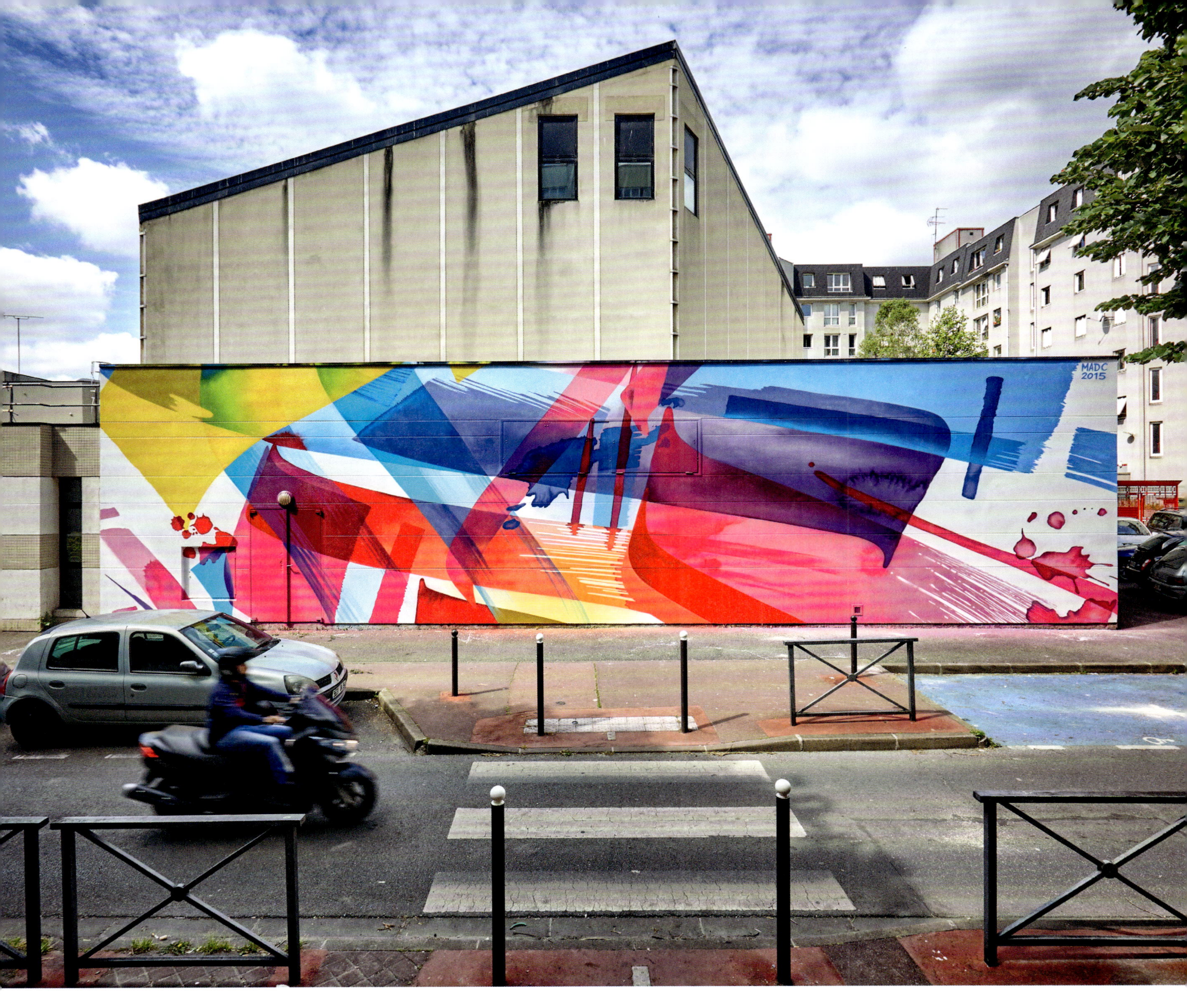

95–97 (this spread). Théâtre Jean-Vilar, Vitry-sur-Seine, France, May 2015

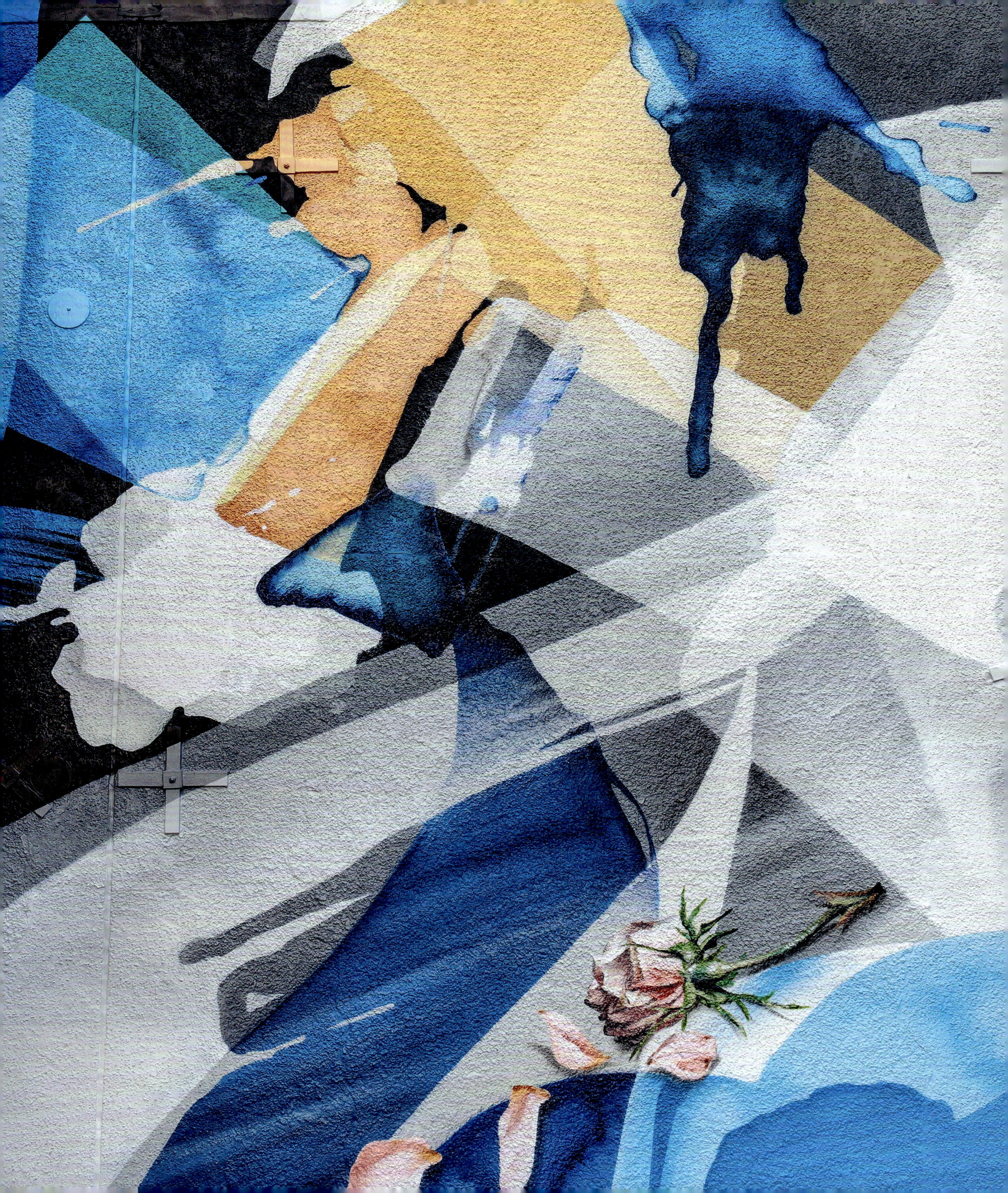

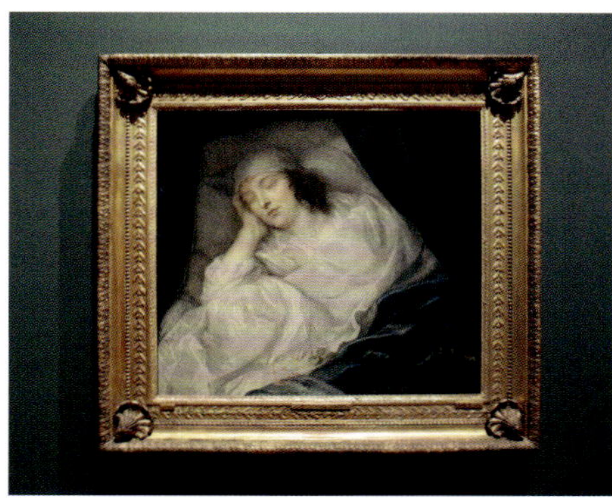

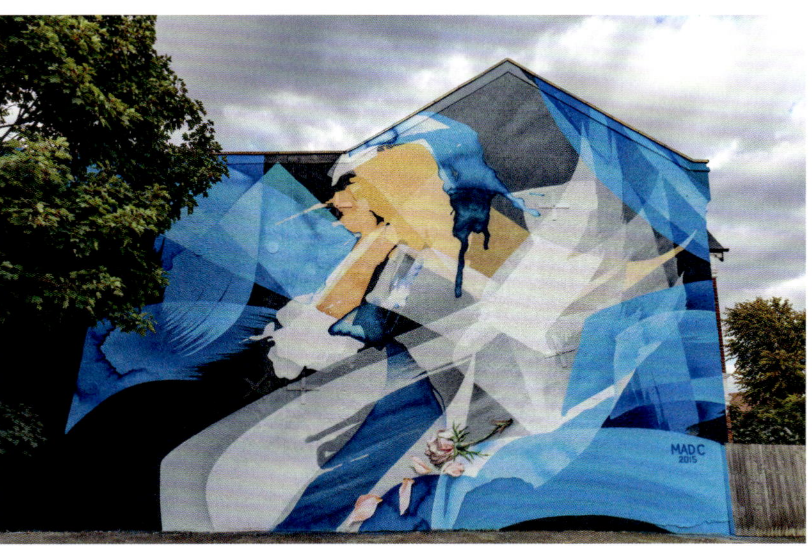

In 2015 MadC worked in London again, this time with a contribution to the Dulwich Outdoor Gallery project in the south of the city. Since the beginning of this project, Dulwich had increasingly developed into one of the most exciting areas in London public art. While in hip Shoreditch the lifespan of murals could often be limited to a few days until others overpainted the works, especially in popular spots, Dulwich developed into an important place for public art. This was thanks to the curator Ingrid Beazley, a pioneer in mediating between the street and the art museum, who worked for the Dulwich Picture Gallery for many years. In 2013 Beazley launched the Dulwich Outdoor Gallery by inviting numerous international mural artists to be inspired by a work from the rich collection of the Dulwich Picture Gallery, and to create a mural on selected walls in public space in the area around the museum in response.

Alongside artists such as Stik, Nunca, ROA, Remi Rough and Conor Harrington, MadC created a work that can still be found on Lordship Lane in Dulwich today. She was inspired by the painting *Venetia, Lady Digby on her Deathbed* from 1633, painted under heartbreaking circumstances **(fig. 99)**. Years before, the commissioner of the work, Sir Kenelm Digby, had fallen madly in love with society beauty Venetia Stanley and married her against his mother's wishes. When she unexpectedly died in her sleep on 30 April 1633, he asked his artist friend, Sir Anthony van Dyck, to capture the beauty of her lifeless body. The painting shows Lady Digby as if she were asleep, her cheeks a delicate pink, her face resting on her hand. Surrounded by the flowing fabrics of the bed and the curtain, she appears to be floating. Despite the calm that emanates from her body, a dynamic composition results through the diagonal lines of the bed sheets, blankets and curtains. It was precisely this composition that MadC took up in her interpretation of the work and transferred to her calligraphic watercolour-like style **(fig. 100)**. Lady Digby is dissolved into flowing forms; beige shapes vaguely indicate her body. The floating quality is captured in the translucent blue, grey and white surfaces. The work slips into abstraction, except for one element that MadC retains. The rose, which was laid on Lady Digby's deathbed as a farewell and which, with the loss of its petals, testifies to the transience of all life, is executed in a realistic manner at the lower edge of the house facade.

The Dulwich Outdoor Gallery is one of the successful projects that narrowed the discursive rifts between graffiti, street art and the art museum. Ultimately, it is people like Ingrid Beazley, who sadly died much too early, who are needed to create new spaces and forms of experimentation and exchange between institutions, artists and the public. This is the only way artistic positions like MadC's can create a new place for themselves between the traditional realms.

98 (opposite). Detail from *Lady Digby, on her Deathbed*
99 (top). Anthony van Dyck, *Venetia, Lady Digby, on her Deathbed*, 1633, oil on canvas, 74.3 x 81.8cm, DPG194. Dulwich Picture Gallery, London
100–103 (bottom and next two spreads). *Lady Digby, on her Deathbed*, 381 Lordship Lane, Dulwich, London, 2015 (Dulwich Outdoor Gallery)

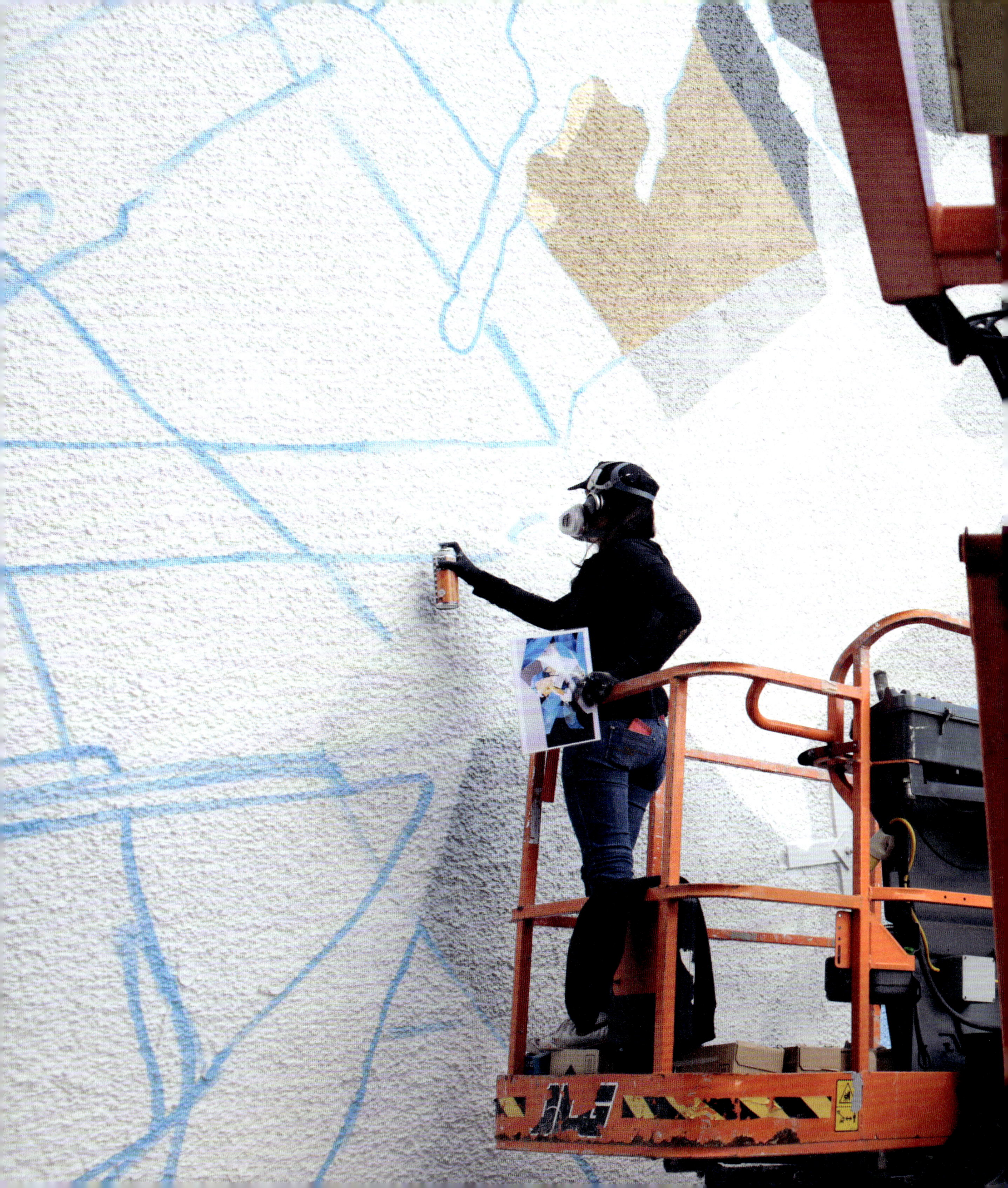

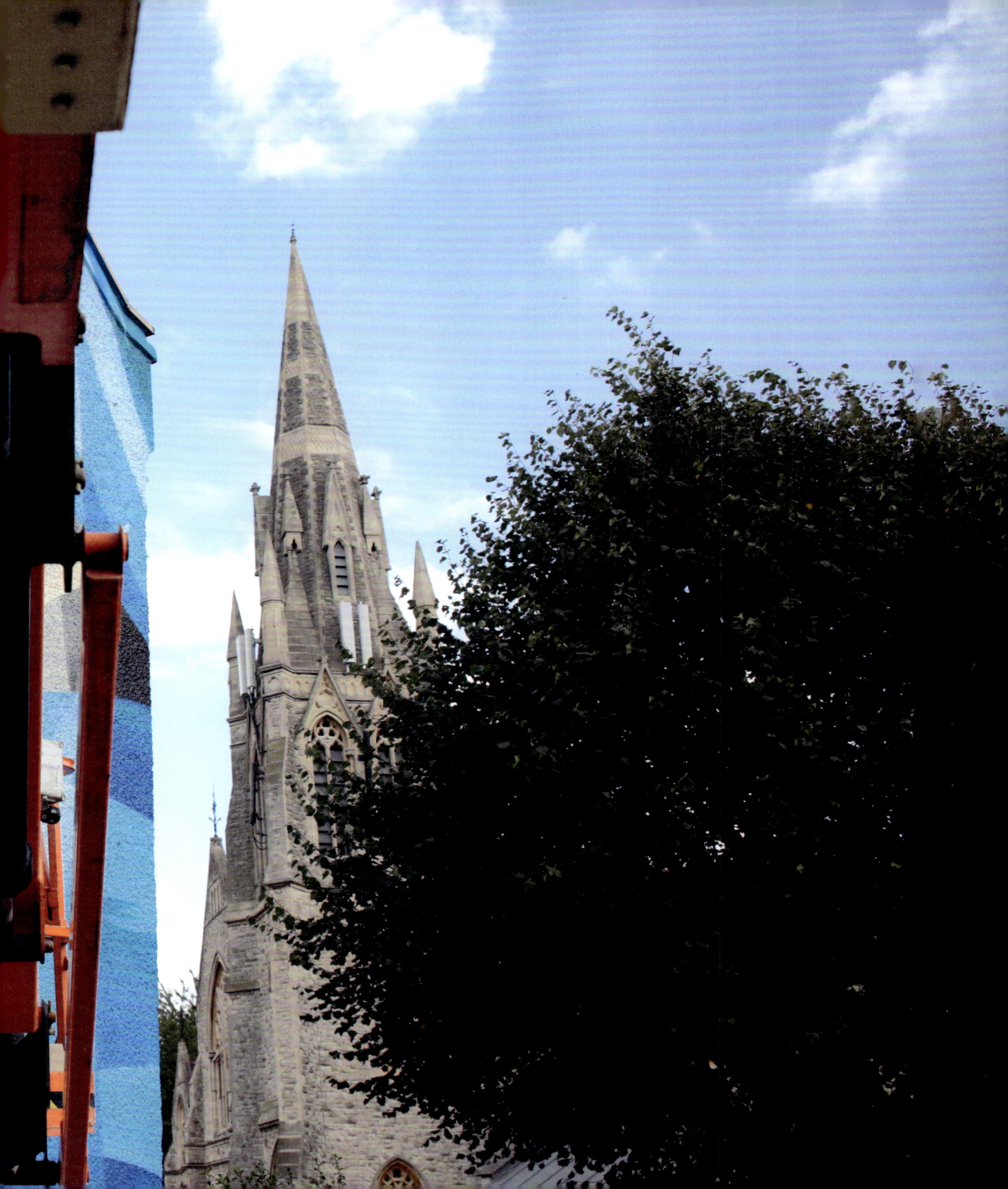

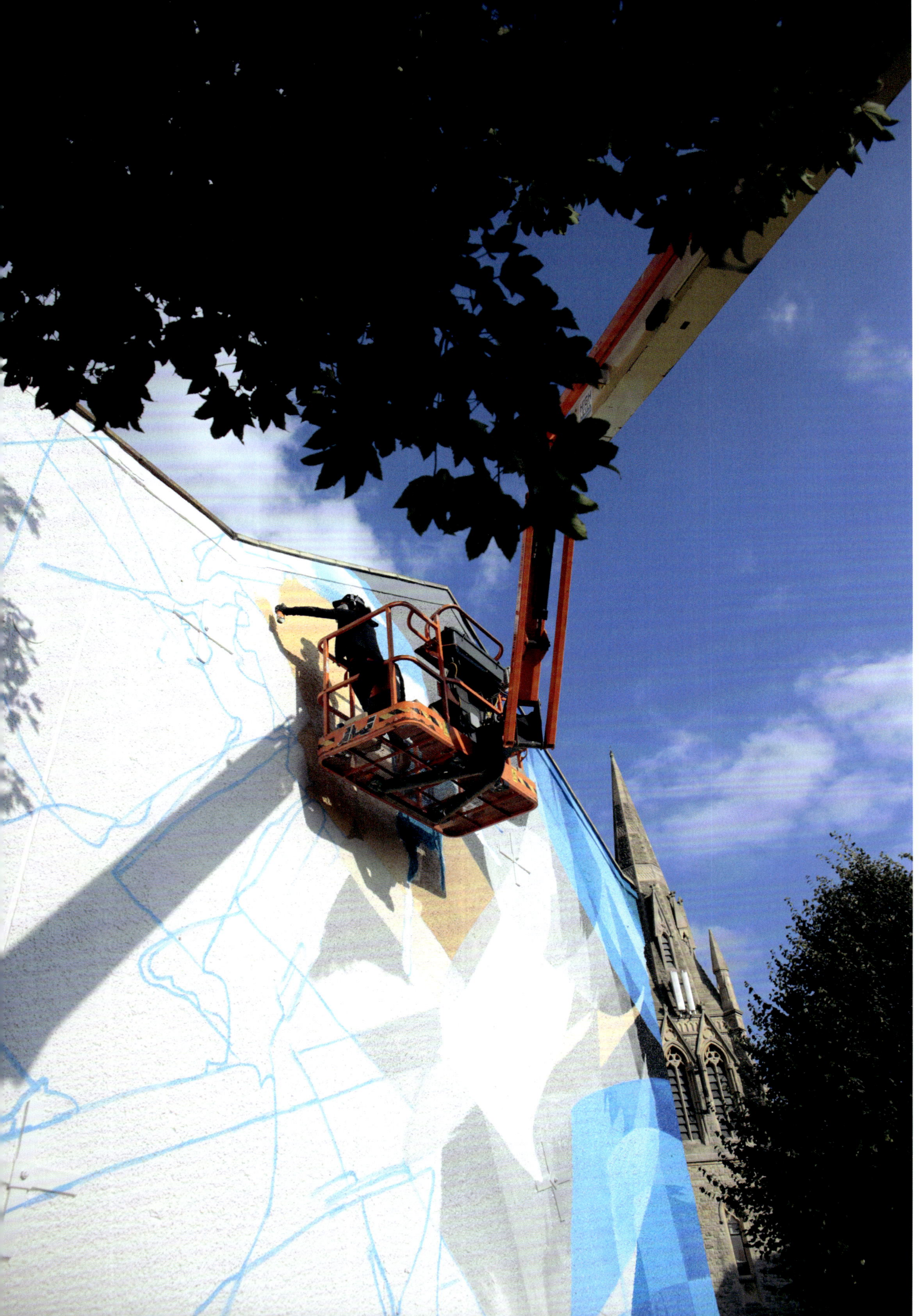

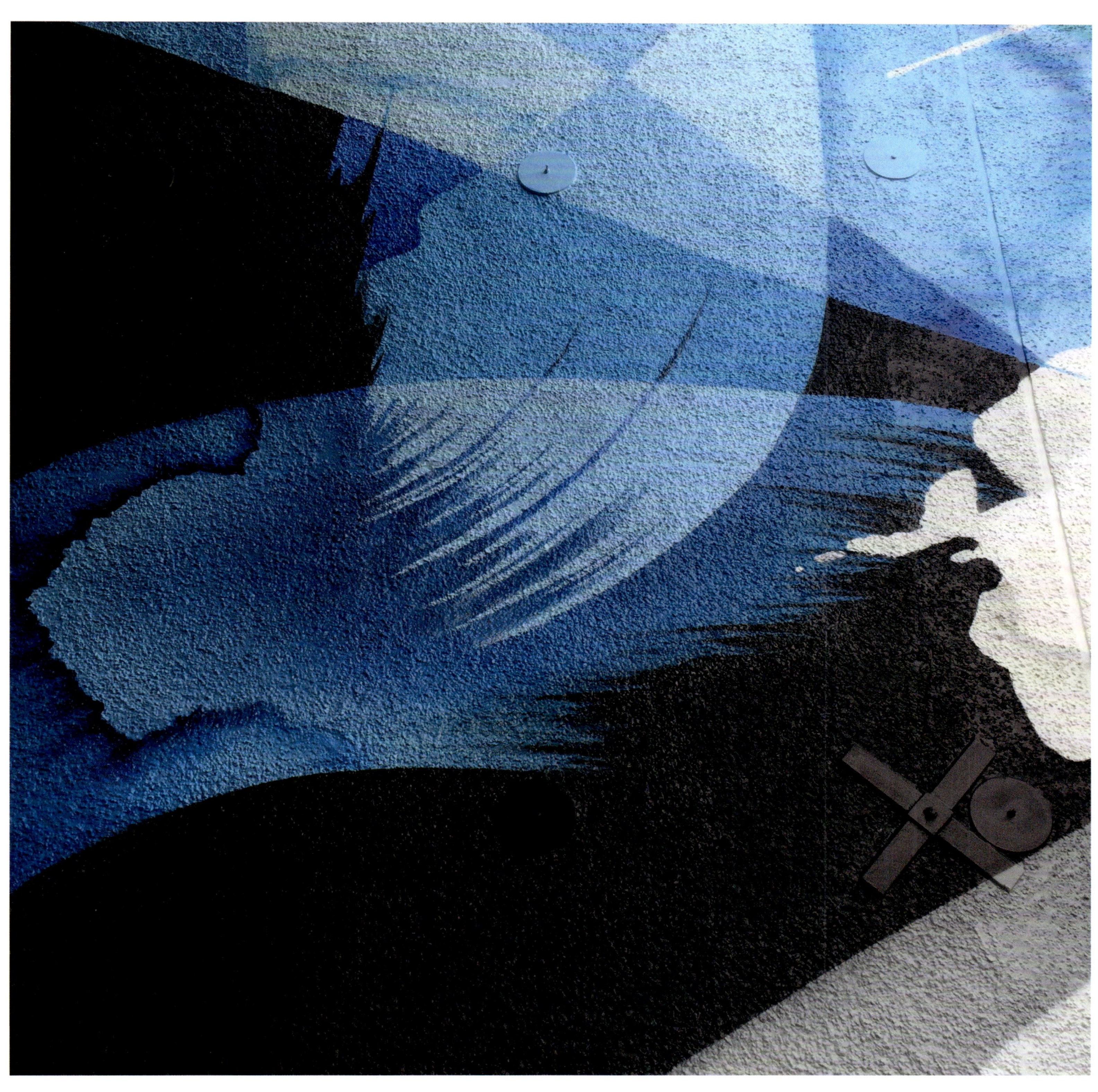

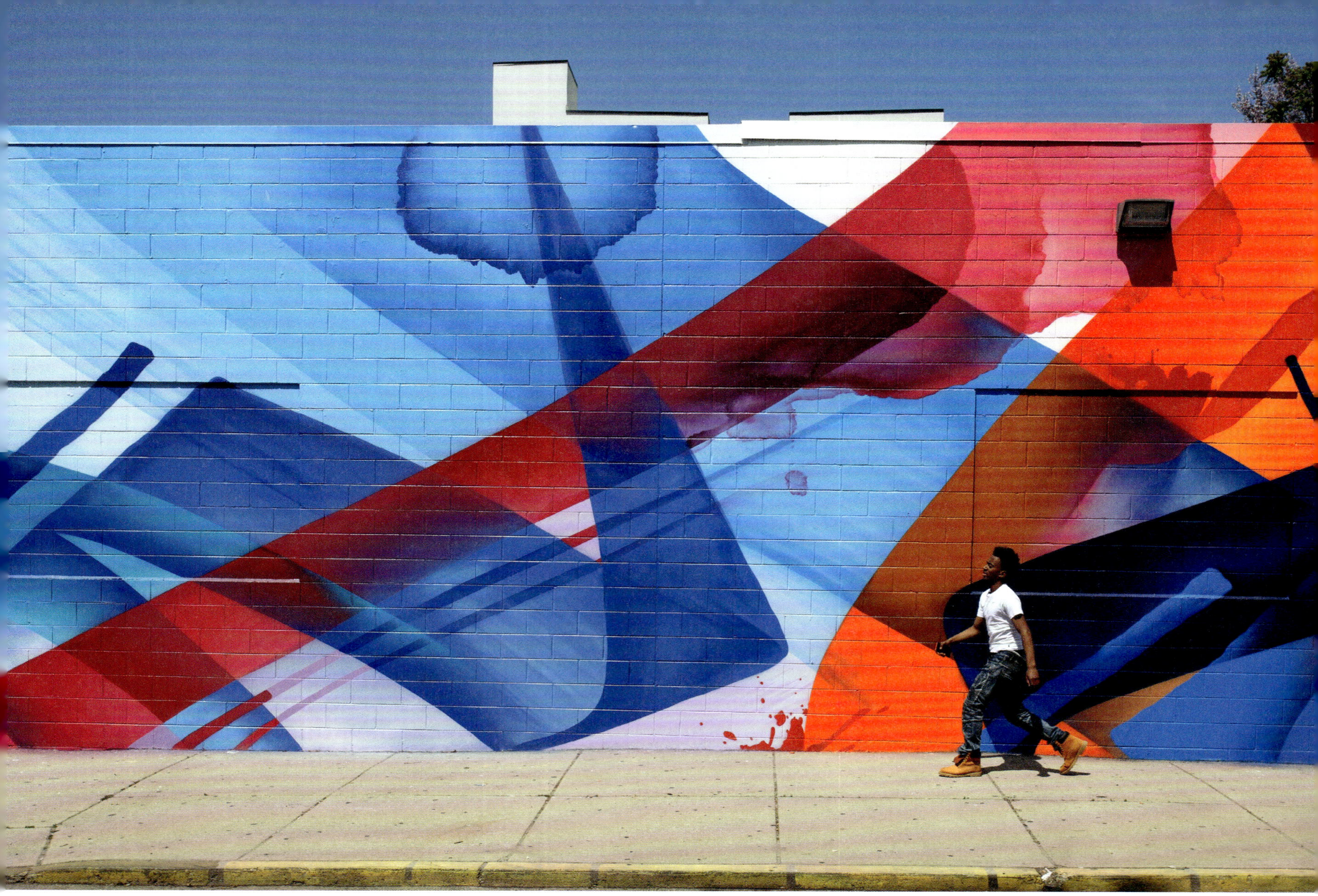

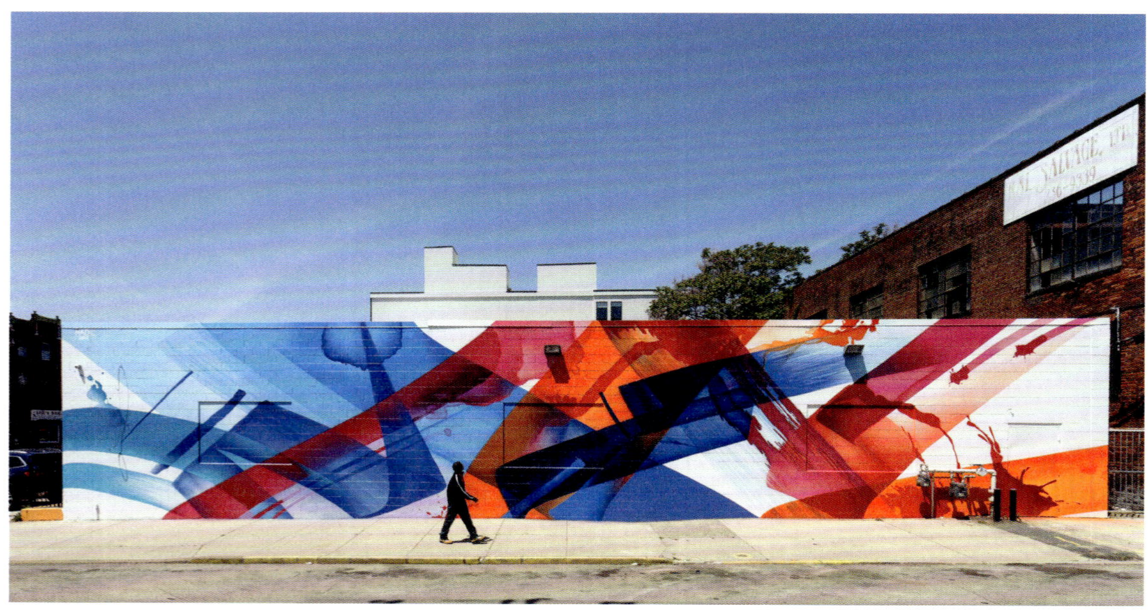

104, 105, 108 (top, bottom and next spread). *Reading between the Lines*, Philadelphia Mural Arts Program, 26th Street and Girard Avenue, Philadelphia, USA, May 2016
106–107 (opposite, top and bottom). Marrakech Biennale, Avenue El Glaoui, Marrakech, Morocco, February 2016

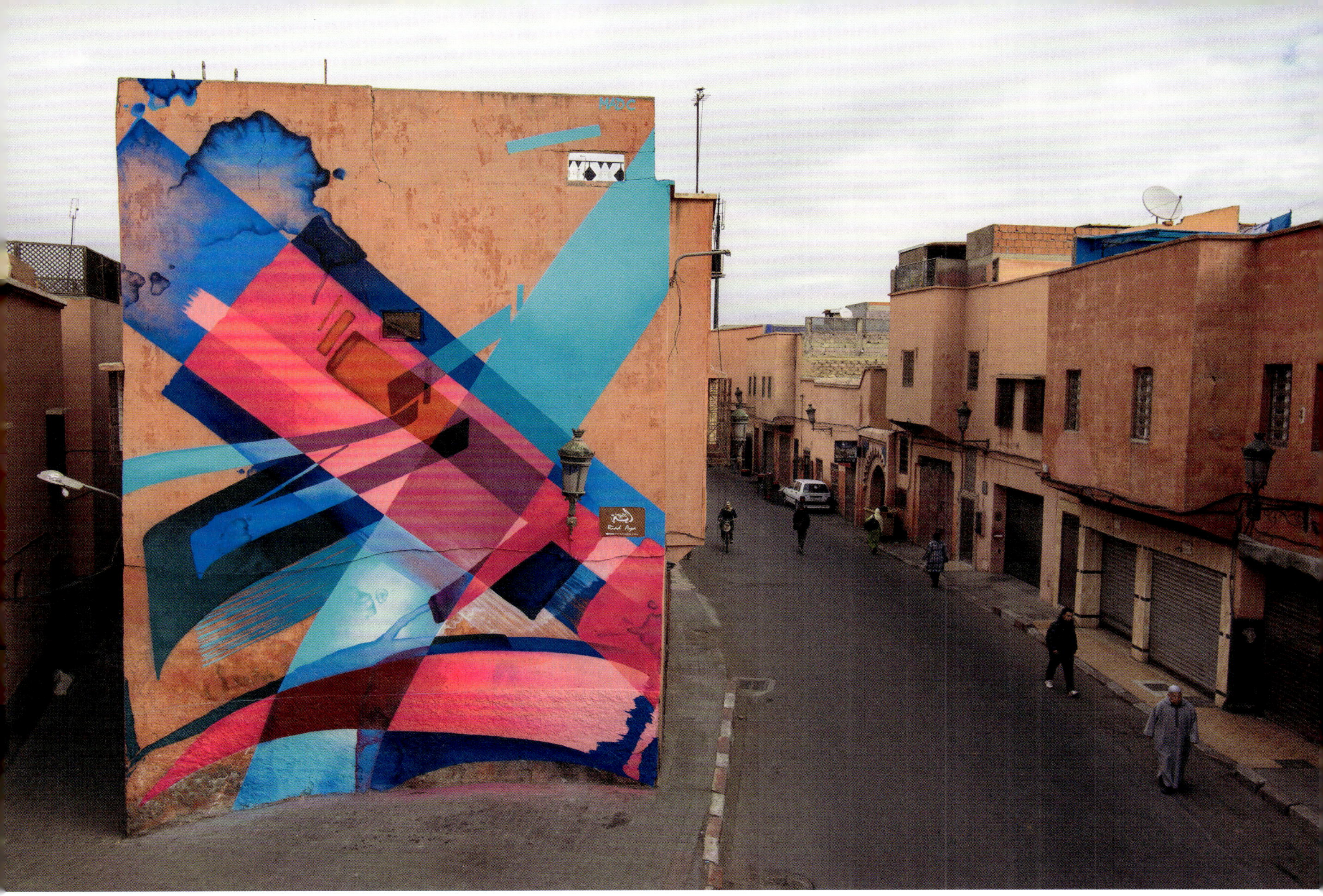

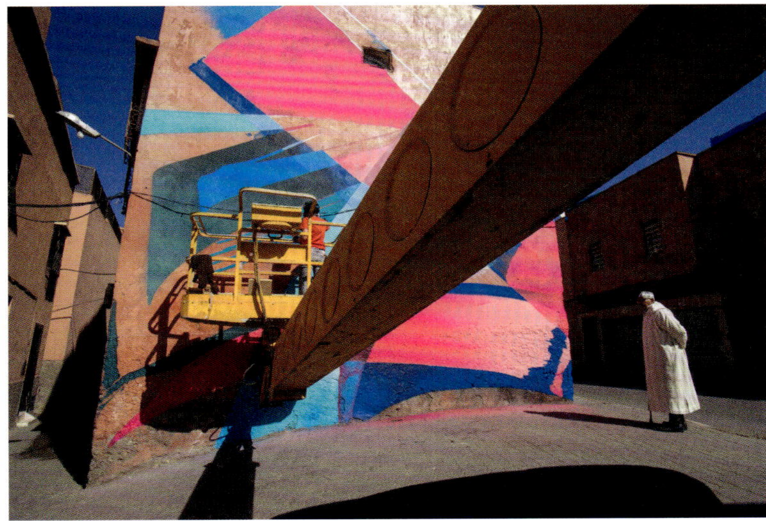

Other projects that followed for MadC were also facilitated by far-sighted people who made spaces of freedom possible. The invitation to the Philadelphia Mural Arts Program in May 2016 was one of the highlights. Jane Golden, hired as a young artist to deal with the graffiti problem in Philadelphia, established in 1984 a unique public art programme which integrated murals as a natural part of the city and local communities. By promoting graffiti writers early on and initiating public contracts, she made a major contribution to making graffiti and murals more widely accepted and of higher quality. In doing so, she created what is now an international model for transforming public space and strengthening communities through art. For MadC, the invitation to Philadelphia was an opportunity to be a part of this story **(fig. 104)**. In the same year, she took part in the MB6 Street Art project, a parallel programme of the sixth Marrakech Biennale in Morocco. Under the artistic direction of Reem Fadda, curator at the Guggenheim Museum in New York, the Marrakech Biennale partnered with this new programme to put further focus on art in public spaces. Working on a wall in the old town of Marrakech was, in many ways, a special experience for MadC **(fig. 106)**.

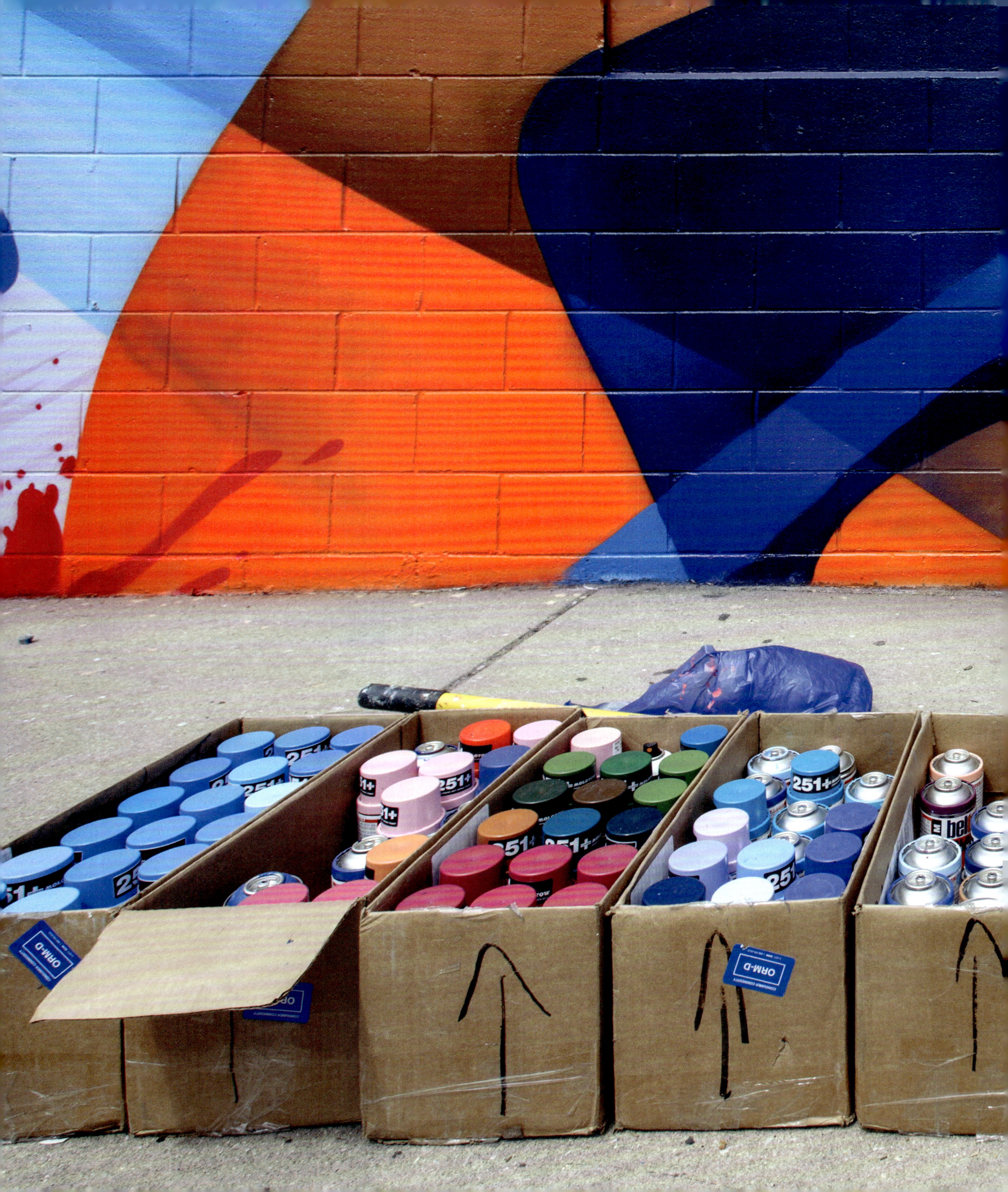
251+
ORM-D

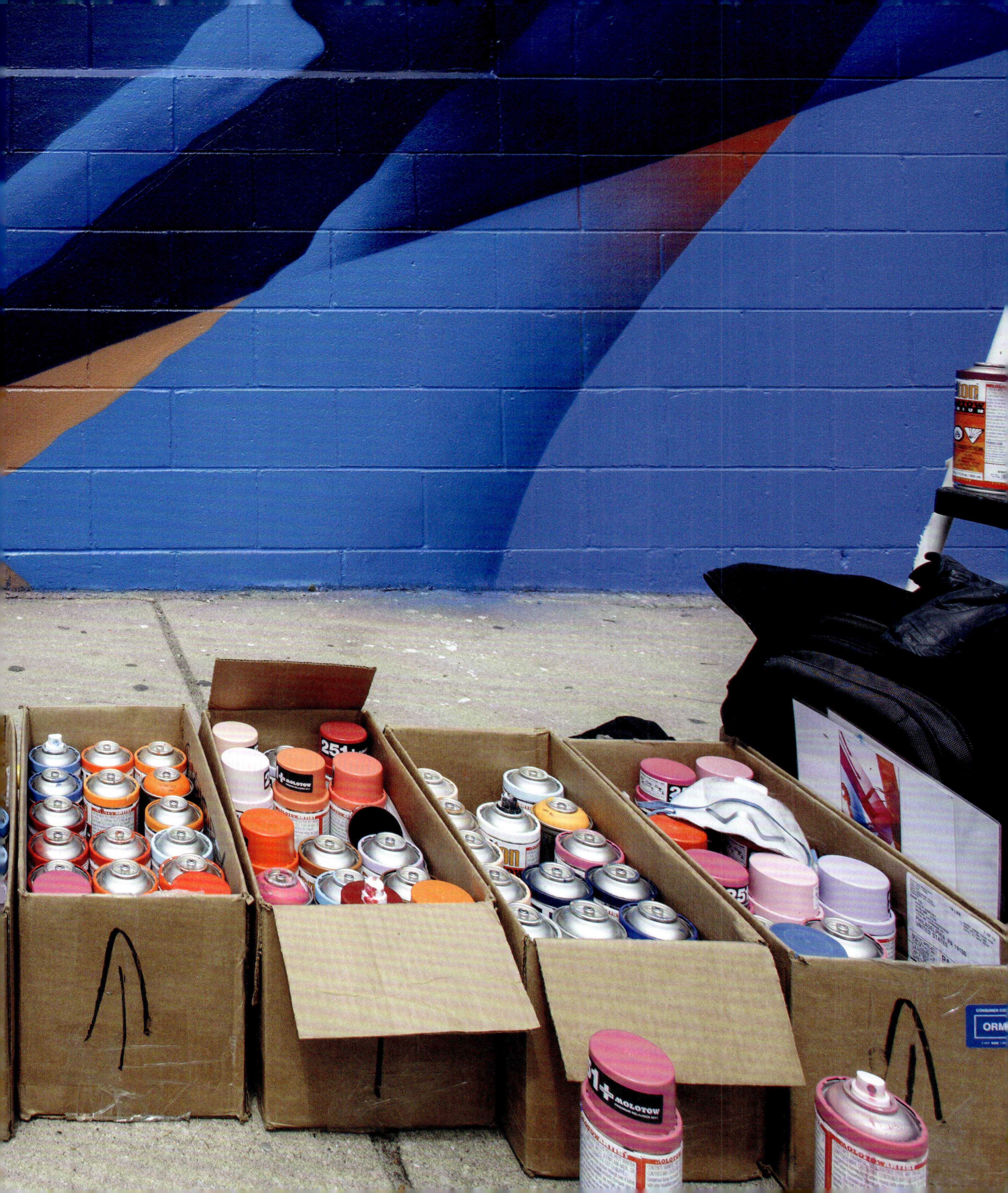
251
MOLOTOW

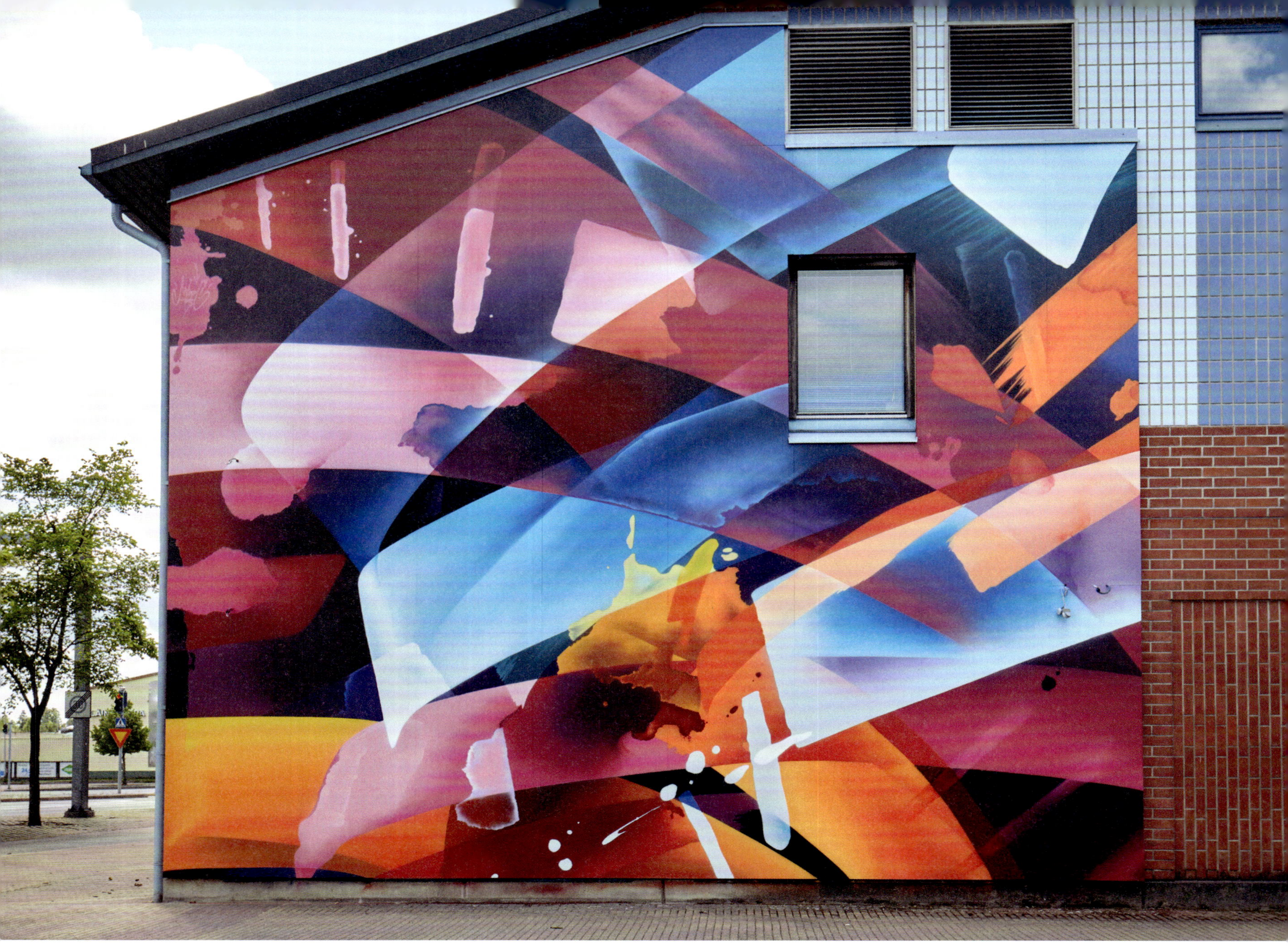

In 2017 she received an invitation which enabled the logical next step in her career – the design of the facade of an art museum and the participation in a simultaneous exhibition. The Art and Museum Centre Sinkka in Kerava was the first museum in Finland to trace their national history of graffiti, and they invited MadC as an international star to present her work. While the exhibition with many of her works on canvas was dismantled after a few months, the mural continues to exist and has graced the face of the museum building ever since (figs. 109–112). Her works no longer needed to shy away from classic visual considerations, as they existed in both discourses – in the visual arts as well as in graffiti art. In her works on canvas, MadC examined fundamental questions of painting, created her own spatial and colour system through her compositions, and explored the visuality of artistic means. She questioned how watercolour paint behaves on paper, how transparent acrylic paint behaves on canvas. A broad brushstroke? A sprayed area? On the canvas, how can energy be conveyed? How can the creative process be seen? How is coincidence used as an artistic method? Here she developed the translucent coats of paint, which were later transferred to the wall as transparent layers.

109–112 (this spread and next spread). *Free at Last*, Art and Museum Centre Sinkka, Kerava, Finland, August 2017. The mural is still gracing the exterior of the museum and has become a landmark in the area

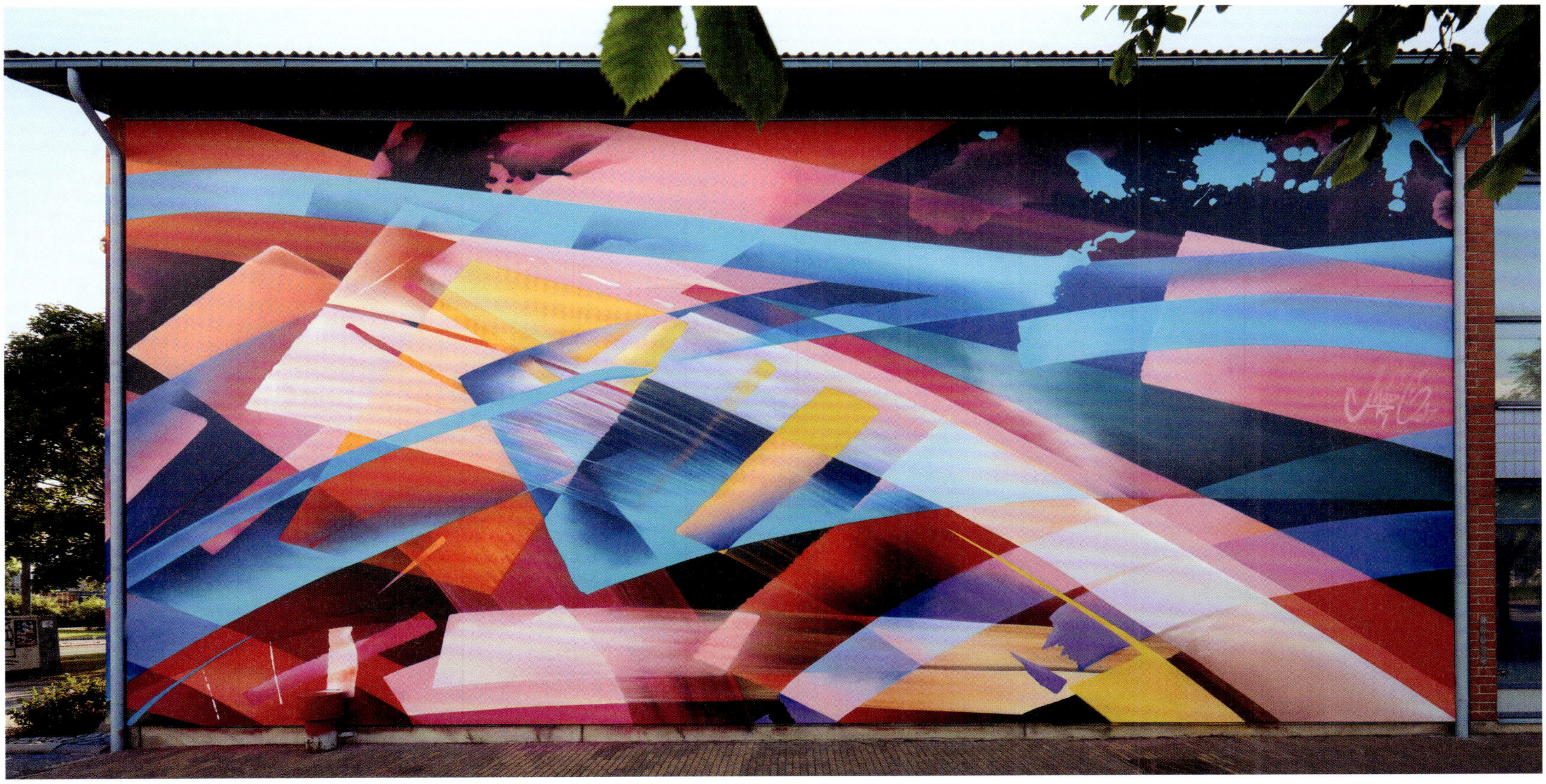

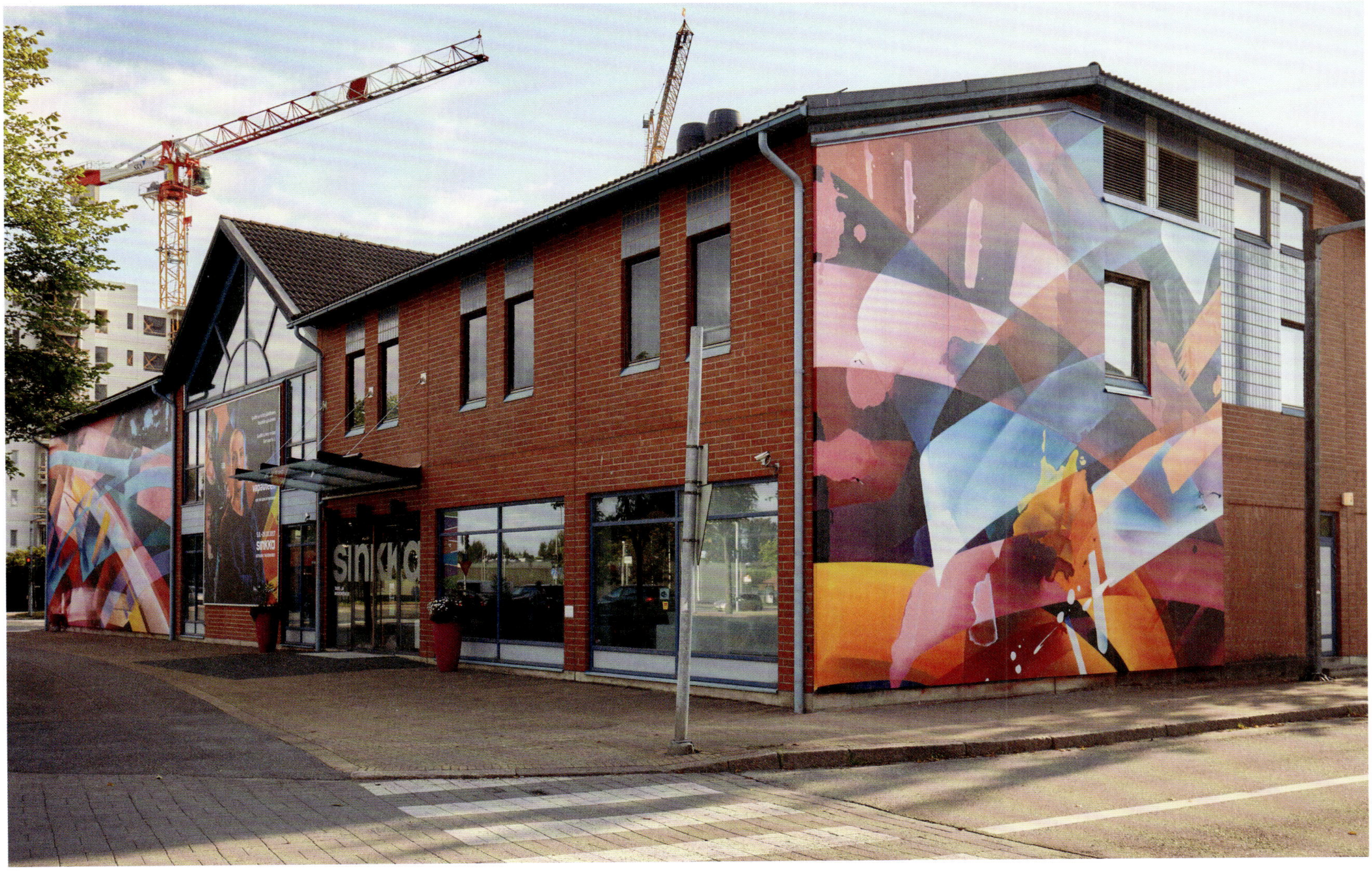

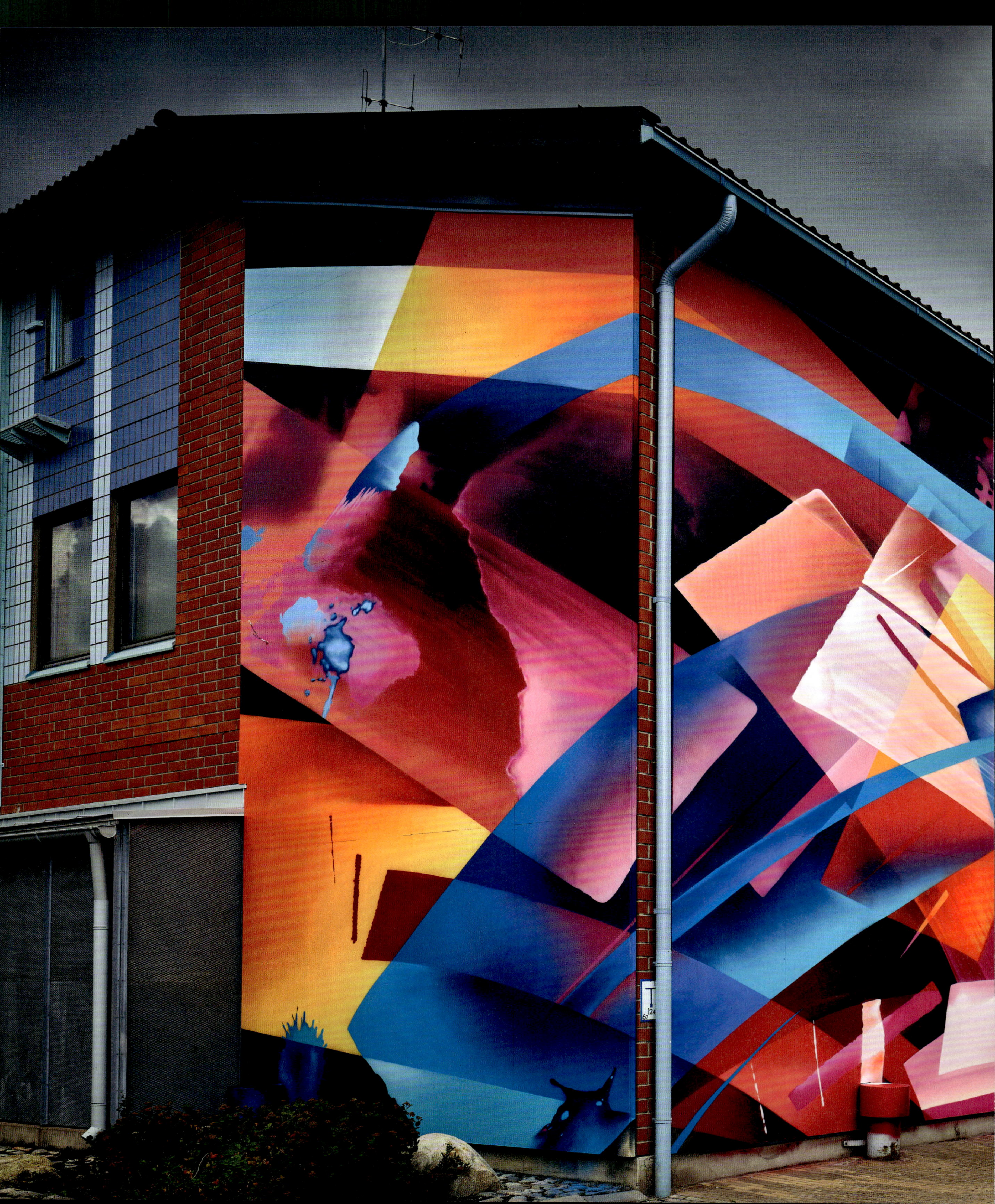

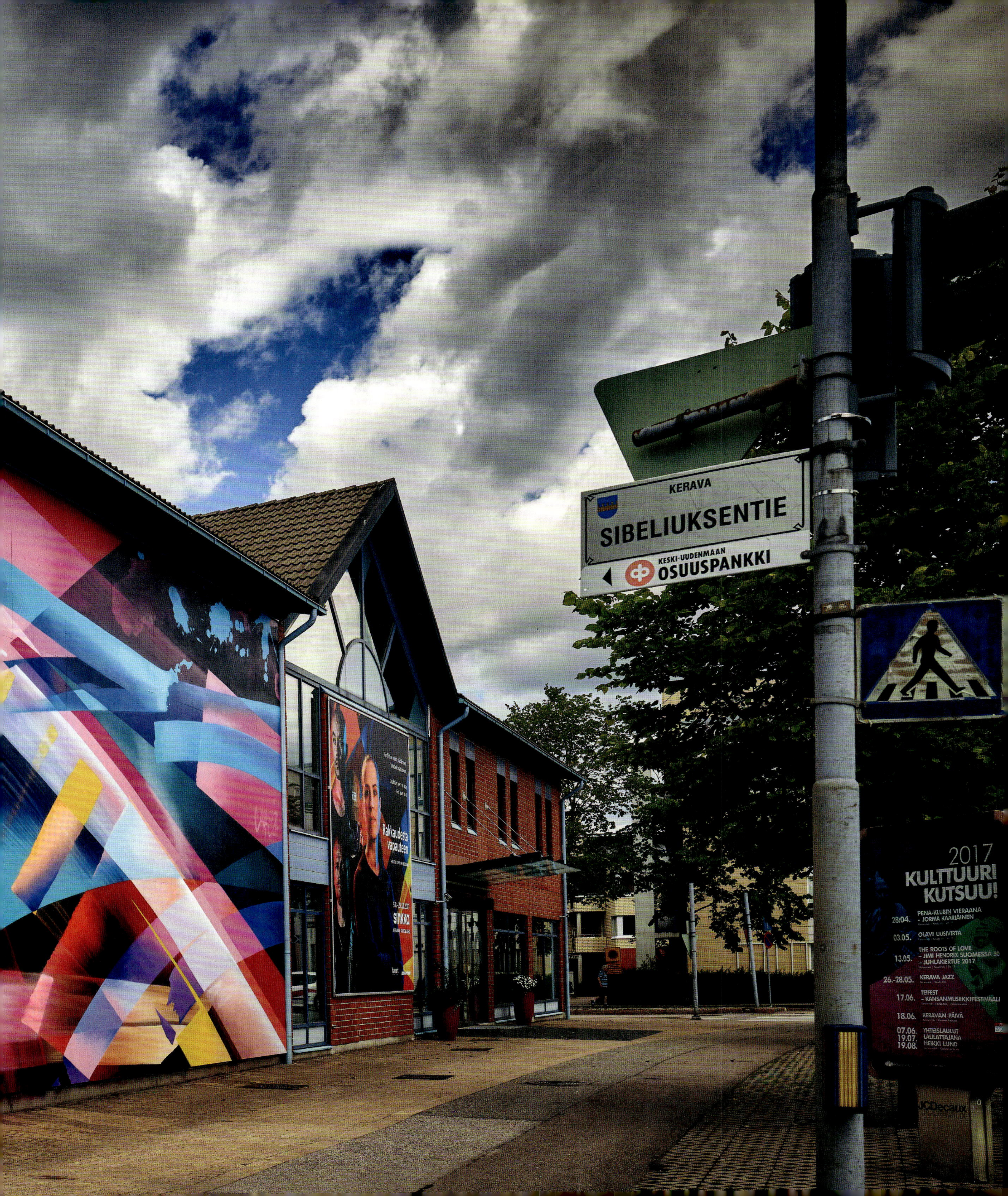
KERAVA
SIBELIUKSENTIE
KESKI-UUDENMAAN
OSUUSPANKKI
Rakkaudesta vapauteen
SINKKO
2017
KULTTUURI
KUTSUU!
28.04. PENA-KLUBIN VIERAANA - JORMA KÄÄRIÄINEN
03.05. OLAVI UUSIVIRTA
13.05. THE ROOTS OF LOVE - JIMI HENDRIX SUOMESSA 50 - JUHLAKIERTUE 2017
26.-28.05. KERAVA JAZZ
17.06. TE!FEST - KANSANMUSIIKKIFESTIVAALI
18.06. KERAVAN PÄIVÄ
07.06. 19.07. 19.08. YHTEISLAULUT LAULATTAJANA HEIKKI LUND
JCDecaux

The work in the studio was characterised by spontaneity, but also by calm, the opportunity to step back and continue after a certain time. Up to several weeks were dedicated to a single work – a period of time that was not available on the street or on large walls. Her compositions came into being through sweeping, precisely set lines. No wild expression, but a dynamic of movement manifested itself here; the images seemed literally to dance (see fig. 113). The numerous glazing layers of paint create a spatial depth that evokes associations with the abstract works of Gerhard Richter. MadC and Richter, however different their approaches may be, share at least some very obvious similarities – the urge to exhaust the means of painting, their focus on the properties of the medium and its translatability, and the dynamic lines in abstract compositions. But unlike Richter, whom MadC admires, her method of layering is not one of hiding. While the relationship between the invisible and the visible plays an important role for Richter, who covers up layers of paint in order to subsequently expose them again, MadC works with the greatest possible transparency – virtually every brushstroke can be traced, every layer shines through. Still, chance also plays an important role for her. Each step follows in response to the previous one. In doing so, she uses intuition instead of calculation in order, like Richter, to achieve results that go beyond what she could have imagined beforehand.

By transferring the compositions to large walls, MadC created a kind of visual oxymoron that drew its strength and its own rhetorical quality from these very differences. With this type of abstraction, she created a visual universe that greatly affected the atmosphere of the places where it can be seen. The formal questions, the universality of the abstract, is of more interest for MadC than territory markings and the dissemination of clear political messages, which in the genre of street art can be found on numerous walls (with Banksy – who also began as a graffiti writer before conquering the field of street art – being just the tip of the iceberg). She steers clear of the display of her own political opinion. Instead, she wants her works to open up spaces in which the beholder can think for themselves and bring their own experience to look at the world slightly differently. Gerhard Richter once said very aptly: 'A picture can help us to think something that goes beyond this meaningless existence. That is something that art can do.'[10] MadC fills her murals with positive energy and a visual language that is no longer closed by semi-secret codes but stands for itself. Here, abstraction is not the opposite of representation, but results from the search for how painting – or art – can express something for which words are insufficient.

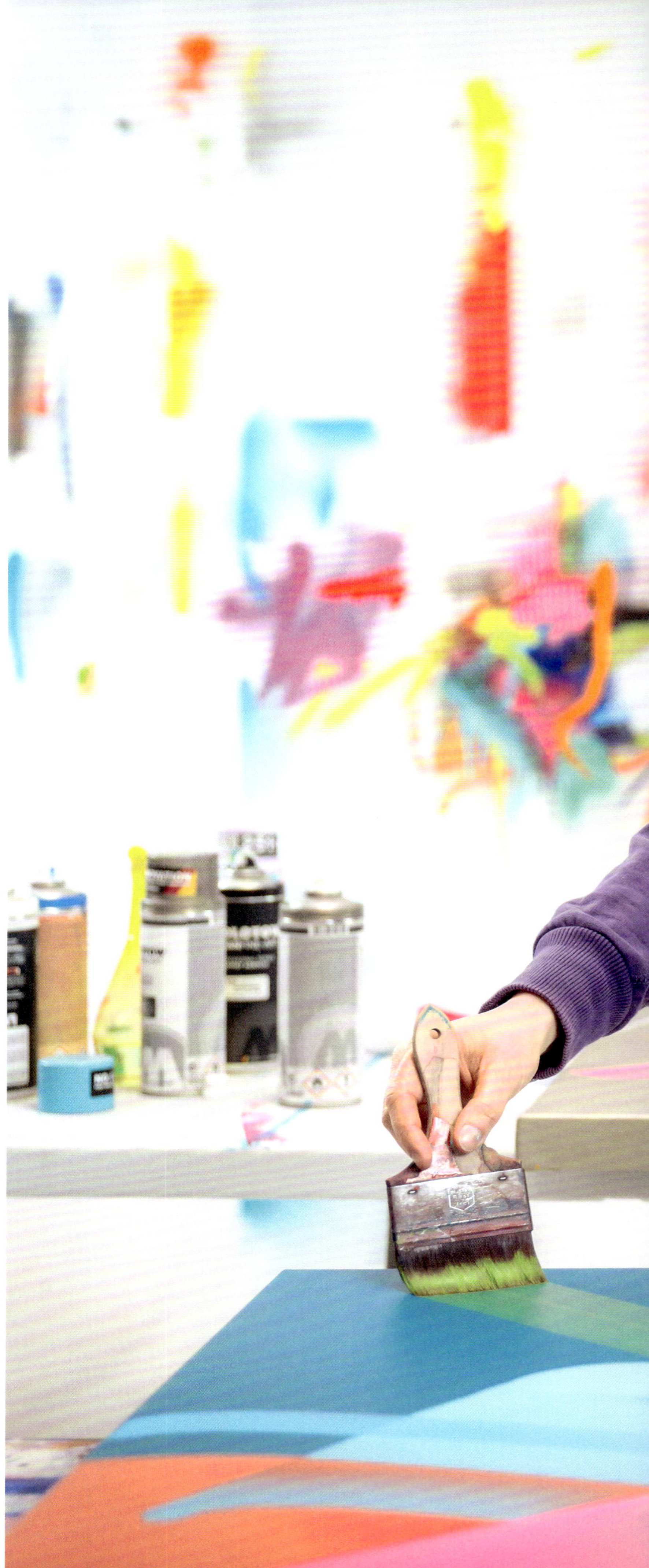

113. MadC studio, Halle, Germany, 2018

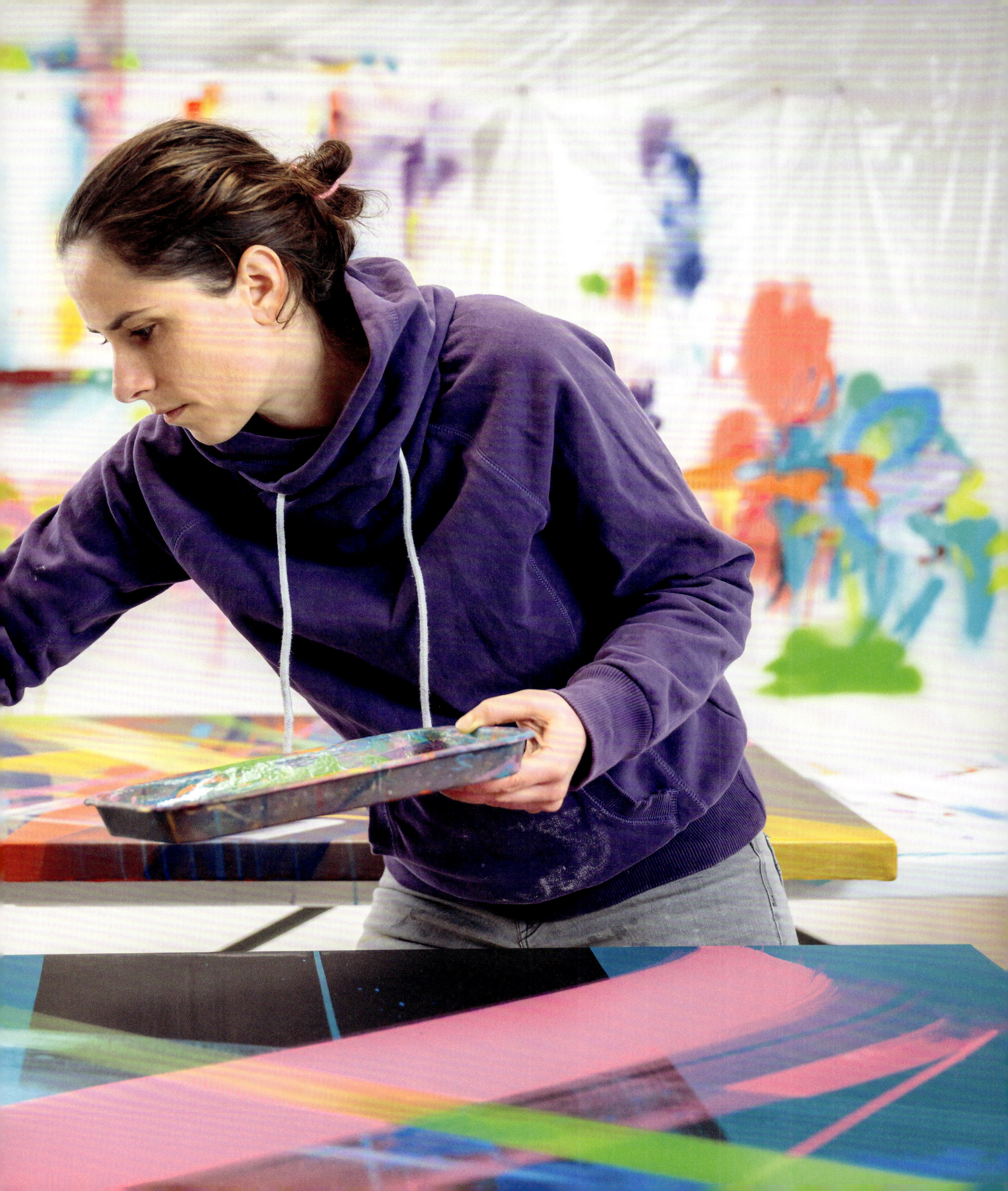

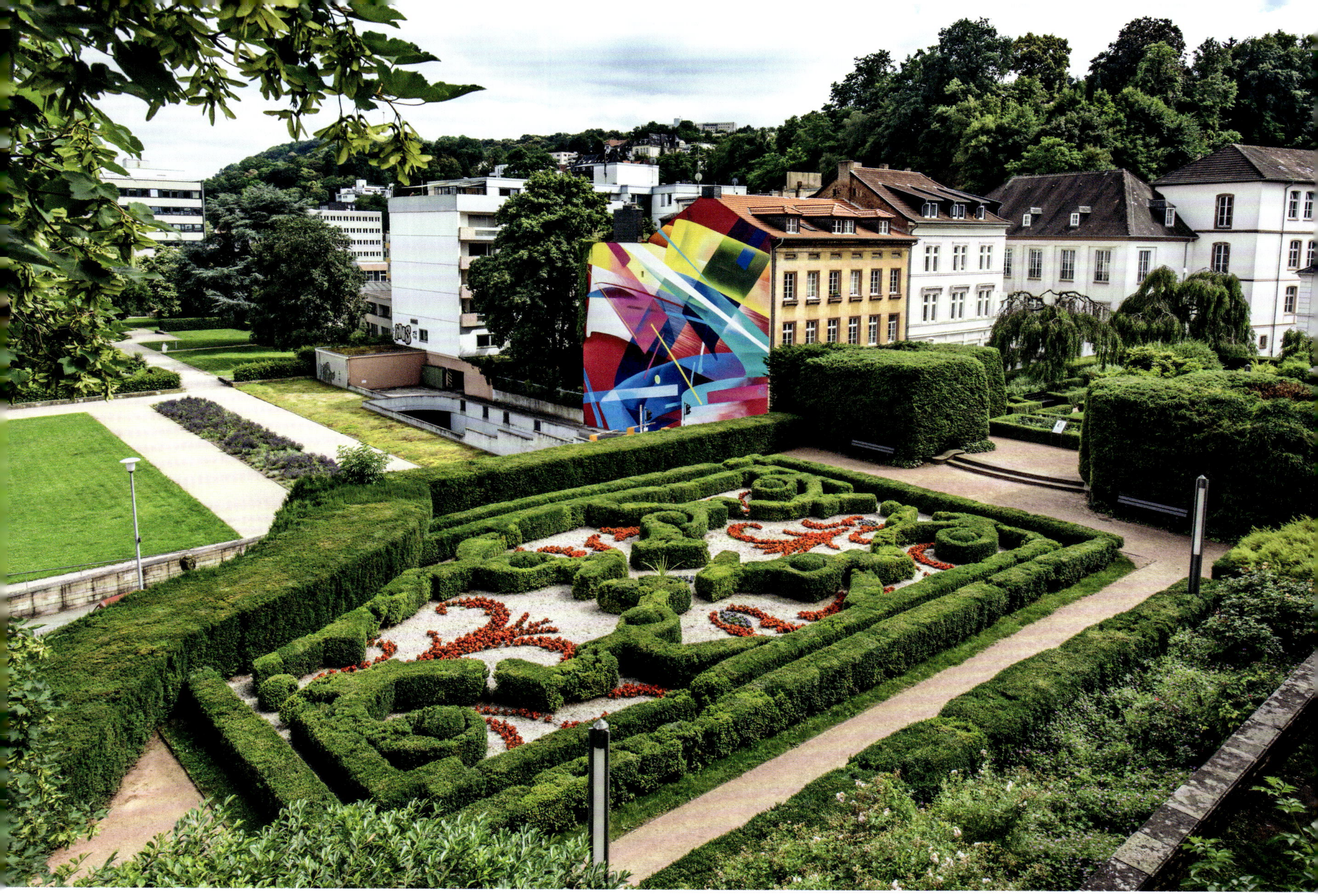

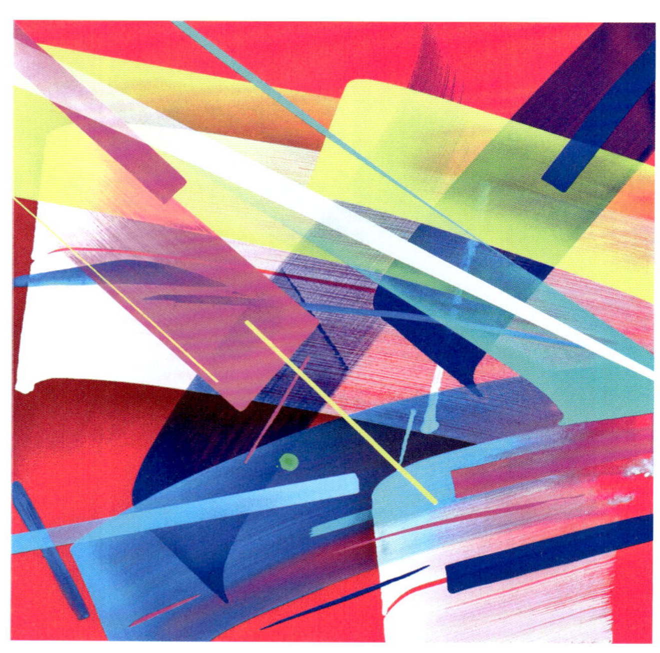

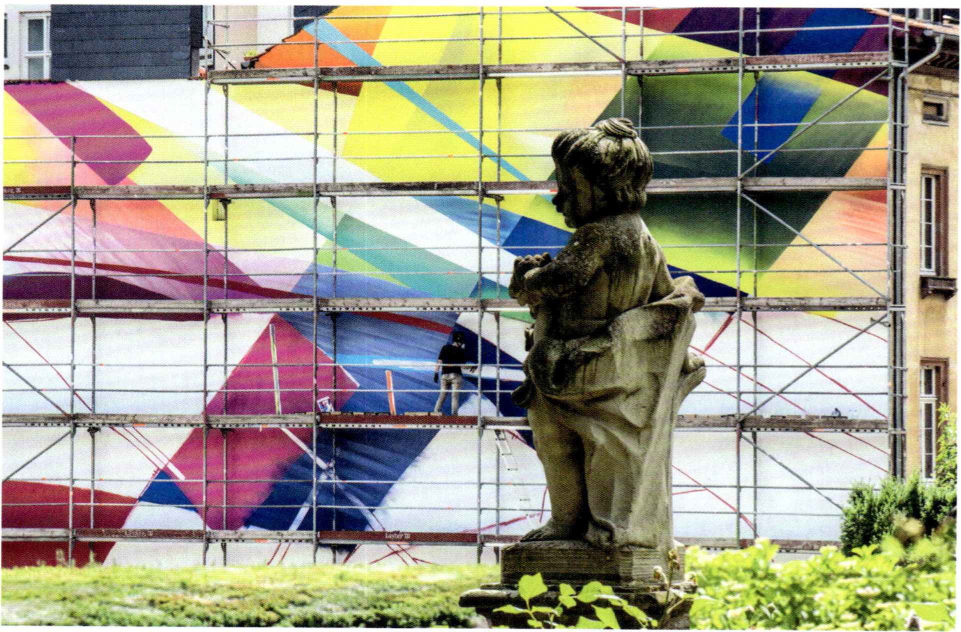

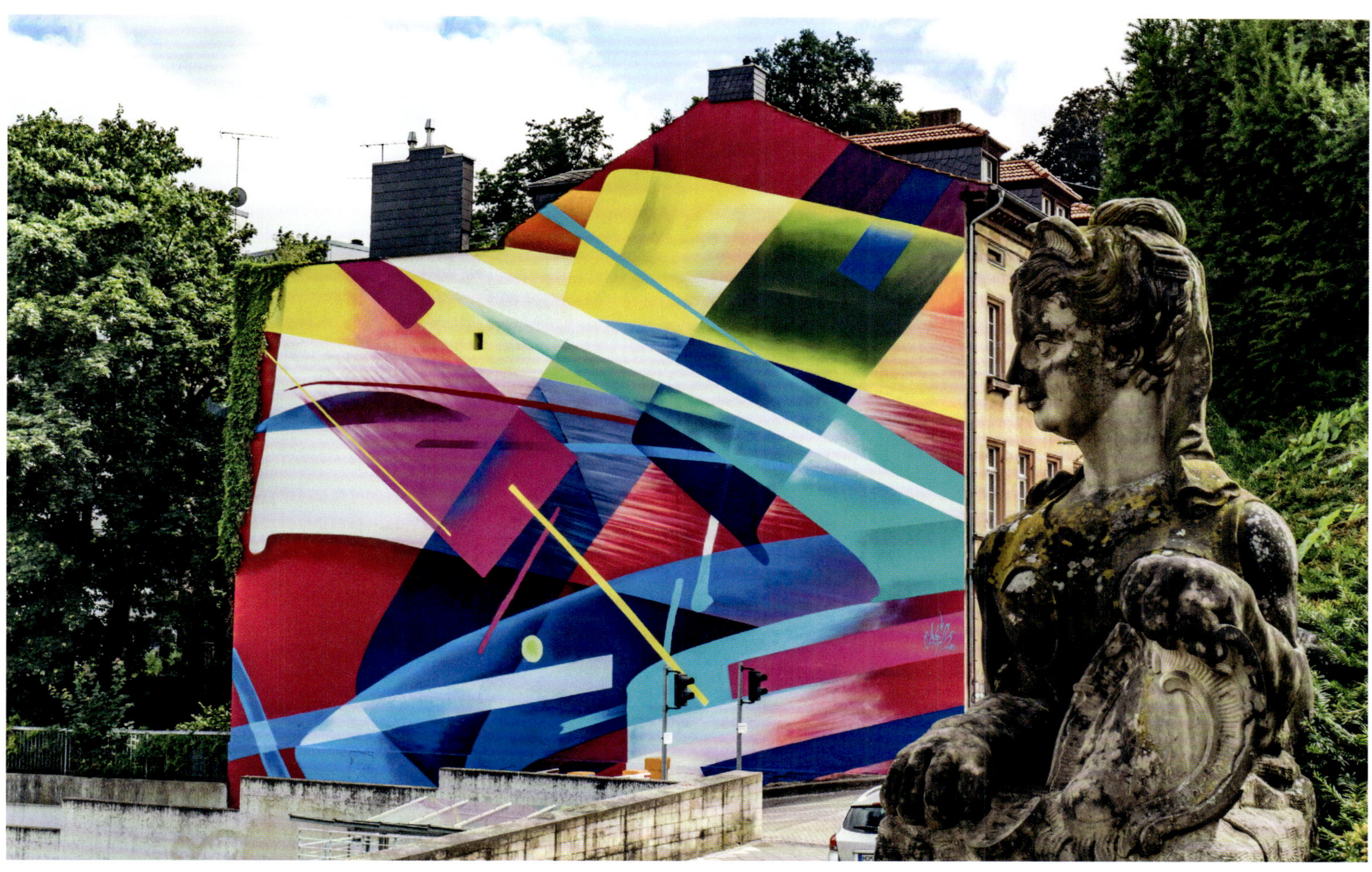

The fact that a work of art free of ideological messages nevertheless can become political in the public space was evident in Saarbrücken, Germany, in 2018. Invited to participate in the ArtWalk Saarbrücken, organised by the Saarland Ministry of Culture, MadC created a wonderfully colourful mural on a house wall in the Spichererbergstrasse, directly adjacent to the palace garden **(fig. 114)**. It didn't take long for a heated discussion to spark on social media and in the local newspaper as to whether this was the right work in the right place – so much modernity on the fringes of a Baroque ensemble (mind you, this was one of the few buildings in Saarbrücken that was spared in World War II). This discussion drew even bigger circles, which can be read in the local press: 'A Saarlander who finds the work of art too flashy and unsuitable for the ensemble of the palace, palace garden, state parliament and state parliament garden has gone one step further. He has filed a complaint with the local supervisory authority.'[11] The responsible persons in the ministry had, of course, obtained the necessary permits and were rather relaxed about the situation, as can be seen in a statement by spokeswoman Marija Herceg: 'In this democratic approach to art, a controversial discussion is not only consequential but even an integral part.'[12]

It didn't remain only a matter of words. A graffiti writer, who, based on his style, was probably a toy in the hierarchy, bombed several of the works only two weeks after the creation of the ArtWalk, maybe expressing his own disapproval of the programme. The murals were restored, but shortly afterwards, MadC's work was threatened with another horror scenario. Discussions began about a possible house construction on the site, which would have covered the mural completely. But these plans were discarded, and so, despite all the debate, the work can still be admired on the edge of the palace park. One may feel reminded of *The 700 Wall*, in which ships fight against various dangers on the raging sea – even 'officially' commissioned works are not immune from destruction, although in most cases, the lifespan is significantly longer. Ultimately, this development also shows how close art can be to everyday life, something museums can only wish for their artworks. But it also demonstrates how close it is to disappearing when in the public arena.

Another testament to disappearance was MadC's project realised in 2019 in the old terminal building of Dresden Airport **(figs. 118–128)**. This retrospective of her work of the past two decades was a celebration of transience. Spread out over the walls of the 8,000-square-metre hall, it told MadC's artistic and personal story. Her development from classic graffiti pieces and throw-ups to blockbusters to works with transparent surfaces and watercolour elements, as well as the path from clearly recognisable and legible letters to abstraction, was recreated. For a short period of time, she transformed the hall into a huge temporary work of art, documented by the filmmaker René Kästner. The time-lapse recordings are all that remains. The hall was demolished a short time after, without the public having been able to experience the entire work on-site beforehand. But this was the deal.

10 Gerhard Richter, quoted in Jiří Fajt and Milena Kalinovská (eds), 'Kunst als etwas Menschliches', in *Gerhard Richter*, exh. cat., Prague: Národní Galerie v Praze, 2017, pp. 11–13, here p. 13. Extract translated by Eva Ruschkowski.

11 Buss, Silvia, 'Graffiti-Künstler schaltet Kommunalaufsicht ein', *Saarbrücker Zeitung*, https://www.saarbruecker-zeitung.de/saarland/saarbruecken/saarbruecken/kunstwerk-von-madc-in-saarbruecken-erregt-die-gemueter_aid-23986365 (accessed 14 March 2021). Extract translated by Eva Ruschkowski.

12 Ibid.

114 (opposite, top and bottom right). ArtWalk Saarbrücken, Spichererbergstrasse 9, Saarbrücken, Germany, June 2018
115 (opposite, bottom left). *10:50-03042018*, 100 x 100cm, acrylic, watercolour and spray paint on canvas, 2018. This was the sketch for the mural in Saarbrücken, Germany
116. ArtWalk Saarbrücken, Spichererbergstrasse 9, Saarbrücken, Germany, June 2018

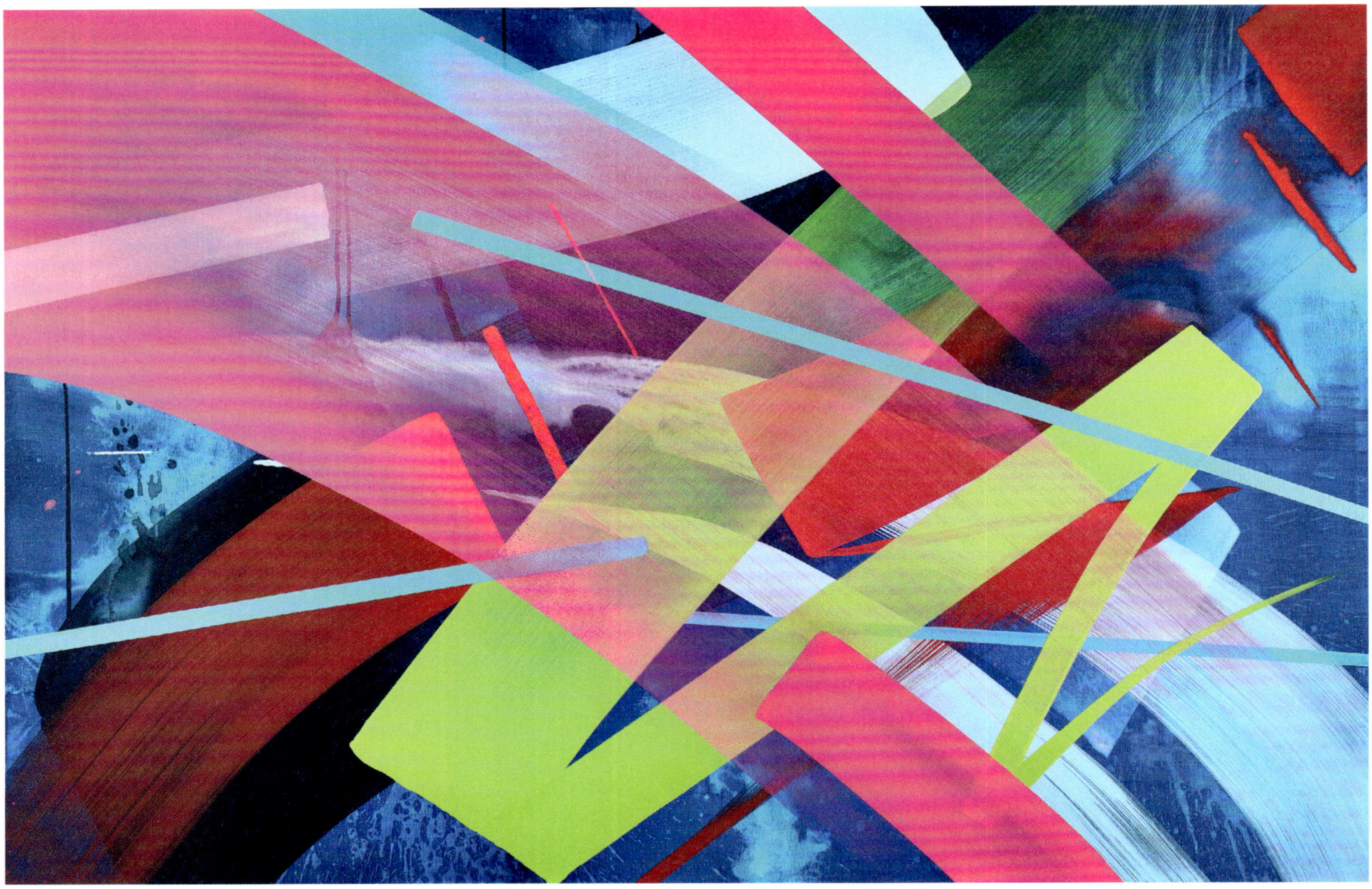

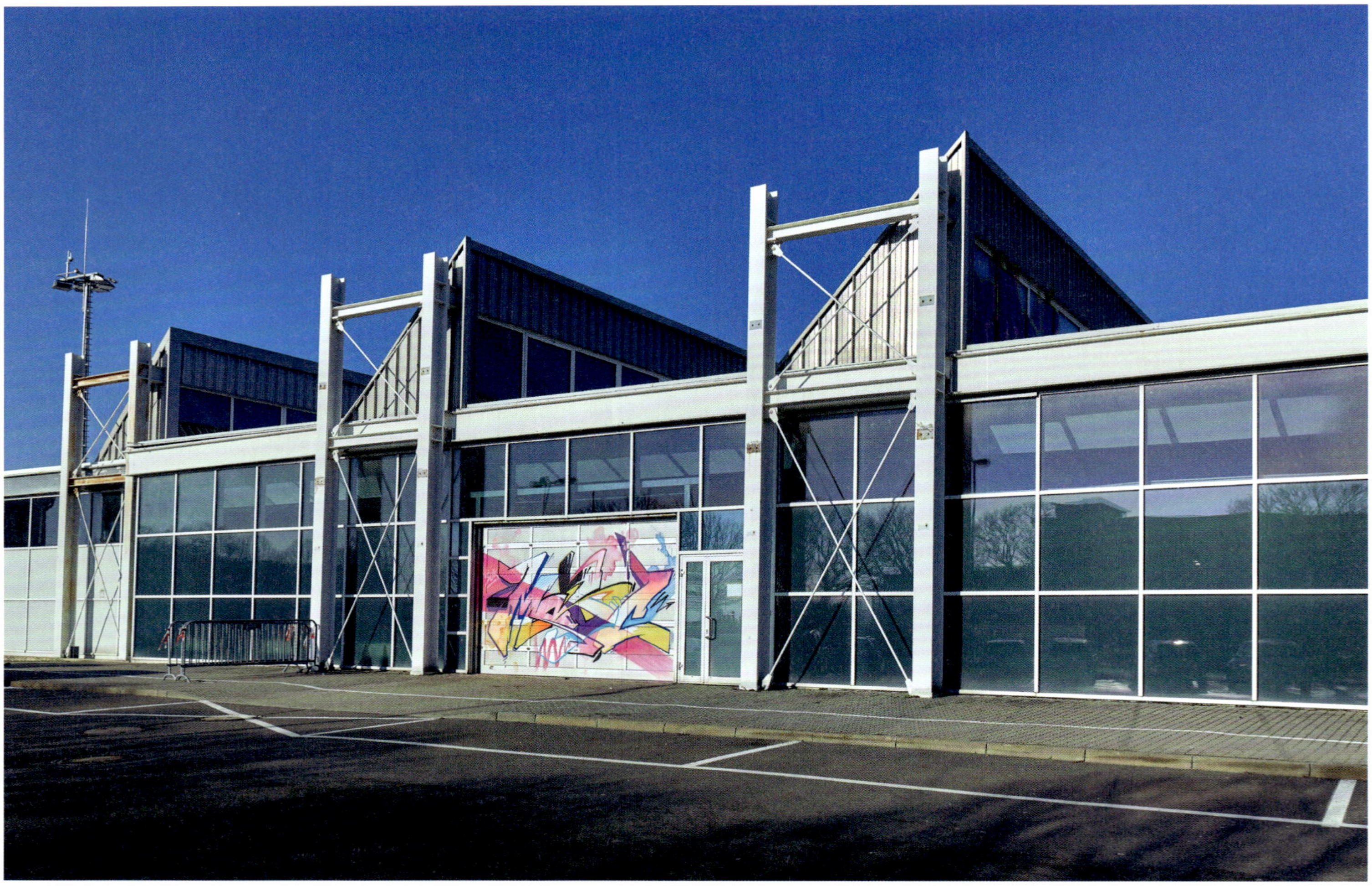

117 (opposite, top). *DRS Gateway 2018-2019*, 100 x 150cm, acrylic and spray paint on canvas, 2018. This canvas was the basis for the mural in Dresden, Germany

118–128 (opposite bottom, this page and next three spreads). *DRS Gateway*, Dresden International Airport, Germany, January 2019. The mural was painted at minus degrees, so the bucket paint didn't dry for many days. MadC's original plan was to paint the floor, ceiling and walls of the main hall to create the complete canvas in an overlarge size. Because the paint didn't dry within the 12 days of completion, the plan had to be changed on the spot

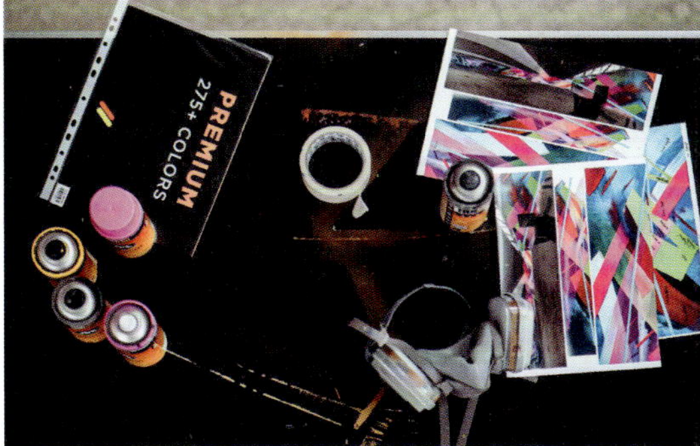

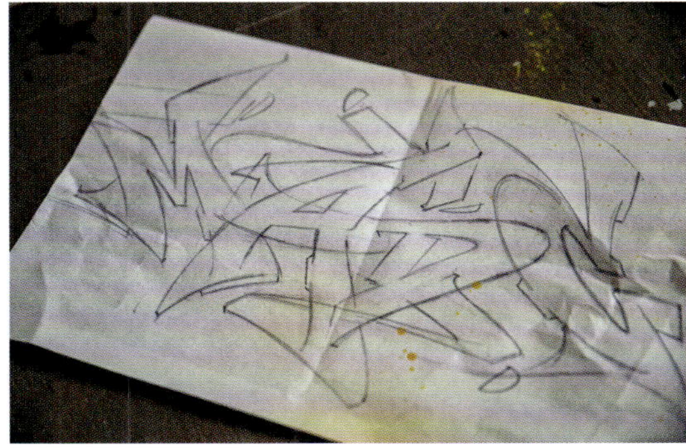

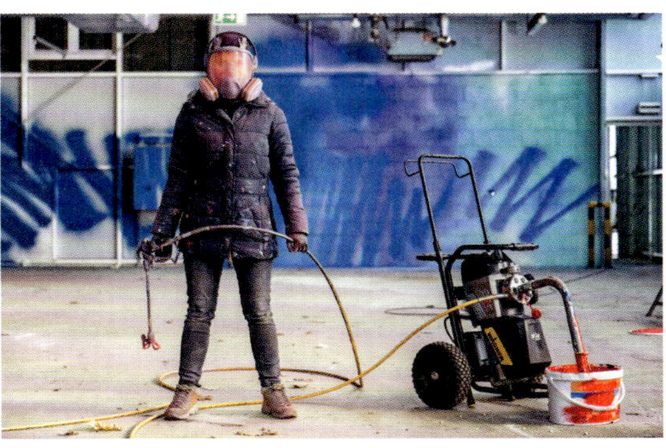

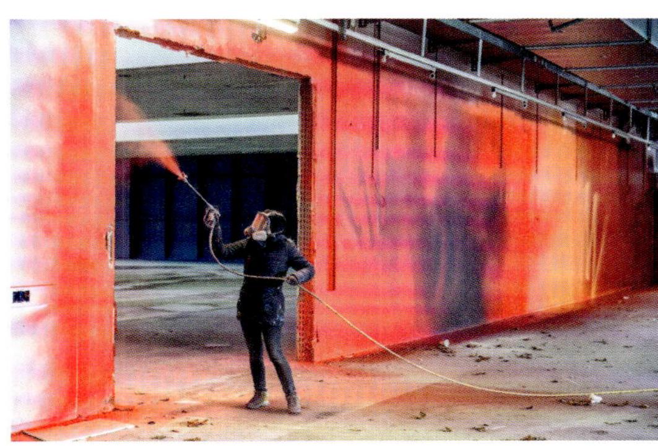

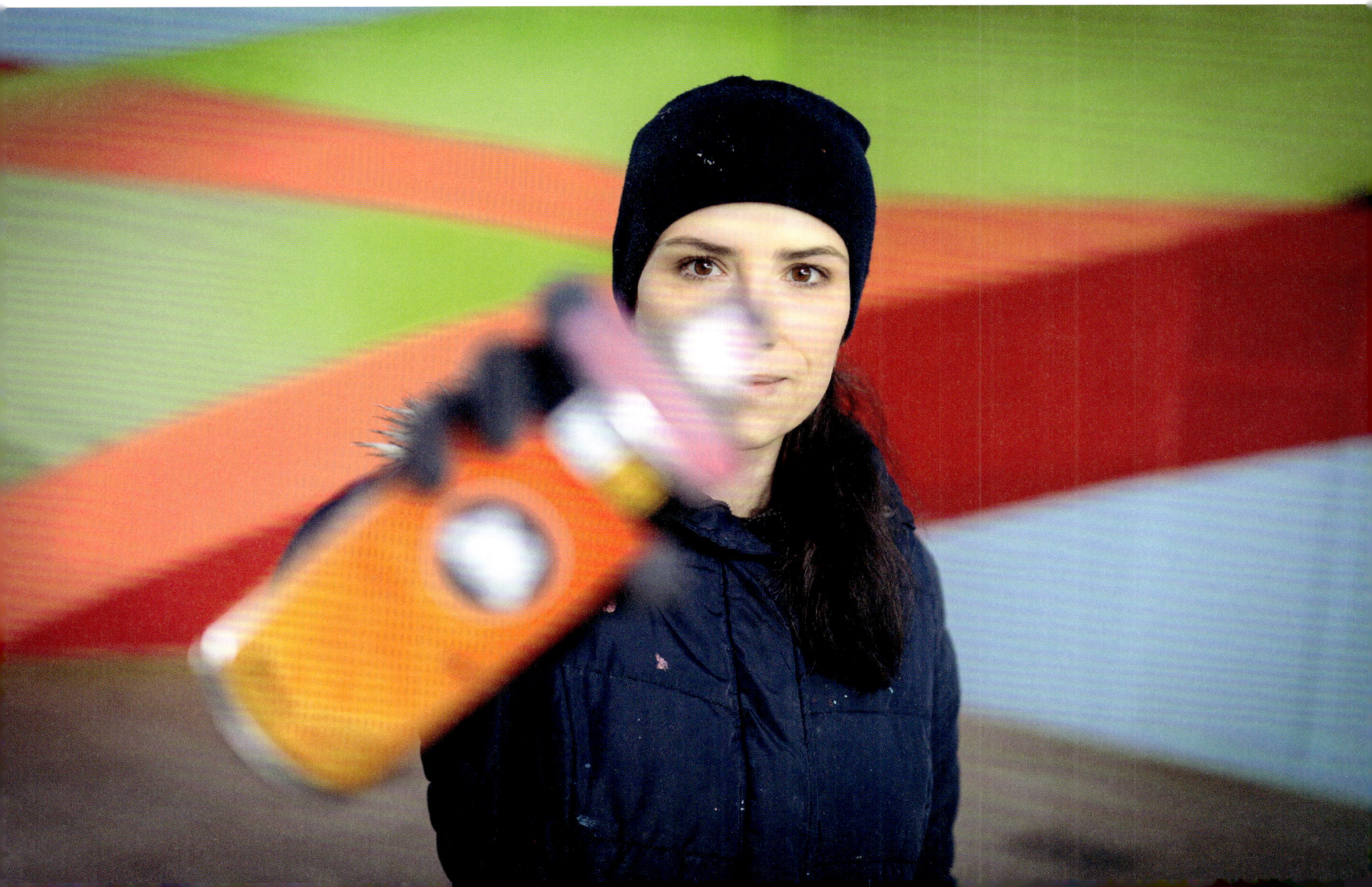

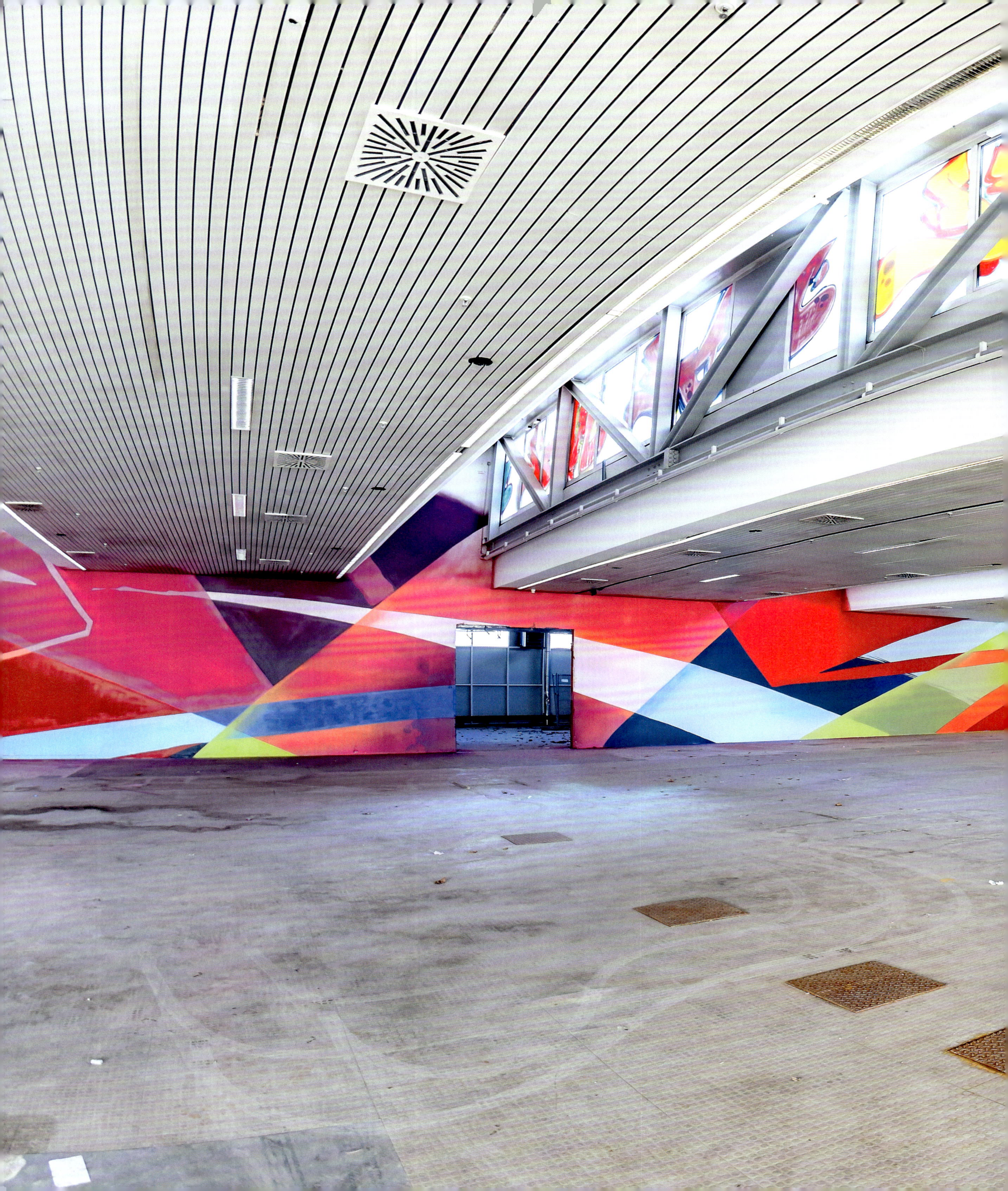

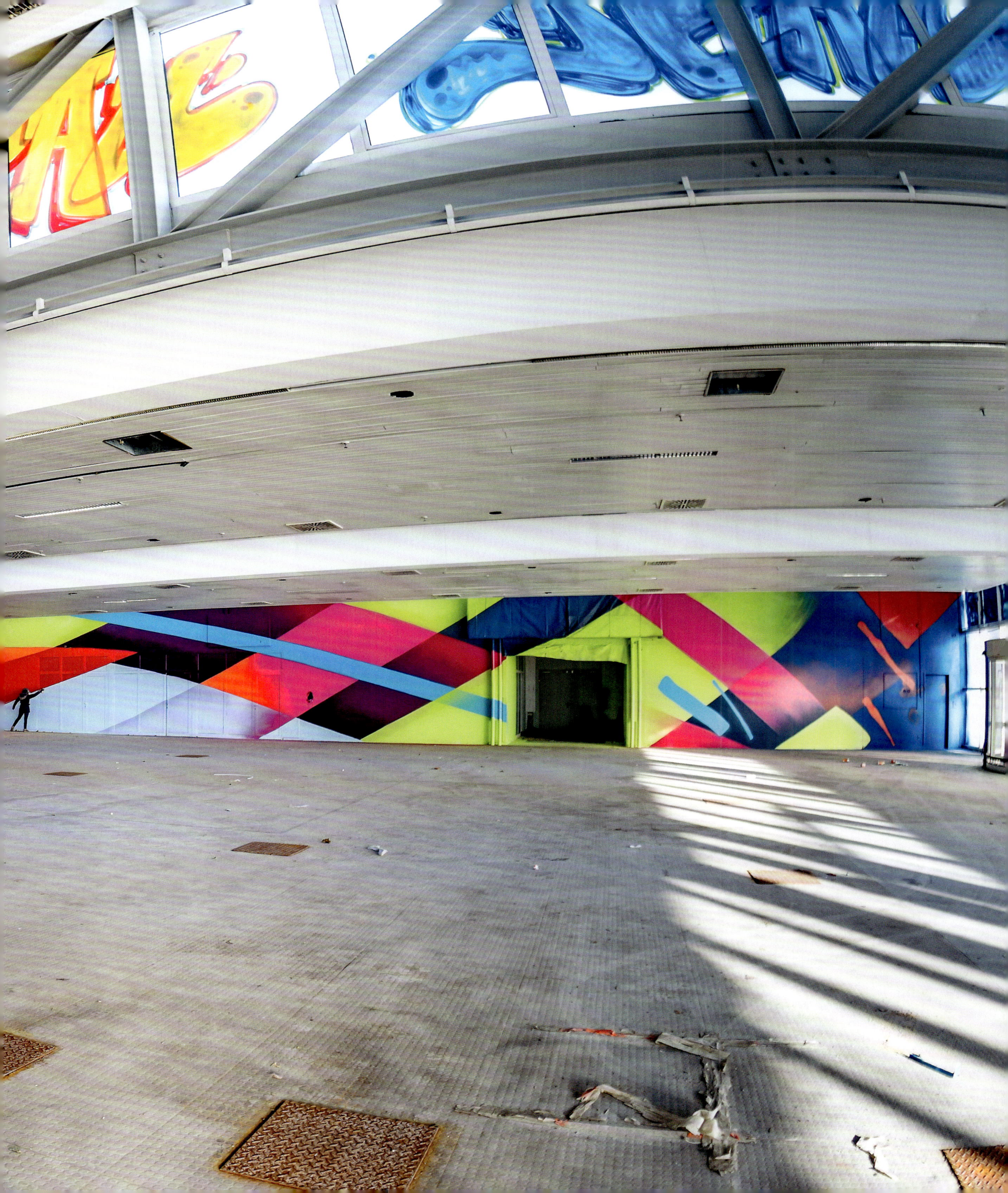

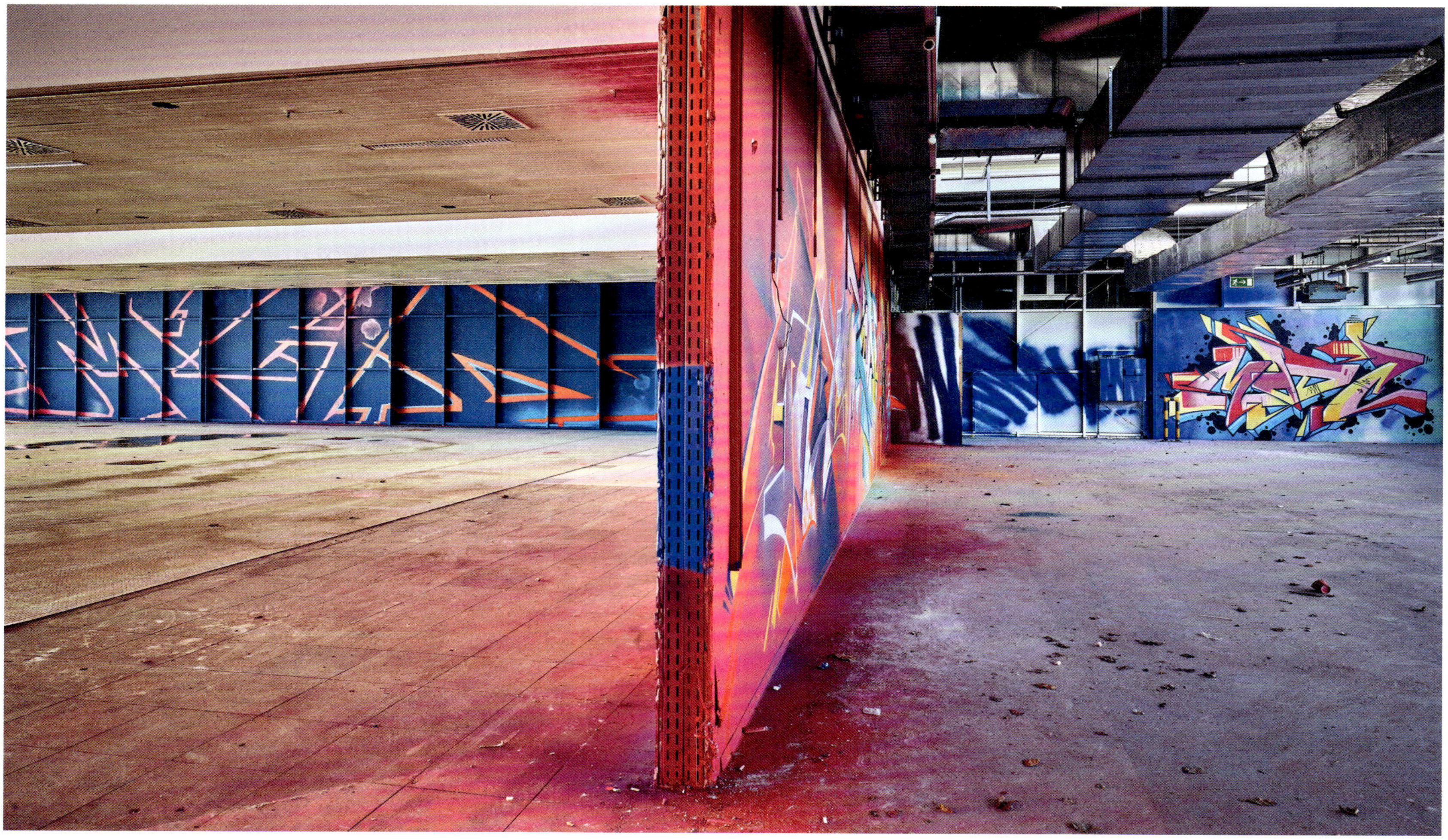

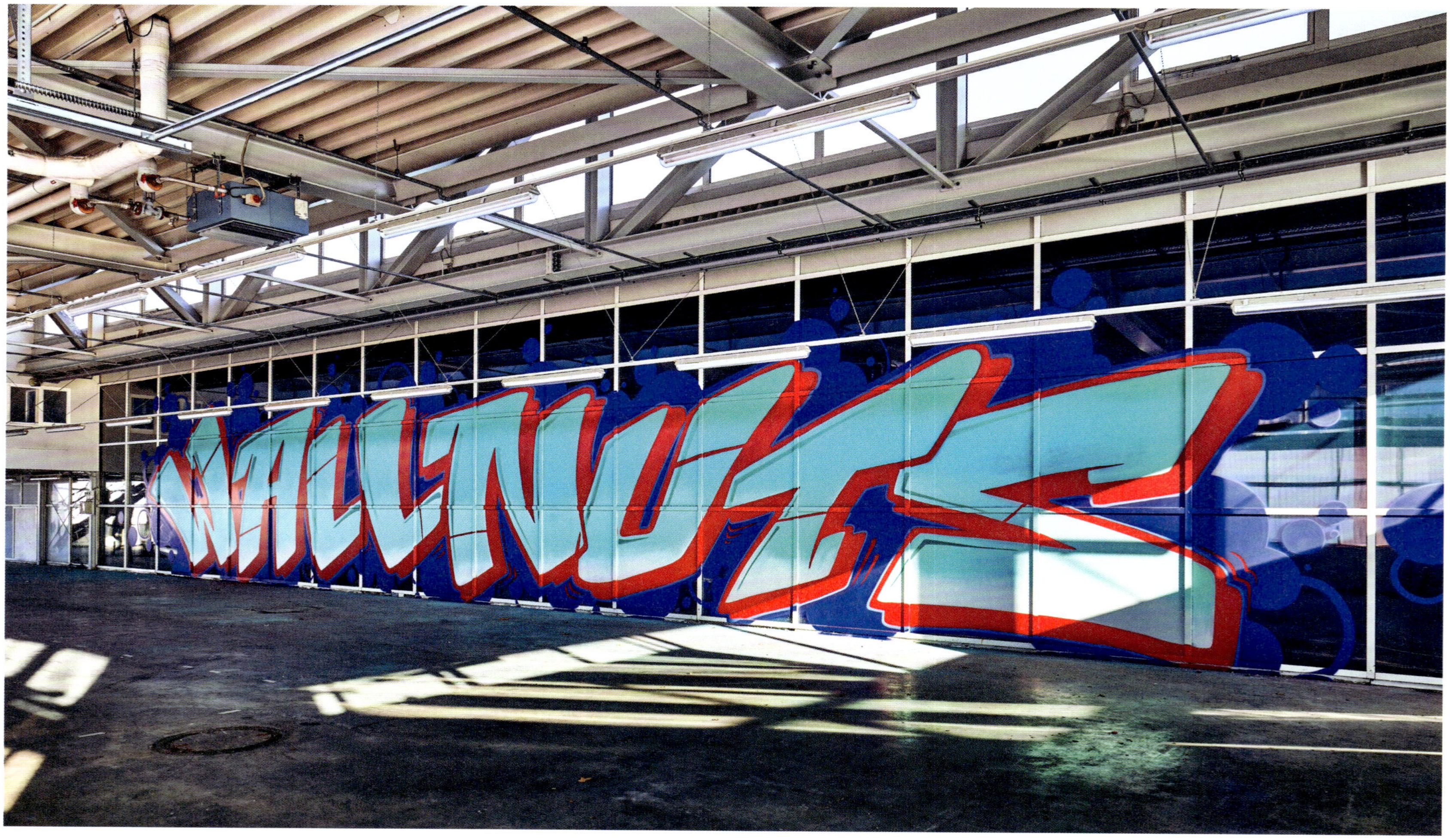

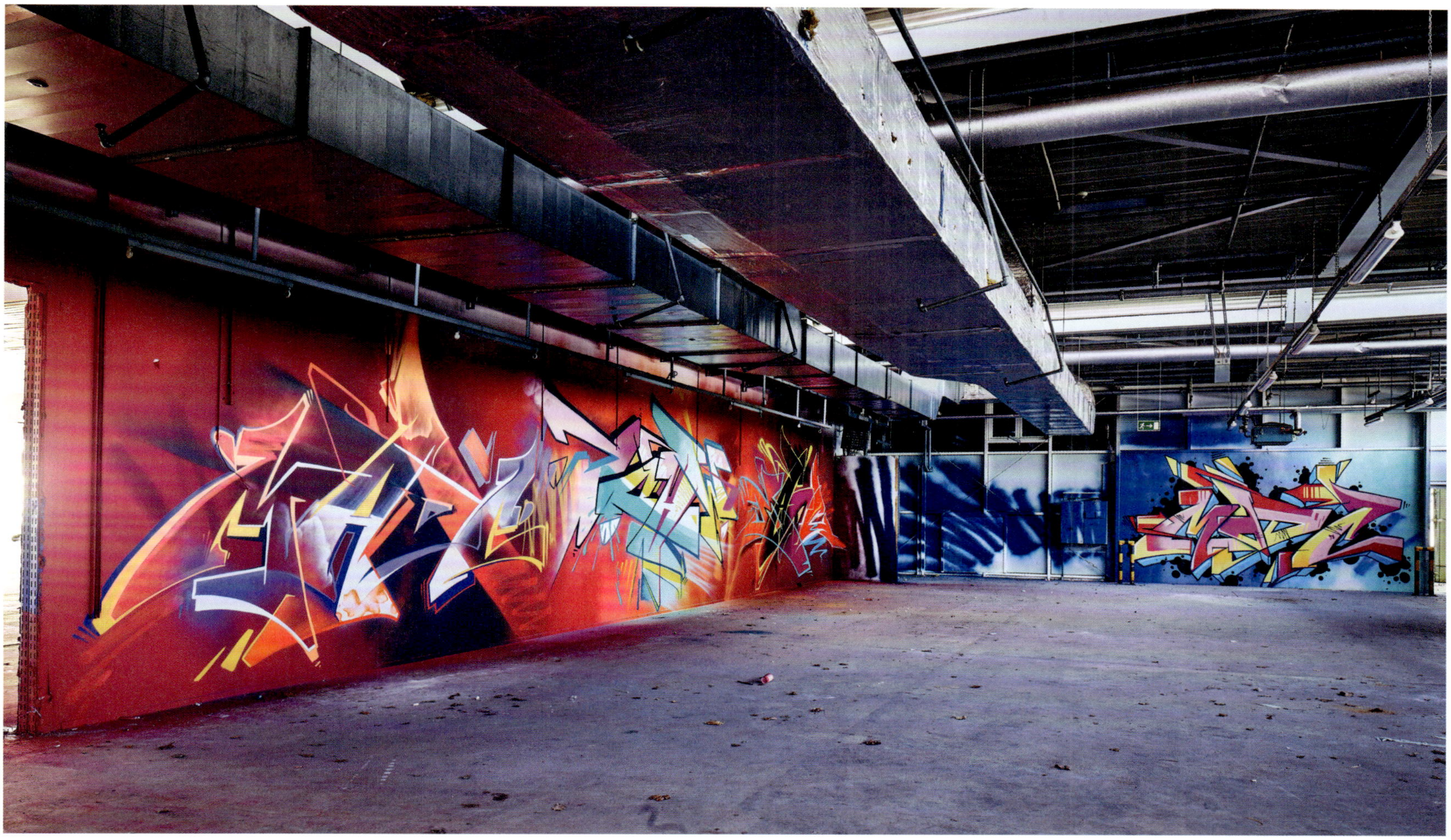

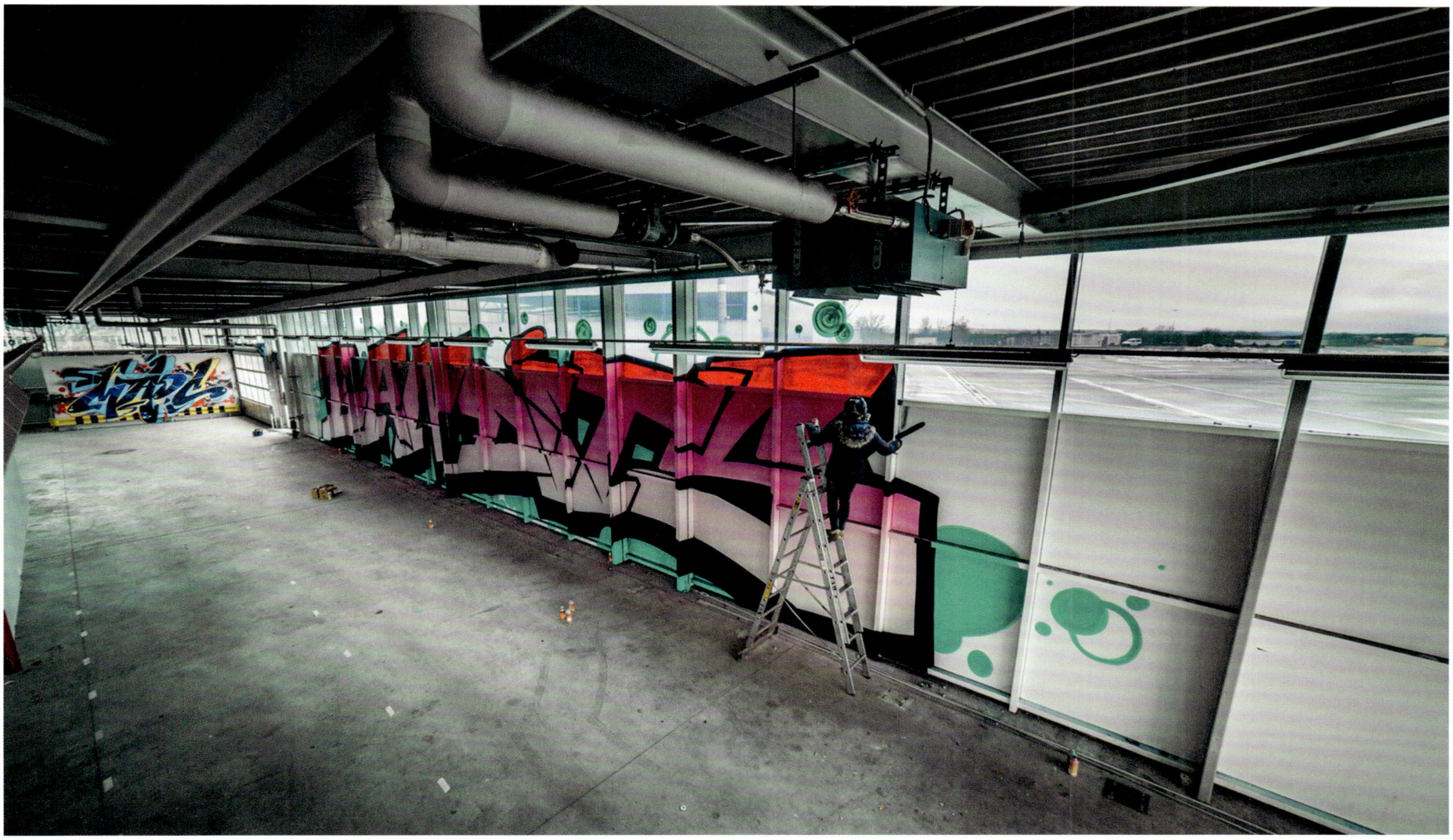

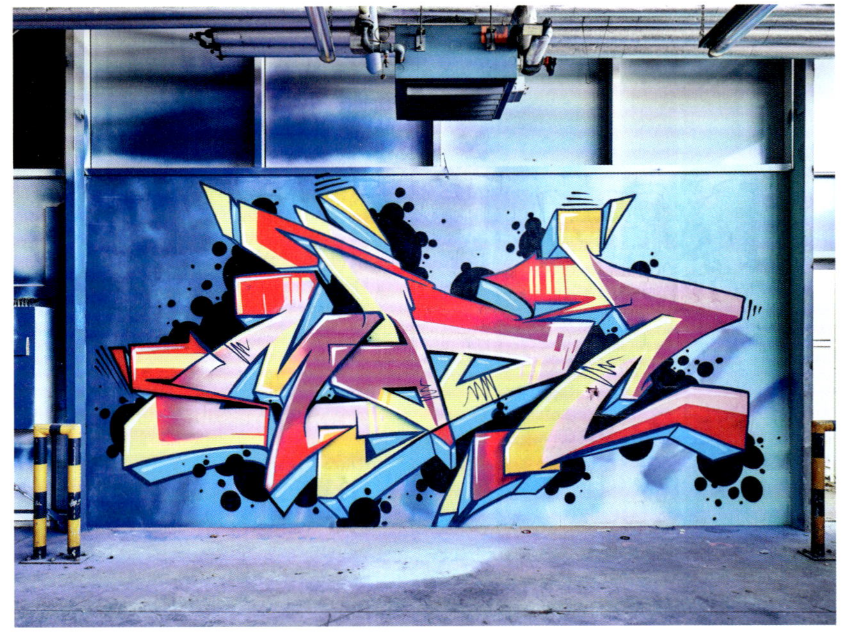
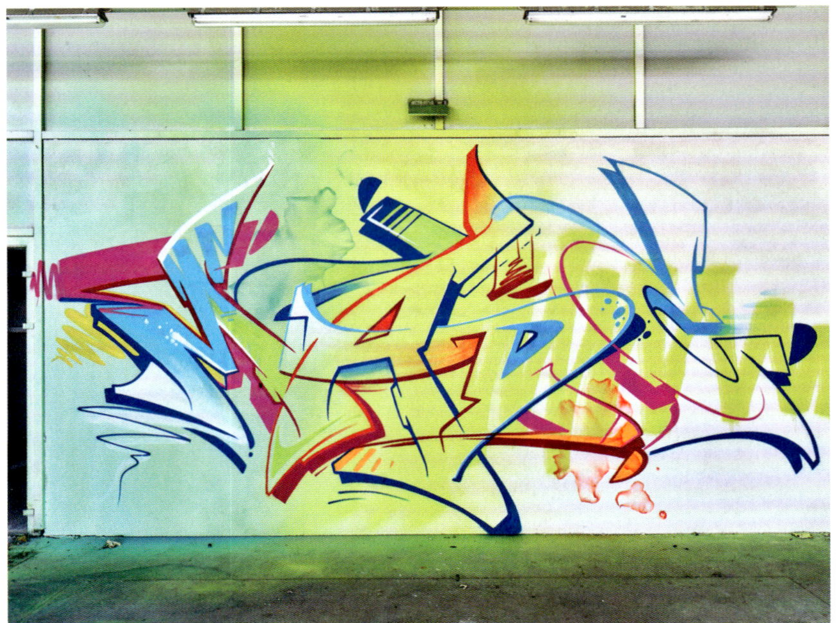
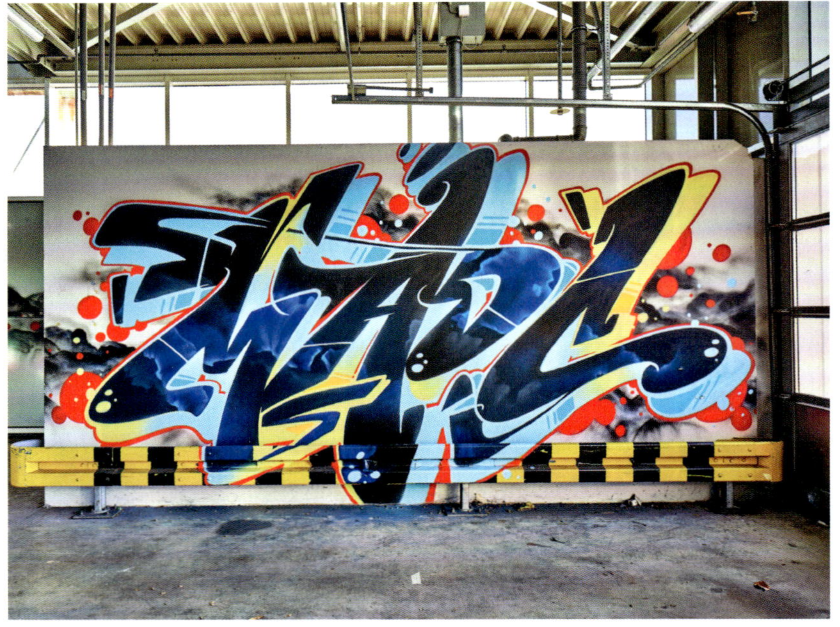
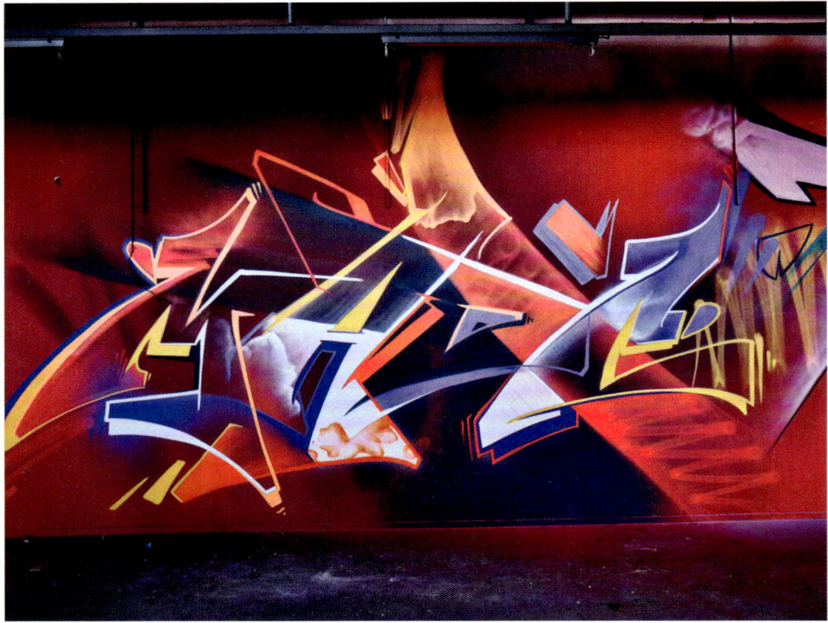
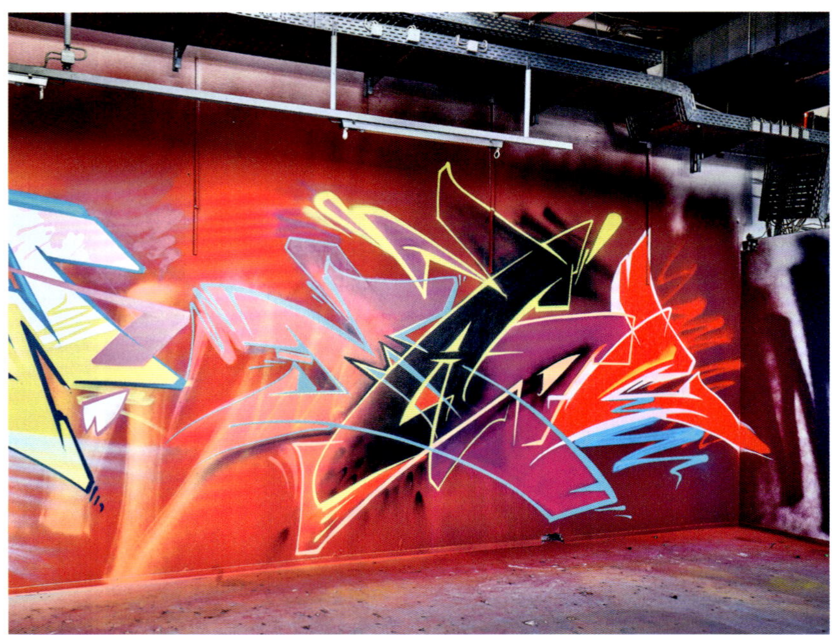
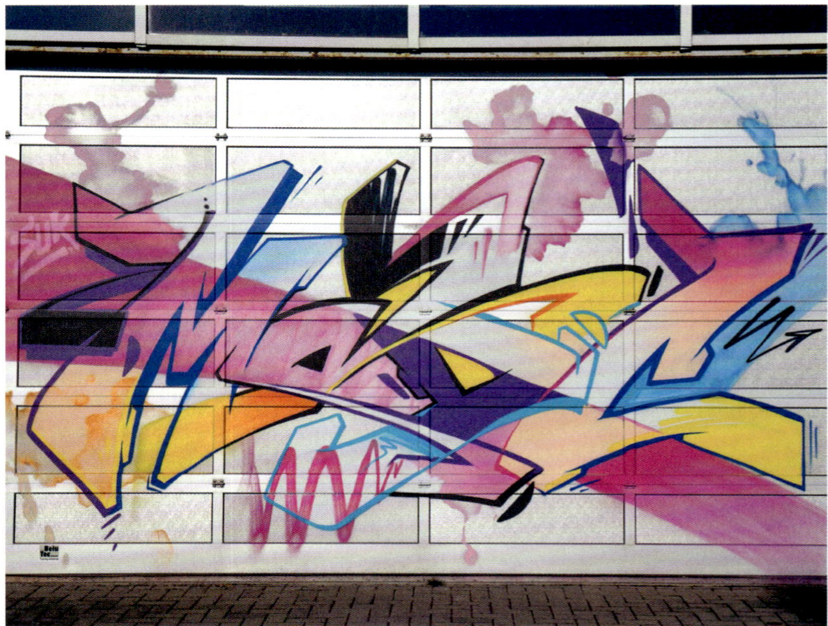

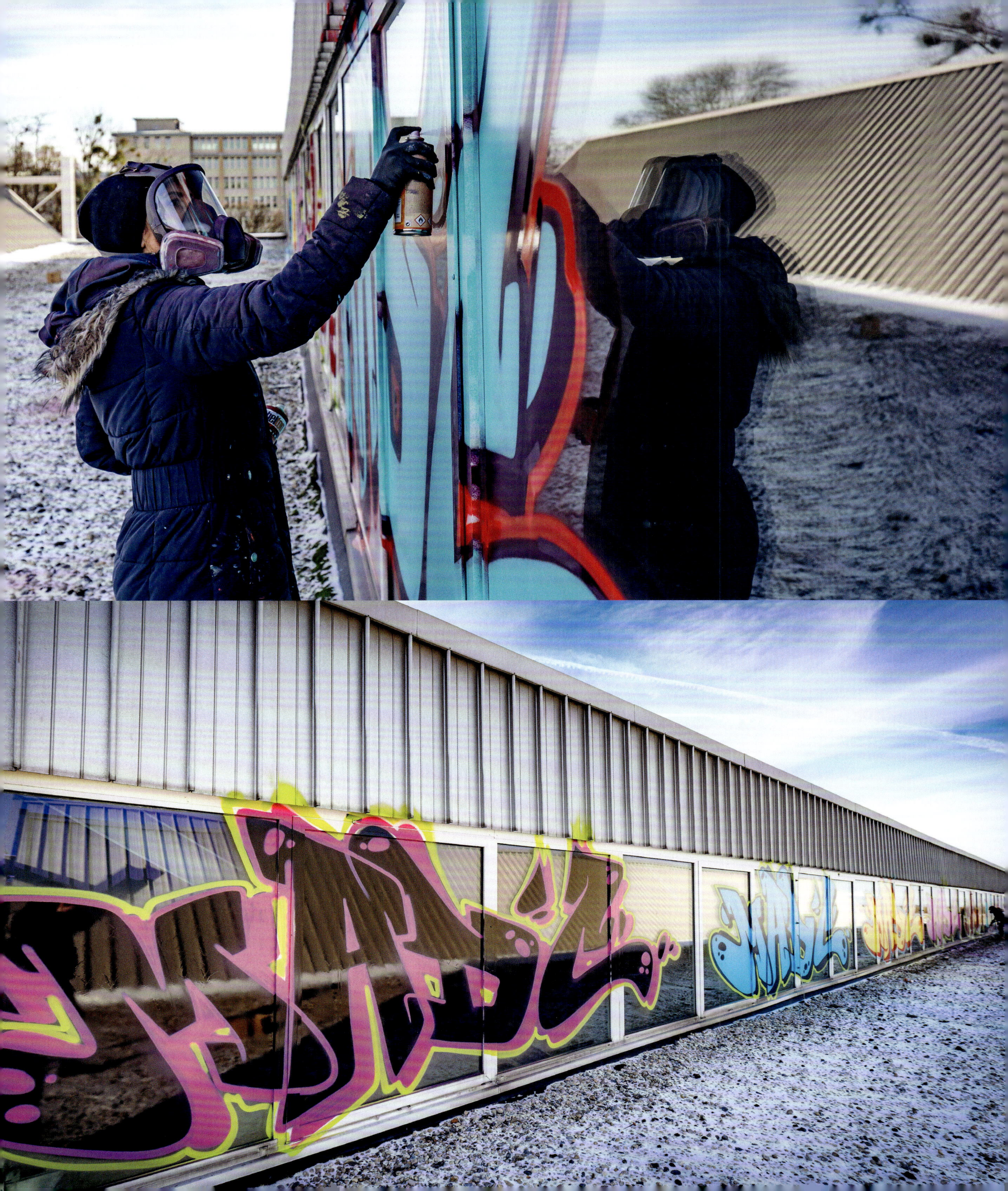

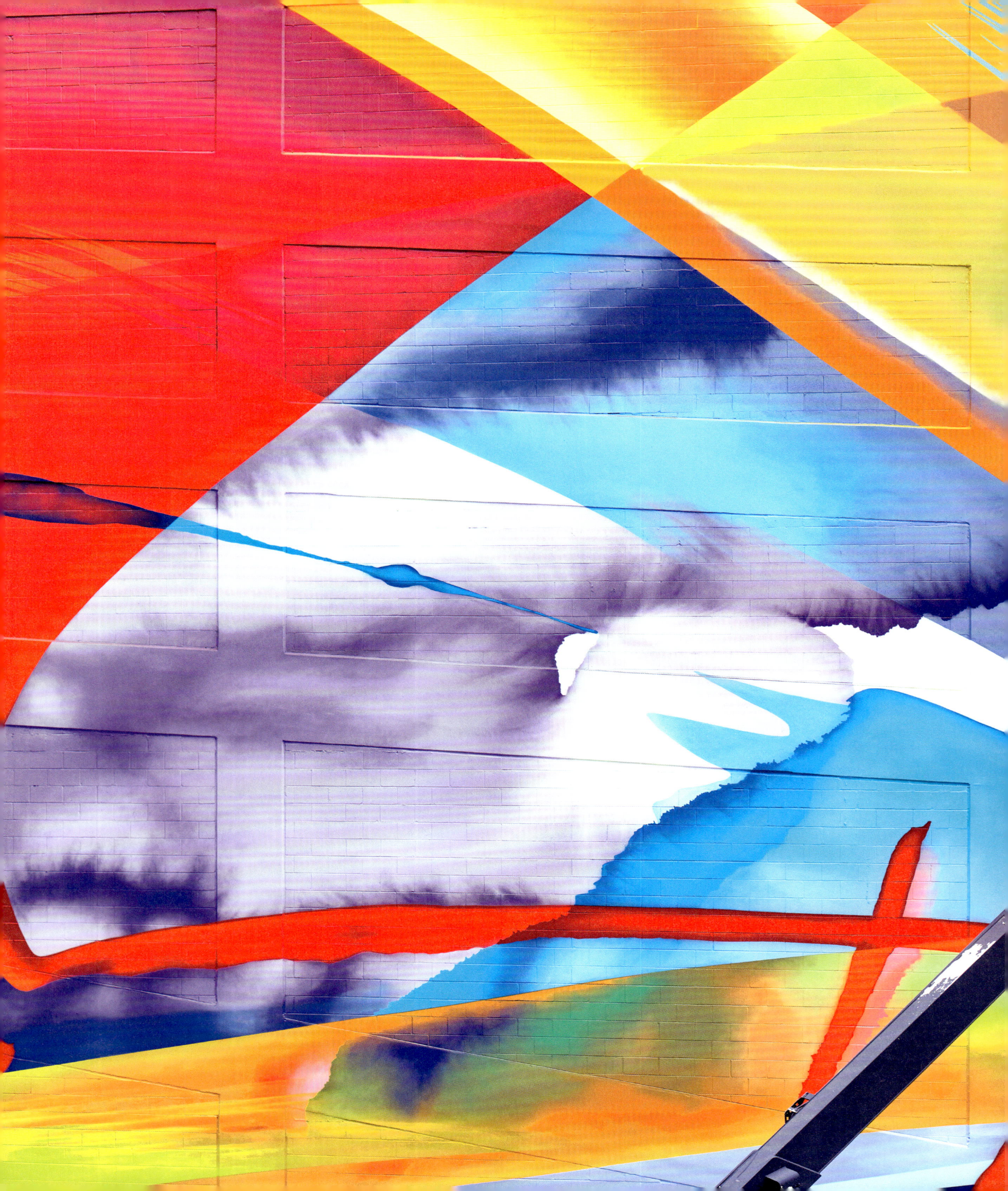

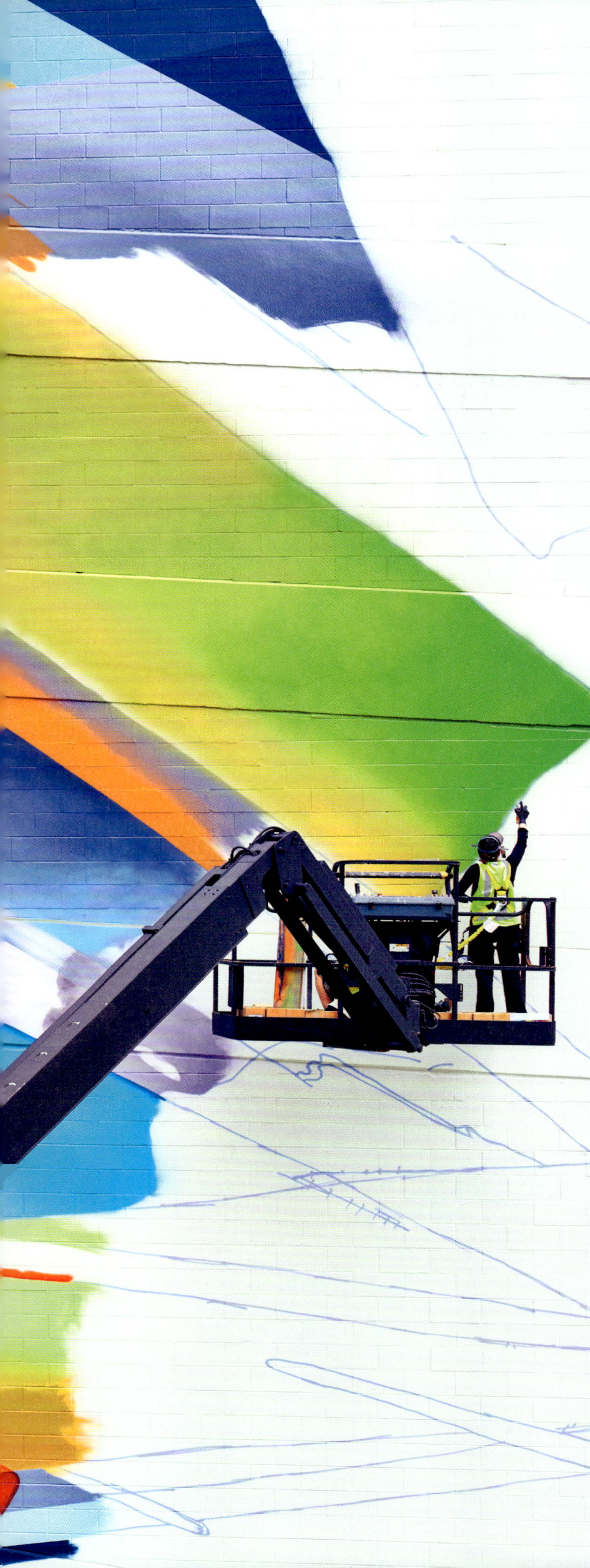

GOING BIG

In recent years, MadC's murals have grown bigger in size. Having found the required techniques to tackle vast surfaces with *The 500 Wall* in Leipzig, she was able to further refine and optimise them. In 2018, with *The 1000 Wall* in Chicago **(fig. 129)**, she broke her record, and described the impressive experience:

> I was very excited about the opportunity to work with Neysa for the Wabash Arts Corridor of which I had heard quite a bit before already. When she sent me photos and measurements of the wall, I was intimidated by the size, which hasn't happened in a long time. But absolutely everyone on that project was dedicated 100% and made this mural my smoothest painting experience to date. We had no broken lifts, we didn't run out of paint and we were very lucky with the weather. I was even offered a physiotherapist because, after 22 years of painting, this mural had caused me the first sore arm ever.[13]

The sheer vastness of the wall gave the work a new dimension, which in turn is the subject of a book that MadC had published in 2015. Under the title *Mural XXL*, she picked up on a global development that was increasingly becoming a genre of its own, settled between the worlds of graffiti and street art and the visual arts, and which was also a category that applied to her own work. All over the world, there was a growing number of these oversized murals, which were mostly produced with permission and therefore had a longer lifespan than illegally executed or smaller pieces. The visibility of the works was greatly enhanced by their dimensions, while the impact on the urban landscape was also greater compared to smaller works. For *Mural XXL*, MadC had brought together numerous artists who were working in the genre and who had produced magnificent works that expanded the categories in several ways. She also consolidated her role as a close observer of global developments in art in public spaces.

129. MadC working on *The 1000 Wall*, Wabash Arts Corridor, 1326 South Michigan Avenue, Chicago, USA, 2018

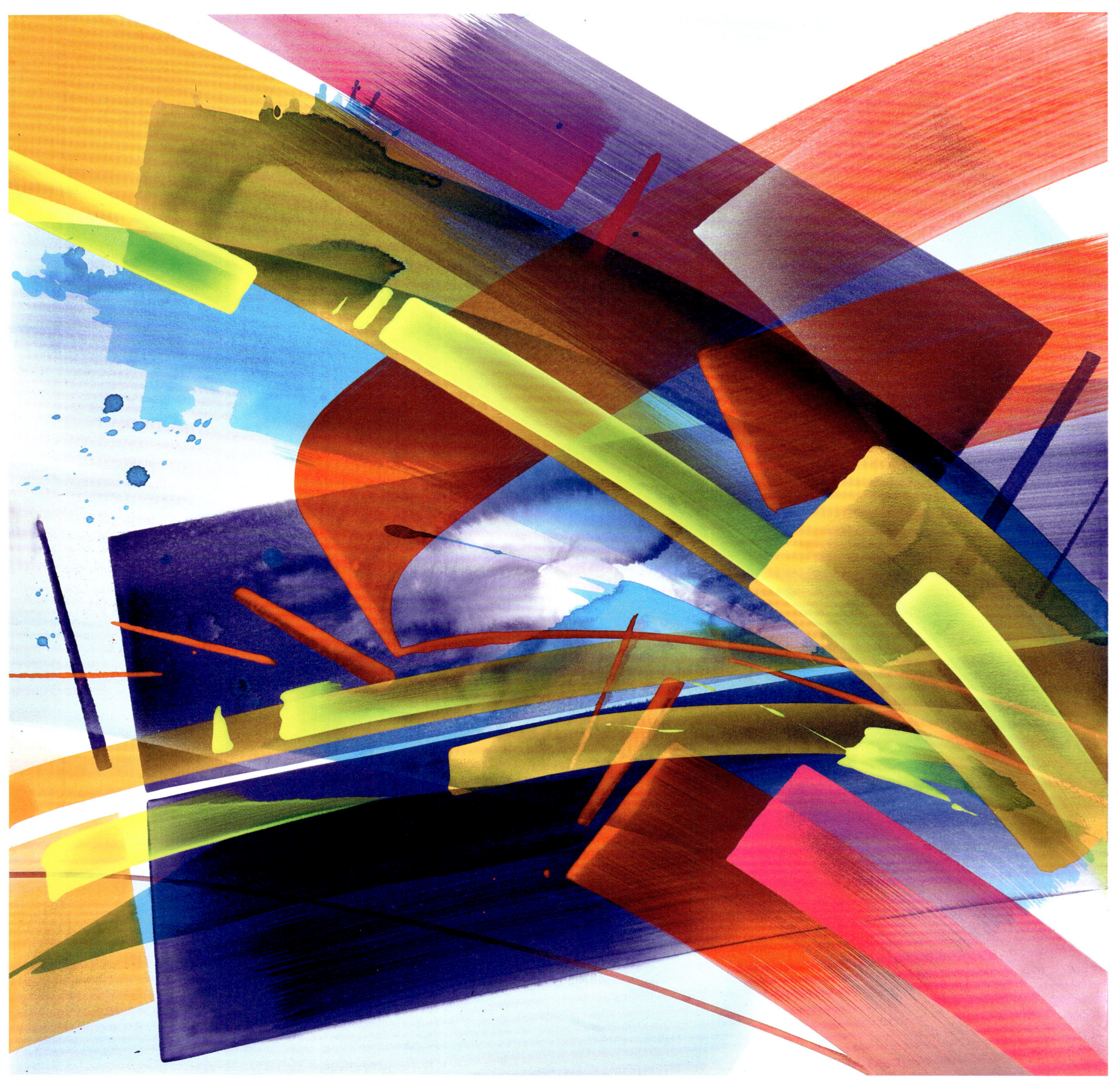

130. *13:47-21102017*, 100 x 100cm, acrylic, watercolour and spray paint on canvas, 2017. This was the sketch for the mural in Chicago, USA
131–136 (opposite and next three spreads) *The 1000 Wall*, Wabash Arts Corridor, 1326 South Michigan Avenue, Chicago, USA, 2018. This wall was the largest surface area MadC had painted to date, and it took her and her assistant, HAKS180, 13 days to complete

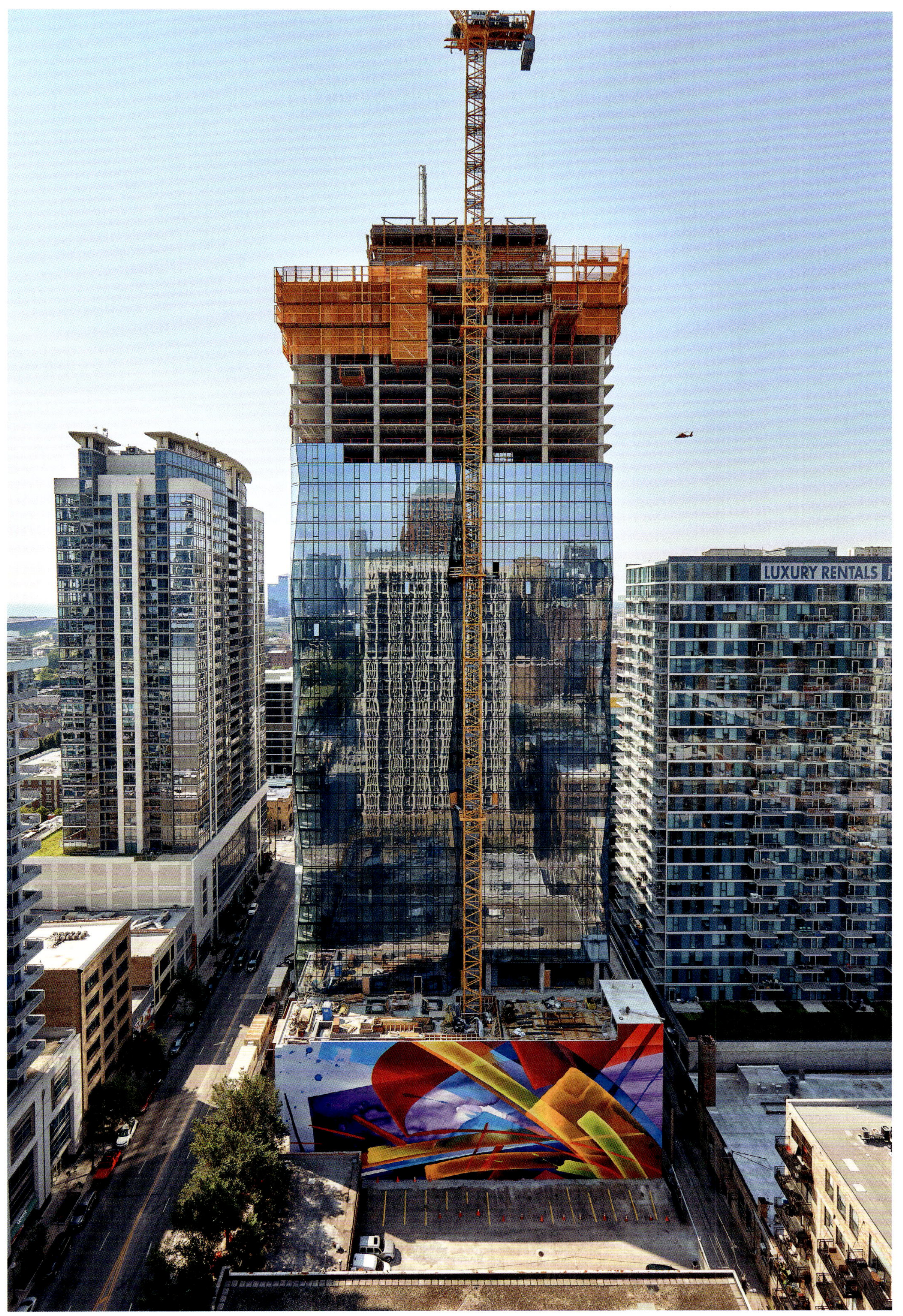
LUXURY RENTALS

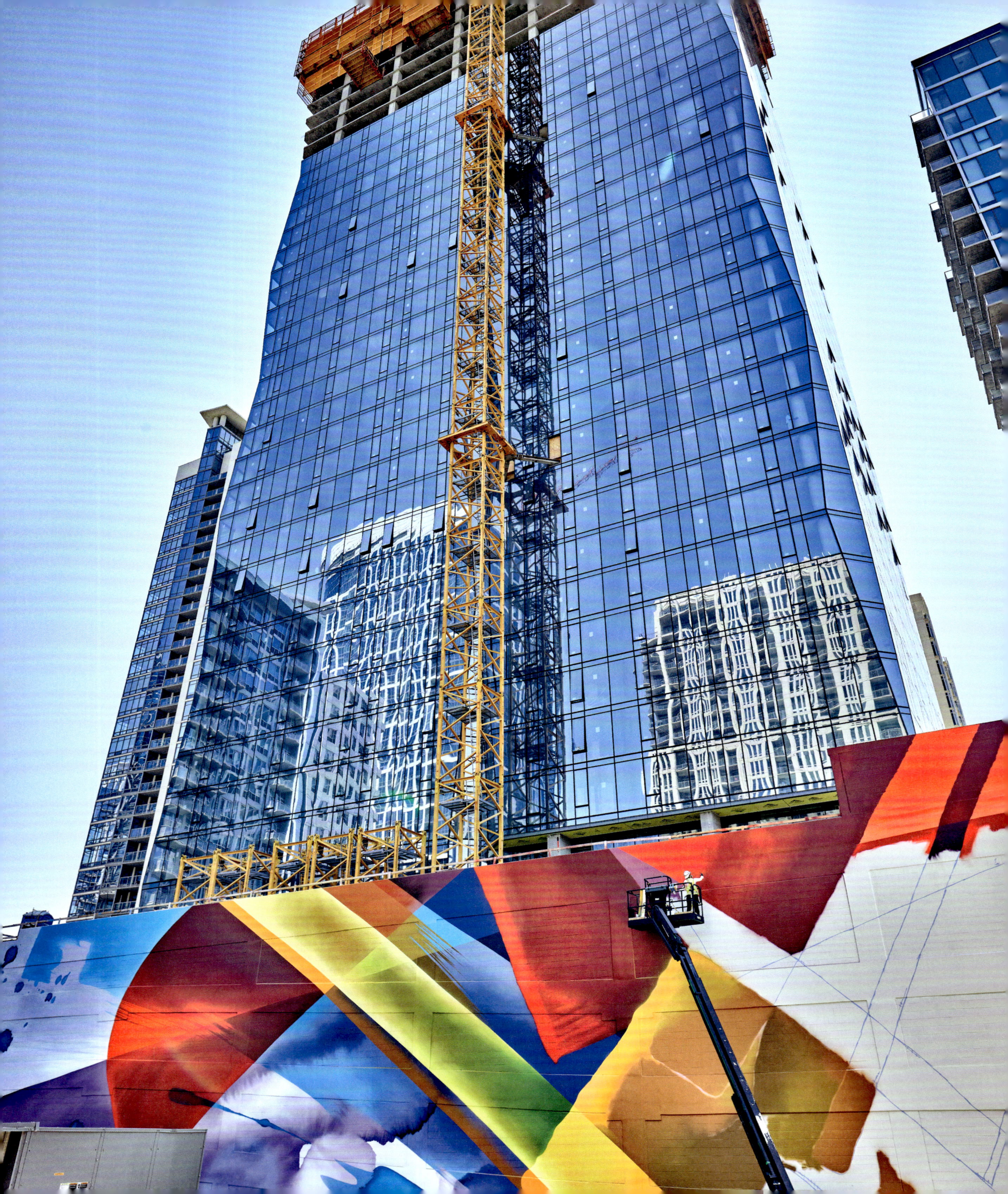

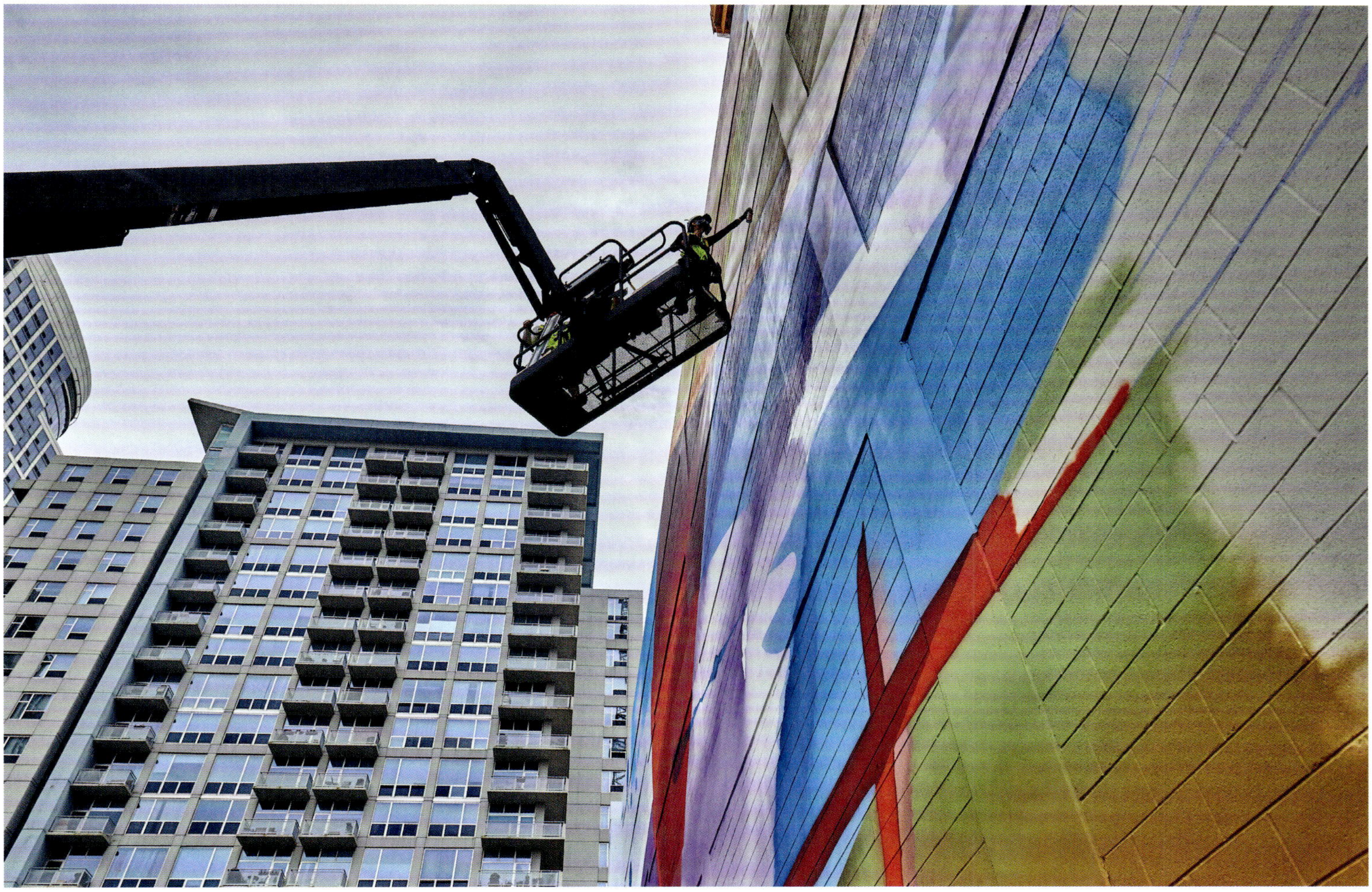

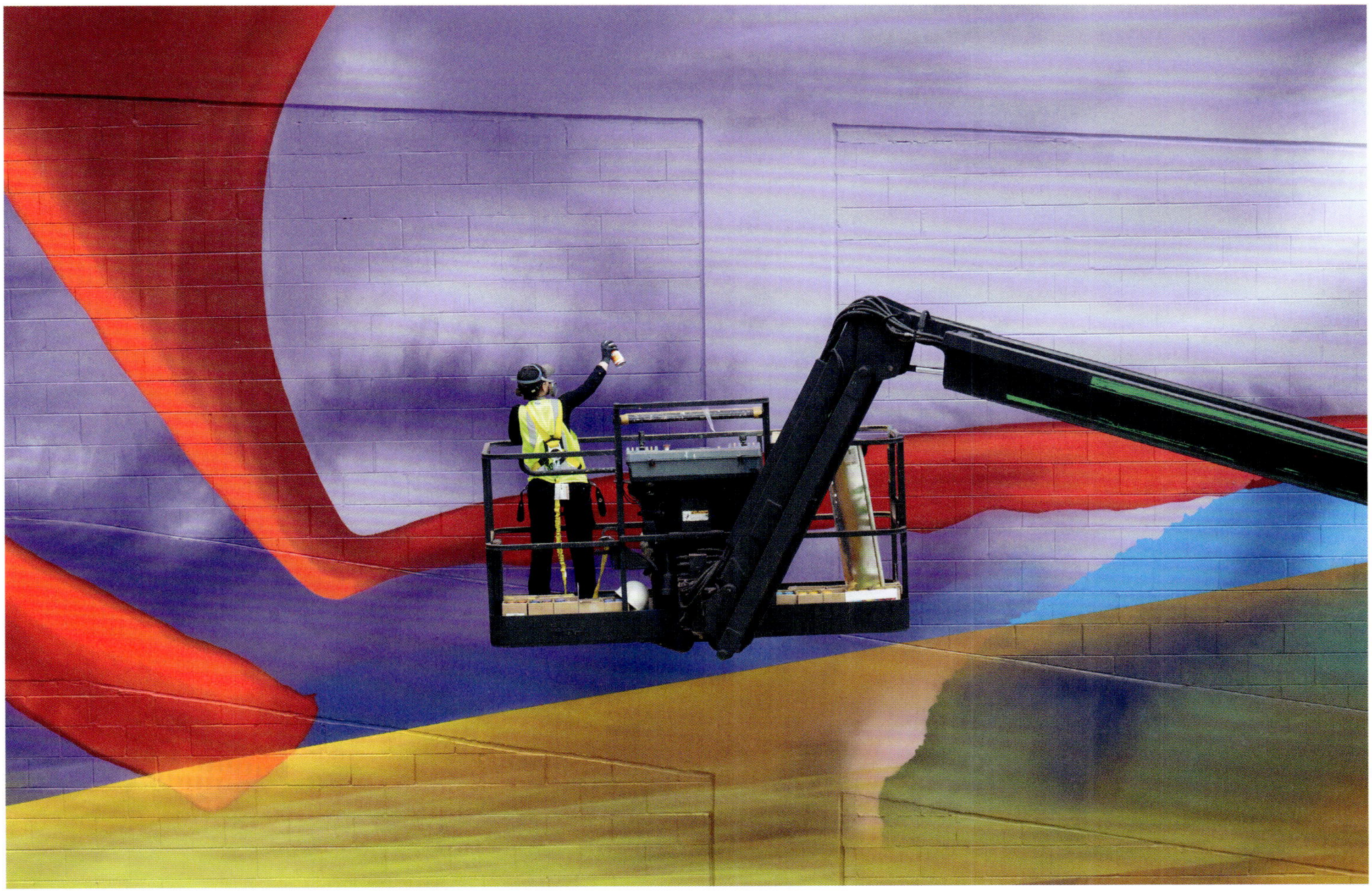

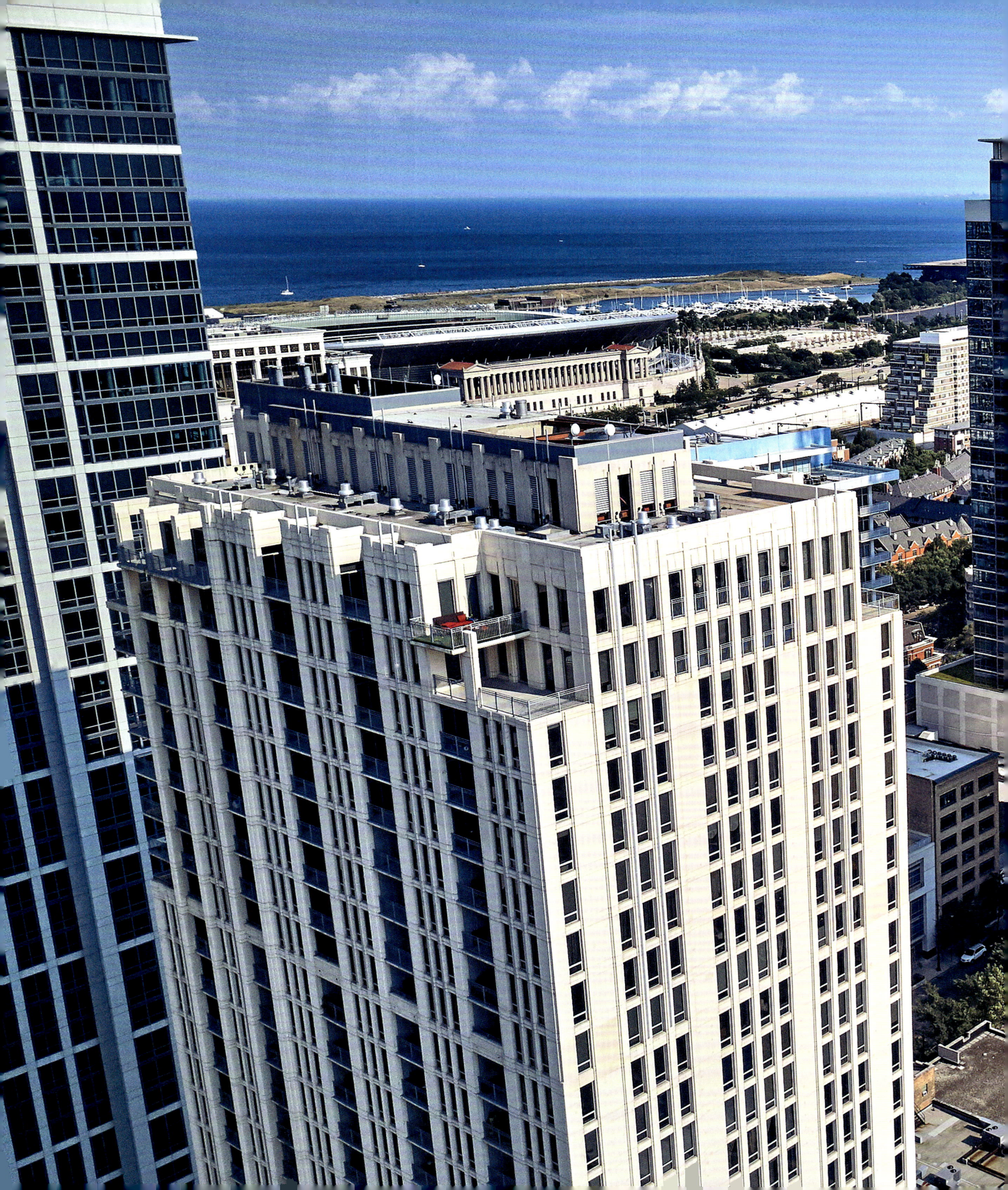

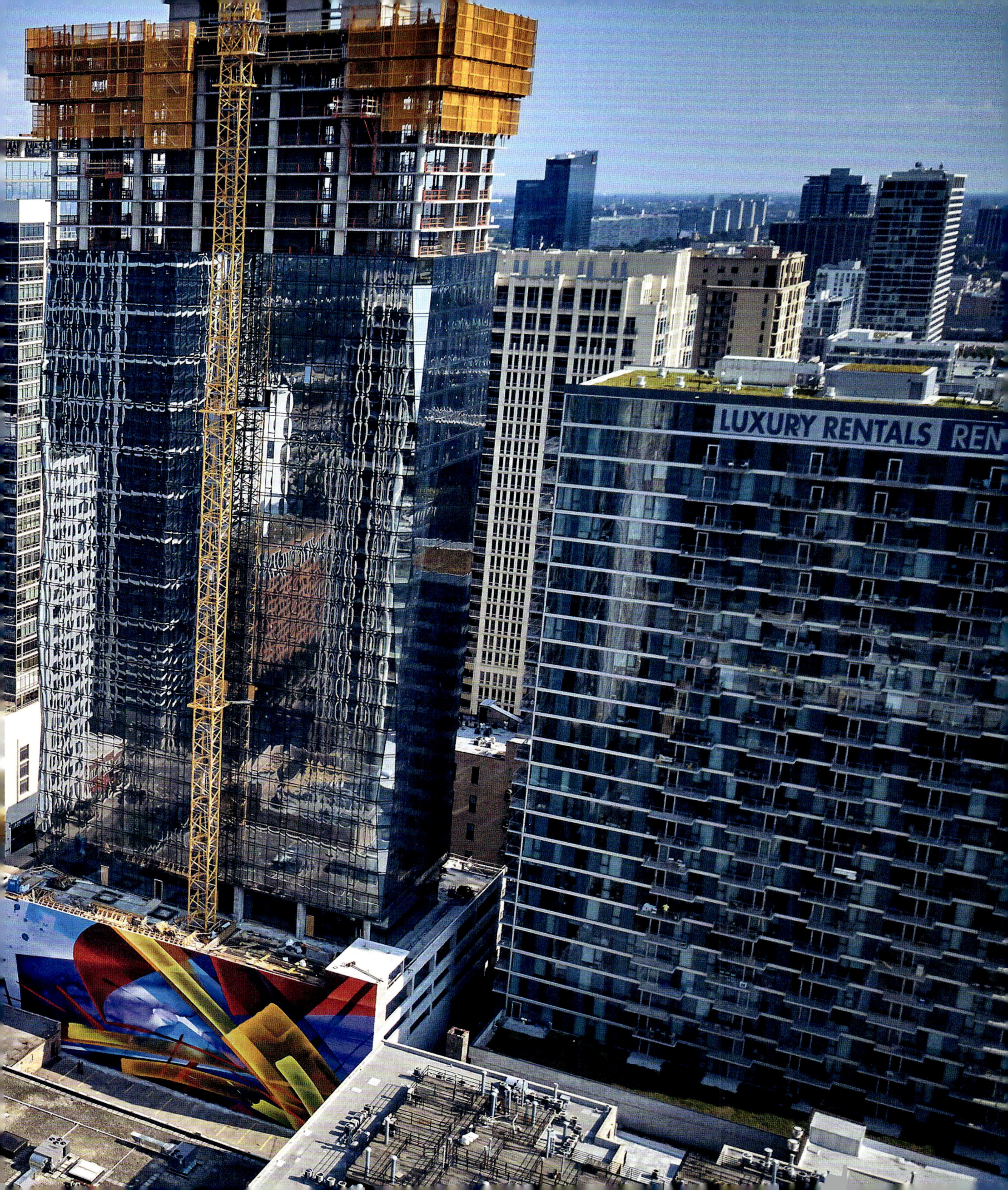
LUXURY RENTALS

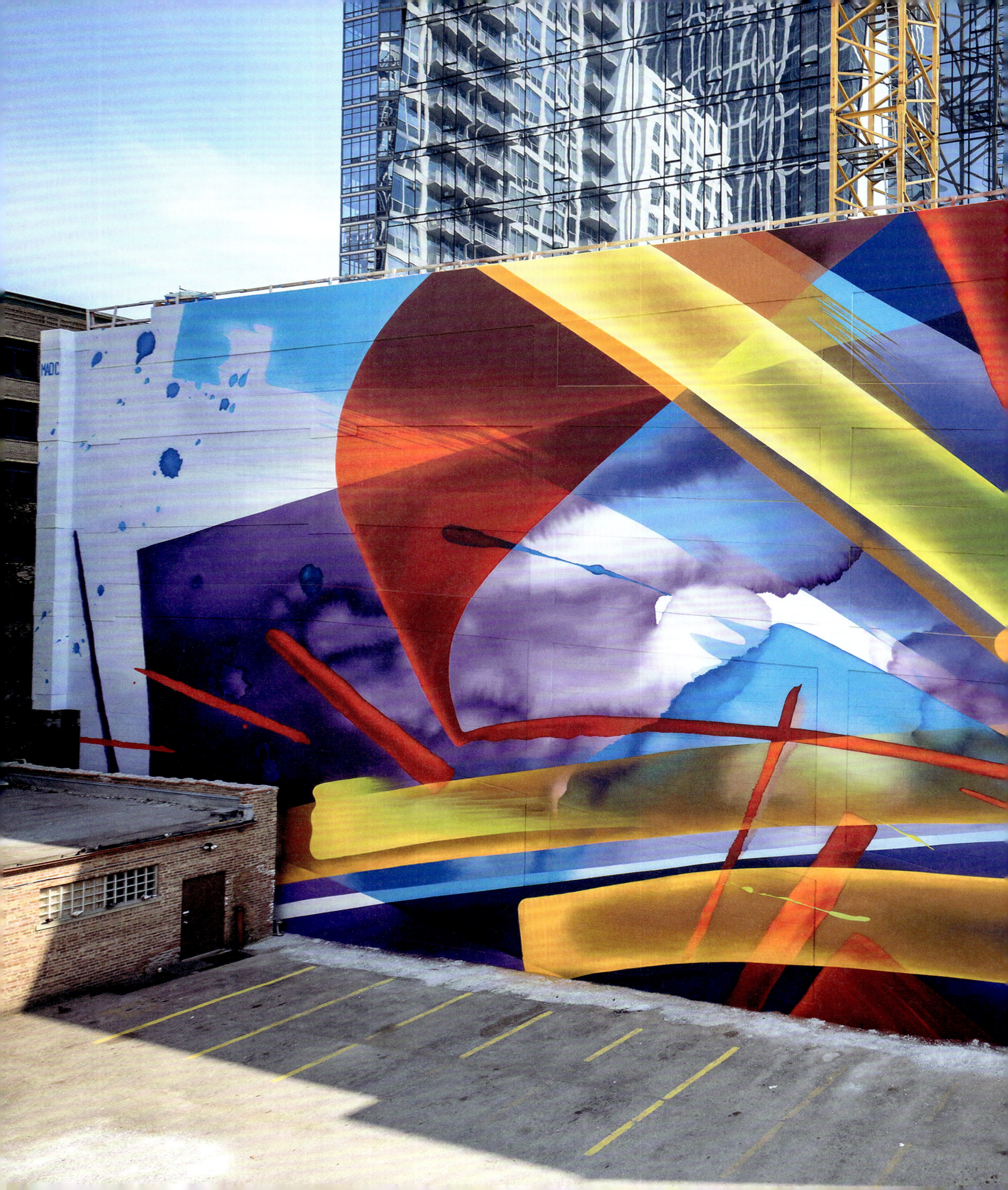
MADC

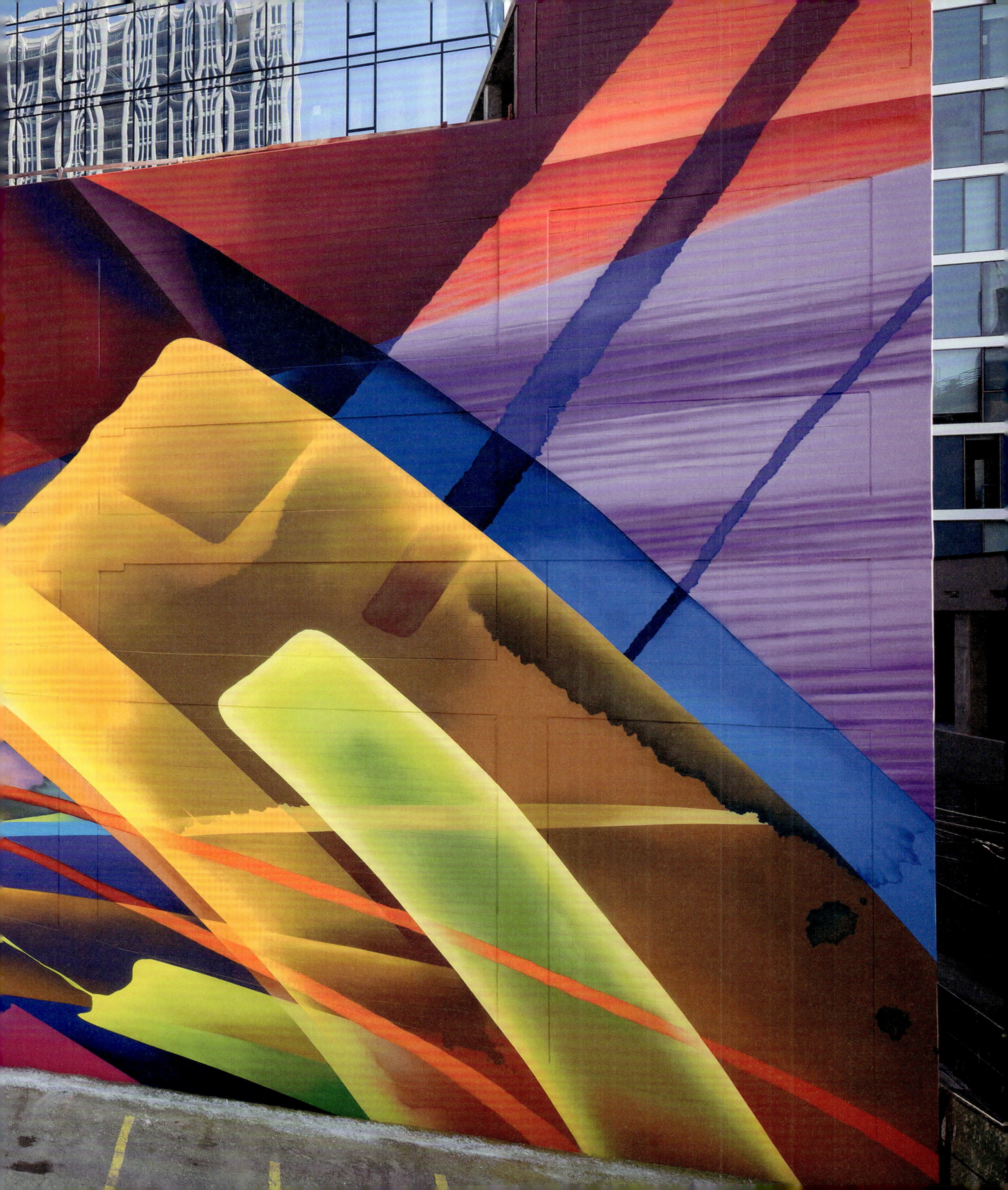

Murals in XXL dimensions became an integral part of MadC's artistic repertoire, resulting in major projects such as the walls in Jersey City **(figs. 150–152)** and Berlin-Hellersdorf **(figs. 164–166)** in 2019, and in Abu Dhabi in 2020, the largest mural to date throughout the Arabian Peninsula **(figs. 173–177)**. While she worked alone for the first large murals, she now has assistants who support her for new projects, for example creating the first grid on the wall or filling uniformly monochrome areas. The essence of her artistic handwriting, transparency and watercolour elements, however, remains firmly in her hands, as she is the only one who has mastered this craft in absolute perfection.

In addition to the large mural projects, MadC remains varied. Her art repeatedly takes her to unusual places such as the Colombian jungle, picturesque Baden-Baden or the Maldives (opposite), where she also experienced the first lockdown of the global COVID-19 pandemic. Shortly before, in January 2020, she had opened her first exhibition in Taiyuan, China, which received an immensely positive response. Currently, she is working on drafts for glassworks that will be integrated into the new building for the Reinhard Ernst Museum in Wiesbaden, Germany. They will be fabricated by the same glass workshop that made the windows designed by Gerhard Richter for Cologne Cathedral.

There are also always opportunities for MadC to spray new style writings, for which she returns again to the classic conventions of graffiti and transfers her energetic abstract lines into wild styles. But what remains particularly exciting are her activities in the studio, which continue to form the epicentre of her artistic work.

13 MadC cited in Haden, Donna, 'MadC Paints Her Largest Mural To Date in the Wabash Arts Corridor!', *Graffiti Street*, 30 August 2018, https://www.graffitistreet.com/madc-paints-her-largest-mural-to-date-in-the-wabash-arts-corridor-chicago-2018 (accessed 14 March 2021). Neysa is Neysa Page-Lieberman, director and curator at Columbia College Chicago.

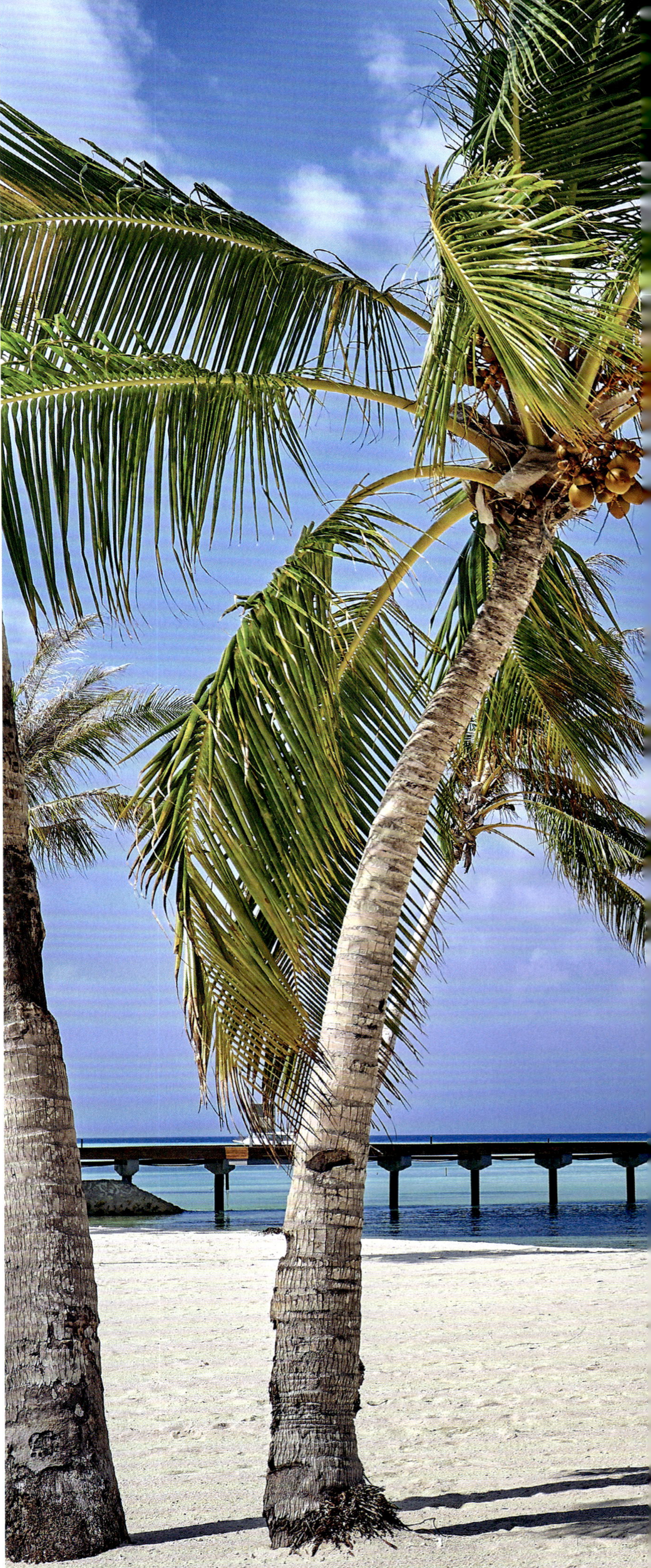

137–145 (opposite and next two spreads). Pullman Maldives, Maamutaa Island, Maldives, September–October 2019

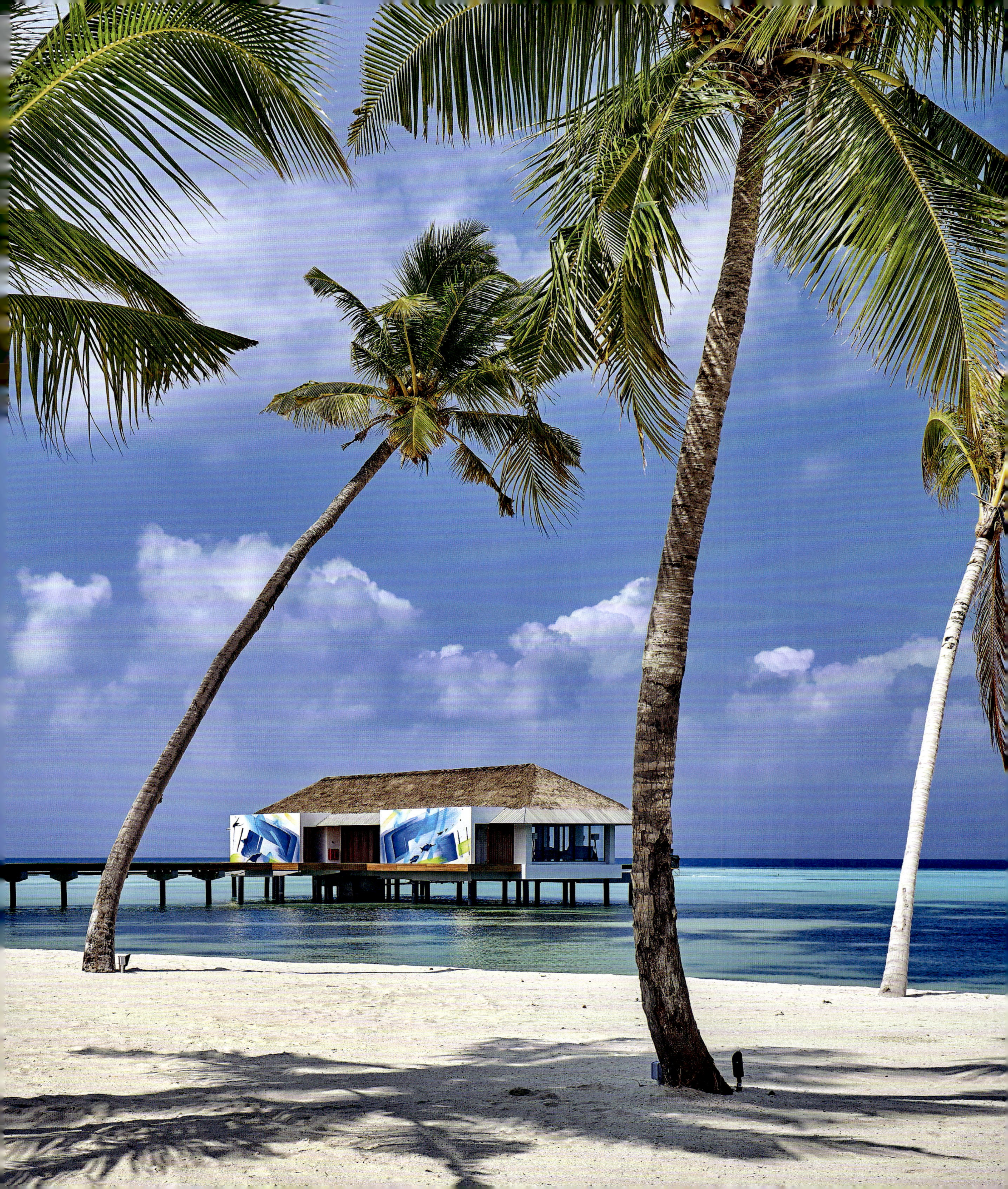

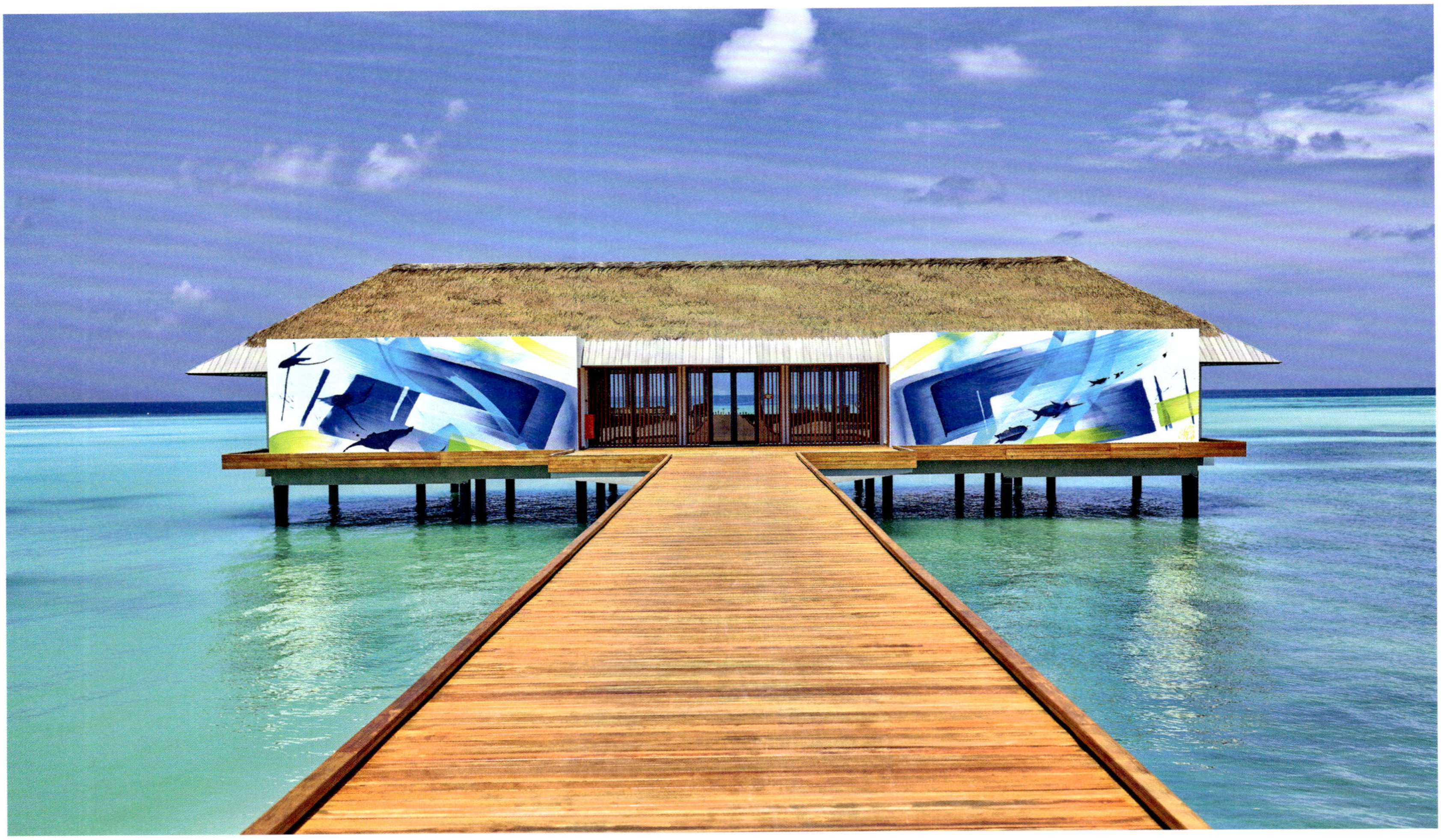

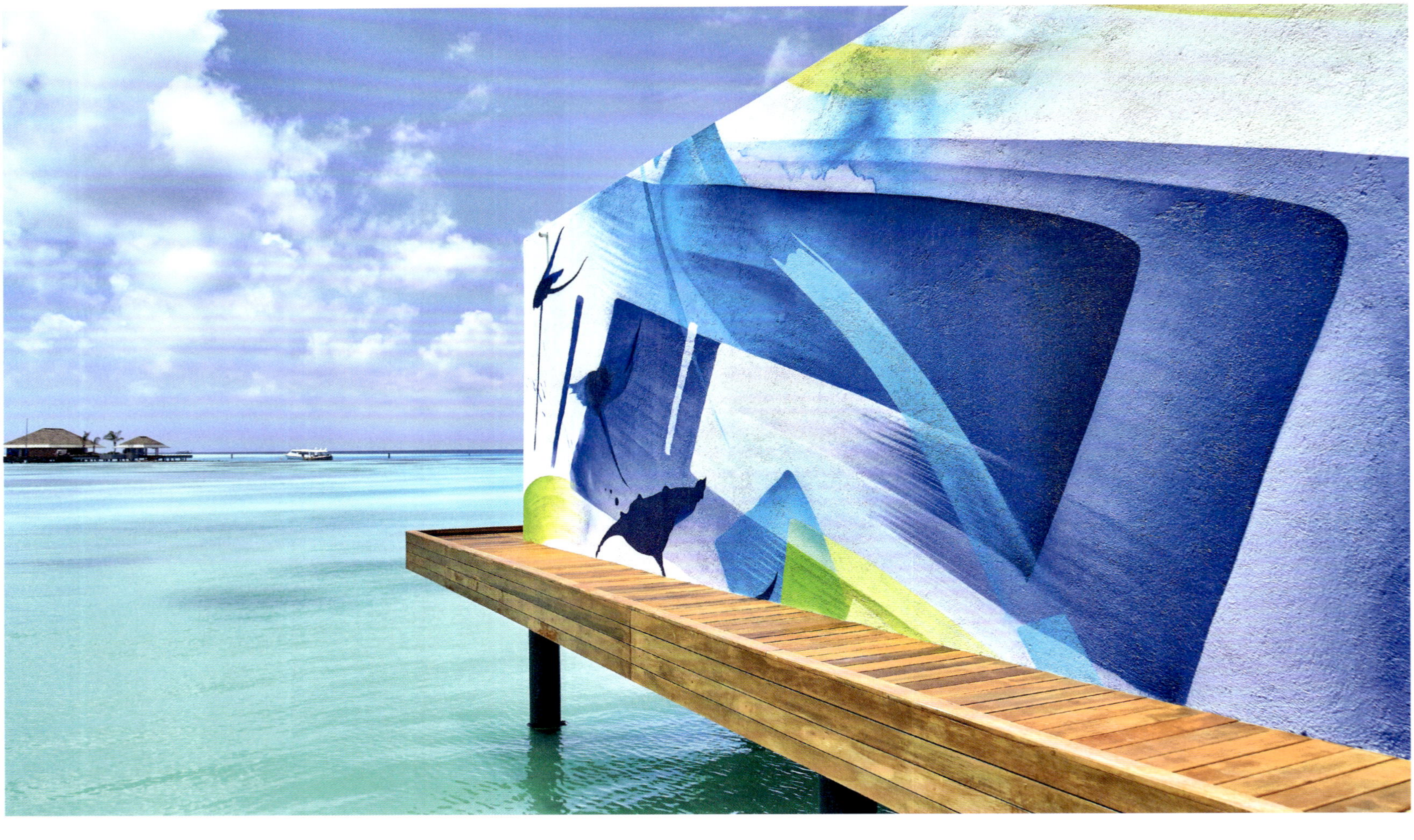

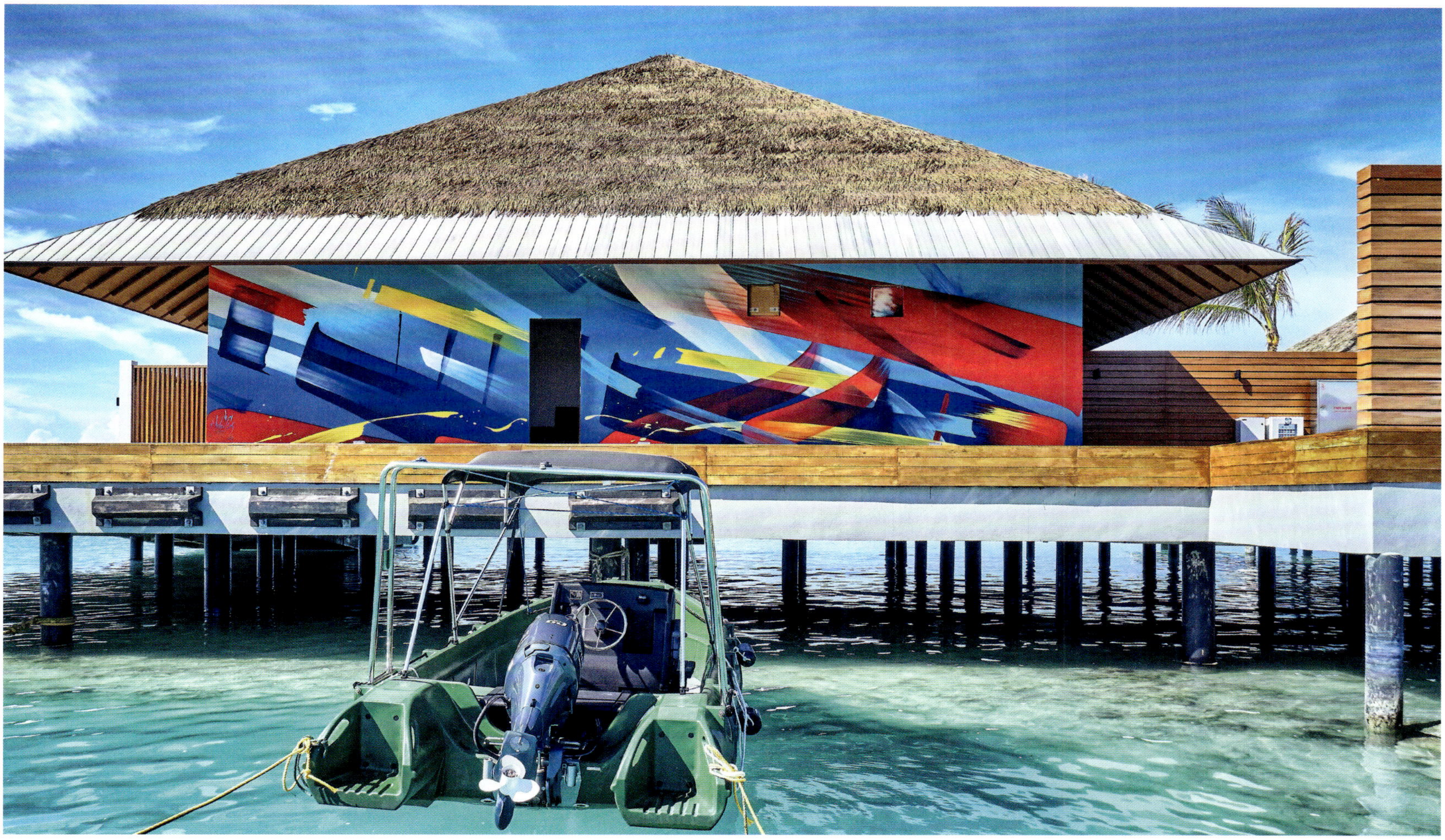

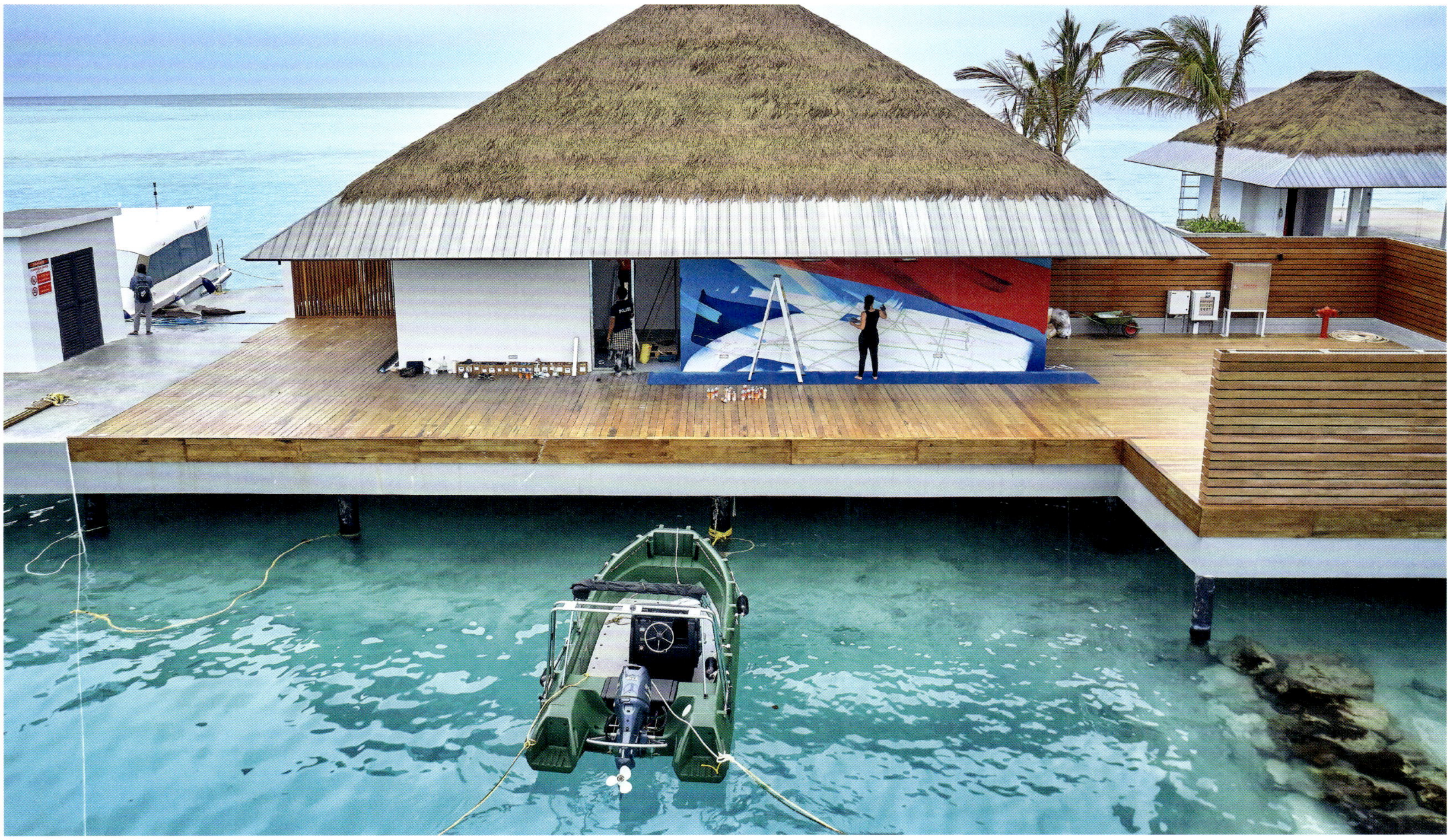

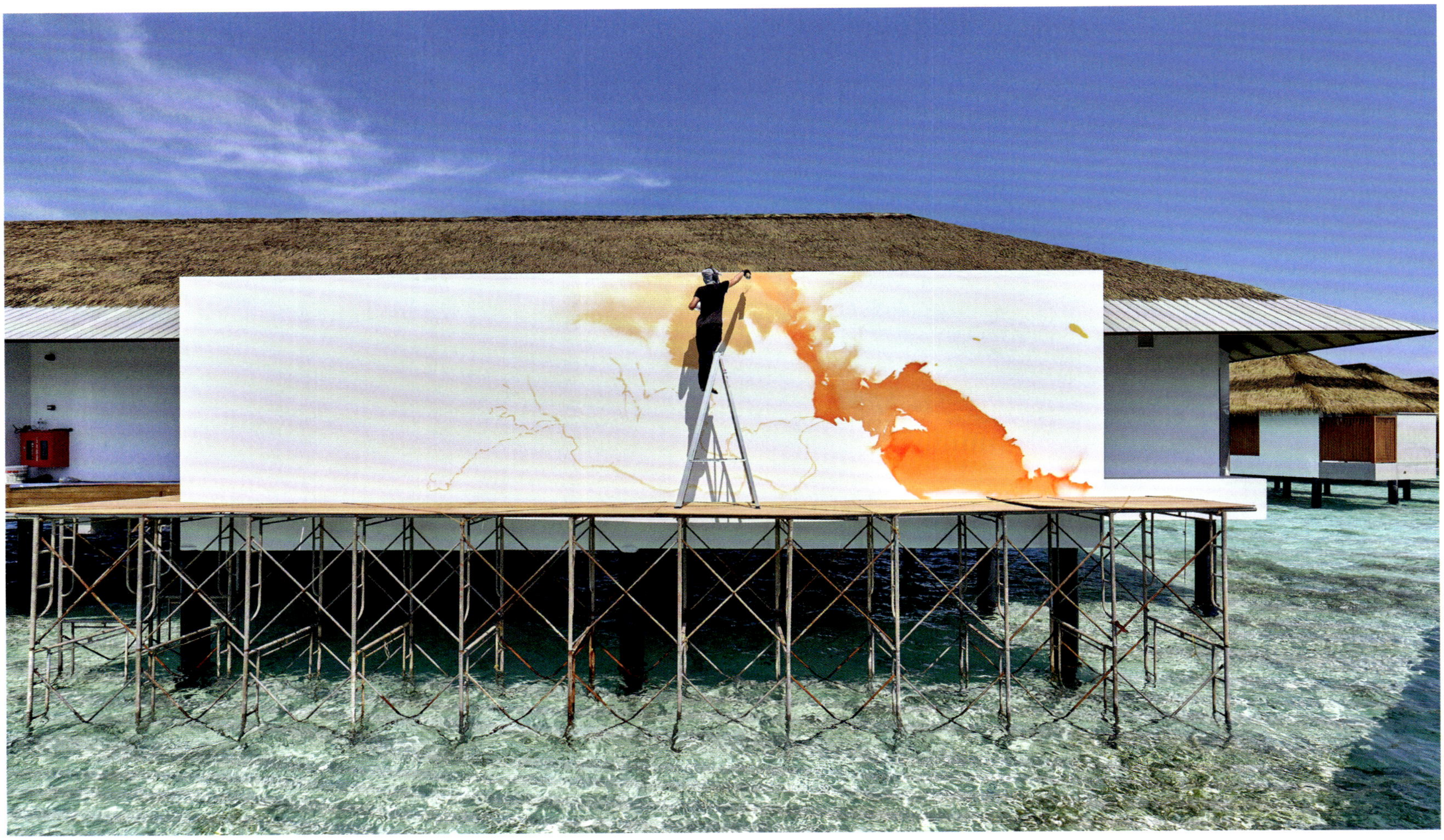

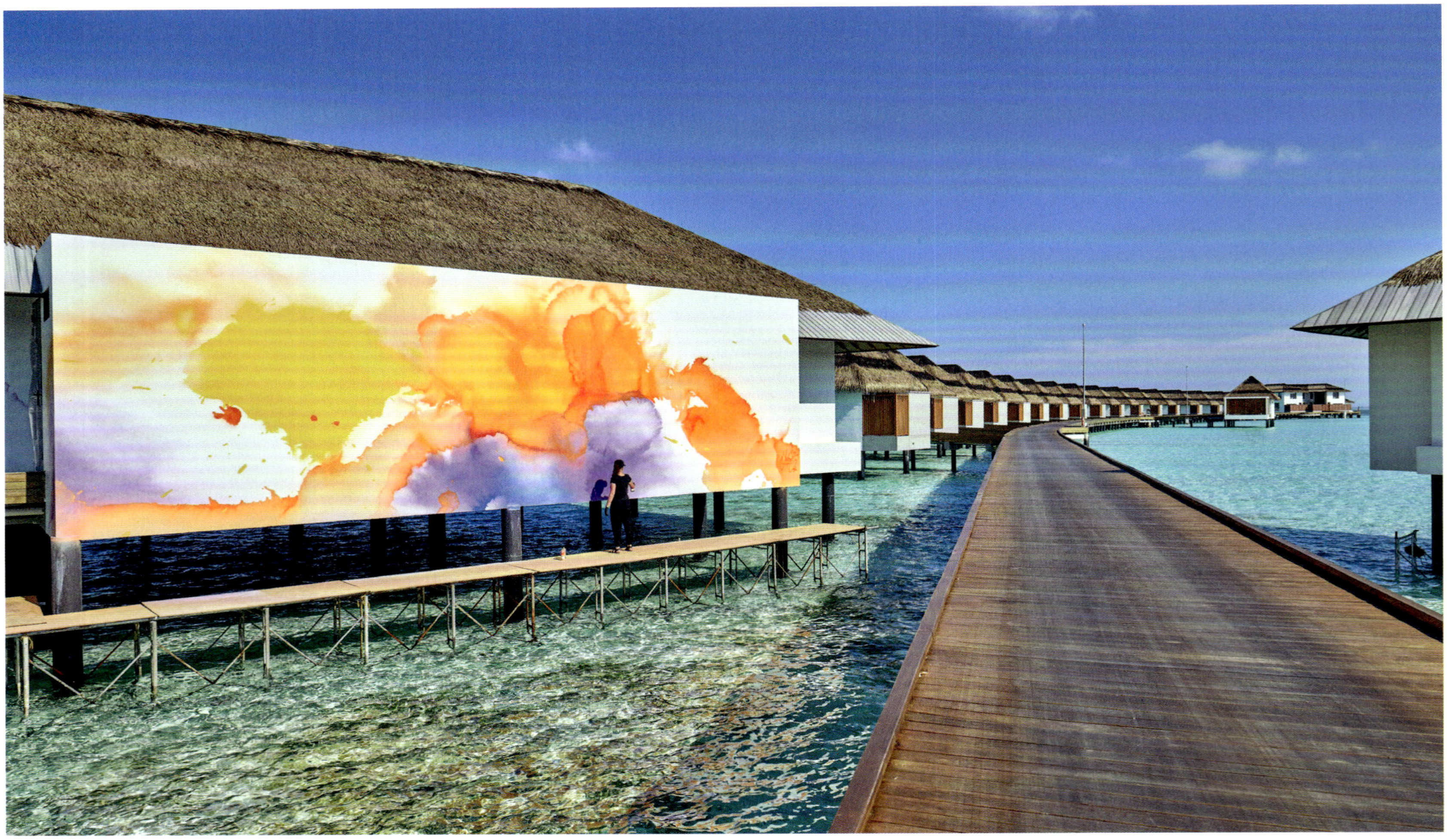

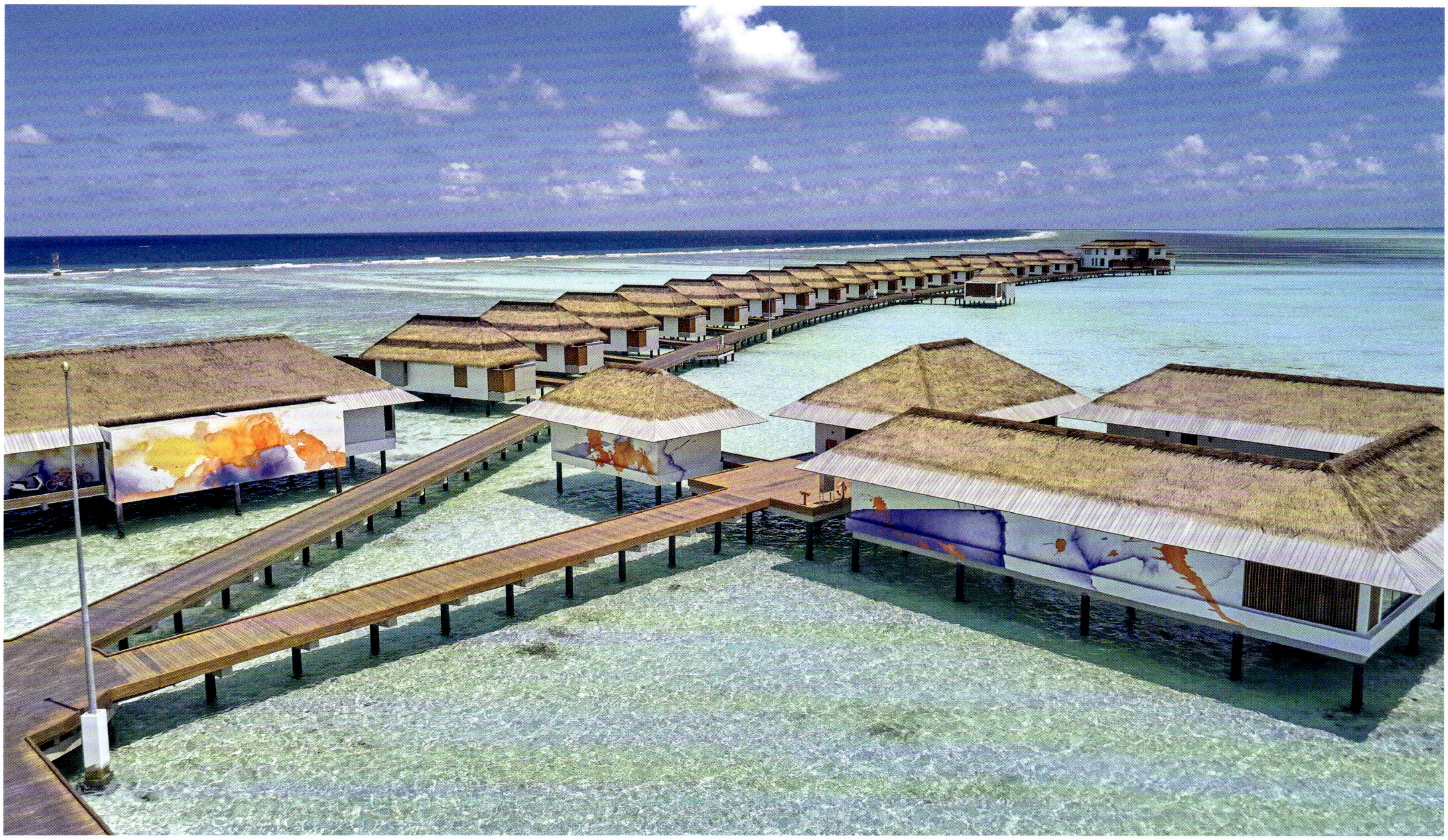

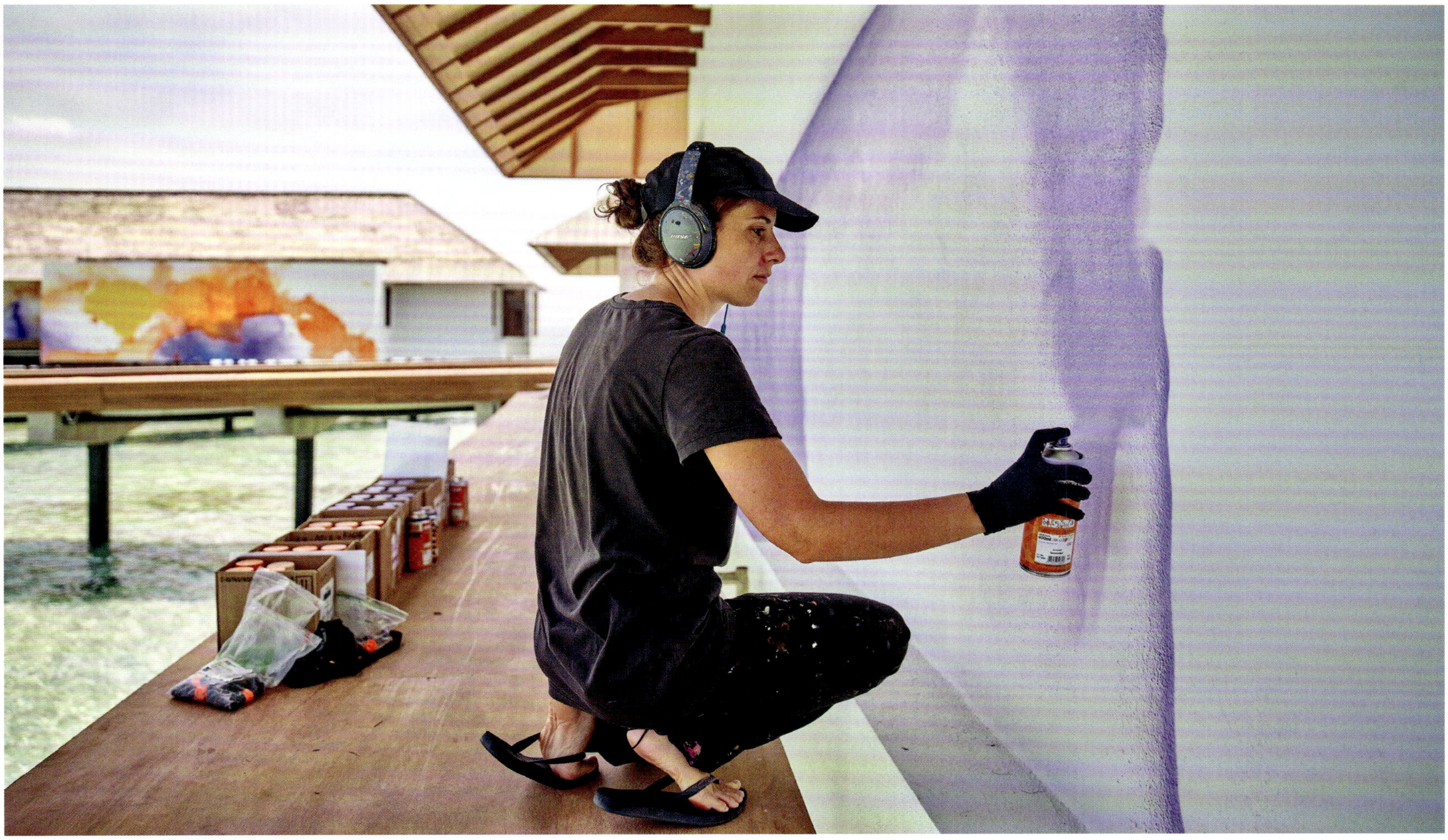

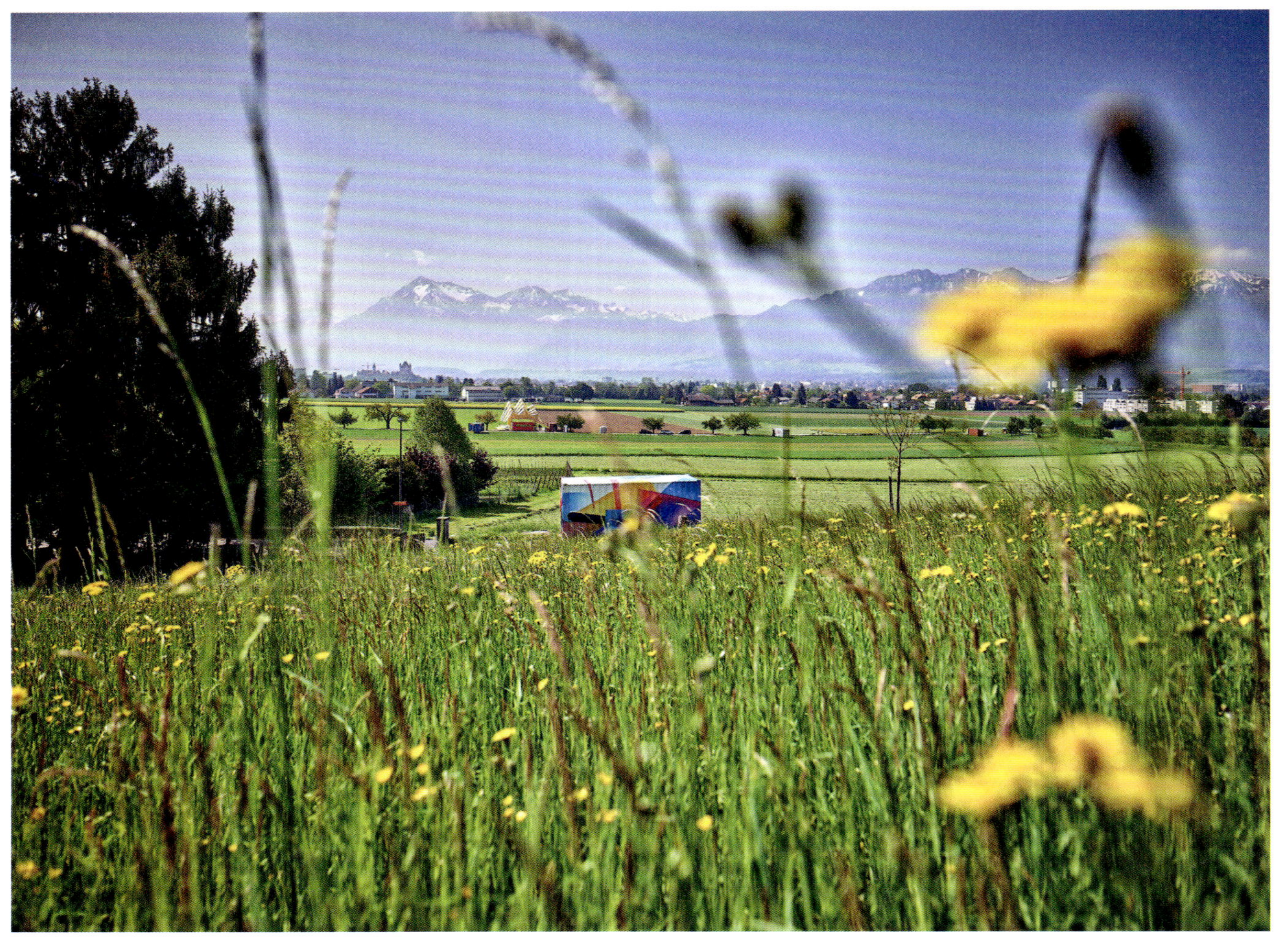

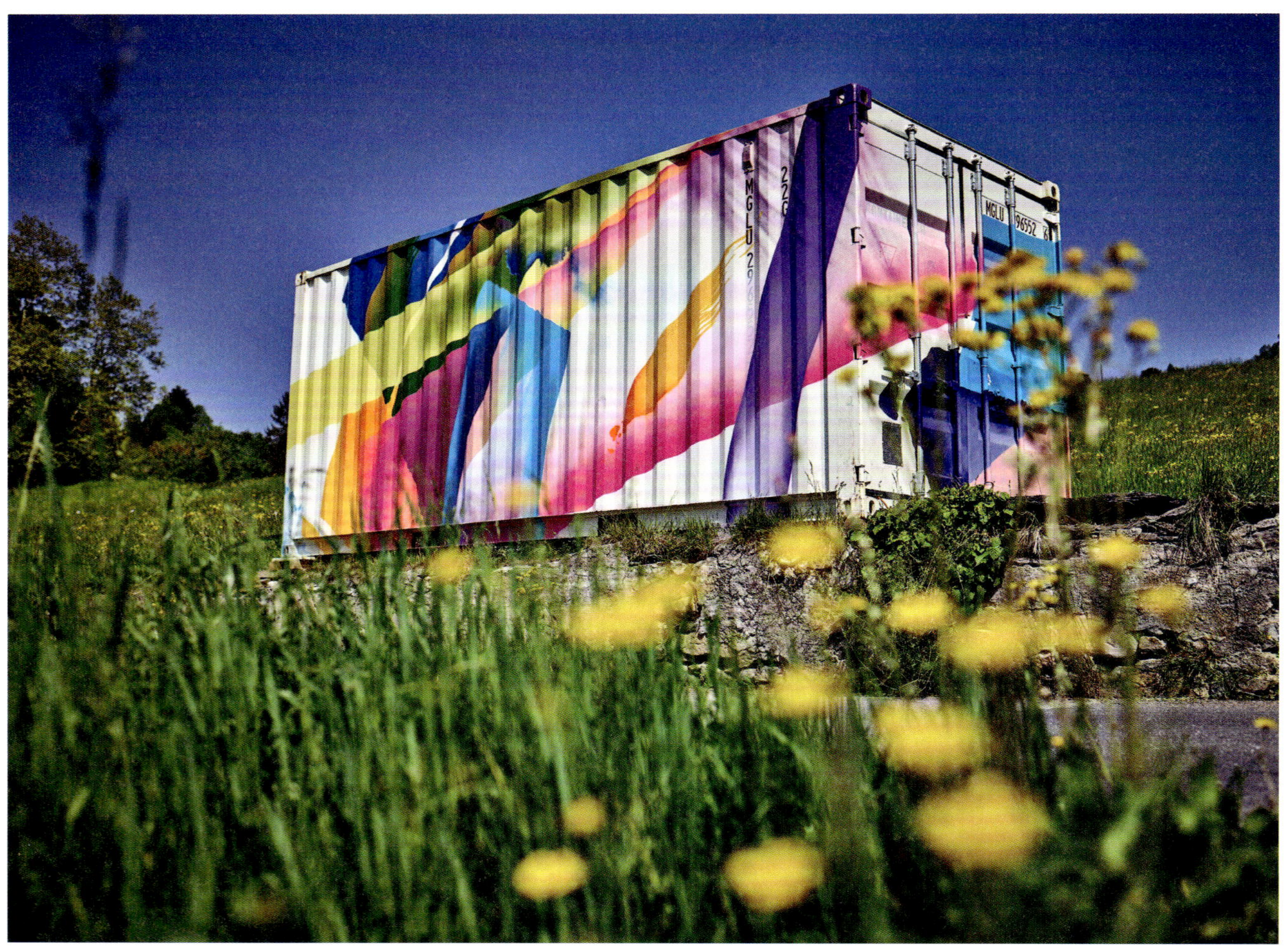

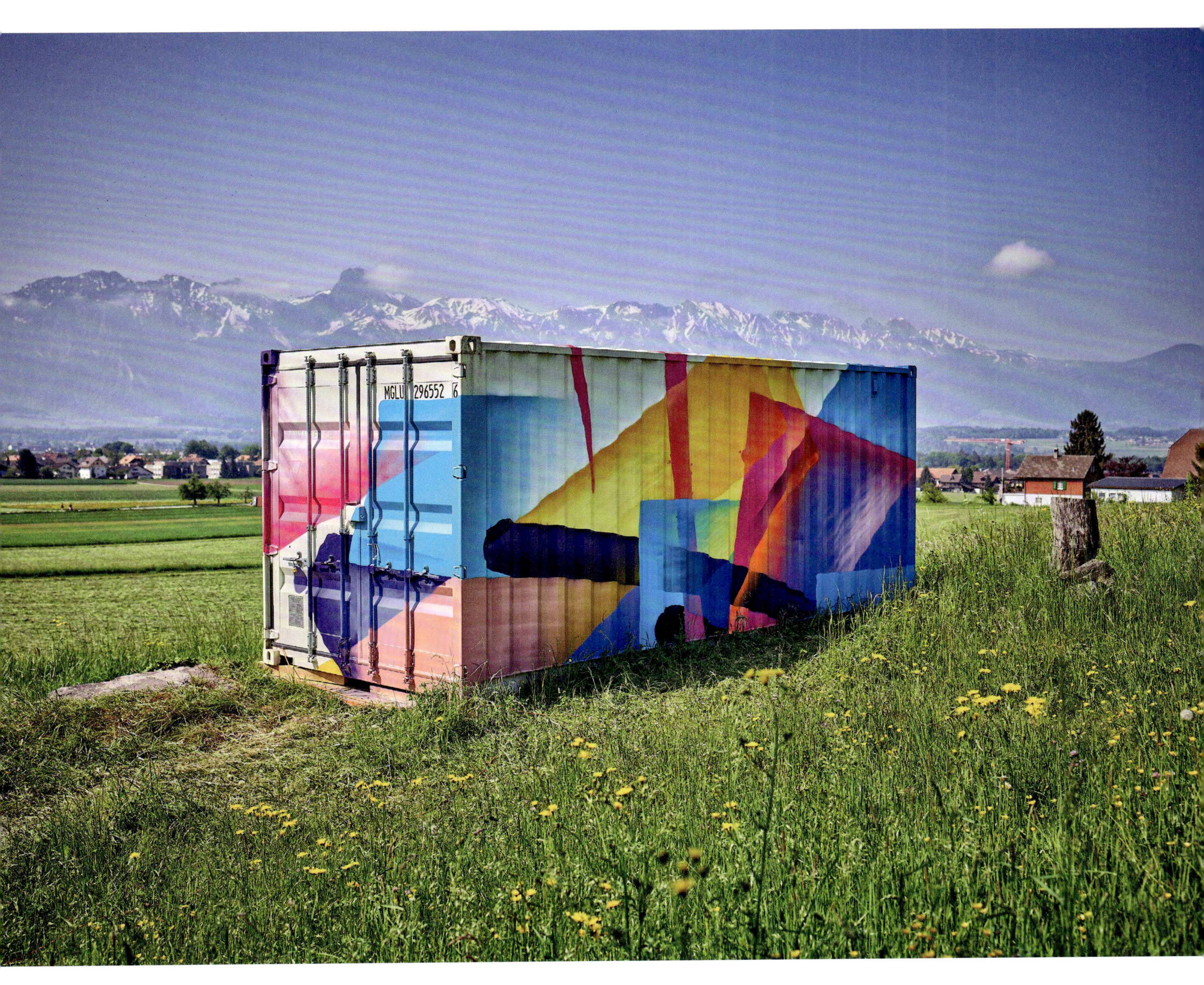

146–148 (this spread). *Art Container*, Steffisburg, Switzerland, 2018.
This was a temporary installation for the summer period

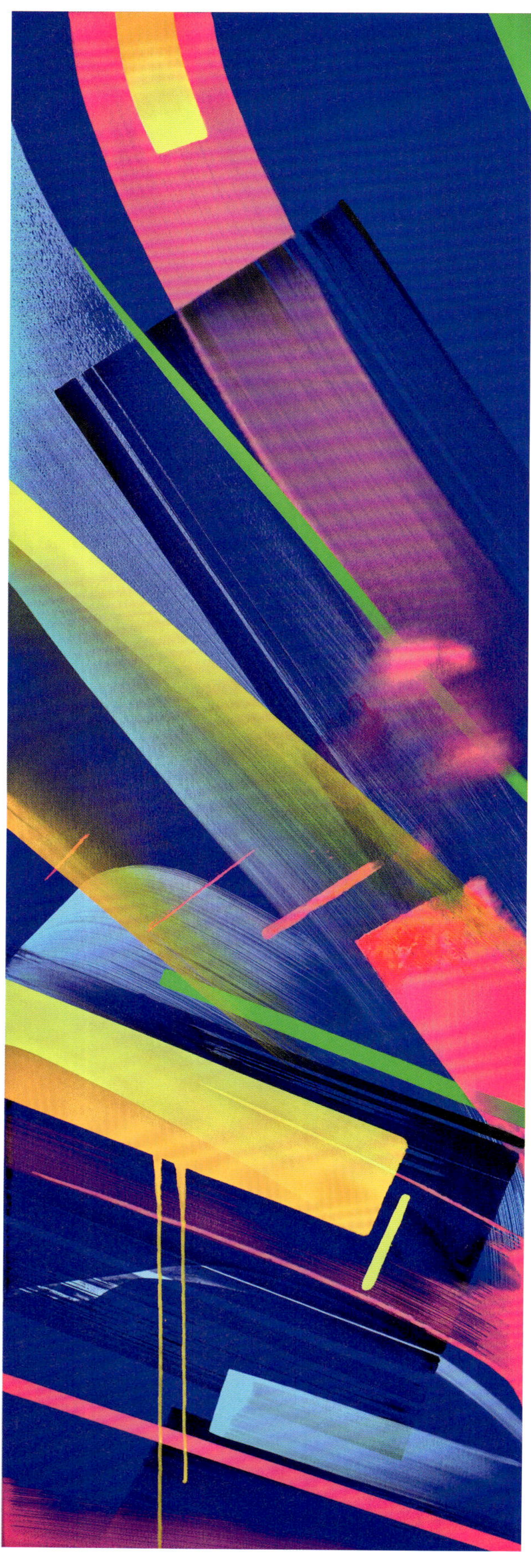

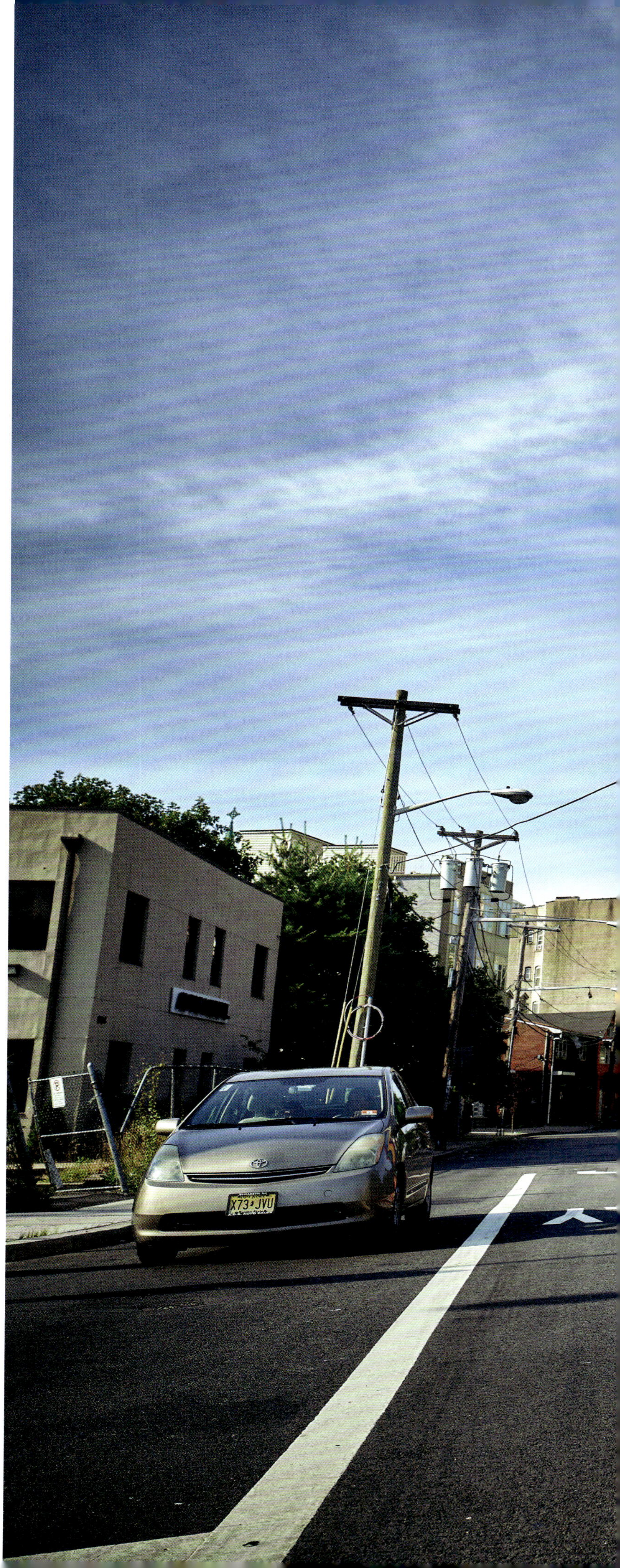

149. *17:39-15052019-JerseyCity*, 180 x 60cm, acrylic and spray paint on canvas, 2019. This canvas was the sketch for the mural in Jersey City, USA (opposite)
150–152 (opposite and next two spreads). *JC 180*, 627 Summit Avenue, NJ 07306, Jersey City, USA, June 2019. At the time, this was the highest mural in Jersey City and the highest that MadC had painted. Due to strong winds and broken engines, the work had to be stopped many times; it took her and two assistants 13 days to finish. Watching the sunrise over Manhattan was, for MadC, an unforgettable memory associated with this wall

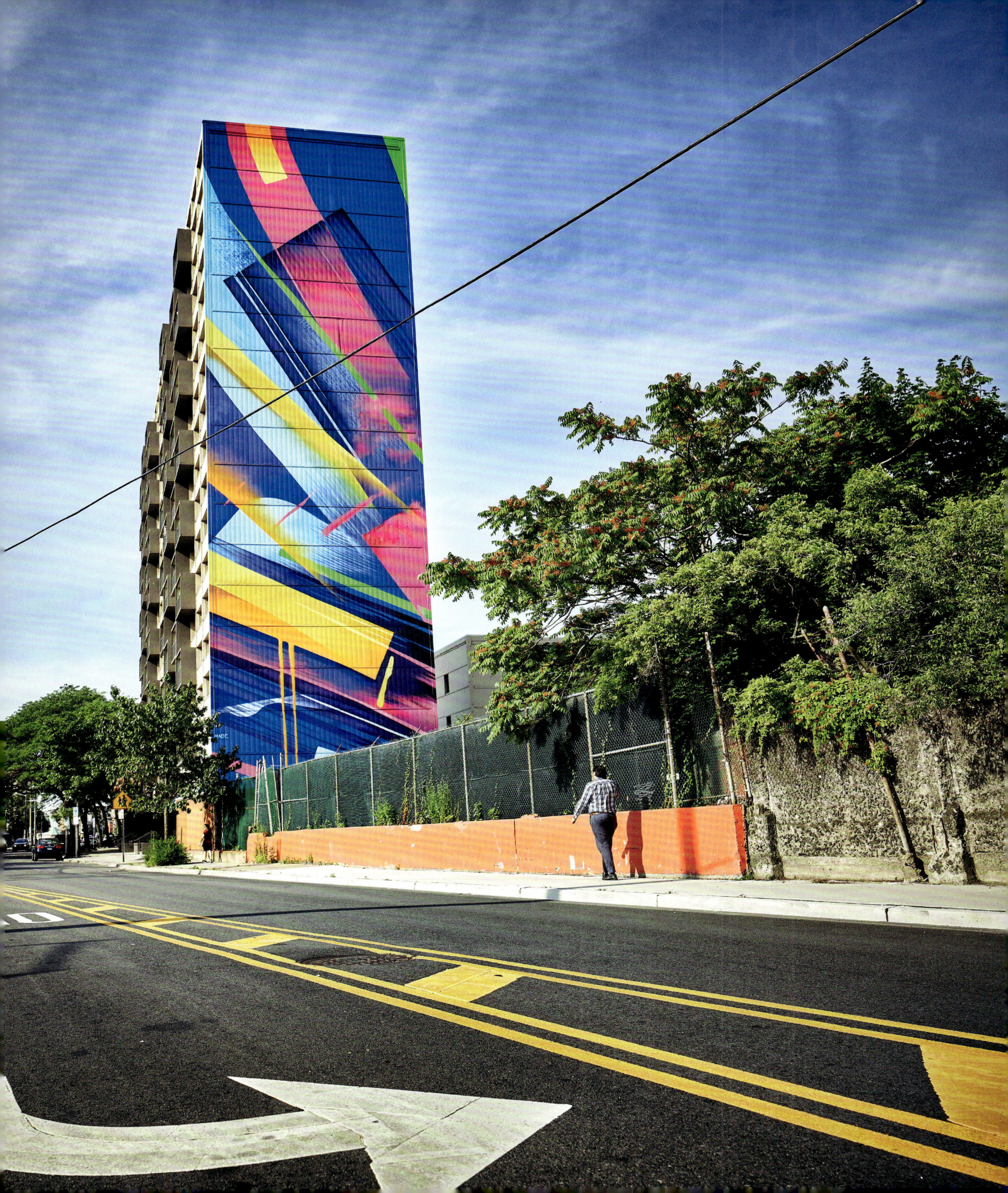
MADC

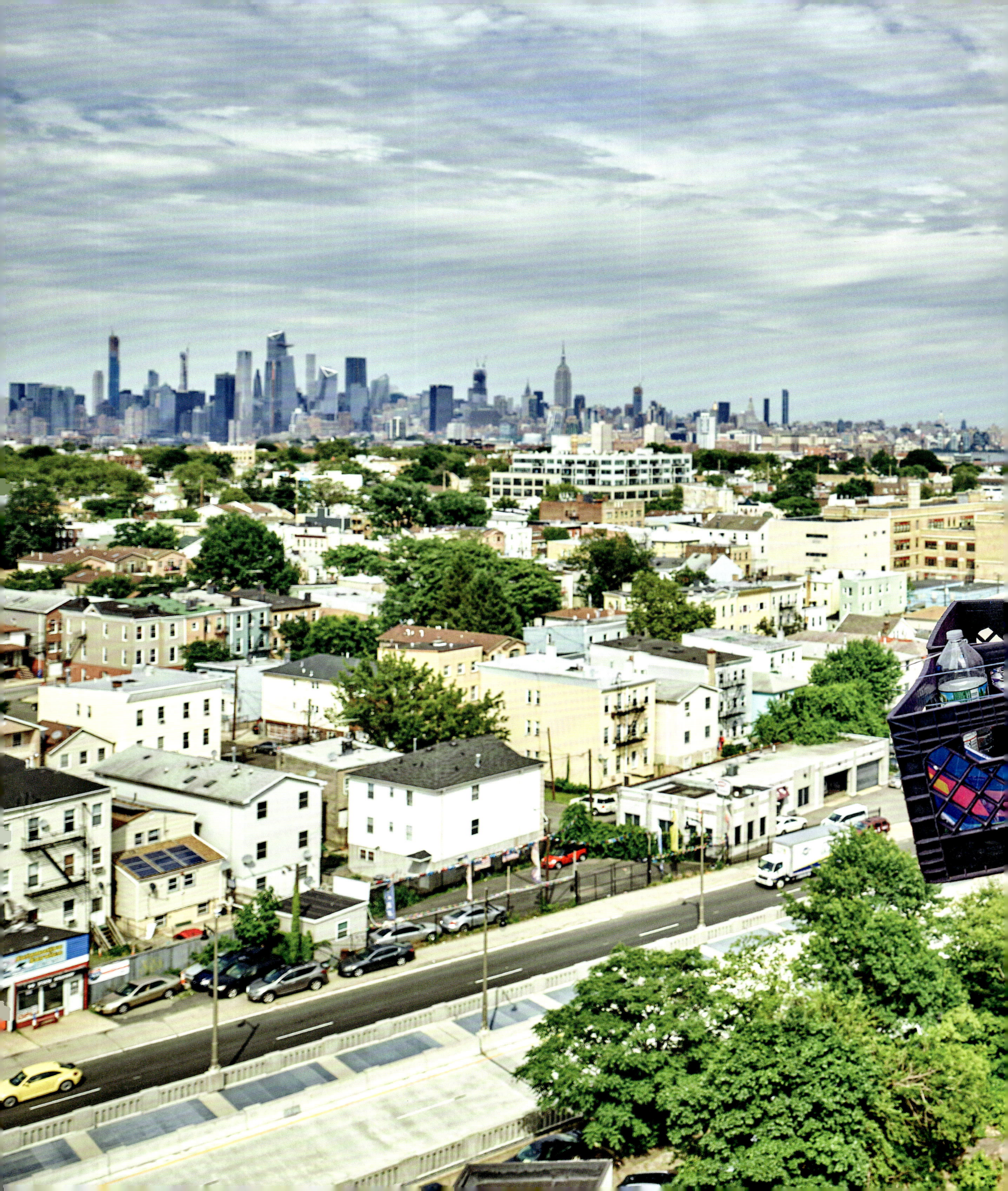

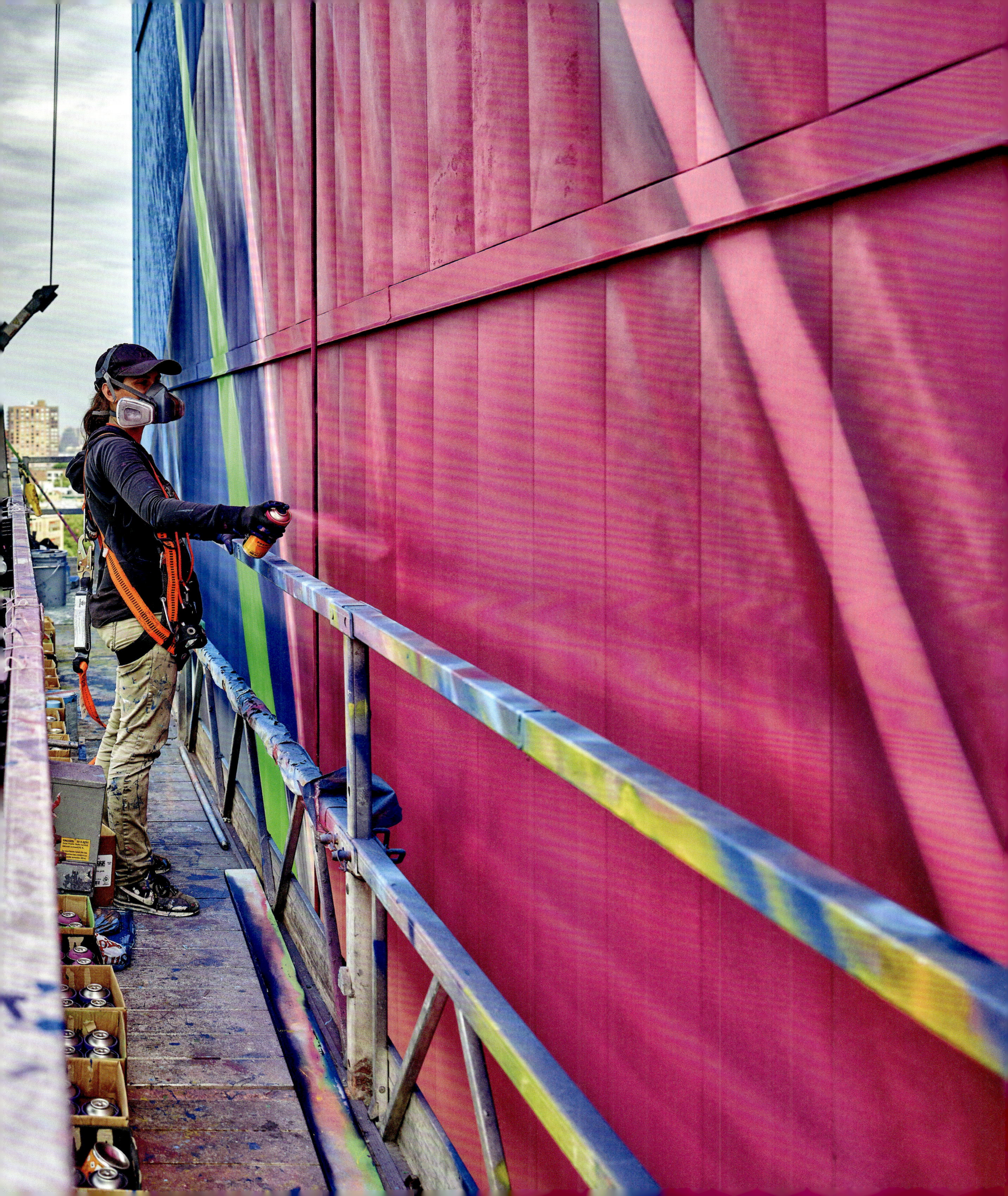

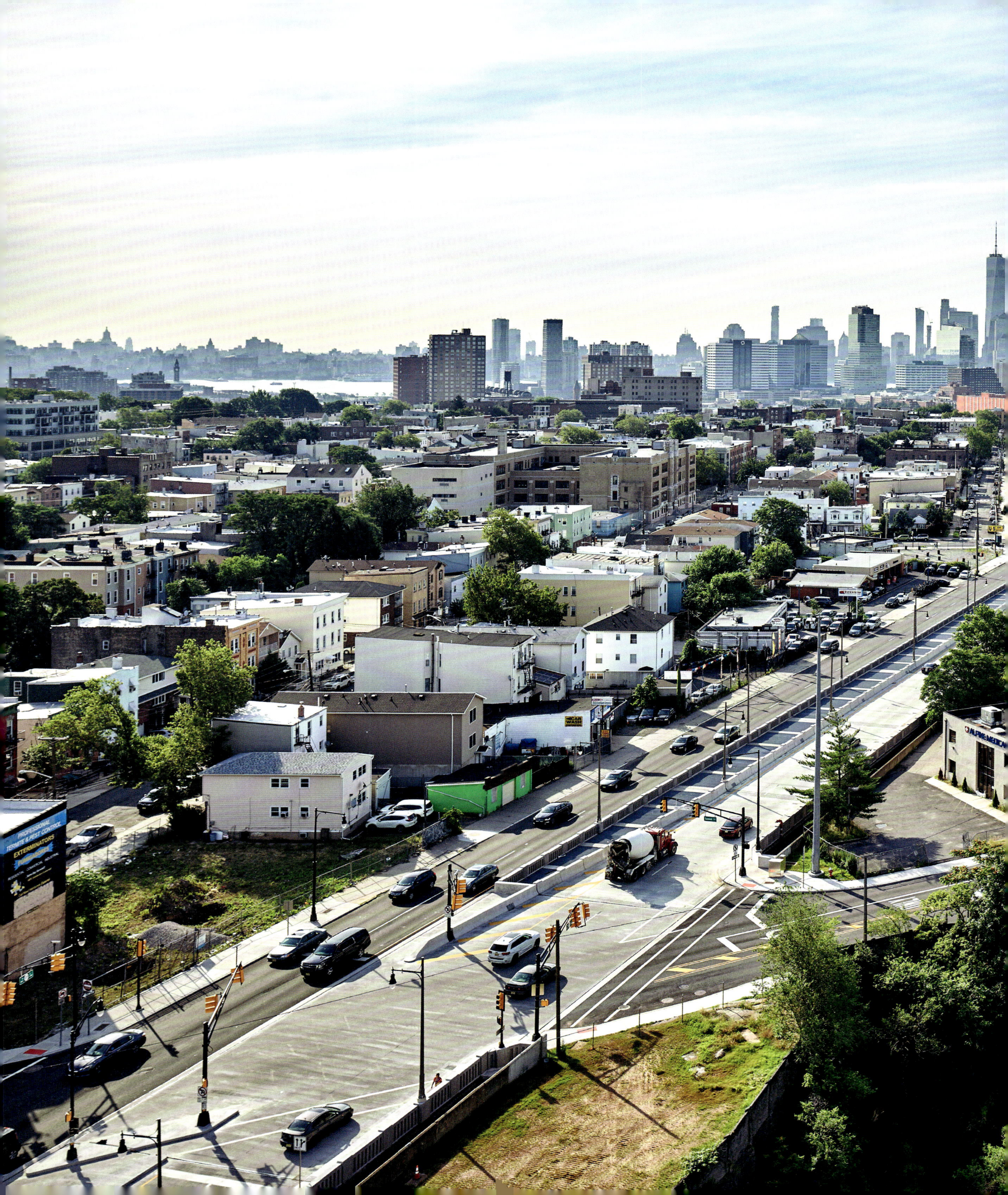
PROFESSIONAL
TERMITE & PEST CONTROL
EXTERMINATORS
ALPINE

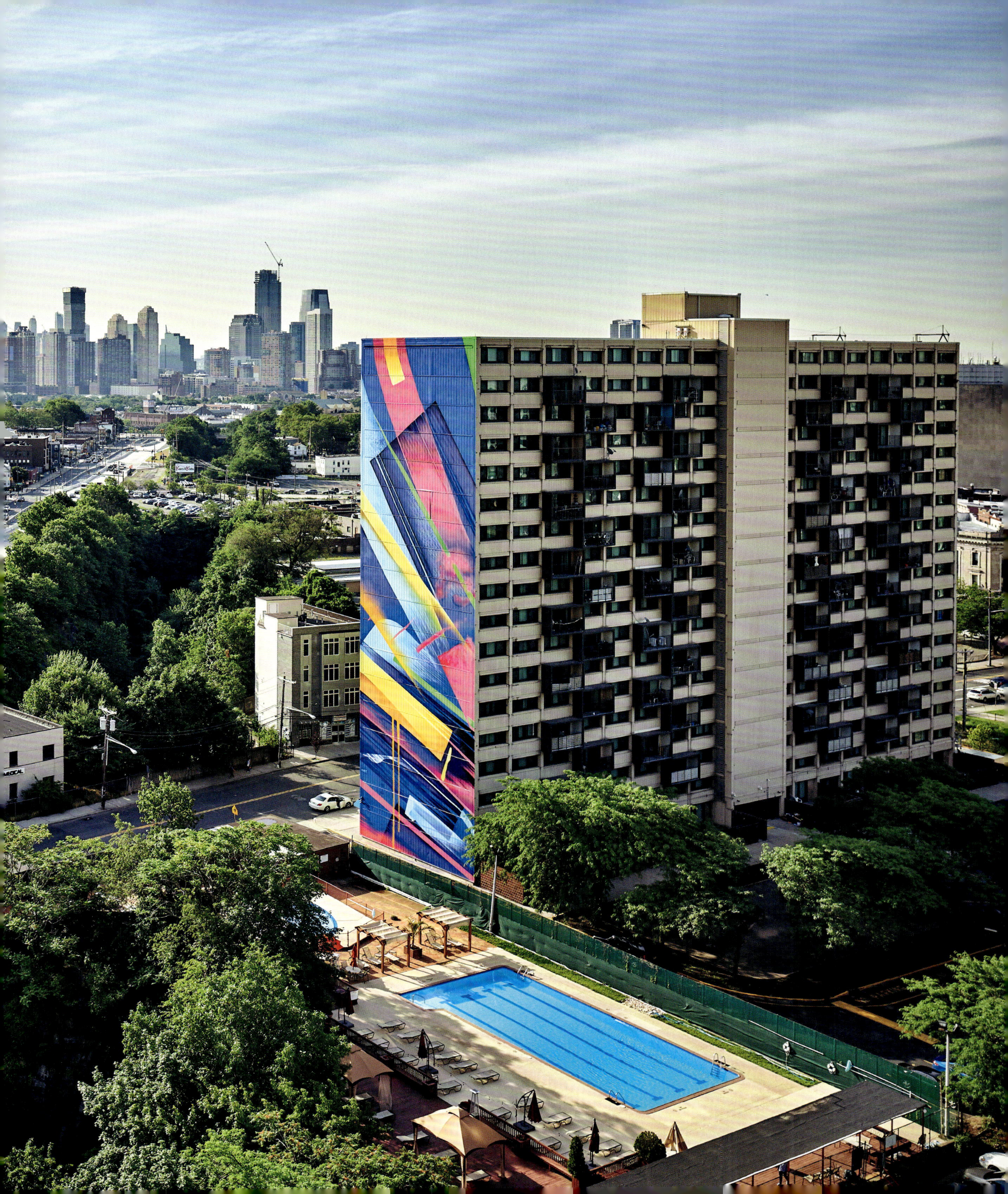

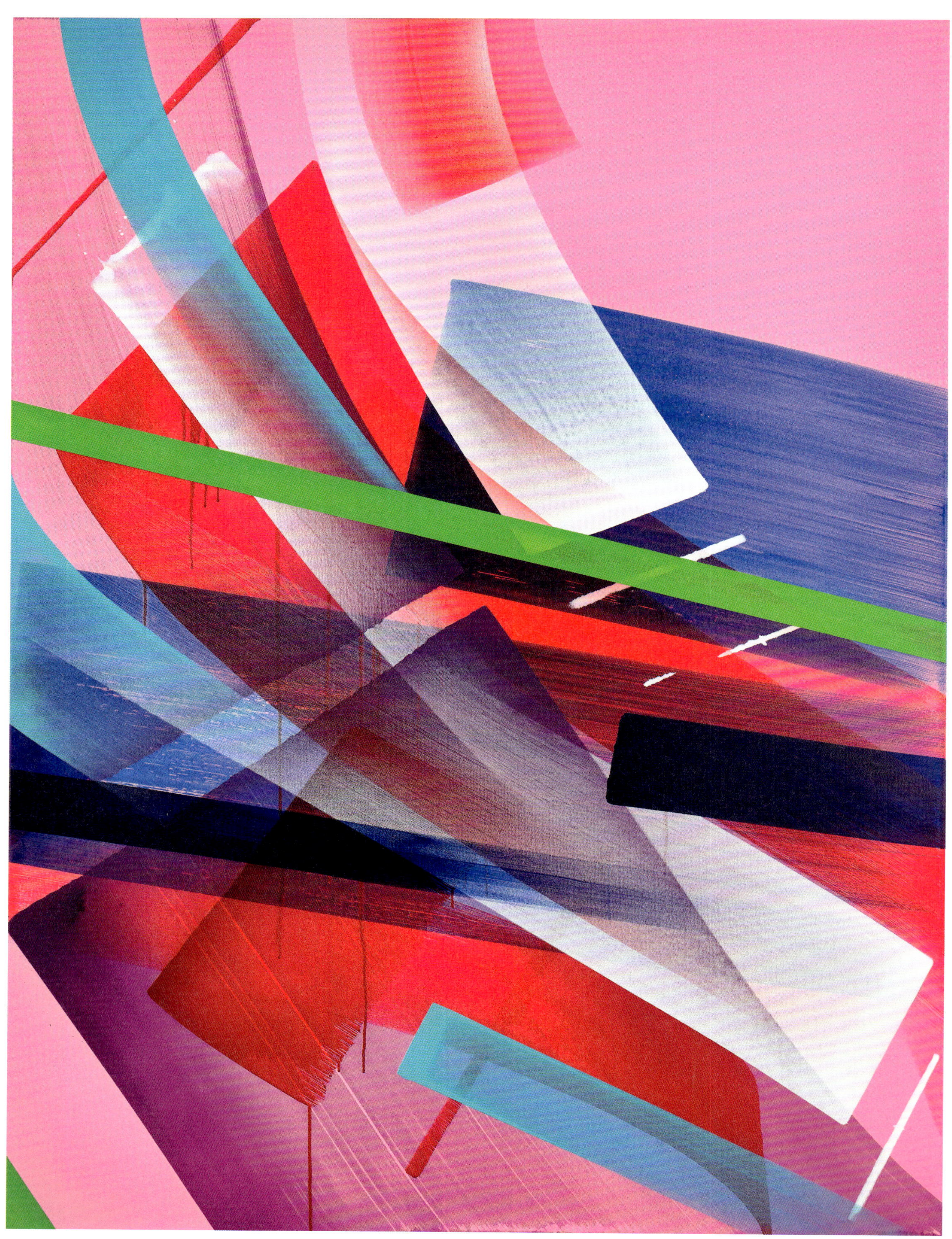

153. *CPH 05-2019*, 160 x 120cm, acrylic and spray paint on canvas, 2019.
This canvas was a sketch for the mural in Copenhagen, Denmark (opposite)

154–157 (this page and next spread). *Rytterbakken 2-20*, 2400 Copenhagen Nordvest, Denmark, April 2019. MadC painted this wall in two days, with spray paint only

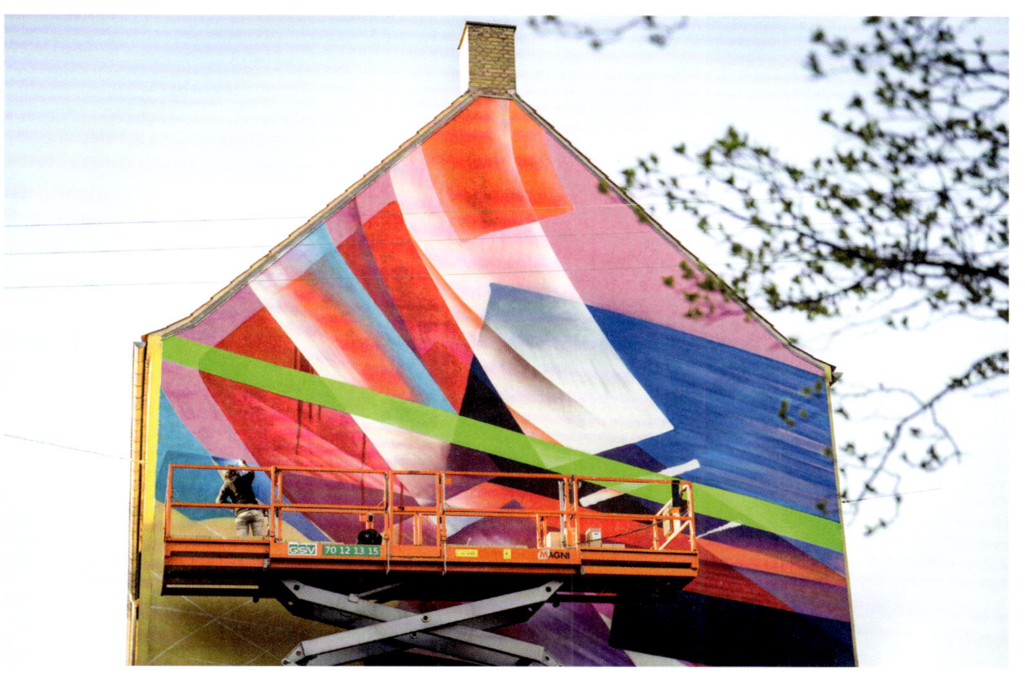

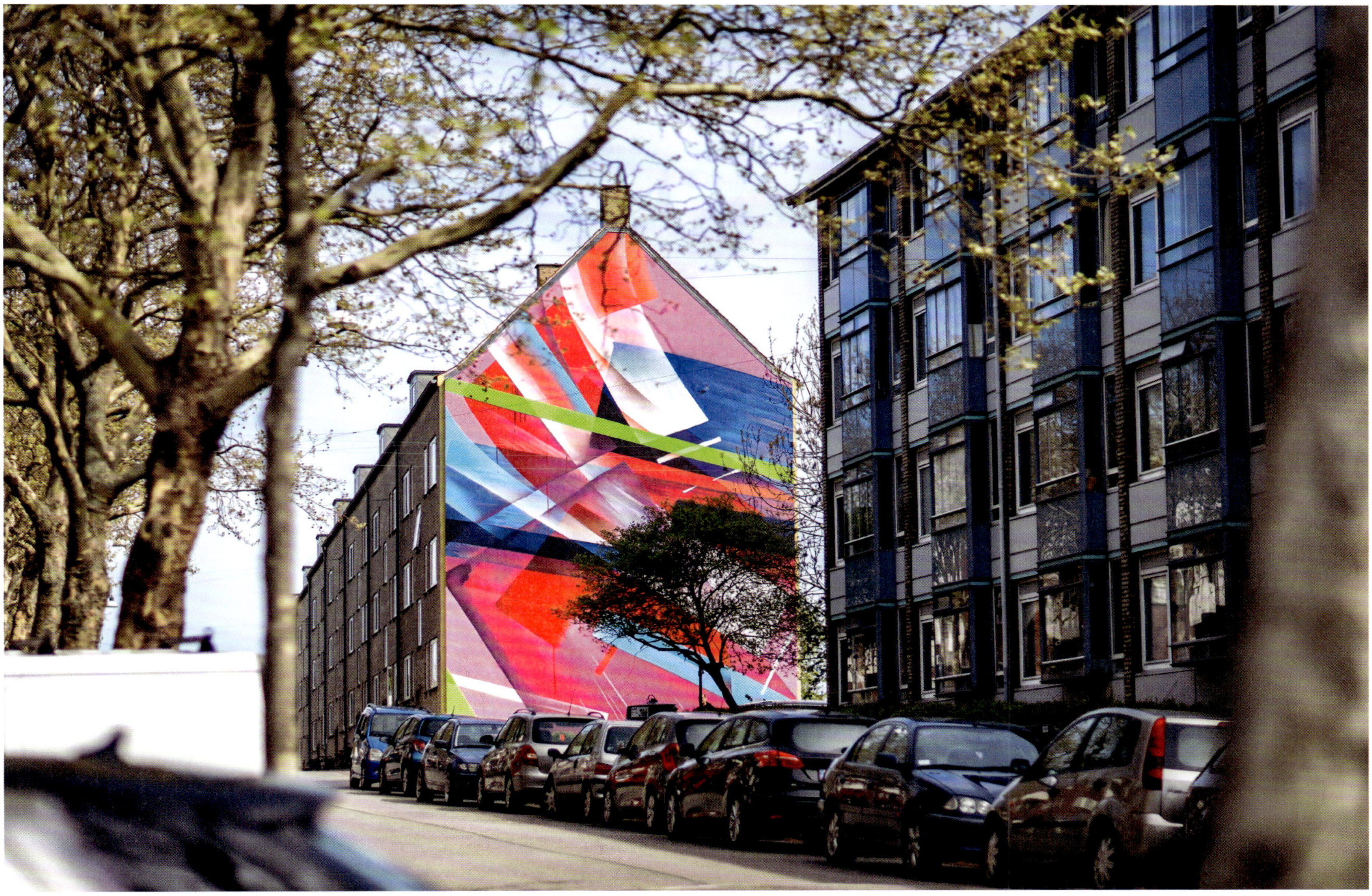

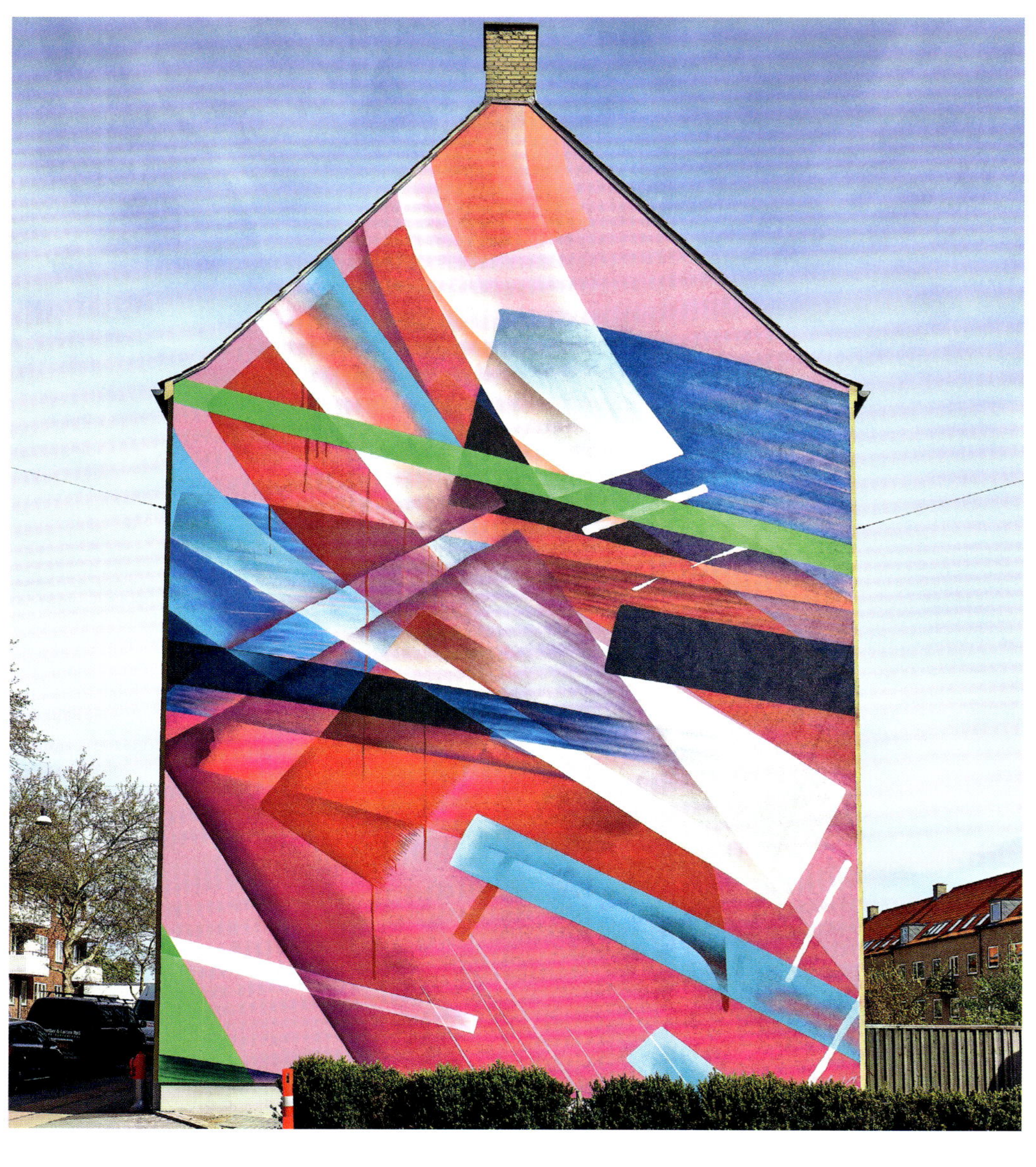

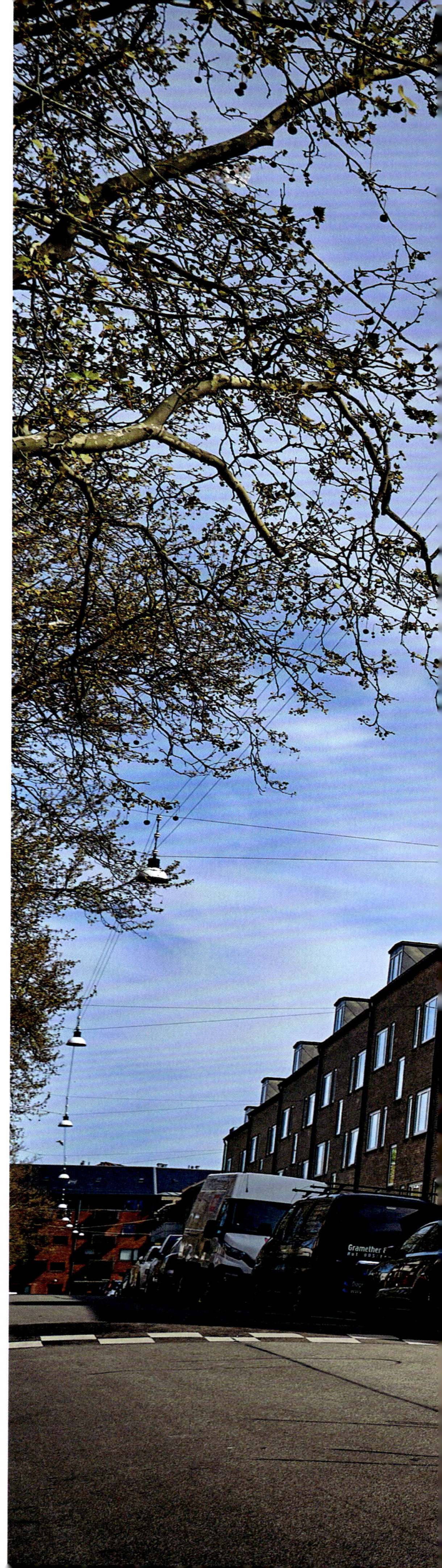

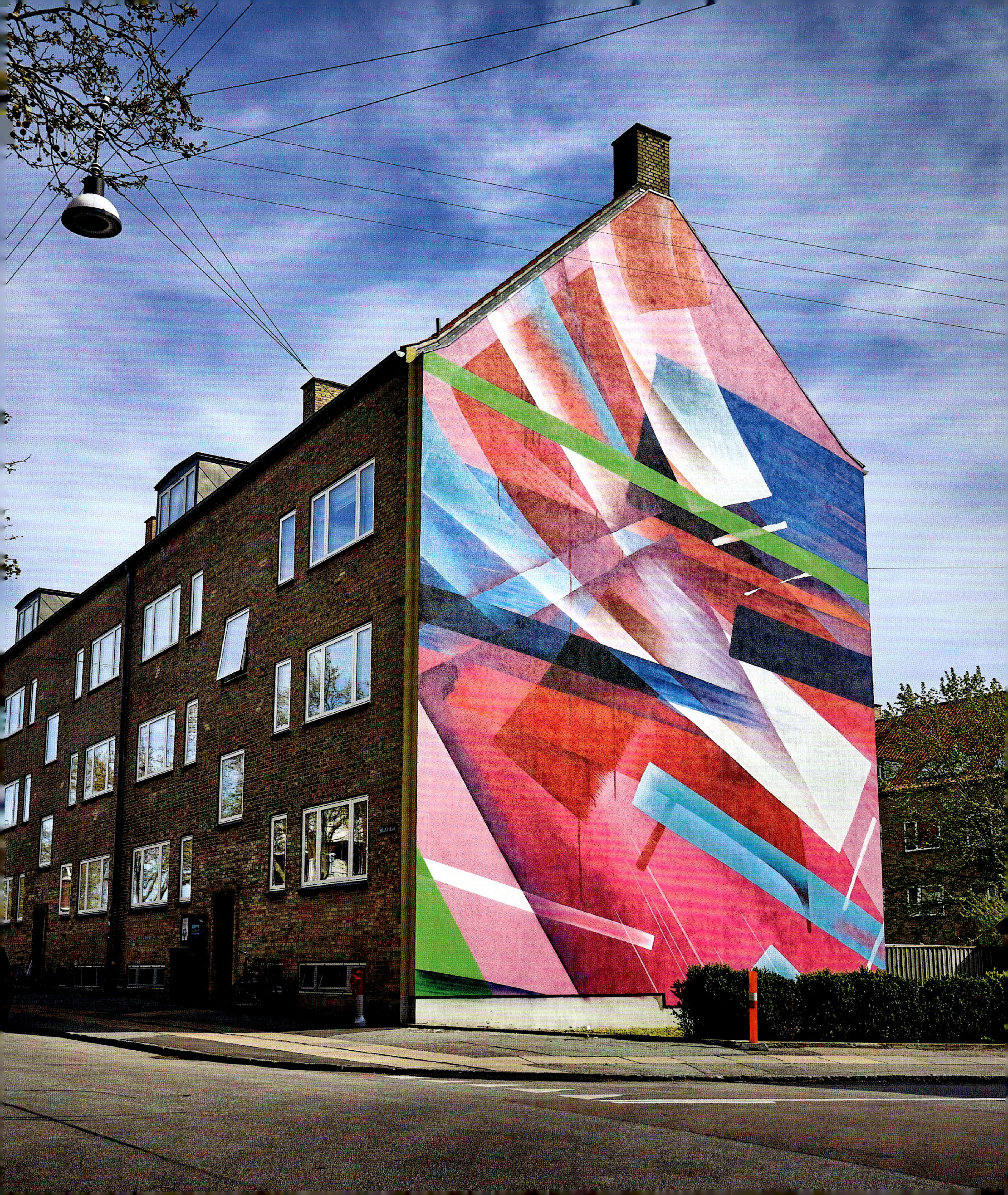

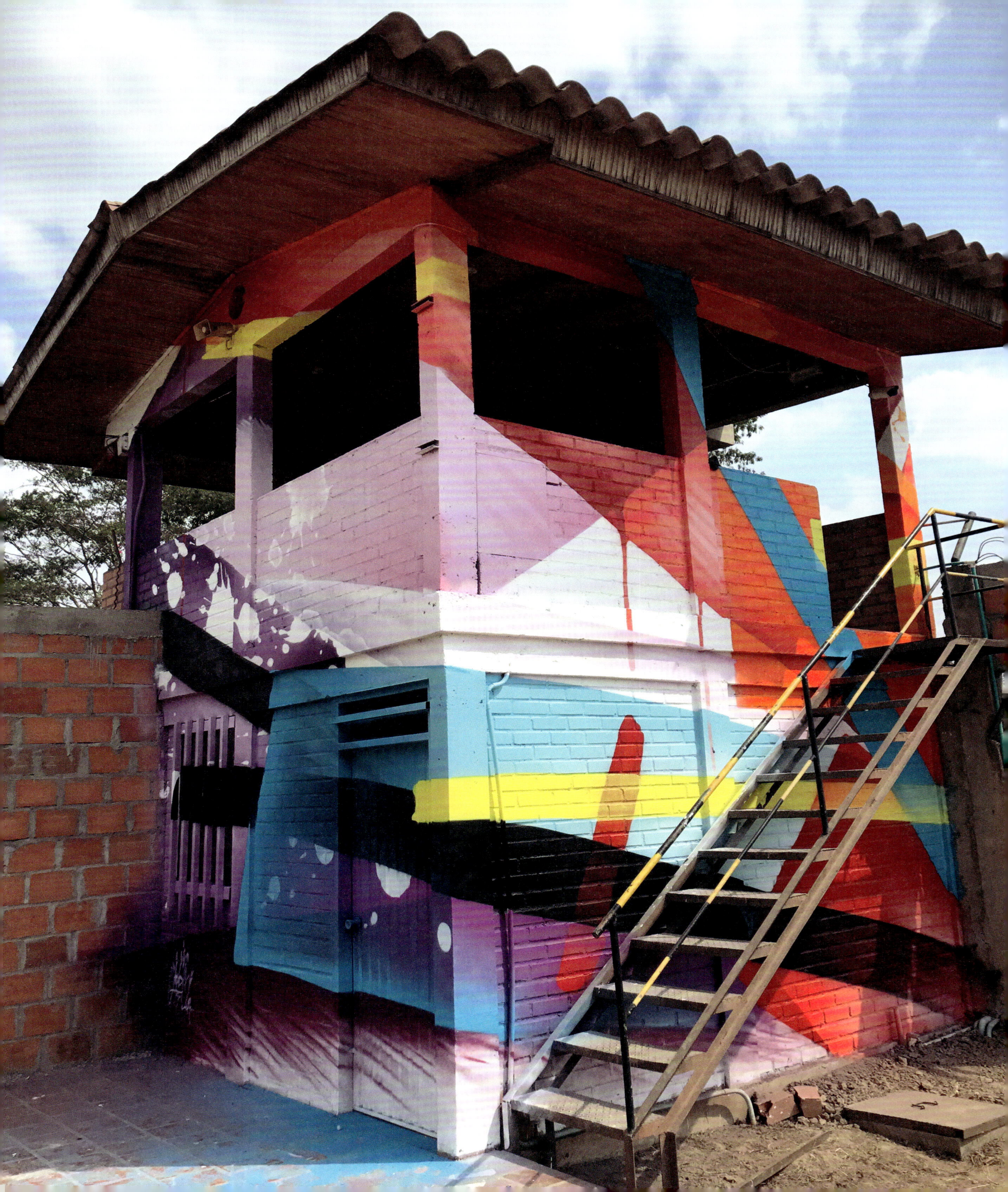

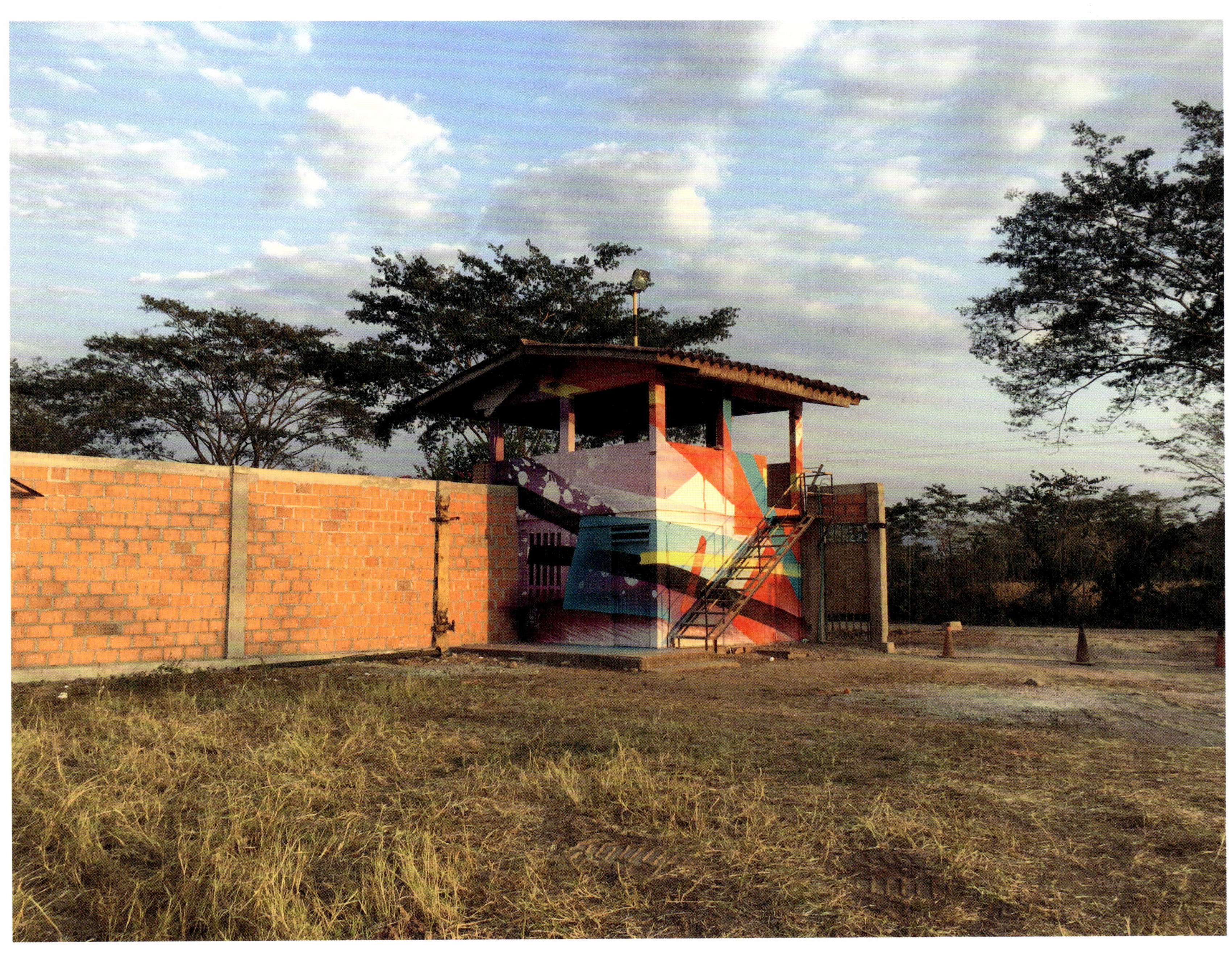

158–159 (this spread). Dictador Art Masters, Valledupar, Colombia, 2019

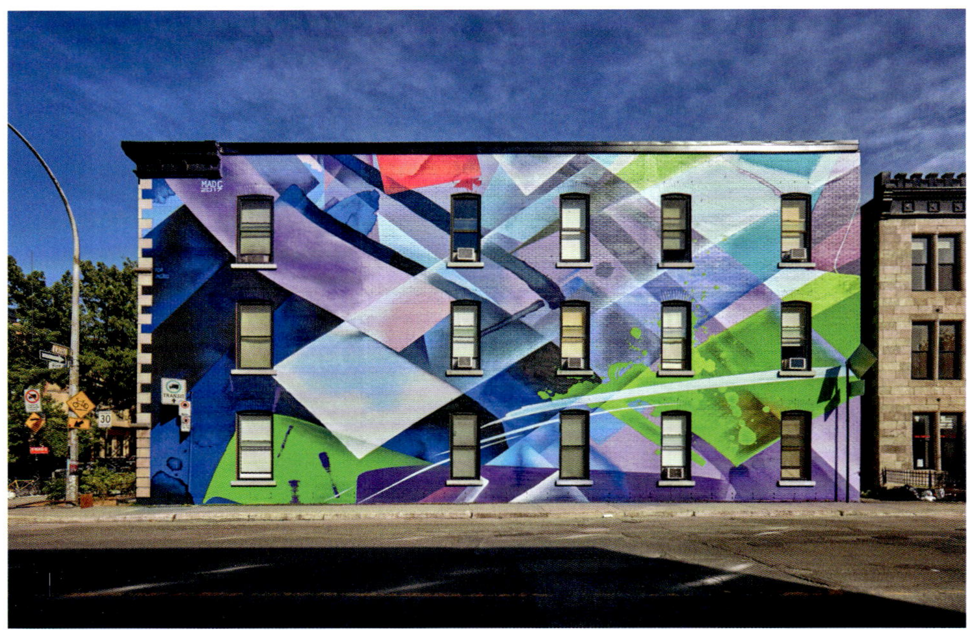

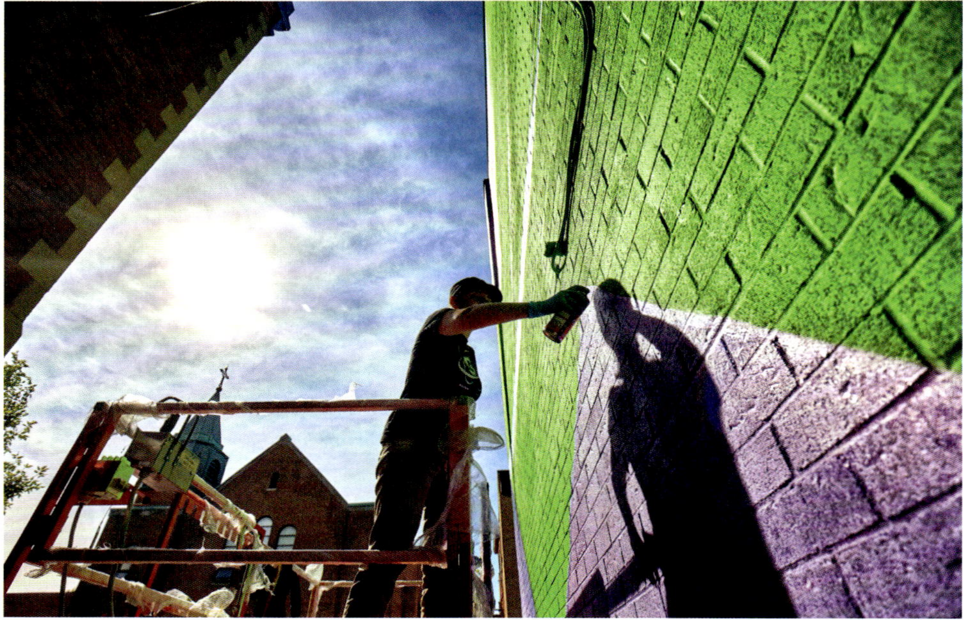

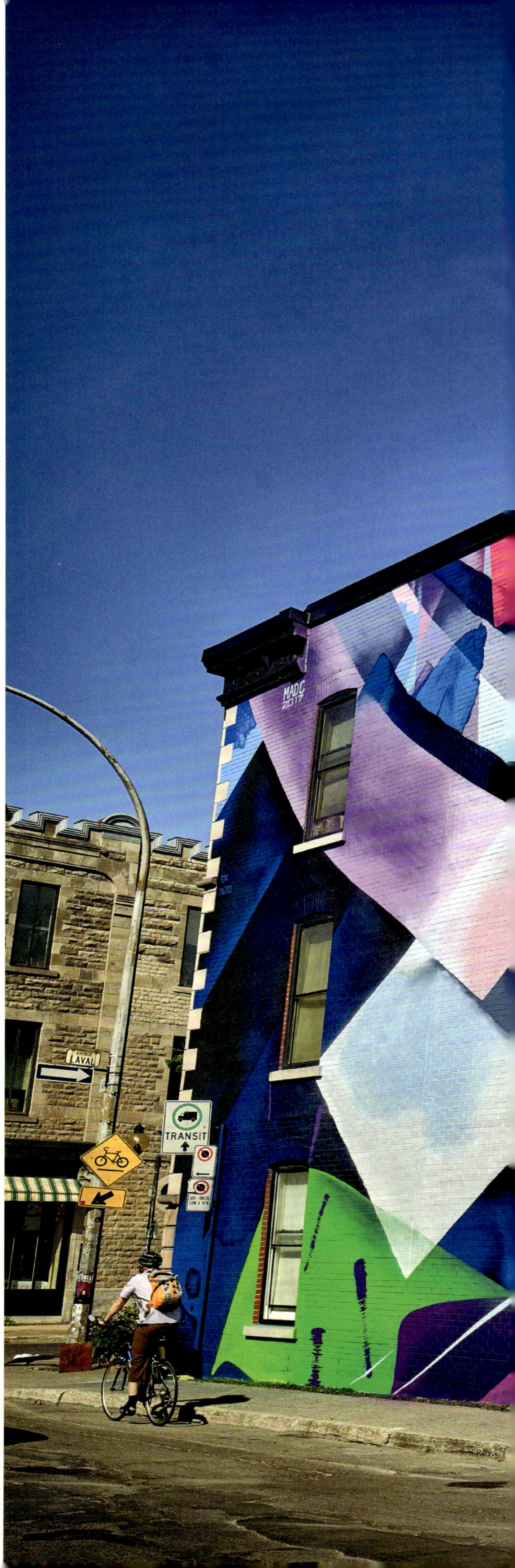

160–162 (this spread). MURAL Festival, Avenue des Pins Est, Montreal, Canada, June 2017

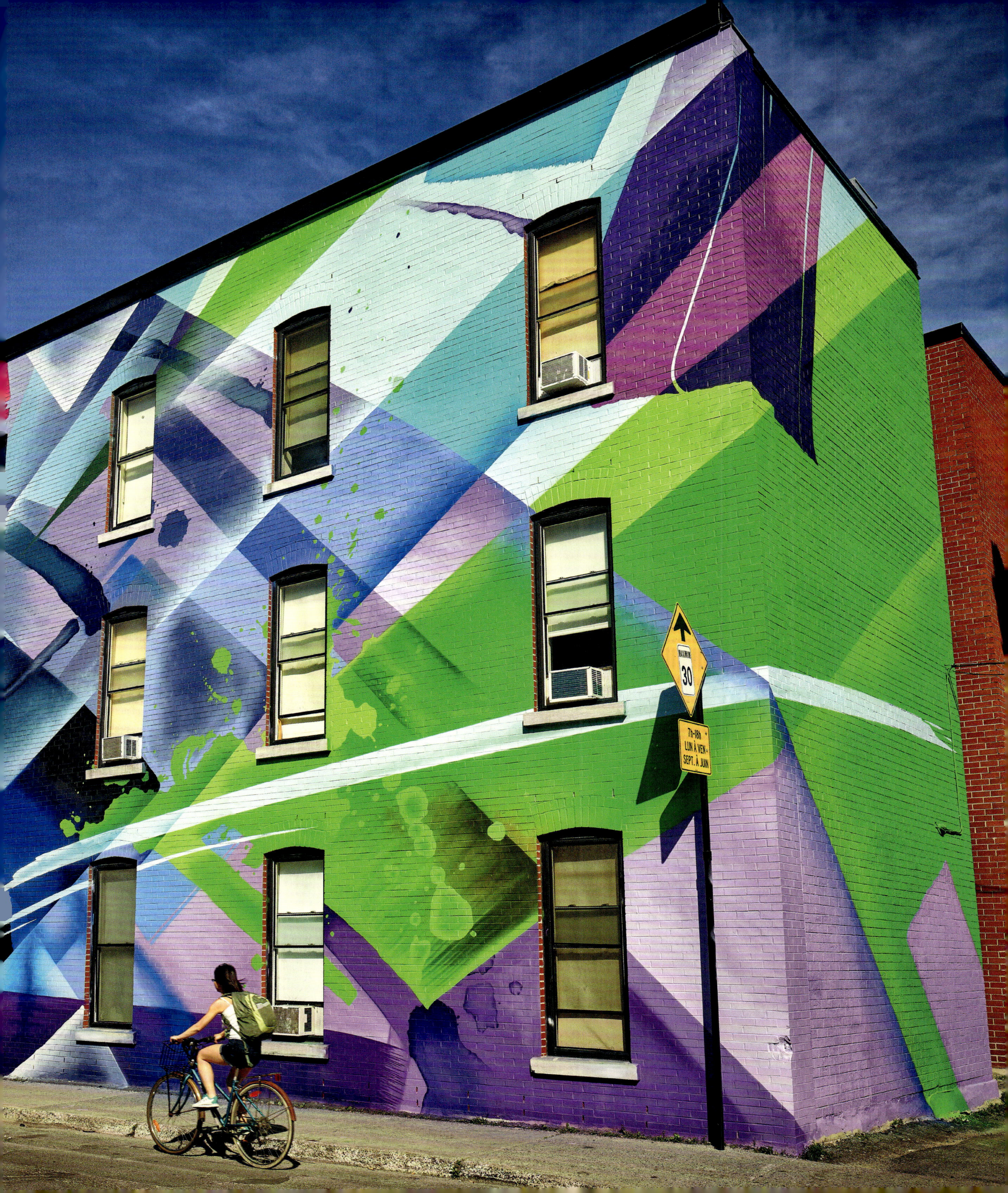
MAXIMUM
30
7h-18h
LUN À VEN
SEPT. À JUIN

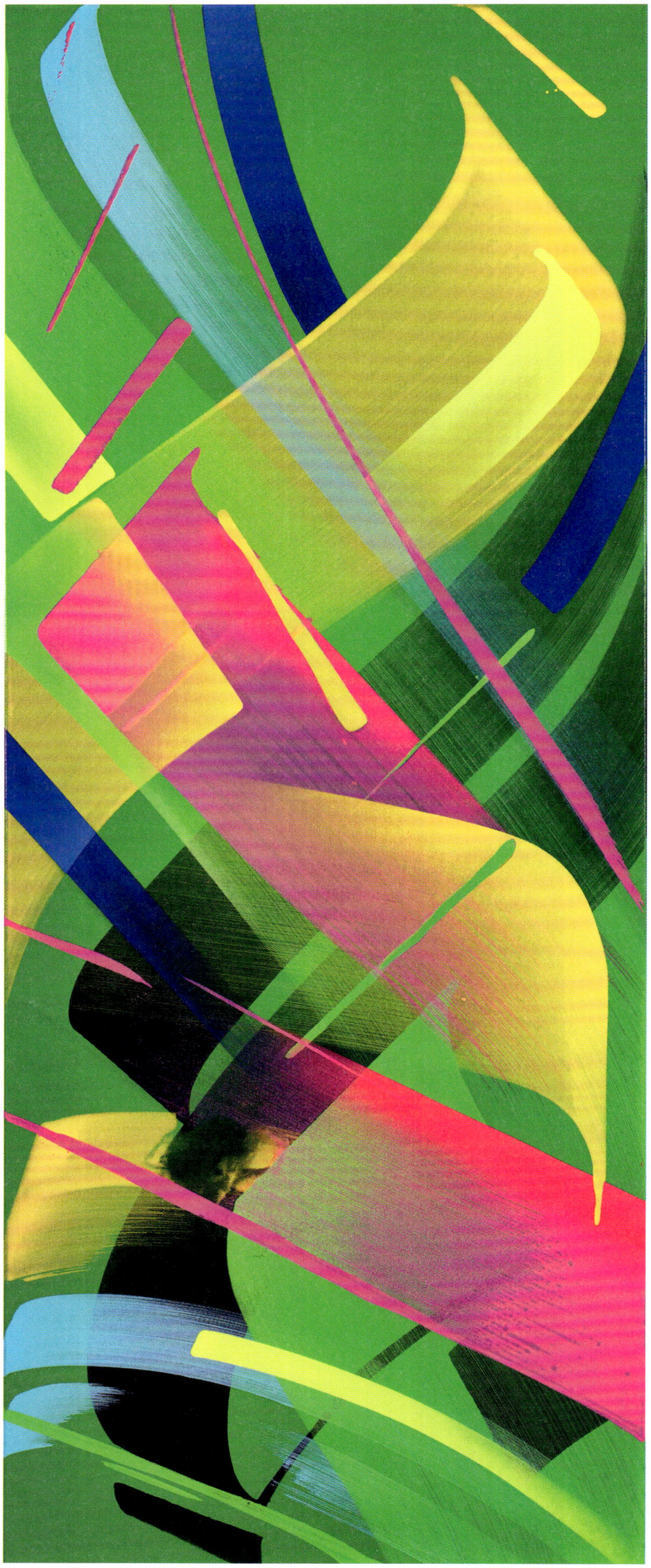

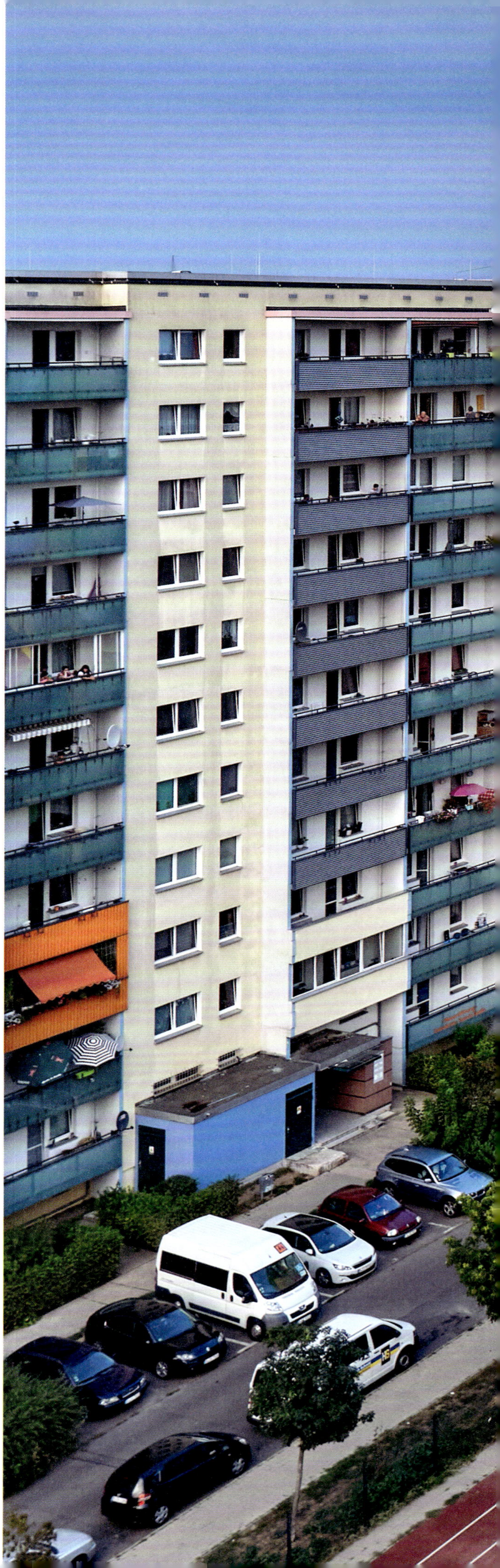

163. *12:05-07062019-Berlin*, 150 x 60cm, acrylic and spray paint on canvas, 2019. This canvas was a sketch for the mural in Berlin, Germany (opposite)
164–166 (opposite and next spread). Berlin Mural Festival, Alte Hellersdorfer Strasse 133, Berlin, Germany, August 2019

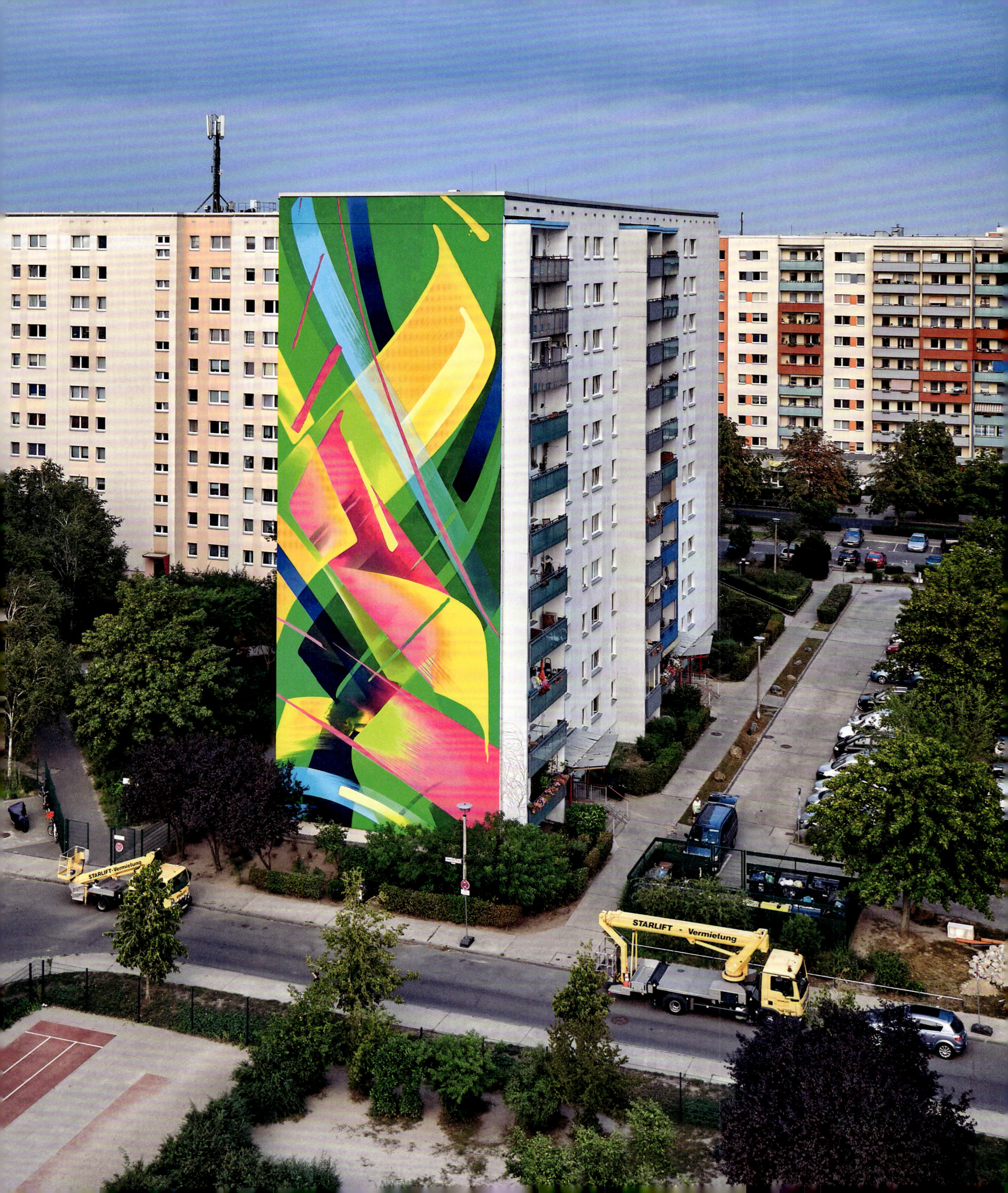
STARLIFT - Vermietung
STARLIFT-Vermietung

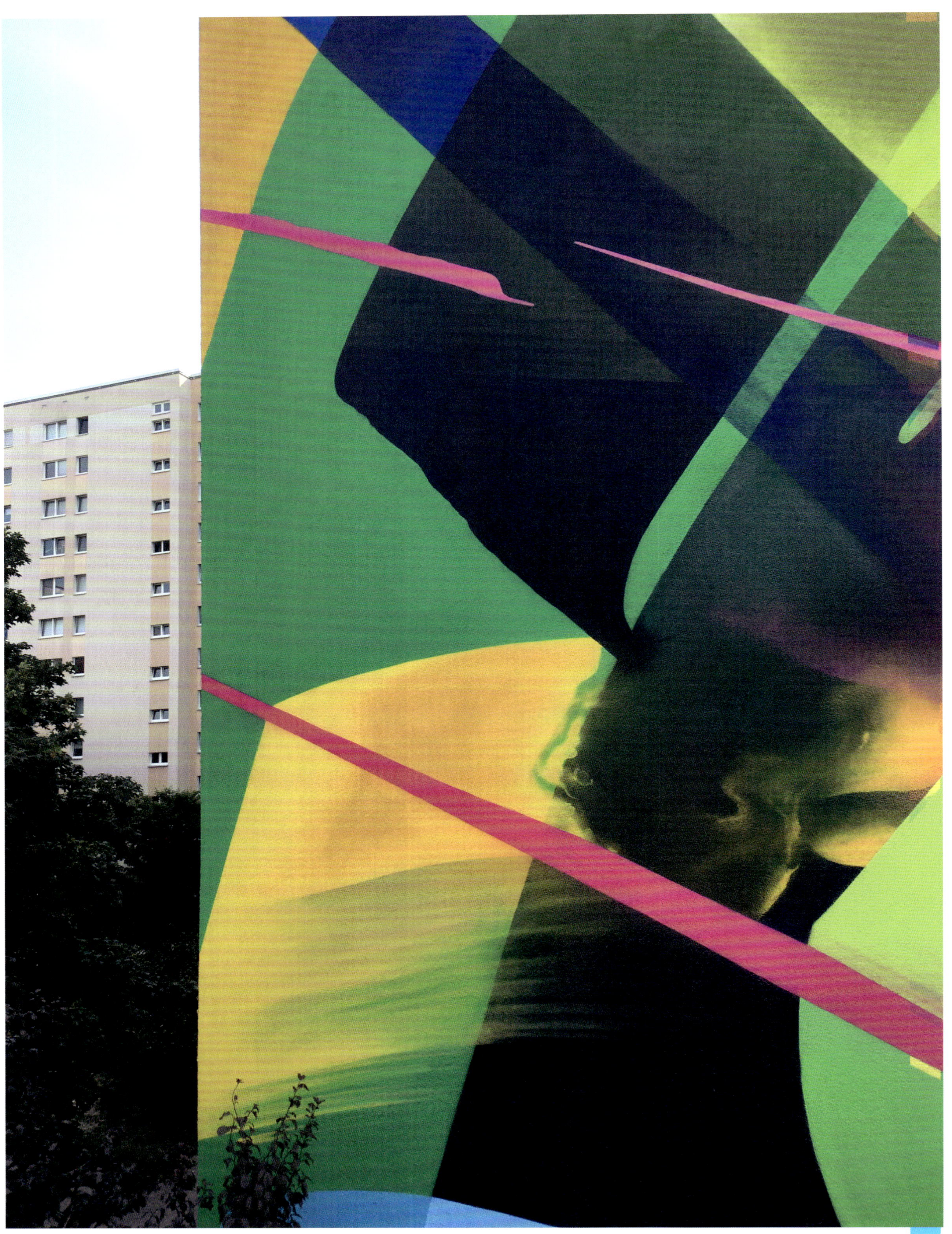

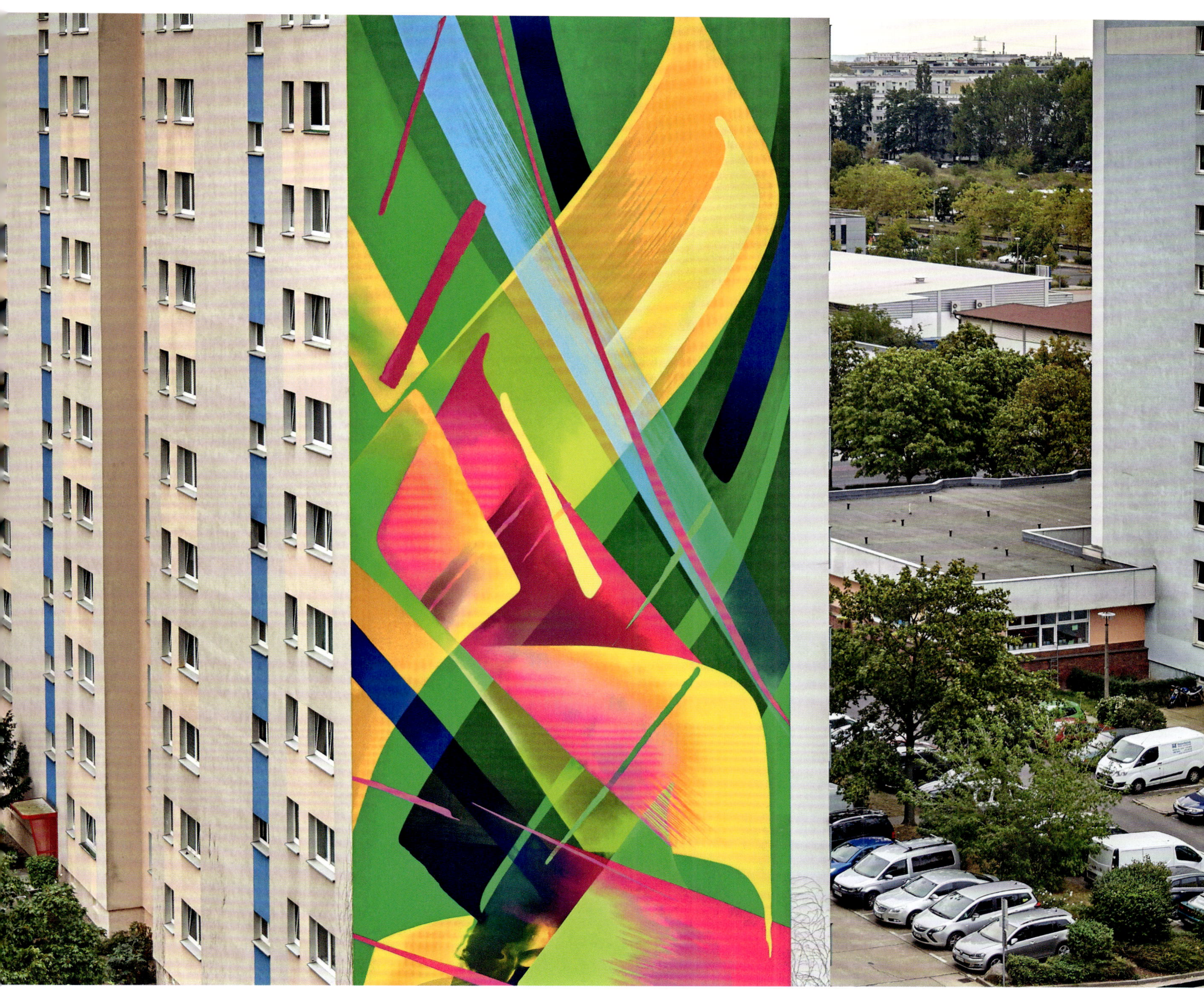

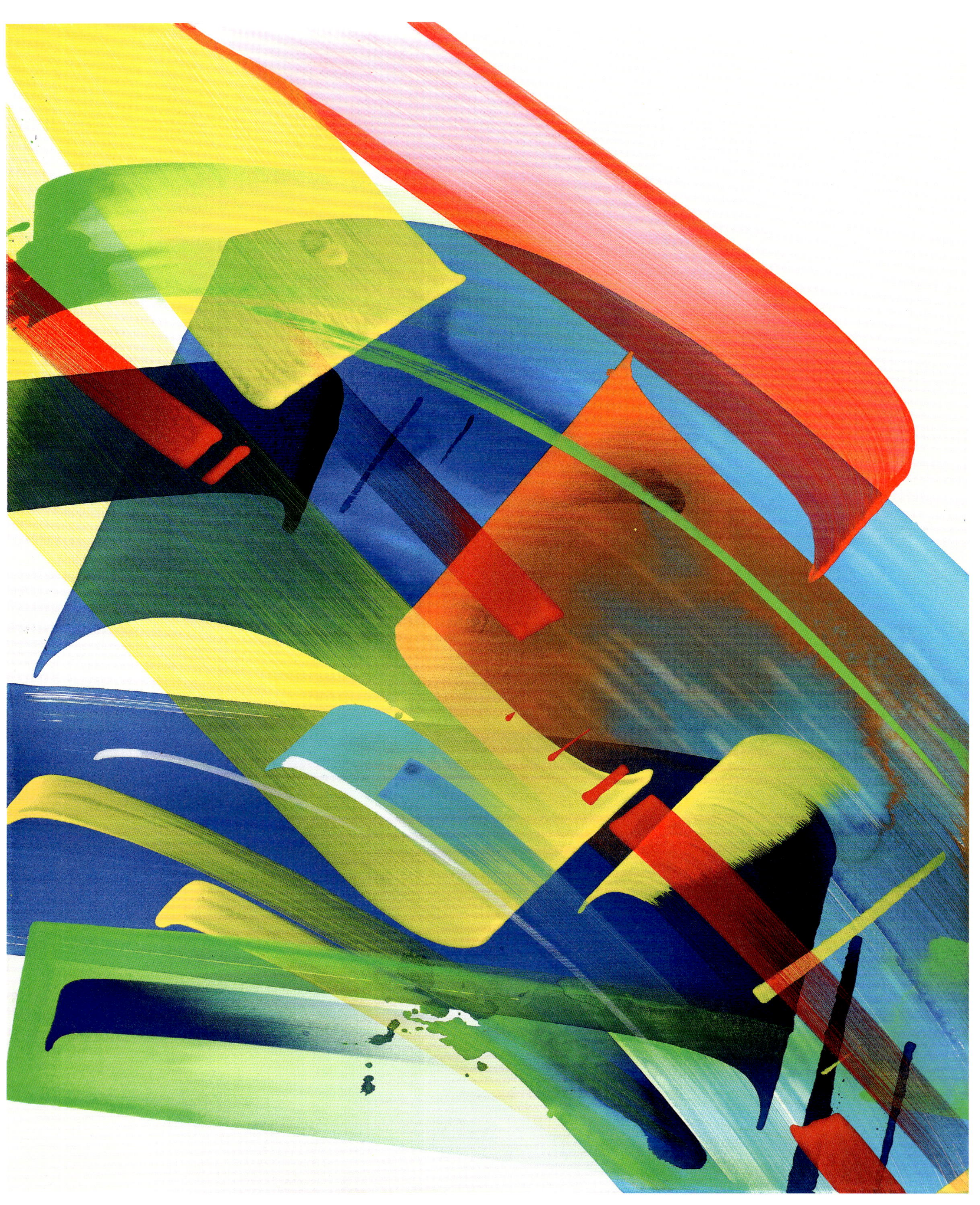

167. *12:06-27112019*, 100 x 80cm, acrylic and spray paint on canvas, 2019.
This canvas was the sketch for the mural in Rheine, Germany (opposite)

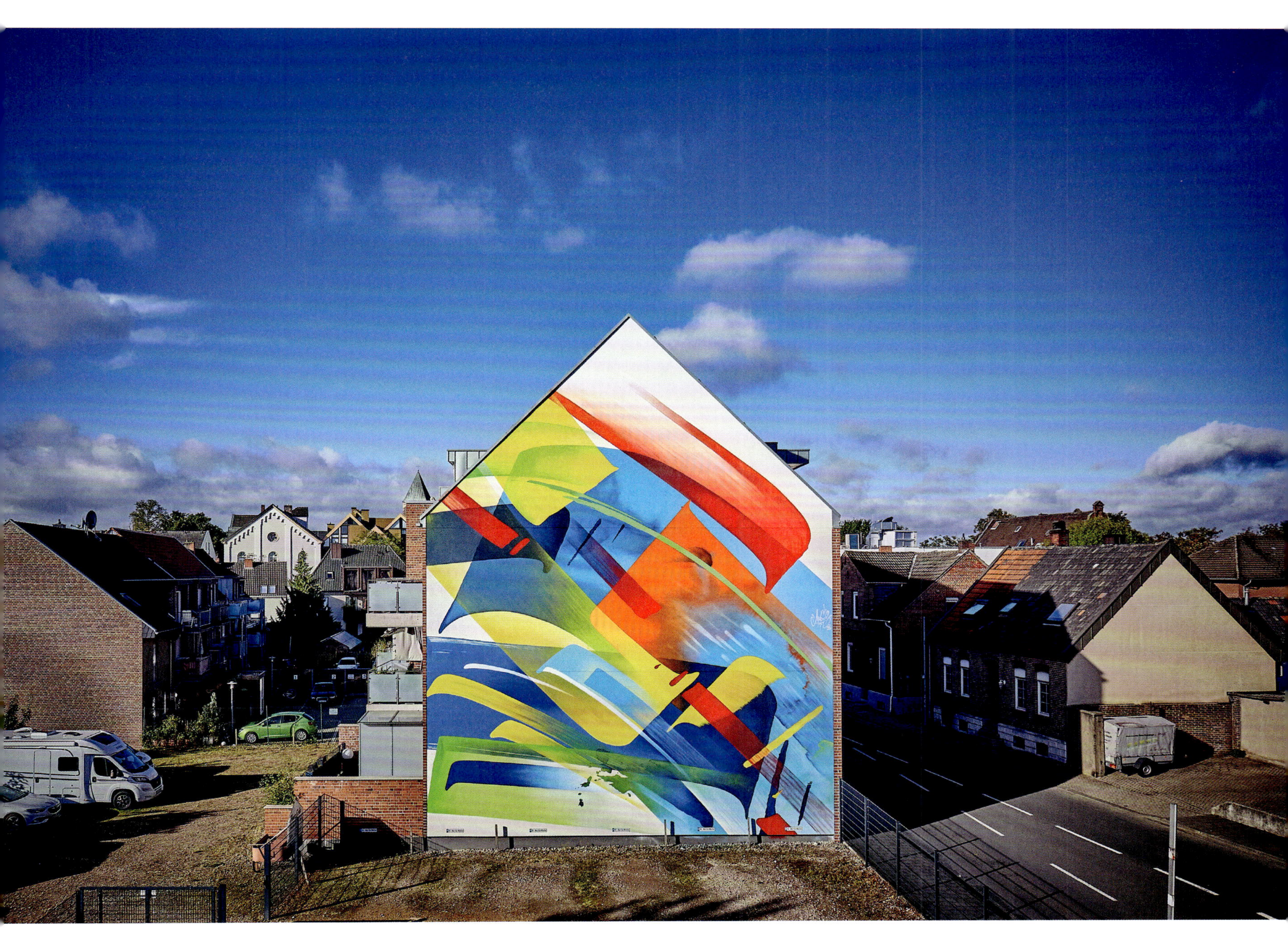

168. Humboldtstrasse, Rheine, Germany, September 2020

170–172 (below, opposite and next spread). London Mural Festival, Chance Street, Shoreditch, London, September 2020

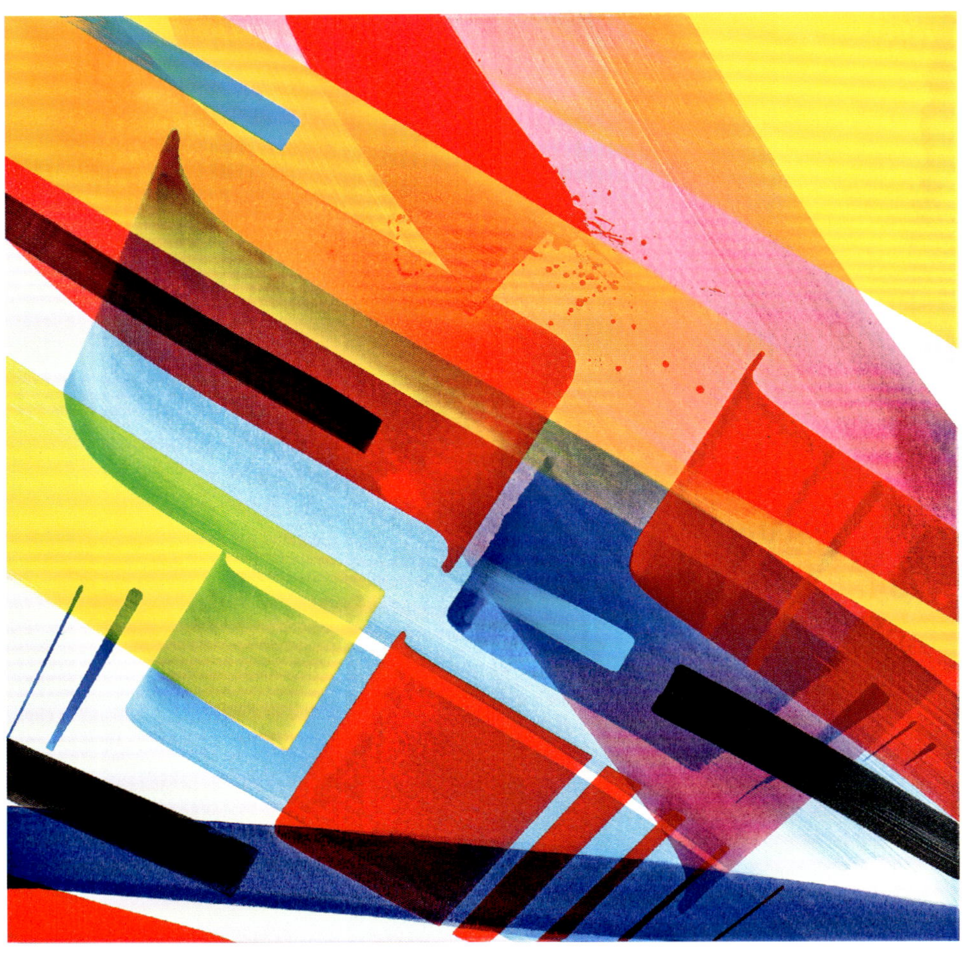

169. *19:01-19052020*, 100 x 100cm, acrylic and spray paint on canvas, 2020. This canvas was used as a base for the mural painted in London, UK (below and opposite)

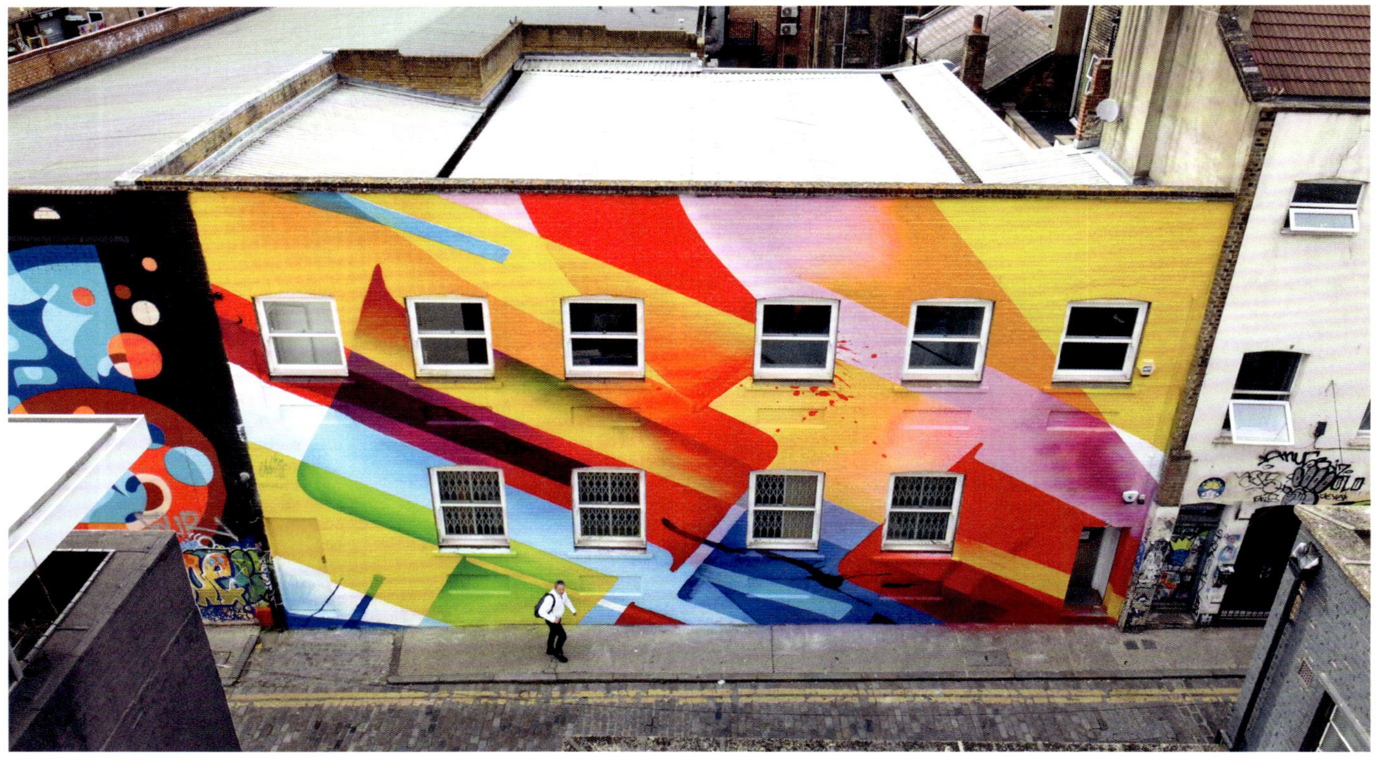

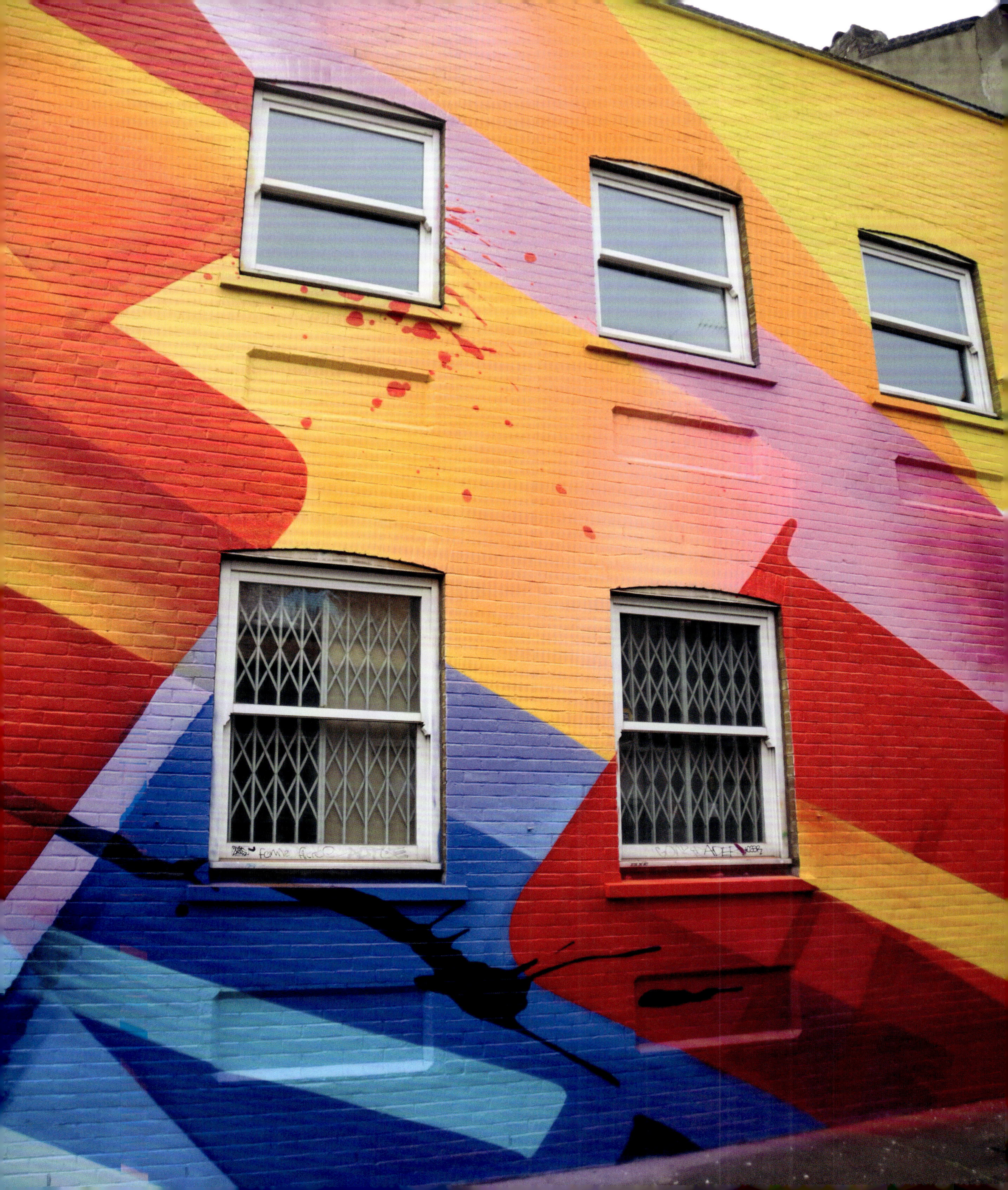

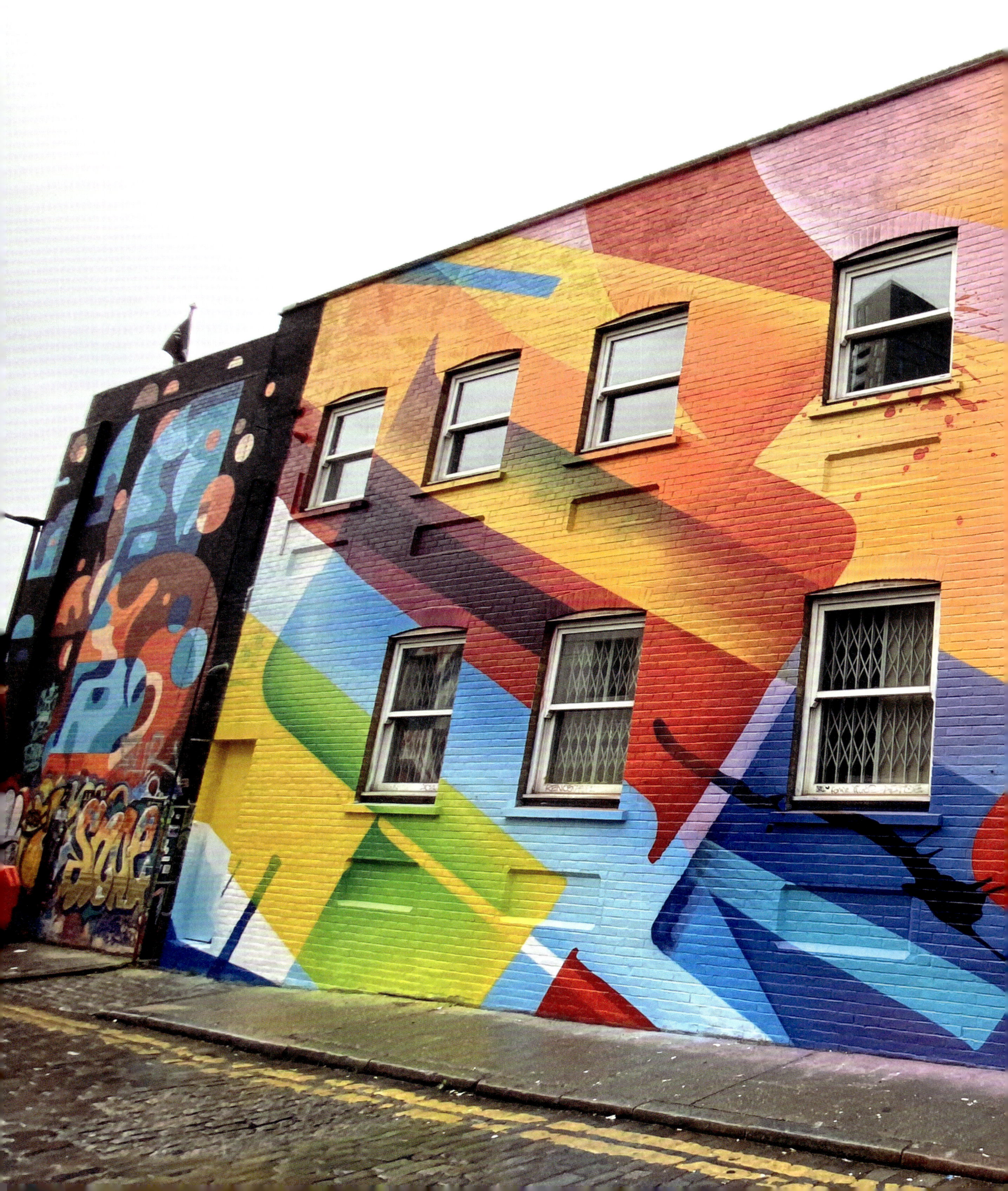

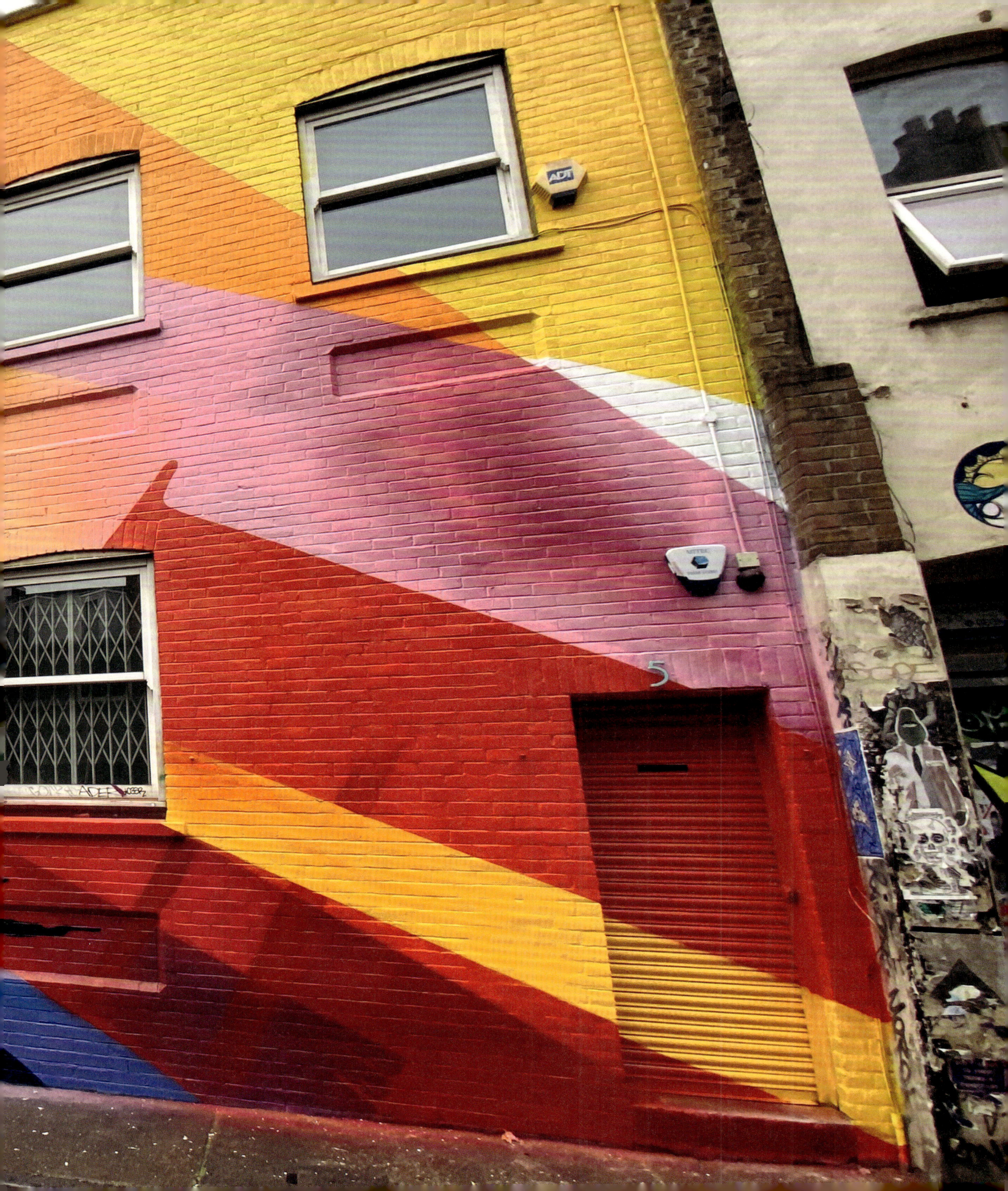
ADT
5

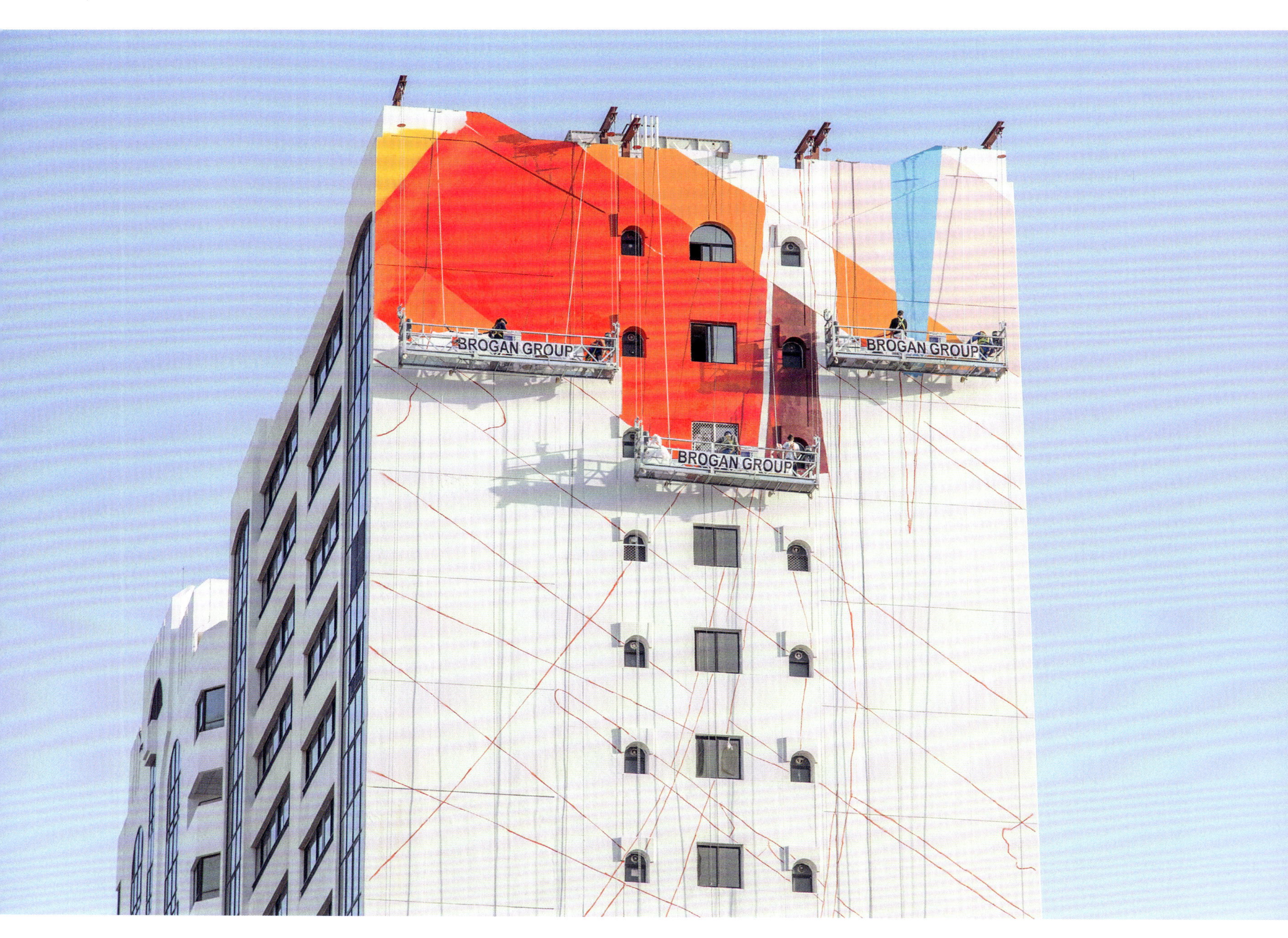

173–177 (this spread and next two spreads). Sheikh Rashid bin Saeed Street, Abu Dhabi, United Arab Emirates, 2020. This is the highest mural in the UAE, and also the highest MadC has painted so far. It was painted for the initiative 'For Abu Dhabi', with the help of an international production team

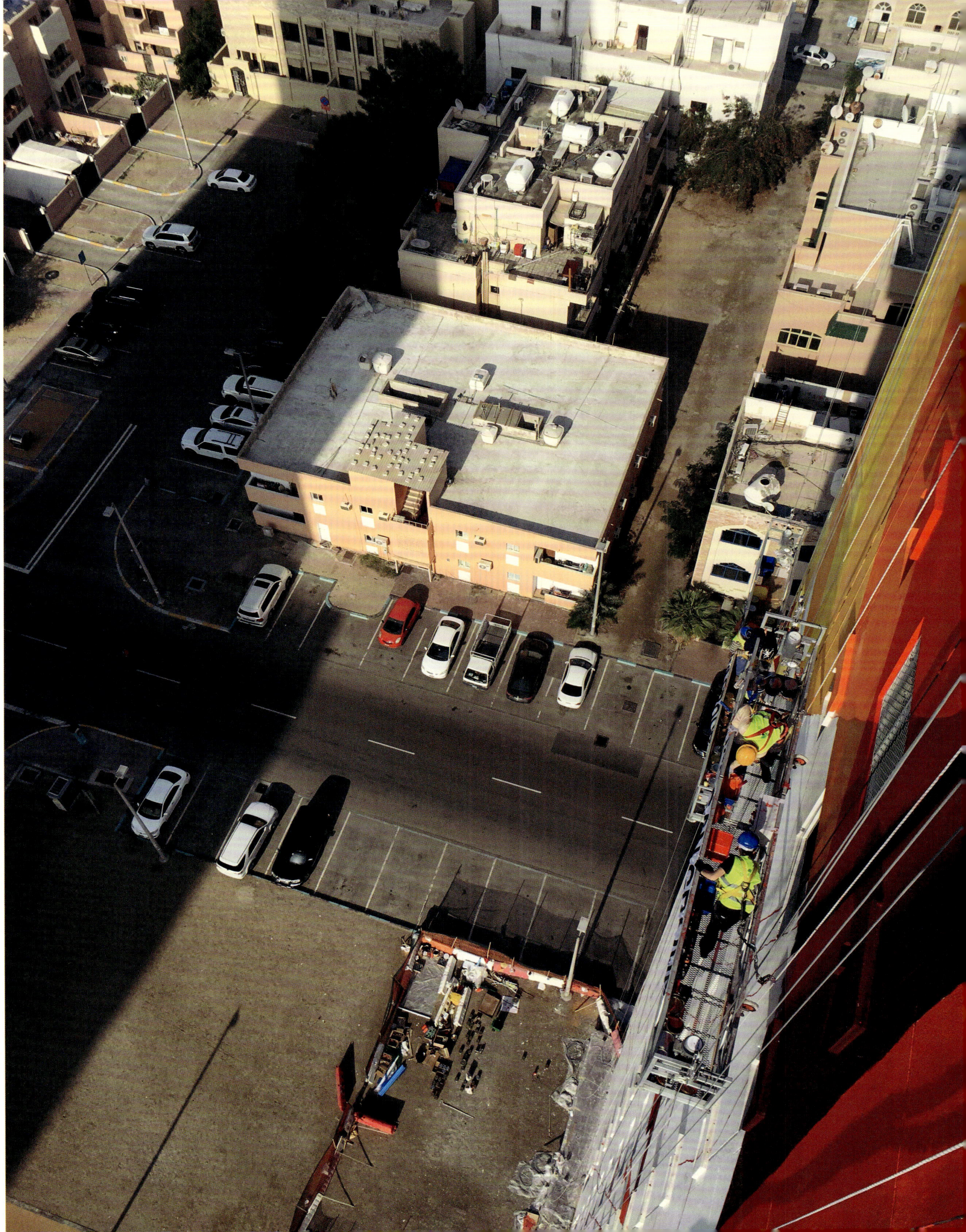

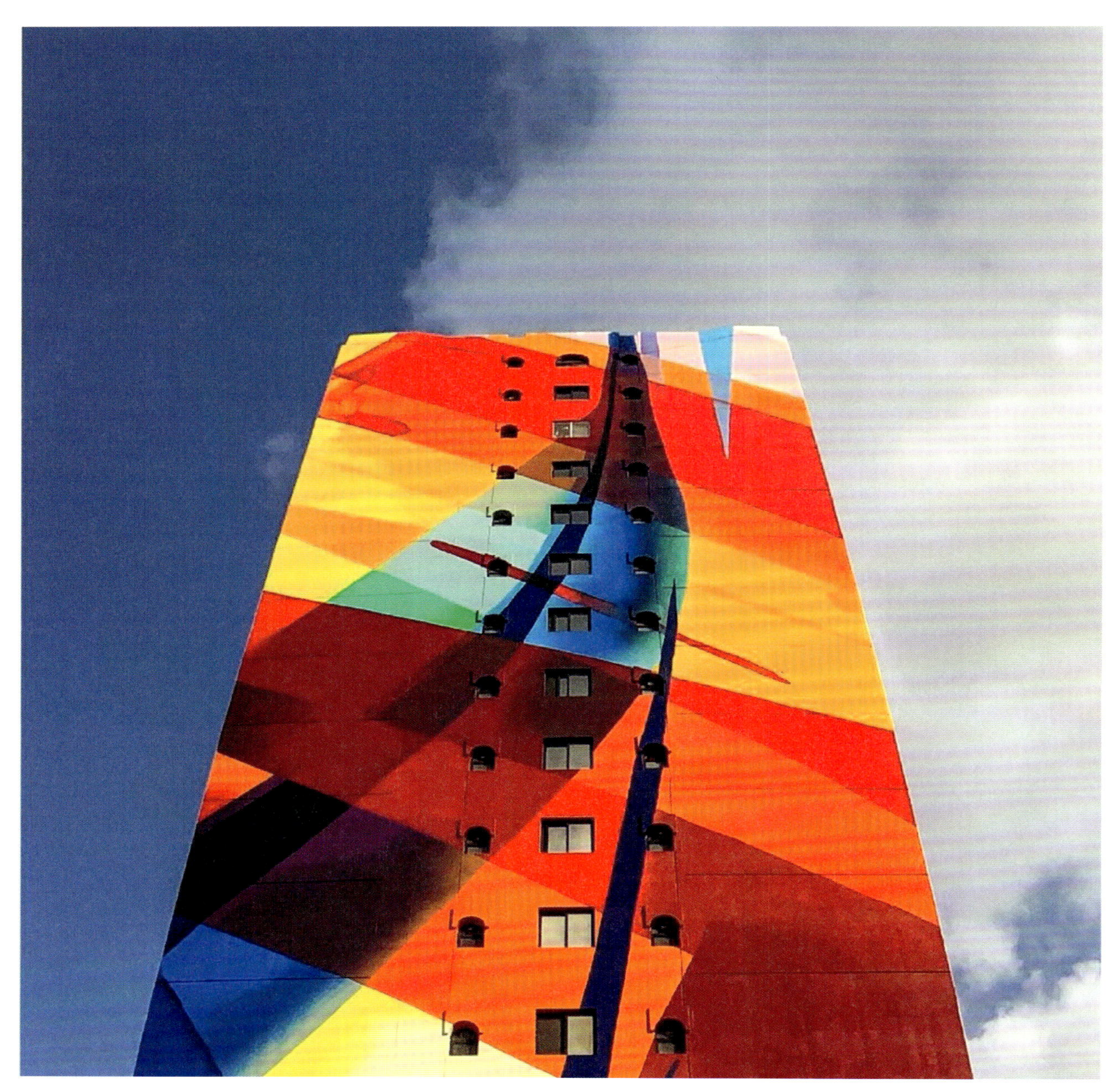

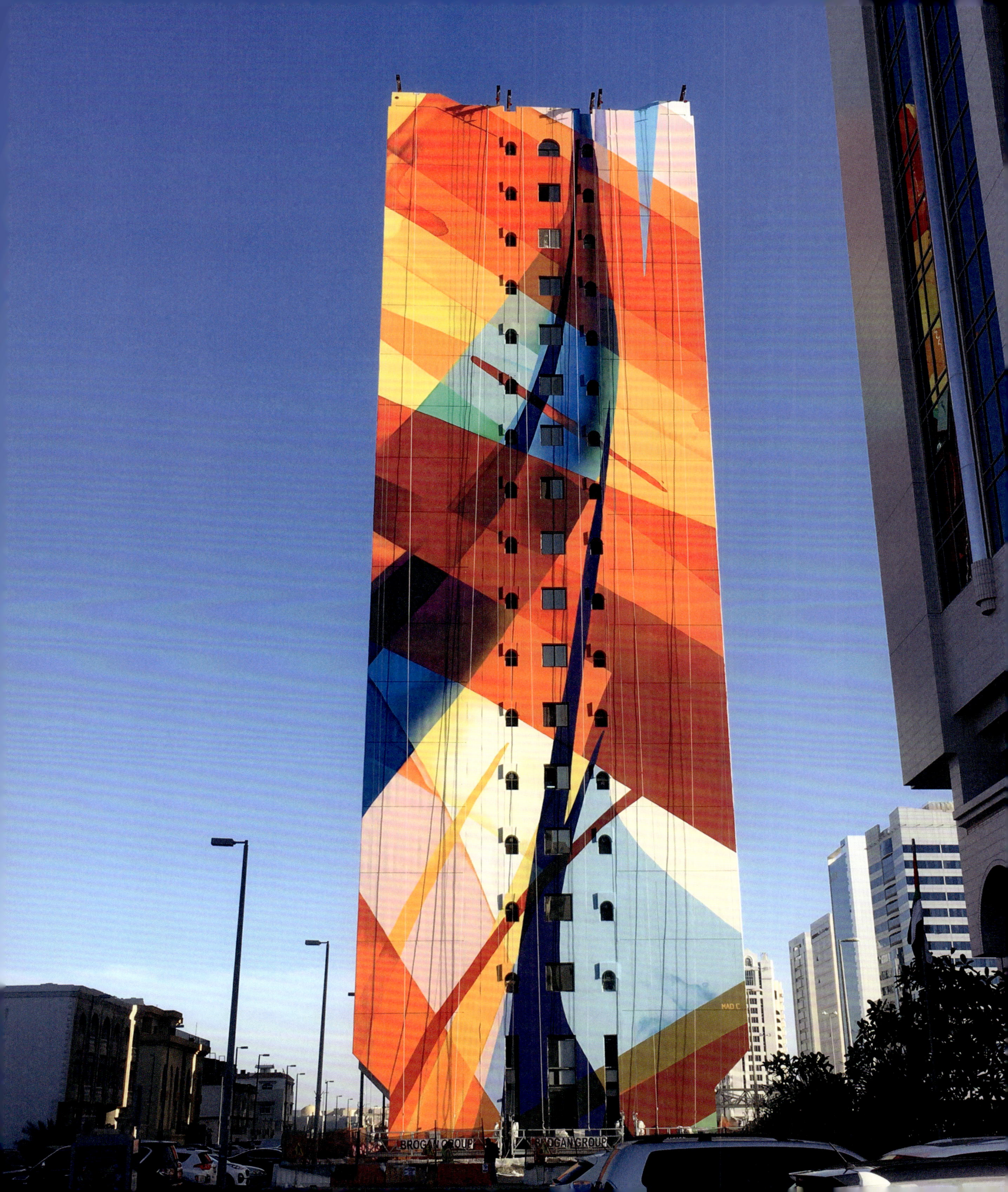
MAD C
BROGAN GROUP
BROGAN GROUP

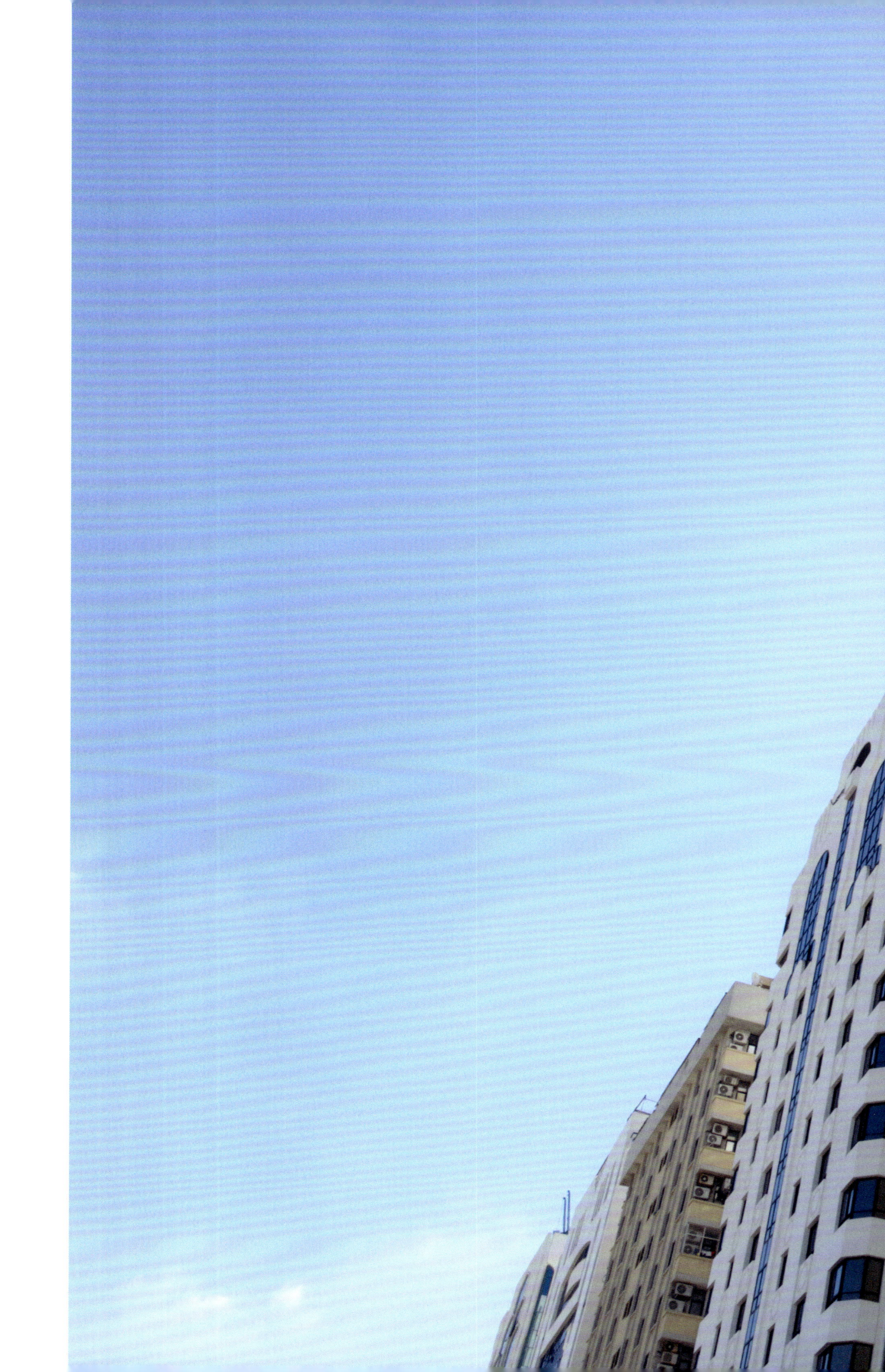

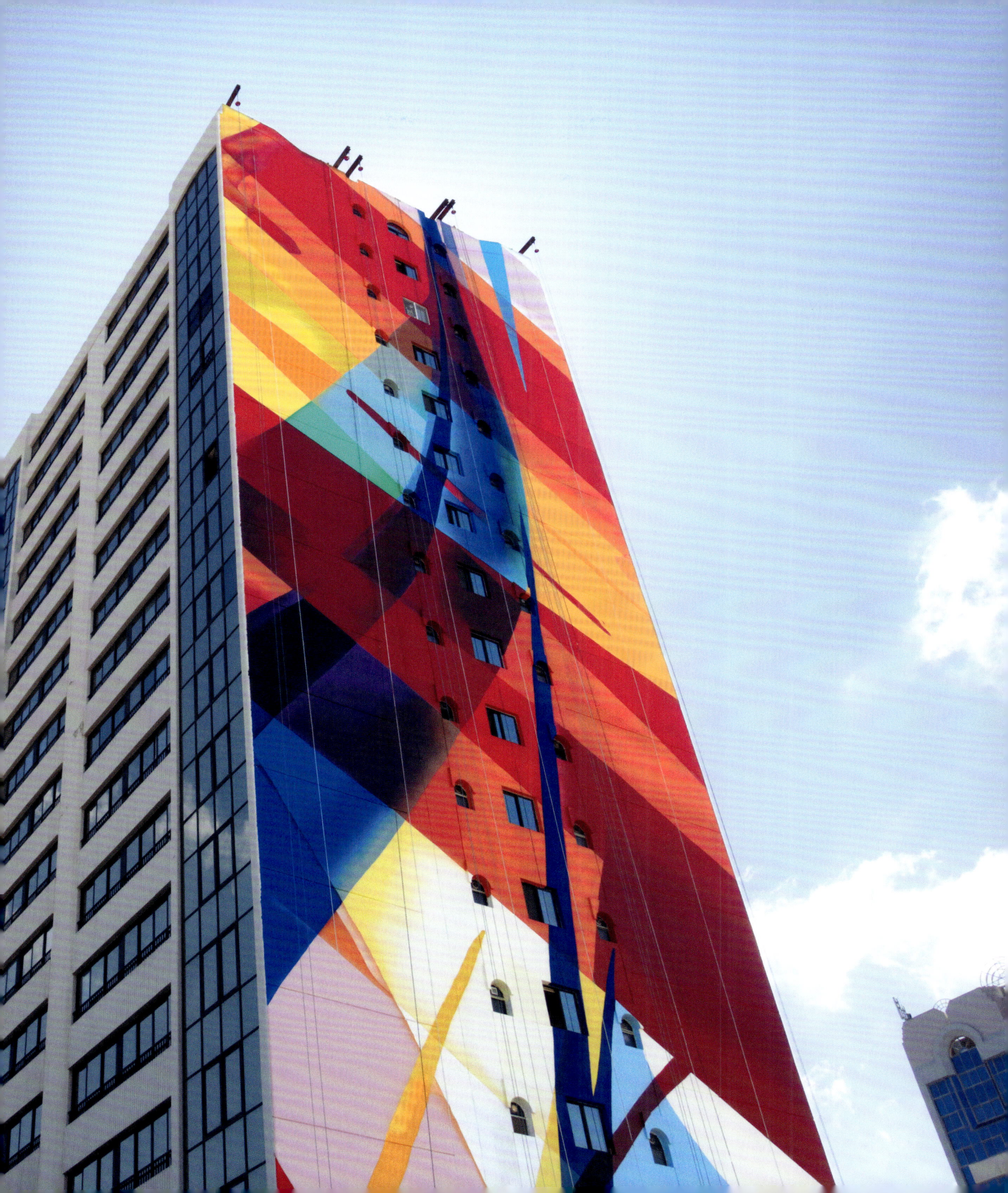

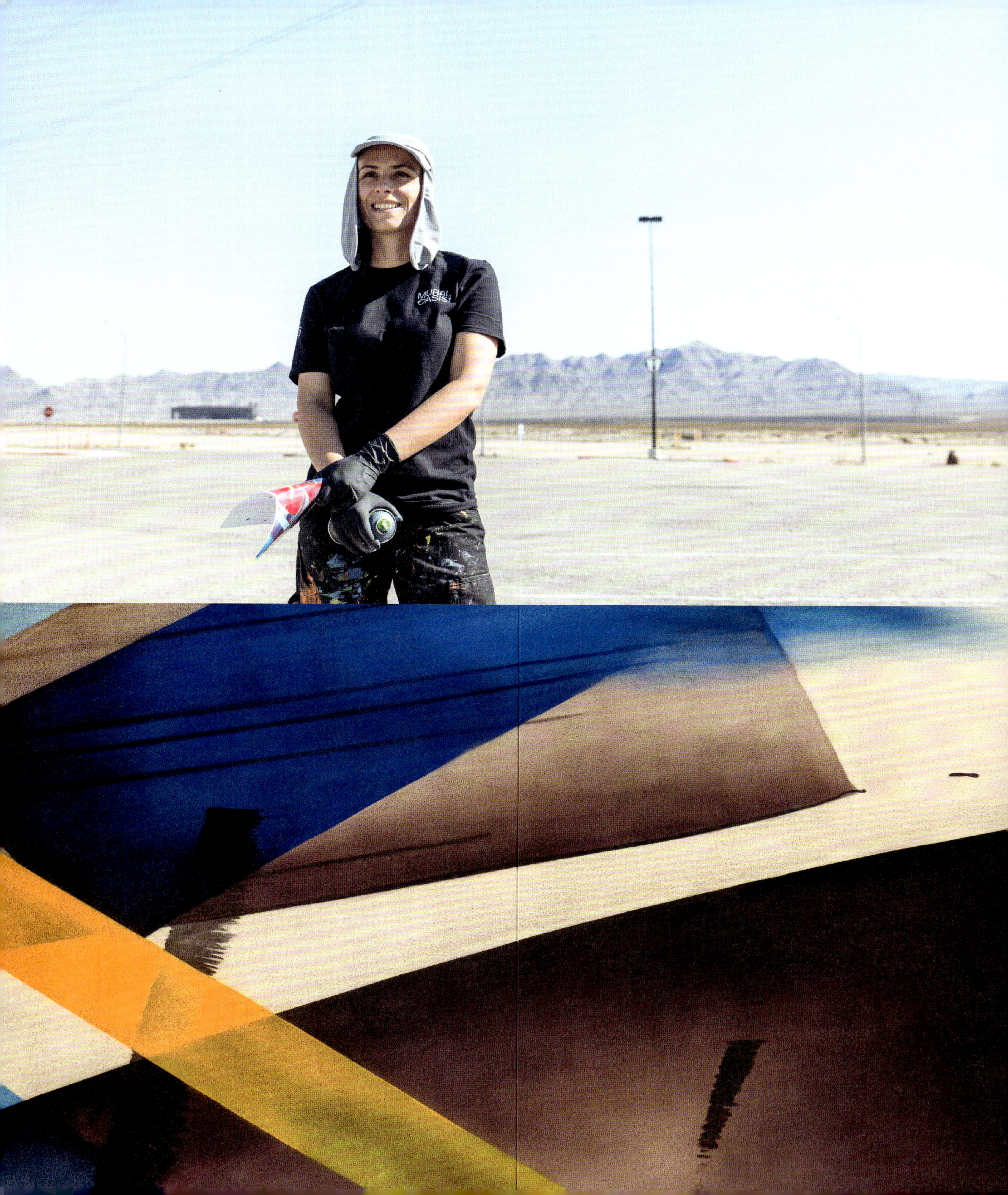
MURAL
OASIS

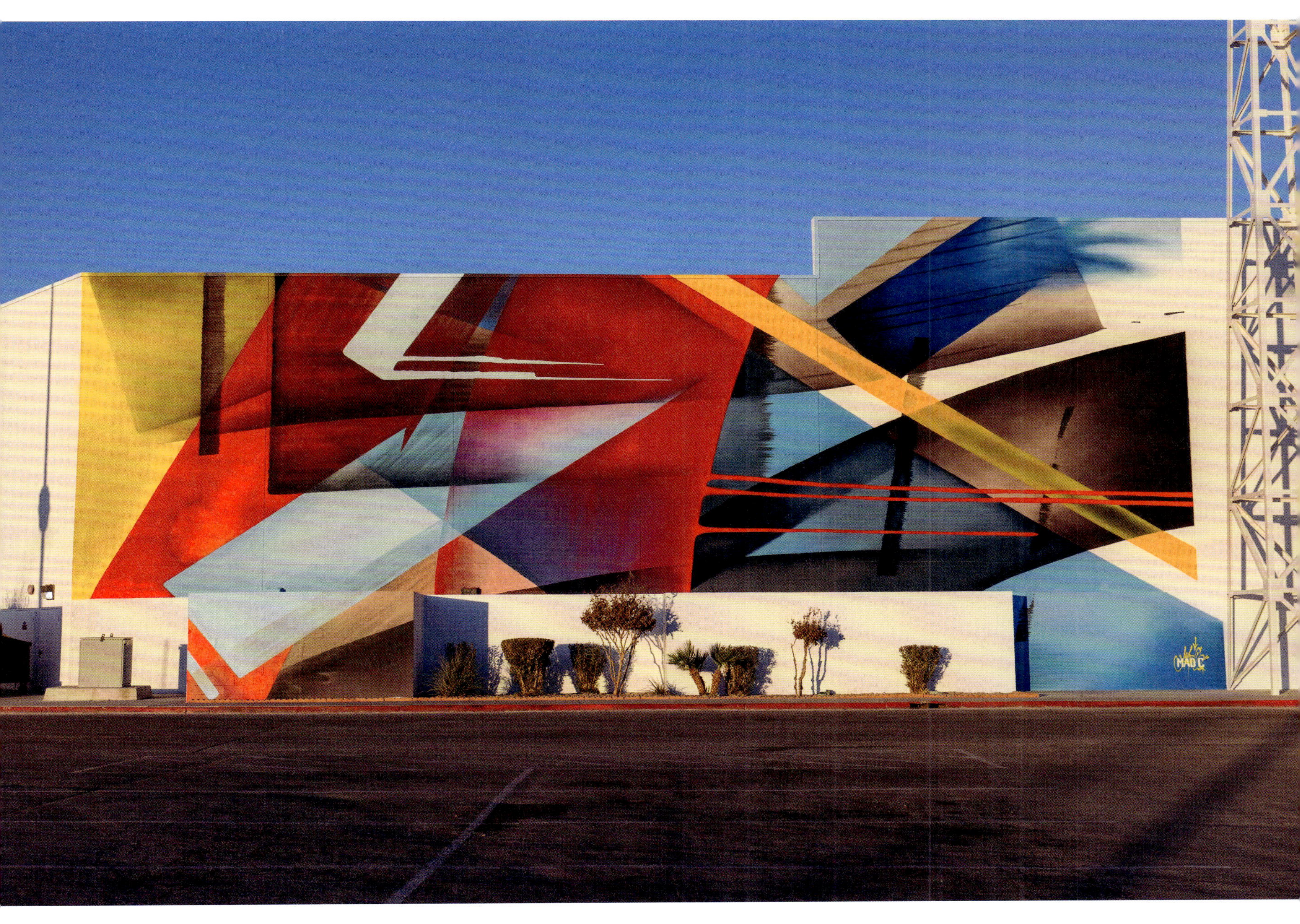

178–180 (this spread and next spread). Mural Oasis,
32100 Las Vegas Boulevard South, Primm, Nevada, USA, 2019

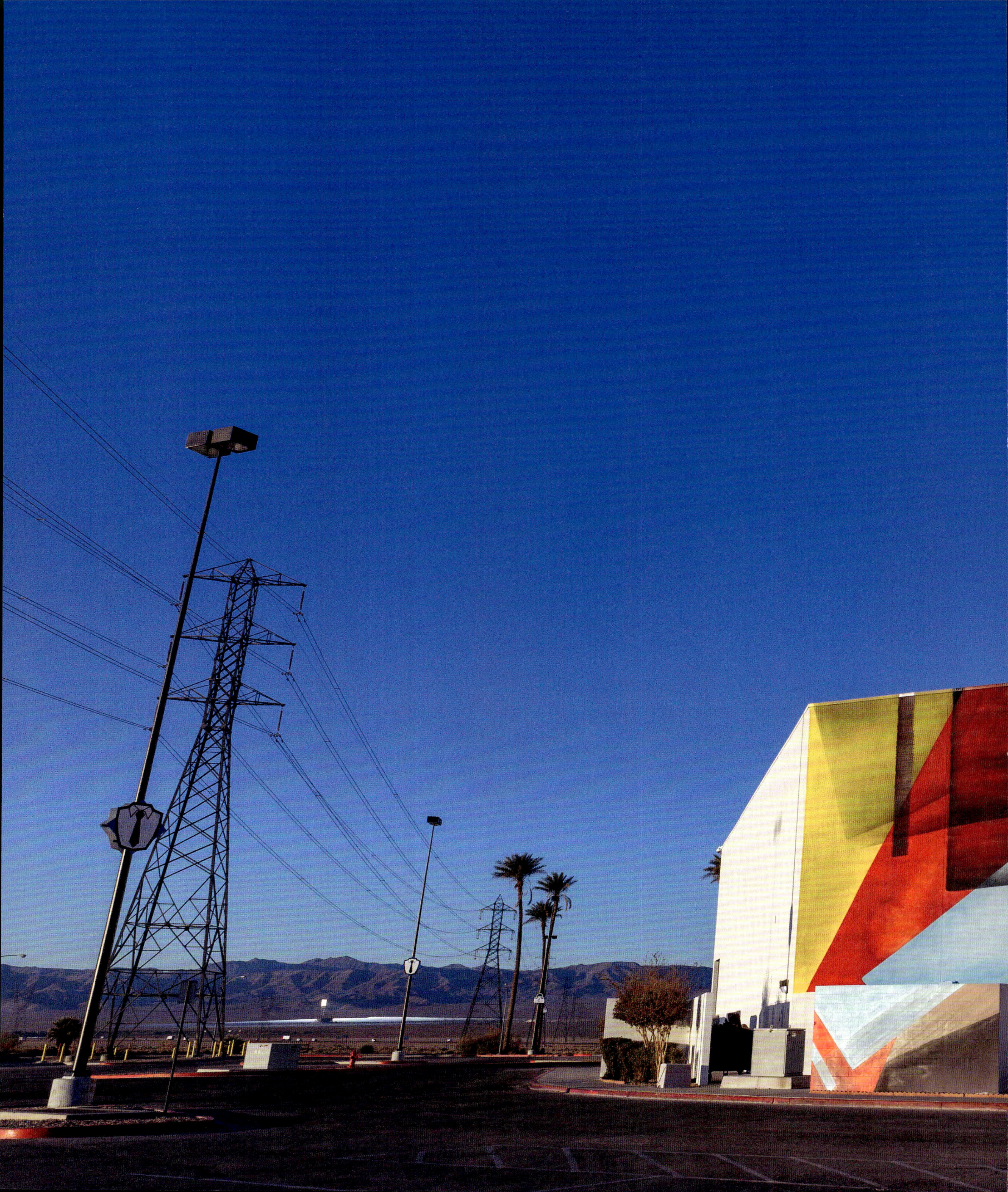

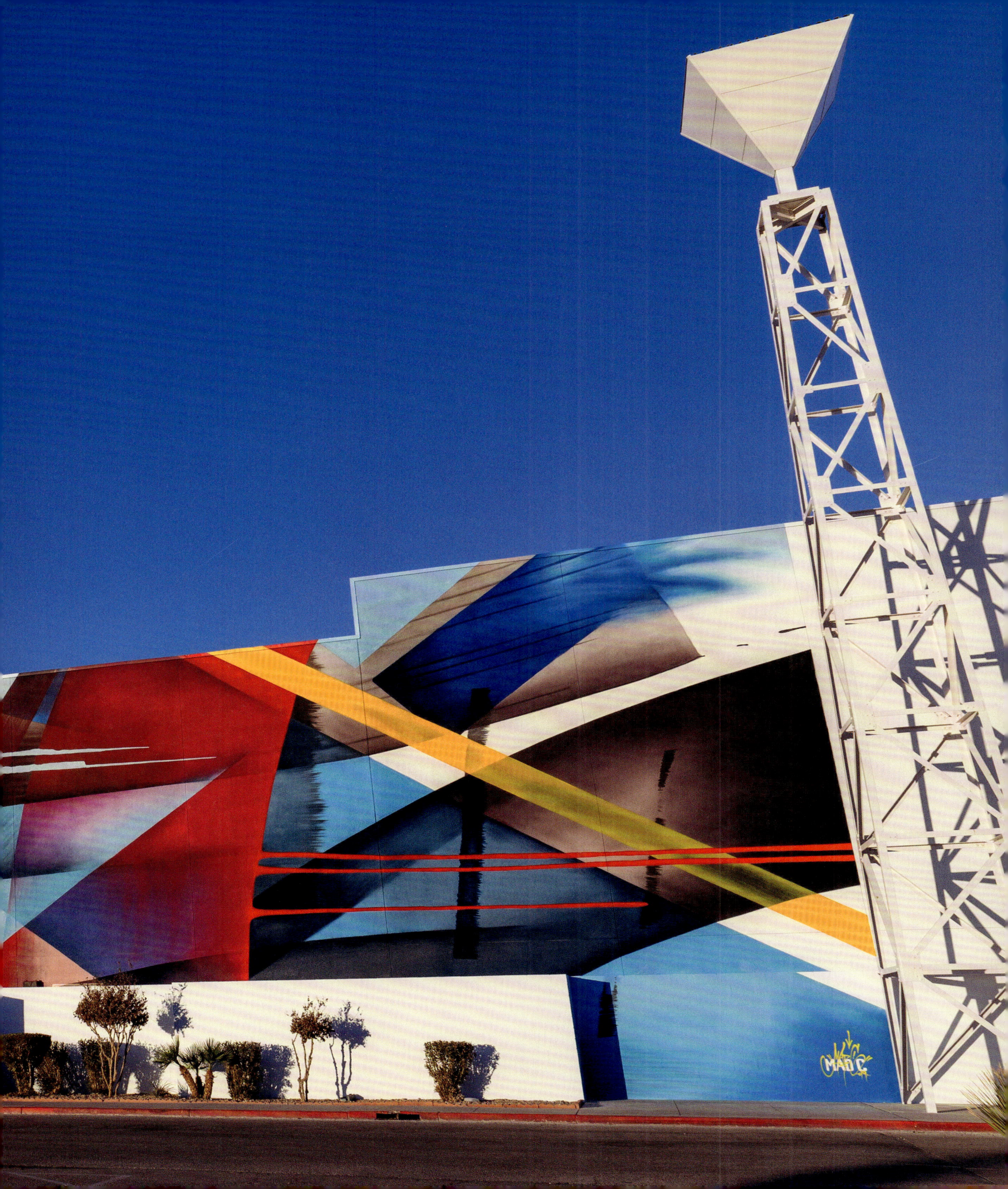
MAD C

STUDIO WORKS

A light-flooded, spacious room opens in front of us, populated by long wall-papering tables with delicate metal frames. On the walls hang assemblies of neatly arranged brushes of various sizes, as well as scrapers and other utensils. A shelf filled with cans of paint and turpentine stands by the wall; rulers, hammers and angles are scattered around the room. Long runs of paper are laid out over the grey floor, which already shows numerous traces of past usage. Canvases of different sizes are spread out on the tables or are hanging on the wall. In different stages of the production process, some are still white, some are already coated with numerous layers of paint. The artist, whose body blurs in motion, roams the room almost like a ghost. However, her presence manifests itself in every object located in the studio.

Photography offers a rare glimpse into this space in which artistic energies materialise for the first time, where MadC is able to experiment, fail, start afresh and repeatedly question her own approaches **(fig. 181)**. Here, in this space of protection and possibility, she continuously develops new forms, continues to experiment intensively with the means and possibilities of the image. In this context, one is reminded of *The 700 Wall*, in which the studio is a central theme (see pp. 40, 42). Frankenstein's monster – a being consisting of different parts and influences – is working there on the 'disegno', the design in the classic art-historical sense, which forms the basis and starting point of the work of art. In the depicted studio, rats are in the process of stealing some designs – a well-known phenomenon in the world of graffiti. Almost 12 years after the execution of *The 700 Wall*, however, it can be said that MadC has developed such a distinctive handwriting, differing so radically from classic graffiti art, that so-called 'bitings', i.e. imitations by other artists, should no longer pose a risk.

A focus of her studio practice is work on canvas. These works not only connect the various artistic spheres in which MadC moves, but also the realms in which they are presented – the street and the gallery. While some canvas works serve as templates for large murals in public spaces, they also stand for themselves and have featured in numerous exhibitions in recent years. With their bright colours they fill the white cubes of the gallery rooms, and are characterised by a strong presence, a distinctive imagery and the deep space that is formed by their glazed layers. They testify to the artist's inexhaustible urge to create, and her desire to let colours, shapes, surfaces and levels converge in ever new constellations on the canvas.

The exhibition *Street to Canvas*, taking place in the gallery of HENI Artists Agency in London alongside the publication of this book, gets to the heart of MadC's studio practice by offering a broad insight into her current oeuvre. Featuring many of her most recent canvas works, the exhibition can also be seen as an analogy of the last chapter of this book. This presentation of her newest works accentuates the intensity of her exploration of modes of expression, and bears witness to energies that manifest themselves on the canvas – sometimes rather controlled, sometimes slightly untamed.

Above all, the works show how MadC continues to pursue a tireless search to implement her own visions. The fact that she repeatedly crosses the borders of art categories and discourses remains an important, if not fundamental, characteristic of her artistic approach. Thus, the position as an outsider that MadC has taken again and again – be it her childhood in Ethiopia, her experience of returning to the GDR, being a woman in the graffiti scene, being an artist with a graffiti background in the visual arts – has helped her work to achieve its freedom of unique expression.

181. MadC studio, Halle, Germany, 2014

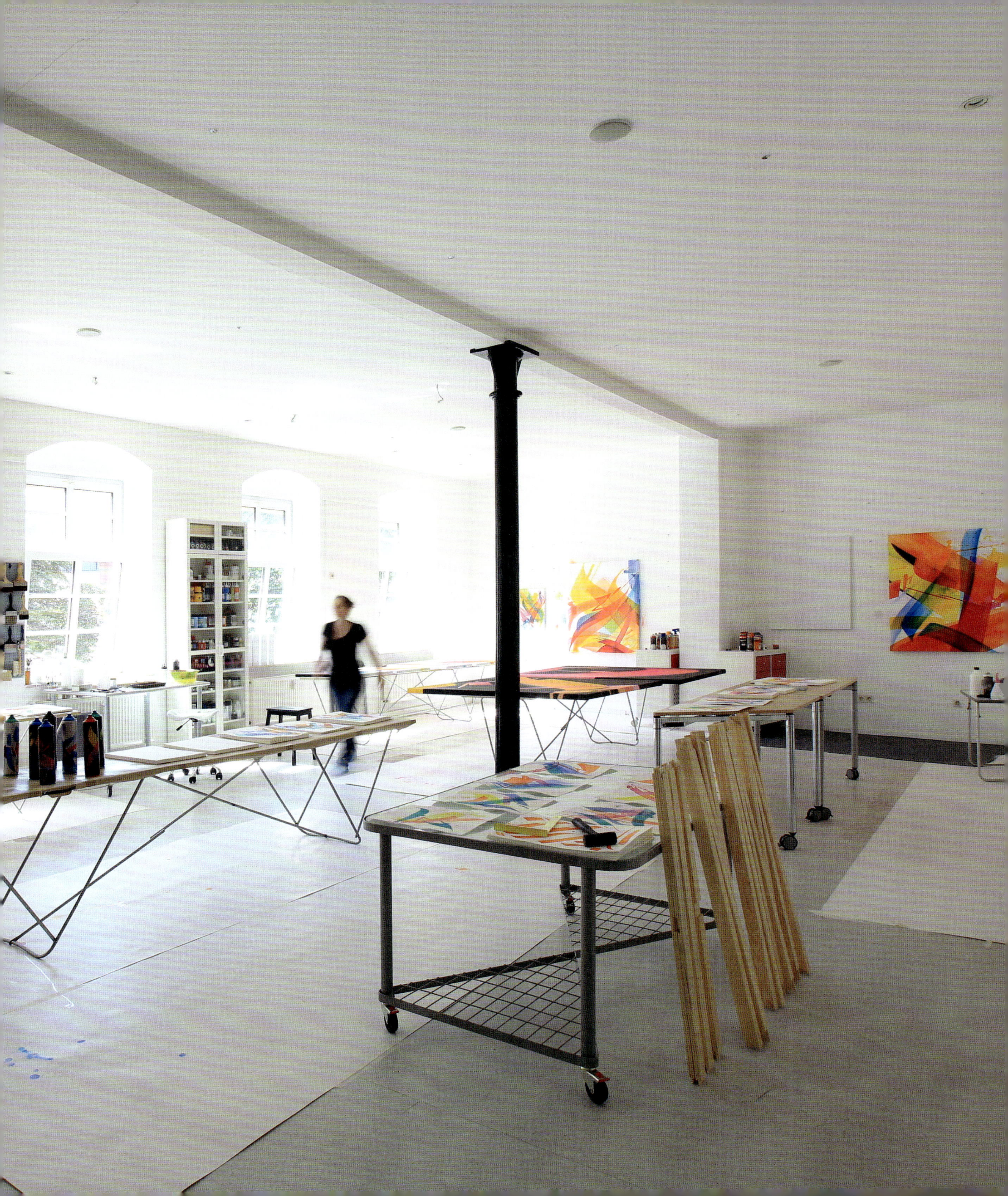

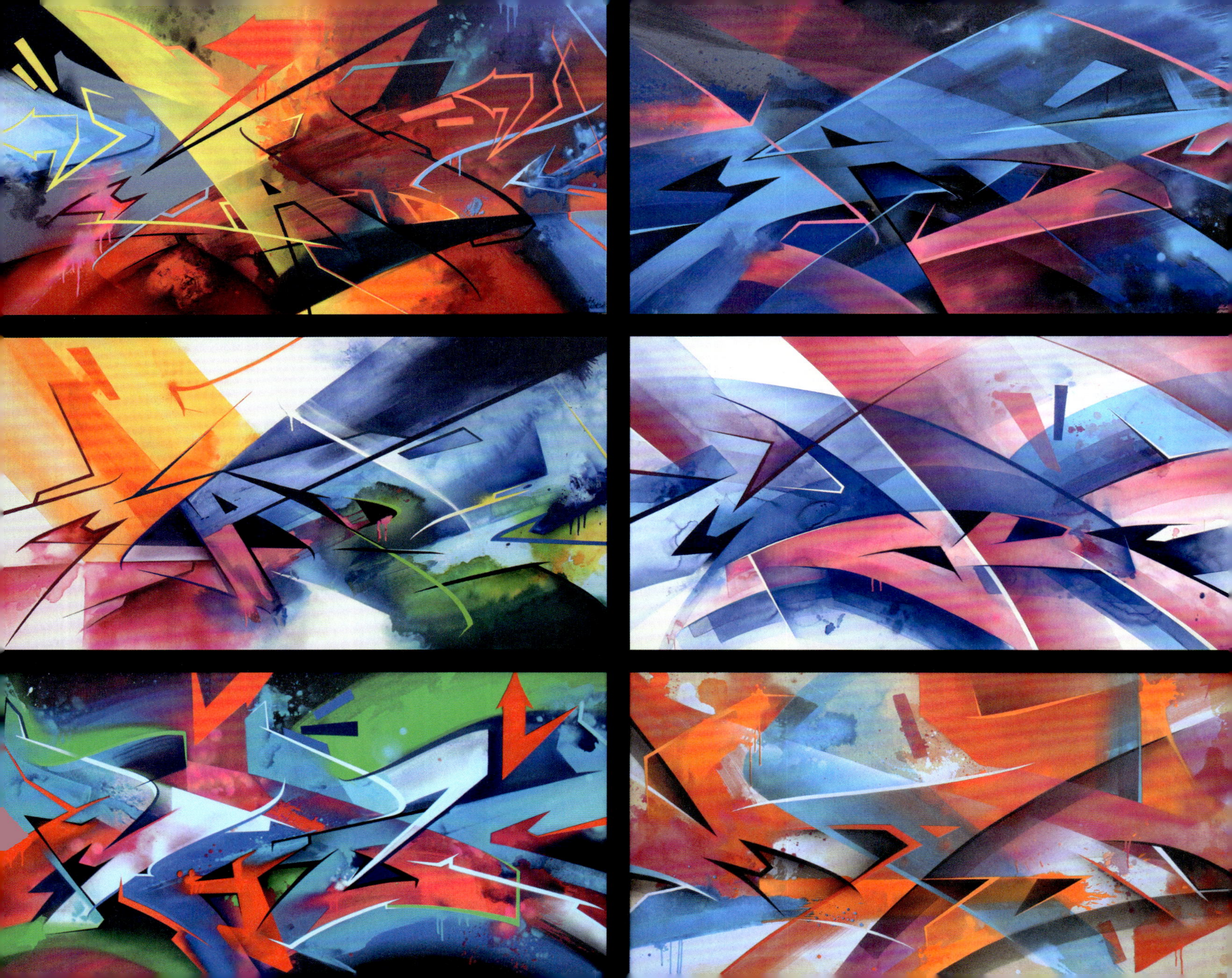

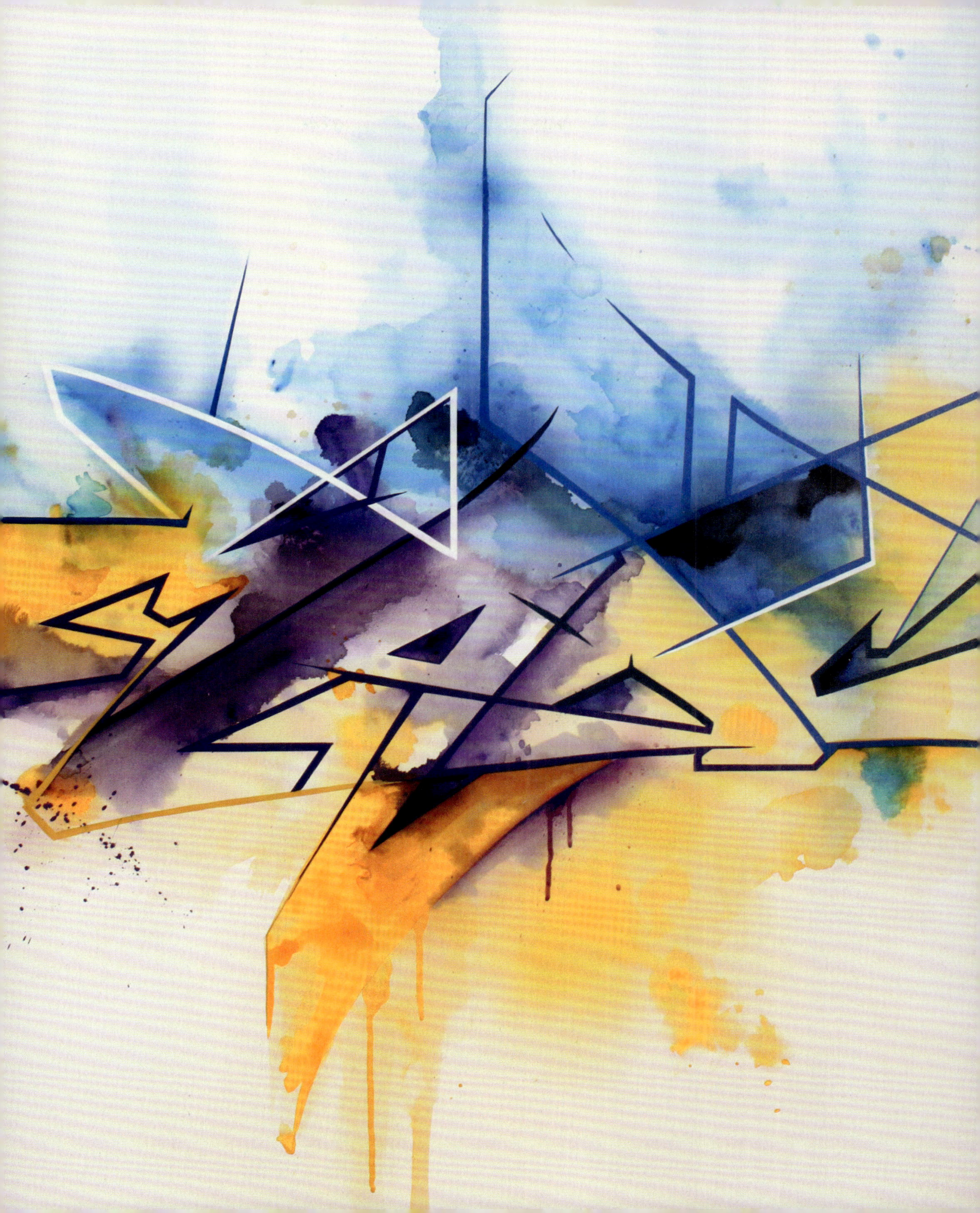

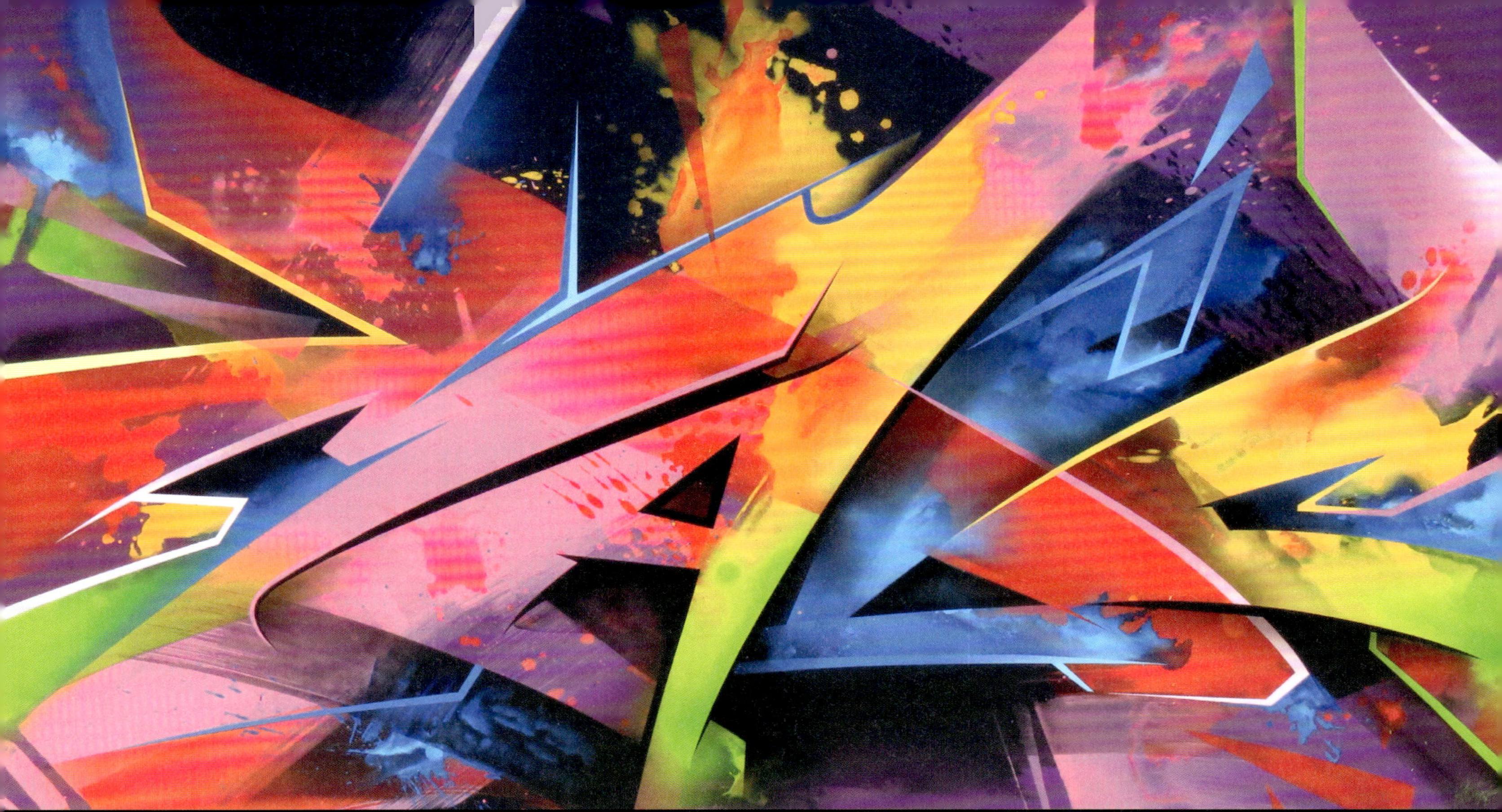

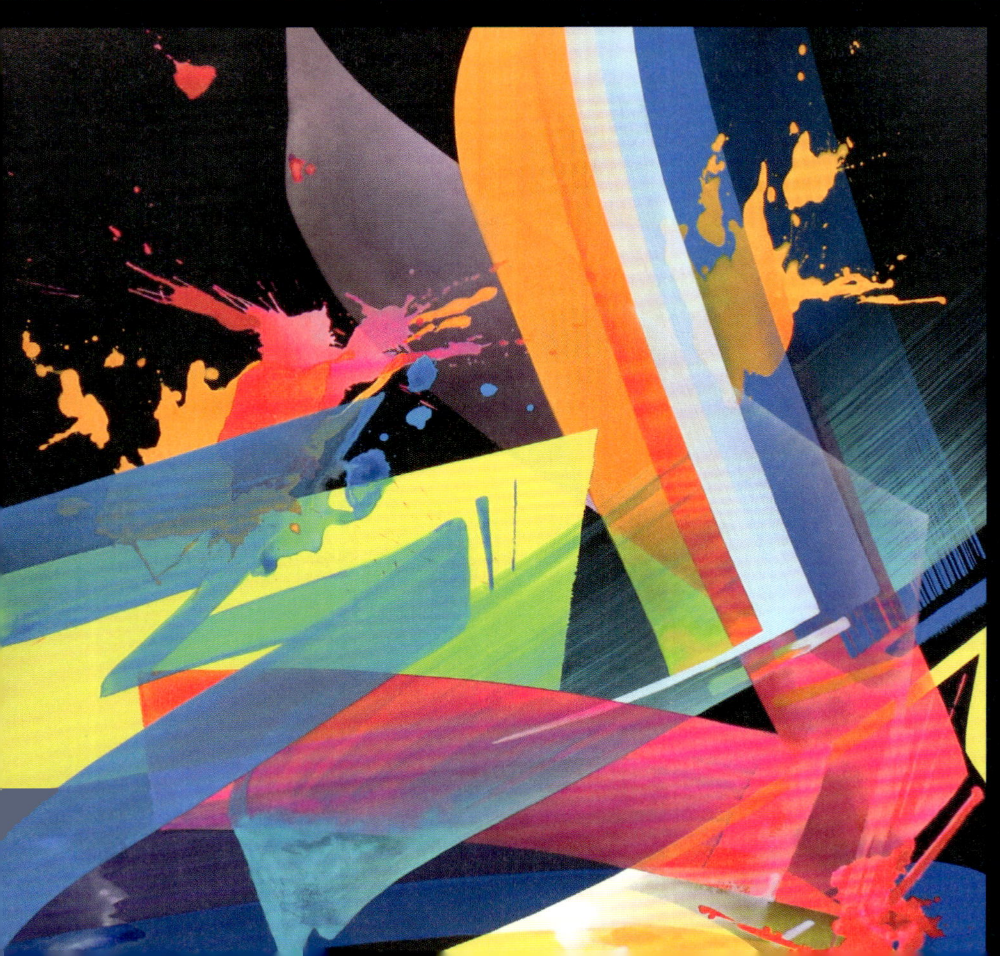

189 (top). *nineteen-forty-nine*, 100 x 180cm, acrylic and spray paint on canvas, 2013
190 (bottom). *fourteen-thirty*, 120 x 120cm, acrylic, watercolour and spray paint on canvas, 2013
191 (opposite). *sixteen-fourteen*, 150 x 120cm, acrylic and spray paint on canvas, 2013

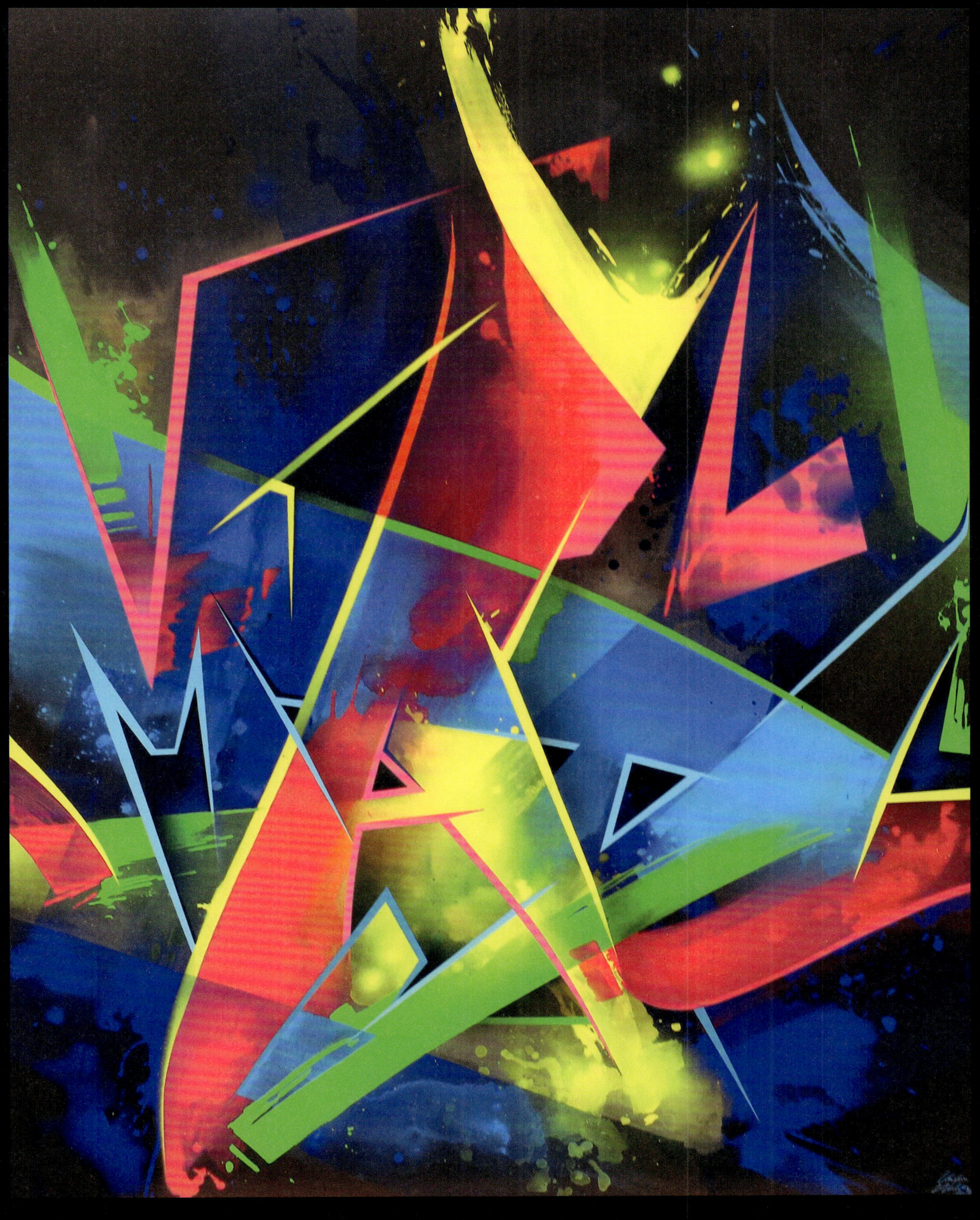

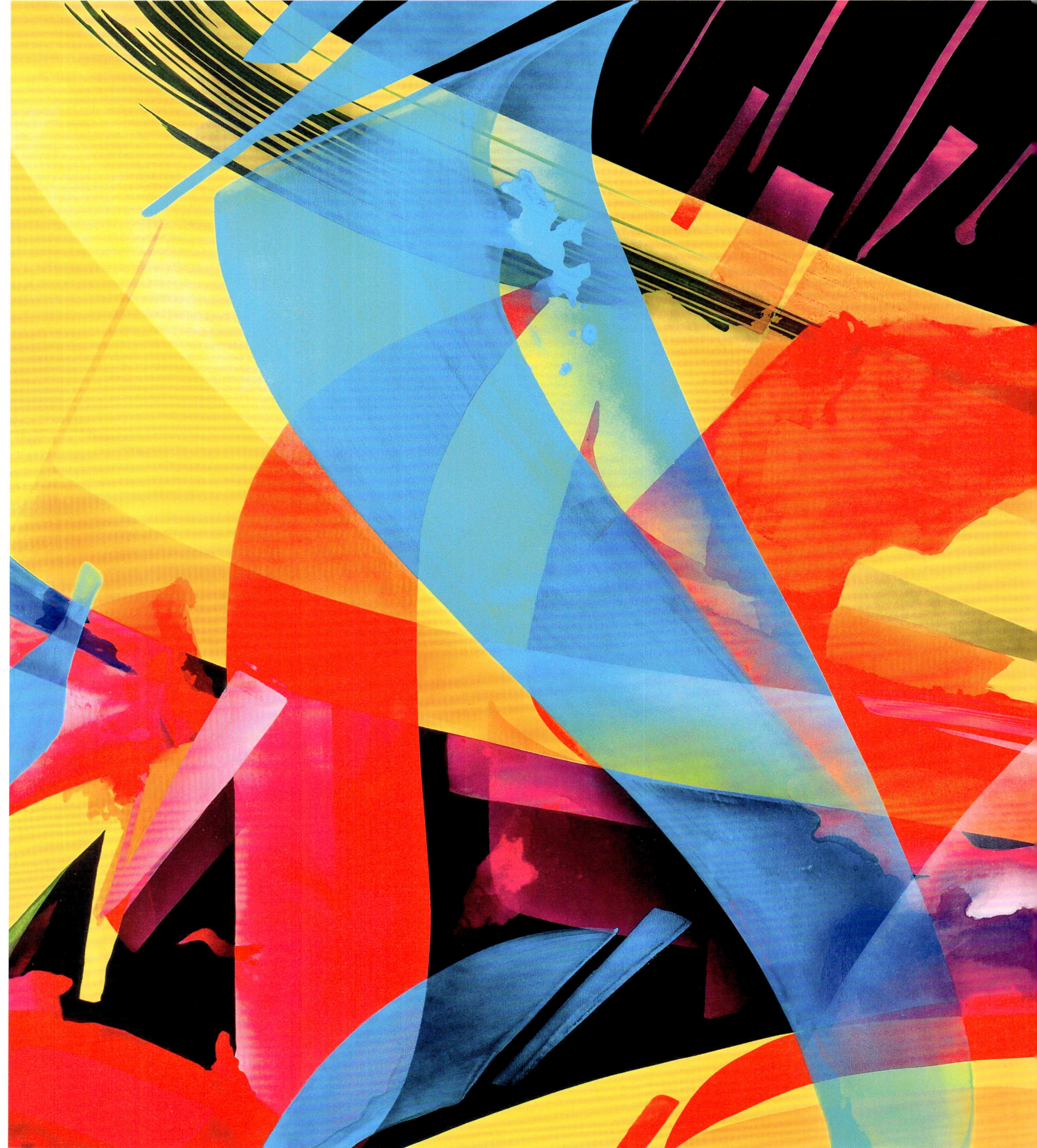

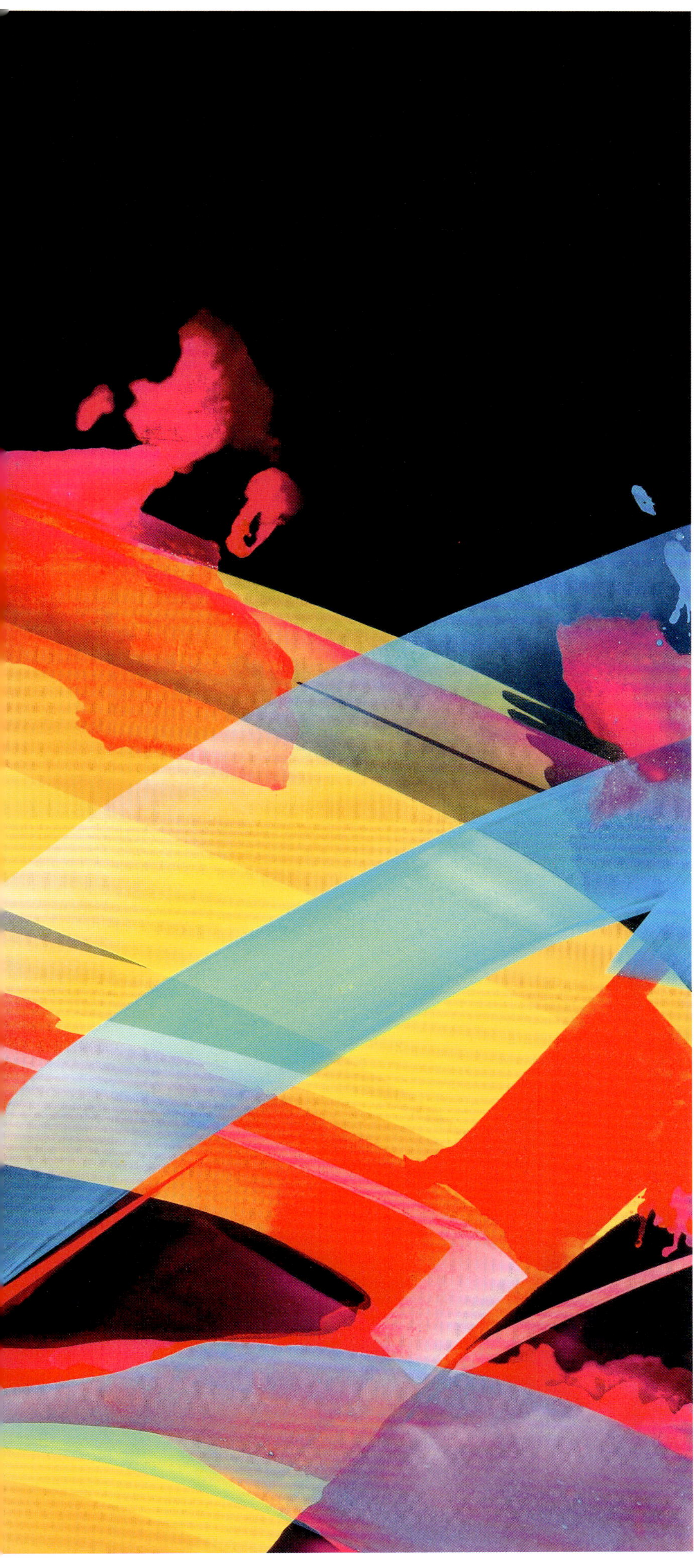

192. *eighteen-twenty*, 180 x 250cm, acrylic, watercolour and spray paint on canvas, 2014

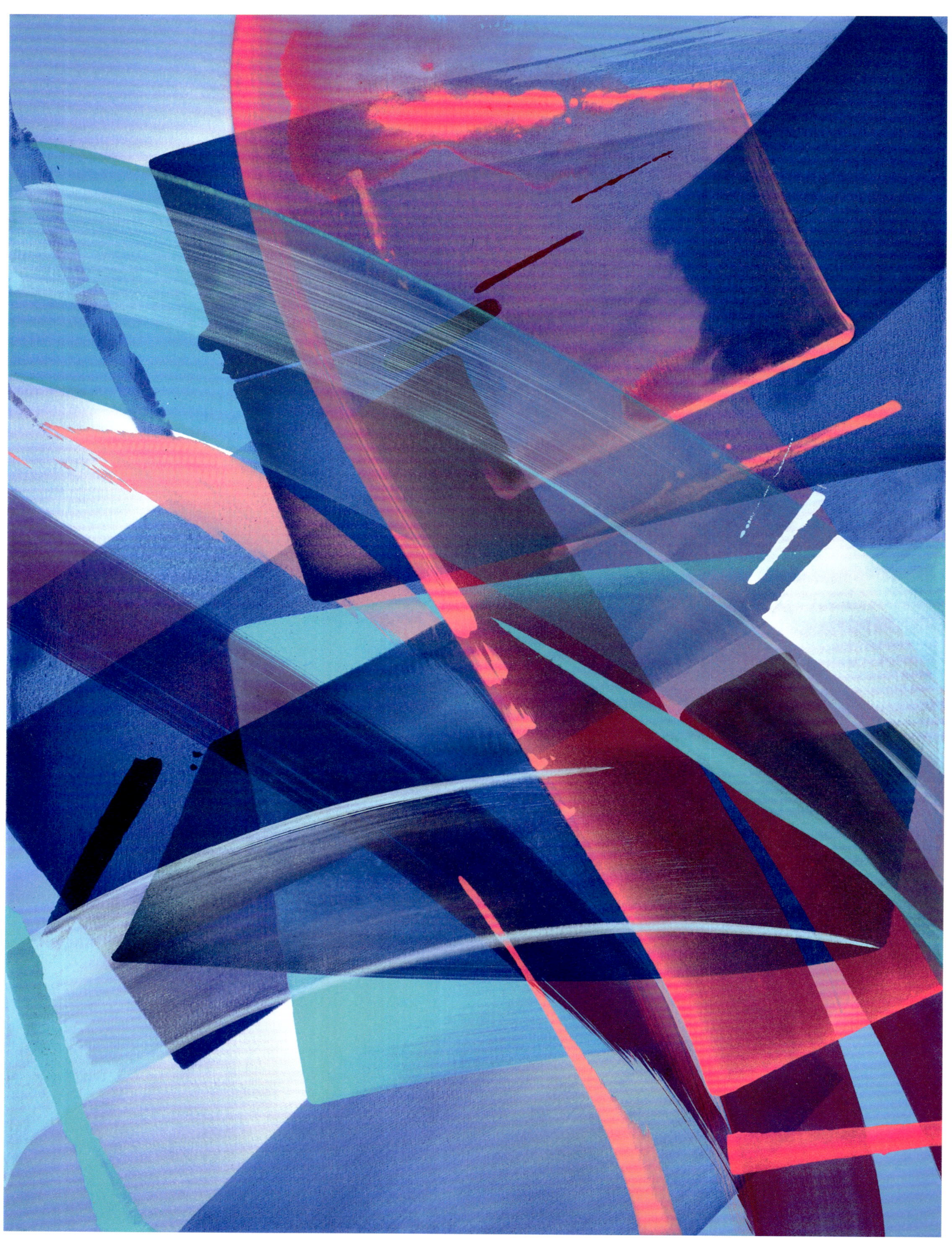

193. *10:54-25112017*, 80 x 60cm, acrylic, watercolour and spray paint on canvas, 2017

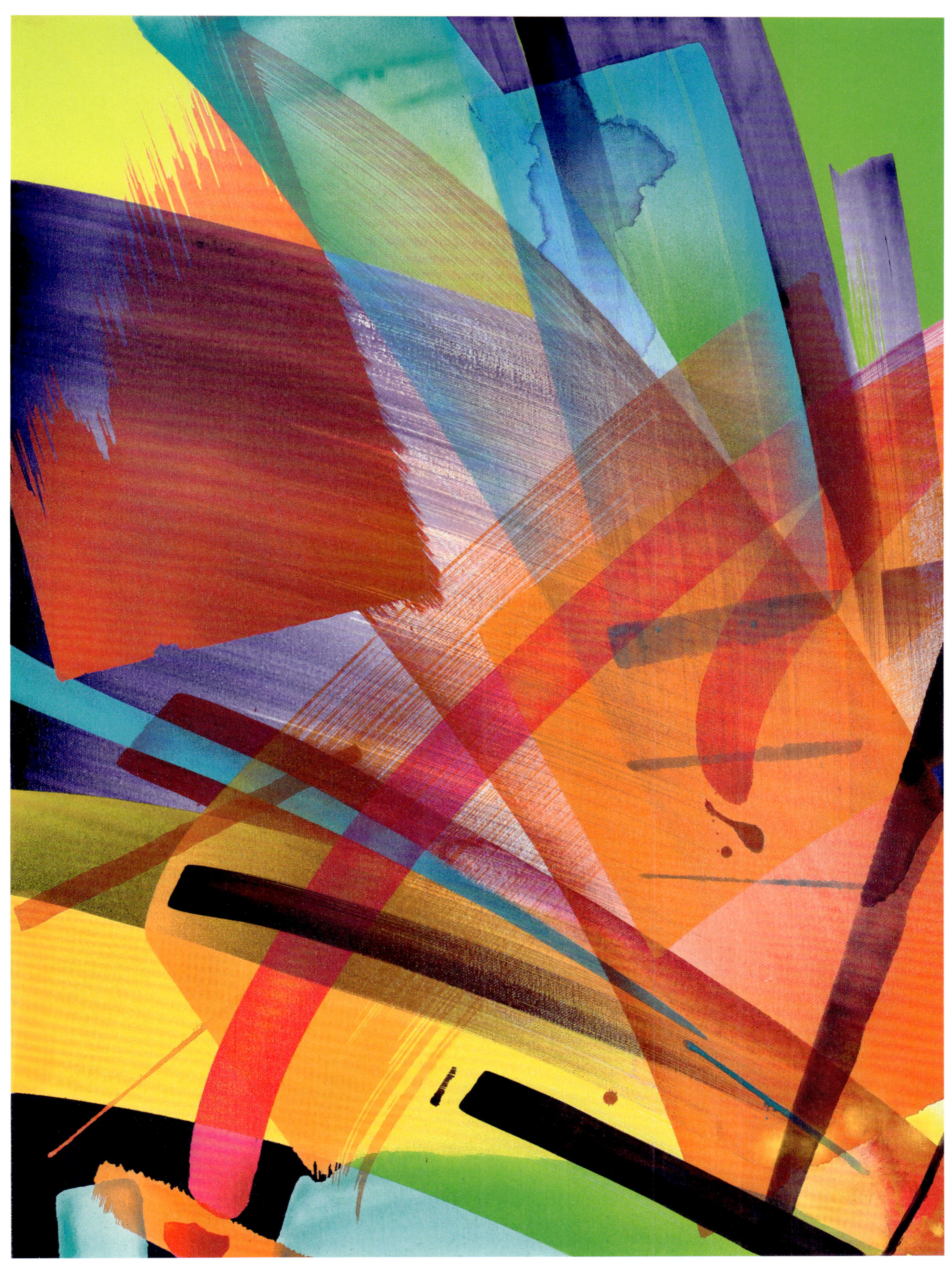

194. *13:56-26052017*, 80 x 60cm,
acrylic and spray paint on canvas, 2017

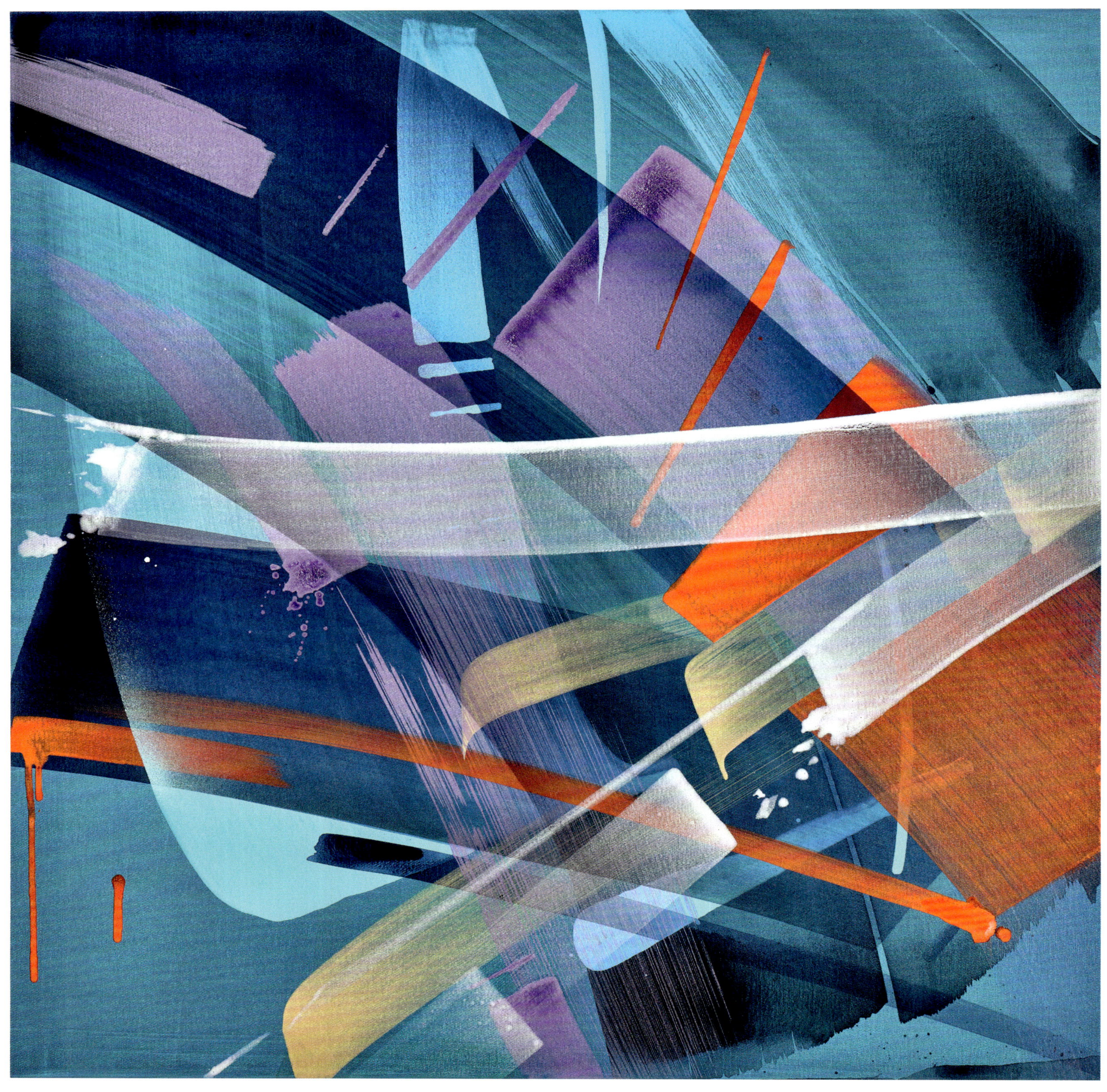

195. *12:53-19102017*, 80 x 80cm, acrylic and spray paint on canvas, 2017. Canvas was part of the show *Conquête Urbaine*, Musée des Beaux-Arts, Calais, France, 6 April–3 November 2019

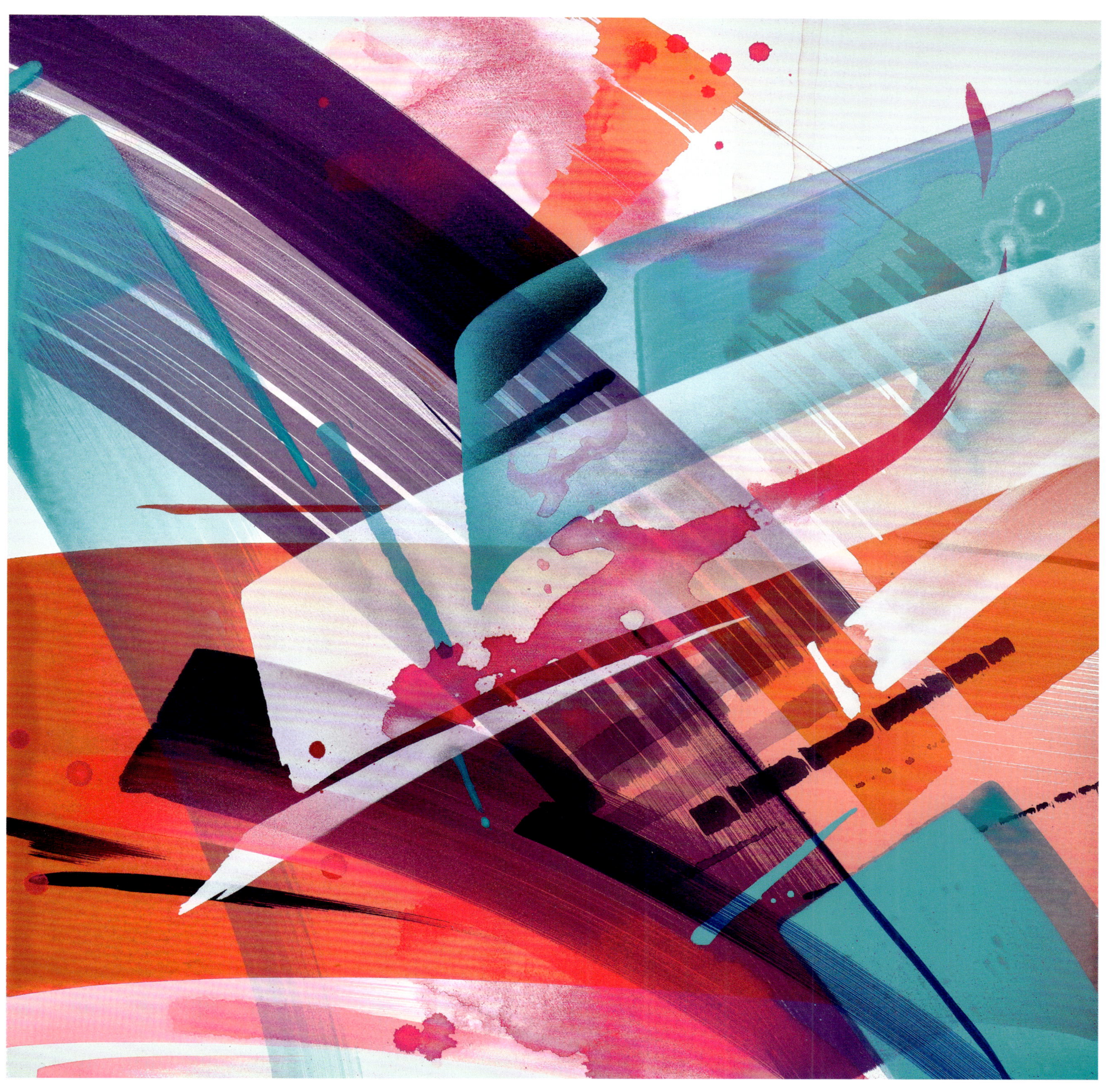

196. *11:14-29052017*, 60 x 60cm, acrylic, watercolour and spray paint on canvas, 2017

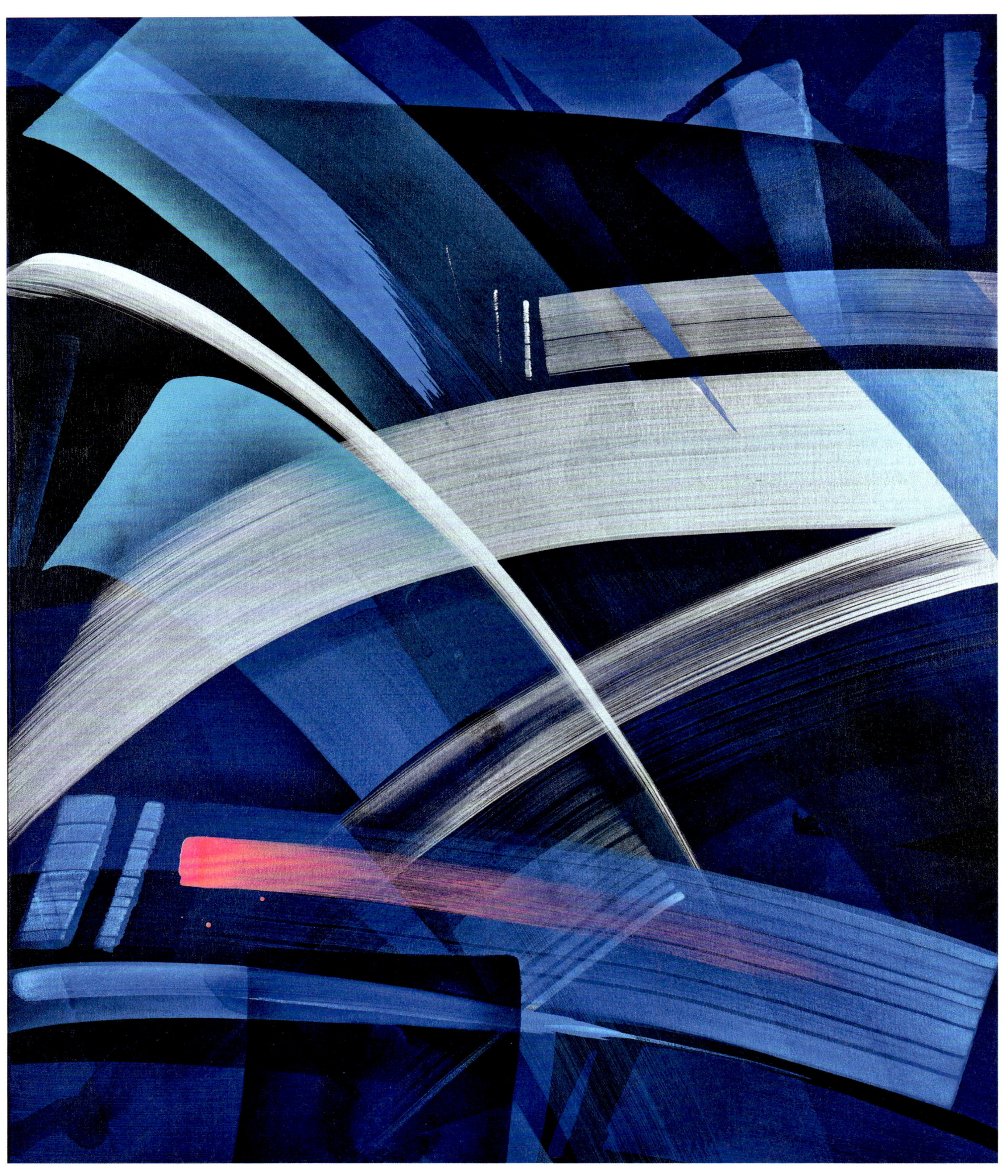

197. *20:12-25112017*, 120 x 100cm,
acrylic and spray paint on canvas, 2017

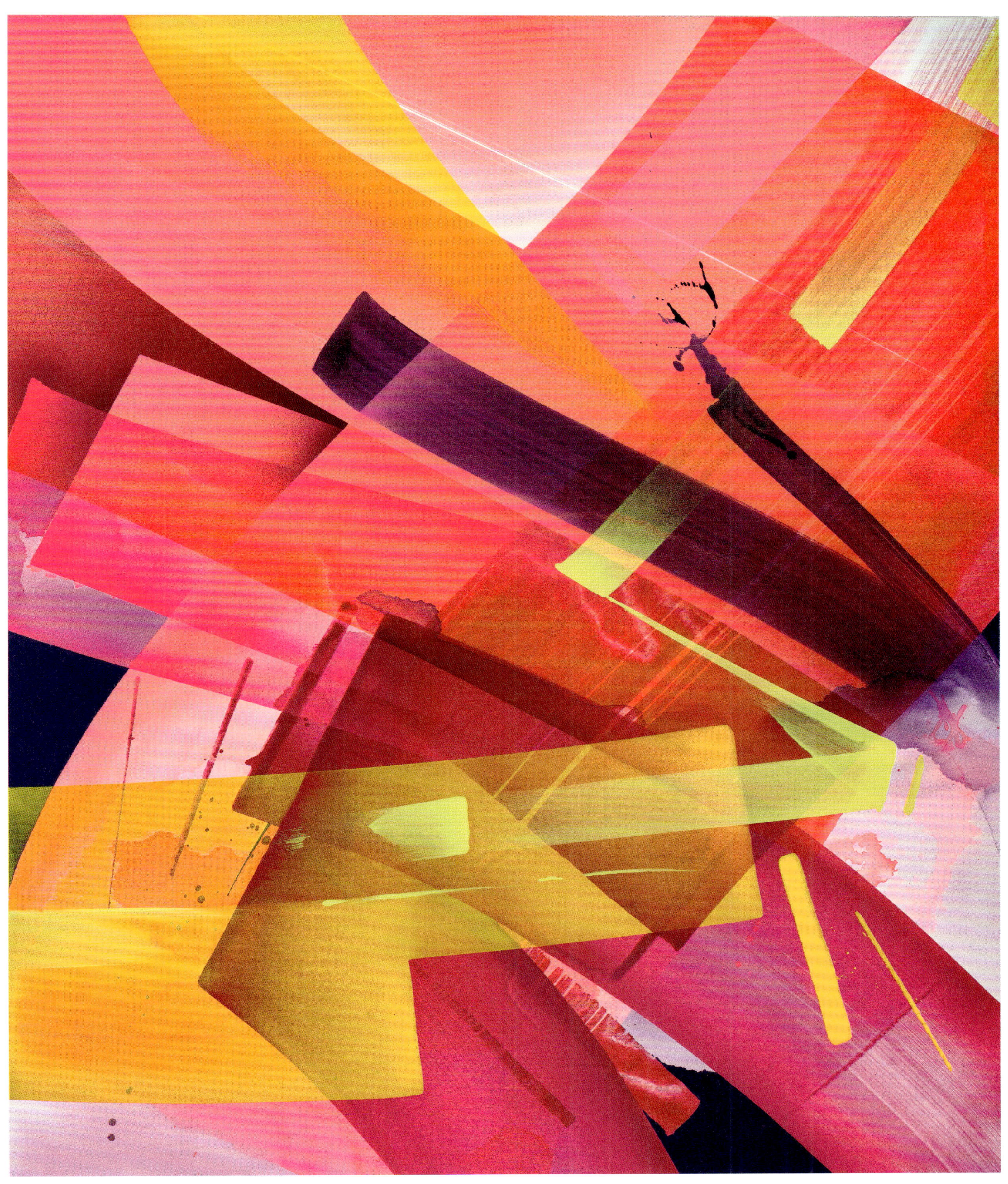

198. *09:40-22052017*, 120 x 100cm, acrylic, watercolour and spray paint on canvas, 2017

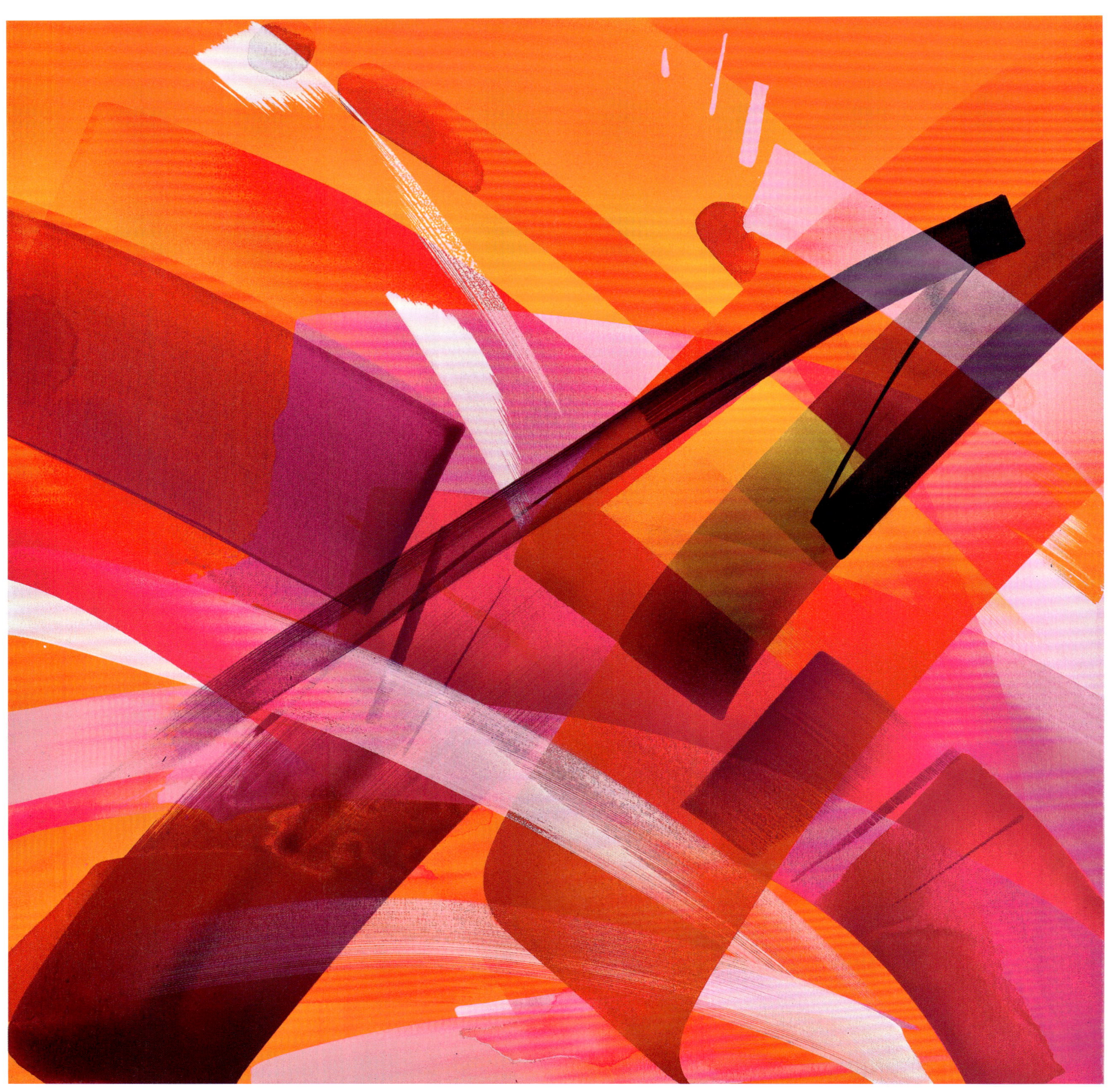

199. *17:18-21-03-17*, 100 x 100cm,
acrylic and spray paint on canvas, 2017

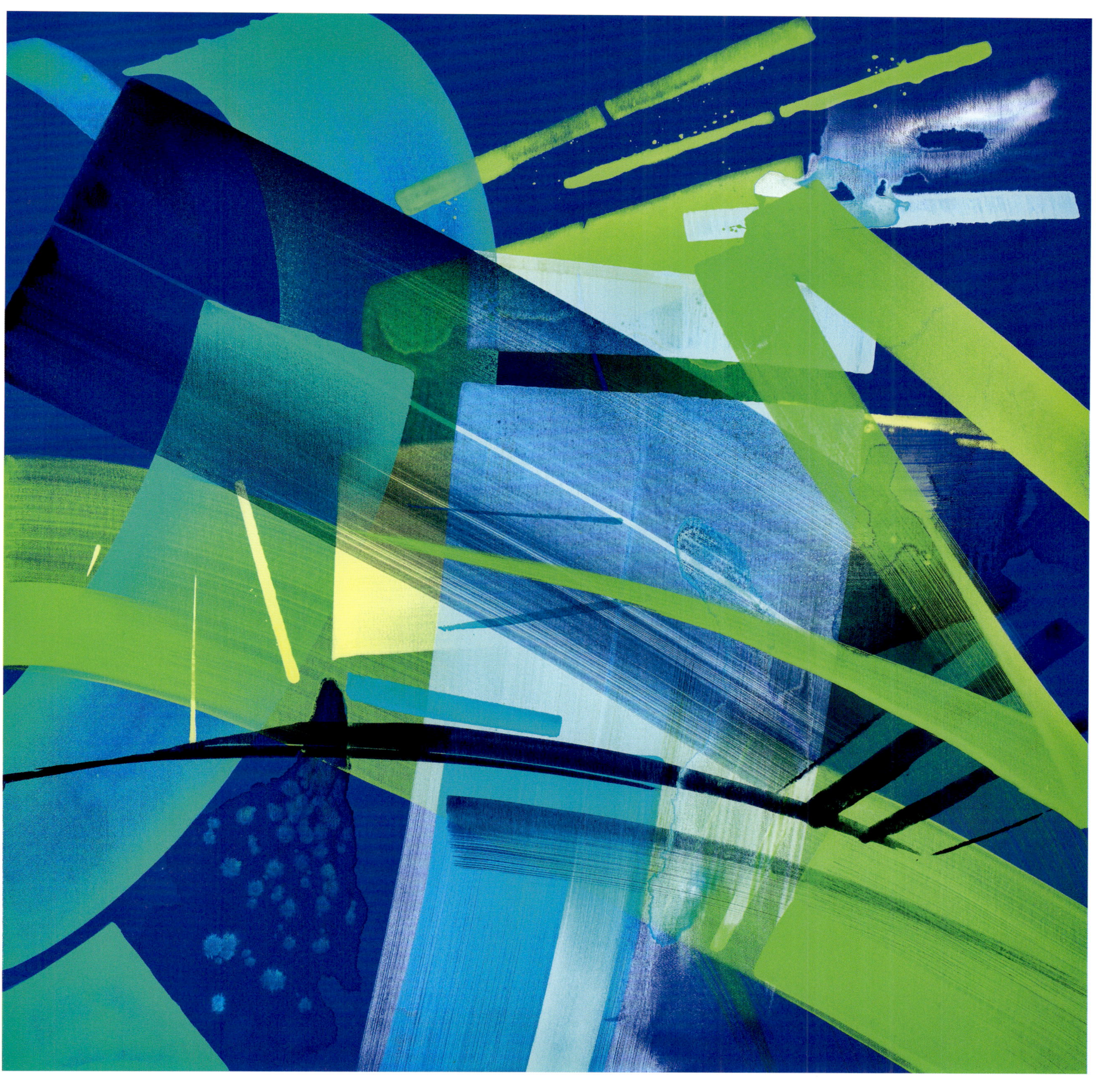

200. *15:28 2017-10-04*, 100 x 100cm,
acrylic and spray paint on canvas, 2017

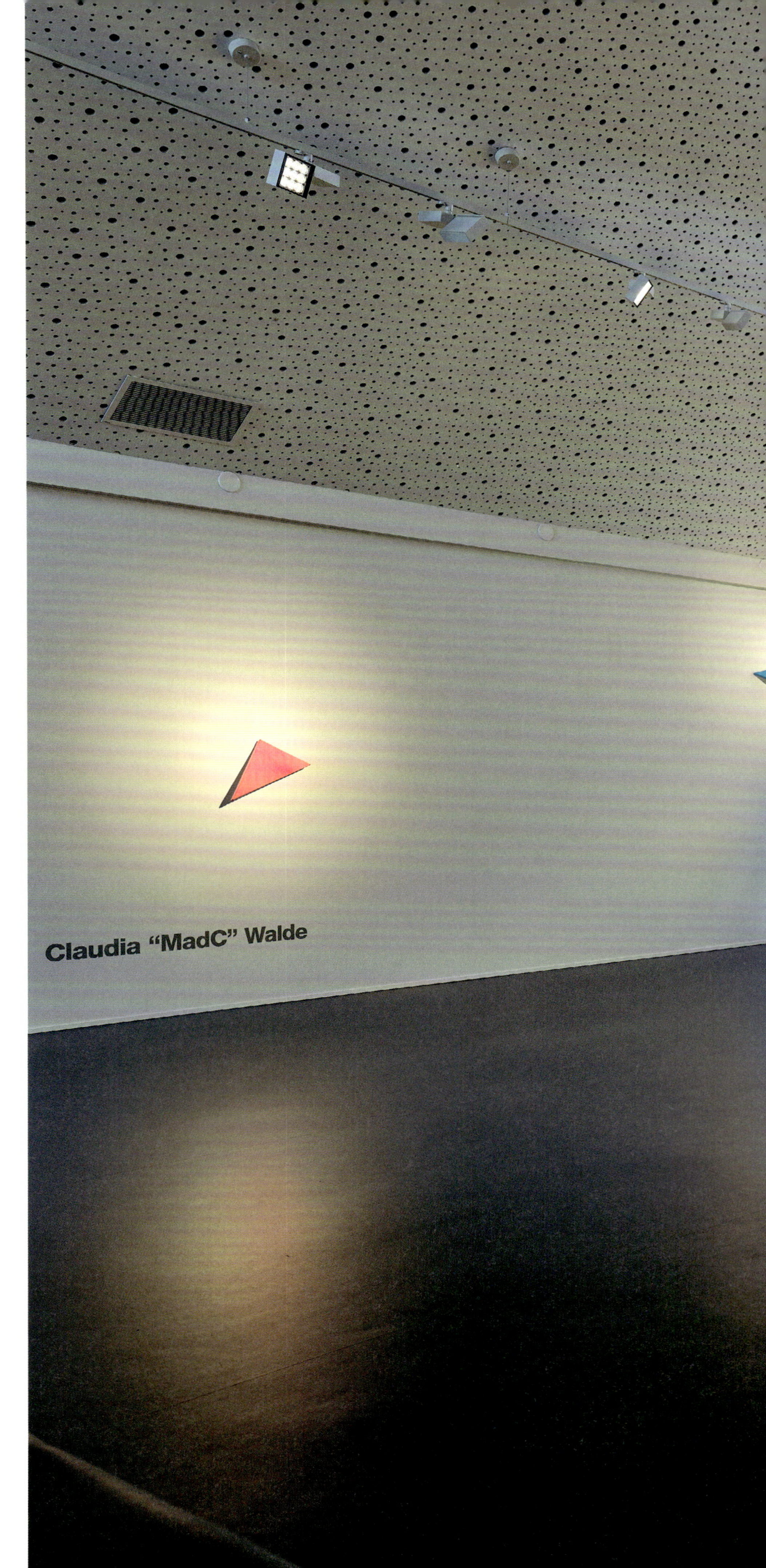

201. *For the Love of Freedom*, group show at Art and Museum Centre Sinkka, Kerava, Finland, 5 August–29 October 2017

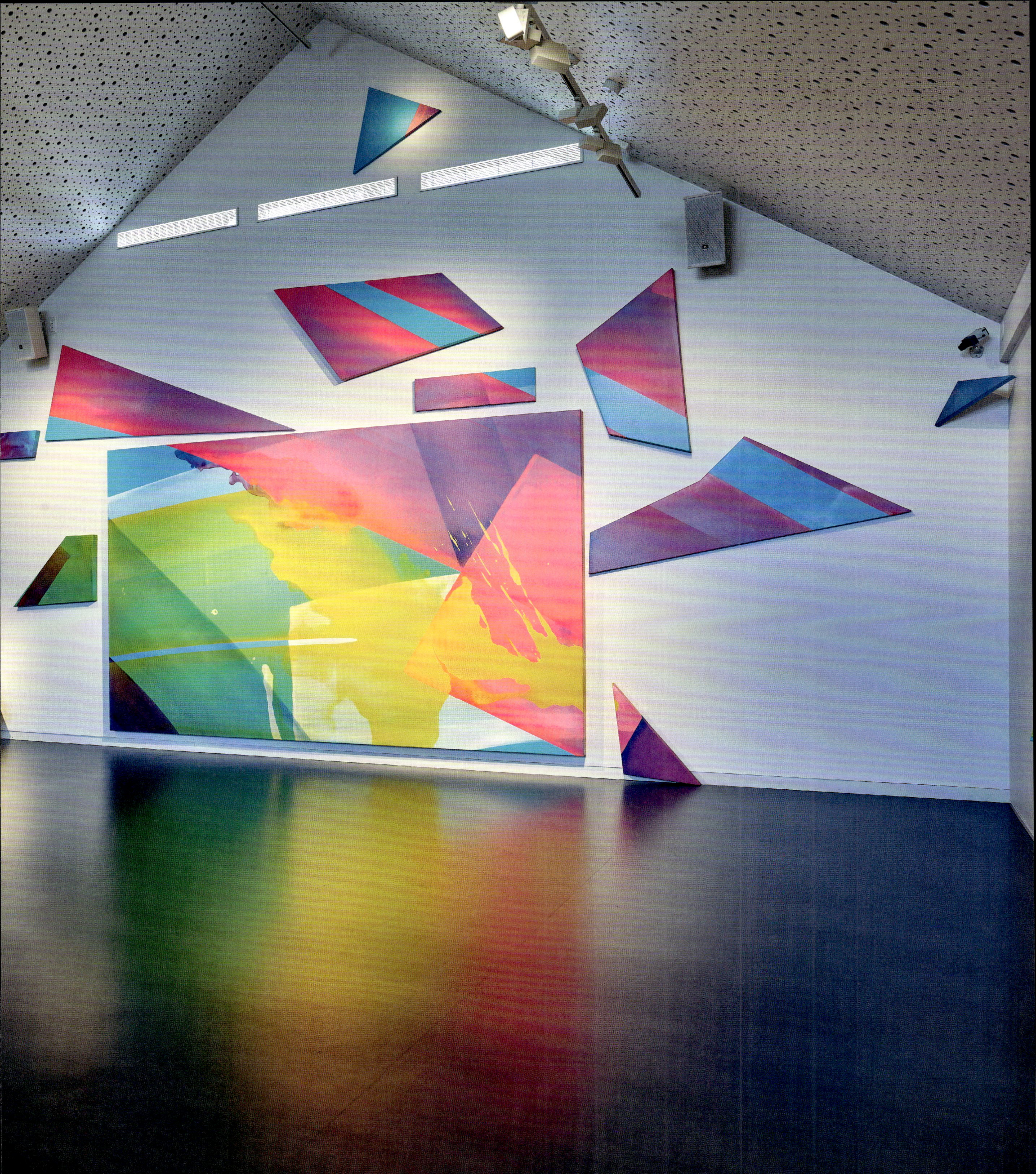

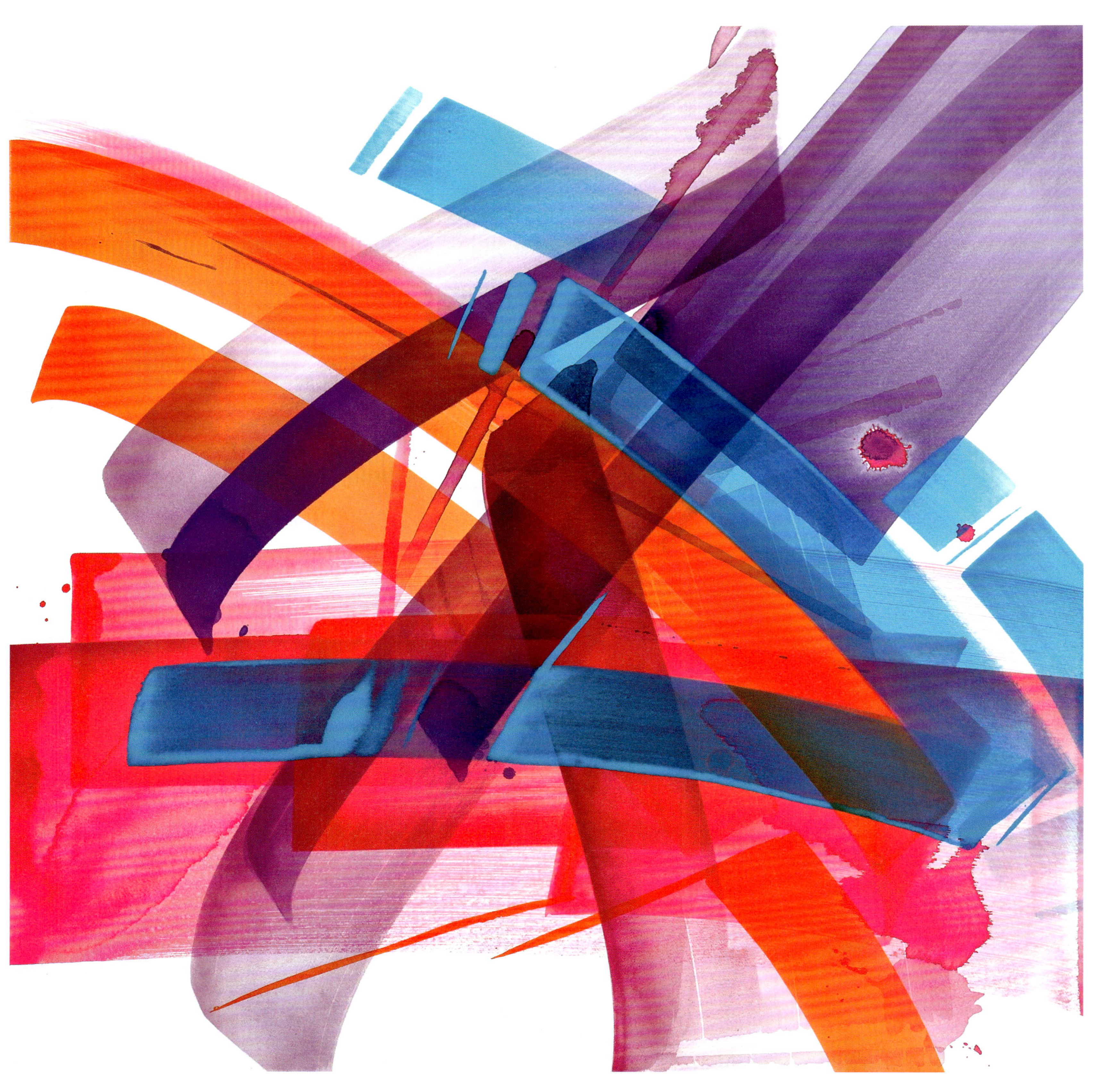

202. *12-39*, 80 x 80cm, acrylic, watercolour and spray paint on canvas, 2015

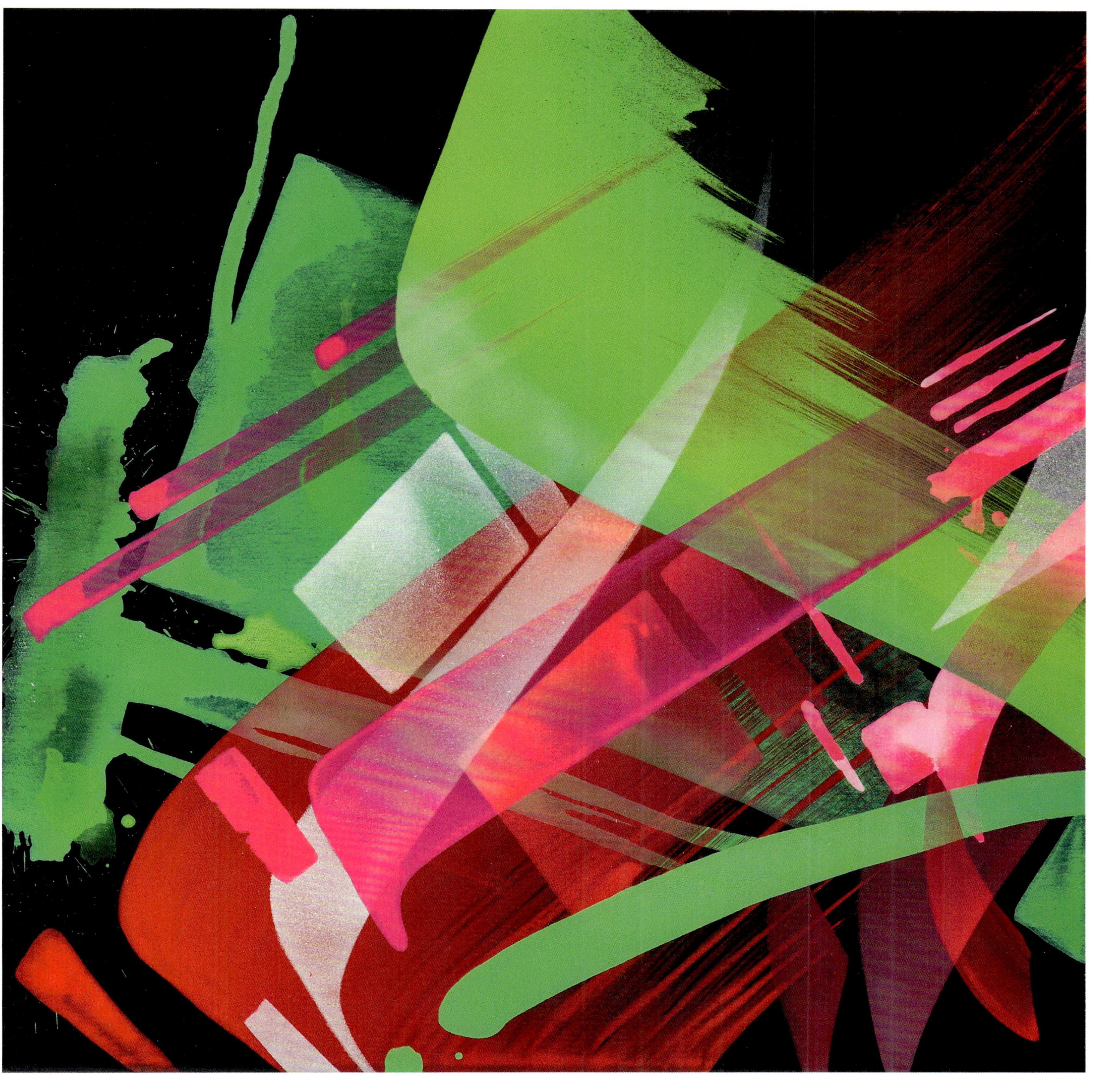

203. *10-20*, 60 x 60cm, acrylic, watercolour and spray paint on canvas, 2015

204 (next spread). *15-35*, 120 x 220cm, acrylic, watercolour and spray paint on canvas, 2015

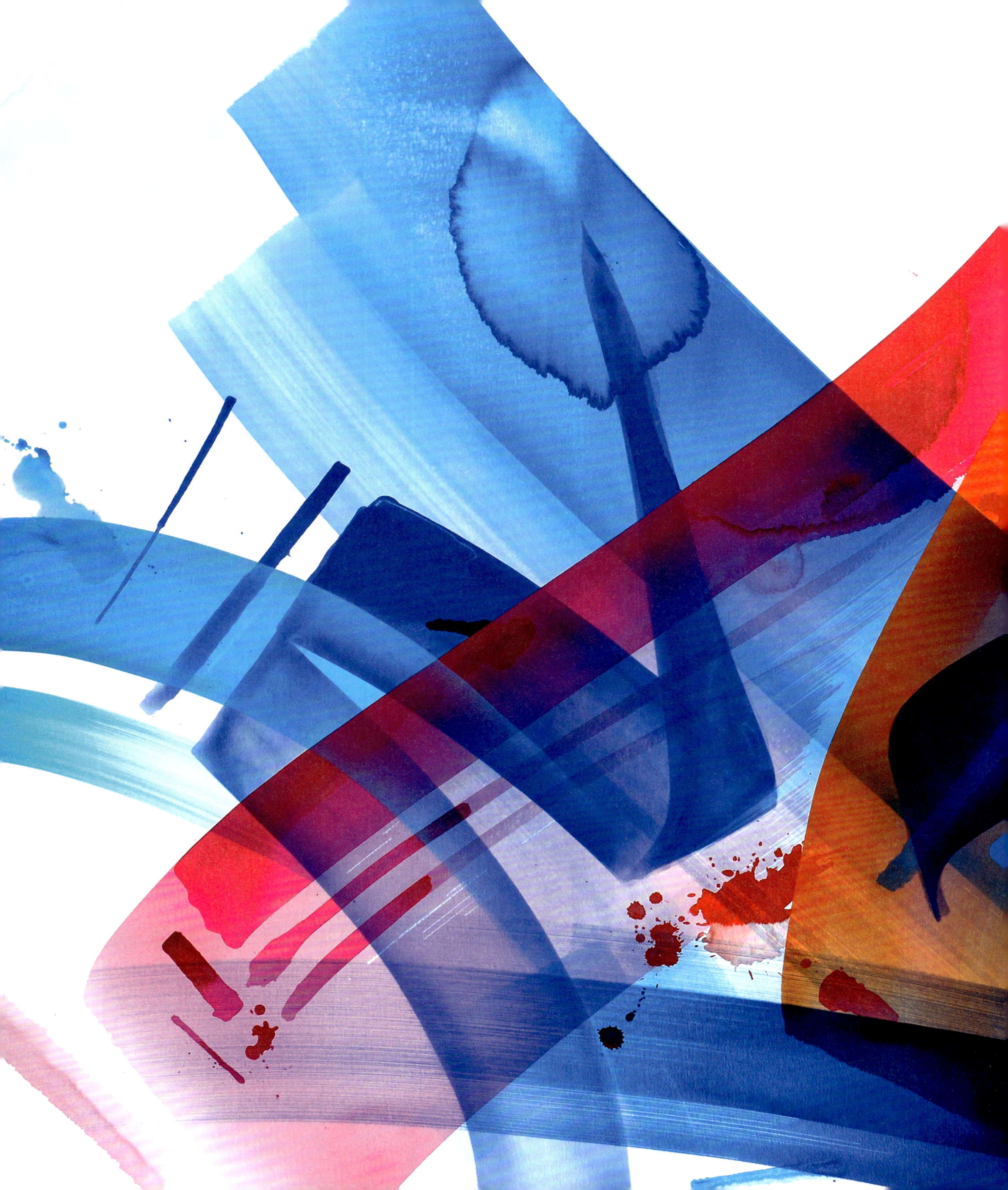

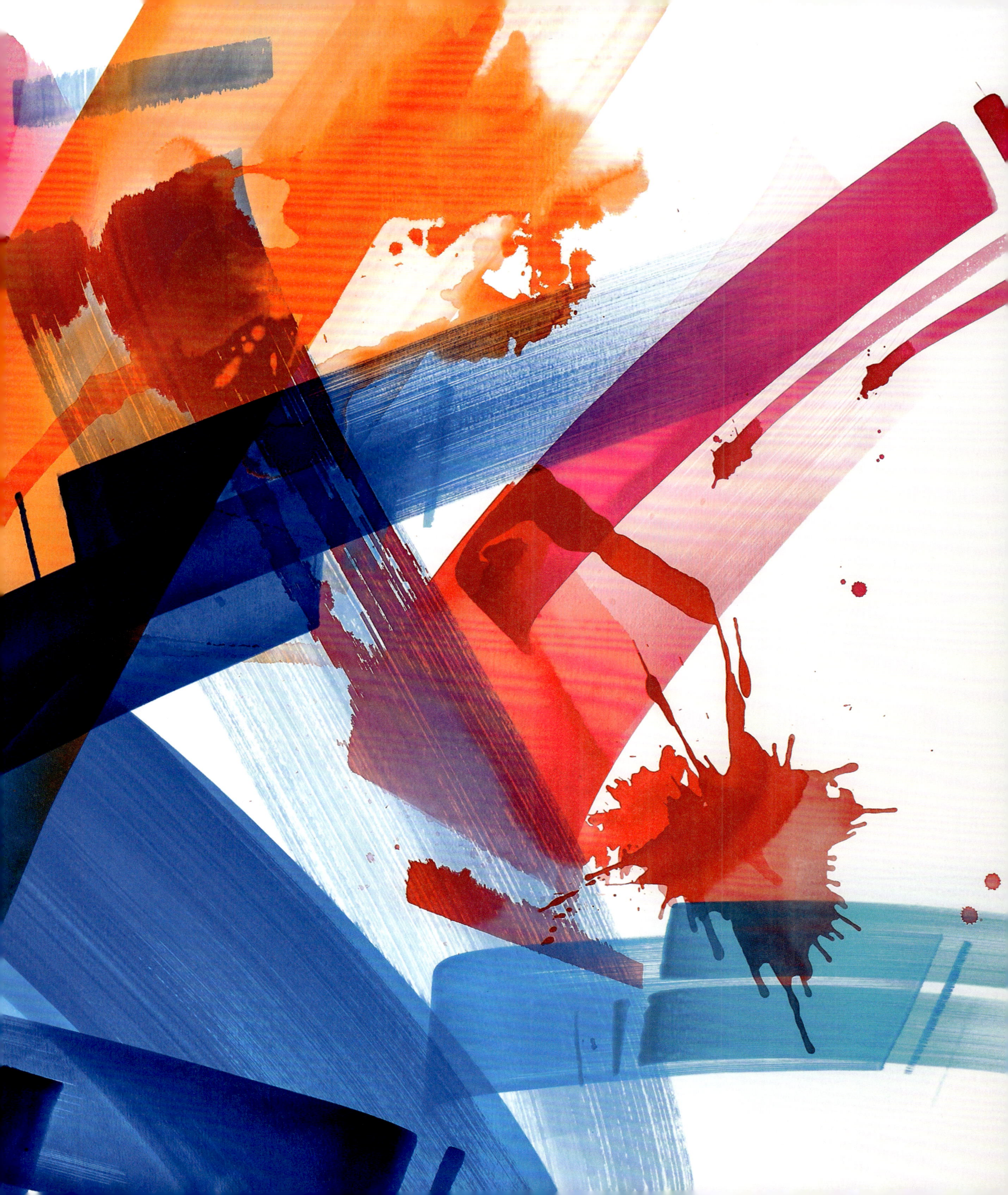

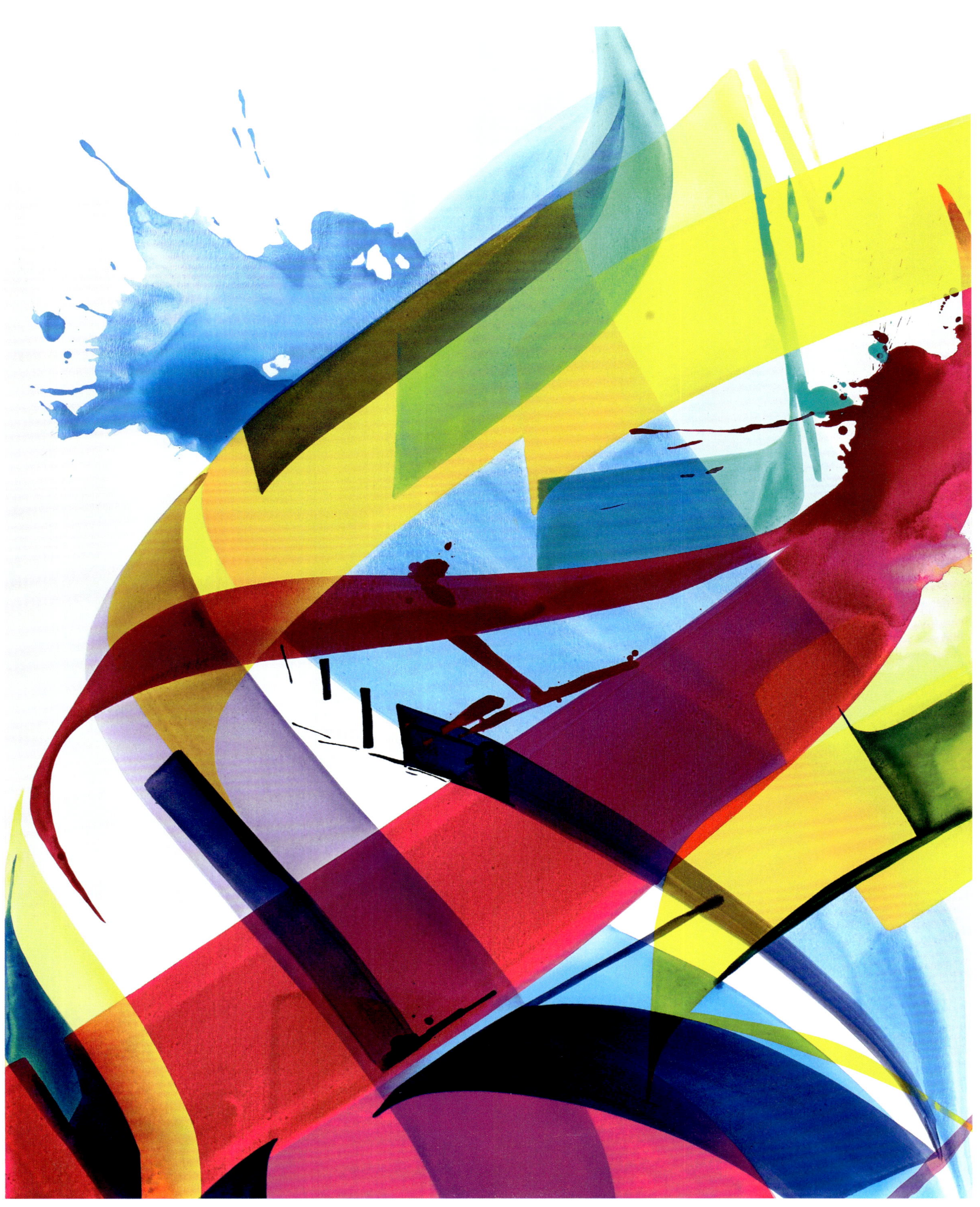

205. *nine-forty-nine*, 162 x 130cm, acrylic, watercolour and spray paint on canvas, 2014

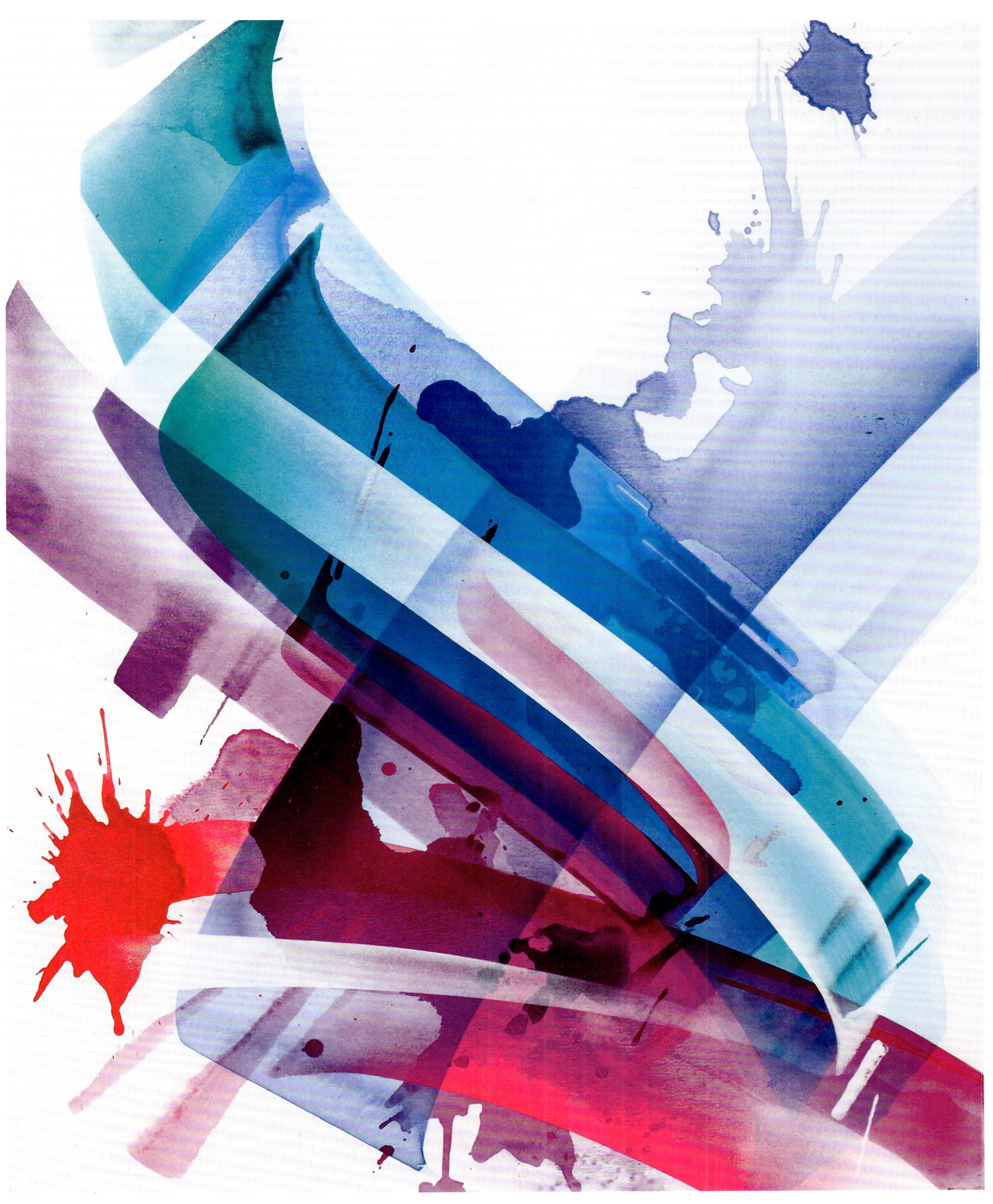

206. *18-32*, 100 x 81cm, acrylic, watercolour and spray paint on canvas, 2014

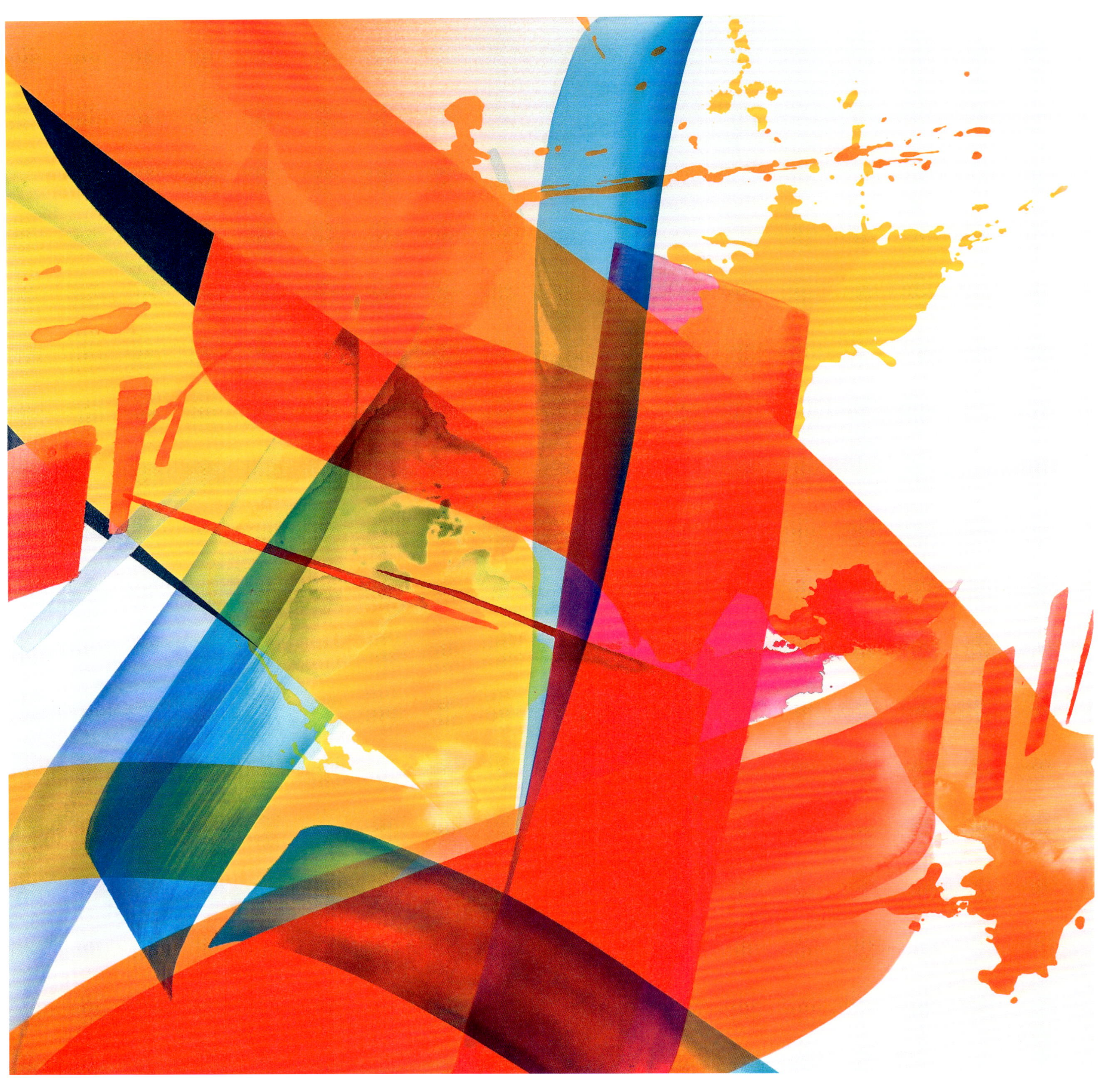

207. *eighteen-twenty-eight*, 120 x 120cm, acrylic, watercolour and spray paint on canvas, 2014

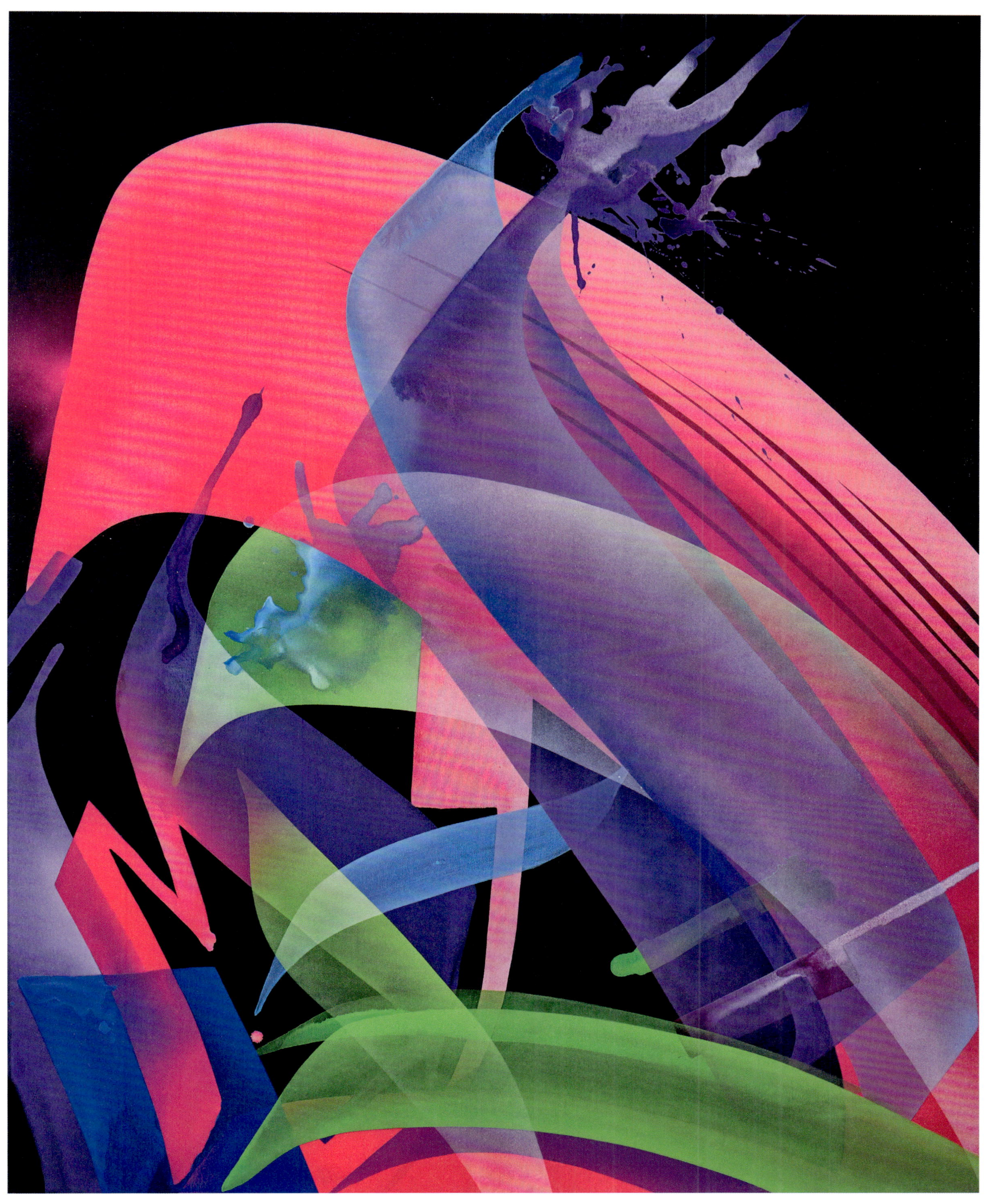

208. *thirteen-sixteen*, 162 x 130cm, acrylic, watercolour and spray paint on canvas, 2014

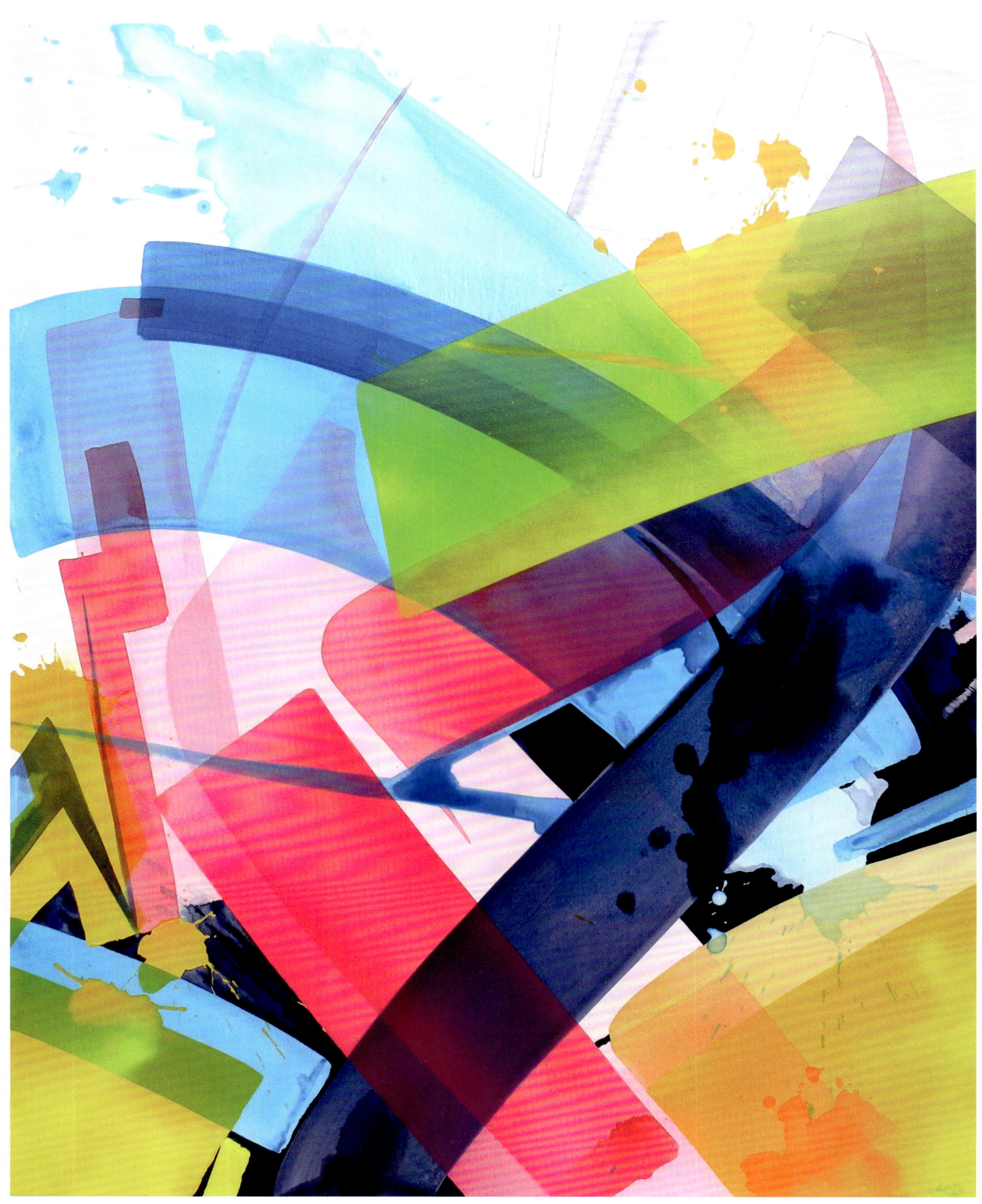

209. *nineteen-seven*, 100 x 81cm, acrylic, watercolour and spray paint on canvas, 2013. This canvas was used for the Art Rock festival, Saint-Brieuc, France, 13–15 May 2016

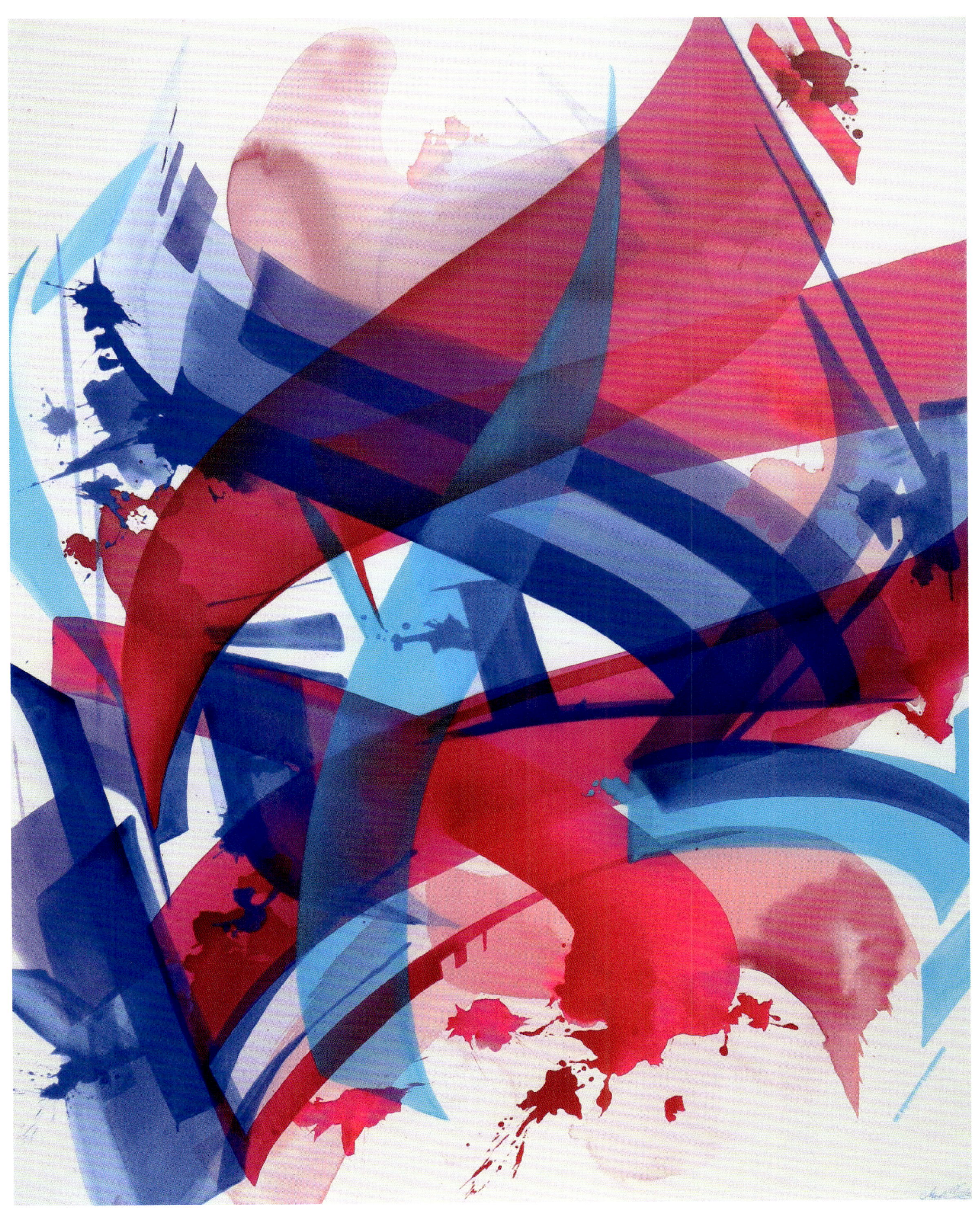

210. *twelve-thirty-one*, 150 x 120cm, acrylic, watercolour and spray paint on canvas, 2013

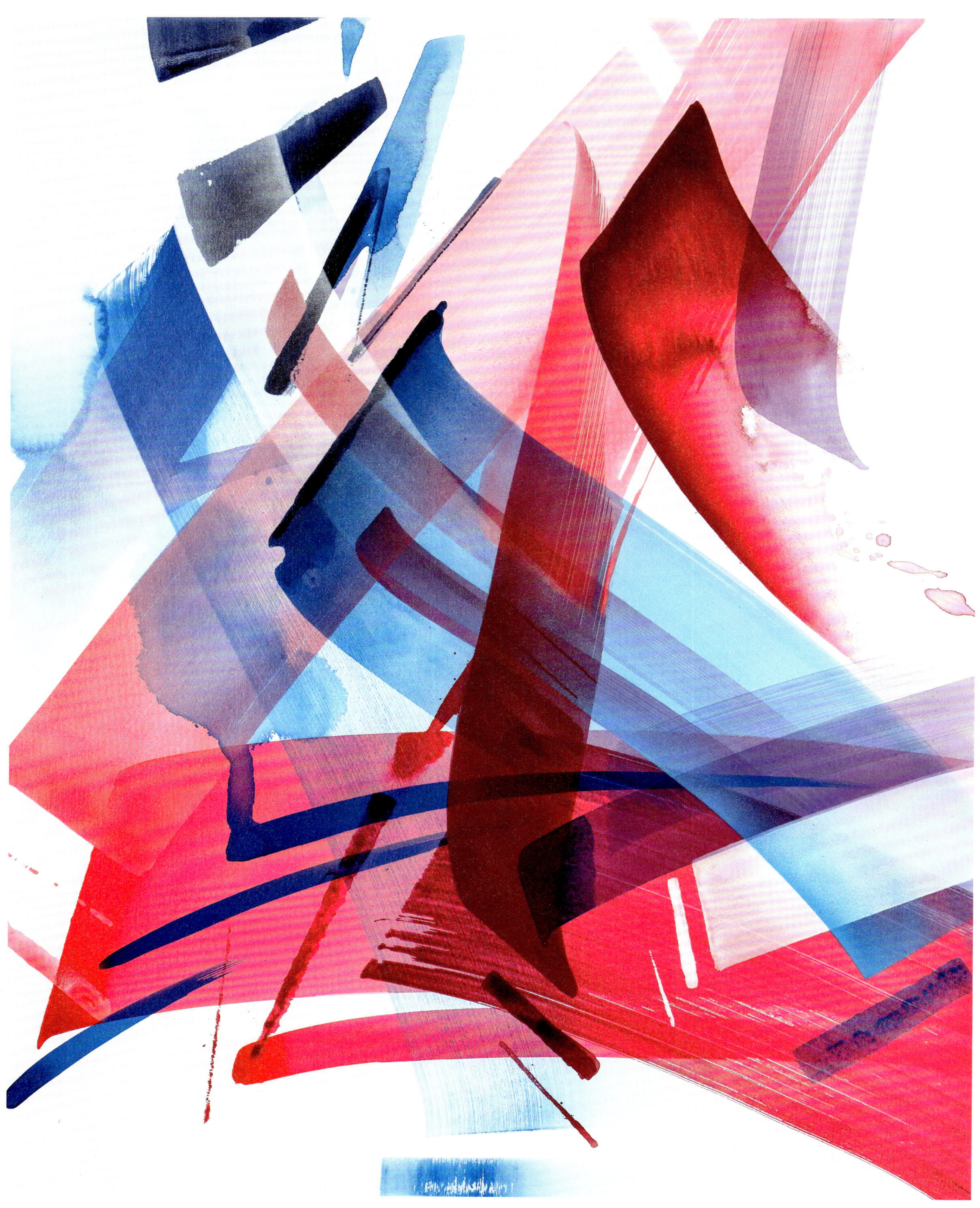

211. *10-11*, 100 x 81cm, acrylic, watercolour and spray paint on canvas, 2015

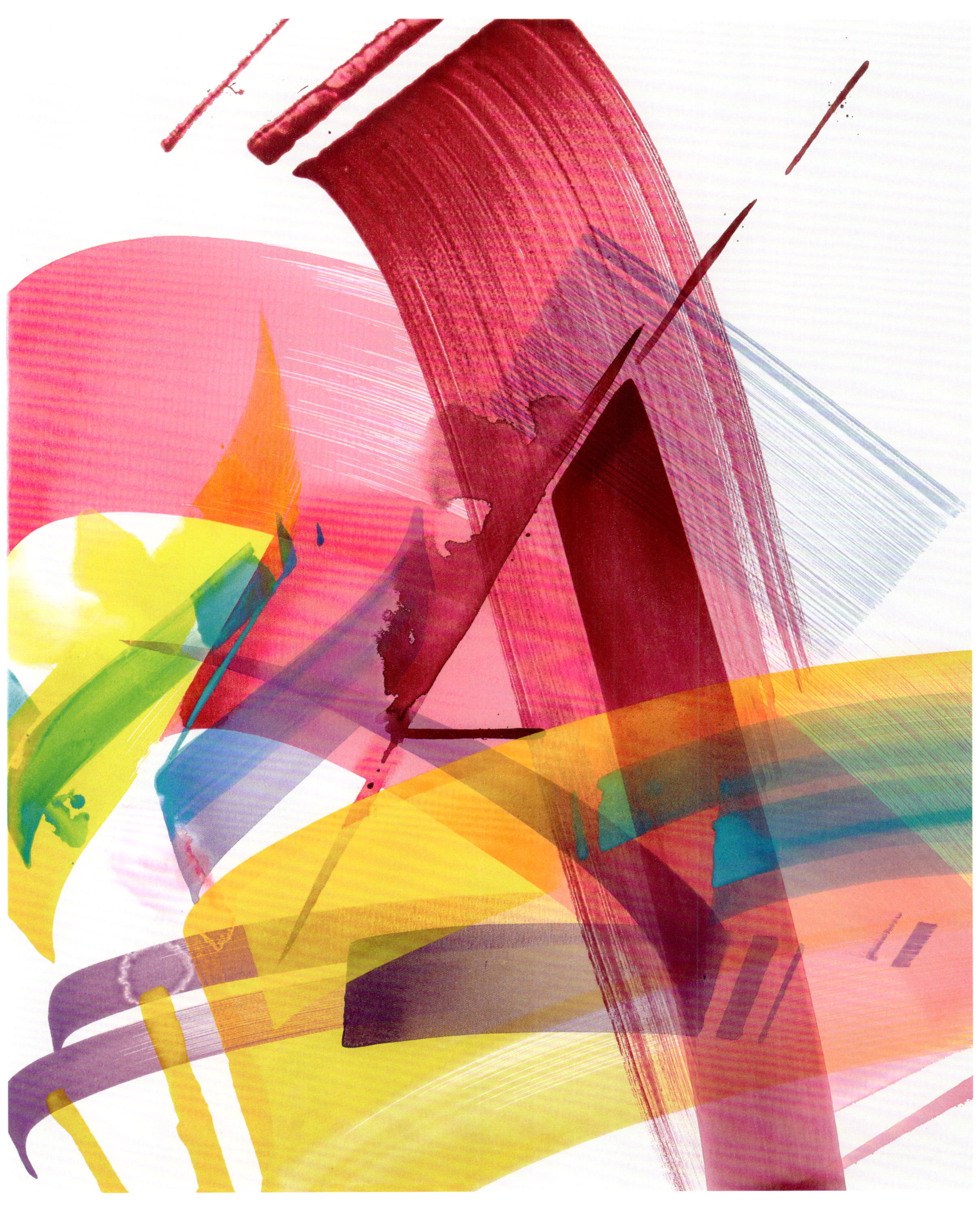

212. *1833-2015*, 100 x 81cm, acrylic, watercolour and spray paint on canvas, 2015

213 (next spread). Detail from *15:08-22042018*, 200 x 200cm, acrylic, watercolour and spray paint on canvas, 2018

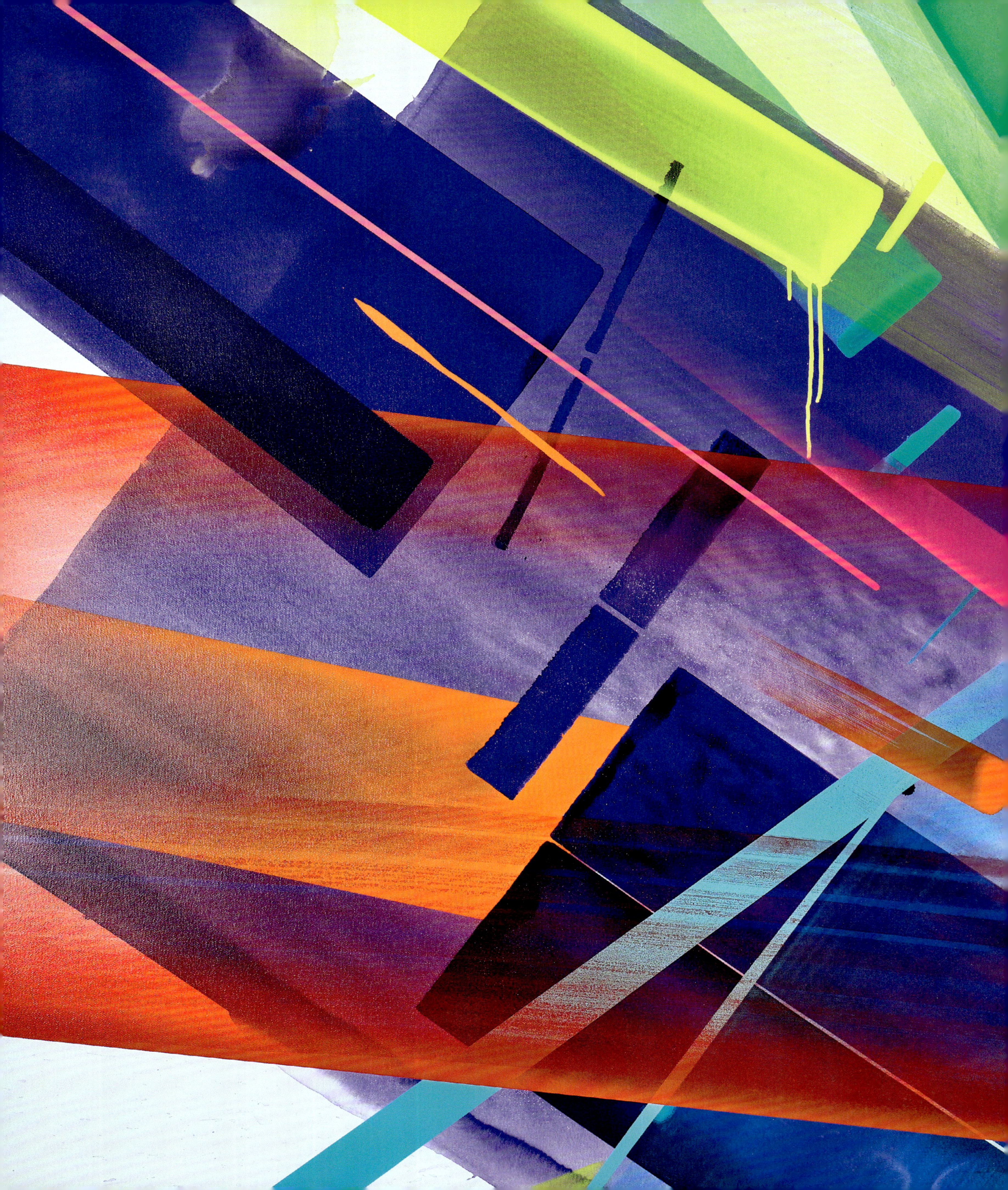

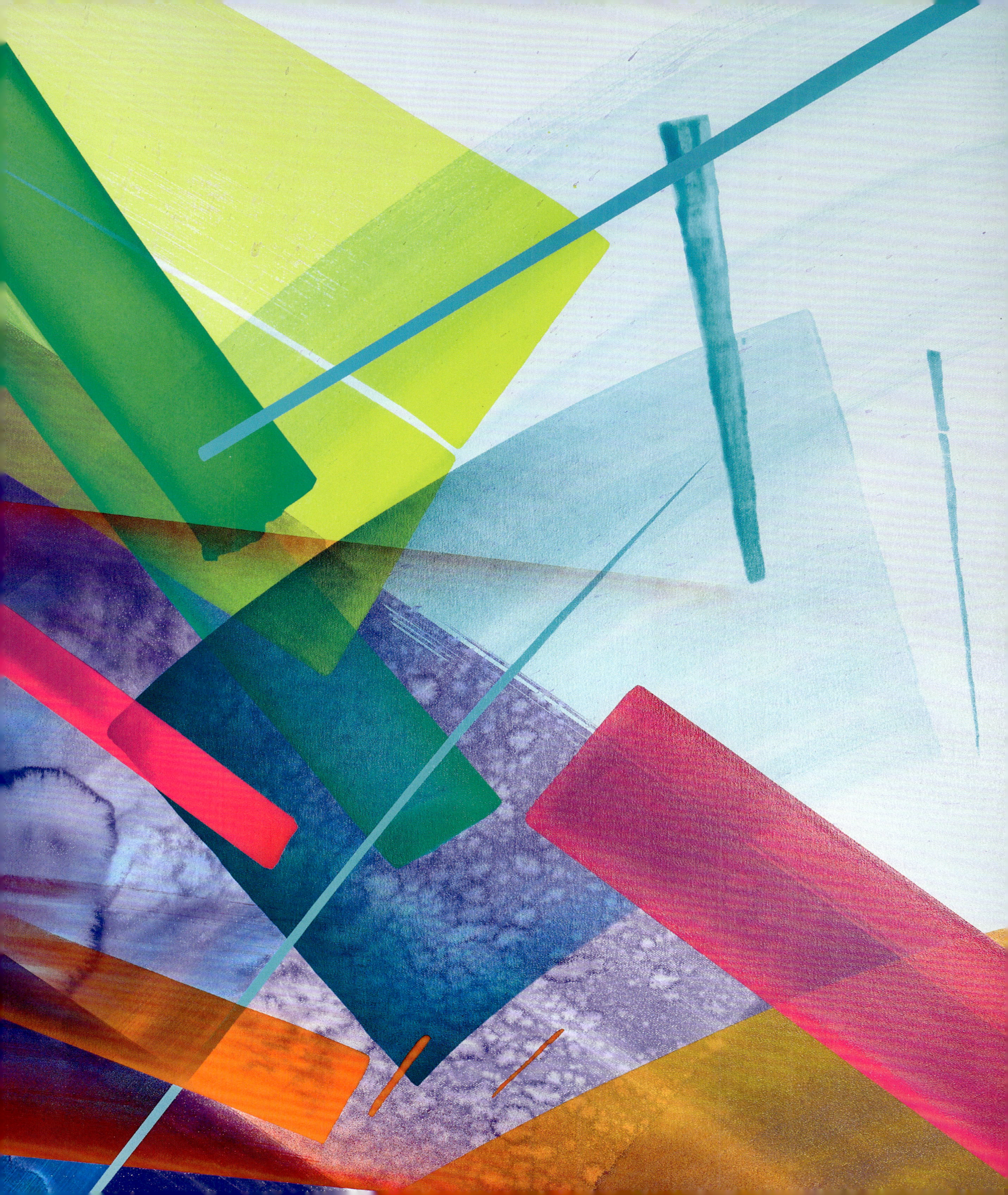

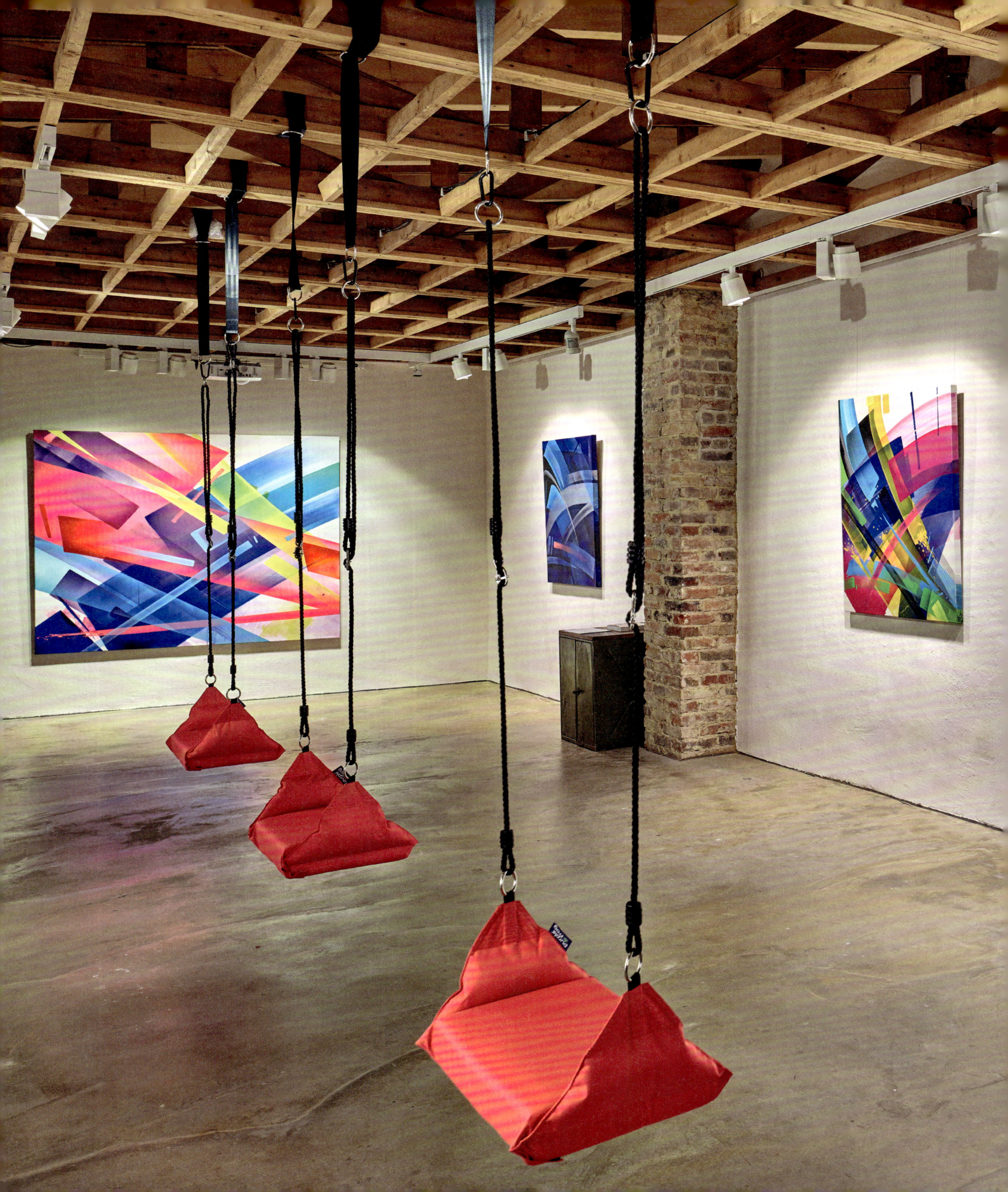

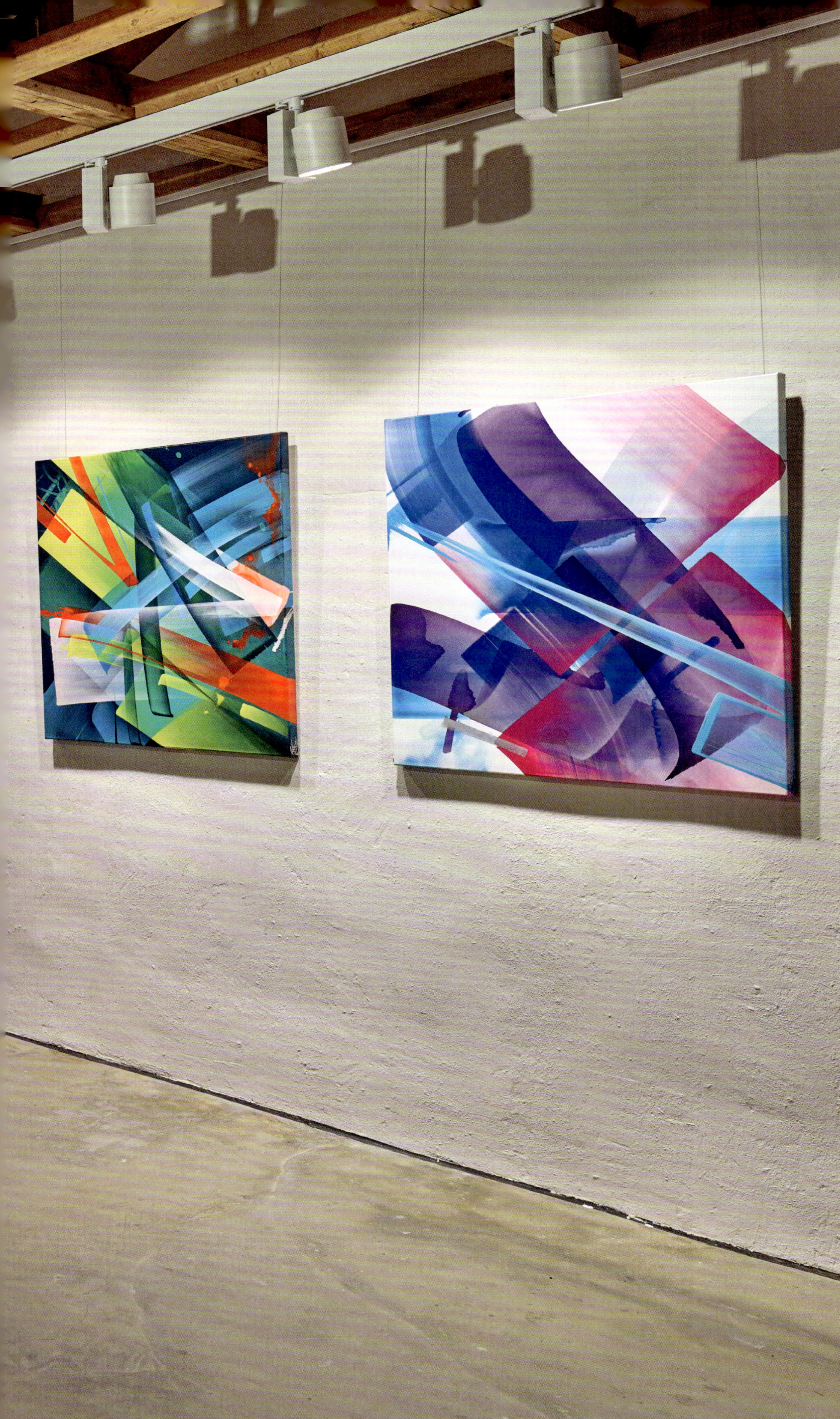

214. *Daydreaming*, solo show at 44309 Gallery, Dortmund, Germany, 13 January–24 February 2018

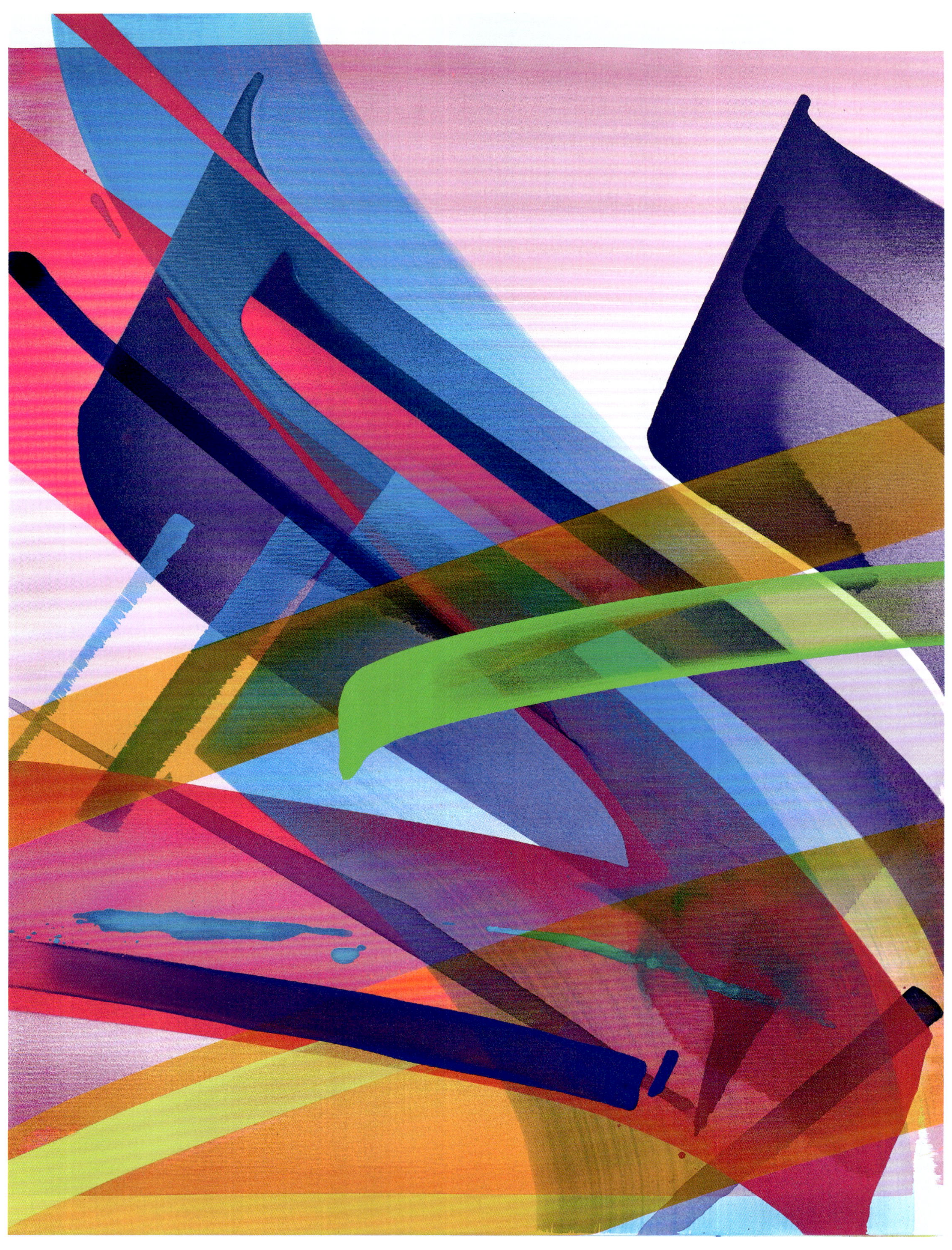

215. *12:35-03032018*, 80 x 60cm, acrylic, watercolour and spray paint on canvas, 2018

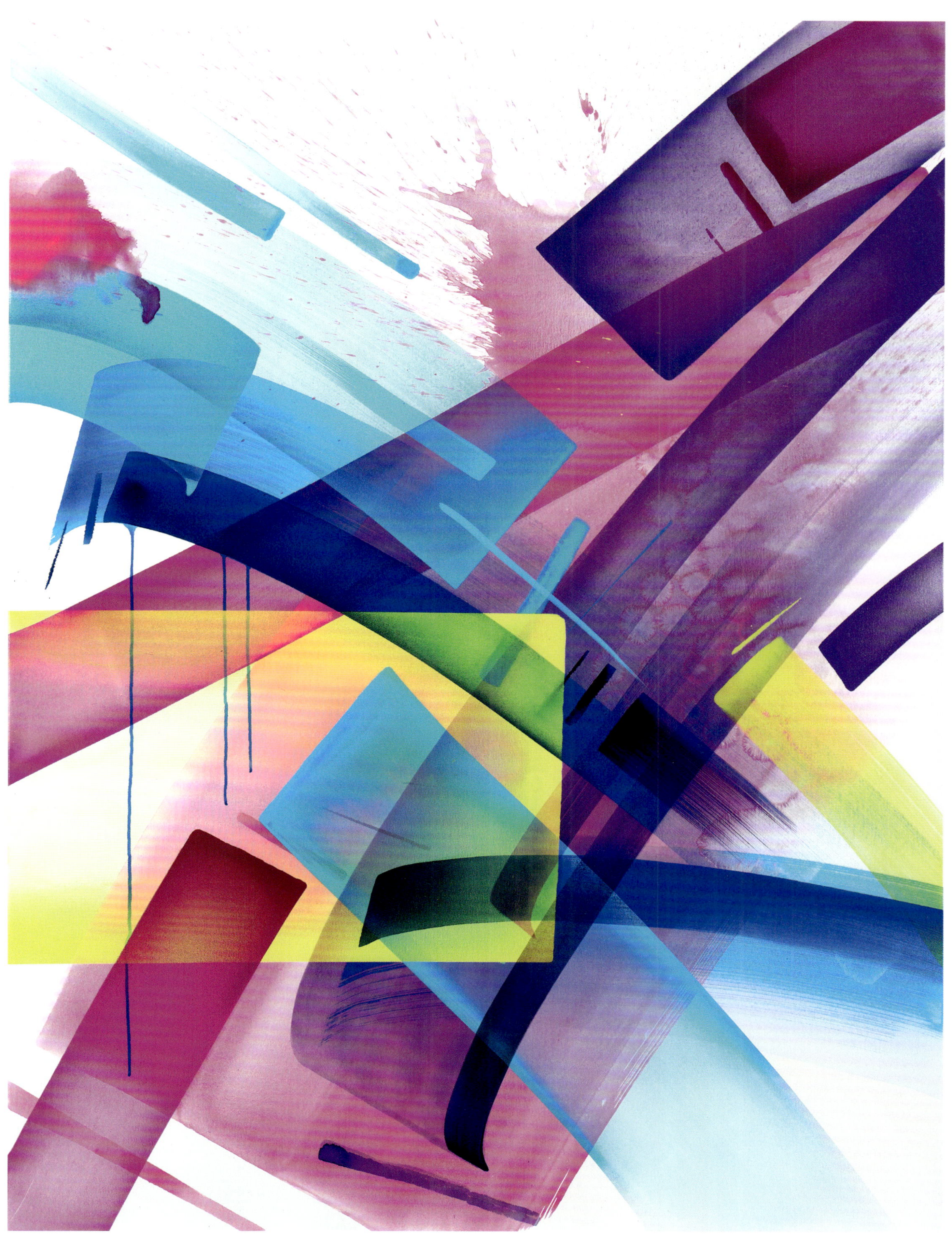

216. *16:59-29032018*, 160 x 120cm, acrylic, watercolour and spray paint on canvas, 2018

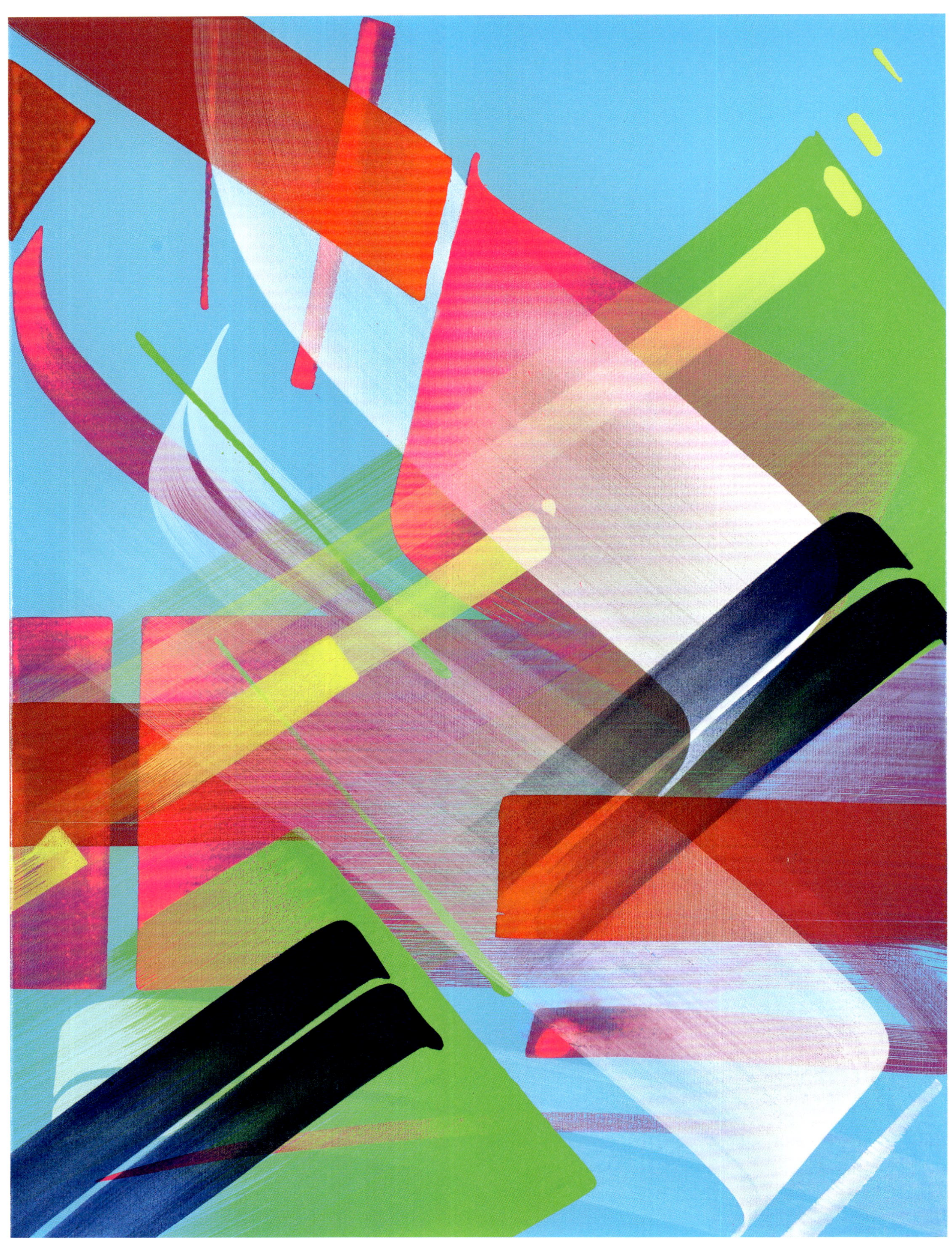

217. *11:45-06092019*, 80 x 60cm, acrylic,
watercolour and spray paint on canvas, 2019

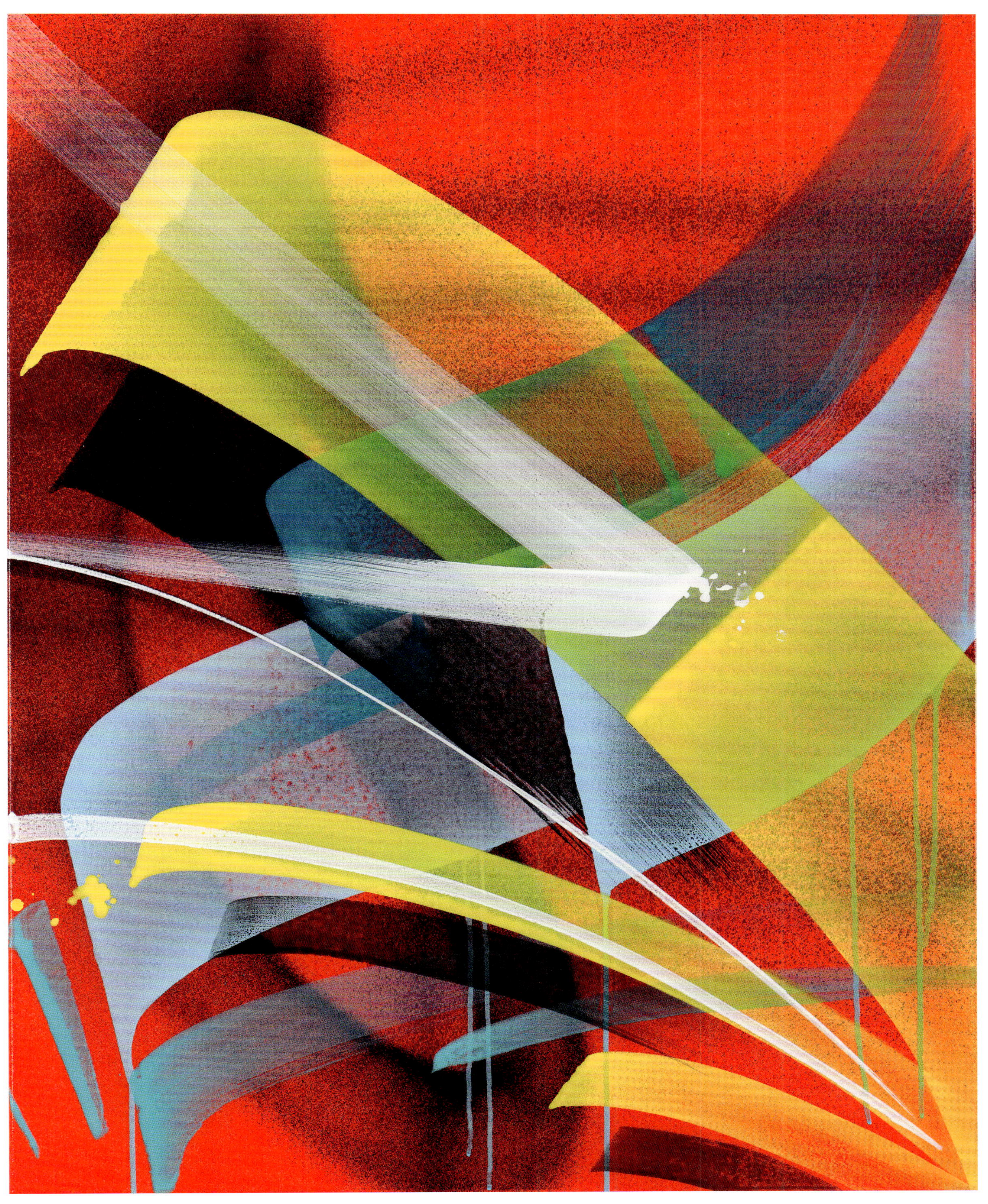

218. *19:22-09062021*, 100 x 60cm, acrylic and spray paint on canvas, 2019

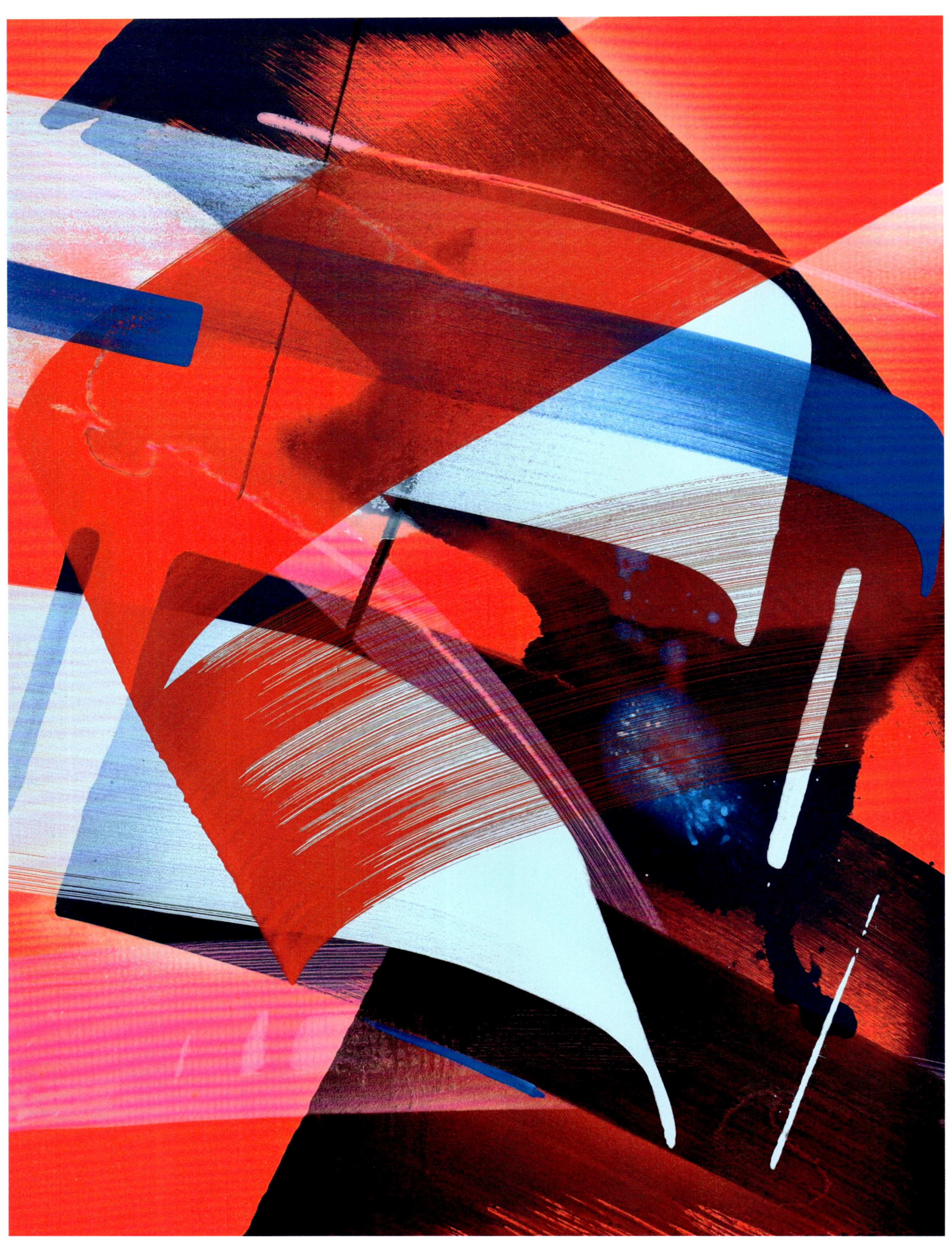

219. *17:13-15022019*, 80 x 60cm, acrylic and spray paint on canvas, 2019

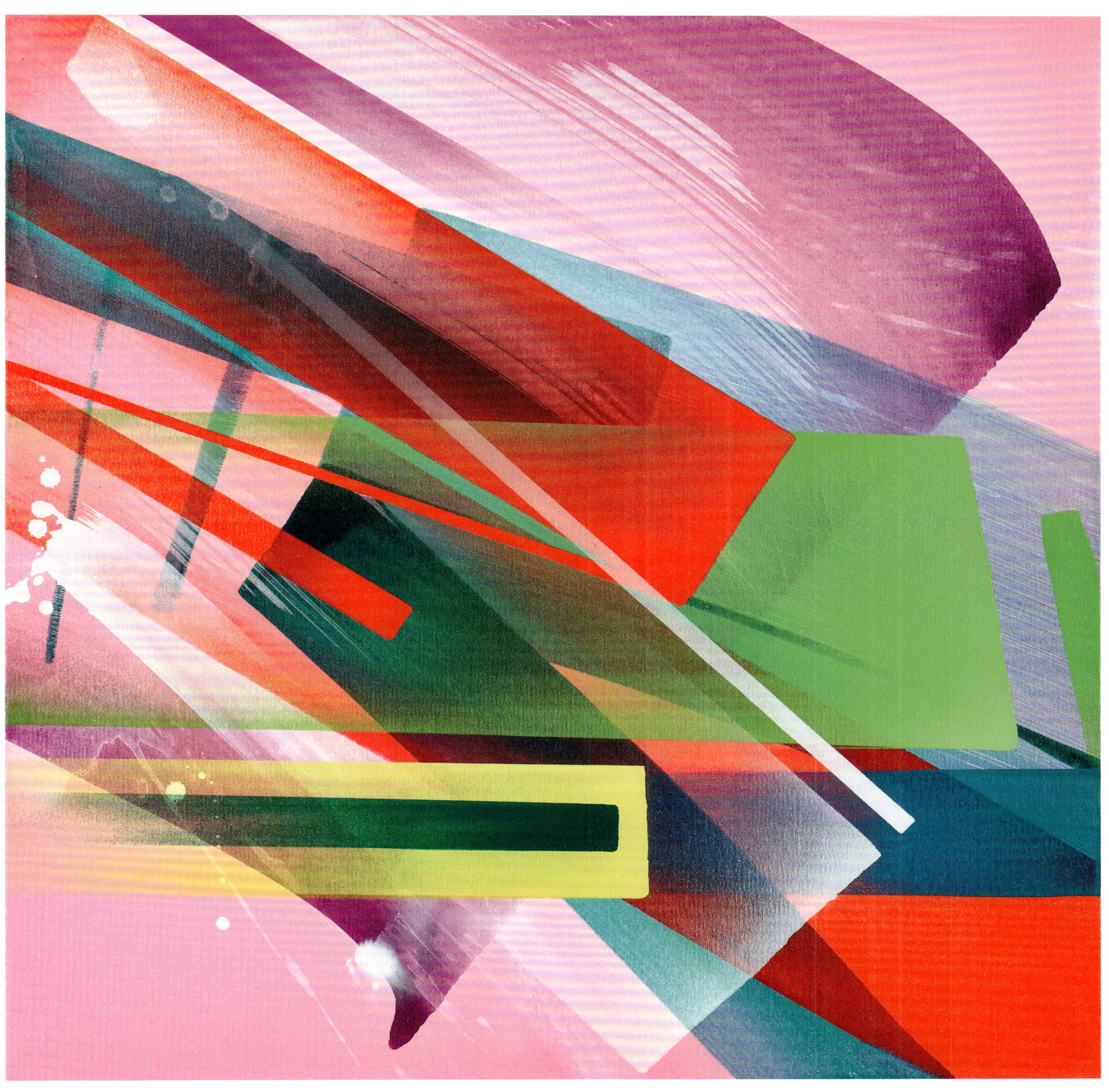

220. *14:42-04042019*, 80 x 80cm, acrylic, watercolour and spray paint on canvas, 2019

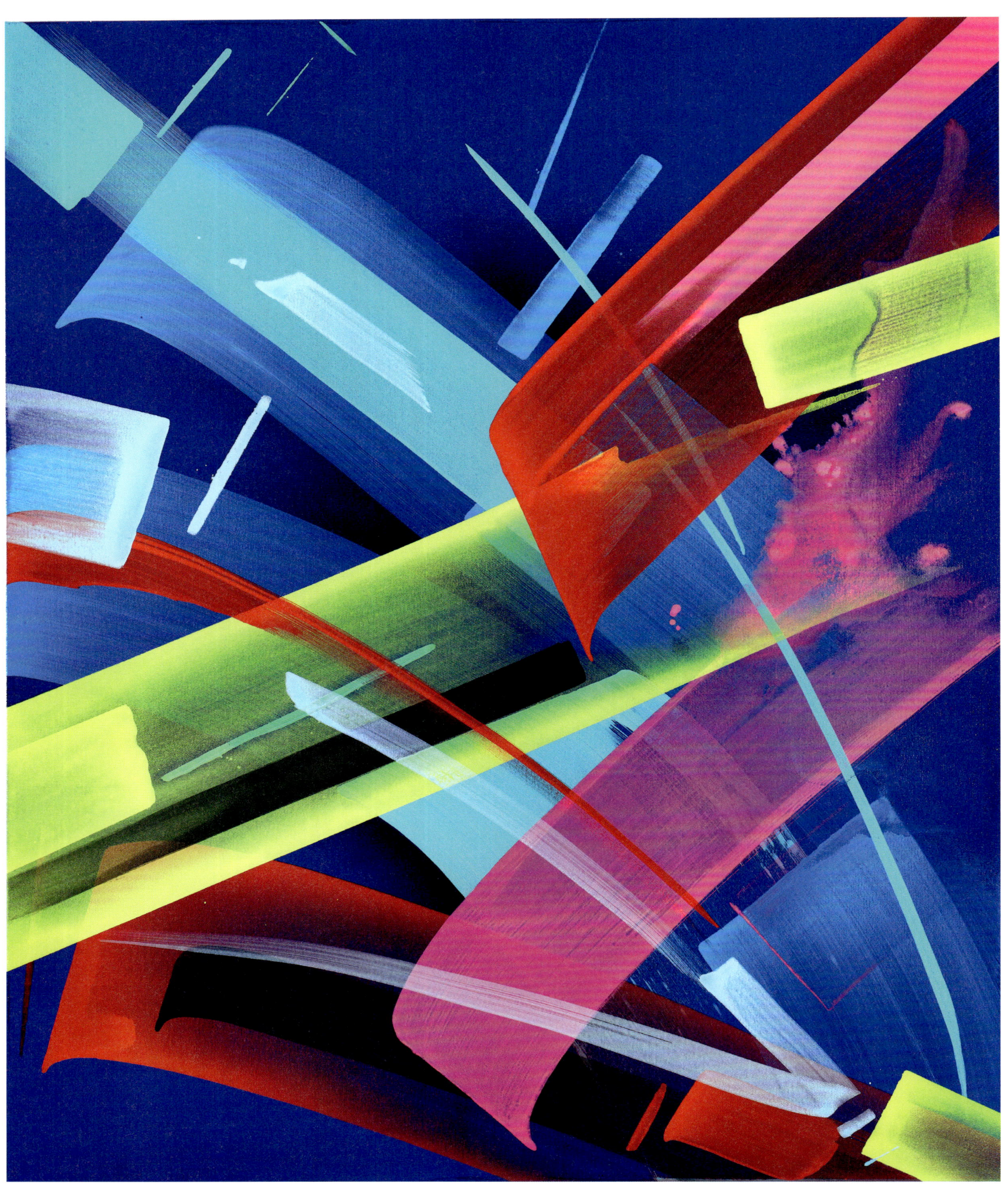

221. *09:08-07042018*, 120 x 100cm, acrylic, watercolour and spray paint on canvas, 2018

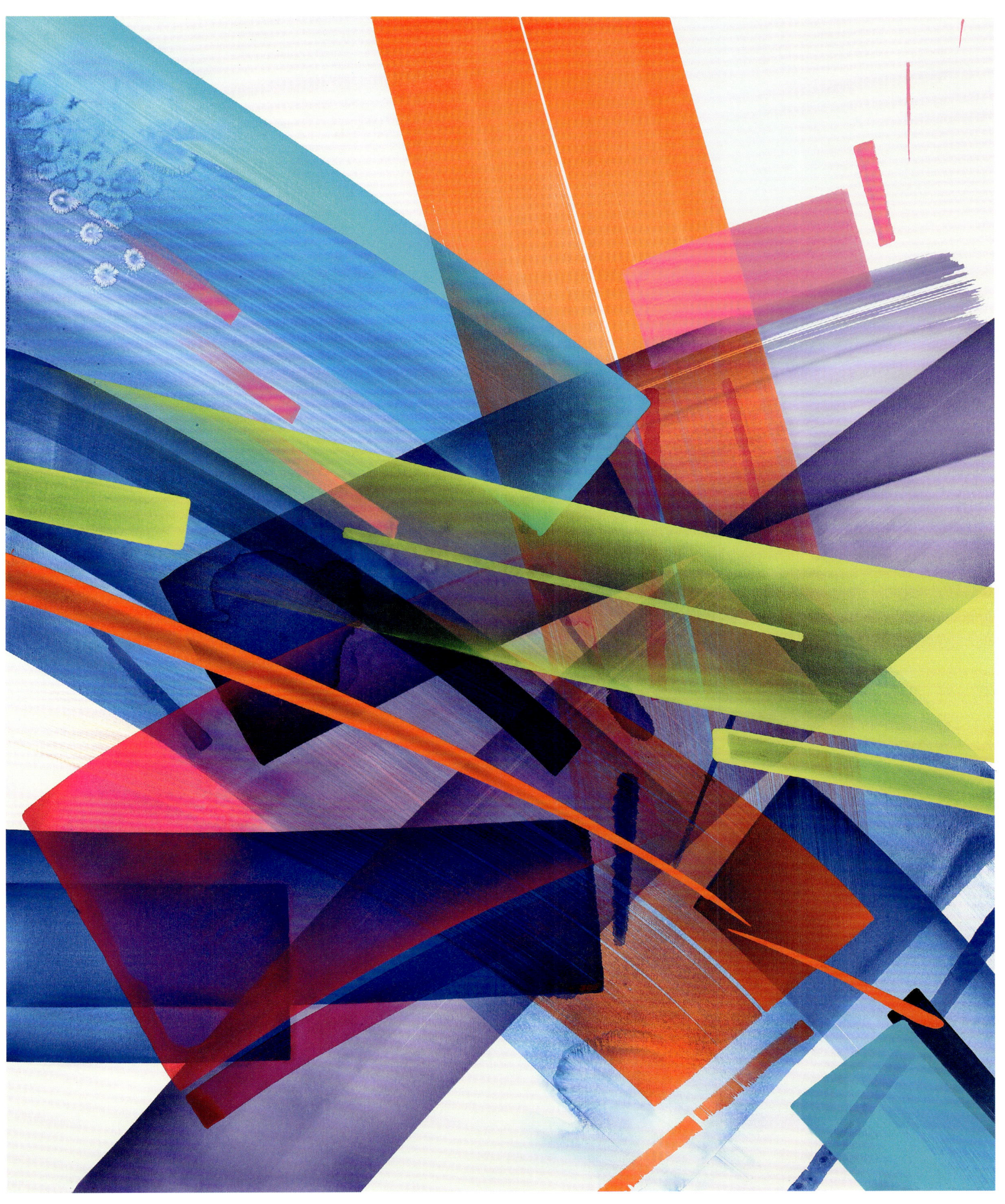

222. *10:25-15032018*, 170 x 140cm, acrylic, watercolour and spray paint on canvas, 2018

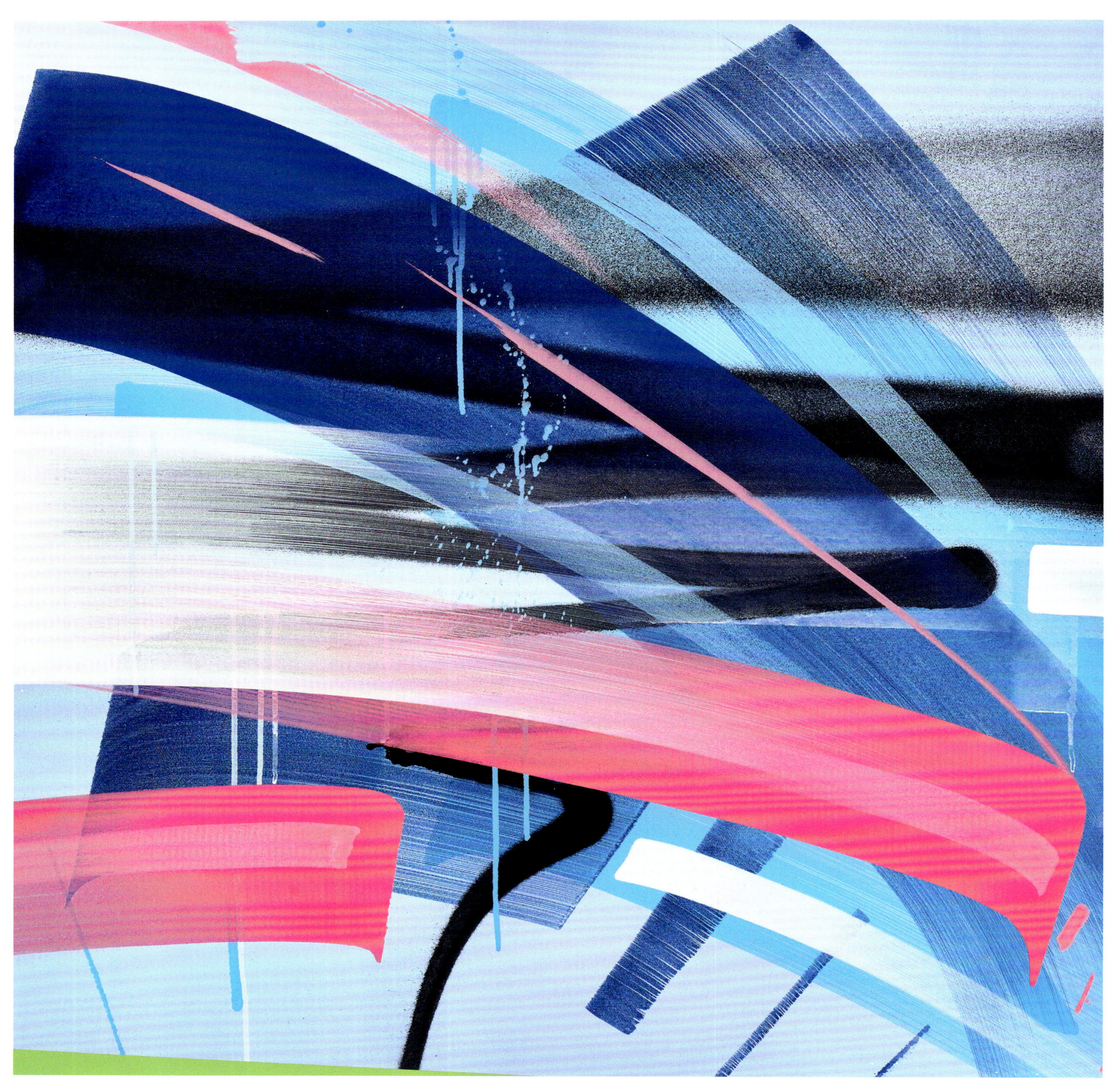

223. *18:18-05042019*, 80 x 80cm, acrylic, watercolour and spray paint on canvas, 2019

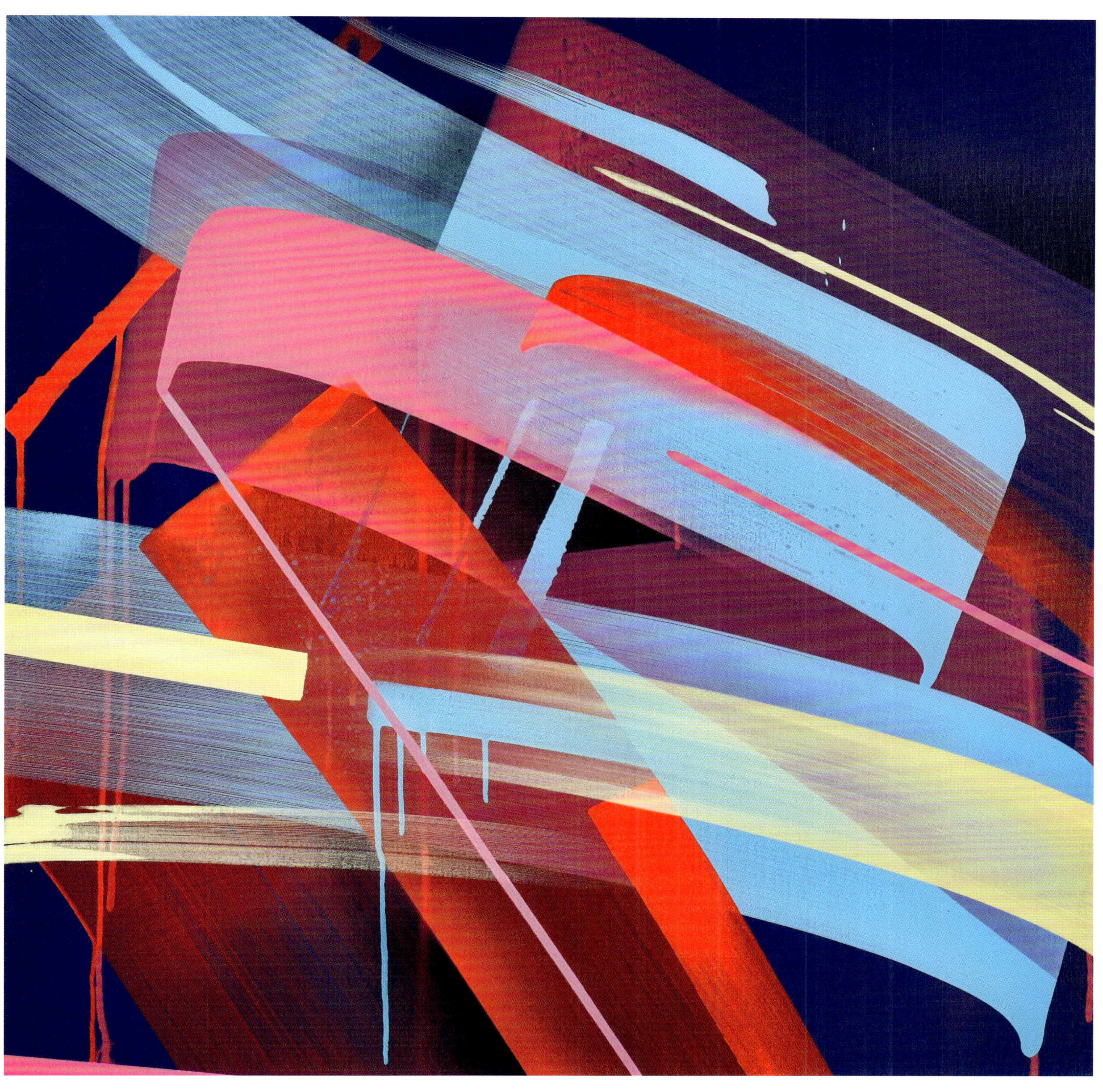

224. *15:18-05042019*, 80 x 80cm, acrylic, watercolour and spray paint on canvas, 2019

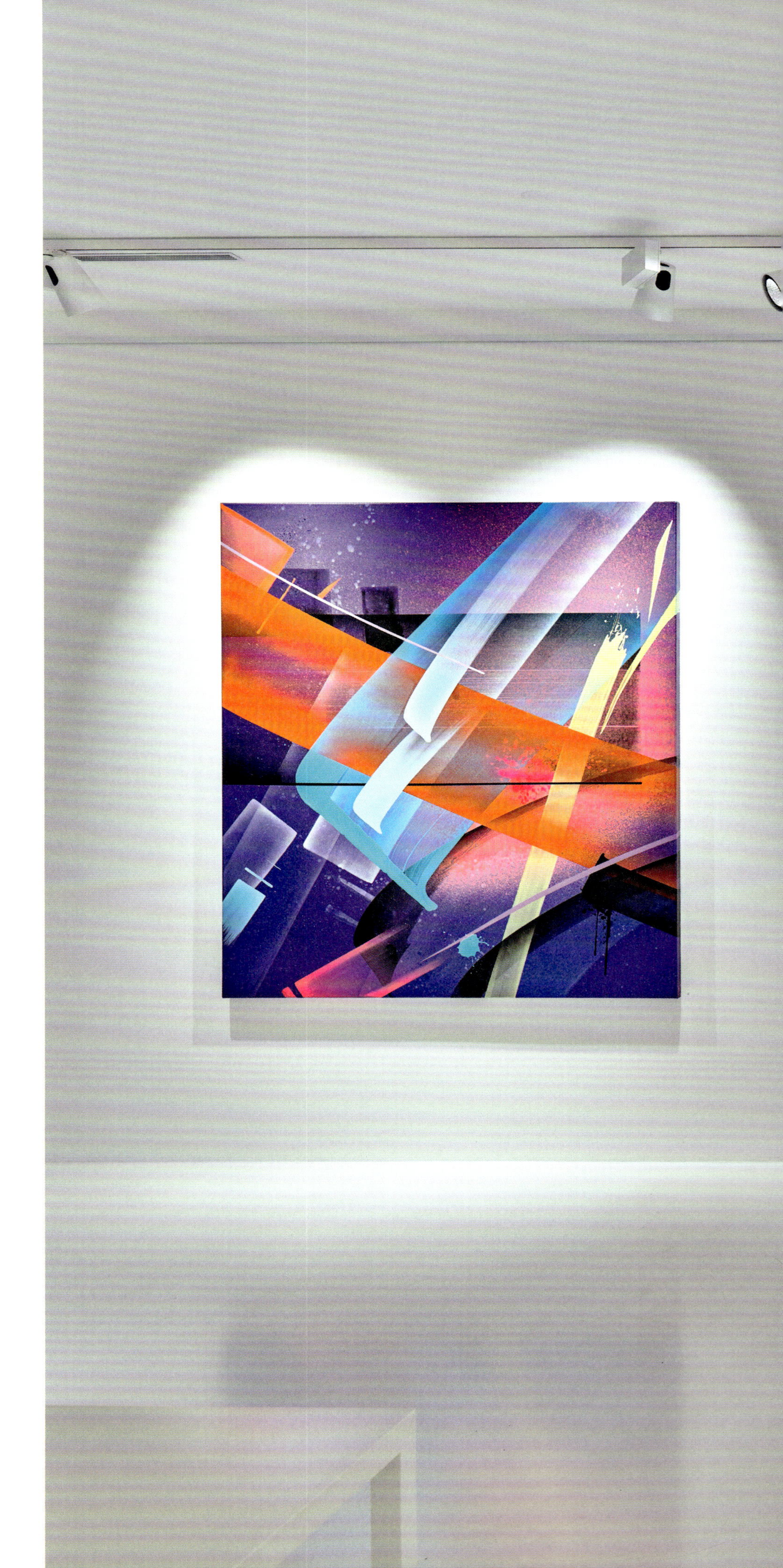

225–228 (opposite and next two spreads). *Pink Power*, solo show at Kolly Gallery, Zurich, Switzerland, 25 October–20 November 2018

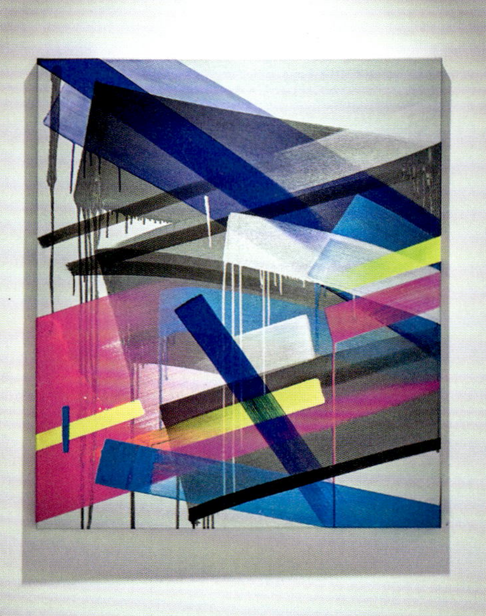

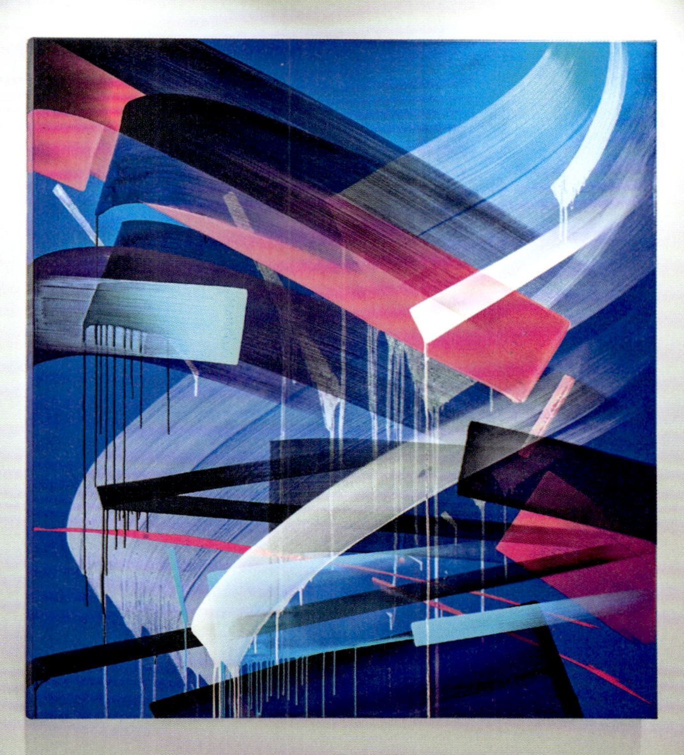

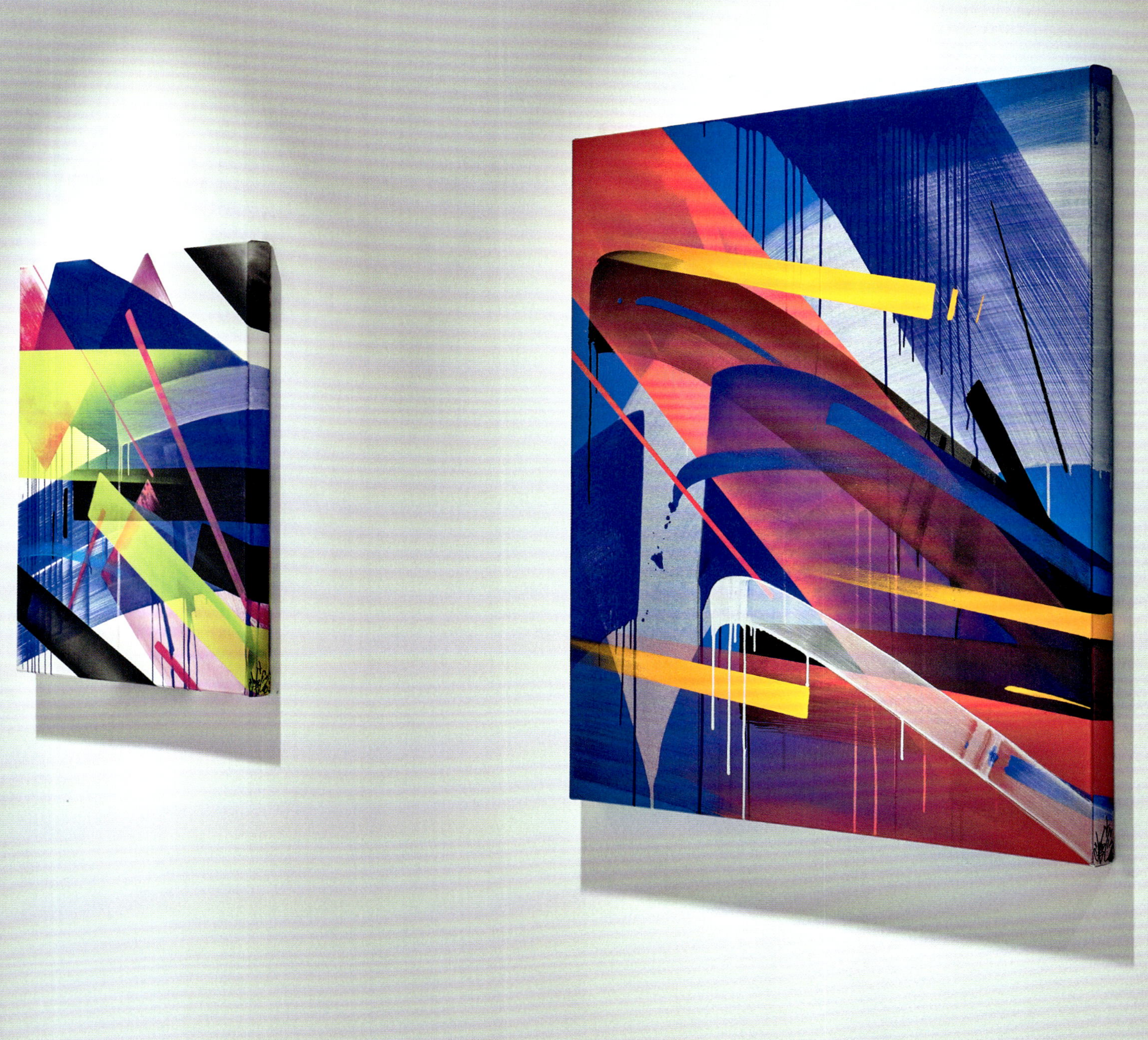

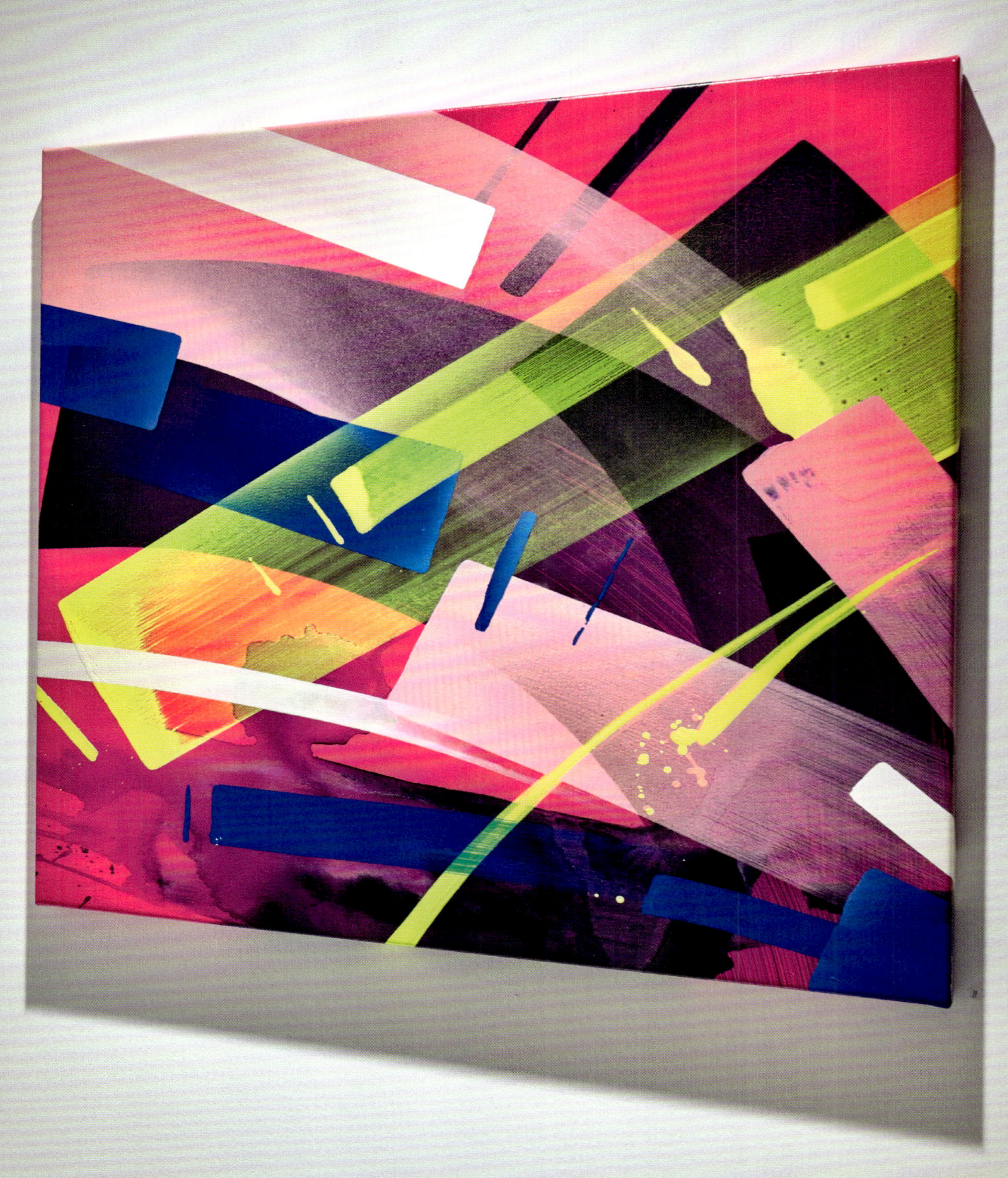

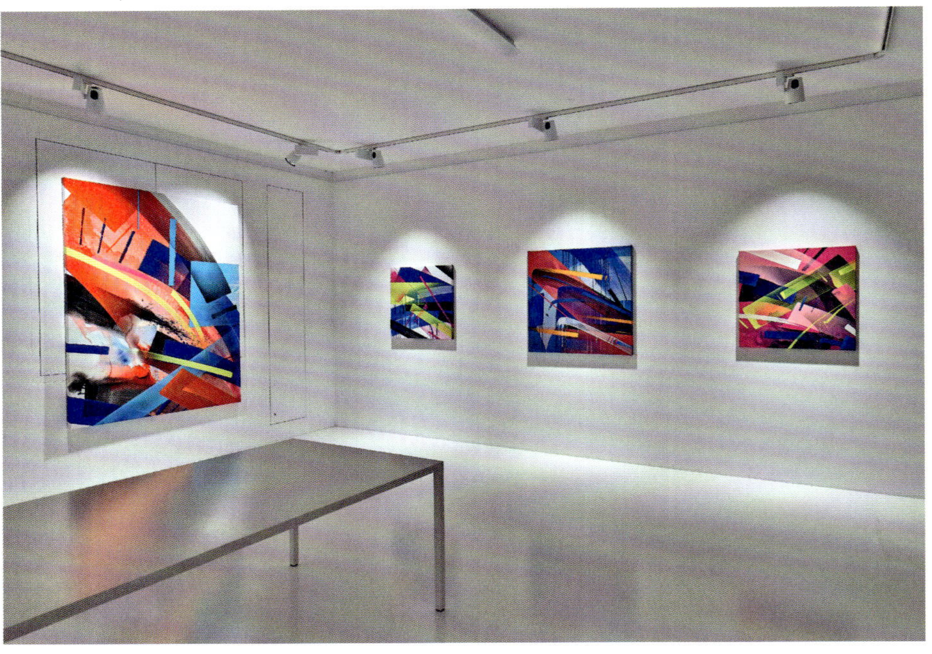

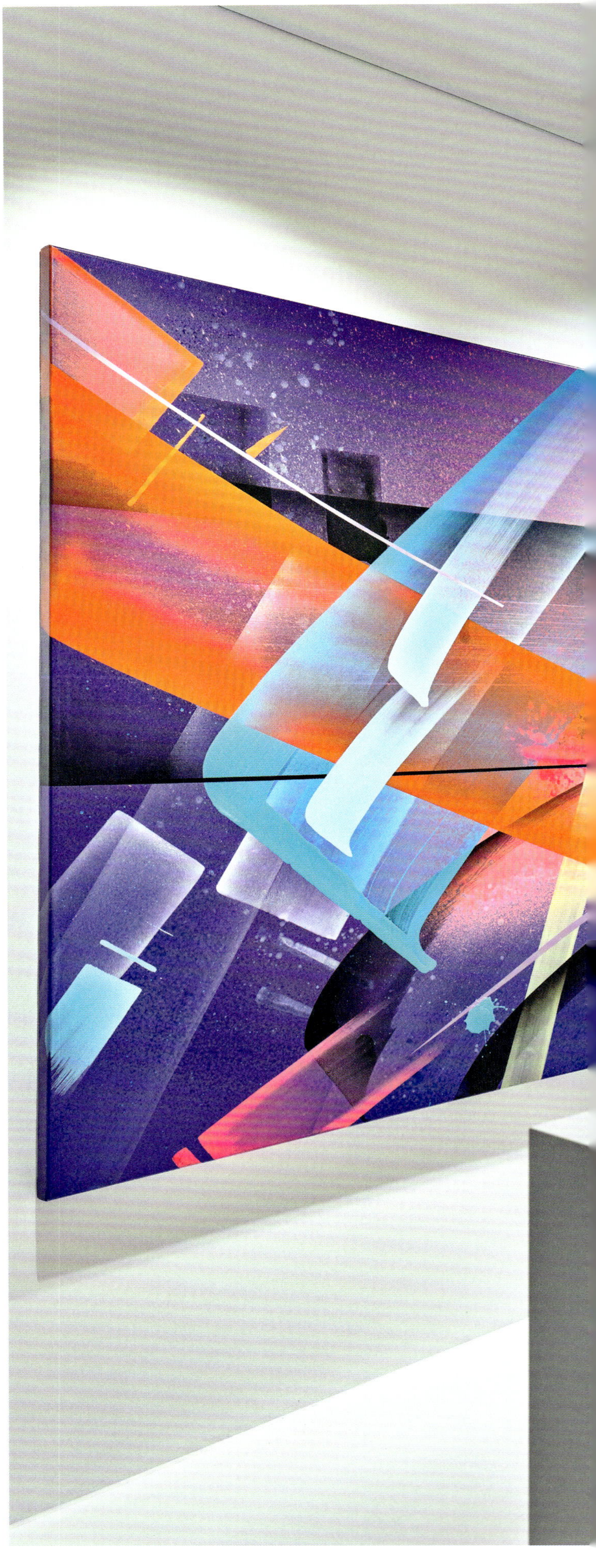

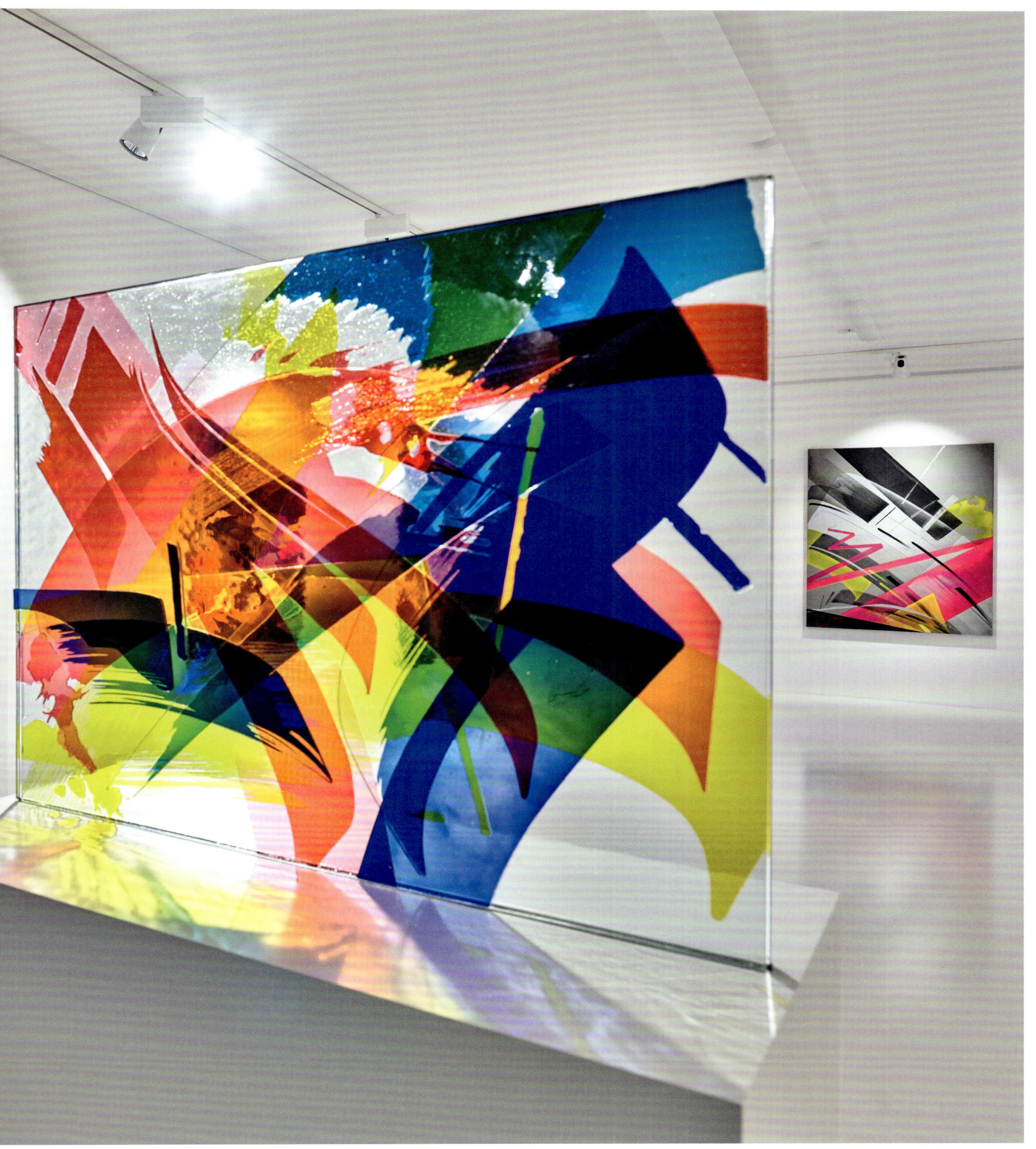

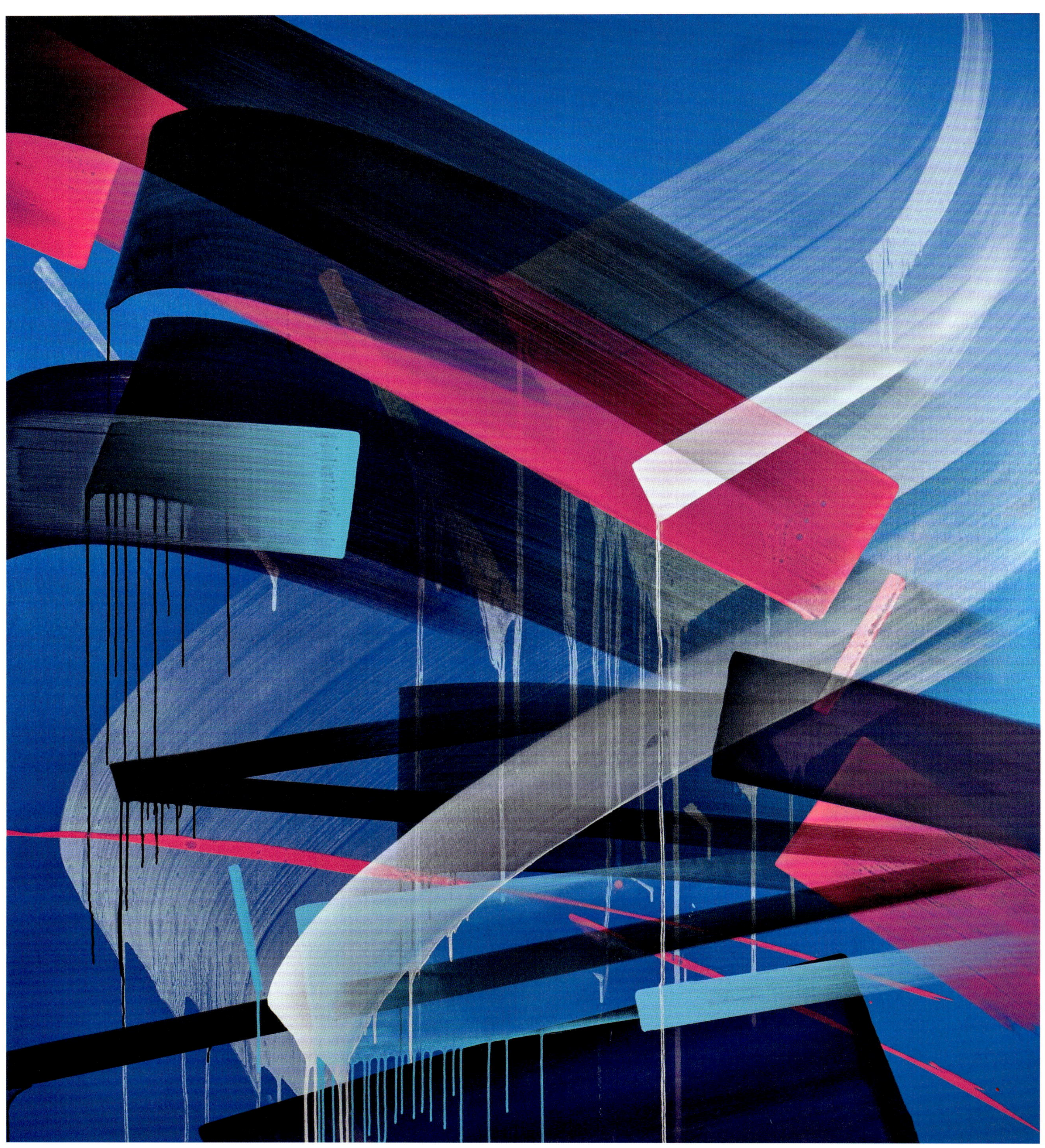

229. *Blue Steel*, 180 x 160cm, acrylic and spray paint on canvas, 2018

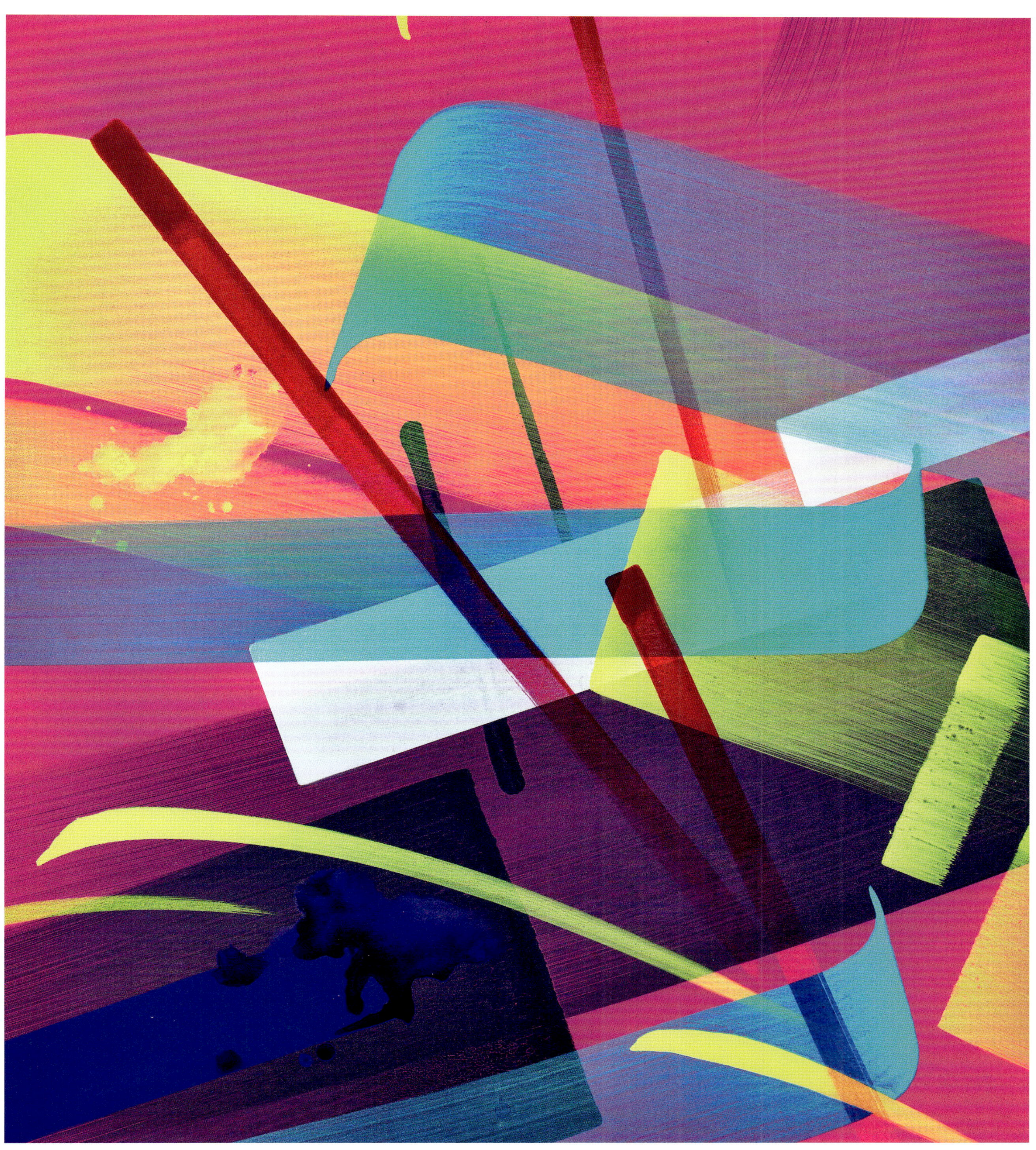

230. *Pink Power*, 90 x 80cm, acrylic, watercolour and spray paint on canvas, 2018

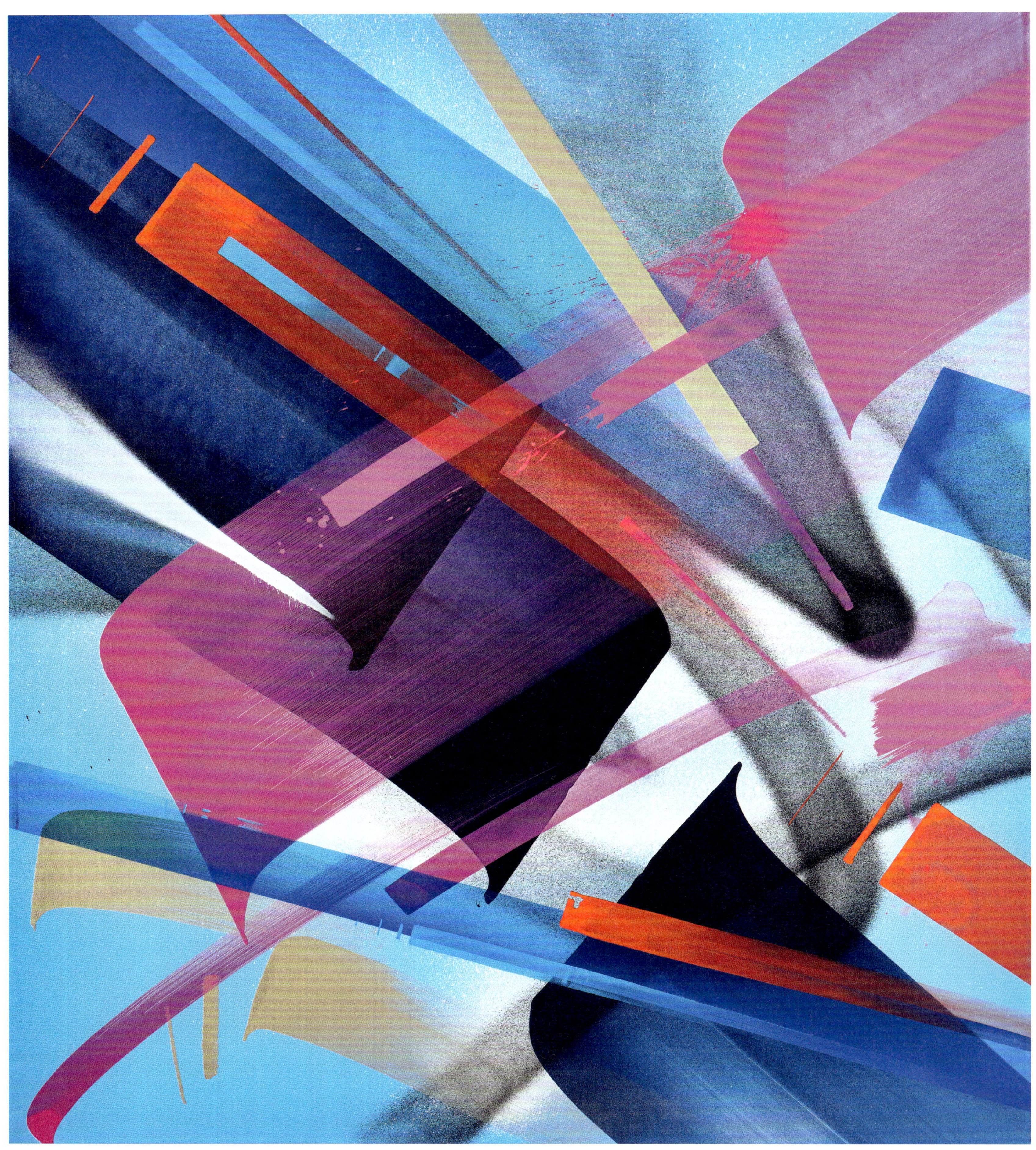

231. *10:18-15112018*, 180 x 160cm, acrylic, watercolour and spray paint on canvas, 2018

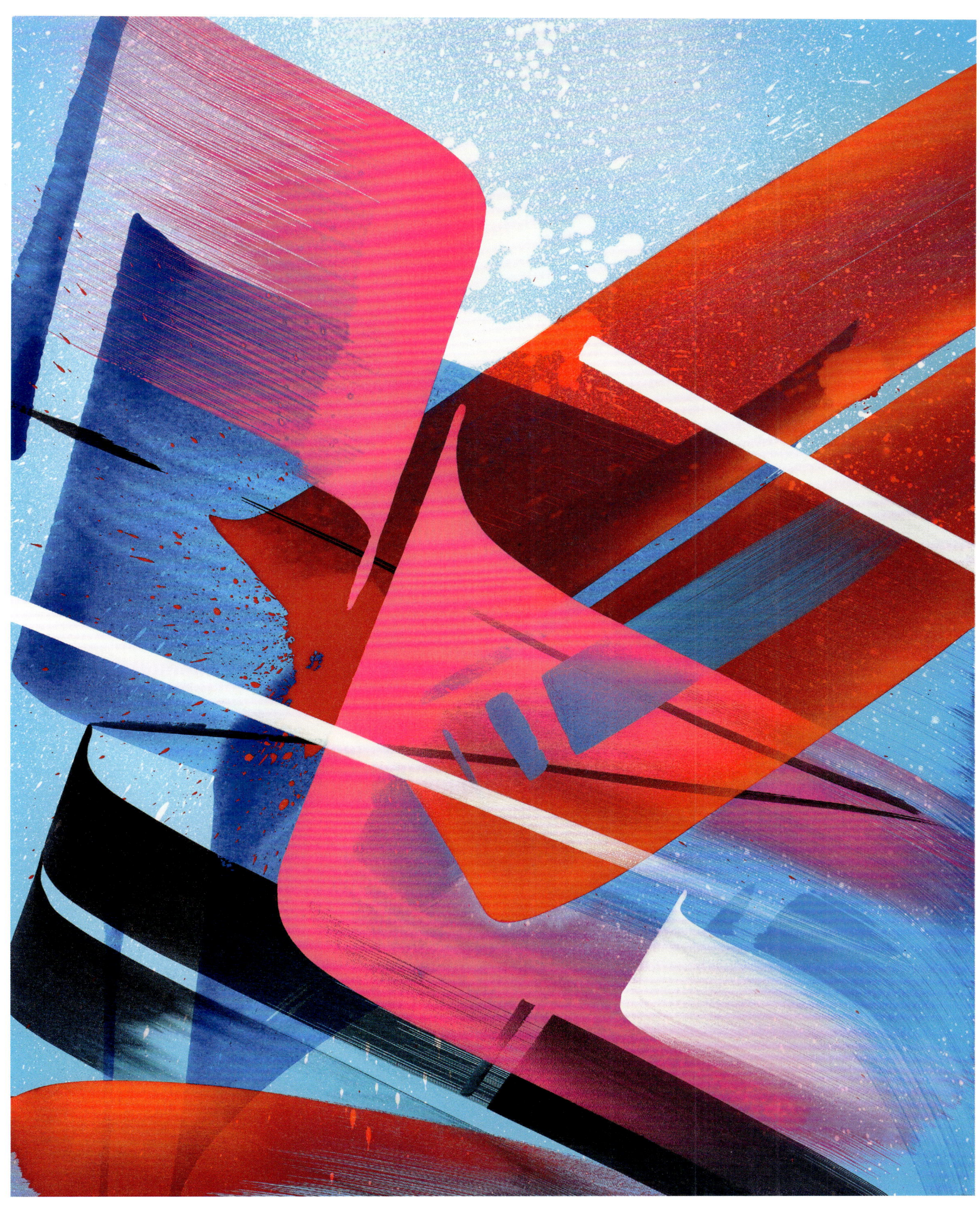

232. *14:16-19082019*, 100 x 80cm, acrylic, watercolour and spray paint on canvas, 2019

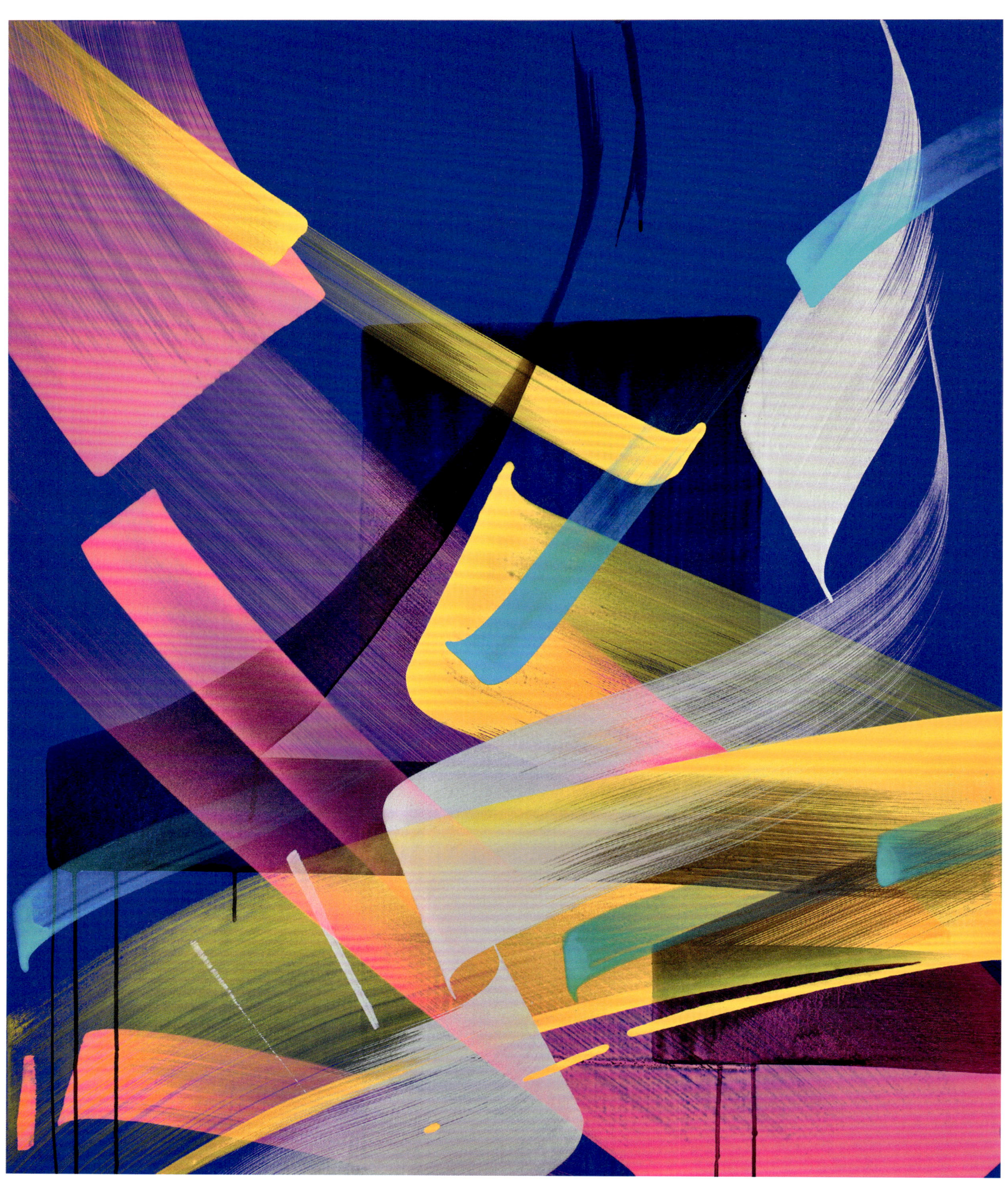

233. *14:01-20102019*, 120 x 100cm, acrylic, watercolour and spray paint on canvas, 2019

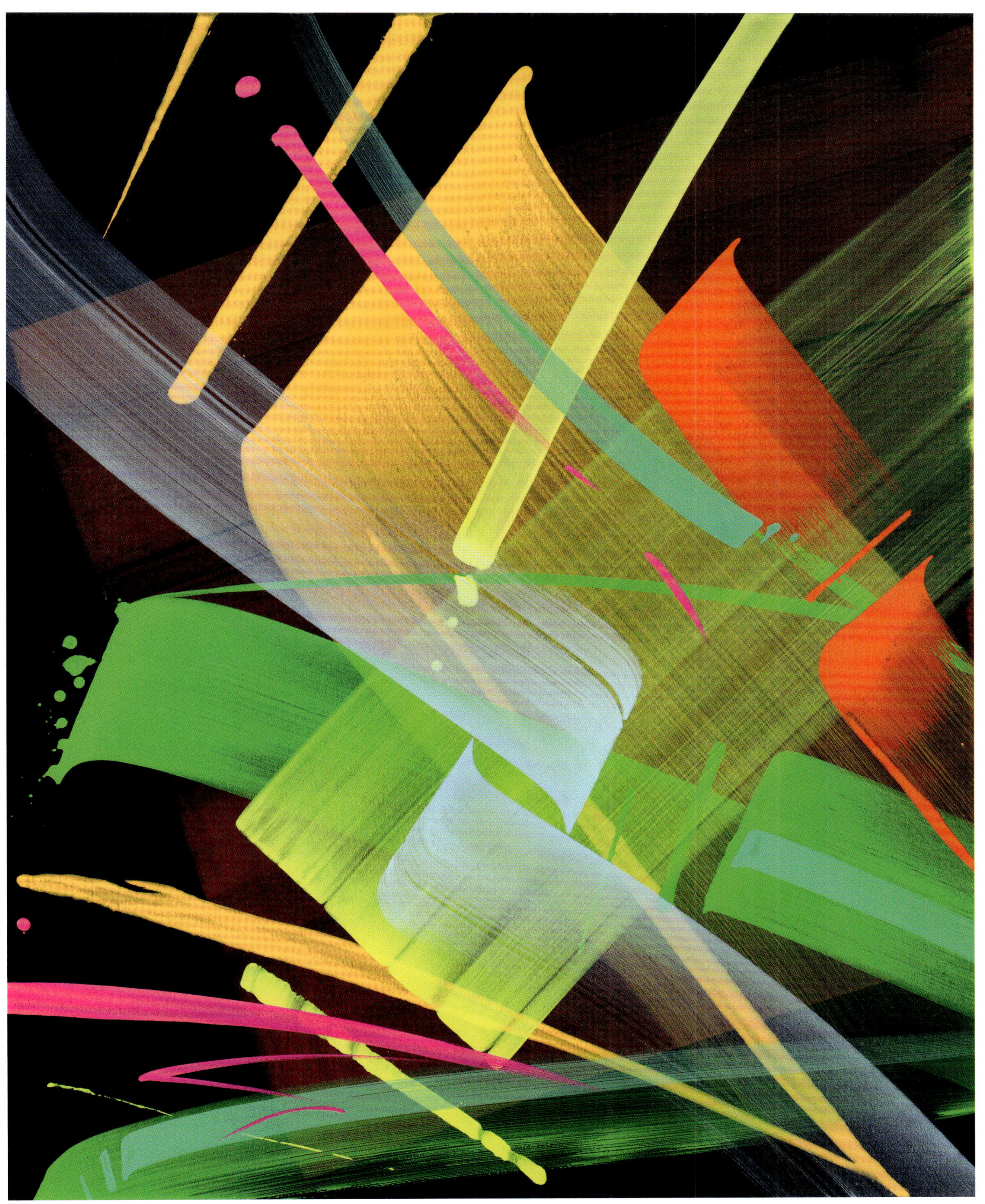

234. *13:27-12072021*, 100 x 80cm, acrylic and spray paint on canvas, 2021

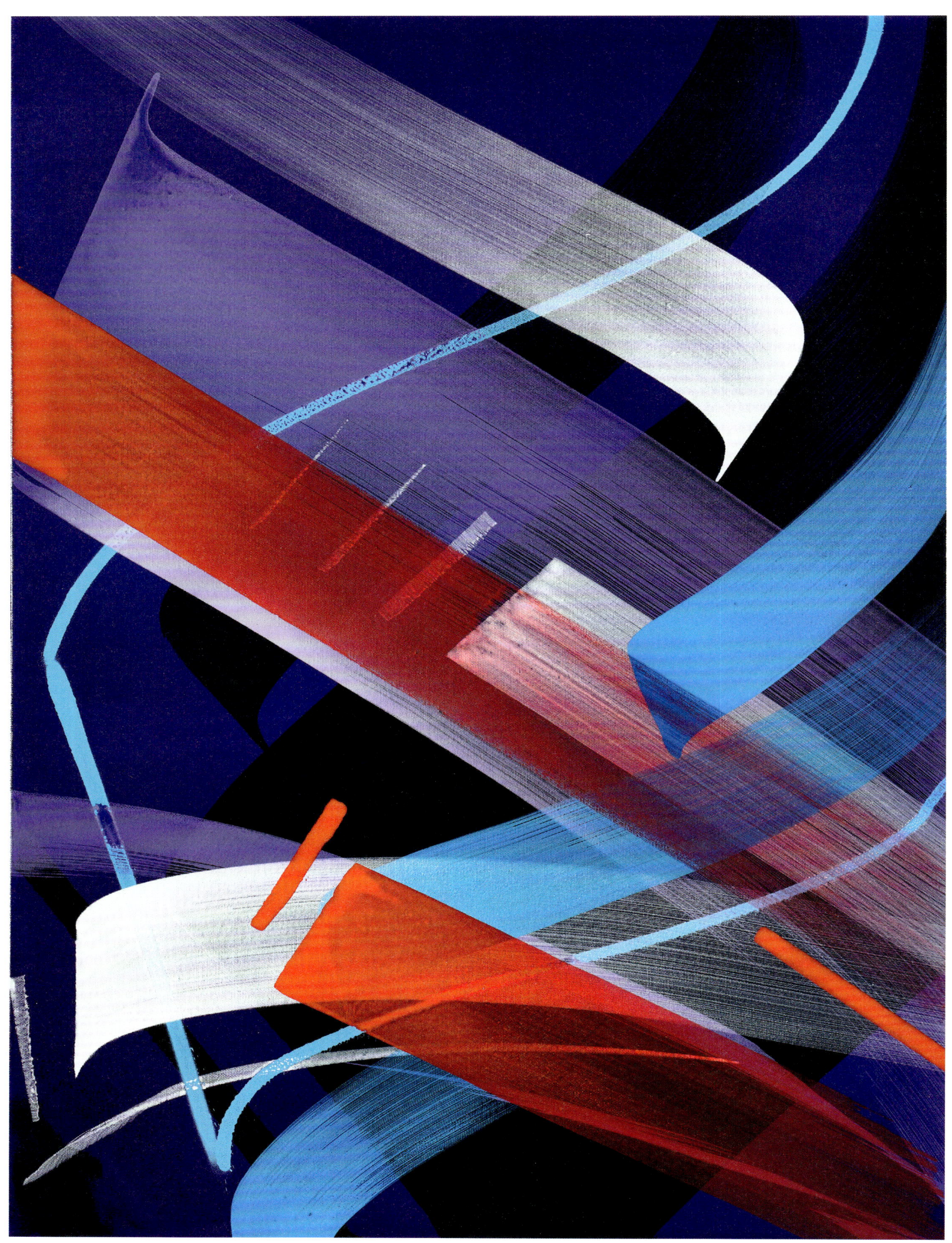

235. *13:29-20082019*, 80 x 60cm,
acrylic and spray paint on canvas, 2019

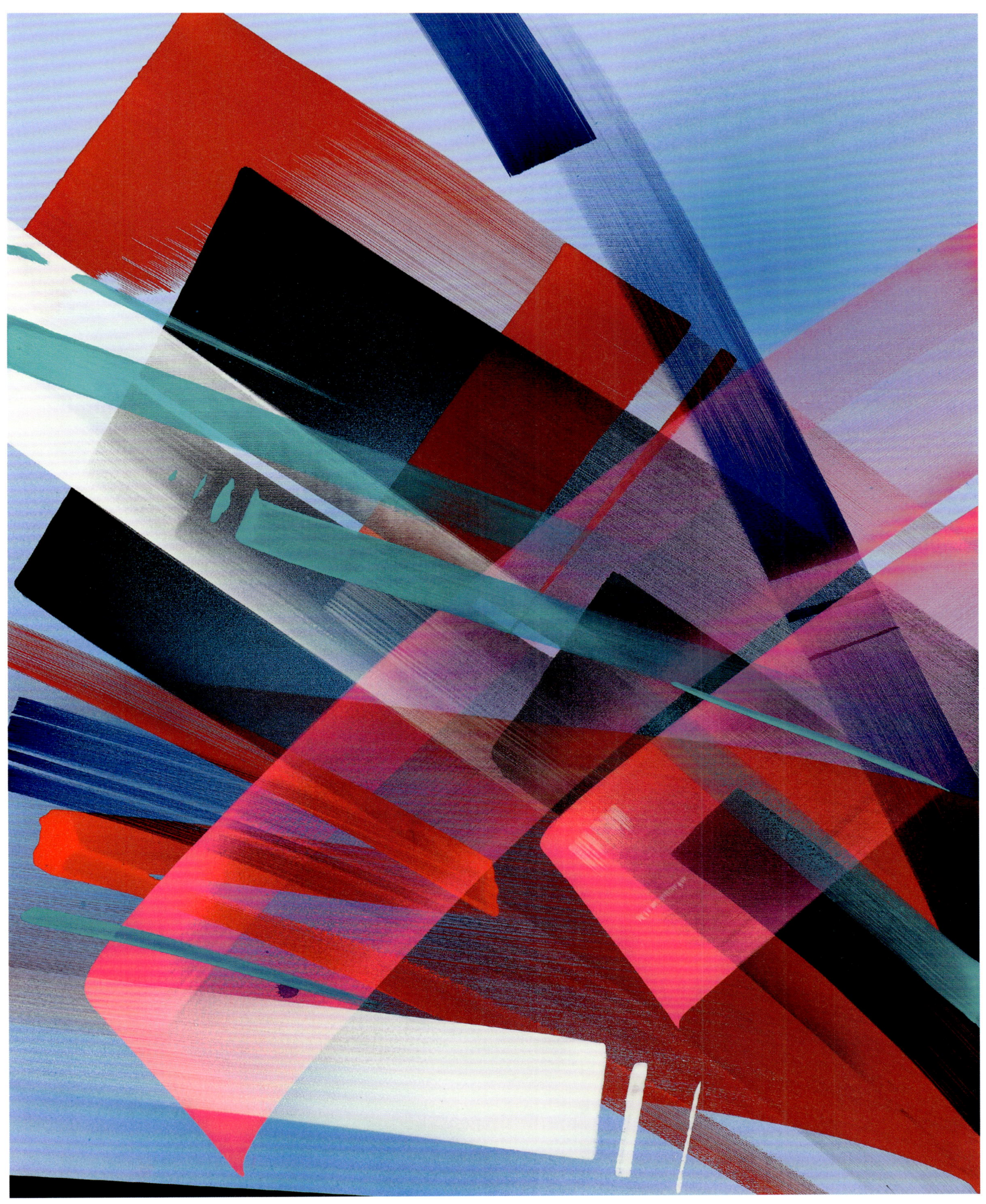

236. *13:23-29112019*, 100 x 80cm, acrylic, watercolour and spray paint on canvas, 2019

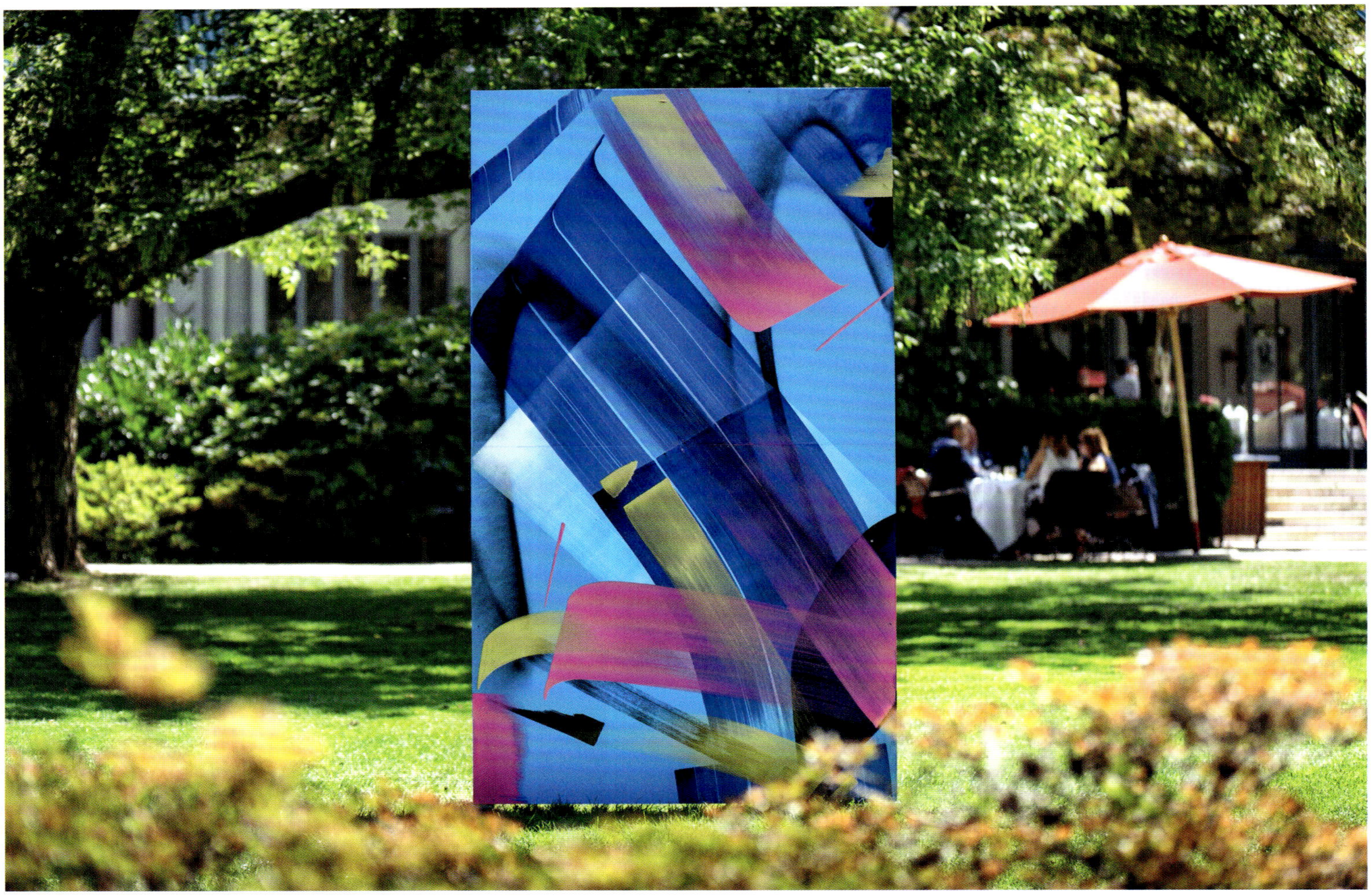

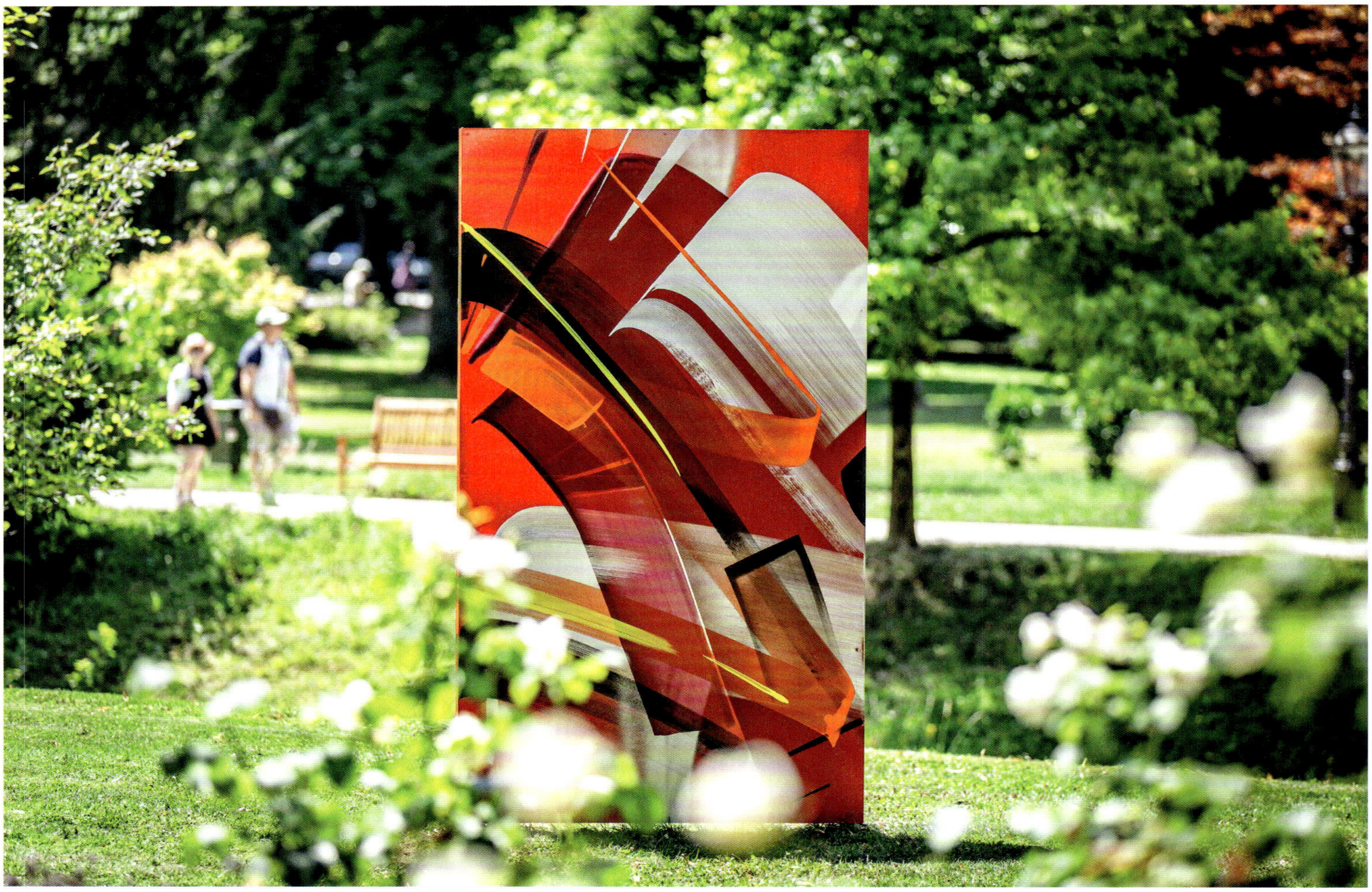

237–240 (this spread). Brenners Park-Hotel and Spa, Baden-Baden, Germany, 2019. MadC painted metal panels in memory of her graffiti past and installed them in the park around Brenners Park-Hotel and Spa, to create a dialogue between two worlds that were far apart

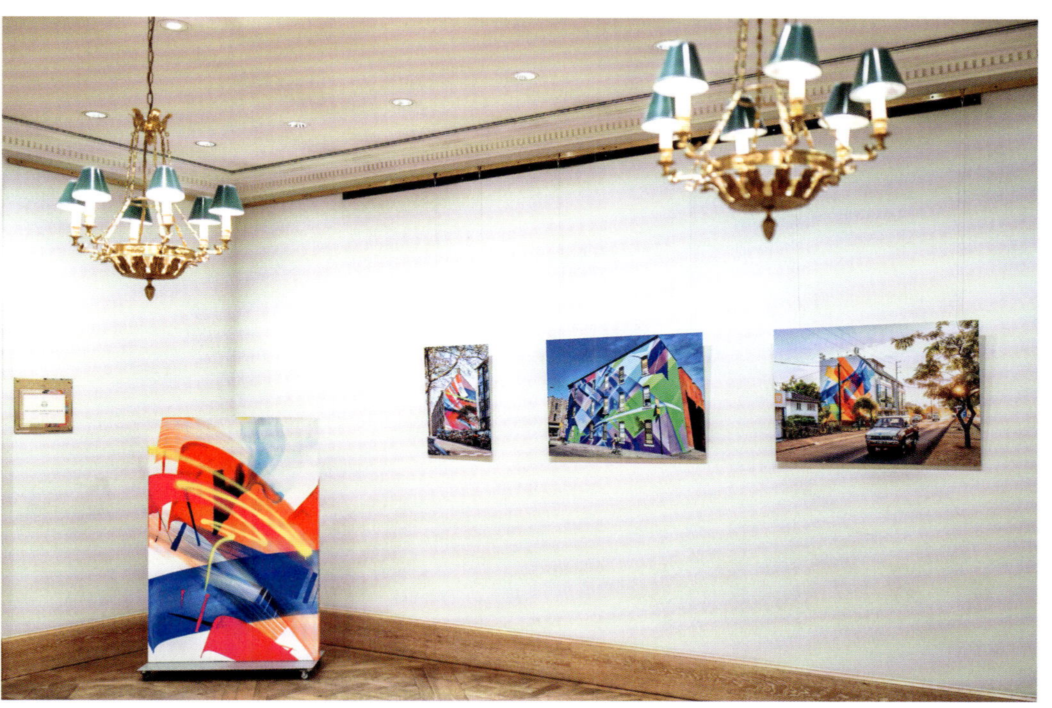

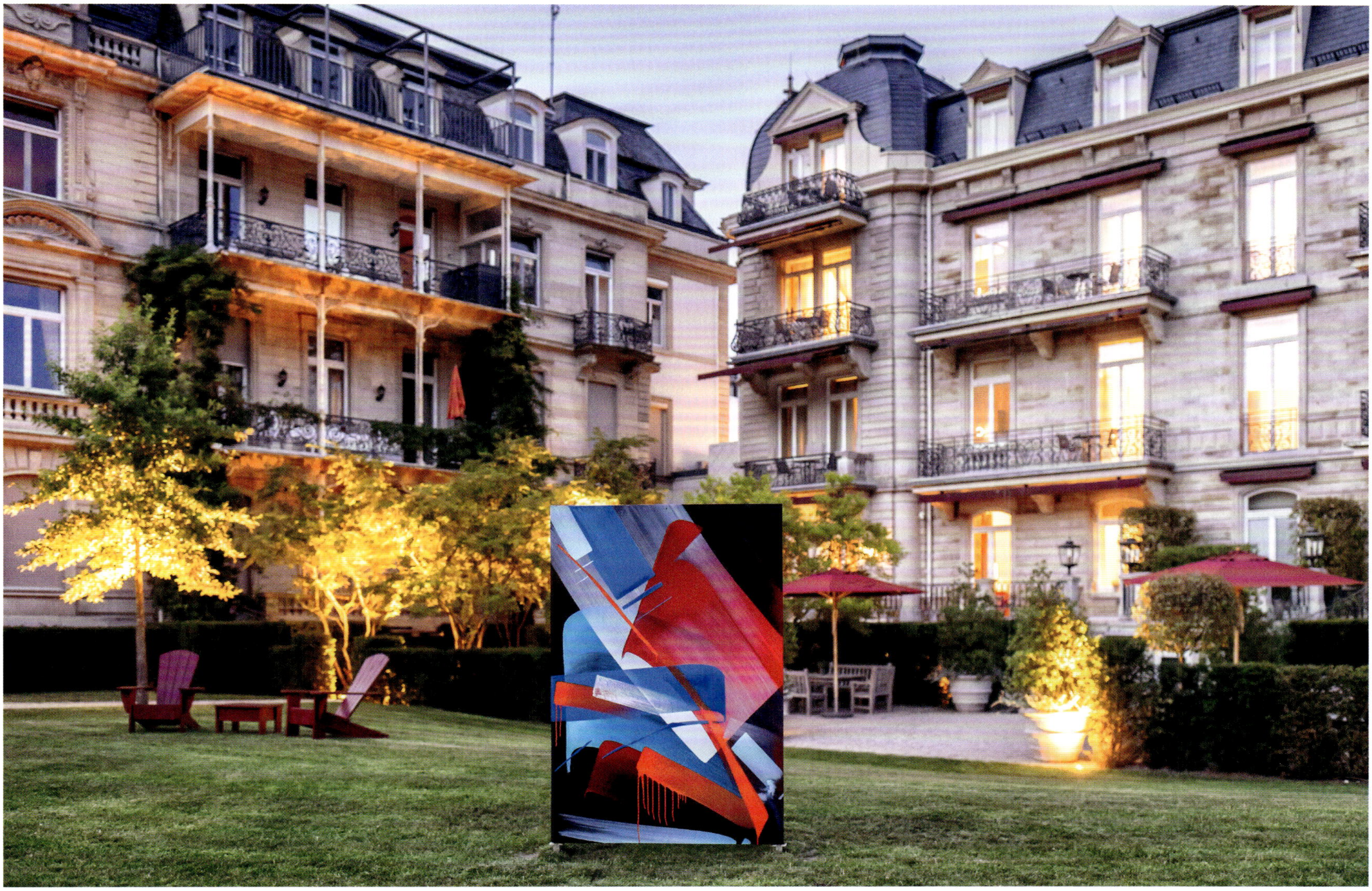

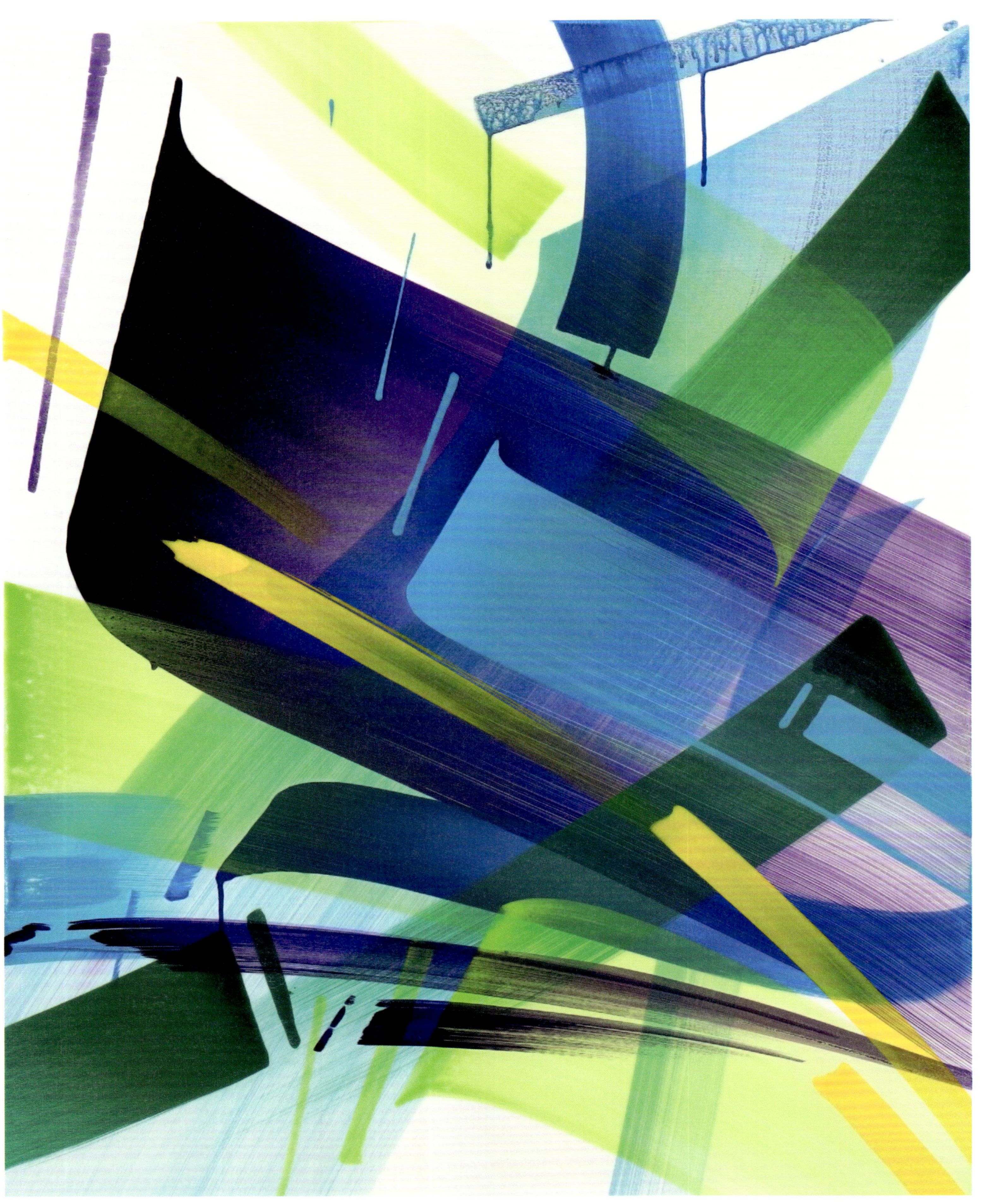

241. *15:01-26112019*, 100 x 80cm,
acrylic and spray paint on canvas, 2019

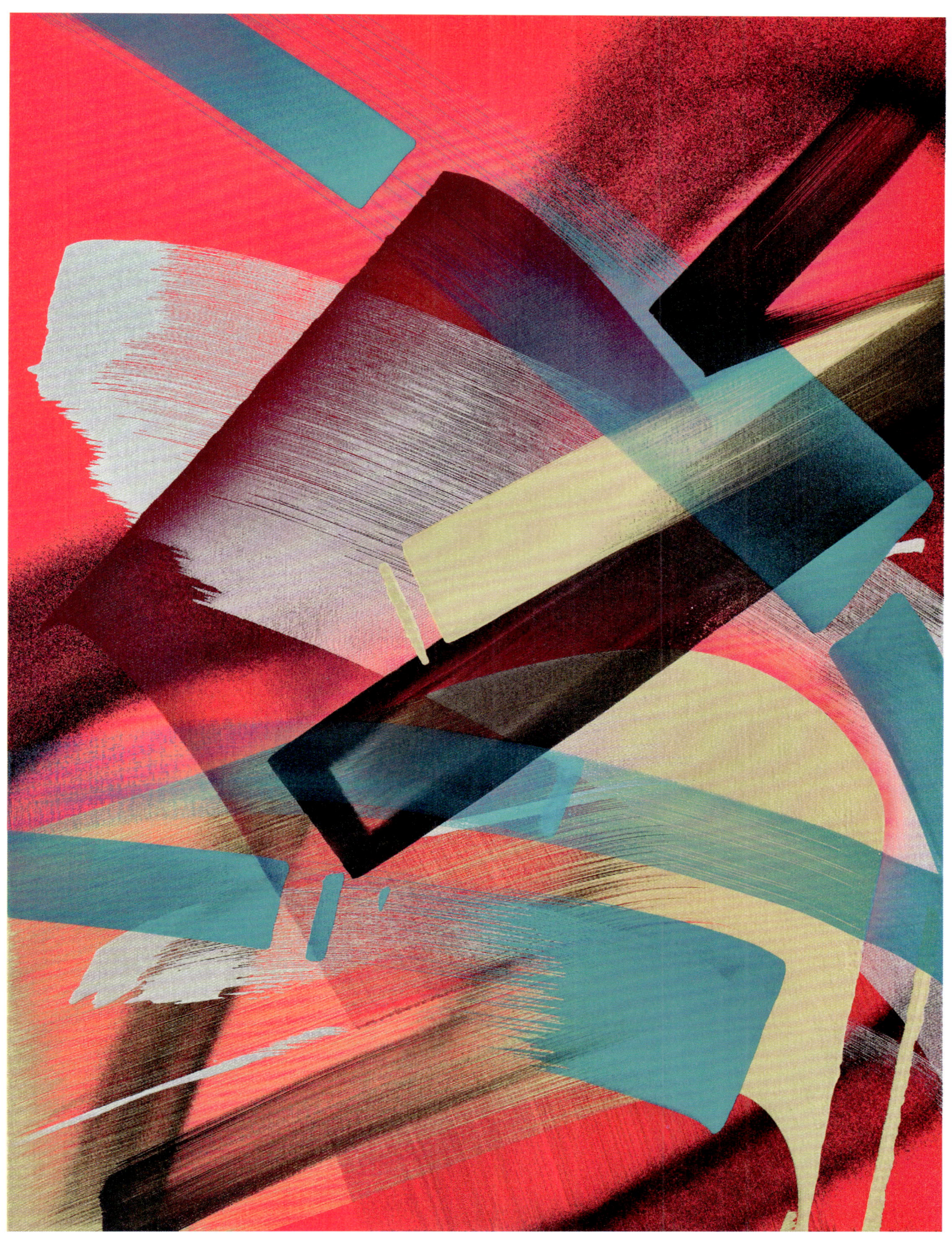

242. *09:08-15102019*, 80 x 60cm,
acrylic and spray paint on canvas, 2019

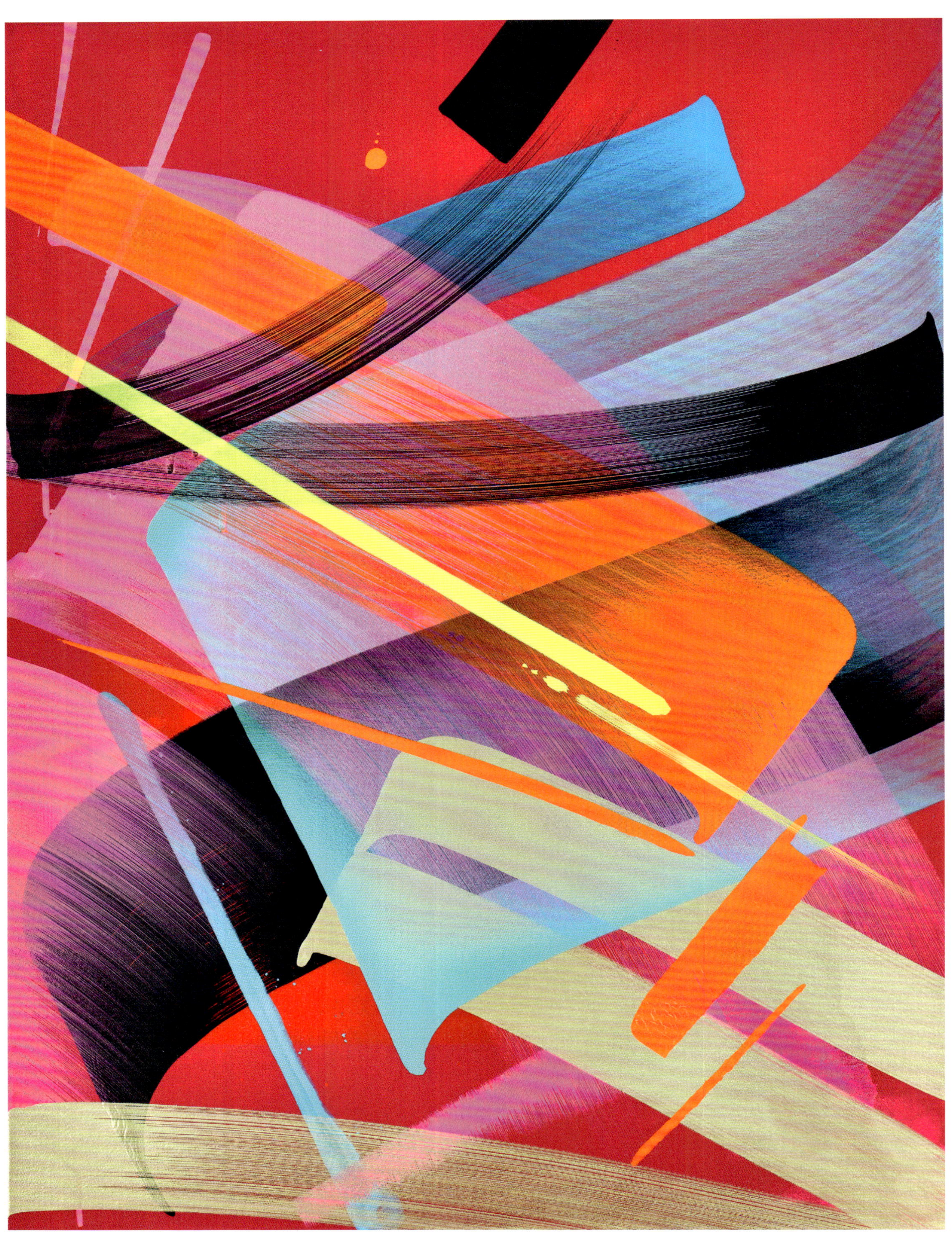

243. *17:36-19102019*, 80 x 60cm, acrylic, watercolour and spray paint on canvas, 2019

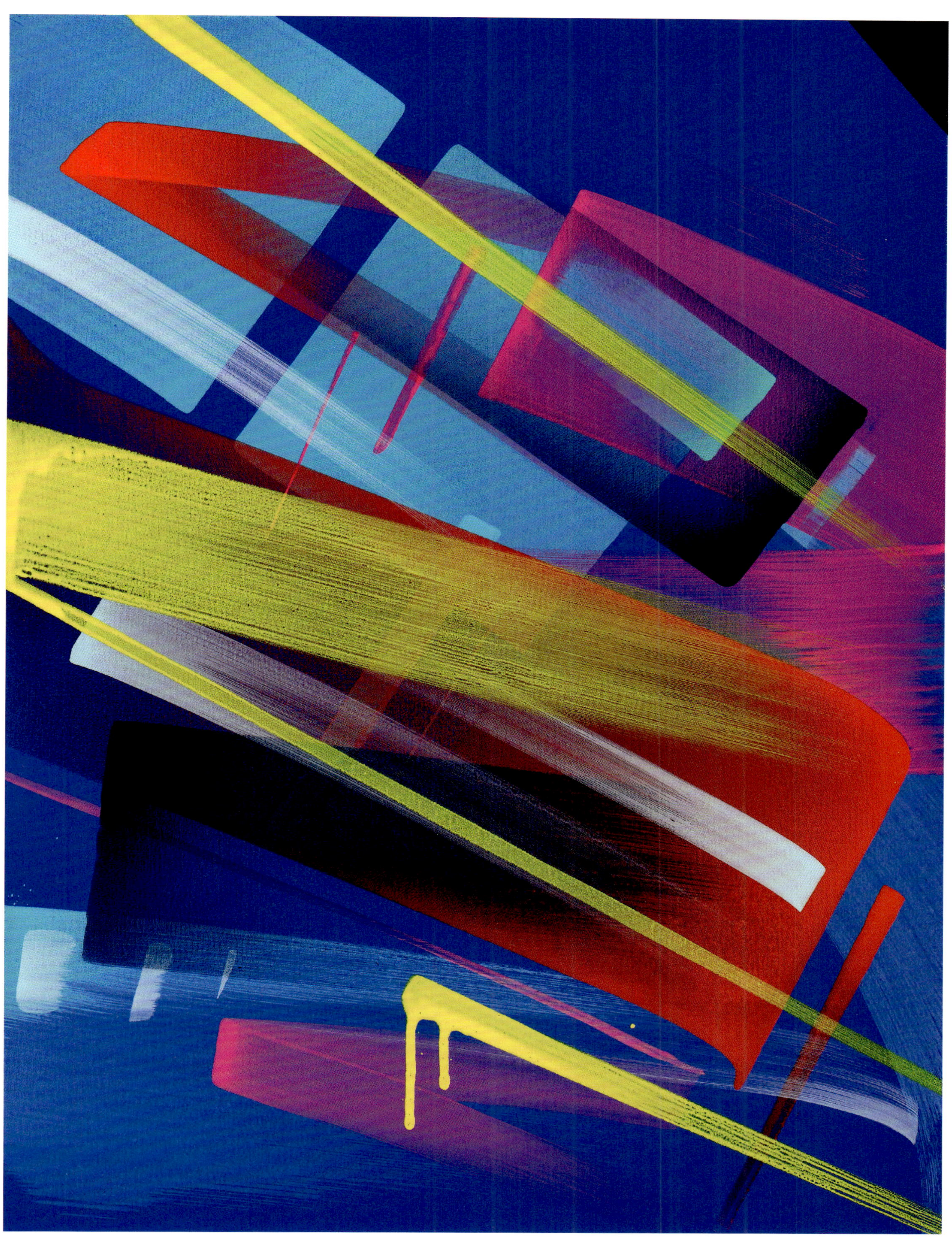

244. *10:18-03062019*, 80 x 60cm, acrylic, watercolour and spray paint on canvas, 2019

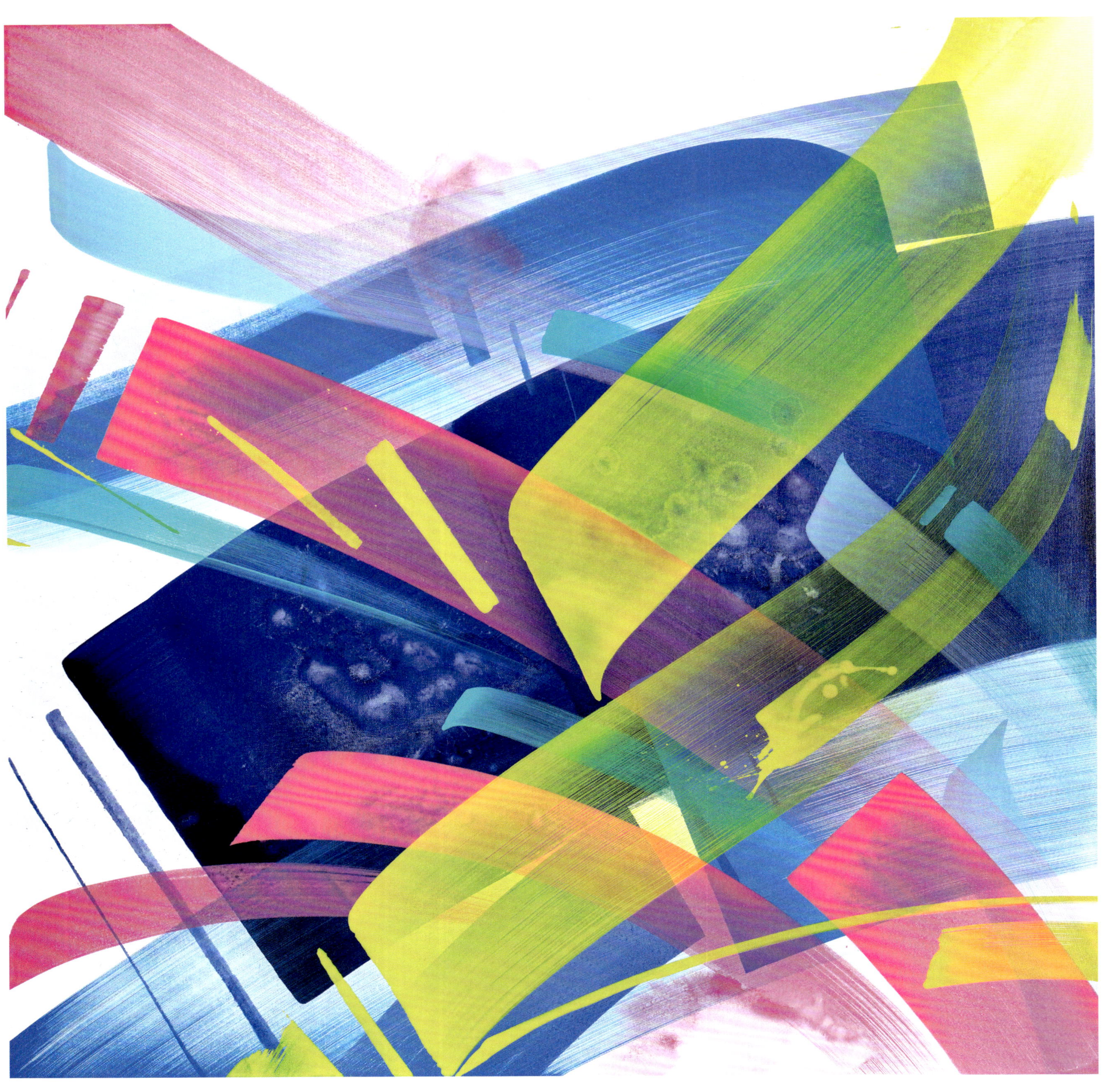

245. *11:24-22072020*, 100 x 100cm, acrylic, watercolour and spray paint on canvas, 2020

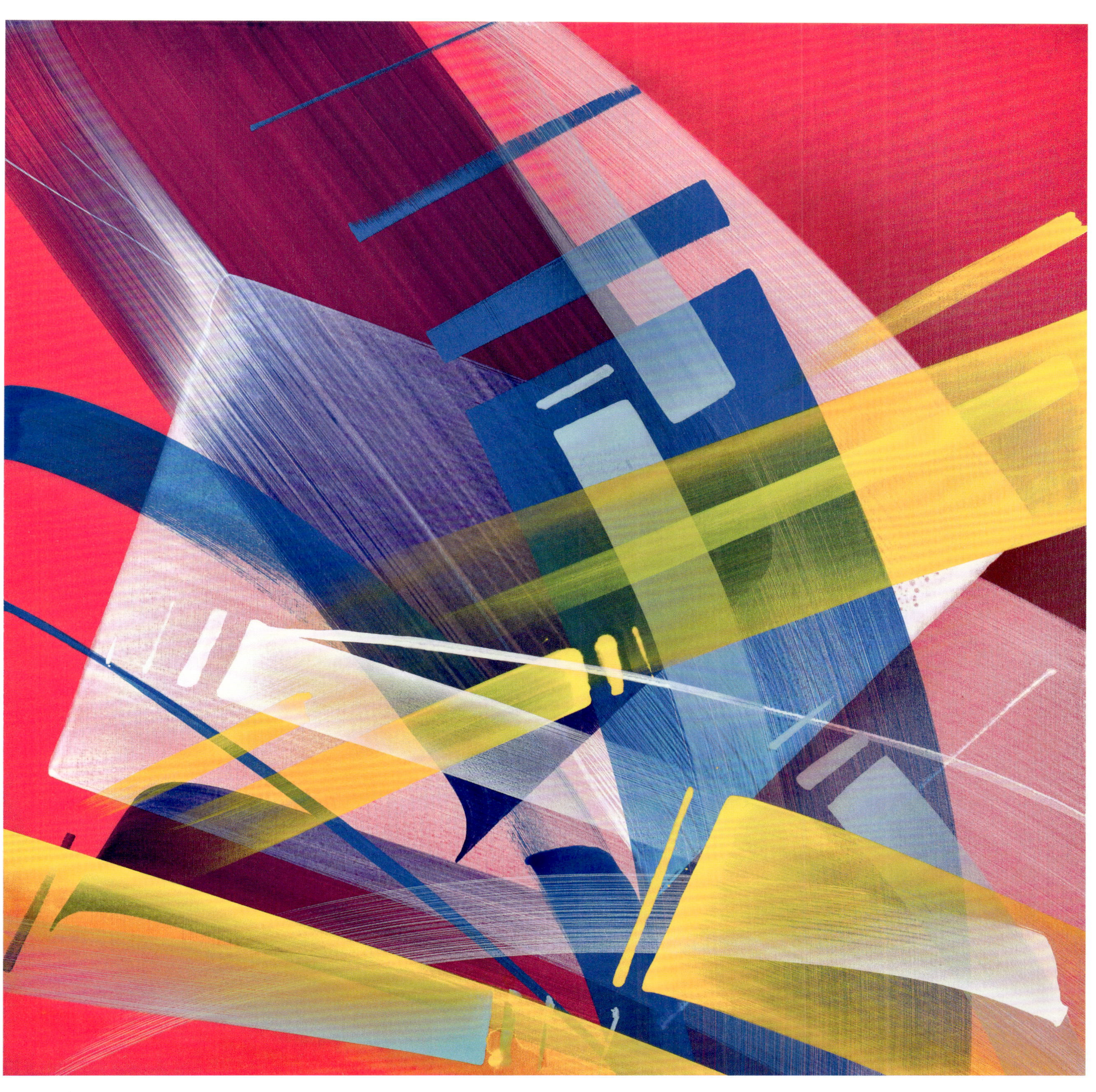

246. *09:15-20072020*, 100 x 100cm, acrylic and spray paint on canvas, 2020

247 (next spread). *14:28-17072020*, 100 x 150cm, acrylic and spray paint on canvas, 2020

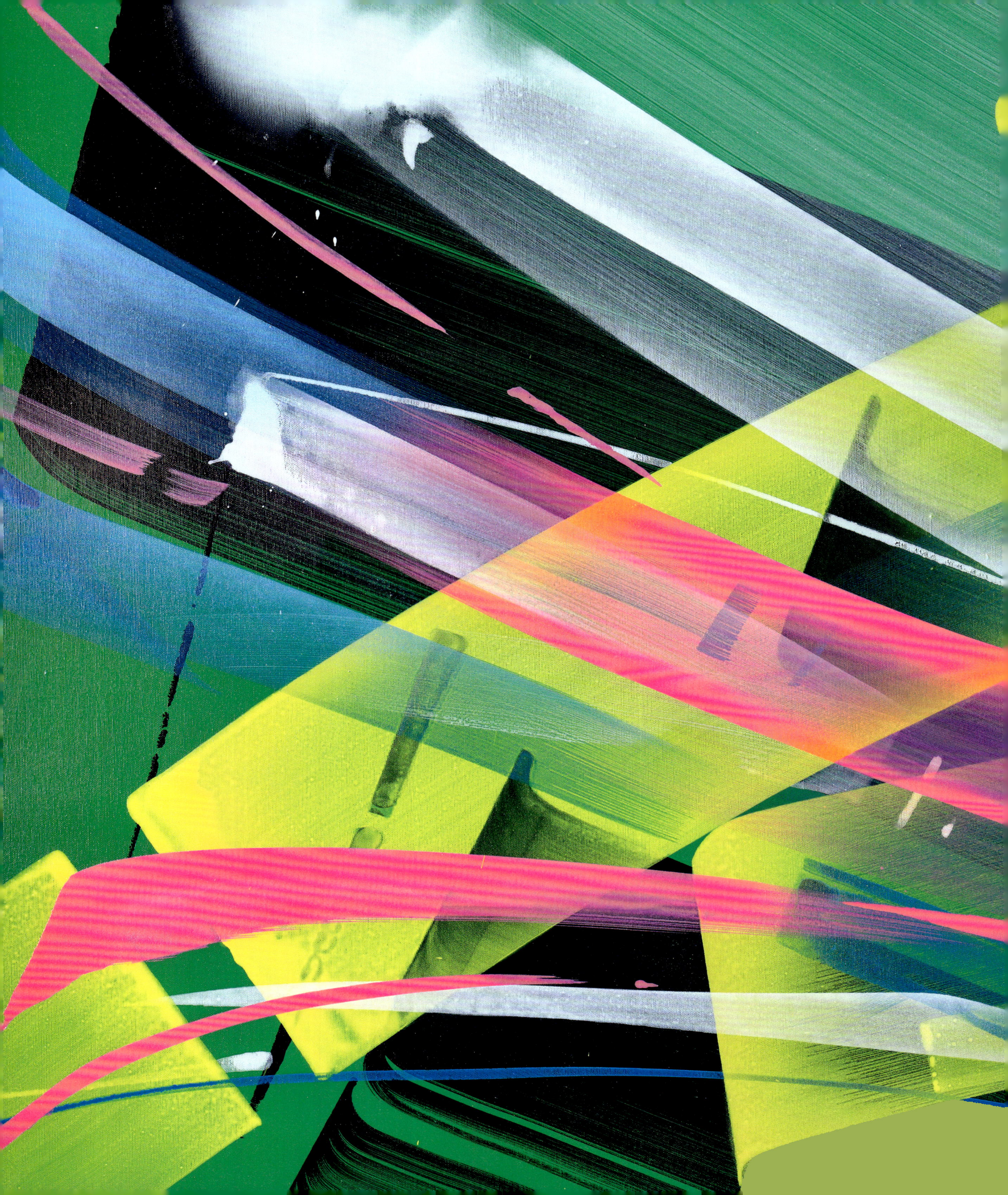

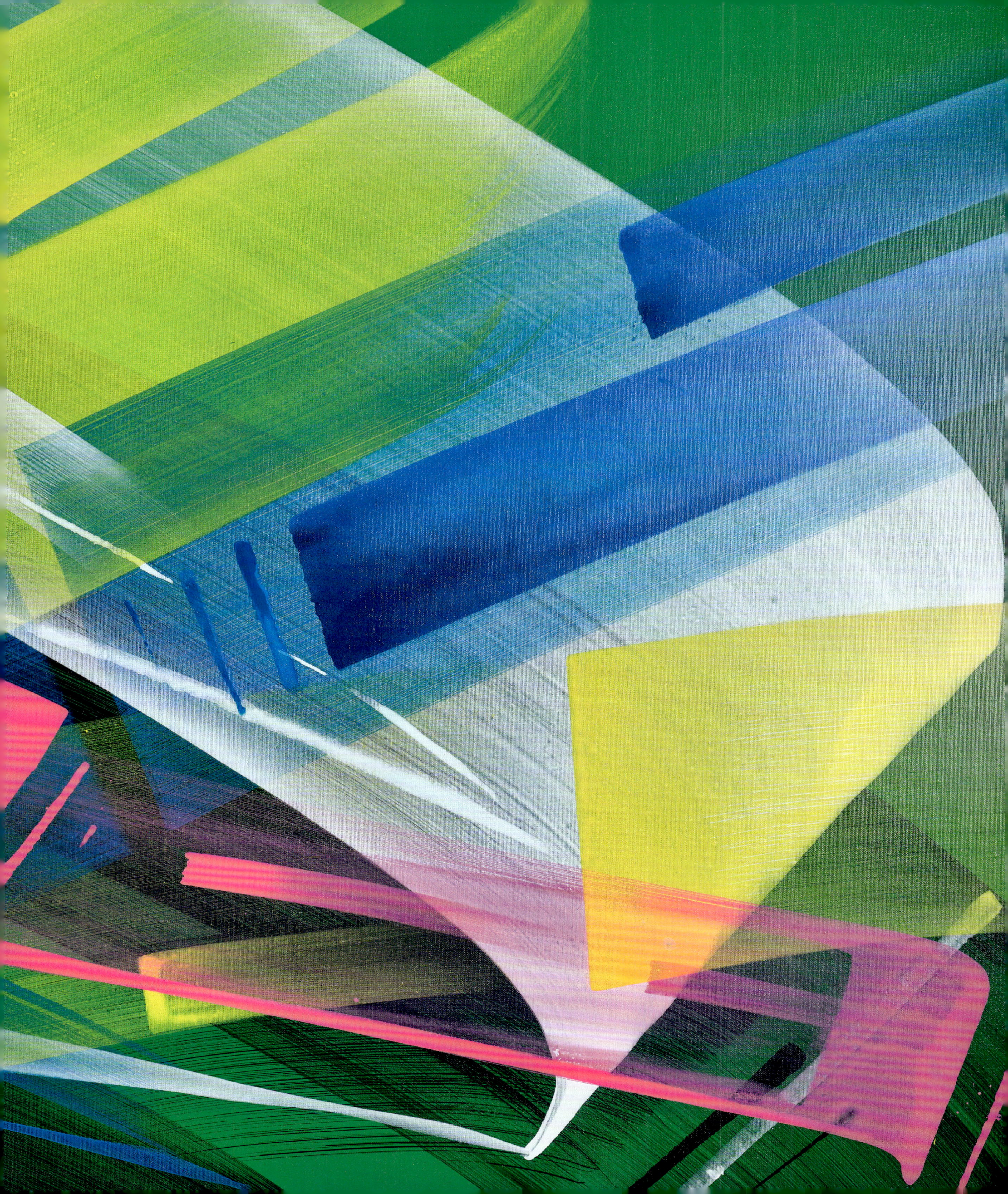

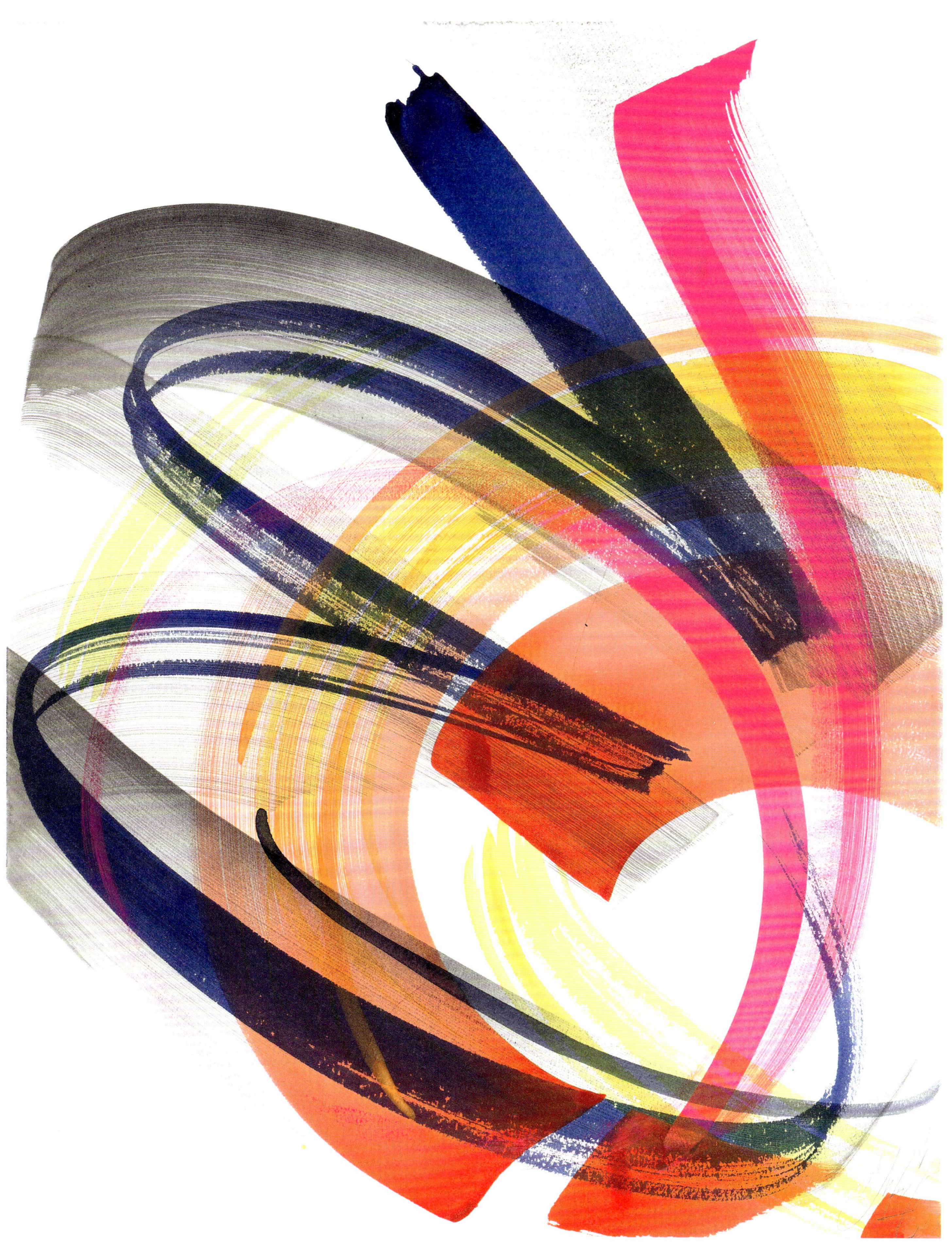

248. *paint and paper Five*, 77.5 x 56cm,
watercolour and spray paint on paper, 2020

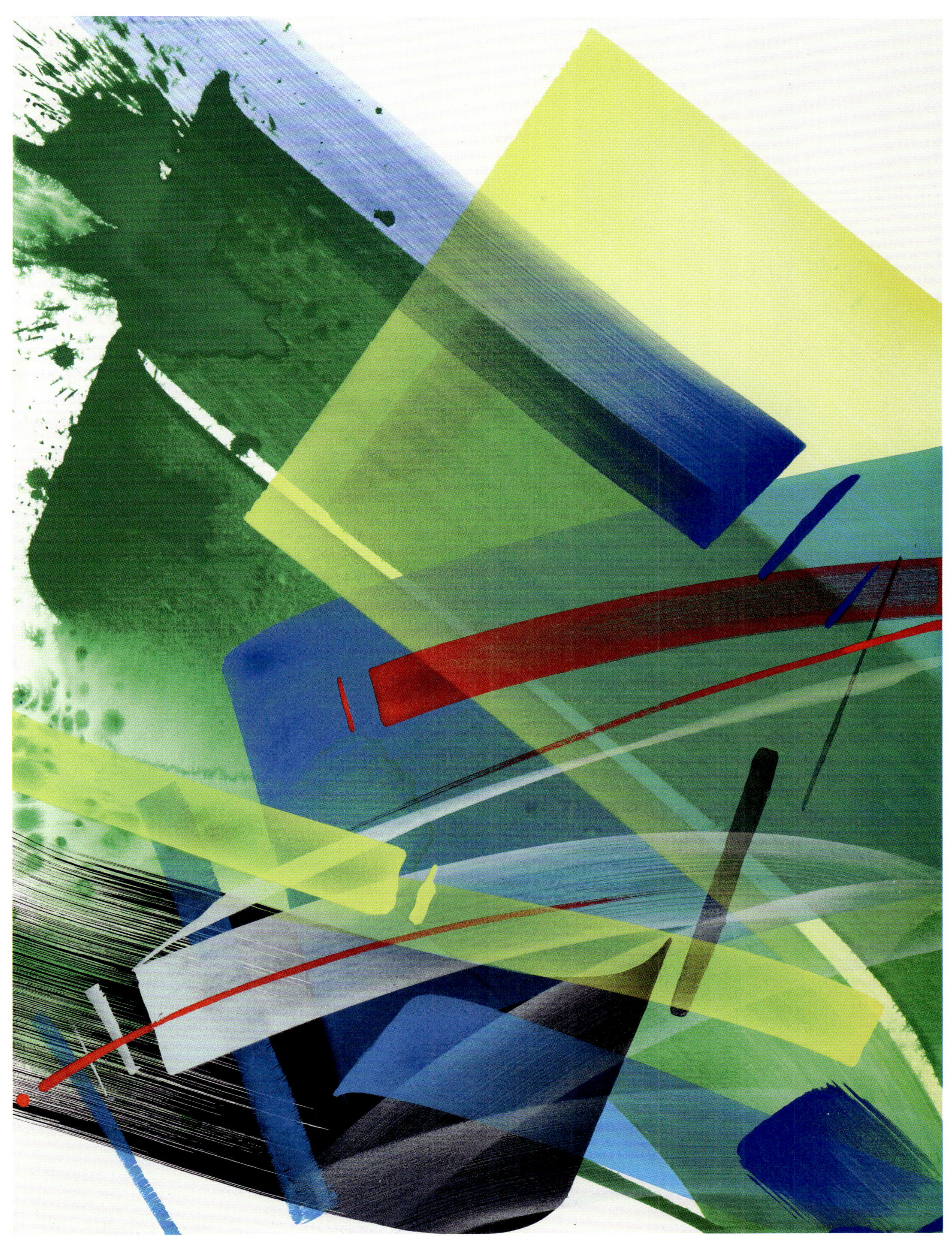

249. *17:52-01042021*, 80 x 60cm, acrylic and spray paint on canvas, 2021

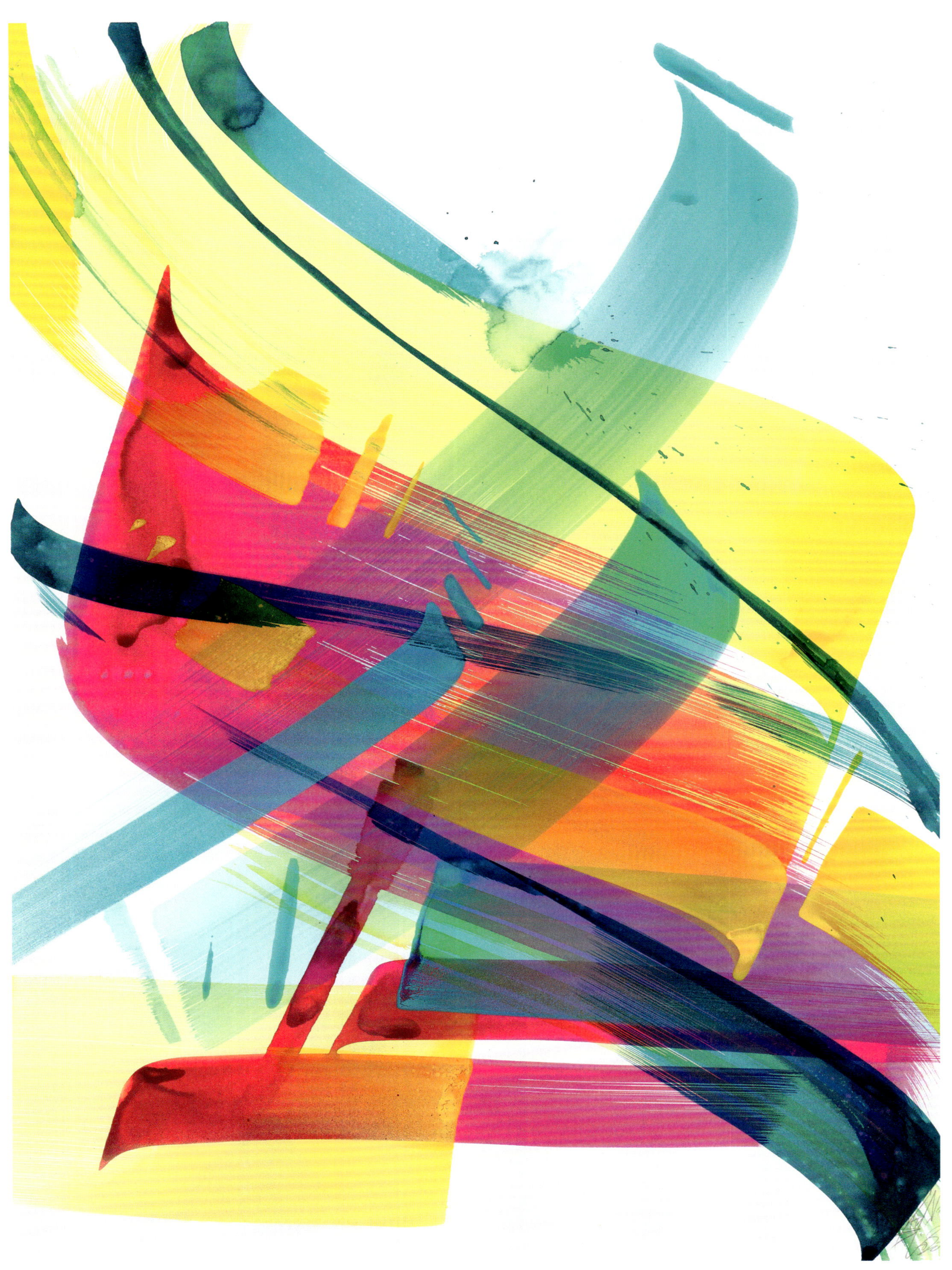

250. *paint and paper One*, 77.5 x 56cm,
watercolour and spray paint on paper, 2020

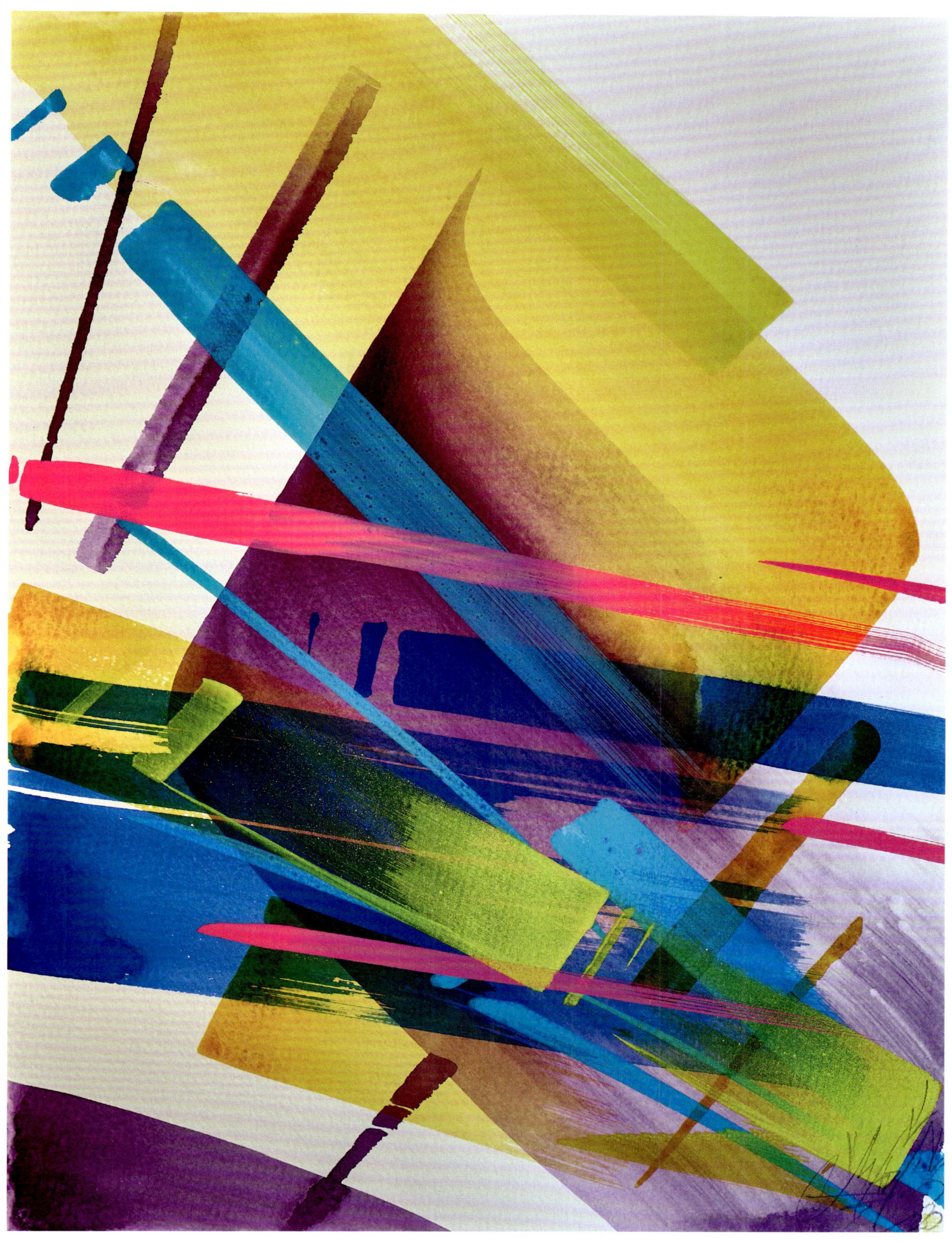

251. *Quarantine Day 6*, 40 x 30cm,
watercolour and spray paint on paper, 2020

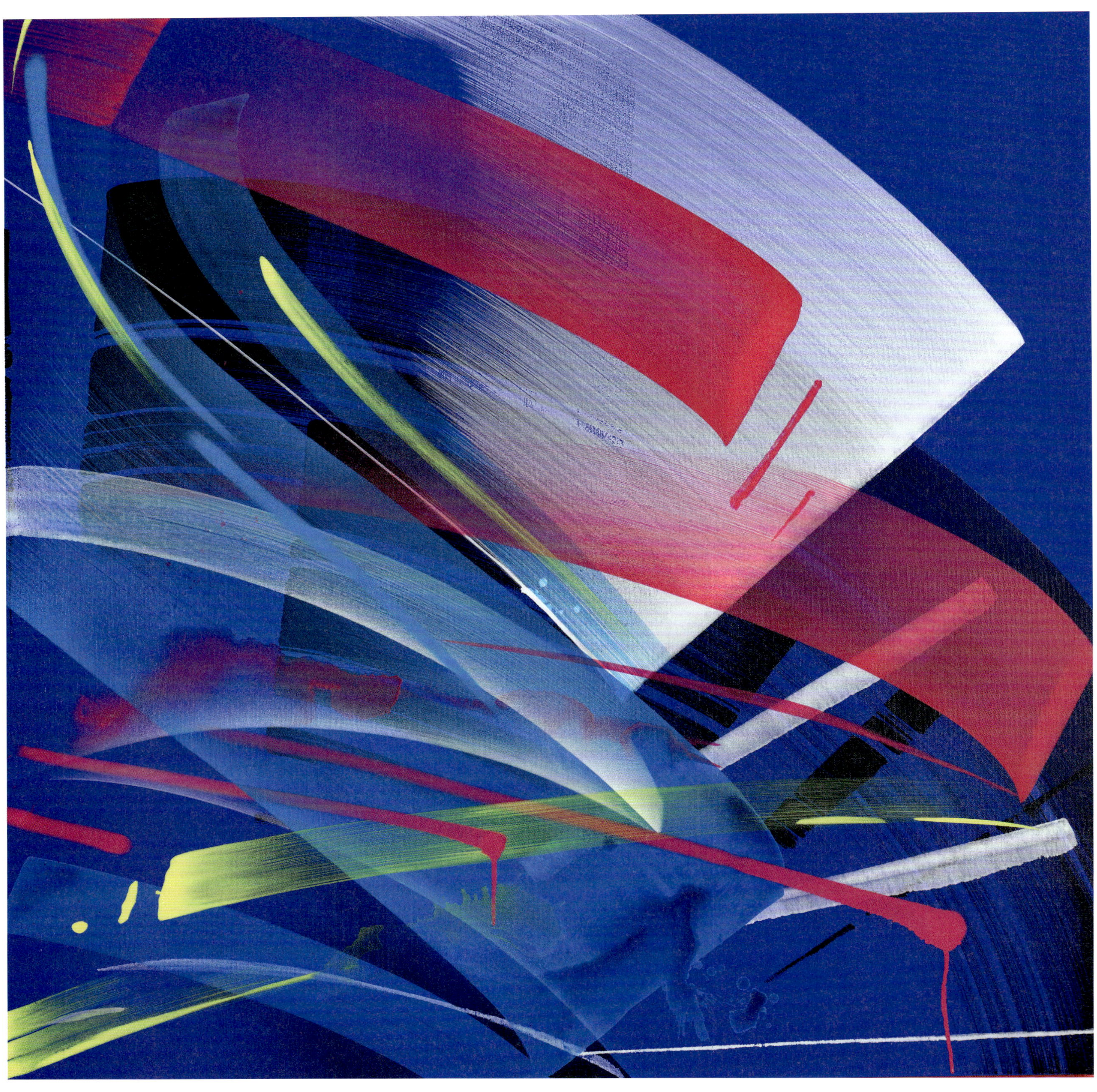

252. *15:53-21072020*, 100 x 100cm,
acrylic and spray paint on canvas, 2020

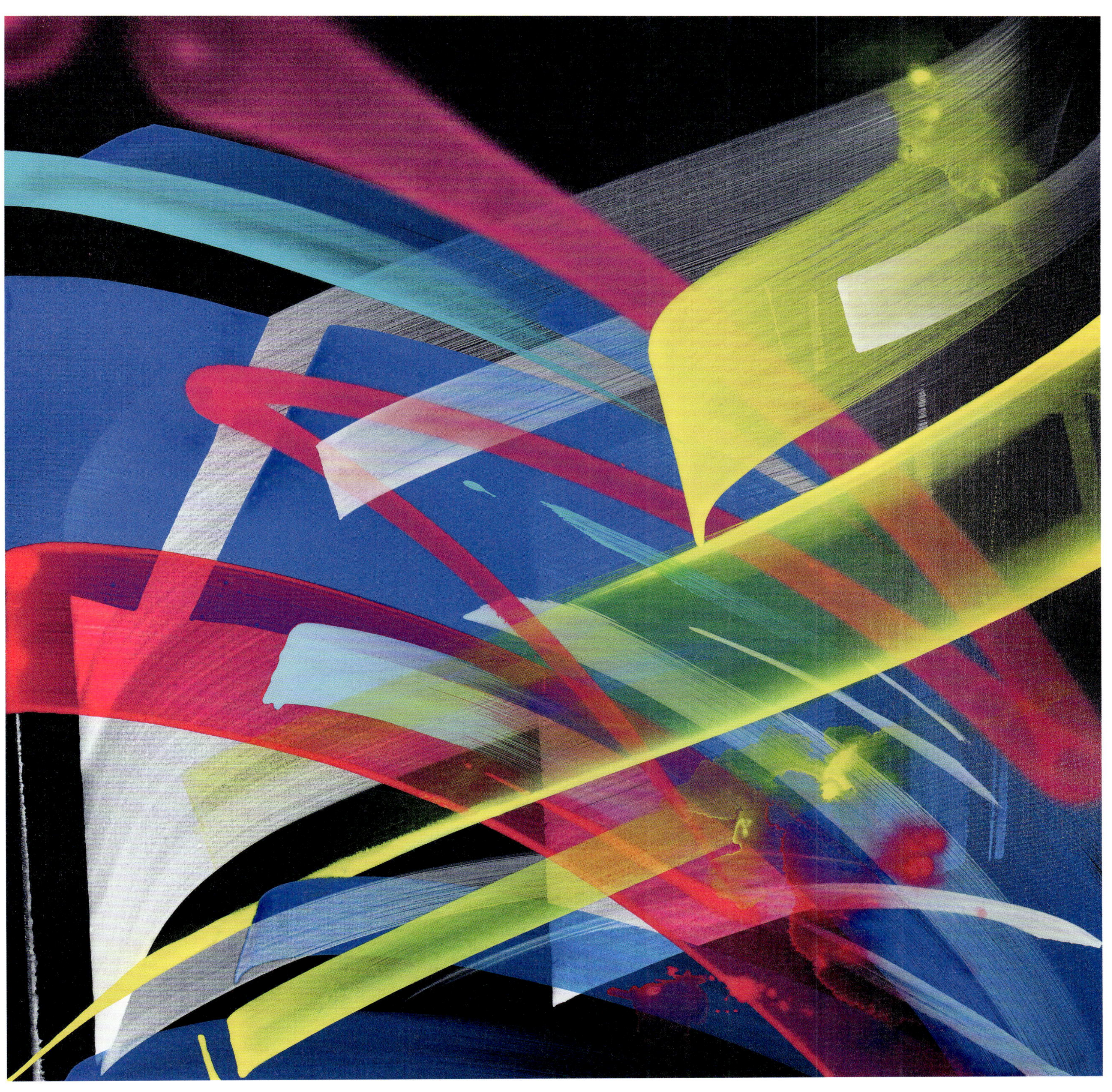

253. *10:34-22072020*, 100 x 100cm,
acrylic and spray paint on canvas, 2020

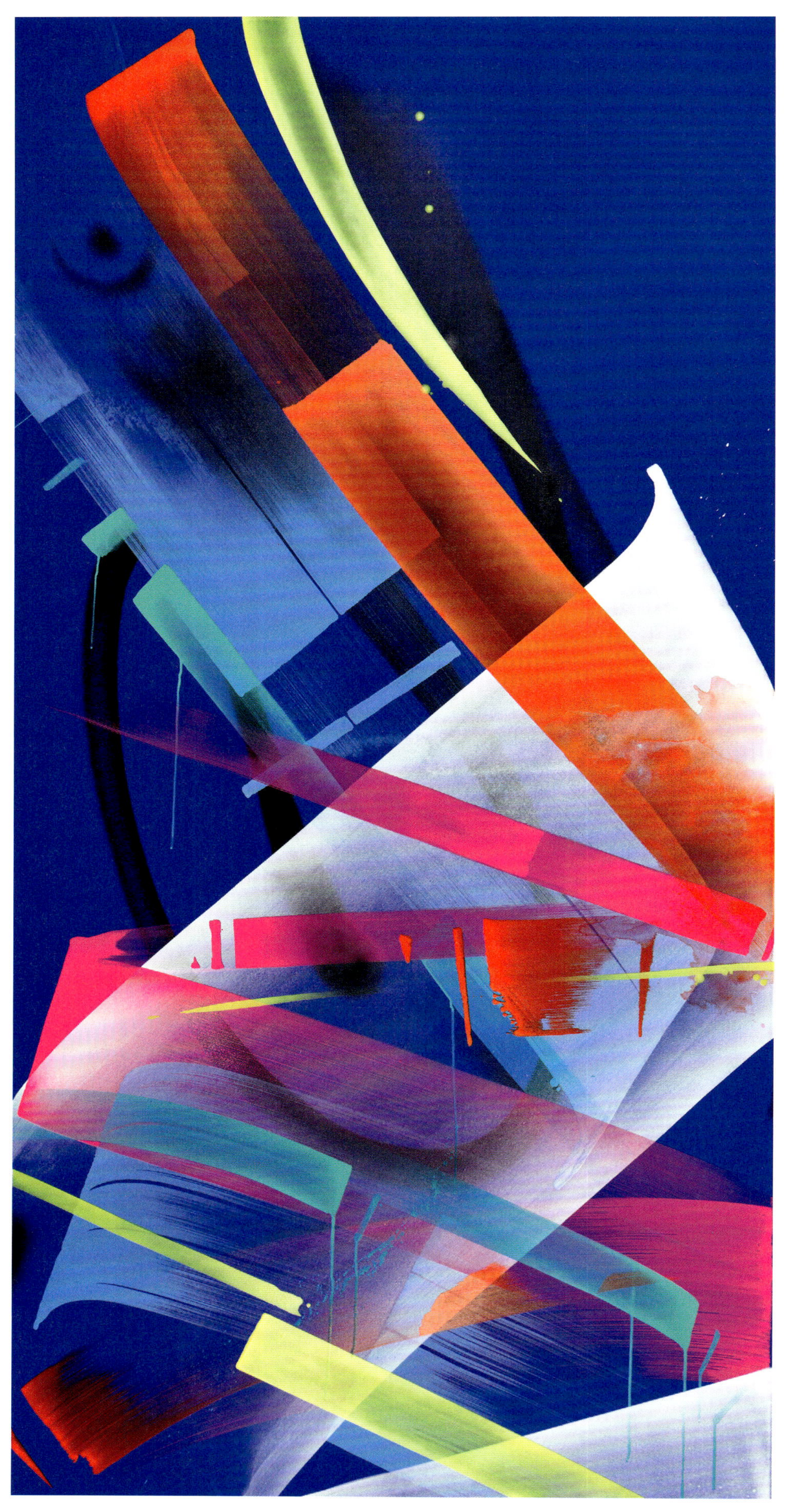

254. *16:47-11082020*, 240 x 120cm, acrylic, watercolour and spray paint on canvas, 2020

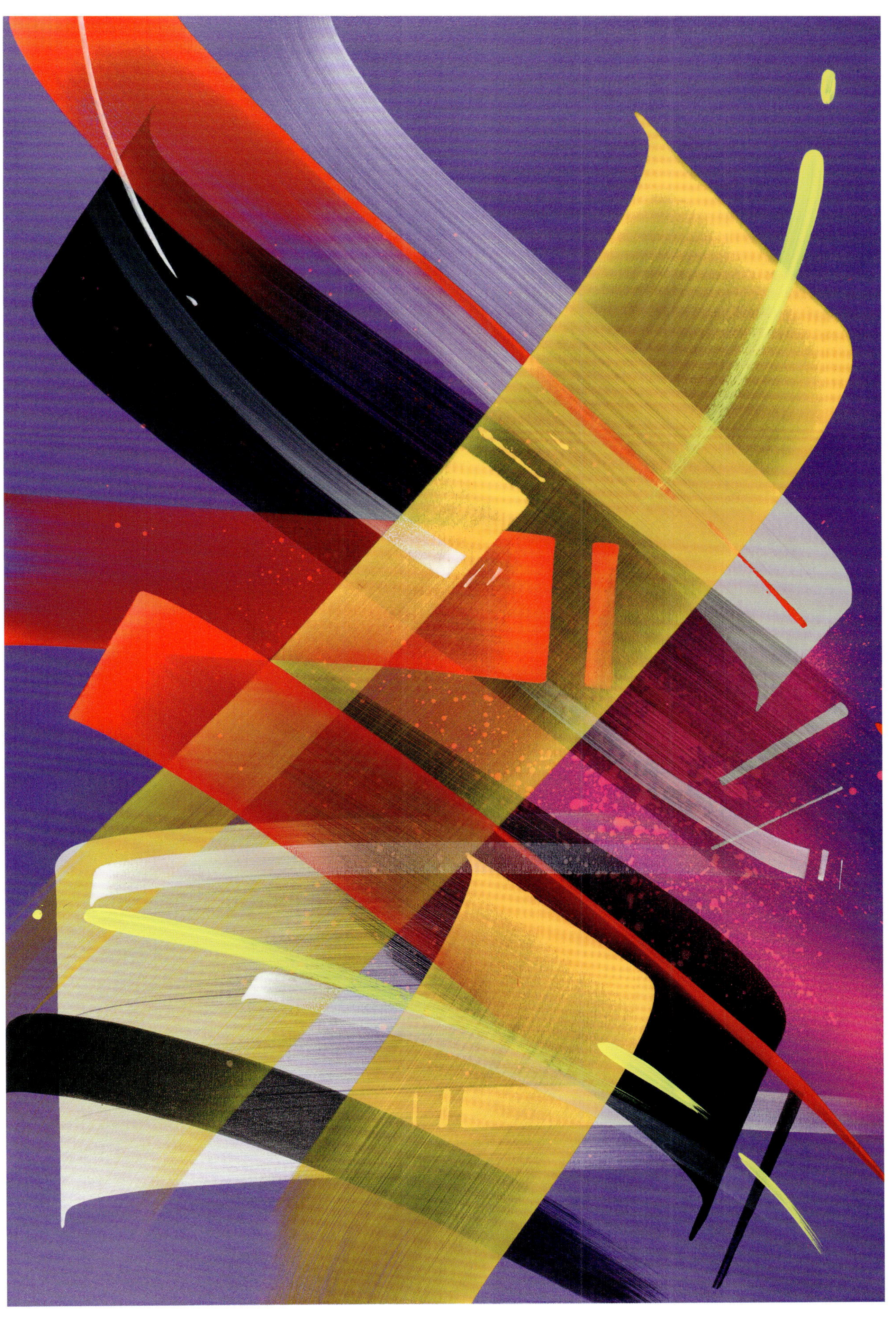

255. *19:17-13072021*, 180 x 120cm, acrylic, watercolour and spray paint on canvas, 2021

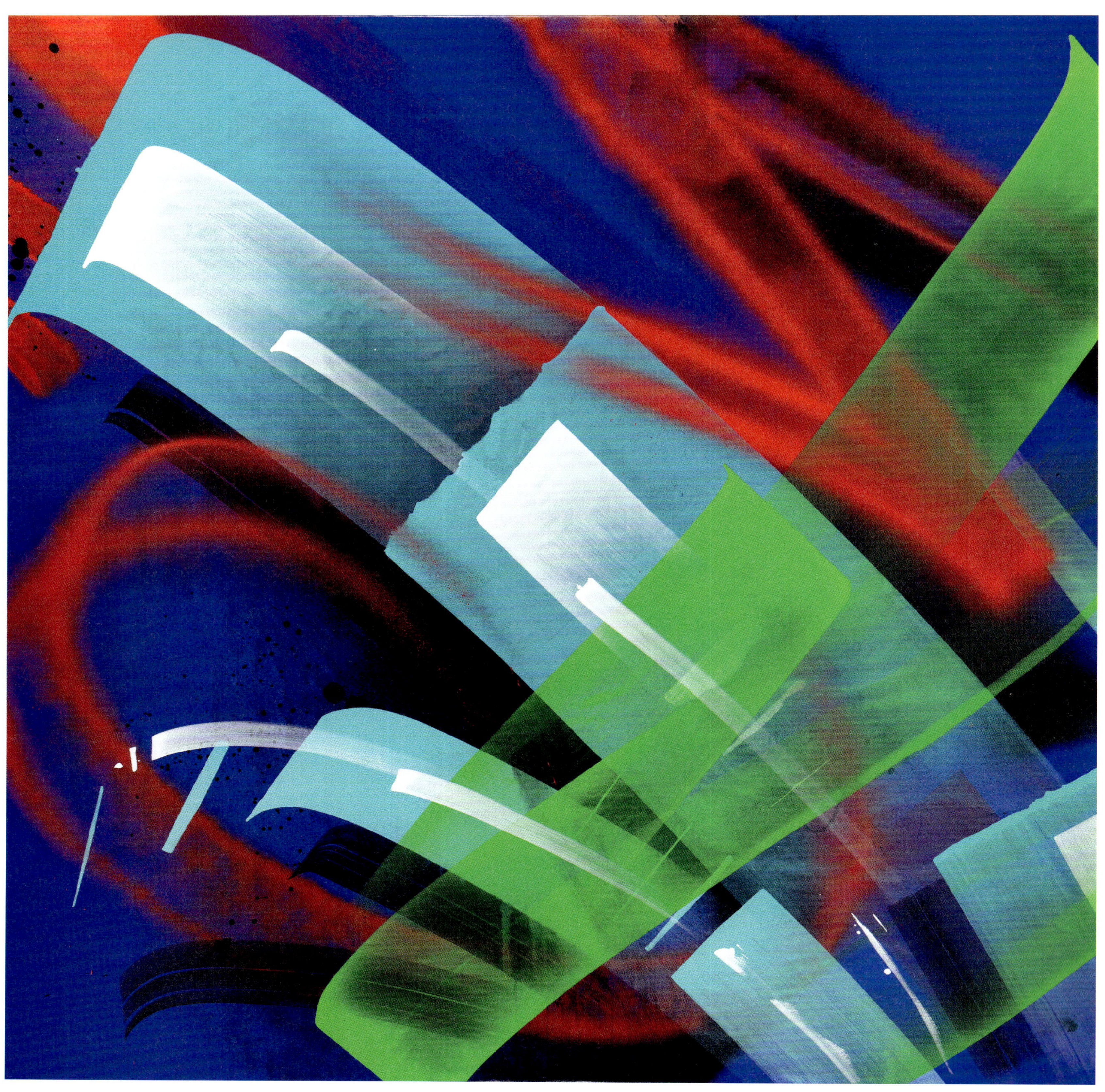

256. *18:32-04072021*, 250 x 250cm, acrylic and spray paint on canvas, 2021

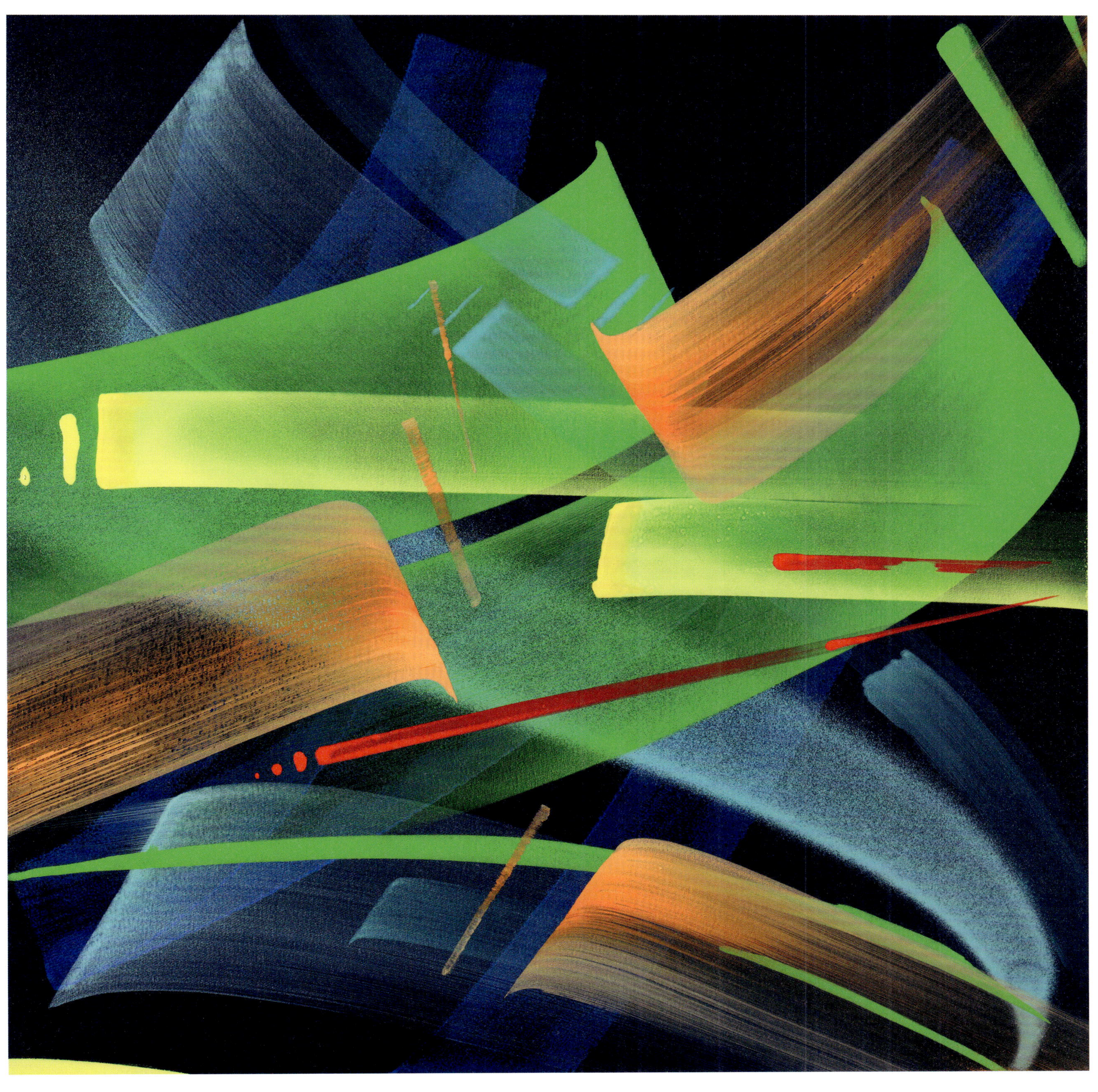

257. *22:09-09062021*, 80 x 80cm, acrylic and spray paint on canvas, 2021

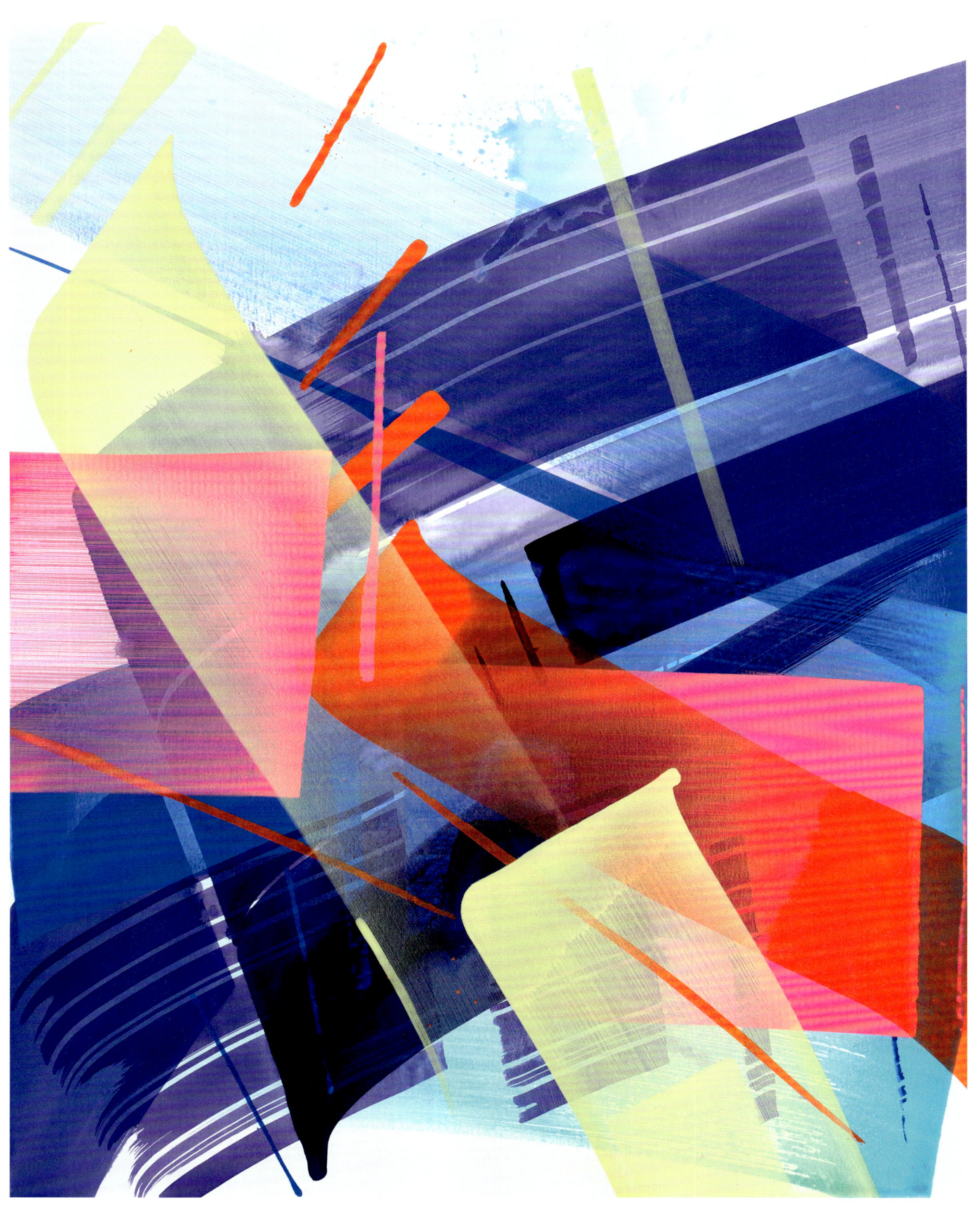

258. *13:22-15042021*, 100 x 80cm, acrylic, watercolour and spray paint on canvas, 2021

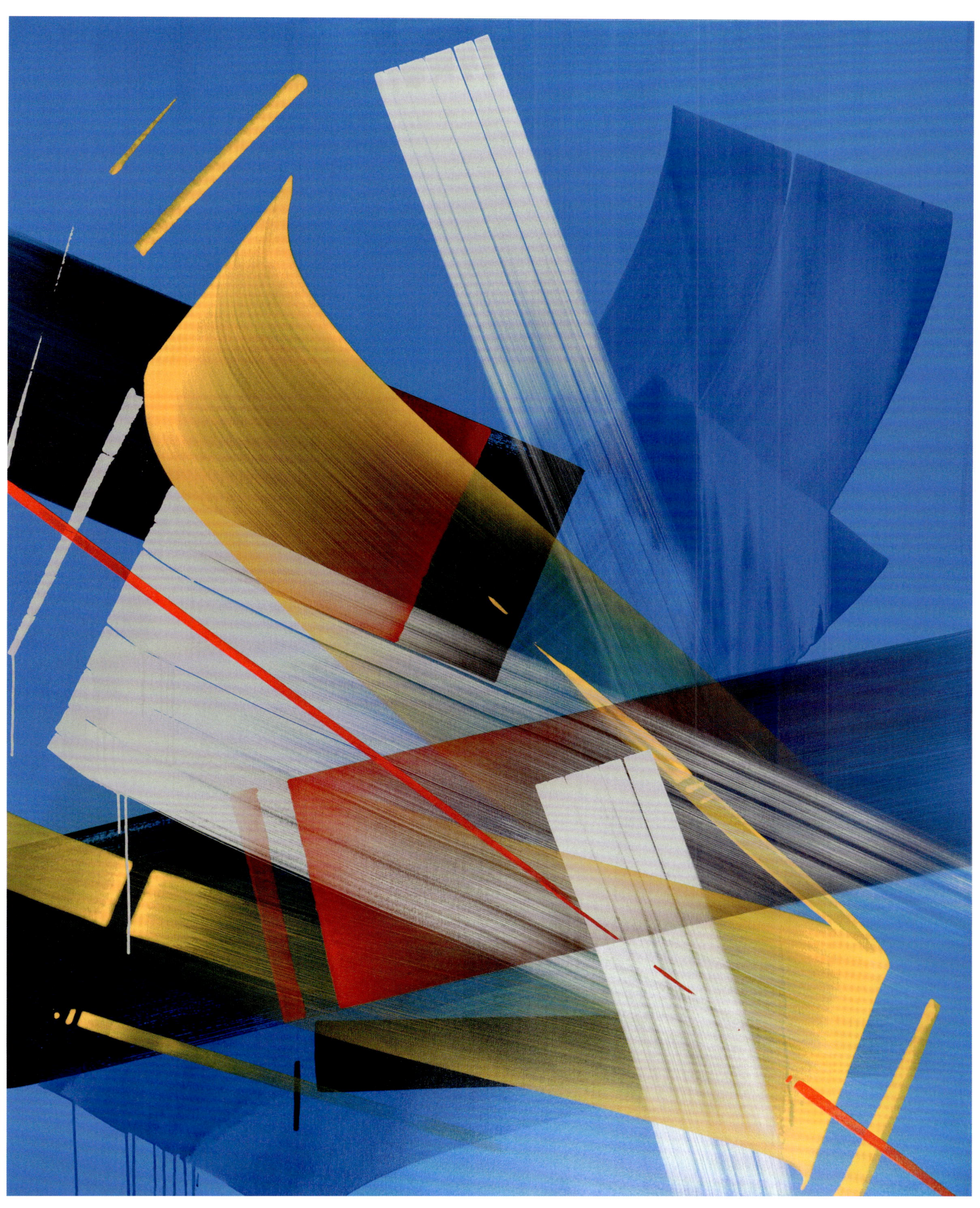

259. *12:27-07072021*, 200 x 160cm, acrylic and spray paint on canvas, 2021

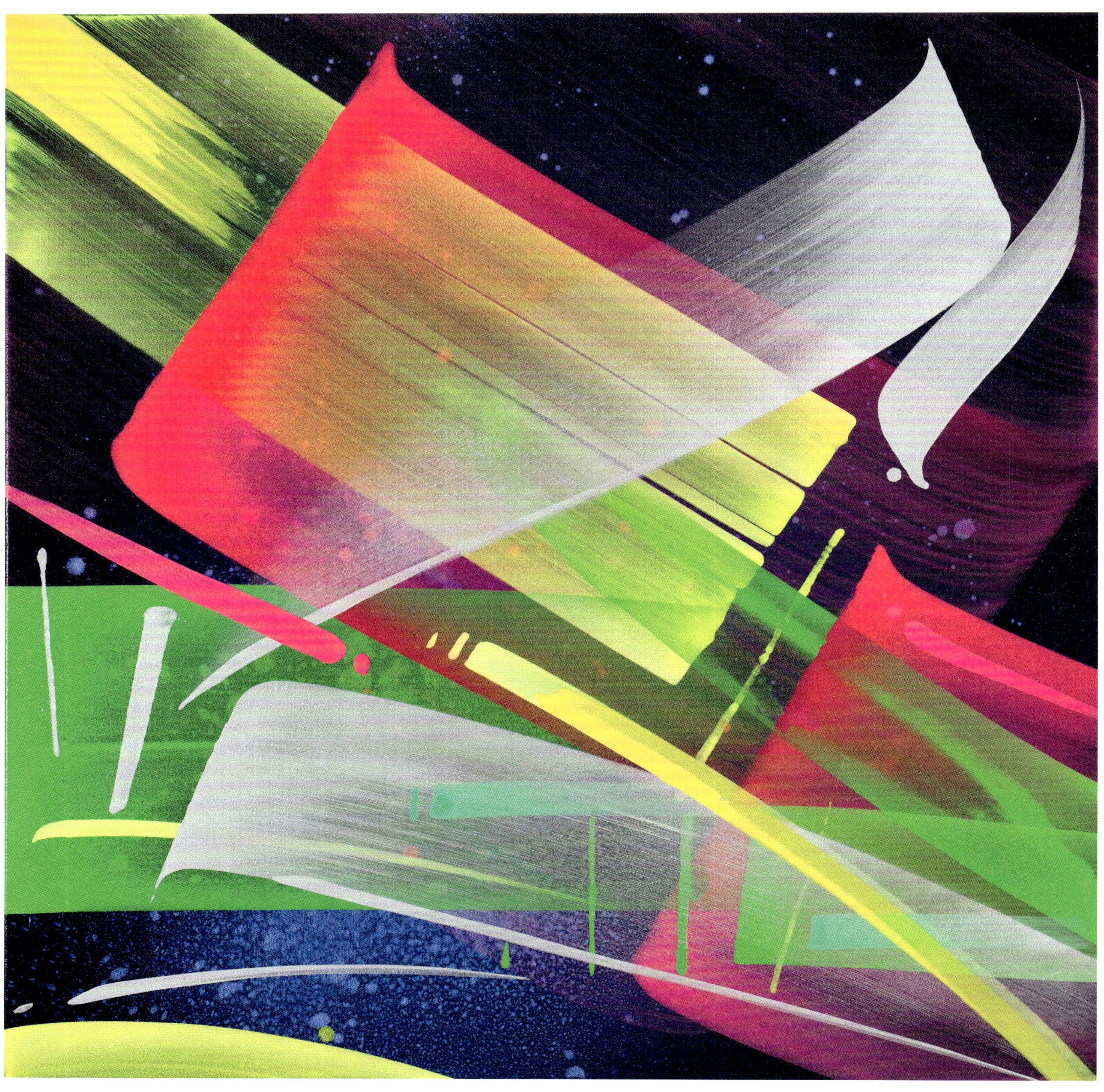

260. *10:21-13072021*, 100 x 100cm, acrylic, watercolour and spray paint on canvas, 2021

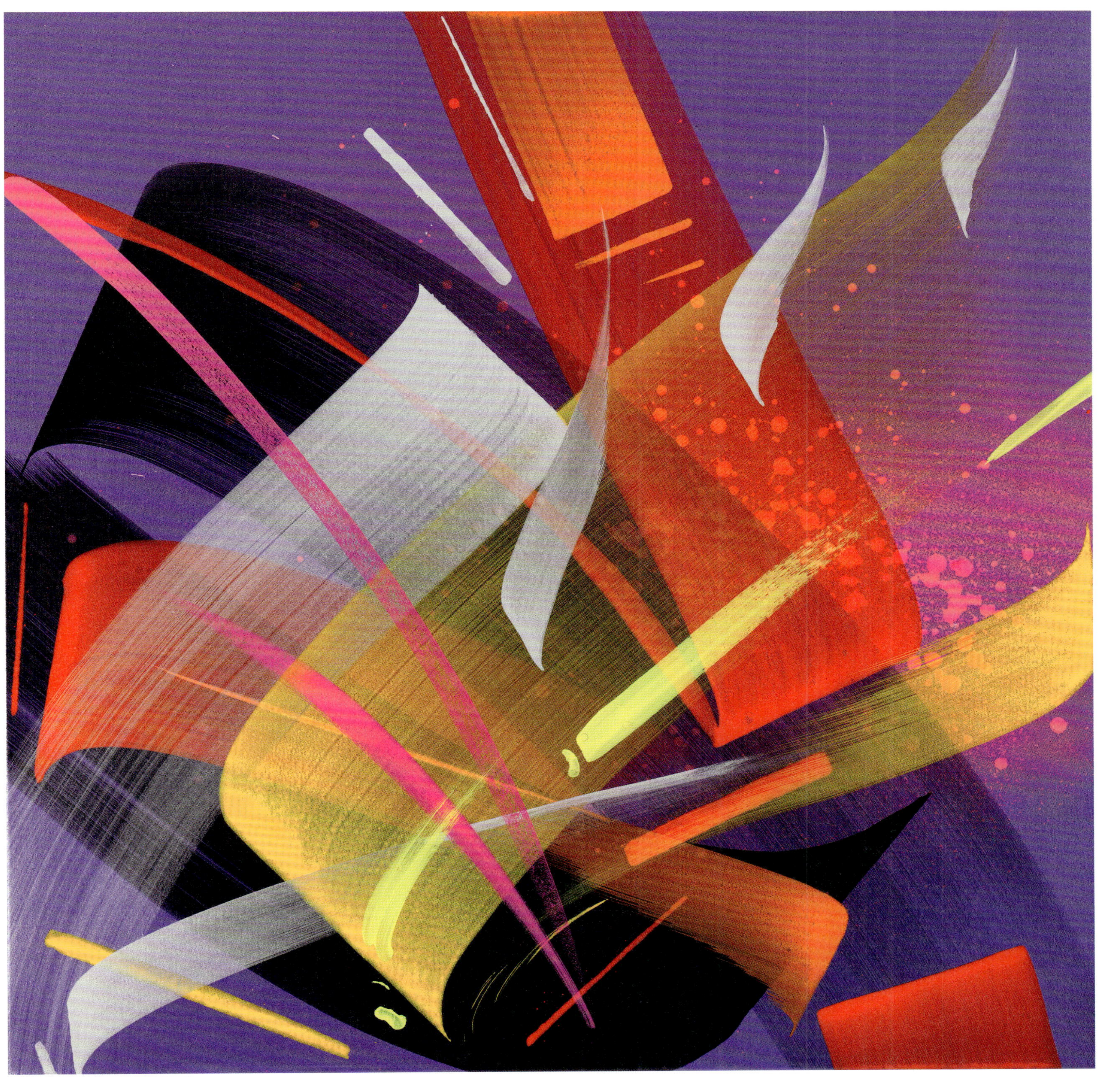

261. *10:29-12072021*, 100 x 100cm, acrylic, watercolour and spray paint on canvas, 2021

262 (next spread). Detail from *13:51-09082020*, 240 x 120cm, acrylic, watercolour and spray paint on canvas, 2020

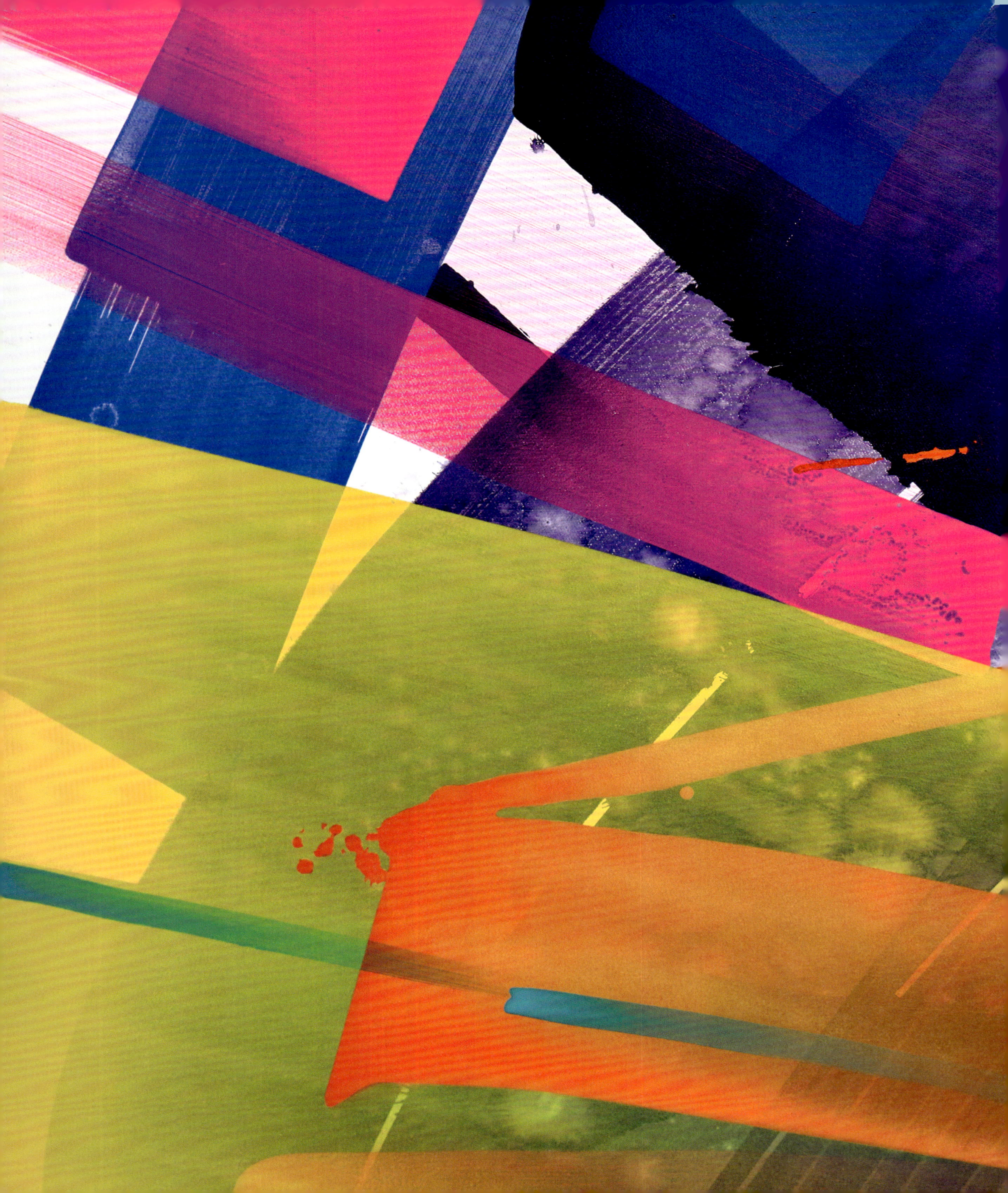

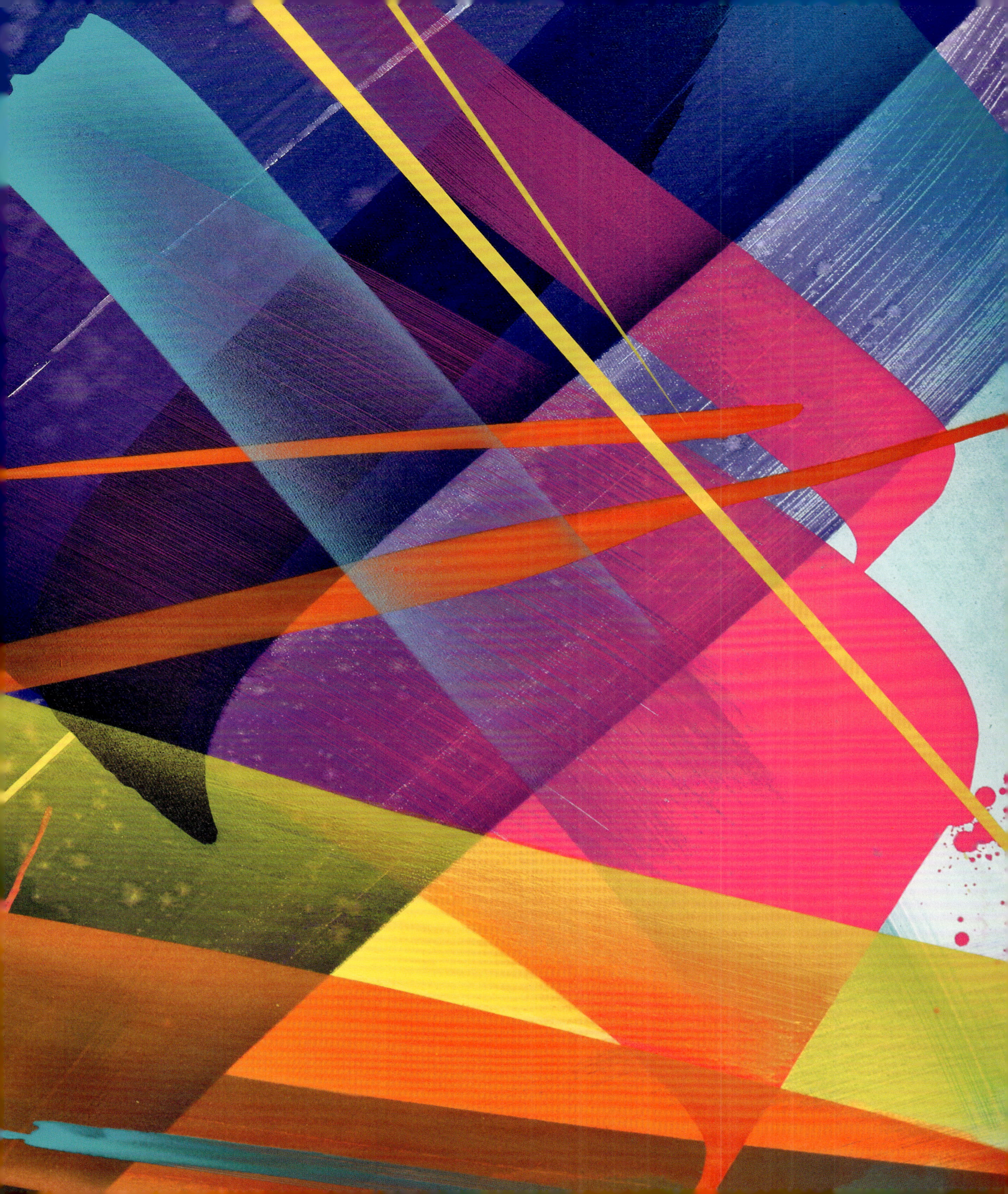

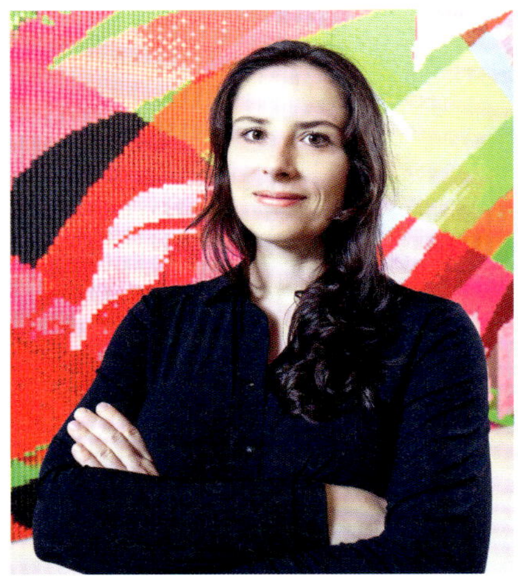

MadC

MadC (Claudia Walde, b. 1980) is a world-renowned visual graffiti artist, muralist and designer. She was born in Bautzen, Germany, and is best known for her large-scale murals. She studied at Central Saint Martins College of Art and Design, London, and Burg Giebichenstein University of Art and Design, Halle, and has a master's degree in Graphic Design. Her canvases are exhibited in solo and group shows worldwide. Mural commissions include Art and Museum Centre Sinkka, Kerava, Finland (2017); The Wynwood Walls Museum, Miami, USA (2017); The Marrakech Biennale, Morocco (2016); Dresden Airport, Germany (2019); and the 'For Abu Dhabi' Project, UAE (2020).

Her artistic style is based in graffiti art, resulting in vividly coloured, dynamic calligraphy and transparent layers. Through kinetic movement, MadC captures the energy of painting on a massive scale. In every painting, from street to canvas, her unique use of colour and composition is layered with the spontaneous movement of lines produced by spray cans or brushstrokes.

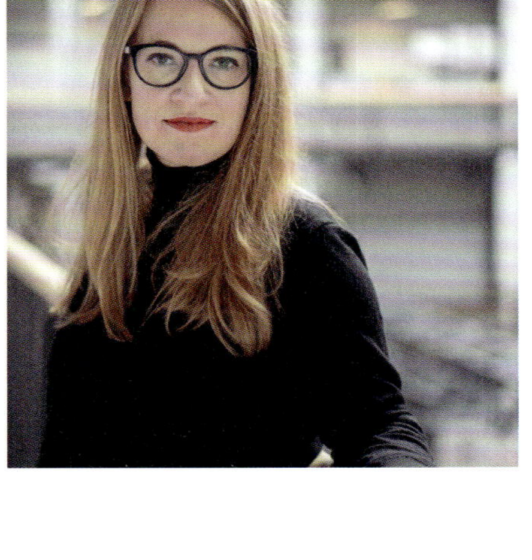

Luisa Heese

Luisa Heese (b. 1984) is a writer and curator based in Germany. She has written widely on contemporary art, and has worked on curatorial projects with institutions such as Musée des Beaux-Arts de Nancy, France, and Staatliche Kunsthalle Baden-Baden, Germany, where she has also held numerous editorships and had essays published on a wide variety of international artists. Since 2020 she has been the director of the Museum im Kulturspeicher Würzburg, Germany. From 2006 Heese has presented lectures on contemporary art at Braunschweig University of Art, Germany; University of Würzburg, Germany; and Universidade Nova de Lisboa/Centro de Arte Moderna, Portugal.

EXHIBITIONS LIST

SOLO SHOWS

2020 *Paint on Paper*, Kolly Gallery, Zurich, Switzerland
2020 *First Lines*, Kolly Gallery, Zurich, Switzerland
2020 *Goddess*, GAO's Fine Art, Taiyuan, China
2019 *Inside/Outside*, Galerie Brugier-Rigail, Paris, France
2019 *Sequence*, Kolly Gallery, Zurich, Switzerland
2019 *Dialog*, Brenners Park-Hotel and Spa, Baden-Baden, Germany
2019 *Cherry Blossom*, Kolly Gallery, Zurich, Switzerland
2018 *Pink Power*, Kolly Gallery, Zurich, Switzerland
2018 *Rush Hour*, WallWorks NY, New York City, USA
2018 *Southern Lights*, Galerie Nicolas-Xavier, Montpellier, France
2018 *Night and Day*, 44309 Gallery, Dortmund, Germany
2016 *Home Sweet Home*, Galerie Brugier-Rigail, Paris, France
2016 *Kaleidoscope*, Kolly Gallery, Zurich, Switzerland
2015 *Bits and Pieces*, WallWorks NY, New York City, USA
2015 *Night and Day*, 44309 Gallery, Dortmund, Germany
2015 *Character*, Pure Evil Gallery, London, UK
2015 *The Bright Side of Life*, Galerie Brugier-Rigail, Paris, France
2014 *Reflections*, Kolly Gallery, Zurich, Switzerland
2013 *Over the Edge*, 1AM, San Francisco, USA
2012 *Layers*, 44309 Gallery, Dortmund, Germany
2012 *Between the Lines*, La Grille, Yverdon, Switzerland
2011 *MadABC*, Pure Evil Gallery, London, UK
2009 *Pretty/Ugly*, Galeria BARAKA, Kraków, Poland

SELECTED GROUP SHOWS

2020 *Art Basel on Beach Street*, WallWorks NY/212 Arts, New York, USA
2020 *Roads of Abstraction*, CultureInside Gallery, Luxembourg
2020 *Page Blanche*, Galerie Nicolas-Xavier, Montpellier, France
2019 *Iconoclast*, Miaja Art Collections, Singapore
2019 *Variations*, Galerie Nicolas-Xavier, Montpellier, France
2019 *Conquête Urbaine*, Musée des Beaux-Arts, Calais, France
2019 *Bronx Pride*, WallWorks NY, New York City, USA
2018 *Street Colour*, Institut Bernard Magrez, Bordeaux, France
2017 *Searching for Surfaces*, Vertical Gallery, Chicago, USA
2017 *Compendium*, Treason Gallery, Seattle, USA
2017 *For the Love of Freedom*, Art and Museum Centre Sinkka, Kerava, Finland
2017 *Abstract Forum*, Forum Przestrzenie, Kraków, Poland
2017 *Adventures in Modern Abstraction*, StolenSpace Gallery, London, UK
2017 *Abstract Realism*, Affenfaust Galerie, Hamburg, Germany
2017 *Who's Your Daddy?*, Kolly Gallery, Phnom Penh, Cambodia
2017 *Radius*, Urban Nation, Berlin, Germany
2017 UrbanArt Biennale, Völklinger Hütte, Germany
2016 *Magic City*, Dresden, Germany
2016 Marrakech Biennale, Marrakech, Morocco
2015 *Who's Your Daddy?*, Kolly Gallery, Lausanne, Switzerland
2015 *Red One*, Jardin Rouge, Marrakech, Morocco
2015 *Fifty Fifty*, Kolly Gallery, Geneva, Switzerland
2015 *Urban Pott*, 44309 Gallery, Dortmund, Germany
2015 *Past & Future*, Kolly Gallery, Zurich, Switzerland
2015 *Revolution*, 1AM, San Francisco, USA
2014 *Miami*, Library Street Collective, Art Basel Miami, USA
2014 *First Taste*, WallWorks NY, New York City, USA
2013 *Urban Contemporary Art*, Galerie Le Feuvre, Paris, France
2013 *Billboard Painters*, Galleri NB, Viborg, Denmark
2013 *Innovative Art*, Reutov Museum, Reutov, Russia
2012 *Paper Party*, Galerie Le Feuvre, Paris, France
2012 *Team Rex*, Red Gallery, London, UK
2012 *Art & Sole*, Lab Art Gallery, Los Angeles, USA
2011 *Urban Art EFX*, CBK Gallery, Amsterdam, Netherlands
2011 *Public Provocations III*, Carhartt Gallery, Weil am Rhein, Germany
2011 *Hallenkunst*, Chemnitz, Germany
2010 *Dalla A alla Z*, touring exhibition, Italy
2010 Underground Arts Collective, New York City, USA
2010 *Tribute to DARE*, K31 Gallery, Lahr, Germany
2010 *Hallenkunst*, Chemnitz, Germany
2009 *Piece Out*, Belleville, USA
2008 *Heart & Soul*, New York City, USA
2008 *Sneaker Galaxy*, New York City, USA
2007 *White Gallery*, Leipzig, Germany
2006 *Flour 'n' Sugar – Flavoured Streets*, Leipzig, Germany

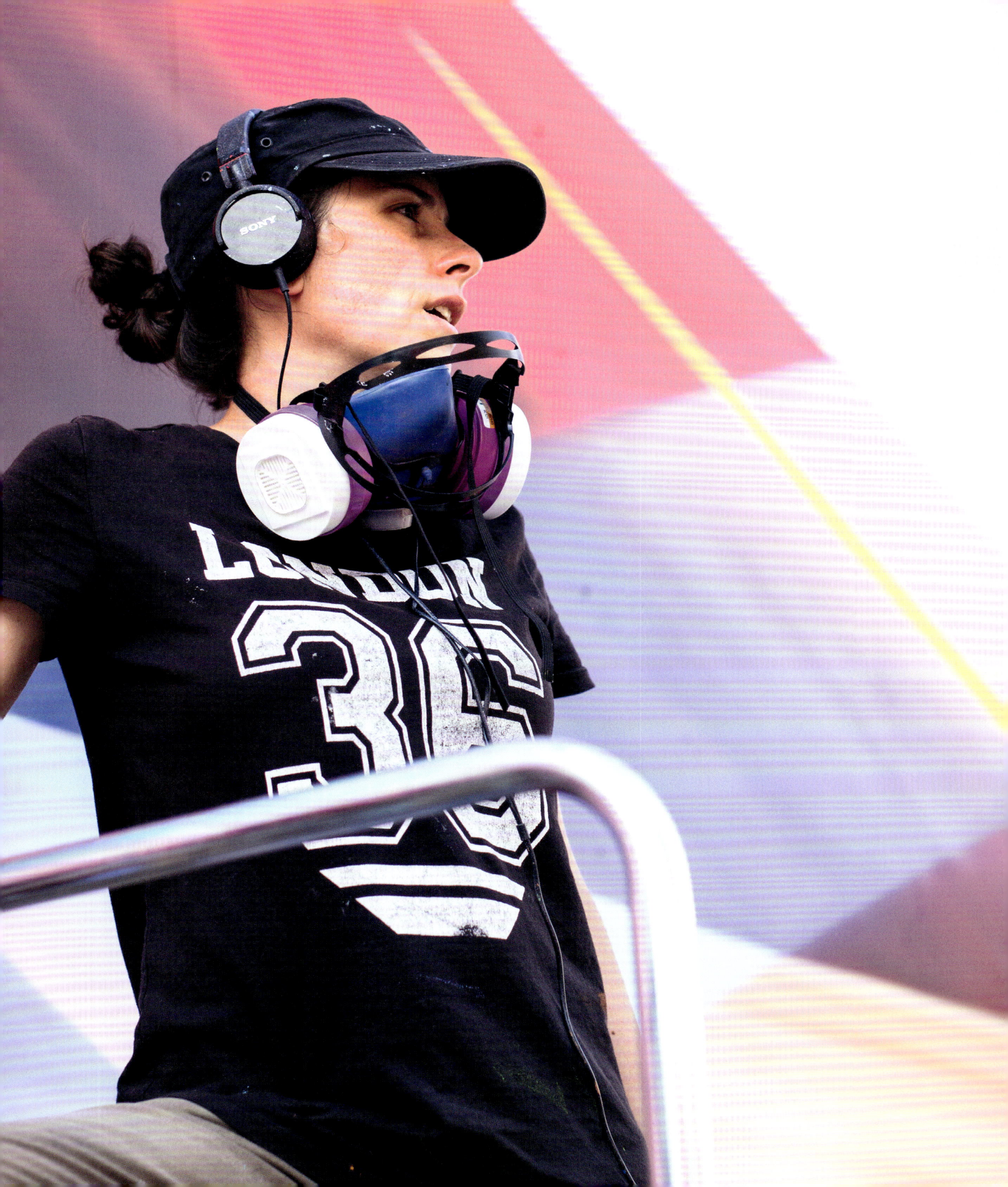
SONY

ACKNOWLEDGEMENTS

Thanks to everyone who was a part of my journey, to everyone who supported me through the years and helped me grow. I'm grateful to be surrounded by good people with positive energy. Special thanks to:

Emily & Pauline, Marco Prosch, Stephan Walde, my parents, grandparent, aunt and uncle, Sascha Sasse, Jürgen Feuerstein, Reno Rössel, Julien Kolly, Dr Rightnow, Joe Hage, Olaf Ginzel, René Kästner, Thomas Stønjum, Luisa Heese, Thomas Deichsel, Jamie Camplin, Frederik Richter, Reinhard Ernst, Barbara Römer, Neysa Page-Lieberman, Ingrid Beazley, Remi Rough, Annelies Maenhout, John 'Crash' Matos, Frank Marrenbach, Kiki Kausch, Jack Aguirre, Marite Iglesias, Steven van der Kruit, Laurent Rigail, Eric Brugier, Thomas Thompson, André Cardinali, Isabelle Miaja, Jacob Kimvall, Jens-Peter Brask, Giancarlo Petrucci, Hendrik Rümenap, Magda Rümenap, Dr Denis Pfister-Grune, Bob Zeltman, family Lecke, Clara, Philipp & Carina Stahl, Mathias Kaßner, Tasi, Iryna Shulikina, Johanna, Theresa, Lotte, Lilly, Jette, Sophia, Valentina, Pure Evil, Marco Lauber, Andrea Timillero, Nicolas Xavier, Jouni Väänänen, Arja Elovirta, Niki Schilling, Karl-Hermann Schmiing, Frank Wend, Michael Kretschmer, Maciej Frej, Luicho Delgado, Luicito Nazario, Lars Oschatz, Mathias Göbel, Shahed Naji, Julian Ziege, Natalie Roesner, Rye Quartz, Soten, Dare, HAKS180, Klöver, Slider and the Bandits crew, Wallnuts crew, Can2 and Stick up Kids crew, S.kape, Mare139, JonOne, Been3, Klark Kent, Robert Cantor, Newkon, Faith47, Lady Pink, Miss Klor, Dalek, Gaia, Blek le Rat, Alexone, Symbiz, Amok, Chromatics, Team Red Tower, Justin BUA, Michael De Feo.

PICTURE CREDITS

All photographs in this book are © Marco Prosch, unless otherwise stated below. Images listed below which appear in the opening and final pages of the book are unnumbered and are cited by page reference; all other images are cited by figure number. Grateful thanks to all contributors.

Martha Cooper: fig. 2
Ian Cox: figs. 106, 107
Dare: fig. 29
Dulwich Picture Gallery, London: fig. 99
Fokke Hassel: fig. 119
For Abu Dhabi: fig. 175
Tim Hughes: *JC 180*, pp 12–13
Holger Kiefer: figs. 114, 116
Jayson de Leon: fig. 135
Red Tower Films / Michael Schmidt: figs. 46, 128
Reno Rössel: figs. 80, 81, 82, 83, 84, 98, 100, 101, 102, 103, 168
Luke Shirlaw: figs. 178, 179, 180
Karolina Sobel: *Luisa Heese*, p.232
Tost Films: figs. 173, 177
Jouni Väänänen: *Free at Last*, pp 4–5 and 234
Steve Weinik: figs. 104, 105, 108, and pp 238–239

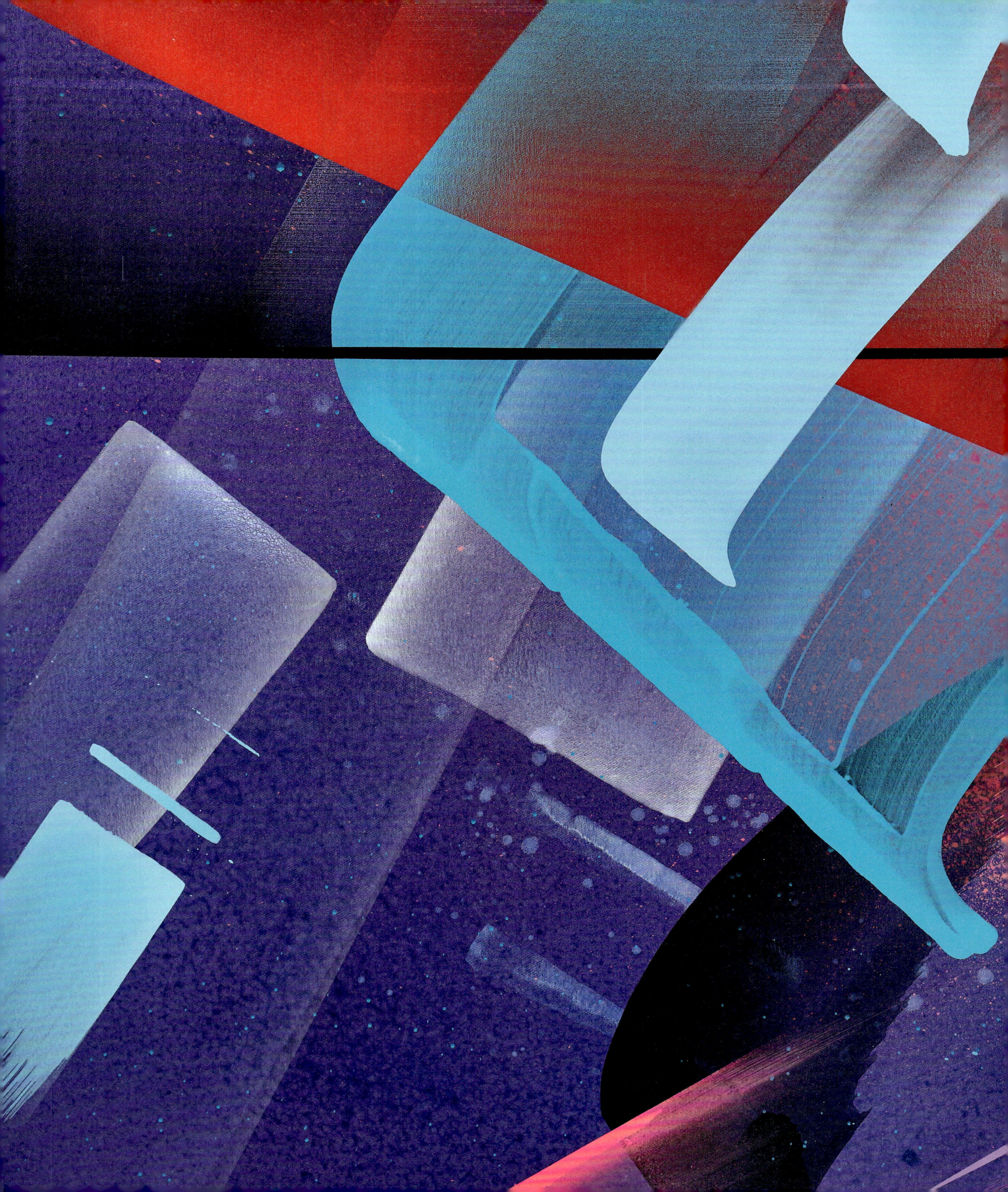

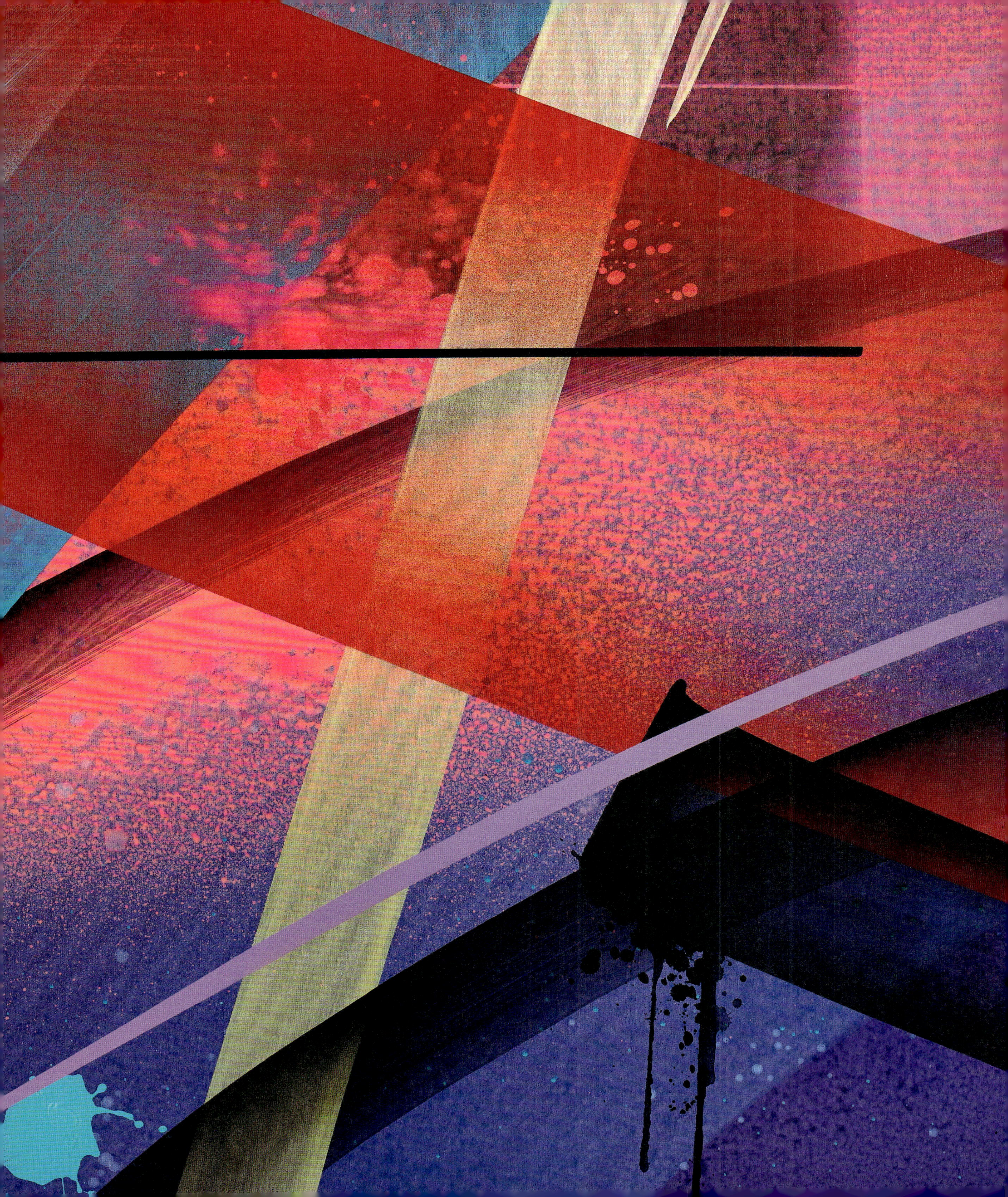

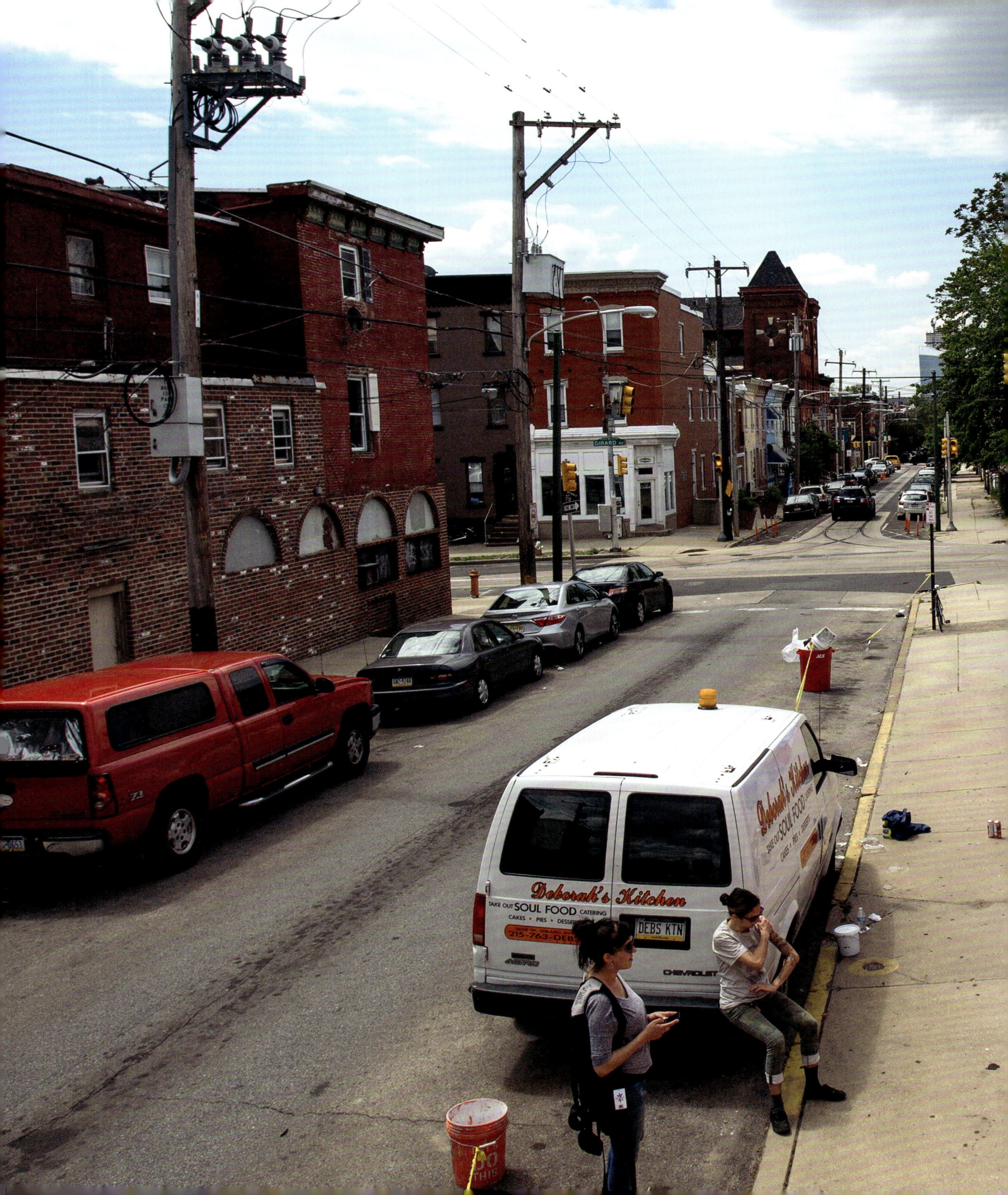
GIRARD AV
Deborah's Kitchen
TAKE OUT SOUL FOOD CATERING
DEBS KTN
CHEVROLET

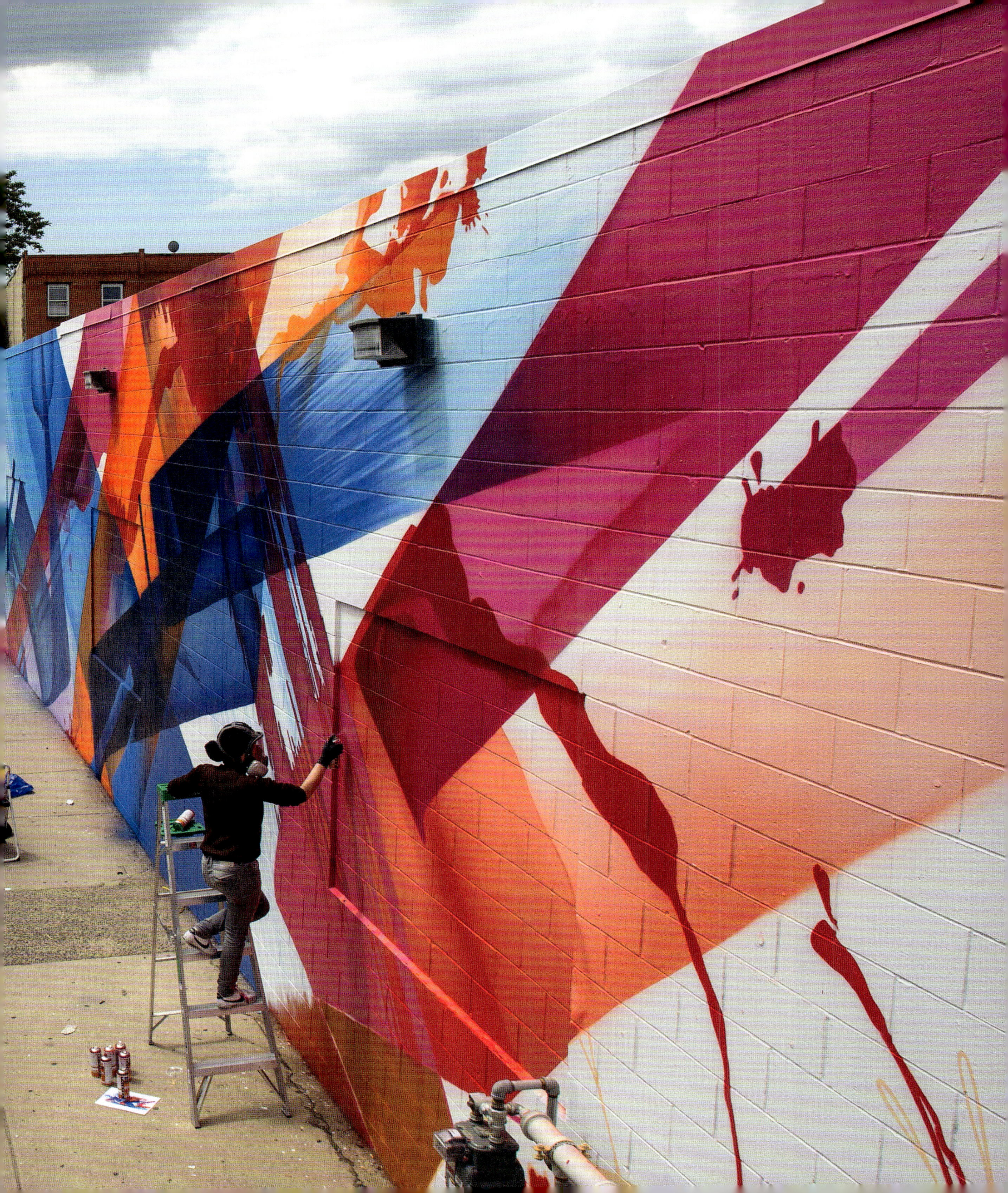

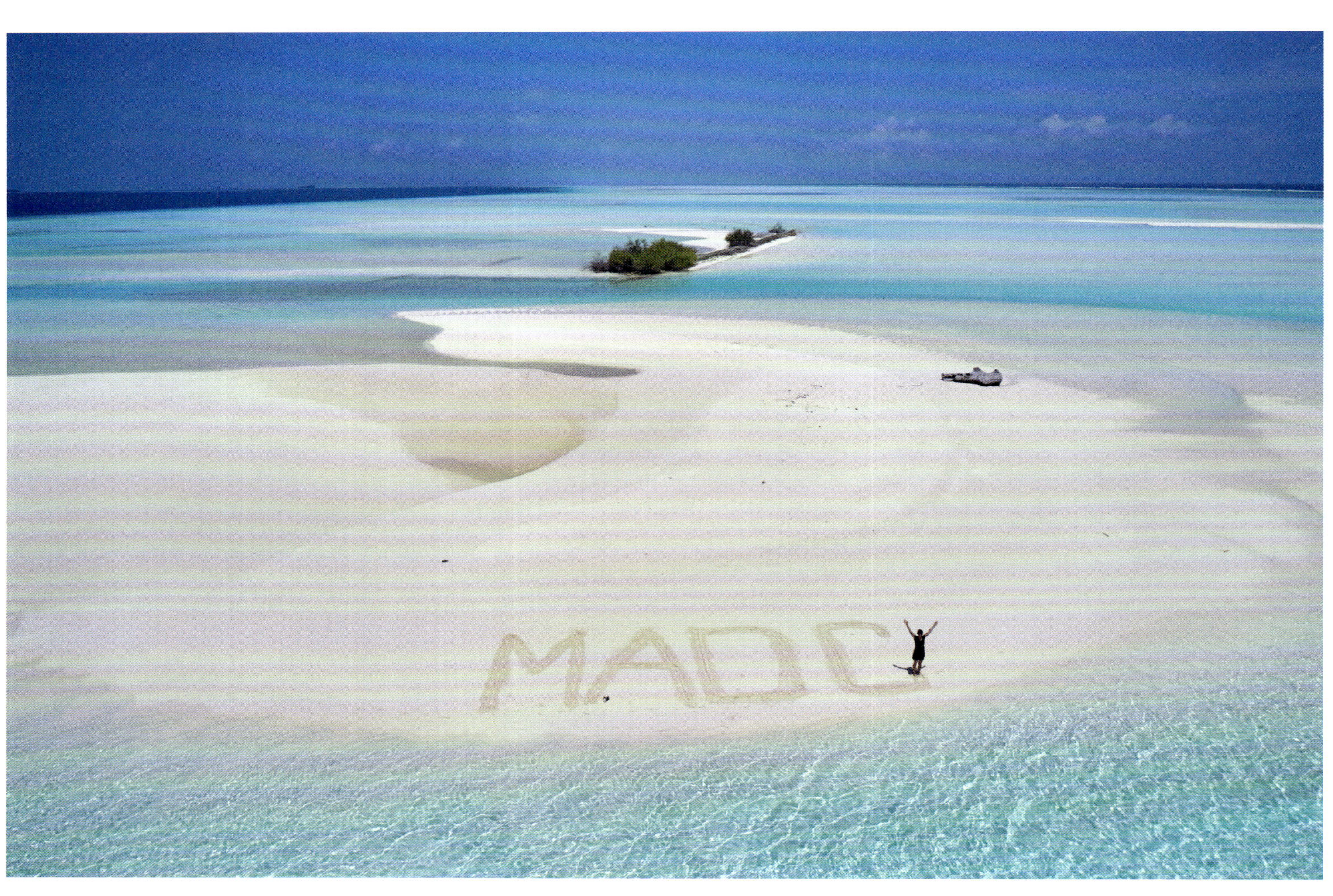